36: *British Novelists, 1890-1929: Modernists,* edited by Thomas F. Staley (1985)

37: *American Writers of the Early Republic,* edited by Emory Elliott (1985)

38: *Afro-American Writers After 1955: Dramatists and Prose Writers,* edited by Thadious M. Davis and Trudier Harris (1985)

39: *British Novelists, 1660-1800,* 2 parts, edited by Martin C. Battestin (1985)

40: *Poets of Great Britain and Ireland Since 1960,* 2 parts, edited by Vincent B. Sherry, Jr. (1985)

41: *Afro-American Poets Since 1955,* edited by Trudier Harris and Thadious M. Davis (1985)

42: *American Writers for Children Before 1900,* edited by Glenn E. Estes (1985)

43: *American Newspaper Journalists, 1690-1872,* edited by Perry J. Ashley (1986)

44: *American Screenwriters,* Second Series, edited by Randall Clark, Robert E. Morsberger, and Stephen O. Lesser (1986)

45: *American Poets, 1880-1945,* First Series, edited by Peter Quartermain (1986)

46: *American Literary Publishing Houses, 1900-1980: Trade and Paperback,* edited by Peter Dzwonkoski (1986)

47: *American Historians, 1866-1912,* edited by Clyde N. Wilson (1986)

48: *American Poets, 1880-1945,* Second Series, edited by Peter Quartermain (1986)

49: *American Literary Publishing Houses, 1638-1899,* 2 parts, edited by Peter Dzwonkoski (1986)

50: *Afro-American Writers Before the Harlem Renaissance,* edited by Trudier Harris (1986)

51: *Afro-American Writers from the Harlem Renaissance to 1940,* edited by Trudier Harris (1987)

52: *American Writers for Children Since 1960: Fiction,* edited by Glenn E. Estes (1986)

53: *Canadian Writers Since 1960,* First Series, edited by W. H. New (1986)

54: *American Poets, 1880-1945,* Third Series, 2 parts, edited by Peter Quartermain (1987)

55: *Victorian Prose Writers Before 1867,* edited by William B. Thesing (1987)

56: *German Fiction Writers, 1914-1945,* edited by James Hardin (1987)

57: *Victorian Prose Writers After 1867,* edited by William B. Thesing (1987)

58: *Jacobean and Caroline Dramatists,* edited by Fredson Bowers (1987)

59: *American Literary Critics and Scholars, 1800-1850,* edited by John W. Rathbun and Monica M. Grecu (1987)

60: *Canadian Writers Since 1960,* Second Series, edited by W. H. New (1987)

61: *American Writers for Children Since 1960: Poets, Illustrators, and Nonfiction Authors,* edited by Glenn E. Estes (1987)

62: *Elizabethan Dramatists,* edited by Fredson Bowers (1987)

63: *Modern American Critics, 1920-1955,* edited by Gregory S. Jay (1988)

64: *American Literary Critics and Scholars, 1850-1880,* edited by John W. Rathbun and Monica M. Grecu (1988)

65: *French Novelists, 1900-1930,* edited by Catharine Savage Brosman (1988)

66: *German Fiction Writers, 1885-1913,* 2 parts, edited by James Hardin (1988)

67: *Modern American Critics Since 1955,* edited by Gregory S. Jay (1988)

68: *Canadian Writers, 1920-1959,* First Series, edited by W. H. New (1988)

69: *Contemporary German Fiction Writers,* First Series, edited by Wolfgang D. Elfe and James Hardin (1988)

70: *British Mystery Writers, 1860-1919,* edited by Bernard Benstock and Thomas F. Staley (1988)

(Continued on back endsheets)

DICTIONARY OF LITERARY BIOGRAPHY
DOCUMENTARY SERIES
AN ILLUSTRATED CHRONICLE

VOLUME SEVEN

Depicting The Lives And Work Of Authors—Including Photographs, Manuscript Facsimiles, Letters, Notebooks, Interviews, And Contemporary Assessments

DICTIONARY OF LITERARY BIOGRAPHY

DOCUMENTARY SERIES

AN ILLUSTRATED CHRONICLE

VOL. SEVEN

MODERN AMERICAN POETS

JAMES DICKEY
ROBERT FROST
MARIANNE MOORE

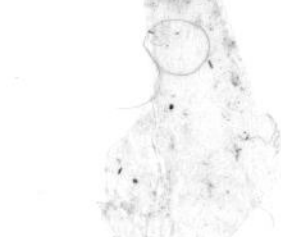

EDITED BY KAREN L. ROOD

A BRUCCOLI CLARK LAYMAN BOOK

GALE RESEARCH INC.
DETROIT, NEW YORK, FORT LAUDERDALE, LONDON

Matthew J. Bruccoli and Richard Layman, *Editorial Directors*
C. E. Frazer Clark, Jr., *Managing Editor*

Manufactured by Braun-Brumfield
Ann Arbor, Michigan
Printed in the United States of America

Gale Research Inc.
835 Penobscot Bldg.
Detroit, MI 48226-4094

ISBN 0-8103-2782-1

Library of Congress Cataloging-in-Publication Data

(Revised for vol. 7)
Dictionary of literary biography documentary series.

"A Bruccoli Clark Layman book."
"A Bruccoli Clark Layman book"–v. 6-7 t.p.
Includes index.
Contents: v. 1. Sherwood Anderson, Willa Cather, John Dos Passos, Theodore Dreiser, F. Scott Fitzgerald, Ernest Hemingway, Sinclair Lewis / edited by Margaret A. Van Antwerp–v. 2. James Gould Cozzens, James T. Farrell, William Faulkner, John O'Hara, John Steinbeck, Thomas Wolfe, Richard Wright; edited by Margaret A. Van Antwerp–v. 7. Modern American poets. James Dickey, Robert Frost, Marianne Moore / edited by Karen L. Rood.
1. Authors, American–Biography–Sources. 2. American literature–History and criticism. I. Van Antwerp, Margaret A. II. Bruccoli, Mary. III. Johns, Sally. IV. Title: Documentary series.
PS129.D48 1982 810'.9 82-1105

ISBN 0-8103-1112-7 (v. 1)

PERMISSIONS

JAMES DICKEY

TEXT: All previously unpublished material by James Dickey is from the author's private papers and is published here by his permission. P. 4, "James Dickey, Hurdler and I," p. 117, "James Dickey Induction–Academy of Arts and Letters" and "Review: *Wayfarer: A Voice from the Southern Mountains*," by permission of the *James Dickey Newsletter*. P. 14, "A Too-Sure Hand," © 1953 by the *Houston Post*; used by permission. P. 18, letters by Dickey from "Ezra Pound and James Dickey: A Correspondence and a Kinship," by permission of James Dickey; letter by Pound, p. 20, by permission of New Directions, Inc. P. 22, excerpt from "University Influence on Poetry," reprinted from *Prairie Schooner*; by permission of University of Nebraska Press; copyright © 1961 University of Nebraska Press. P 24, excerpt from "Things, Voices, Minds," © 1962 by the Yale Review; used by permission. P. 25, "Your Next-Door Neighbor's Poems," © 1864 by the University of the South; reprinted by permission of the editor. P. 35, "James Dickey's New Book," © 1964 by the Modern Poetry Association; reprinted by permission of the editor of *Poetry* and Wendell Berry. P. 35, "Oriented by Instinct by Stars," © 1964 by the Modern Poetry Association; reprinted by permission of the editor of *Poetry* and the Estate of Robert Duncan, New Directions, Inc., Executor. P. 37, "To Dream, To Remember: James Dickey's *Buckdancer's Choice*," by permission of the editor of the *Northwest Review*. P. 42, "James Dickey on Poetry and Teaching," and p. 43, "James Dickey's NBA Remarks," © 1966 by R. R. Bowker Company; reprinted by permission. P. 43, excerpt from "The Way of Exchange in James Dickey's Poetry," © 1966 by the University of the South; used by permission of the editor. P. 46, "Robert Frost, Man and Myth," by permission of the *Atlantic Monthly*. P. 50, "Inventing the American Heart," © 1967, and p. 62, "Resurrection for a Little While," © 1970, by permission of the *Nation* Magazine/The Nation Company, Inc. P. 54, " 'Dazzingly Simple' Poetry is Predicted for the Future," and p. 106, "James Dickey's Odyssey of Death and Deception," © the *Washington Post*. P. 55, "James Dickey as Critic," © 1968 by the *Chicago Review*; used by permission. P. 65, "Art and Immediacy, James Dickey's *Deliverance*," by permission of Donald W. Markos.] P. 73, "Promised Land or Paradise Lost: The South Beheld," © 1975 by the University of Georgia, reprinted by permission of the *Georgia Review*. P. 78, "James Dickey," © 1977 by *Agenda*; reprinted by permission of *Agenda*. P. 82, "The Most Dangerous Game of the Poet James Dickey," by permission of the *South Carolina Review*. P. 86, excerpt from "Exchanges: Inventions in Two Voices," © 1980 by the University of the South; used by permission of the editor. P. 88, "A Radical Departure for James Dickey," © 1982; reprinted by permission of *The State*, Columbia, S.C. P. 93, excerpt from "James Dickey Symposium: A Celebration," edited by W. Thorne Compton, Associate, Institute of Southern Studies; used by permission of the Southern Studies Program, University of South Carolina. P 101, review of *Night Hurdling*, © 1984 by the University of Georgia; reprinted by permission of the *Georgia Review*. P. 108, "James Dickey as Southern Visionary," by permission of the *Virginia Quarterly Review*.

PHOTOS: Pp. 5, 6, 7, 9, 11, 13, 16, 18, 23, 26, 33, 44, 60, 61, 66, 67, 69, 73, 74, 80, 81, 85, 87, 89, 91, 98, 110, 111, courtesy of James Dickey. Pp. 52, 54, 57, 76, courtesy of University of South Carolina. P. 79, Columbia Newspapers photo by Steve Hunt. P. 83, © 1979 by Terry Parke. P. 94, © by Terry Parke. P. 95, photo by Leonard Copeland. P. 105, illustration © 1986 by Richard Jesse Watson.

ROBERT FROST

TEXT: All letters by Frost from *Selected Letters of Robert Frost*, ed. Lawrence Thompson, © 1964 by Holt, Rinehart & Winston; reprinted by permission of Holt, Rinehart & Winston. Letters from Frost to Louis Untermeyer, Sylvester Baxter, and Wilbert Snow reprinted by permission of Alfred C. Edwards, Trustee and Executor for the Estate of Robert Lee Frost. Letters from *Family Letters of Robert and Elinor Frost*, ed. Arnold Grade, © 1972 by the State University of New York Press; reprinted by permission of the State University of New York Press. P. 133, excerpt from "How a Columbus Mother Inspired Her Son," by permission of the *Columbus Dispatch*. P. 140, excerpt from "Freshman Days," by permission of *Dartmouth Alumni Magazine*. P. 170, "The Golden Room," by permission of the *Atlantic Monthly*. P. 182, review of *North of Boston*, reprinted by permission of the *New Republic*, © 1915 by the New Republic, Inc. P. 185, excerpt from *Bygones*, copyright © 1965 by Louis Untermeyer; reprinted by permission of Harcourt, Brace & World. P. 191, excerpt from "Editor's Easy Chair," by permission of *Harper's Magazine*. P. 194, "Poetry of Axe Handles," by permission of the *Philadelphia Inquirer*. P. 197, "Frost and Masters," © 1917 by permission of the Estate of Harriet Monroe. P. 217, "Recruit Legislator," © 1936 by the *Baltimore Sun Company*; used by permission. P. 218, "The Instincts of a Bard," © 1936, and p. 235, "The Other Robert Frost," © 1947, by permission of the *Nation* Magazine/The Nation Company, Inc. P. 227, "Robert Frost, Dean of American Poetry," and p. 246, "Poems That Soar and Sing and Charm," I.H.T. Corporation; reprinted by permission. P. 234, "A Few Personal Memories of Robert Frost," by permission of the *Southern Review*. P. 235, "Still Further Range," by permission of the *Yale Review*. P. 238, T. S. Eliot toast, © 1976 by Valerie Eliot; used by permission of Valerie Eliot and Faber & Faber, Ltd. P. 241, "Robert Frost Pays Visit as New 'Poet Laureate,'" p. 245, "Frost's Poem Wins Hearts at Inaugural," and p. 250, "Kennedy Leads World Eulogies of Poet Robert Frost, Dead at 88," © the *Washington Post*. P. 249, "Frost Calls K Generous Ruffian," by permission of the Associated Press.

PHOTOS: All Frost photos and manuscripts are used by permission of Alfred C. Edwards, Trustee and Executor for the Estate of Robert Lee Frost. Houghton Library, Harvard University, from the copies at the University of Virginia Library: pp. 128 (top l.) and 134 (bottom). Robert Frost Collection, Clifton Waller Barrett Library, Special Collections Department, Manuscripts Division, University of Virginia Library: pp. 128 (top r., 6538, N45-1788-I; bottom r., 6261-ad.1, N45-1778-D), 130-132 (6261), 138 (top, 6261-ad.20, N45-1788-C), 139 (6261-a, N45-1788-A), 148 (l., 6261, N45-1478-E), 153 (top, 6538, N45-1788-P; bottom, 6261, N45-1478-A), 156-157 (6261), 159 (top, 6538, N45-1788-R), 160 (bottom l, 6261, N45-1478-E), 164 (6261), 165 (6261, N45-1788-L), 170 (6538, N45-1788-J), 186 (6261-ad.14, N45-1788-O), 191 (6538, N45-1788-F), 200-201 (6261-c.), 209 (6261), 213 (6538, N45-1788-P), 217 (6538, N45-1788-G), 226 (6261), 228 (top, 6261; bottom, 6261, N45-1788-M, photo by Jacob Lofman), 230 (6261), 231 (6261), 232-233 (6261), 241 (6538, N45-1788-H). Robert Frost Collection, Clifton Waller Barrett Library, Special Collections Department, Division of Rare Books, University of Virginia Library: pp. 138 (bottom), 146, 166-167, 247. Lawrance Thompson-Robert Frost Collection, Clifton Waller Barrett Library, Special Collections Department, Manuscripts Division, University of Virginia Library: pp. 159 (bottom l, 10,044-a, N45- 1668-A; bottom r., 10,044-a, N45-1477-B). The Jones Library, Inc., Amherst, Mass.: pp. 134 (top), 160 (top and bottom r.), 183 (from the copy at the University of Virginia Library), 202, 207, 208, 222, 237, 240. Henry E. Huntington Library and Art Gallery: pp. 144, 145 (l.), 154, 155, 158, 178, 179, 196, 215, 219, 223. Dartmouth College Library: pp. 148 (r.), 150, 151. Robert Frost/George H. Browne Collection, Plymouth State College Library: p. 162. Lilly Library, Indiana University: pp. 172, 251. Middlebury College News Bureau: p. 221. Amherst College Library: p. 239. Copyright Warren Rothschild, from the copy at the University of Virginia Library: p. 242. UPI/Bettmann Newsphotos: p. 245. Stewart Udall: p. 249.

MARIANNE MOORE

TEXT: P. 254, "Durable Poetry in Our Time," © 1958 by the Christian Science Publishing Society; used by permission of the *Christian Science Monitor*. P. 258, interview with Marianne Moore, from *Writers at Work: The Paris Review Interviews, Second Series*, © 1977 by the *Paris Review*, Inc. all rights reserved. Reprinted by permission of Viking Penguin, a division of Penguin Books, USA, Inc.; used by permission. P. 273, review of *Others: An Anthology of New Verse*, used by permission of New Directions, Inc. P. 276, "A Symposium on Marianne Moore," used by permission of the Estate of Harriet Monroe. P. 287, "Miss Moore's Art Is Not a Democratic One," © 1925 by the *New York Times* Company; reprinted by permission. P. 295, "Introduction" to *Selected Poems*, reprinted with permission of Macmillan Publishing Company; copyright 1935 by Marianne Moore, renewed 1963 by Marianne Moore and T. S. Eliot. P. 299, excerpt from "New Verse," by permission of the *Spectator*. P. 304, "Marianne Moore," by permission of the Estate of William Carlos Williams, New Directions, Inc., Executor. P. 306, "A Poet on Pavlova Photographs," and p. 313, "A Sampler of Delights," I.H.T. Corporation, reprinted by permission. P. 307, "Marianne Moore and E. McKnight Kauffer: Two Characteristic Americans," by permission of *Twentieth-Century Literature*. P. 310, "Thou Art Translated," by permission of the *Observer*. P. 311, "Medley of Marianne Moore," by permission of the Estate of Babette Deutsch. P. 314, "Telephone Interview with Busy Poet Produces Her Views on Baseball, Floyd Patterson, and Verse Style," © 1962 by the *New York Times* Company; p. 319, "What the Angels Missed," © 1966 by the *New York Times* Company; p. 322, "Straight Lines over Rough Terrain," © 1967 by the *New York Times* Company; p. 324, "Marianne Moore, Pulitzer Poet, Dies" and "Shaper of Subtle Images," © 1972 by the *New York Times* Company; all reprinted by permission. P. 316, "Reminiscence," by permission of Anatole Pohorilenko, Executor for the Estate of Monroe Wheeler. P. 318 "Speech Delivered at Dinner Meeting of the National Institute of Arts and Letters on the Occasion of Marianne Moore's 75th Birthday, November 15, 1962," by permission of the Estate of Malcolm Cowley.

PHOTOS: Pp. 254, 256, 259, 261, 272, 277, 291, 303 (photo by Arthur Steiner), 308, 326 (photo by Esther Bubly), used by permission of Marianne Craig Moore, Literary Executor for the Estate of Marianne Moore, and the Rosenbach Museum & Library. Pp. 270, 277, 294, 297, 305, 315, 317, Rosenbach Museum & Library. P. 257, Bryn Mawr College Archives. P. 311, Culver Pictures, Inc. P. 319, 321, Black Star. P. 323, UPI.

CONTENTS

PREFACE ix

ACKNOWLEDGMENTS xi

JAMES DICKEY (1923- 3
Ronald Baughman

ROBERT FROST (1874-1963) 127
Karen L. Rood

MARIANNE MOORE (1887-1972) 253
Patricia C. Willis

CUMULATIVE INDEX 331

For
Ella Lane King

PREFACE

DLB: Documentary Series is a reference source with a twofold purpose: 1) it makes significant literary documents accessible to students and to scholars, as well as to nonacademic readers; and 2) it supplements the *Dictionary of Literary Biography* (1978-). The *Documentary Series* has been conceived to provide access to a range of material that many students never have the opportunity to see. By itself it is a portable archive. Used with *DLB*, it expands the biographical and critical coverage of the essays by presenting key documents on which these essays are based. *DLB* places authors' lives and works in the perspective of literary history; the *Documentary Series* chronicles literary history in the making.

Each volume in the *Documentary Series* concentrates on the major figures of a particular literary period, movement, or genre. *DS 7* is restricted to three modern American poets–James Dickey, Robert Frost, and Marianne Moore–whose careers span the twentieth century. They have been selected for their influence on literary history and because their careers generated documents of enduring interest. Wherever possible, letters, notebook and diary entries, interviews, and book reviews are included in *Documentary Series* entries. Each document is chosen to illuminate a notable event in a writer's personal or professional life or to reveal the development of his reputation. Entries vary in length and content according to the author's writing habits, the availability of his or her papers, and the amount of attention given him or her in the literary press.

Beginning in the late nineteenth century, one after another of the assumptions about the order of the universe was destroyed, and with those losses came a corresponding diminution of shared values and beliefs. Frost and his contemporaries, who had inherited traditional poetic forms that no longer reflected the world as they saw it, were the first to face the modern poet's dilemma: the need to write poems that both mirrored the world's chaos and imposed a momentary order upon it. Each poem written is a small man-made form placed against a background of "hugeness and confusion shading away from where we stand into black and utter chaos," Frost wrote in 1935. Yet the breakdown of the old order also brought a new freedom. Each of the major modern poets, including the three treated in this volume, devised a highly individual poetic style, bringing to the raw materials of the modern world a personal sense of the need for form and how to achieve it.

Robert Frost, the earliest of the poets covered in *DS 7*, is also the most traditional. Yet, when Frost's second book, *North of Boston*, was published in 1914–after a poetic apprenticeship of two decades–reviewers hailed it as revolutionary. Frost himself said with pride, "I dropped to an everyday level of diction that even Wordsworth kept above." He discovered in the irregular accents of everyday speech a metaphor for the world's disorder, and by imposing these "sounds of sense" upon the regularity of traditional forms, he found a way to create an uneasy equilibrium between order and chaos–a "momentary stay against confusion."

Marianne Moore, fifteen years younger than Frost, began her career in 1915, but received little recognition as a poet until her second book, *Observations* (1924), won the Dial Award in 1925. Like Frost, she was acquainted with and encouraged by poets of the Imagist movement, but, again like Frost, she followed her own dictates in shaping a poetic style. She shared with Frost a strong distaste for falsely "poetic" language. "I too dislike it," she wrote in "Poetry" (1919), in which she said poets should create "imaginary gardens with real toads in them." Yet she went beyond Frost by rejecting traditional meters and verse forms and creating her own elaborate poetic patterns.

James Dickey, one of the new generation of poets who emerged after World War II, is also disdainful of pretentious, "poetic" language, which he finds often in his contemporaries' work, along with an over-concern with elegance of technique at the expense of vision. Dickey's own technique has evolved from recognizable stanzaic units to the "open" poem, in which the placement of lines and spaces on the page is his attempt to illustrate how the mind functions, with thoughts and feelings occurring in clusters and bursts, leaping from one association to another. "The poet must evoke a world that is realer than real," he has written. "This world is so real that the experienced world is transfigured and intensified, through the poem, into *itself*, a deeper *itself*, a more characteristic *itself*. If a man can make words do this, he is a poet." Rather than seeing the poem as means of escaping from personality, as T. S. Eliot has suggested, Dickey glories in the self's response to and involvement with his world.

Literary documents often convey messages beyond the words they employ. The surviving manuscripts from the nearly two decades between the first appearance of one of Frost's poems in a national magazine (1894) and the publication of his first book, *A Boy's Will* (1913), are concrete evidence of the large stockpile of early poems on which he drew for the rest of his long career–often revising the poems in ways to heighten their dramatic qualities. Early drafts by Dickey and Moore attest to the care they took in creating the "intensified" worlds of their poems. Dickey, for example, has often written many drafts for a single work, sometimes making extensive revisions but at other times changing little.

Letters often record an author's personal responses to the events of his life and his private observations about his work. Unlike Dickey and Moore, Frost tried to avoid writing prose for publication, but he often used letter writing as a means of working out his poetic theories. Dickey's correspondence with Ezra Pound documents a link between two generations of poets, but it also shows Dickey's refusal to follow the man he has described affectionately as being "like someone's crazy uncle."

Notebook and diary entries also present the observations, experiences, and ambitions that shaped the writer's career. Excerpts from Dickey's notebooks–published here for the first time–provide significant insights into his development as a writer. Entries in his notebooks often include a line or idea that is later enlarged into a series of drafts for a poem or a novel. In addition to writing in a notebook, Moore also kept a file of clippings from newspapers and magazines, which she drew on for images in her poems.

Interviews contribute to the formulation of an author's public image, as he speaks directly to readers, often attempting to define and secure his place in literature. After some early experiences of seeing himself misrepresented in print, Frost became adept at hiding behind the farmer-poet mask he created. Yet, in interviews he did provide valuable information about his life and his poetic theory and practice, as did Marianne Moore, who revealed as well her interest in baseball and other nonliterary topics. Dickey often uses interviews to explore his ideas about his own work and to clarify his critical stance toward the work of others. Much of the available biographical information about him comes from his interviews.

Book reviews by influential critics, contemporaries of the author, evoke the literary atmosphere of the era. Reviews influence public opinion as they chart the course of an author's critical reception. They are invaluable for the understanding of a writer's reputation, providing the basis from which subsequent assessments of his work evolved.

Pictures from an author's life may often clarify the reader's perception of his work. The *Documentary Series* provides photographs of the author, his family, friends, and associates throughout his life.

Each author entry in *DLB: Documentary Series* is therefore a concise illustrated biography as well as a sampling of the diverse materials that have heretofore been accessible only to a limited group of researchers. Too often readers see only the results of an author's painstaking toil and hear only the conclusions of others about the merits of his work. They rarely have the opportunity to glimpse a writer's work in progress, to consider firsthand the judgments of his contemporaries, and to examine extracts from his personal papers. *DLB: Documentary Series* offers these opportunities, facilitating the study of an author's life and career from a variety of perspectives, each of which enriches the appreciation and understanding of his enduring achievements.

ACKNOWLEDGMENTS

This book was produced by Bruccoli Clark Layman, Inc. Karen L. Rood is senior editor for the *Dictionary of Literary Biography* series.

Production coordinator is James W. Hipp. Systems manager is Charles D. Brower. Photography editor is Susan Todd. Layout and graphics supervisor is Penney L. Haughton. Copyediting supervisor is Bill Adams. Typesetting supervisor is Kathleen M. Flanagan. Typography coordinator is Sheri Beckett Neal. Charles Lee Egleston, Laura Ingram and Michael D. Senecal are editorial associates. The production staff includes Helen Baucum, Rowena Betts, Anne L. M. Bowman, Joseph M. Bruccoli, Teresa Chaney, Patricia Coate, Sarah A. Estes, Willie M. Gores, Cynthia Hallman, Susan C. Heath, David Marshall James, Kathy S. Merlette, Ellen McCracken, Laura Garren Moore, and Jack Turner. Jean W. Ross is permissions editor.

Walter W. Ross and Jennifer Toth did the library research with the assistance of the reference staff at the Thomas Cooper Library of the University of South Carolina: Lisa Antley, Daniel Boice, Faye Chadwell, Cathy Eckman, Gary Geer, Cathie Gottlieb, David L. Haggard, Jens Holley, Jackie Kinder, Marcia Martin, Jean Rhyne, Beverly Steele, Ellen Tillett, Carol Tobin, and Virginia Weathers. Clara Colby helped with research at the University of Virginia Library.

Special thanks are also due to Richard H. F. Lindemann at the University of Virginia Library, Sara S. Hodson at the Henry E. Huntington Library and Art Gallery, and the staff at the South Caroliniana Library, University of South Carolina.

We are especially indebted to James Dickey, who advised Ronald Baughman and made his private papers available.

DICTIONARY OF LITERARY BIOGRAPHY

DOCUMENTARY SERIES

AN ILLUSTRATED CHRONICLE

VOLUME SEVEN

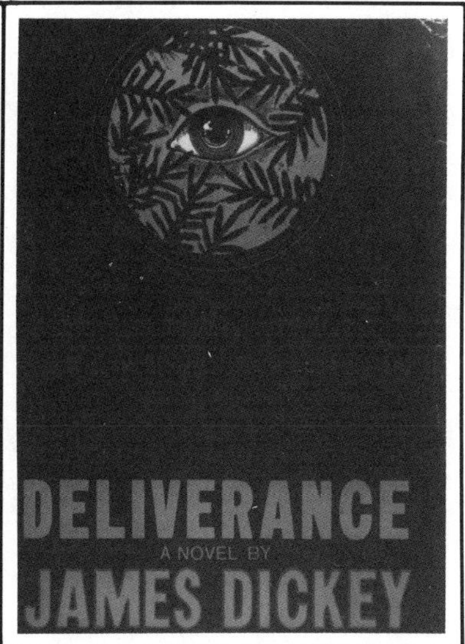

JAMES DICKEY

(2 February 1923-   )

Ronald Baughman
University of South Carolina

See the James Dickey entries in Dictionary of Literary Biography, *volume 5,* American Poets Since World War II, *and* Dictionary of Literary Biography Yearbook: 1982.

MAJOR BOOKS:

Into the Stone and Other Poems, in *Poets of Today VII,* edited by John Hall Wheelock (New York: Scribners, 1960);

Drowning with Others (Middletown, Conn.: Wesleyan University Press, 1962);

Helmets (Middletown, Conn.: Wesleyan University Press, 1964; London: Longmans, Green, 1964);

The Suspect in Poetry (Madison, Minn.: Sixties Press, 1964);

Two Poems of the Air (Portland, Oreg.: Centicore Press, 1964);

Buckdancer's Choice (Middletown, Conn.: Wesleyan University Press, 1965);

Poems 1957-1967 (Middletown, Conn.: Wesleyan University Press, 1967; London: Rapp & Carroll, 1967);

Spinning the Crystal Ball (Washington, D.C.: Library of Congress, 1967);

Babel to Byzantium: Poets and Poetry Now (New York: Farrar, Straus & Giroux, 1968);

Metaphor as Pure Adventure (Washington, D.C.: Library of Congress, 1968);

Deliverance (Boston: Houghton Mifflin, 1970; London: Hamilton, 1970);

The Eye-Beaters, Blood, Victory, Madness, Buckhead and Mercy (Garden City, N.Y.: Doubleday, 1970; London: Hamilton, 1971);

Self-Interviews, recorded and edited by Barbara and James Reiss (Garden City, N.Y.: Doubleday, 1970);

Exchanges (Bloomfield Hills, Mich.: Bruccoli Clark, 1971);

Sorties (Garden City, N.Y.: Doubleday, 1971);

Jericho: The South Beheld, text by Dickey, illustrations by Hubert Shuptrine (Birmingham, Ala.: Oxmoor House, 1974);

The Zodiac (limited edition, Bloomfield Hills, Mich. & Columbia, S.C.: Bruccoli Clark, 1976; trade edition, Garden City, N.Y.: Doubleday, 1976);

The Strength of Fields [single poem] (Bloomfield Hills, Mich. & Columbia, S.C.: Bruccoli Clark, 1977);

God's Images, text by Dickey, etchings by Marvin Hayes (Birmingham, Ala.: Oxmoor House, 1977);

The Enemy from Eden (Northridge, Cal.: Lord John Press, 1978);

Tucky the Hunter, text by Dickey, illustrations by Marie Angel (New York: Crown, 1978; London: Macmillan, 1979);

Veteran Birth: The Gadfly Poems 1947-1949 (Winston-Salem, N.C.: Palaemon Press, 1978);

In Pursuit of the Grey Soul (Bloomfield Hills, Mich. & Columbia, S.C.: Bruccoli Clark, 1978);

Head-Deep in Strange Sounds (Winston-Salem, N.C.: Palaemon Press, 1978);

The Water-Bug's Mittens: Ezra Pound: What We Can Use (Moscow: University of Idaho, 1979; Bloomfield Hills, Mich. & Columbia, S.C.: Bruccoli Clark, 1980);

The Strength of Fields [collection] (Garden City, N.Y.: Doubleday, 1979);

Scion (Deerfield, Mass. & Dublin, Ireland: Deerfield Press/Gallery Press, 1980);

The Starry Place Between the Antlers: Why I Live in South Carolina (Bloomfield Hills, Mich. & Columbia, S.C.: Bruccoli Clark, 1981);

Deliverance [screenplay] (Carbondale & Edwardsville: Southern Illinois University Press, 1982);

Puella (Garden City, N.Y.: Doubleday, 1982);

Värmland (Winston-Salem, N.C.: Palaemon Press, 1982);

False Youth: Four Seasons (Dallas: Pressworks, 1983);

Night Hurdling: Poems, Essays, Conversations, Commencements, and Afterwords (Bloomfield Hills, Mich. & Columbia, S.C.: Bruccoli Clark, 1983);

Bronwen, the Traw, and the Shape-Shifter, text by Dickey, illustrations by Richard Jesse Watson (San Diego, New York & London: Bruccoli Clark/Harcourt Brace Jovanovich, 1986);

Alnilam (Garden City, N.Y.: Doubleday, 1987);

Wayfarer: A Voice from the Southern Mountains, text by Dickey, photographs by William A. Bake (Birmingham, Ala.: Oxmoor House, 1988);

MOTION PICTURES:

Deliverance, screenplay by Dickey, Warner Bros., 1972;

Call of the Wild, screenplay by Dickey, Charles Fries, 1976.

OTHER:

Yevgeny Yevtushenko, *Stolen Apples,* includes twelve poems adapted by Dickey (Garden City, N.Y.: Doubleday, 1971);

INTERVIEWS:

The Voiced Connections of James Dickey: Interviews and Conversations, edited by Ronald Baughman (Columbia: University of South Carolina Press, 1989).

BIBLIOGRAPHIES:

Jim Elledge, *James Dickey: A Bibliography: 1947-1974* (Metuchen, N.J. & London: Scarecrow Press, 1979);

Elledge, "James Dickey: A Supplementary Bibliography, 1975-1980: Part I," *Bulletin of Bibliography,* 38 (April-June 1981): 92-100, 104;

Elledge, "James Dickey: A Supplementary Bibliography, 1975-1980: Part II," *Bulletin of Bibliography,* 38 (July-September 1981): 150-155;

Matthew J. Bruccoli and Judith S. Baughman, *James Dickey: A Descriptive Bibliography* (Pittsburgh: University of Pittsburgh Press, 1990).

LOCATION OF ARCHIVES:

Major collections of manuscripts are found in the Washington University Library, St. Louis; and the Library of Congress.

MEMOIR:

Robert S. Lowrance, Jr., "James Dickey, Hurdler and I," *James Dickey Newsletter,* 1 (Fall 1984): 8-9.

Dickey's well-known love of athletics, particularly track and football, has often appeared as a subject in his poetry and fiction. In the inaugural issue of the James Dickey Newsletter, *Dickey's high-school track coach provided his recollections of the poet's athletic achievements. Following his graduation from North Fulton High School, Dickey spent one year at the Darlington School in Rome, Georgia, and then enrolled at Clemson.*

James Dickey was born in Buckhead, Georgia, to Eugene and Maibelle Swift Dickey. When asked by an Atlanta magazine for reminiscences of early Christmases, Dickey provided this photograph and wrote, "Christmas memory? Grammar school . . . fifth grade . . . old enough to have a racing bike . . . fantasized about it. . . . Living at 166 W. Wesley Road in Atlanta. . . . Mother had spectacular Christmases. . . . Coming down to see it there . . . there it was–two-wheeled magic! The magic the machine can have only for the child. . . . I'm still riding it in my memory . . . into another life."

James Dickey's *Night Hurdling* (1983) takes its title from one of its stories which describes his overcoming a champion and setting a new hurdling record. It was my privilege to be Jim's track coach at that time, which was during his four years at North Fulton High School in Buckhead.

The school was new. I had organized a track team, secured county aid in having a track constructed around the football field, and had placed the first trophy in the school's trophy case. Considering the quality of the athletes and their determination to win, this last is not surprising. I can still clearly see Jim as he called to me.

"Coach, come over here and see that I am doing this right."

I squatted beside the hurdle and watched him barely clear the crosspiece and slap his forward foot as close to the hurdle as possible, then stride on to the next one. Jim was "doing it right." His championships testify to that. Although slightly tall for the low hurdles, Jim was a strong, intelligent athlete, and he adapted his stride to a conquering length and pace. He was demonstrating even at that time his dedication to the finer details that result in a quality product in any field. In college he continued his record-setting form.

The teams won six championships in the seven years I coached. In one North Georgia Interscholastic Conference meet with ten teams entered in ten events, the North Fulton team won nine first and one second place. My hurdler (not

Dickey participated in football and track throughout his high-school and college careers. This photograph is from the Darlington School yearbook for 1941-1942.

Jim) was defeated by a boy from Athens who had been coached, we were told, by Spec Towns! My runner felt he had failed the team and would not speak to the others for two weeks.

A few years ago I secured a publisher for my first book of poetry, *Fountain of Youth.* I had seen Jim on several occasions at the Buckhead Boys' annual gathering. (His poem about North Fulton graduates gave them their name.) Such is the camaraderie of these graduates that when I called Jim to ask him if he would write an introduction to my book, his response was prompt and generous. This is the introduction he sent me:

"Forty years ago when I had only been running races in tennis shoes with neighborhood friends, I bought my first pair of 'spikes' and experienced with frustration and excitement the bite of my feet–intended now to run *meaningfully* fast–into a prepared surface: a real track. At that moment I came under the direction of the track coach of North Fulton High School in Atlanta, Robert Lowrance, and began to learn what running is all about: *really* about. For many painful afternoons I struggled with the problem of Form, and under the eye and mind and gentle incisive concern of Lowrance came to find out something about it, and how to use it. As the poet Allen Tate has said, 'In art all roads are long, and they all lead to the problem of Form.' When later I transferred my energies from the track onto a more dangerous surface, the written page, I came to see that, although the medium was different, the basic situation was the same: how best to use what one had. I now find that Bob Lowrance has gathered together the poems he has written over the years between, and I am delighted–but

Dickey left Clemson in late 1942 to serve in the 418th Night Fighter Squadron, U.S. Army Air Corps.

not surprised–to find that the same qualities with which he imbued me and my fellows forty years ago have now, for him, been transferred into this other medium, the page: my 'track' is now his. These poems exhibit all the tact, all the care for measure, for tolerant exactness, for human limitation and possibility, that I have always associated with Lowrance. I am happy to introduce this book, and to call attention to these good things. James Dickey, Carolina Professor and Poet in Residence, University of South Carolina, National Book Award Winner in Poetry, Poetry Consultant to Library of Congress"

I am proud to have James Lafayette Dickey as introducer of my poetry, and I am proud to claim him as a friend.

COMBAT MISSION LOG:
"418th Night Fighter Squadron (SEP), APO 180," unpublished, author's private papers.

After graduation from high school, Dickey attended Clemson University, where he played football during the fall 1942 semester. At the end of that semester he left school to join the U.S. Army Air Corps. During World War II he served in the South Pacific. The 418th Night Fighter Squadron, of which he was a member, participated in more than one hundred missions, including major battles on Okinawa and mainland Japan. This section of the squadron's log of sixty-seven missions, in many of which Dickey took part, conveys in its terse factuality only the merest suggestion of the drama involved. Throughout his writing career, Dickey has repeatedly explored the war's impact on him both in his poetry and fiction.

Mission 1.
Type of mission - Patrol and Reconnaisance Jap Convoy.
Nil interception.
Date - 26 December 1944.
Area - Mindoro.

Mission 2.
Type of mission - Patrol.
One Tony destroyed.
Date - 27 December 1944.
Area - Mindoro.

Mission 3.
Type of mission - Patrol.
One Betty probably destroyed.
Date - 27 December 1944.
Area - Mindoro.

Mission 4.
Type of mission - Patrol.
Destroyed two Tonys.
Date - 27 December 1944.
Area - Mindoro.

Mission 5.
Type of mission - Recco.
Nil Interception.
Date - 28 December 1944.
Area - Mindoro.

Mission 6, 7.
Type of mission - Recco.
Nil interception.
Date - 28 December 1944.
Area - Mindoro.

Mission 8, 9, 10.
Type of mission - Patrol.
Nil interception.
Date - 28 December 1944.
Area - Mindoro.

Mission 11, 12, 13.
Type of mission - Patrol.
Nil interception.
Date - 29 December 1944.
Area - Mindoro.

Mission 14.
Type of mission - Recco.
Nil interception.
Date - 29 December 1944.
Area - Calamain Route.

Mission 15.
Type of mission - Convoy cover.
Nil interception.
Date - 29 December 1944.
Area - Mindoro, to 9° 50'N, 121° 50'E

Mission 16.
Cover L-3 Resupply Convoy.
Two Irvings destroyed.
Date - 29 December 1944.
Area - Kill made 15 miles south convoy.

Mission 17, 18, 19.
Type of mission - Cover L-3 Resupply Co.
Nil interception.
Date - 29 December 1944.
Area - Mindoro-Lingayen route.

Mission 20.
Type of mission - Patrol.
Nil interception.
Date - 29 December 1944.
Area - Mindoro.

Mission 21, 22.
Type of mission–Convoy cover.
Nil interception.
Date - 30 December 1944.
Area - Mindoro-Lingayen route.

Mission 23.
Type of mission - Patrol.
One Rufe destroyed.
Date - 30 December 1944.
Area - Mindoro.

Mission 24.
Type of mission - Patrol.
Nil interception.
Date - 30 December 1944.
Area - Mindoro.

Mission 25.
Type of mission - Convoy Cover.
Nil interception.
Date - 30 December 1944.
Area - Mindoro-Lingayen Route.

Mission 26.
Type of mission - Patrol.
One Rufe & one Frank destroyed.
Date - 30 December 1944.
Area - Mindoro.

Mission 27, 28, 29, 30.
Type of mission - Patrol.
Nil interception.
Date - 30 December 1944.
Area - Mindoro.

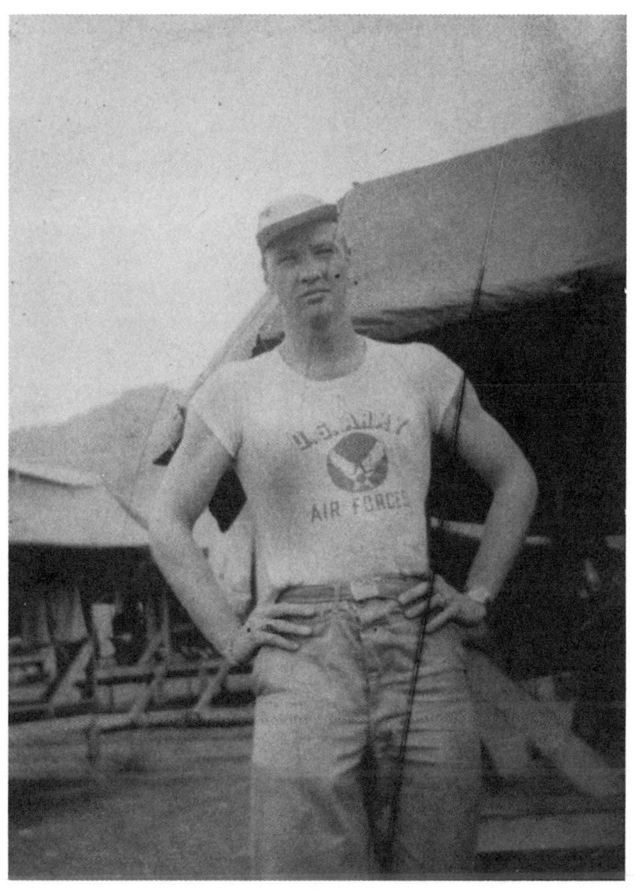

During World War II, Dickey served in the South Pacific. This setting and experience later inspired such major poems as "The Performance," "The Firebombing," and "Victory."

Mission 31, 32, 33, 34, 35.
Type of mission - Patrol.
Nil interception.
Date - 31 December 1944.
Area - Mindoro.

Mission 36, 37, 38, 39.
Type of mission - Patrol.
Nil interception.
Date - 1 January 1945.
Area - Mindoro.

Mission 40, 41.
Type of mission - Patrol.
One interception, no kill.
Date - 1 January 1945.
Area - Mindoro.

Mission 42, 43, 44, 45.
Type of mission - Patrol.
Nil interception.
Date - 2 January 1945.
Area - Mindoro.

Mission 46, 47, 48, 49.
Type of mission - Patrol.
Six interceptions, no kill.
Date - 3 January 1945.
Area - Mindoro.

Mission 50.
Type of mission - Patrol.
Two float planes destroyed.
Date - 4 January 1945.
Area - Mindoro.

Mission 51.
Type of mission - Patrol.
Fired on possible Frank, no kill.
Date - 4 January 1945.
Area - Mindoro.

Mission 52, 53, 54.
Type of mission - Convoy Cover.
Nil interception.
Date - 4 January 1945.
Area - Mindoro-Lingayen Route.

Mission 55.
Type of mission - Patrol.
Nil interception.
Date - 4 January 1945.
Area - Mindoro.

Mission 56, 57, 58.
Type of mission - Convoy Cover.
Nil interception.
Date - 5 January 1945.
Area - Mindoro-Lingayen route.

Mission 59.
Type of mission - Patrol.
Two interceptions, no kill.
Date - 5 January 1945.
Area - Mindoro.

Mission 60.
Type of mission - Convoy cover.
One Val destroyed.
Date - 5 January 1945.
Area - Mindoro-Lingayen route.

Mission 61, 62.
Type of mission - Patrol.
Two interceptions, no kill.
Date - 6 January 1945.
Area - Mindoro.

Mission 63, 64, 65.
Type of mission - Patrol.
One interception, no kill.
Date - 7 January 1945.
Area - Mindoro.

Mission 66.
Type of mission - Convoy Cover.
Two twin engine bombers destroyed.
Date - 8 January 1945.
Area - 205 miles northwest of base.

Mission 67.
Type of mission - Convoy Cover.
Nil interception.
Date - 8 January 1945.
Area - Mindoro-Lingayen Route.

JOURNAL ENTRY:
"Sketch for the building of the rational poem," unpublished, mid-February 1952; author's private papers.

Dickey married Maxine Syerson on 4 November 1948. He attended Vanderbilt University in Nashville, Tennessee, earning a B.A. with honors in 1949 and an M.A. in 1950. He began teaching at Rice Institute in Houston, Texas, but was soon recalled to active military service during the Korean War. Returning from Korea, Dickey resumed teaching at Rice. While there he wrote extensive journal entries in large, hardbound ledgers. The entry transcribed here, from pages 5-9 of one ledger, offers insight into his early preparation for writing poetry. His approach to the "rational" elements of writing poetry is strikingly similar to his approach to learning to play the guitar, shoot a bow, play football or run track, and fly an aircraft. His first impulse is to devise a "rational" set of skills by which he can become accomplished enough in verse to answer the question: "What is to be done with impulse, or whatever arrives from 'inspiration.'" As a self-described "romantic" poet who relies on and believes in feeling more than reason, Dickey indicates in this early statement his care in preparing himself to allow the heart to take dominion over the mind.

5

Sketch for the building of the rational poem–
These must be answered

Question: 1. What is the subject?

a. What is the *general* subject? Grief, joy, renunciation, acceptance, avowal, love, lust, hatred, death, life? A combination? Antithesis? Development from (through) to

2. What attitude toward the subject is to be expressed? Confusion, understanding, immersion, helplessness before or under? (Conversion from one thing to another?) Awakening?

3. With the first two clearly defined, the *method* begins to make itself clear. The burden of the poem is thrown wholly onto an answer to the question: What devices will best get this said? Be most vivid, powerful, moving and profound? This perhaps is something like the objective correlative. The correlative, however, is only "objective" in order finally to reside in the imagination. Its "objectivity" is simply a making available of a certain image or train of images to the individual imagination to "mean" what it will & does.

The questions may then be subdivided into the "personal" characteristics of the particular

5

Sketch for the building of the rational poem –
These must be answered
Question: 1. What is the subject?
a. What is the general subject? Grief, joy, renunciation, acceptance, arousal, love, lust, hatred, death, life? A combination? Antithesis? Development from (through) to?
2. What attitude toward the subject is to be expressed? Confusion, understanding, immersion, helplessness before or under? (Conversion from one thing to another?) Awakening?
3. With the first two clearly defined, the method begins to make itself clear. The burden of the poem is thrown wholly onto an answer to the question: What devices will best get this said? Be most vivid, powerful, moving and profound? This perhaps is something like the "objective correlative." The correlative, however, is only "objective" in order finally to reside in the imagination. Its "objectivity" is simply a making available of a certain train of images to the individual imagination to "mean" image or what it will & does.

The questions may then be subdivided into the "personal" characteristics of the particular poem, all to turn round the considerations: what devices will best make available the decided-upon attitudes –
a. Who is speaking? What voice? Active or passive? Where
1. First person
2. Second person (very limited use) addressed
3. Third person
These considerations require considerable exploration.
b. Why is he speaking?
1. Usually implicit in the poem, but may be used as a deliberate device: ("Because I do not hope to turn again" –)
c. What is the setting?
Some setting, to be related intimately to the imagery,
(see Bottom next page: 6)

Early in his career Dickey sought a theoretical foundation for his poetry. This page from one of his notebooks reveals his search for techniques to convey his poetic vision (Author's private papers).

poem, all to turn round the considerations: what devices will *best* make available the decided-upon attitudes–

a. Who is speaking? What voice? Active or passive? Where?
1. First person
2. Second person (very limited use) addressed
3. Third person

These considerations require considerable exploration.

b. *Why* is he speaking?
1. Usually implicit in the voice, but may be used as a deliberate device: ("Because I do not hope to love again"–)
c. What is the setting?

Some setting is to be linked . . . to the imagery (See bottom of page 6)

6

by comparison and/or contrast, is a part of the poem. It is either stressed, to be let emerge, or implicit.: ("Silk bars the road, a spider rope") Is it a reflection, reminiscence, an anticipation? How combine these.

Now a gathering up:

Take stock: line up and integrate what has thus far been achieved. Follows

(a) a rehearsal of possibilities as to

Imagery–or is the poem to be relatively imageless, conceptual?

1. Kind:
a. Active (violent)
b. Passive (still)
and combinations
c. Sight (predominant), sound, smell, touch–taste–

d. What is the *context* of the imagery; what is to *link* the images? A knowledge of the genius operative beneath mediaeval statuary? Physics (Empson)? Freud? Mythology? All men's grief, joy, common knowledge? Or no context: an interplay?

e. See section on "words." How may the image best be verbalized? Best be integrated with, moved *through* the language, words of the poem, best be *expressed by* them?

Stanza form, or form in general

This a difficult thing to determine:

1. a. May the poem best be expressed through a series of linked (imagery, concepts) and developing packages (stanzas)? Or does it *seem to want to* flow a long way at once, without conceptual or syntactical break?

Setting: Something moved through? In? Or static (as a still life)? How, how much moved through or static? *Why*?

7

Narrative, etc. meter, syntax, words, revision, sound (symbol, allegory & imagery)

b. If a stanzaic form is to be used, *which stanzaic form? Rimed? Unrimed? How many feet to which line?*

Rime as organizational factor–

1. If a rime scheme suggests itself, are the rimes to be full rimes, or slant or assonantial rimes? Rimes as I see them are by nature "clinchers," intensifiers. The harder the conclusion is to be made, the harder the rime should be struck. (This rather a shallow notion, but a fair beginning). What do we rime *for*? Simply to satisfy an essentially meaningless convention? Assonantial or slant rime a kind of sub[t]lety device, making us realize connections where there apparently were none, work "under cover."

Is the rime to be feminine? What are the uses of these? Look up. Feminine: inconclusive, delicately unbalanced.

2. How may the stanza rime? Couplets? It is possible, although considerable mastery is involved, to make a convention of rime work against itself; to make the heroic couplet non-epigrammatic, and to express a slow-paced movement of the emotions in tetrameter couplets.

Must the rime of the stanza recur like a memory (a repetition of an early line end in a late) or must it bang closed like a gate (closing couplet, full-rimed). Must it be touched very lightly (slight slant rime, early-late repeated), a faint gong or whisper?

These things must be worked out

Enjambment? Where? Use sparingly.–

Meter

a. What is the metric to accomplish? Is it to dance? Or plod? Shake? Be firm, conclusive? Is it to tear along (Tourneur, Roy Campbell) or be struck off slowly, like bells?

8

b. At what stage of the game is the meter to do exactly what? What syllable is to be empha-

NOTES FOR PROJECT

I am interested in developing toward poetic structure a series of notes which I have been engaged upon for the last two years. When completed this should run to several thousand lines. The poem has not yet taken form, except in the details of a few sections. With a view toward the working out of an adequate technique for encompassing the difficult and rather divergent strains of this poem, I have also in mind the writing of two or three poems of several hundred lines each as necessary exercises, as well as several lyrics I have from time to time drafted.

In regard to the long poem I can say only that I intend it to make use of "cinematic" devices (panning, montage) interspersed with narrative sections, and cut back and forth in time and from place to place, threading together certain personal associations and historical events. It will deal in some fashion with the theme from crime, with the air war in the Pacific, and possibly with civil war, with athletics and business. I do not believe that it will possible for me to complete this poem during the year of my possible tenure in fellowship; however, the year would give me the opportunity for a great deal of the spade-work and experimentation necessary to its writing.

Of the preliminary poems, I wish particularly to recast and implement some notes on a long elgy on my friend Walter Armistead, killed recently in an aircraft accident.

In the lyrics I wish to attempt to put into practise a system of metrics I have already experimented with to some extent, and wish also to place the lyric centrally in some meaningful human situation, in opposition to the current practise of " getting a poem up out of something" simply because one sees a set of verbal (and imaginal) relationships as amenable to poetic usage.

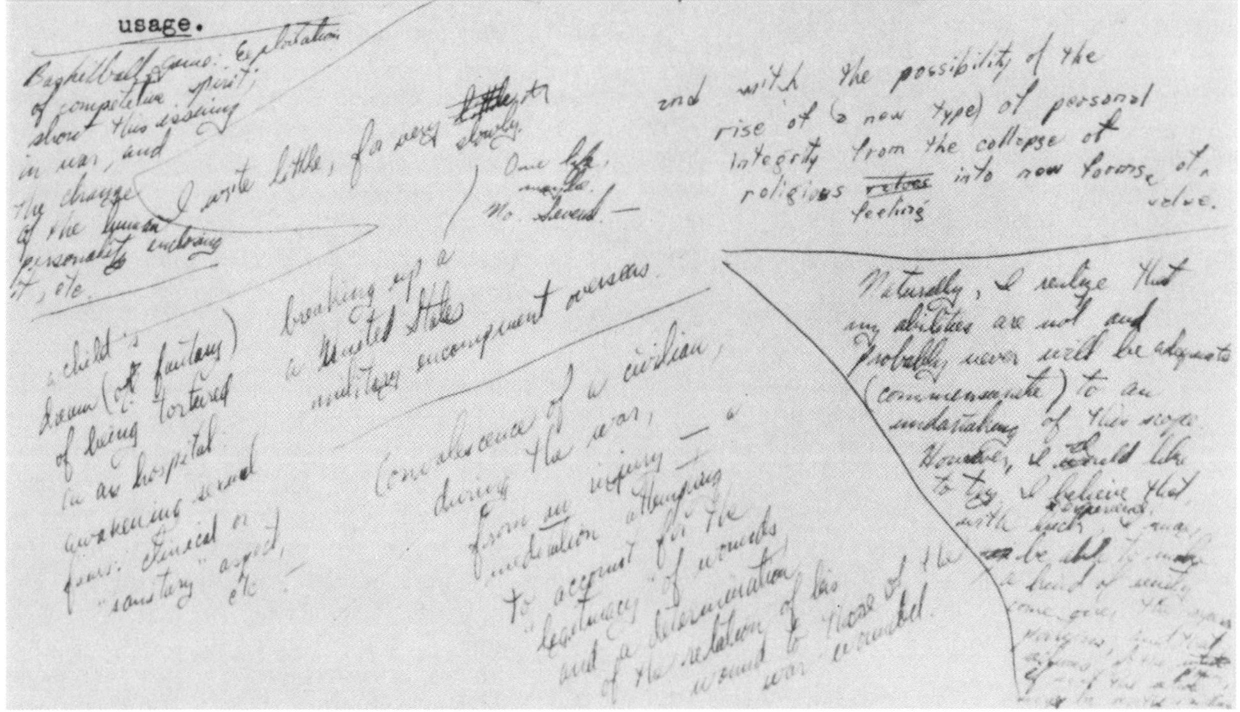
and with the possibility of the rise of (a new type) of personal integrity from the collapse of religious feeling into new forms of value.

Naturally, I realize that my abilities are not and probably never will be adequate (commensurate) to an undertaking of this scope. However, I should like to try.

Page from an early draft of Dickey's application for a Sewanee Review *fellowship (Author's private papers)* sized, what balance or imbalance of weights to be achieved? Where do we need a foot substituted, the spell retarded, impelled forward, made to sink, rise, circle, hover, stop, begin again? Dance music or dirge or any balance?

Syntax

1. Is the poem to be expressed logically, conceptually, syllogistically (Overt, or motivating undisclosed?)

2. What syntactical distortions, if any, are justified, and why?

3. Declarative sentences? Questions? (Rhetorical or really questions?) Balanced or loose sentences? How do these several jibe with other technical considerations? (Meter, stanza-length, etc.)

Sound

a. What sound pattern for any given territory of the poem? An overall pealing-together of sounds? Opposition, contrast? Overall slow weaving or staccato breakage all along a given line in contrast? Sound as device for congruence, emphasis, re-emphasis. As mood-establisher, dispeller. How does the sound go with the other considerations (Meter, imagery)? A development of one kind of sound-pattern (also with imagery, syntax, meter) into another? A displacement in favor of another? Why? What is accomplished?

Symbol, Allegory–to what extent are the images to be "more than themselves," to stand for, represent, be replaced by, evoke? How precisely establish *this* degree? (Tone, emphasis by the various technical devices).

Analogy? Metaphor? Simile? Local or extensive (Metaphysicals)? Linked? Progressive? Digressive? Unravelling?

9

Read Theory of Literature; Stauffer–

To what extent is narrative to be employed?

How is the poem to proceed, develop? By what means? Logic? Illogic? Association? Repetition (Of what?) Dream? The subconscious? Conceptually? Train of images? Development of one central image? Metamorphosis of image, sound?

Words:

1. What word had better be used here? Why? How much strength to give to adjectives, adverbs, etc., under the self-developing laws of the poem's problem? How do the words ride under the (now) existing laws?

Revision: How to take out, put in, so that the whole rides together, addles the imagination and resettles it, by its variously-wrought magics, into more permanent forms?

This whole diagram is directed toward developing a program of action to answer: What is to be done with the impulse, or whatever arrives from "inspiration"? It is impossible that a good poem should develop out of the impulse unaided.

Make a marriage between meaning & sound, & experiment with interplay–

Try always to encourage the exploratory sense of language, in every phase–

Out of a careful rendition & exploration of these possibles the poem develops–

I wish a subtle introverted poetry, nuanced well and strongly subtly, sensitive where Graham is heaving & rockbound–

BOOK REVIEW:

"A Too-Sure Hand: Clarksville Man Competent Stylist," *Houston Post*, 12 April 1953, VII: 7.

While teaching English composition courses at Rice Institute in Houston and working on his early poetry, Dickey wrote eleven book reviews that appeared in the Houston Post *between 12 April 1953 and 6 June 1954. These reviews primarily treated American and European fiction, although some focused upon works in other genres, including Conrad Aiken's* Collected Poems, *Dylan Thomas's* Under Milkwood, *and a collection of essays by Sacheverell Sitwell. This first review for the* Post *evaluates William Humphrey's* The Last Husband and Other Stories.

William Humphrey's first book of stories is very nearly a model of its kind: The stories are quiet, well-constructed, rather unimaginative, and combine easily the elements of competent naivete, casual observation, and "real" interest in people which the various writing workshops of universities urge on their talented students. Mr Humphrey uses the material, presumably, he is most familiar with; though one of the stories deals with an artists' colony and another with New York and commuter towns, all the rest are set in the country, in the author's native Texas (he's from Clarksville), and are concerned with family situations.

The last two stories, "A Fresh Snow" and "The Hardys," are by far the most successful in the book, though the former is stylistically very much in the debt of James Joyce's "The Dead." (Joyce: "A few light taps upon the pane made him turn to the window. It had begun to snow again." Humphrey: "A sudden darkening of the light made her turn to the window. The snow was thickening.")

"A Fresh Snow" skillfully plays off against each other the South of tradition, still preserved in rural areas through custom, the observance of kinship lines, family gatherings, and the land, and the industrial North, where custom plays no part in the lives of the people, who understand nothing of such observances and regard them as useless ornamentations of the spirit, or as "living in the past." These elements are caught up together and presented, moved through the mind of a young southern girl who has married an unimaginative northern boy during the war, and now lives with him in a northern city.

In the four pages which comprise the story, the girl's reflections as she waits for her small son to come home from school, a whole configuration of misunderstanding, of not wanting to understand, is projected through the evocation of the husband, who never appears, and another, of longing, of remembering a kind of childhood never, now, possible to other children is opened up to enfold the little boy as he comes in, "his cheeks red with cold," covered with the snow of the great city.

"The Hardys" is almost as successful, though it suffers to some extent from lack of concentration. Here, an old farmer and his wife, his second one, prepare to sell the house in which he has lived for 53 years, and she for almost as long. As they move about the rooms, putting price-tags on articles of furniture, estimating the prices they should ask, and culling from their effects those things which have become too meaningful to leave behind (she wishes to take everything; he, only a sixpence and a jack-knife), Humphrey underlines the woman's growing dissatisfaction with her life: Though her husband is considerate, kind to her, and presumably loves her, in his uncommunicative way, she cannot forego her obsession with his dead first wife, Virgie, "safe in Heaven these 50 years, safe in Mr Hardy's mind, forever, young and pretty." Having borne Mr Hardy's 10 children, she sits, "her backbone like spools on a thread," thinking, "surely, when the Lord called you you didn't have to come as you were. What else could Hell be?"

Though there are passages elsewhere in the book which are well thought-out, none of the other stories is as successful as the two mentioned. Humphrey does not seem to be sufficiently involved in, committed to, his material, seems rarely to look on it as anything other than material. He is a little too studiedly casual, detached, demanding of his prose only a small part of what it should give, setting up his effects carefully and then leaving the room and turning the lights down to the right intensity. Reading Mr Humphrey, one wishes for one story at least (the story is almost "A Fresh Snow") to take the easy-going author by the throat and jerk him bodily into it, so that later, when he stares in amazement and some horror at the page, he (and the reader) may discover that the thing, the experience, is there, in words, for good, happening again and again.

FELLOWSHIP APPLICATION:
"Project Notes" (draft), circa 1953, unpublished; author's private papers.

These previously unpublished "Project Notes" are a draft for part of Dickey's application for a Sewanee Review *writer's fellowship, outlining the goals he intends to pursue in Europe. His comments provide insights into his early concerns with theme and structure in "the long poem," a form in which he produced some of his best-known work during the mid 1960s. "A Vision of the Sprinter" may have become "The Sprinter's Mother," published in the Spring 1955 issue of* Shenandoah, *Dickey's first appearance in that journal. Dickey received the fellowship, and for a year, beginning in August 1954, he and his family lived in France and Italy.*

I am interested in developing toward poetic structure a series of notes which I have been engaged upon for the past two years. When completed the poem should run to several thousand lines; at present only a few of the details of individual sections have taken form. With a view toward working out an adequate technique for encompassing the difficult and rather divergent strains of this poem, I have also in mind writing two or three poems of several hundred lines each as exercises, as well as finishing ten or twelve lyrics I have from time to time drafted, in different forms.

In regard to the long poem, I can at present say only that I intend it to make use of de-

Dickey married Maxine Syerson in 1948, while he was a student at Vanderbilt. The mother of his two sons, she died in 1976.

vices adapted from both cinema and "still" photography and from painting, that it will include a good many narrative passages, and will cut back and forth in time and from place to place, threading together certain personal associations and historical events in a manner which I hope will produce something of a "timeless" perspective, and that it will deal in some fashion with a theme from athletics, one from crime, with the air war in the Pacific, and with the possibility of the rise of a new type of personal integrity from the collapse of religious feeling into new forms of value. I believe that, with time, luck, and experience, I may be able to produce a really good long poem. I do not believe that it will be possible for me to complete the poem during the year of my possible tenure in fellowship; however, the year would give me the opportunity to do a great deal of the spade-work and experimentation necessary to its writing.

Of the preliminary poems, which I would expect to complete during the year, I wish particularly to write an elegy on my friend Walter Armistead, killed recently in an aircraft accident. I wish also to finish a rather difficult and odd poem on classical Greek athletics, called "A Vision of the Sprinter," for which I have never been able quite to find a suitable form.

In the shorter poems, I should like an opportunity to experiment with a system of metrics based on a specialized use of vowels. Up to this time I have not been able to sustain a poem using this technique above seven or eight successive lines without stiffness or mannerism, but the last stanza of my poem "The Childing Autumn" may suggest that the experiments are of possible value.

Because I write slowly, and have therefore not produced a great deal, I have as yet given little thought to publishing a book. Should a year of leisure result in a sufficient number of satisfactory poems, and in one or more self-contained portions of the long one, I should naturally be interested in finding someone to bring them out together. However, my main concern at present is with formal rather than "public" relations: with writing poems that shall be organically and humanly experiencable: with finding for each poem that system of words that shall sing most clearly and closely still about the subject insofar as this is known to me.

LETTER:

To Andrew Lytle (draft), 1954, unpublished; author's private papers.

After receiving news that he had won the Sewanee Review *fellowship, Dickey expressed his thanks to Andrew*

Lytle and others, including Allen Tate and Monroe Spears, who recommended him for the award. This letter conveys Dickey's jubilation at the prospect of making his writing career become a reality. The "Angel" poem referred to in the letter is "The Angel of the Maze," which appeared in the June 1955 issue of Poetry.

Dear Mr. Lytle,

I am sorry I am a little late in answering your letter, which was one of the finest things I ever read, but since Tuesday my wife and I have been walking back and forth, passing each other with dazed looks, under the shadow of a great happiness trembling to be solid. We heard that day from Mr. Spears that we had been given the fellowship, which confuses and excites us progressively as the belief becomes more acceptably true to us. I think we both really *believe* it now, though it was very hard at the beginning. Allen Tate writes (Spears tells me): "Dickey seems to me to be one of the most original young poets I have read since the war." All this good fortune is a pretty terrible burden on the vanity of one who has not, until now, had much contact with people whose opinion on literary matters he respects. With luck I may, though, assimilate it in a valuable way toward a productive self-confidence, instead of, as now, feeling as though I have been given momentarily a marvellous kind of dream-strength with which to set the cloud-capp'd palaces and towers of the earth in a shrewder and more releasing light, but suspecting all the time that the strength will be rescinded, and I, waking, shall see that I have done or earned nothing. I am terribly happy, with only the fear that I shall not justify what seems to you and the other *Sewanee* editors to be worth encouraging.

Your remarks on "The Angel" poem are very much "on target": the two mazes do need to be dramatized; the poem needs something else: more strength, more clarity, at that point. But I have lost contact with the poem; it has set, like concrete or mud, and my efforts to tamper with it have not come out of a deep enough center: they miss in one way or another touching the other parts of the poem. So I shall have to wait a little, always bearing your comments in mind. Someone (Elizabeth Bowen, I think) says that the essential problem of t[he] novelist is "how to convey." This seems to me to be equally true of any art. There is always the problem of *means*, and of the employment of what one hopefully takes for possible means: the problem of selection.

I have always believed in the artist as much as in art, and in the freedom which to him is such a deep erecting of limits, through all of which he may once or twice burst, past all planning or preconception. It is not possible for anyone who has once had the feeling that a phrase, a set of two words in combination, even, is uniquely his, and is of possible value to other people, to be happy without trying to extend and complete what you call his subject, the one that is his rightly by birth, persuasion, and the slant of the blood as it runs. It is wonderful to know that you are working; I have not read anything new of yours since *A Name For Evil* (*The Long Night* has always seemed to me the best novel ever to come out of the South, Faulkner's not excluded). When I read "The Guide" in *A Southern Vanguard*, I somehow got the idea that it might be part of a novel. Is that the case?

My own novel is pretty much complete in my mind, but there is the problem of performance, yet, of course. I am a very wasteful worker, and spend too much time trying to salvage or transmute what I have made unsalvagable, or what was no good in the first place. I don't want to work myopically on one phrase for hours without knowing at all what I want it to contribute to. To avoid doing this, I have blocked out the book fairly rapidly, and accomplished a kind of first draft, trying out a few alternative possibilities along the way. Because of this, I feel that the novel has a better chance to hold together; if the individual sections stand up, the whole thing ought to. But there is all that to do, yet.

We shall be leaving Texas right around the first of June, to avoid having to pay rent on the apartment. After that until we sail for England early in August, we'll be in Atlanta, where my parents live. I think, if you could manage it that way, that it would be easier for us to meet there, especially since Dallas is around 270 (instead of 30) miles from Houston. I shall hope very hard that you'll be able to stop off.

I'd like to try to stand up, here, and say without embarrassing either of us that I thank you from the strength of all the accumulated silences I have lived under and tried to articulate, for your part in giving me the opportunity that the fellowship allows: to pick up all this crippled shrillness of words and throw it with both hands to-

Dickey reading to his sons, Kevin (born 1958) and Christopher (born 1951)

ward the light, where the thing can truly be made.

Yours,

LETTERS:

From Lee Bartlett and Hugh Witemeyer, "Ezra Pound and James Dickey: A Correspondence and a Kinship," *Paideuma,* 2 (Fall 1982): 290-312.

Upon his return from France and Italy in 1955, Dickey and his friend William Pratt visited Pound, who was confined to St. Elizabeths Hospital in Washington, D.C. Pound had been confined there in 1946, after having been found mentally incompetent to stand trial on treason charges stemming from anti-American, pro-Fascist radio broadcasts he had made from Italy during World War II, and he was not released until 1958. The exchange of fifteen letters and cards between the two writers from 29 August 1955 to 7 November 1958 connects two divergent generations of American poets. Dickey's culminating appraisal of Pound's influence on contemporary poetry occurred in his 1979 University of Idaho Pound lecture, "The Water-Bug's Mittens: Ezra Pound: What We Can Use," collected in Night Hurdling.

29 August 1955
Atlanta

Dear Mr. Pound,

A few weeks ago Bill Pratt and I came out to see you; I have been meaning to write to you ever since, though I have nothing particular to say beyond mentioning that I enjoyed meeting you and your wife very much, and that I should like very much to hear from you.

Now that "l'année de la poésie" is over and we have re-entered the buried life via the gates of the University of Florida, American life has us by the throat again, as before we discovered Europe, stuffing a tiny salary into one hand and nailing the other to the blackboard. Europe seems very far away and inaccessible, and poetry has come again to have the attributes of a personal weapon rather than those of artisanship. All this has no real cause to interest you, but I hope it does, for I remember the time spent talking with you and Mrs. Pound as somehow indicative of a new orientation toward America for me, coming down as we had done through the vast, lucid (but withal bewildering, despite everything) tangle of highways and super-highways out of New York.

My best regards to Mrs. Pound. Meanwhile, I plunge through the brick-work and cactus-blossoms of the University of Florida, in search of the Head of the English Department. Ave Caesar, morituri te salutant!

Write, if you wish.

Yours,
James Dickey

1720 N.W. 7th Place
Gainesville, Fla.

Pound responded with a request for Pratt's address. The "Gaudier sketch" to which Dickey referred in his next letter is Henri Gaudier-Brzeska's drawing of Pound.

30 September, 1955
Gainesville, Fla.

Cher Maître,

Bill Pratt's address (after so long a time) is Box 41, Station B, Nashville, Tennessee. I hope to be forgiven for the delay. There are reasons, but I don't believe in reasons, really, and feel that I should have written straight through the middle of them, and shall, from this on.

We hear it is cold in Washington, though nobody in Florida would ever believe it, or gets cold in Winter. My wife and I are collaborating on a kind of project (she works, and I goad) to knit you a sweater, or I guess it will be a kind of sweater, though at the present stage it knows more what it is trying to be than we do. Would you like the Gaudier sketch worked in, if we can (we can't guarantee artistry, but can fumble at similarity) work it in? It will be a heavy sweater, anyway, so that if it really does get cold there, it can go ahead and do so.

My regards to René Crevel, if he should happen to wander in, dressed as a ghost. I am reading Mon Corps et Moi.

I have written a long, over-violent and pretty good poem, which I shall send you after a few more weeks, if you like.

My best to Mrs. Pound.

Yours,
James Dickey

The correspondence with Pound continued, and by February 1956 Dickey was under fire at the University of Florida after he read his poem "The Father's Body" to a local women's group.

20 February, 1956
Gainesville, Fla.

Dear Uncle,

I render herewith the annual report of Florida sweater-growers, to say the one we (my wife, especially, but myself also, to some extent: you will recognize the holes) have been most concerned with. The winter is nearly gone now, and we are still "making progress"; that is, we aren't through with it yet. But it will be a warm one when finished, and you can use it forever. And it *is* almost finished.

There is not much else to say from here, except that a whole generation of Florida students is being brought up on the *ABC of Reading*, much to the astonishment of the Cerberi of the English Department. Also, I lectured, I mean "lectured," to the American Pen Women's Society so furiously (and, I guess, controversially) that their National President wrote to the president of *this* place and demanded that I be kicked out. I haven't been, yet, but the U. of Florida may martyr me still. I rather hope so, though it may just be possible that I am doing one or two people some good here.

There is a poem of mine to appear in the *Partisan Review* you may want to look at. It is the only one that comes anywhere near doing what I want to do. Others have appeared, but on reading them over I can't for the life of me think they're what I want. But there are some new ones still baking that seem to have some of it. Also, there is a long omnibus review of poets in the Spring *Sewanee* that gets in some good licks against a man by the name of Jarrell, whose work has been to some extent influential, in a bad and sentimental way, here for the last few years. He should read Bunting, and either change or kill himself.

All my love to Mrs. Pound. We think of you often, up to our waists in sand, and burned by the winter (for it is a hot one here.) And we *will* finish the sweater, if I have to wear out a wife a day working on it.

By the way, is there any news of Pratt? He won't write to me, though I heard some way or other that he now has a child, a girl, specifically.

Yours,
James Dickey

1720 N.W. 7th Place
Gainesville, Florida

15 August, 1956
Atlanta, Ga.

Dear Uncle,

We mailed the sweater we made, and you should have it in a few days, if you don't already. It is good and strong, and should keep the *Cantos* warm this winter, and thereafter. I reckon it is heresy of some kind to send a *sweater* in this kind of season, but when you unstow it this fall I hope it will go round you warmly, and with the other kind of warmth, too.

I left the University of Florida *in medias res,* "all accusations refuted but that of being the bohemian type." I am in Atlanta working, and teaching and I (at least in the sense of my getting paid for it) are through. It is probably a good thing for both of us.

Can you get me in touch with Bunting?

My love to Mrs. Pound.

I have read the last ten *Cantos* and they are mighty good. But you sure don't need me to tell you that.

Have not heard from Pratt in five months.

Work going well. Book promised (tentatively) in Spring.

Yours,
Jim Dickey

Pound responded with a typically eccentric effusion.

Thanks for information that the sweater has been swatted.

As for touching the Bunting
his address is

242 New Burn Rd. Throckley, Northumberland
(wich iz in England)

the best way is with a bag of oatmeal. (*)

Further details on why those who can't, teach
might be added to gramp's anthropoligical data,
or as hist/moeurs contemp/

no need for laconism on part of the Dickey

as yr/ correspondence is de SULTory, I take it yu
letch not for numerous pen pals.

(*)

all depending on how serious you are AND on what you work FOR, in terms of currency.

After working at the McCann-Erickson Agency in New York, Dickey returned to Atlanta in 1956 where he continued in the advertising business until 1961. He had not written to Pound for nearly nine months because of his distaste for the anti-Semitism expressed in some of Pound's letters. Pound resumed the correspondence with a letter about Edge, *an Australian little magazine published by writers sympathetic to Pound. Dickey's response was his last letter to Pound.*

5 June, 1957
Atlanta, Ga.

Dear Uncle,

Good to hear from you. I will write the *Edge* people and see what they have.

I don't know whether I told you, but I am out of teaching. Had bad luck there and a passel of "Pen Women" got me booted. I am now making a living by half-successfully disguising myself as a "business man," coming down town to work in an office from nine to five each day, and banging away at lunch hour and evenings at poems and a few reviews. *Partisan Review* people say they will bring out a book for me if I can finish a manuscript by Nov. 15th, and I tell myself I am working toward that, though it goes very slowly.

Have a good letter from Bunting, though he sounds discouraged and says he cannot write because of the work he has to do. He says there is no more of his work besides the Galveston volume you sent and a long poem a few years ago in *Poetry*. It is hard to think that *he* thinks there will be no more. Can you prevail on him to get going on some new stuff ? I would like to, but since I don't know him, can't really.

Rock-drill good. I think the image about the water-spider (or whatever) and the flower of shadow on rock is the best single image in Cantos. Would not want to stand off Kenner and the others on this, but will hold to opinion anyway.

Nothing "cultural" here. Have a house where I can put books. Should like to read up on monetary reform. Can you recommend? I know

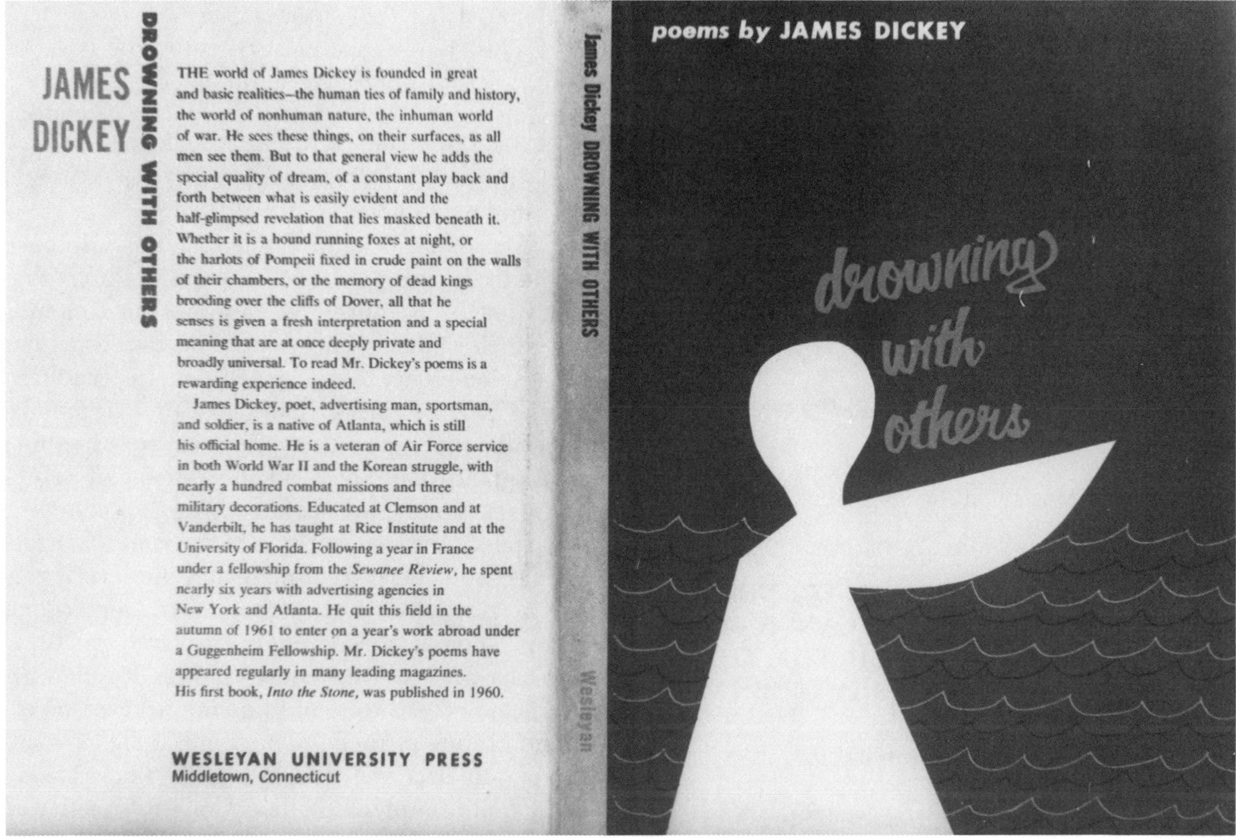

Dust jacket for the first book-length collection of Dickey's poems (1962). It was preceded by Into the Stone, *which appeared in* Poets of Today VII *(1960) along with works by two other poets.*

nothing about money except that it is hard to come by, but not so hard as when teaching gave it.

Heard from W. Pratt. He tells me you say good things about Lloyd Frankenberg's poems. Have F's "Red Kite." The stuff is good, but strikes me as more or less usual. Has Pratt got the name right?

Good, again, to hear from you. Let me know what you need, and wife and I will try to supply.

My best to Mrs. Pound. Thank her (belatedly) for sending me the Angold. I had not known him. Some very good clumsyish poems.

Can't find anything of René Crevel.

Yours,
James Dickey

2930 Westminster Circle
Atlanta, Ga.

JOURNAL ENTRIES:
From Dickey's notebooks, late 1950s, unpublished; author's private papers.

Throughout his writing career, Dickey has used his personal journal as a repository for ideas to be developed; comments to himself; insights, snatches of songs or images or lines that come to him; and for more extensively developed meditations on his own poetic and critical stances. Dickey's notebook entries, which take a variety of forms (handwritten, typed, tape-recorded for a secretary to type), often reappear years later in finished, polished works. The following notes from three separate pages probably date from the late 1950s.

To be the poet of the passionate, unresigned middle age!
The "second wind"–Also: the poet of the *aging process*

the *wildness* of things!

get the *new metric* going!
(For Blood)

1. Transferrence of qualities!
2. Cause & effect!

!!! Energy, energy! true energy!

TRADITIONAL POETRY IS STILL ONLY TRADITIONAL POETRY, NO MATTER HOW GOOD IT IS. I AM AFTER SOMETHING ELSE.

To make amazing, simple statements!
To discover the lie that puts the truth to shame!!

Shrödieger:
"*I* am the world."

I want the naked vision, not the tricks–
The "second innocence"–

If you *do* it right, It will be *done* right.
It will *be* right.

MY WHOLE POETIC WORK IS FOUNDED ON THE NOTION THAT YOU CAN HAVE *VISIONS* OF THINGS, THOUGH THE THINGS THEMSELVES BE OUTWARDLY ORDINARY.

Theme of *rebirth* (Squires review)

My approach to poetry is *physical*–bodily–

Naturalness! Naturalness!

I want to *engulf* the reader in the poem–

BOOK REVIEW:
From Oliver Evans, "University Influence on Poetry," *Prairie Schooner,* 35 (Summer 1961): 179-180.

Dickey's Into the Stone and Other Poems, *a collection of twenty-four poems, was published in* Poets of Today VII *(1960), along with collections by Paris Leary and Jon Swan. Dickey's poems were attacked by some reviewers for excessive adherence to an academic formalism on one hand and an excessive use of a personal voice on the other. Later, the poet's use of the personal voice was cited as part of his poetic strength.*

On the basis of Into the Stone *Dickey received a Guggenheim Fellowship that allowed him to live with his wife and two sons, Christopher and Kevin, in Italy during 1961-1962. Following their return from Italy, Dickey began a series of poet-in-residence positions: Reed College, 1963-1964; San Fernando Valley State College, 1964-1965; and the University of Wisconsin at Madison, 1966. In 1966 he was appointed Consultant in Poetry for the Library of Congress.*

This volume, the most recent in the Poets of Today Series published annually by Scribner's, presents, together with the customary prefatory essay by John Hall Wheelock (editor of the series), the work of three poets: James Dickey, Paris Leary, and Jon Swan.

Mr. Wheelock, in discussing the influence of the universities on modern poetry, admits that it has not been entirely wholesome, but contends nevertheless that "The poetry of our time has greatly benefited by the more general erudition on the part of poets." This may or may not be so; it depends upon the value that one is willing to assign to that which, in the pursuit of erudition, is so frequently sacrificed: *e.g.,* spontaneity, directness, lyricism, elevation of the kind that characterizes the best of Whitman, and the sort of verbal magic–there is no other word for it–that Dylan Thomas so dazzlingly displayed on occasion. To find satisfactory substitutes for these is for me no easy matter, and I do not believe that erudition is one of them. Sometimes, to be sure, little or no sacrifice was involved–there having been, quite simply, little or nothing to sacrifice *ab initio;* and it is precisely here, for the unwary reader, that the danger lies: the danger, that is, of being deceived by the poet who is merely erudite. Such a poet will frequently have recourse to the obscure, for it is the most obvious means of concealing a talent.

I do not mean that the poets presented here exhibit obscurity of this sort, though there is some evidence of it in Mr. Dickey; nor do I wish to imply that the fact that two of them (Mr. Dickey and Mr. Leary) hold graduate degrees disqualifies them as authentic talents. But there is a disturbing tendency in both these poets toward the merely ingenious and the deliberately complex. Those poems of Mr. Dickey which are wholly successful, like "The Underground Stream," do not reveal this tendency, and display frankly the talent that is there–a talent, however, that as yet is not fully formed. His frame of reference is rather narrowly personal (most of the poems are autobiographical in a literal sense), and there are instances of imprecise epithet ("dog-eye colored land") and infelicitous sound effects ("As the trees free-fall / Into their green"). Occasionally, however, one finds a line so simply effective as almost to compensate for these deficiencies: "The whole field stammers with gold." . . .

Poem

On the Inundation of
the Coosawattee Valley

No way out, unless (Lewis) (Lord) King could find a way in.
Sheer gorges, and at the end
A forty-foot double fall
Falling out of life in purity (cloudlike)
There was no road, but he got in.

where we were in danger
is buried, both in us
And in the land. Below the water-skiers
Braselton braces both feet on the canoe
With his hurt back on a rock
~~And I sit~~ Lewis King climbs the last ridge of the gorge
And, ~~a moment~~ a second before deliverance,
I sit with my head in my hands.

Early draft for a poem Dickey published in the December 1962 Yale Review. *Retitled "The Inundation," the poem was collected as the third part of "On the Coosawattee" in* Helmets *(1964). "On the Coosawattee" treats material more fully developed in Dickey's 1970 novel* Deliverance *(Author's private papers).*

Book Review:

From Thom Gunn, "Things, Voices, Minds," *Yale Review,* 52 (October 1962): 129-138.

In his review of Drowning with Others *(1962), Gunn is one of the earliest reviewers to recognize Dickey's visionary quality.*

In spite of his distrust of concepts and his concentration on the physical, James Dickey can be connected in scarcely any way with [William Carlos] Williams. *Drowning with Others* reminded me once or twice, on the contrary, of such fantasists as Paul Klee and Jean Cocteau. Unlike as he is to them in temperament, his effects are sometimes similar to theirs, in that he builds fantasy on a basis of solid physical detail. "The Heaven of Animals" could be the title of a picture by Klee, for example, and such lines as "My green, graceful bones fill the air / With sleeping birds" form a Klee-like image, while the melting of human figures with forms chalked on a blackboard (in "Between Two Prisoners") is similar to the semi-hallucinatory devices in Cocteau's movies.

His is, by choice, an almost entirely sensuous imagination. On the first page of the collection occurs this description of a lifeguard swimming under water searching for a body.

> Like a man who explores his death
> By the pull of his slow-moving shoulders,
> I hung head down in the cold,
> Wide-eyed, contained, and alone
> Among the weeds,
>
> And my fingertips turned into stone
> From clutching immovable blackness.

The passage pivots on the fourth line, but the rest supports it with the strength of accurately evoked sensation. There are many such passages in the book: description charged with feeling, the words sharp, precise, and hard.

If the basis of fantasy is here firmer and more muscular than it is in Klee or Cocteau, the nature of the fantasy is different also. Dickey's is an effort to make fantasy meaningful, to turn it into vision. The subject of the vision could be very loosely described as the rhythm of the universe, in which death and violence are as important a part as their opposites. The image of the hunter, whether human or animal, recurs frequently. And the basic vision is maybe of participation in this rhythm, a participation which involves a simultaneous loss of identity and a keen awareness of the total process. In fact, Dickey implies that the awareness results from the loss. It will be seen not only how such ideas connect with his dependence on images but also with what other writers of the past he is aligned. A key poem is "The Heaven of Animals," which is executed with a beautiful simplicity and concision, and is probably the best poem in the book.

> For some of these,
> It could not be the place
> It is, without blood.
> These hunt, as they have done,
> But with claws and teeth grown perfect . . .
>
> And those that are hunted
> Know this as their life,
> Their reward: to walk
> Under such trees in full knowledge
> Of what is in glory above them,
> And to feel no fear,
> But acceptance, compliance.
> Fulfilling themselves without pain
>
> At the cycle's center,
> They tremble, they walk
> Under the tree,
> They fall, they are torn,
> They rise, they walk again.

It is an almost feudal vision of order: the hunted are as satisfied with their place in creation as the hunters, they are part of "the cycle." Yet the poem is executed with the tenderness of conviction, and one willingly suspends one's disbelief.

There are two weaknesses to this collection. The more serious is that the meter, as in the first quoted passage but not in the second, is almost consistently anapestic tetrameter. Dickey often handles it astonishingly well, but it is a limiting and monotonous meter at best, and I am unable to see why he considers it so attractive. The other weakness arises from his distrust of conceptual language: he makes something of a fetish of images (images are, after all, merely a rhetorical device), and at times one senses that an idea which occurred to Dickey in abstract terms is being *translated,* too deliberately, into images. The effect in such cases is of indirection, almost of preciosity. Moreover the images sometimes accumulate too rapidly, and the result of such rapidity is that the accumulation tends to lack meaning as in much of the lengthy "Dover: Believing in Kings."

It would be a mistake to make too much of the resemblances between Levertov, Creeley, and Dickey, but it seems as if their attitude to style results from an attitude to life, from their trust in "a wise passiveness." . . .

BOOK REVIEW:
"Your Next-Door Neighbor's Poems," *Sewanee Review,* 72 (April-June 1964): 307-321.

Between 1956 and 1965, Dickey earned a reputation as a perceptive and exacting poetry reviewer for prestigious literary journals. During this period most of his critical writings (often omnibus reviews) appeared in the Sewanee Review *and* Poetry; *but he also provided significant appraisals of poetry for the* Virginia Quarterly Review, *the* Hudson Review, Shenandoah, *the* Kenyon Review, American Scholar, *and the* New York Times Book Review. *Some of these reviews were later collected in* The Suspect in Poetry *(1964) and* Babel to Byzantium *(1968). In the following previously uncollected omnibus review, Dickey evaluates Charles Edward Eaton's* Countermoves, *Anthony Ostroff's* Imperatives, *Robinson Jeffers's* The Beginning and the End, *Robert Hazel's* Poems 1951-1961, *Allen Grossman's* A Harlot's Hire, *Paul Roche's* The Rank Obstinacy of Things, *Robert Pack's* Guarded by Women, *Anne Ridler's* Selected Poems, *Richard Eberhart's* Collected Verse Plays, *and translations of Octavio Paz's* Sun-Stone.

If you live in one place long enough, and the fact that you write poetry gets around, things happen that you wouldn't believe. First, the neighbor that you borrow the hedge-clippers from tells you that his wife–or secretary, or sister, or mother-in-law, or, very rarely, his son–has written some poems. What can you do but look at them? He brings them; sometimes they *are* by his sister-in-law or his wife, but more than likely they are by him, and have lain furtively, radiating a queer, muffled light, at least for their author, in the bottoms of drawers and filing cabinets or in the side-pockets of golf bags, the course being his most reliable contact with nature. (And who can say that he is not adding up his score when he pauses thoughtfully, looks off into space, squints as though estimating a distance, writes something down, and goes on, smiling a little absently?) The man who has *published* poetry, and perhaps also reviews it for journals–in a word, the man who is conceded to have a visible stake in the game–comes to glimpse a side of American life that most people don't really think exists, as manuscripts come in from all over: perfectly terrible manuscripts, written for all the wrong reasons, most of them sounding like the wish-fulfillment musings of decent folk anxious to show that they have the right feelings about things, the feelings that God and country–and the popular press–decree that one should have. They are desperate displays of attitudes that no one ever really has, for who can be *that* sure of God's love? They are also full of feelings that other poets have had: those poets read years ago in high school texts where the only modern poem comes on little cat feet and Hemingway's photograph looks like a mustached college boy.

The poet–the bedevilled and desperately sympathetic one, the one with a vested interest in the Word–wonders why these offerings are in *verse,* or mean to be in verse, and concludes vaguely that their authors must believe that putting sentiments into verse confers on them a kind of dignity and worth that they otherwise would not have: that the mere fact of employing the same mode of address as famous poets like Carl Sandburg and James Metcalfe and Shakespeare and Longfellow gives one's poor ideas enormously increased value. Even in the worst of these hand-written or too-neatly typed pages, though, there is likely to be something that the poet–the self-styled pro–could not have thought of, and the variety, even in badness, is huge. And occasionally there is something–not a whole poem, but a phrase, an idea, rarely a line–that is really arresting. Perhaps your neighbor tells you, looking apologetically straight at you with his mild home-owning American eyes, that, yes, he wrote that on a sales trip to Natchez: you see, there were these big barges on the river, and on past them the mist was rising up and the water had this kind of hazy look that . . . that was like . . . well, it tells you, right here in the poem. One's eyes sting, and one knows that here is a glimpse of the thing itself: a fragment of the world *owned* by its perceiver, the essentially personal comparison having been made. Later, drinking the neighbor's martini–for revelations of this kind frequently lead to closer relations–one thinks that even in an unpassionate, attenuated life like the mid-twentieth century American's there is still all kinds of room for passionate private views, the sort from which poems are made. One is led also to pleasant speculations on the unkillableness of the poetic impulse as well as on the strange forms it takes, the places where it appears, and above all on its necessity. When the poet goes back to his study to review books of poems, he carries something of all this with him, and, together with his fierce and secret joy over

Mary Sheffield

I believe that she would normally be loving
Wherever green water would run.
I can still see the river move clearly
Around her singing stone.
With her leg dividing the current
She drew from the country the words

To sing the intended warmth
Out of the brutal sunlight
As I rifled the deepest chords
From the strained breast of the guitar.
I can still see the river part
And her leg disappear into foam;

I can still feel the sun grow gentle
As I touch the assembling strings.
O children in California,
Hear how your mother is singing
When the sun disappears,
And feel the Salinas River

Divide at your bed.
I believe that she would normally be loving
Wherever green water will run,
But that the afternoon
When she and a thin boy waded
Into the heart of the current

He holding by the neck his guitar.
Is lost everywhere but in song.
I am content with that, and with knowing
That she will normally be loving
~~With the sun, with green water, and song.~~
Wherever green water will run.

Early draft for a poem published in the Winter 1964 Shenandoah *and collected in* Poems 1957-1967 *(Author's private papers)* the Natchez barges, he is also aware of a new conviction that the books he reviews, the dozens of slim volumes, are written by substantially the same kind of people who shove their manuscripts under his office door and run, or tell him that their grandmother wrote them: they are people who write mostly for the wrong reasons, but in doing so have an occasional flash of what the right reasons might be like. The poets who "see print" are really little different from those others, except that they have read more books: the books that *their* mentors and guardians, who are not the pages of newspapers and popular magazines and old high school textbooks but those of the critical quarterlies and the intellectual periodicals, say they must read; instead of being influenced by Edgar Guest and Robert Service, they are influenced by Yeats and Dylan Thomas. This is admittedly a great advance, but in many or even most cases the allegiance to Yeats and Thomas is just as blind as to Kipling or Service, and the reasons for it are just as wrong. For every really original writer–and originality is little more than developing one's own mode of observation and evaluation: everyone has these qualities, though some have them buried deep–there are dozens who prefer to use someone else's literarily successful manner of writing, and one concludes that what some poets want is not to communicate but to be praised: that poets of such persuasion do not really believe in their own responses, or at least do not believe in them nearly enough. One would not swap, for dozens of these tame, predictable books, the one half-good observation of a battery-salesman's life, when for a moment or two, as he watched barges on the Mississippi, an idiosyncratic observation of the real world temporarily overthrew Ella Wheeler Wilcox. The printed poets very seldom overthrow Wallace Stevens so decisively.

When one picks up the first of many review volumes, one is likely to be thinking of all this: the first thing to be decided about the book of, say, Charles Edward Eaton, is whether or not Eaton is fighting for his identity in a way that matters poetically: whether or not Mr. Eaton has seen those barges in the fog. Mr. Eaton's previous books are remembered, particularly one called *The Shadow of the Swimmer,* some of the poems in which have meant a good deal to at least one reviewer, principally because of their direct and sumptuous muscle-sinew-water-and-sunlight quality of unashamed male athleticism, a subject crying for the right kind of treatment in a culture where it has become *chic* to look at athletes as being suspect in some way, if not actually sinister. Eaton's swimmer poems were a joyful and healthy kicking-over of this attitude; one felt again what a beautiful thing it is to see blue water flowing over live flesh, how strange and right-feeling the naked sun can be. There is in those poems a sense of live heat and direct light and whole health that is incomparably valuable in this age of sedentary subtleties, and one finds that one has been looking forward for a long time to Mr. Eaton's later development of these themes. And here, when one comes on a poem at the beginning of the book which speaks of "the animal-human dream," one is sure, one is almost sure, that this is the book one had hoped for. Yet it is not, quite. Somewhere or other Mr. Eaton has taken a wrong turn. He has taken thought too much, he has gone complex and cultural, in love with art and artists, and in doing so he has declined and become suffused in pointless conjecture and distant musings. One reads with a shudder a description–by Mr. Eaton–of what has happened to Mr. Eaton since *The Shadow of the Swimmer:*

> So it had happened. He had toyed with the real too long–
> He had made it almost livable, four walls
> Of ripening vines, flowers, racing animals:
> It was time to give his lessons in an unknown tongue.

I would like to think that Eaton will ponder that quotation, and that he will find the unknown tongue in the head of a man in the blazing sunlight, naked, looking at the horizon with his lungs full of air, preparing to submerge in a blue sea. That is the Eaton I care about, and not this one full of tedious, assiduously spun-out arguments in clumsy rhymes, heartlessly displaying the Southerner's vagueness and rhetorical hopefulness, believing he is saying something magnificent when it is just vague, serious-sounding, and sonorous. The clumsiness here is not that of the untutored amateur, but the more disheartening clumsiness of botched art, of technical skill tried-for and missed. None of this need be. Eaton's mind is single, direct, and very sensuous. Let him rejoice in these qualities and return to them.

Anthony Ostroff does very well what Eaton is trying to do, but this is not cause for celebration. As the slip-cover says, Mr. Ostroff 's voice is "unassuming and conversational": it is so much so, in fact, that listening to Mr. Ostroff is not much different from listening to your neighbor when he is at his most ordinary–when he is playing golf in earnest. The easy tone is fine when you have something to say, as, for example, William Stafford almost always does, but it is soporific if it just goes on and on without rising to any intensity at all, as in the case of Mr. Ostroff. *Imperatives* are about the last things his pleasant and rather empty poems are. Talent Mr. Ostroff has, but it is inconclusive and probably of no great consequence. His work is themeless; though the words "real" and "unreal" recur with sufficient frequency to allow the reader the surmise that some debate may be going on between them, it is a debate that would rather play with the issues than grapple with them, commit to them emotionally and perhaps lose everything: lose the pleasant, non-abrasive wit and easy conquest of inconsequentials which constitute almost all of Mr. Ostroff 's work. There is nothing much here, but what there is is often nicely turned, well-mannered, and readable on a nothing-else-to-do summer evening. It can't hurt you, unless you are persuaded that it is poetry.

Mr. Ostroff writes:

The fog's great evening swell against the house,
The heavy, impalpable lowering on piercing woods,
The sick tide moaning for its invisible moon,
The cliffs groping through their deep night . . .

Where in all this disconsolate music
Is there room for other wars?

Robinson Jeffers could tell him.

I saw a regiment of soldiers shuffling and stumbling,
Holding onto each other's hands for guidance
Falling into the ditches, falling on the plain road,
Under orders to garrison the empty city.
The furious light of what killed the city had killed their eyes

At three hundred miles' distance. Oh faithful ones
Do you still make war?

Whether or not one assents to him–whether one turns from it with a shudder as from the most blatant kind of self-righteous verse journalism, or whether one feels that a chilling and incontrovertible vision of the twentieth-century fate has been delivered–there is little doubt that one is likely to be affected strongly in some way: a characteristic tone, both grand (or grandiose) and oddly terse, has been encountered; an image dealing with something of consequence has been called up. The words are those of someone telling you–trying to tell you–what you *must* hear. Despite his much-cited impurity and his excesses, Jeffers does have something that all poets probably need and few have: a life-view, a hard core of utter belief, a perspective against which things are measured, a place to stand from which the poet cannot be dislodged, a temper of mind and will that enters into everything the poet writes, conditioning it, accounting for its unique weather–in a word, creating it as a coherent and immediately recognizable world. This position–walled-off with Pacific rock–is responsible for many of the shortcomings of Jeffers' verse: his inverted moralizing, his over-violence, his theatricality (as bad at times as Poe's), his slovenly diction, and his grand *impatience* with the craft (he would have said "trickery") of verse. But it is also responsible for his ultimate strength, against which the tiny surprises of cleverer poets seem so many lost triumphs of interior decorators in forgotten suburban houses. Jeffers is a tragically flawed but incontrovertibly *big* writer: sometimes awful, but still one who will be heard when the well-tuned scrannel-pipes of lesser men die out about him. The present book, taken from manuscript drafts found among his papers, is both good and bad Jeffers, like all his other books. He might have worked on these pieces a little more, had he lived, but I suspect not much; they are like the others. Jeffers has always been preoccupied with death, but over this book there is such a feeling of its actual presence that the reader can almost smell it. Those who have accused Jeffers of posing–those who felt that his austere philosophy of "inhumanism" would fail him at the end–should read this volume. No such failure is indicated; Jeffers contemplates the decay of his own flesh with a detachment that is both inspiring and so indifferent as to verge on the monstrous.

Fallen in between the tendons and bones
It looks like a dead hand. Poor hand a little longer
Write, and see what comes forth from a dead hand.

It is easy to cry Jeffers down in favor of the poet of the moment–there are lots of moments every year, lots of poets–but he cannot finally be dismissed either as a poet or as a prophet, for his poems are intimately tied in with the obsessive drives of mankind, and especially those of the twentieth century. He is a product, not of Greek tragedy or of the Border Ballads of murder, fratricide, and incest–these are only themes–but of science, telling us that the end, the ultimate vision, of science is not the comfort we all want, but tragedy: tragedy without catharsis, and to be alleviated only by the bitterest stoicism. The conviction gathers, as one reads Jeffers' work, that it is the poet's business to present a powerful image, a compulsively powerful one, and that it matters far less than one had previously thought just how this is presented. This is of course an overstatement: it does very much matter how the image is given, and Jeffers' worst passages are very good testimony to that fact. Nevertheless, it does seem to be true that a certain kind of writer is probably better off in complete submission to his view, concentrating on that rather than on the literary means of expressing it. It would be fine, of course, if he were to concern himself with both–if Jeffers had concerned himself with both–but it is also very important that Jeffers had, all his life, a profound concern with *one* of these attributes. What other man in our time has dealt with such enormous spaces, with suns and galaxies, with light-years and the birth and death of star-systems? Who but a madman or Jeffers would risk the inflation and the inevitable lapses-from-grandeur that such subjects inevitably entail? Who would risk it, when it is so much easier to write about your second wife's freckles, about children playing games in public parks? "Vision itself is desperate," Herbert Read has said, and few visions have been so large or so desperate as Jeffers'. But in the end–and, really, long before the end–it was not desperate but serene, not frenetic but as calm as the stone that Jeffers always aspired to be, not inhuman but as near as it is possible for a man to get, through contemplation of universes, seas, and the superb non-caring abandon of the natural world, to being superhuman, the last survivor, the proud and resigned one. He is in many ways a great modern man, and sometimes almost a great poet.

II

> Hear dark the priestly insects of my endless summer coast down to cells of wax,
> and kind weeds bend my flowers to their colors' end;
> in my thin acres hear time burn stones deaf
> and radium's fine ticking to my flaunted ironweeds' blooms
> stop in amazement at rough measures, twined of handclasps
> and the rule of hammer-bruised thumb. . . .

Who in the hell wrote that? one asks, turning back to the cover to see. Well, it develops that Robert Hazel wrote it. Who then is Hazel, with his country-boy's down-home surrealist kit, writing about "windlasses of light" and "gold sawdust"? Is he the worst poet alive, of all those many? Or is he something else, as yet unclassified? The passage above, now: it is surely much too busy, with the slam-bang get-it-all-in approach to the line that tends to pass for imaginative energy among the very young. In his generous and understanding introduction, Allen Tate speaks of Mr. Hazel's "revolt against the well-made poem," and I find myself nodding at the ideal expressed therein. But is *this* the way to revolt against the well-made poem: by writing ill-made poems? Is the Method, then, the great revolt, no more than a kind of frantic rural surrealism, a license to be more arbitrary than anyone else? A method where all things mean or suggest (or *are*) so many other things freely associating with each other in long nervous strutting sentences, in a kind of youthful self-bluffing aggressiveness, that the reader can't for love or money find a single *thing* that asserts its own identity, that really matters in itself, not for what it suggests but for what it is? One gets awfully tired awfully quickly of Hazel's striving–as obvious as a weightlifter's efforts to surpass himself–to say something simply amazing, to come upon some irrational audacities more irrational and audacious than any yet thought of. Yet despite all this–and despite his technical incompetence, wherein his long, long lines invariably lose sight of their poem's intent in their own wilful and hopeful intricacies–Robert Hazel is one of the most interesting young poets now writing, and is almost alone in what he is doing. His political poems are devastating statements, as cuttingly crazy as can be imagined: the kind of thing that freedom of speech makes possible: the kind of thing that it is worth fighting wars to guarantee.

> Dear Myself,
> Today
> I heard music, drowned
> in sunlight and slaughterhouse blood
> and a strange sense of rubber
> tires rolling around
> the speedway without cars
> or drivers, because tonight
> after Hoagy Carmichael went back
> to the piano in the gym
> and Wendell Willkie returned
> to the Law library

my father called me in
from a war to put on the earphones
and listen to Berlin . . .

Mr. Hazel frequently connects in strange, hidden, and illuminating ways with the public and political life; about these matters he is both devious and direct, and almost always surprising, and surprisingly relevant, as if a kind of inspired numskull or village idiot were cryptically babbling things that everybody had suspected about politics and the international situation, but which no one had dared voice. Such moments are very valuable indeed, and make one reflect bitterly on the obtuseness of large publishers and the integrity of (some) small ones. Mr. Ostroff 's pale, decent stuff is deemed worthy of publication by one of the larger houses (albeit one whose poetic fortunes are steadily declining, since the editors have invariably, as by divination, picked the wrong poets of the younger generation), whereas Mr. Hazel's book–ten years of work, and one would think very hard work–comes to us, full of misprints, from some outfit called Eagle Editions in Morehead, Kentucky. Let the right readers now learn of the existence of Morehead, and of eagles.

Allen Grossman's book is also published by a very modest outfit, perhaps even more modest than Eagle Editions. This is from Mr. Grossman:

This is not solitude peopled by phantoms,
Imagined things to which some good adheres,
But rather critical vacancy
In which desire wells as from a sourceless fountain
And spills itself into a cloudy basin.

Notice how the adjectives in the last two lines pair off mechanically and don't do anything, and the superfluousness of "itself." Mr. Grossman is not a very skillful writer, and it would be easy to let that stand as a judgment on his work, were not more important things involved. Though there are many small empty vaguenesses in his book, none of it is slick, and some of it moves in a realm which is altogether Mr. Grossman's, as he takes the glory and the burden of his race on his back. Grossman is not writing deliberate "masterpieces" for seminars to admire, but is using language as a tool in a very difficult and perilous personal quest, which in his case amounts to a religious quest. He is Jewish, and this fact matters to him; it colors his poetry completely: every poem is, in some way, about God. The Prophets keep getting into the poems in odd ways that make one smile and at the same time catch one in a vital place. When Mr. Grossman says "I am a wilderness of springs and fountains," some people are likely to say "Tush," and go back to Mr. Ostroff. They shouldn't. Mr. Grossman is moving where it matters: he is speaking so fast and urgently, in his rather uninventive forms, that he hardly has time to get from one idea to the next, or to put titles to poems. Yet in all his lines there is an open, candid unhesitancy that accords well with the Biblical material, though in fairness it should be said that there is also an unfortunate tendency for internal rhyme to appear in the most unexpected and ill-chosen places. But hear this, especially the end and the things that make the end possible:

A tall woman picks her way among
Rotten stones
Who has minded the cooking pot the ten years
It has had no mistress, and handled the other
Common things, the flesh rake and the iron litter.

She has seen the grave of unknown thousands
Touched with one inadequate wreath, and has not
Stooped to add another flower, and yet
Her face has made a wanderer of me.

Mr. Grossman is not for all readers, but really good readers will find a great deal to move them in his little book.

III

From the first page of Paul Roche's *The Rank Obstinacy of Things,* wherein Mr. Roche refers to a brick (yes, a brick) "contusing the air," the reviewer knows he is in for a hard time: knows he must get ready to fend off wilful brilliances like so many wasps. When you hear someone speak of "tidy buttocks" (even though it is a reference to scissors, of all things), you know you are in the presence of that intolerable patronizing and very ordinary poetical swotting-up that should be stamped out with loggers' boots: you are once again among those little, *little* poems which purport to say infinitely much about small ordinary things, like nail-scissors and hair-brushes, with the poet showing you at every turn how much more he sees in these objects than you do, as he goes on cheerfully writing an endless series of cunning essays on Dean Swift's broomstick. Mr. Roche's work is trim, informed, and full of "examples," these latter being taken from the standard conundrums of scholastic philosophy and a smattering of the sciences, mostly biology and physics at the late high school level. Much of the book is filled with the attention-getting and shocking tastelessness and verbal insensitivity which the bad readers that bad poets deserve take for genius. In addition, Mr. Roche has not yet recovered from the pat playing-with-forms that the young delight and sweat in (to his credit, he delights more than he sweats) and the tendency toward the pat, transparent, solving-everything-solving-nothing ending. But he does have a teasing, perverse, boyish quality that gets to you when it probably shouldn't. This may well be the worst book of a bad year, but Roche himself, for better or worse, is living in it. There is a grinning, unabashed, world-brothering delight in his work that possibly shouldn't be lost; it may in the end come to something, on some other page.

Robert Pack's work has already come to something. Its first and very great virtue is its ability to feel and think at the same time, and its most telling subject is the mysteriousness and increasing depth the world takes on as the adolescent becomes aware of his sexual powers. The book has a strong sexual cast over it, but this subject is treated with tact, and is as far as one can imagine from being sensational. Though these lines are purportedly about Adam, they are really about Pack. The reader may be left to make other applications.

> And then, although he was not superstitious,
> It happened as he always knew it would.
> Beneath the first fruit tree, a draped figure,
> Featureless, shaped as by wind on water,
>
> Drew him down gently, whispering, "Come to me,
> I am the one!" His forked breath parted the wind,
> Like clothes fallen away, and there she lay
> Smiling with his eyes, his lips, and his fierce tongue,
>
> All grown young: his forked breath breathed apart
> Her foaming water-thighs, with the dark clenched between,
> His own, his calling dark, smelling of home,
> Where he leapt in the final spasm of first love.

Though this poem may gain *something* by the reader's holding the Adam-Eve-Snake situation in the back of the mind, it does not really need this; it needs much more the (male) reader's first sexual experience, and the feeling in relation to that is very powerfully and cleanly indicated. Mr. Pack has a fine ear, fine technical resources, a clear, uncluttered mind, and the capacity for both directness and depth. He is not tortured, but curious and responsive, and, above all, honest with and about his subjects. These are sterling qualities, but they would not come to what they do here without the compulsiveness of Mr. Pack's themes. They *make* this book, and the adolescent's deepening and infinitely perilous world is here given a treatment that is as mysteriously true, releasing, and troubling as the experience itself is, or can be. There have been few such convincing examples as *Guarded by Women* that childhood is one thing and adulthood another, but adolescence is a thing apart.

Anne Ridler is as feminine as Mr. Pack is masculine. She is less puzzled and more accepting than he; her pervading tone is that of a gentle, reflective mysticism, somewhat reminiscent of Kathleen Raine's. The danger of writing of this kind, where one automatically hooks up with the seasons, the sun, the stars, and so on, is that such an attitude tends to kill off the tension between opposites that characterizes the best poems and probably creates them. Mrs. Ridler is almost frighteningly undivided and certain of her small but infinitely important place in the general scheme; what her poems gain in assurance and scope, they lose in bite, in the capacity to involve us *in* their themes, for we tend rather to consider them, from a comforting distance, as mildly consoling sermons of no particular urgency or relevance to our real concerns. Her pantheism would be likely to come to more than it does, in my opinion, if it made sharper verbal distinctions. Mrs. Ridler has the unfortunate habit–and it seems like just that–of falling back on heavily emotional but indistinct verbiage which is in no sense worthy of her serene and sometimes profound imagination.

> Lovers whose lifted hands are candles in winter,
> Whose gentle ways like streams in the easy summer. . . .

One sluggishly responds, as one feels one is meant to do, but a yawn is implicit in the response; one longs to get on with it. Yet as a whole Mrs. Ridler's work is very distinguished indeed, with marvelous qualities of wide-awake, self-discovering stillness in it. If she can resist the *habit* of pantheism as a poetic device and explore its human possibilities in a little more telling detail, she will have no peer in the kind of poetry she is best suited to write. In the present book, one is aware that this is a human woman who is

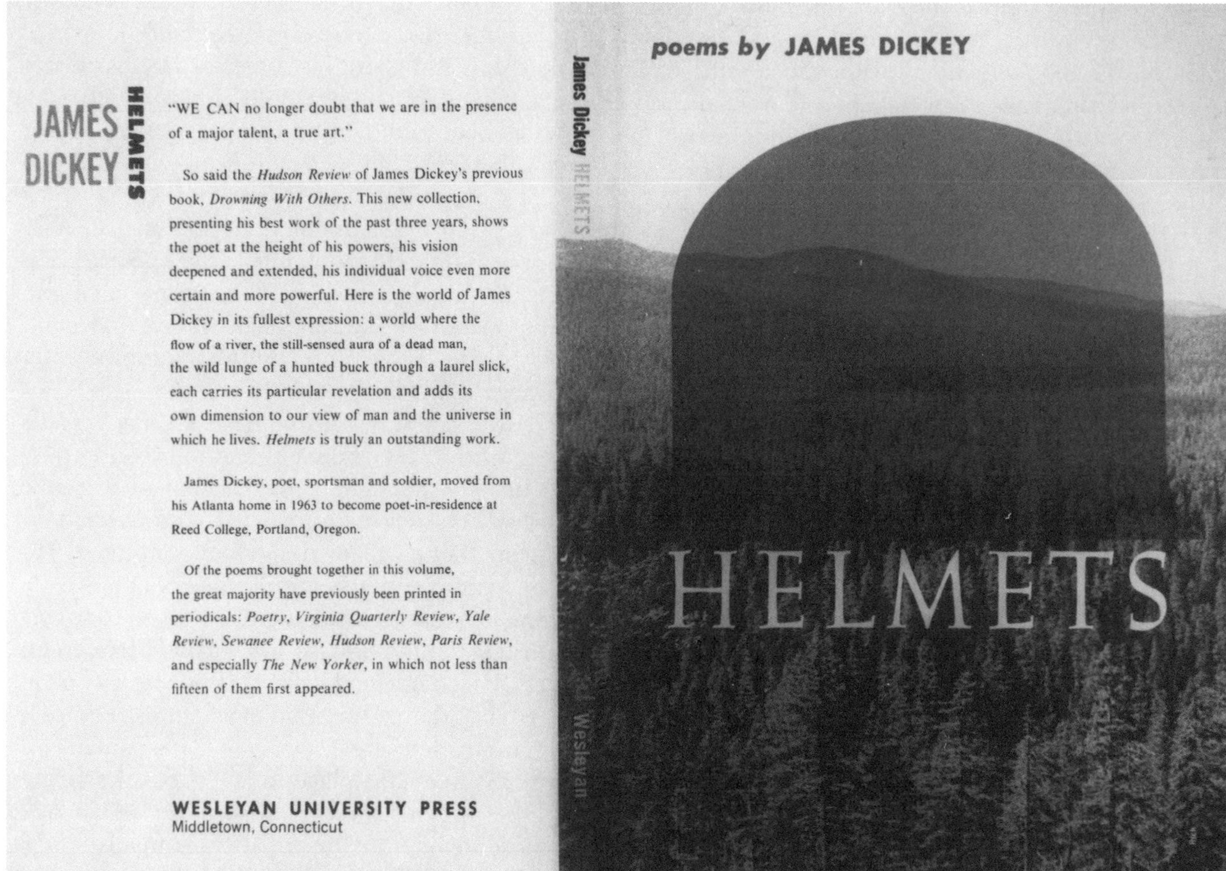

JAMES
DICKEY
HELMETS
"WE CAN no longer doubt that we are in the presence of a major talent, a true art."
So said the Hudson Review of James Dickey's previous book, Drowning With Others. This new collection, presenting his best work of the past three years, shows the poet at the height of his powers, his vision deepened and extended, his individual voice even more certain and more powerful. Here is the world of James Dickey in its fullest expression: a world where the flow of a river, the still-sensed aura of a dead man, the wild lunge of a hunted buck through a laurel slick, each carries its particular revelation and adds its own dimension to our view of man and the universe in which he lives. Helmets is truly an outstanding work.
James Dickey, poet, sportsman and soldier, moved from his Atlanta home in 1963 to become poet-in-residence at Reed College, Portland, Oregon.
Of the poems brought together in this volume, the great majority have previously been printed in periodicals: Poetry, Virginia Quarterly Review, Yale Review, Sewanee Review, Hudson Review, Paris Review, and especially The New Yorker, in which not less than fifteen of them first appeared.
WESLEYAN UNIVERSITY PRESS
Middletown, Connecticut
James Dickey HELMETS
Wesleyan
poems by JAMES DICKEY
HELMETS

Dust jacket for the American edition of Dickey's third collection of poems (1964), the first of his books to have also been published in England

blending with flowers and trees and sea-shells and the cycles of time, but if one were a little more aware of these facts, Mrs. Ridler's position in the poetry of her time would be not only distinguished but triumphant.

IV

The best thing about Richard Eberhart's *Collected Verse Plays* is that there is so much of Eberhart's verse in them. As prolific as he is, Eberhart never writes anything that does not have in it somewhere the spontaneous and wildly intuitive sense of personal discovery. Once one has ceased being irritated by Eberhart's curious and often unfathomable verbal eccentricities, one is delighted to plunge wholeheartedly into his world of furious, half-scholarly, half-primitive speculation: speculation as hilarious and bubbling-spirited as it is entirely serious, where the point is to arrive at the ultimate *reductio ad absurdum* of every idea: the world reduced–or elevated–by imaginative recklessness to its most humorous absurdity and comic seriousness. When one thinks of Eberhart's work, one also thinks of health, vitality, and the best kind of American "accessibility to experience," of an open and candid willingness to meet anything on earth on its own terms, submit to it, live in it recklessly, and write of it even more recklessly, as though there were no difference between the living, the thinking the living occasions, and the writing of it. Though the language in these plays and playlets is put into the mouths of a dozen or so different characters, it is all so obviously Eberhart's–the Eberhart of "The Groundhog" and "The Fury of Aerial Bombardment" we all know so well–that, without *seeing* that there *are* actually different people involved in the action, we are hard put to visualize or believe in their existence. The plays are mostly excuses for talk, for the brilliantly improvised kind of talk on metaphysics, on reality, on the spirit, on good and evil, that Eberhart invents as well as anyone alive. There is a great deal of wit

SCHEDULE OF MR. JAMES DICKEY'S OHIO CIRCUIT

Friday 29 Oct.	3:00 at Cleveland State Univ. Cleveland	Alberta T. Turner
	8:00 at Oberlin College Oberlin	David P. Young
Saturday 30 Oct.	At Kenyon College, Gambier	Robert W. Daniel
Sunday 31 Oct.	4:00 at the College of Wooster Wooster	Raymond G. McCall
Monday 1 Nov.	3:00 at Kent State Univ. Kent	Jacob Leed
Tuesday 2 Nov.	At Ohio University, Athens	Jack Matthews
Wednesday 3 Nov.	3:00 Denison Univ., Granville	Kenneth B. Marshall
	8:00 Ohio Wesleyan Univ. Delaware	Alfred Ferguson
Thursday 4 Nov.	At Miami University, Oxford	William Pratt
Friday 5 Nov.	At Wabash College Crawfordsville, Ind.	Donald W. Baker
Saturday 6 Nov.	At Earlham College Richmond, Indiana	Leigh Gibby
Sunday 7 Nov.	3:00 at Antioch College Yellow Springs	Laurence Eldredge
	Evening: fly to Washington, D.C. from Dayton airport.	William G. Thompson

Schedule of speaking engagements for ten days in 1965, what Dickey described as "Barnstorming for Poetry" in his 1965 essay collected in the 1968 volume Babel to Byzantium *(Author's private papers)* here, too, including some that doesn't come off because it is too crowded with Possibilities to allow its point to come through. The play that comes closest to being a *play* is "The Visionary Farms," a slapstick tragi-farce about big business in the twenties; it has (*I* think) some very effective scenes, and the verse works not only as verse but as dialogue. Yet I must conclude by saying that what matters to me most in connection with this book is that it is by Eberhart, and that the plays display the same qualities as the verse. For those who like Eberhart's mind, his ways with language both good and bad, his daring, his naïveté, and the odd and exhilarating mixture of language that misses but leaves you wishing it hadn't and language that succeeds in ways that nobody but Eberhart could have conceived of, this book is a rare one. There is a lot of Eberhart in it, and if you have this book and his *Collected Poems*, you have just about all of Eberhart. That, it seems, would be the main thing.

V

Lots of people have been to Mexico–I haven't–and have come back full of mysterious talk about it: about the "brooding landscape" so well caught in books like Malcolm Lowry's *Under the Volcano* (and doubtless others), about the odd mixture of cultures, the Indian myths, and so on. The literary travellers are baffled, some of them, by the embarrassment of riches, of material *for* poetry, that exists there. Why, they think, hasn't Mexico produced a poet to match, say, the painter Orozco? To those travellers–as well as to anyone else within earshot–I recommend Octavio Paz's *Sun-Stone*. The edition at hand is issued by the Contact Press in Toronto and translated by Peter Miller, but there is also an edition recently translated by Muriel Rukeyser and put out in New Directions' fine little World Poets series. It is not my wish here to draw comparisons between the two translations, but simply to point a finger at Señor Paz in *any* form (Spanish would be the best form, of course) and say *read*. Like Claudel and Perse, Señor Paz is a diplomat, and like them something of a cosmopolitan. Though he knows European poetry better than most Europeans, he is thoroughly Mexican, and understands his country from every conceivable angle: historical, geographical, psychological, metaphysical. The Sun-Stone of his title (and I am indebted to Miss Rukeyser for this information) is the Aztec Calendar Stone. Structuring his poem around this cyclic form, Paz has written 584 lines–no more, no less–corresponding to the number of days the planet Venus takes to complete its synodic period, and in so doing has attempted to encompass and body forth Mexico itself, the experience, the *meaning* of Mexico, relying largely on a curious and highly visionary surrealism that would not have been possible except for surrealism in its French form, but which Paz's French precursors would never have recognized or been capable of. The finest sections of the poem are not those where Señor Paz is invoking ancient gods and dealing with symbols, but where he envelops himself and the reader in the gorgeous tellurian panoply of the physical Mexico, that ancient new-world ground where life is more than life and the dead are deader than anywhere else.

> –nothing happens, only a blink
> of the sun, hardly a movement, nothing,
> there is no redemption, time does not turn
> backward, the dead are fixed in their death
> and cannot die another death,
> untouchable, nailed in their gesture,
> from their solitude, from their helpless death
> they watch us yet without watching us. . . .

The authority of this comes through even in translation: would come through, I believe, in *any* translation at all. Though my Spanish is not much, it is my impression that Señor Paz is rendered a little better in Mr. Miller's version, which does not try to reproduce the hendecasyllabics of the original. There may be a fable for translators in this opinion, but I am not inclined to point it out. Both translations are good *enough*, and their main point, as well as mine, is to bring you to Señor Paz's Mexico, a place which the literature of the New World will not willingly do without, now that it exists.

VI

The lawns are silent, the books closed, awaiting their placement on the shelves of one's "permanent library," courtesy of the journal that made them available. One drowses, thinking pleasantly of the hundreds of images in the thousands of words one has read, and beyond them to various Truths about the worth of the imagination, the integrity of the mind, of the personal response, but is finally inclined to let all that go, for once. What stays with him, carrying all these other things, is still his ordinary neighbor's image of the barges at Natchez, for the barges are bearing also Eternal Evidence of the secret and idiosyncratic response to things, which books of other people's poems can help and expand, but cannot replace. Growing sleepier and sleepier, the critic hears himself groaning, over and over, "Awakening, awakening." What kind of new life may just possibly lie hidden out *there:* out under the suburban, the American, the world night, under the most impossible circumstances? Impossible, but still conceivable? Sleep comes, and the poet–whoever he may be–steps from a sales convention out onto a river bank. Below him, far below, boats are moving in a fog, like . . . like . . . "I am awake," he says. "At last, by God, I am."

BOOK REVIEW:
Wendell Berry, "James Dickey's New Book," *Poetry,* 105 (November 1964): 130-131.

Berry's review of Helmets *(1964) illustrates both a thoughtful appraisal of Dickey's poems and the growing respect among established poets for Dickey's works.*

Going into this book is like going into an experience in your own life that you know will change your mind. You either go in willing to let it happen, or you stay out. There are a lot of good poems here. *The Dusk of Horses, Fence Wire, Cherrylog Road, The Scarred Girl, The Ice Skin, Drinking from a Helmet,* and *Bums, on Waking* aren't the only poems I thought moving and good, but they are the ones I keep the firmest, clearest memory of.

Thinking just of the poems I've named, I realize to what an extent sympathy is the burden of this book, how much there is of seeing into the life of beings other than the poet. The reader is moved imaginatively and sympathetically into the minds of horses at nightfall, of farmer and animals divided and held together by fences, of a young girl scarred in a wreck, of bums waking up in places they never intended to come to.

Drinking from a Helmet represents not the fact of sympathy, but the making of it. The poet moves from his own isolated experience of war into an almost mystical realization (and assumption) of the life of the dead soldier from whose helmet he drinks. A tense balance is held between the felt bigness of the war and the experience of the one young man.

Cherrylog Road is a funny, poignant, garrulous poem about making love in a junk yard. It surely owes a great deal to the country art of storytelling. It's a poem you want to read out loud to somebody else, and it's best and most enjoyable when you do.

But I think that Mr. Dickey is also capable of much less than his best. There are poems that seem to have been produced by the overstraining of method, ground out in accordance with what the poet has come to expect he'll do in a given situation. *Springer Mountain* will illustrate what I mean. The poem tells about a hunter who, on impulse, pulls off his clothes and starts running after a deer. I can't help believing that the power of insight and feeling that is the *being* of a poem like *The Dusk of Horses* becomes *equipment* in *Springer Mountain.* The poet seems to be using capabilities developed elsewhere, and to be using them deliberately and mechanically. The hunter's gesture, or transport or whatever it is, seems to have been *made* to happen, and isn't seen with enough humor to mitigate its inherent silliness and clumsiness. After a good many readings I don't yet feel I know how it is meant or what it means. And more than that, I have no faith in it, no belief that anybody ever did any such thing. It's like watching a magician's act that, in spite of a certain brilliance, remains flatly incredible.

Usually involved in the weakness of the weaker poems is a dependence on a galloping monotonous line-rhythm (nine syllables, three or four stressed, five or six unstressed, the last unstressed) that can be both dulling and aggravating. The point isn't that this happens, but that it happens often. And when it happens it acts as a kind of fence, on the opposite sides of which the poem and the reader either give each other up or, worse, go on out of duty.

But I want to end by turning back to the goodness of the book. There are poems here of such life that you don't believe they're possible until you read them the second time, and I've got no bone to pick with them.

BOOK REVIEW:
Robert Duncan, "Oriented by Instinct by Stars," *Poetry,* 105 (November 1964): 131-133.

Dickey's increasing exploration of what he called the "open poem" is correctly perceived in Duncan's review of Two Poems of the Air *(1964) as an important change in the writer's voice and works.*

I have been drawn to the poetry of James Dickey by two poems, *The Being* and *Drinking from a Helmet,* which tell of seizures or psychic

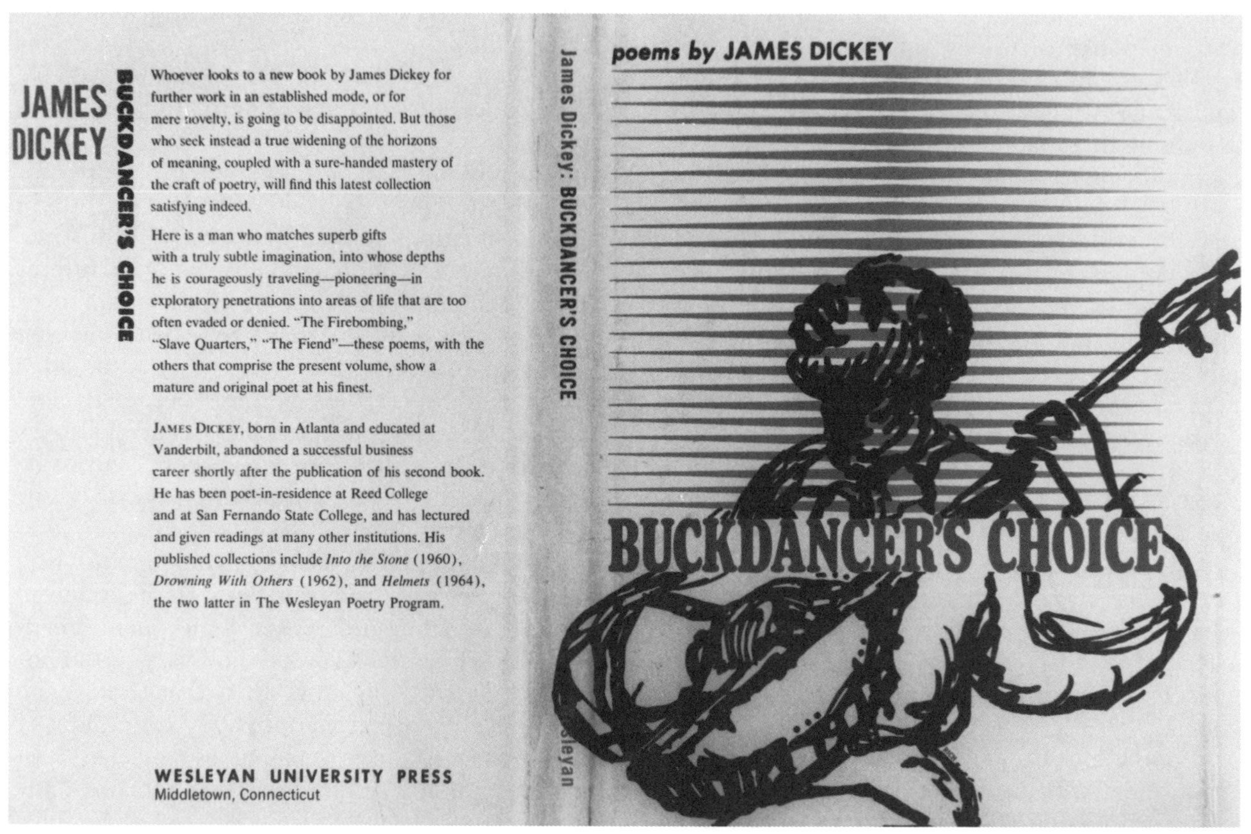

Dust jacket for Dickey's 1965 book, which won the 1966 National Book Award

invasions–"as if kissed in the brain"–where the erotic and the spectral seem to advance an initiation, as if he had passed a shadow-line that gave him a secret commission in poetry; to tell "where I stood, / What poured, what spilled, what swallowed," he resolves in *Drinking from a Helmet,* "And tell him I was the man." Not only in daily life or in dream but in the poetic process, in our art, the real strives to reveal itself to us, to awaken us to its orders. Wasn't that "infinite, unworldly frankness,/Showing him what an entire/ Possession nakedness is" that James Dickey knows in *The Being* a spirit of the same order, advancing from the imagination of his advancing, as that "glitter of a being/which the eye/Accepted yet which nothing understood" whom Stevens raised in *Chocorua to Its Neighbor?* Wherever the thought of the dead, of animal, human or demonic hauntings–the theme of popular spiritism–comes to him, James Dickey's imagination is stirred. In *Drinking from a Helmet,* the poet's prayer "directed to Heaven" goes "through all the strings of the graveyard"; in his earlier *Hunting Civil War Relics at Nimblewill Creek,* he tells us, "But underfoot I feel/The dead regroup"; or, in *The Being,* the visitant is not a living angel but a fallen or dead angel, for it moves "in the heat from a coal-bed burning/Far under the earth"–so, too, the visitant in Stevens's poem had been of a "fire from an underworld,/Of less degree than flame and lesser shine." I am moved by the suggestion throughout of the mysteries of Orpheus, the poet as hero who would charm the dead and the animal world with his music. In *The Being* he is "Given, also, renewed/Fertility, to raise/Dead plants and sleep-walking beasts/Out of their thawing holes."

In these *Two Poems of the Air–The Firebombing* and *Reincarnation*–James Dickey continues in his fascination with the spectral, but he has shifted from the tense verse and concentrated stanza sequence, the direct mode of a poetic experience and commitment, towards a more casual verse following a set story line, allowing even clichés of the supernatural tale: "My hat should crawl on my head/In streetcars, thinking of it,/The fat on my body should pale," the protagonist of *The Firebombing* tells us. The characters of the suburban householder who takes flight in his memory-fantasy of a wartime bombing mission over Japan and the office worker who takes flight in his reincarnation-fantasy as a migratory bird may relate to James Dickey's brief biography given in the Penguin *Contemporary American Poetry:* "He flew in the Pacific during the war and afterwards taught and worked for an advertising agency." But these stories of fantasies are themselves fantasies, where the characters and the things of the suburban world are taken for granted by a mind sophisticated to their advertised values in a commodity world and a wage-slave life "where the payments/For everything under the sun / Pile peacefully up." The firebomber would escape from "twenty years in the suburbs" "Blinded by each and all/Of the eye-catching cans that gladly have caught my wife's eye" into his fantasy of having "secret charge–/ Of the fire developed to cling/To everything" and yet picture his victims, as he pictures himself as householder, as "nothing not/Amiable, gentle, well-meaning/A little nervous for no/Reason." We are no longer here in a world like that of Wallace Stevens's *Chocorua to Its Neighbor,* whose shadow belongs to a poem for "the self of selves" or in the world of James Dickey's *The Being* where he tells us he was true to himself in some way he is not in daily life–"as he/Is only in visited darkness/For one night out of the year." The firebomber and the office worker are not persons of a self but social fantasies of alienation in conformity, of a world like that of Auden's *Age of Anxiety* or Ray Bradbury's fantasy fiction. Here the poet uses the poem to induce flight, as the firebomber induces his fantasy "by whatever means, by starvation visions" or as the office-worker induces his by "a word enabling one to fly/Out the window of office buildings" that "Lifts up on wings of its own/ To say itself over and over." The firebomber has no creative freedom but must carry out the bombing mission his fantasy demands; the sea bird must carry out his migration driven by instinct and directed by the stars, stronger than any self-creation; the poet carries out the story-idea his fantasy demands; immune by the superior orders of military command, mating instinct, or the story to tell, from that "kiss in the brain," the angel or messenger brings, from the creative ground of image, meaning and self, the real world is.

BOOK REVIEW:

William C. Strange, "To Dream, To Remember: James Dickey's *Buckdancer's Choice,*" *Northwest Review,* 7 (Fall-Winter, 1965-1966): 33-42.

Charles Monaghan, in the 15 April 1966 issue of Commonweal, *called* Buckdancer's Choice *the "finest volume of poetry to appear in the sixties," while Joseph Bennett, in the 6 February 1966* New York Times Book Review, *declared, "James Dickey's fourth volume,* Buckdancer's Choice, *establishes him as one of the most important younger poets of our time." Both Monaghan's and Bennett's reviews provide valuable comments, but Strange's review-essay offers a more thorough evaluation of the volume.*

Dream, memory, and poem are an ancient knot in a web of tempting correspondencies: image and event, possibility and necessity, wish and commandment, future and past. At one time or another and in various measure, all of these pairs have been used to explain that tense presence which is a poem, and they are still useful, permitting one to describe handily the tendency of modern poetry as a shift from memory and its coordinates to dream. Of course, there are exceptions. Old Ovid seems a poet of the dream while David Jones clearly writes for us out of a remarkable memory. Still, our time is distinguished by poet-theorists such as André Breton, who talks of *"l'homme, ce rêveur définitif,"* and we support with our prizes the *Seventy-Seven Dream Songs* of John Berryman. And when the drift of western poetry is seen in large perspective, as the pitch of its weight slips from heroic to lyric, then its direction is unmistakable. The Greeks called memory the mother of poetry; we moderns know a deep well of the unremembered where poetry and dreams are born.

James Dickey's most recent book, *Buckdancer's Choice,* stands out sharply in this context as a collection of modern poems in which one can feel both the lure of dream and the thrust of memory. In single poems and in the ordering of the whole, it displays a breadth of concern and a balance of energies that are notable in themselves and full of promise for the future.

Most simply, *Buckdancer's Choice* can be sorted into one set of recognizably modern poems that are dreams in fact or in technique and another set of poems that are "remembered" rather than dreamed. Indeed, this division is so much a part of this book that quite often a poem from one category will be paired off with a poem from the other. "Fathers and Sons," for example, consists of two poems printed together: the first describes a boy asleep and dreaming while his father dies, and the second a father haunted by his memories of a dead son. Other poems may not be so explicitly joined, but they, too, will draw together to enforce a balance between timeless dream and time remembered. "Pursuit from Under" and "Sled Burial, Dream Ceremony" or "Faces Seen Once" and "The Common Grave" cooperate in this way. However, the most striking moments in the dialectic occur when these opposites meet within one large poem such as "The Firebombing" or within a short and remarkably compressed piece like "The War Wound." One comes to read *Buckdancer's Choice* for such compounding poems as these, but the collection is best met in its simples.

Of the two categories, Dickey's dream poems are by far the less impressive. Sometimes they are too dependent upon other poems, even upon poems from other collections. "Sled Burial, Dream Ceremony" is scarcely intelligible without "Pursuit from Under," and "Fox Blood" drives us all the way back to "Listening to Foxhounds" and "A Dog Sleeping on my Feet" in Dickey's second book, *Drowning with Others.*" More often, these poems fail to impress because we know their moves too well. Dreaming transformations of men into appropriate beasts is old hat though Dickey can vary his tired totems effectively, reporting the metamorphosis as fact when it suits him, as in "Reincarnation," or using it boldly in "Gamecock" to stage a conceit. His style, too, is masterful, reaching with suitable ease to the brittle clarity of nightmare. And his bag of dream tricks contains all the turns of a neo-Freudian rhetoric: condensation, displacement, reversal, etc. Indeed, the more clinical these poems are, the more effective they seem to be. Witness the depth and power of Dickey's conception in "Them, Crying" where compulsion is his subject. In something less than eighty lines, he brings to life a truck-driver, "unmarried, unchildlike,/Half-bearded and foul-mouthed," who is drawn irresistibly to the children's ward of a large hospital by the sound of children crying *within him.* Or witness the perfectly realized counterpoint of hallucination and reality in Dickey's presentation of a voyeur in "The Fiend."

He has learned what a plant is like
When it moves near a human habitation   moving
closer the later it is
Unfurling its leaves near bedrooms   still keeping
its wilderness life
Twigs covering his body with only one way out   for
his eyes into inner light
Of a chosen window. . . .

The dreams of damaged minds seldom have been rendered better that this. But the real surprise is to find that Dickey can make of these clinical materials poems that are gracious and charming. Such qualities are not common in those whose work is the dream, be they poets or psychoanalysts, and they have been too rare in Dickey's earlier verse. But he broke through with "Cherrylog Road" in his last collection, *Helmets,* and he breaks through in this book with a poem such as "The Celebration."

This last is as clinical a dream poem as one could wish for. Surely, no tenets are more basic to the art of psychoanalysis than these: We all carry within us a record, written in scars, of the inevitable frustrations met by our growing appetites. Of necessity, these frustrations are usually sexual and often involve our parents. Adjustment, maturity, wisdom, or whatever you choose to call the achievement of a sound life, depends in part upon our becoming aware of past pain and its effects in the present; and this past is recovered most easily through the symbols that we dream. Now, Dickey could have tailored "The Celebration" to these propositions. In it, the poet describes himself moving through symbols to a quite literal anamnesis of his parents as lovers and then back from this vision of the primal scene to a new sense of himself and his responsibilities in the present. What the poet learns, he feels along the body more than knows–"[I] stepped upon sparking shocks/Of recognition when I saw my feet . . . knowing them given"–, but he does try to state what he has recognized as clearly and as directly as he can. He talks of learning to understand

the whirling impulse
From which I had been born,
The great gift of shaken lights,
The being wholly lifted with another,
All this having all and nothing
To do with me.

The final lines of the poem are even more explicit in pointing the moral of all this seeing: the poet sees and becomes as a consequence "a kind of loving,/A mortal, a dutiful son." It is hard to conceive of a poem more properly psychoanalytic in its recognitions and consequent moralizings.

The details which earn this recognition, making the "whirling impulse" known and truly told within the poem, also are heavy with the modern craft of dreams. In its first lines the poem looks like a phantasmagoria of lust:

All wheels; a man breathed fire,
Exhaling like a blowtorch down the road
And burnt the stripper's gown
Above her moving-barely feet.
A condemned train climbed from the earth
Up stilted nightlights zooming in a track.
I ambled along in that crowd. . . .

Most of us have met such carnal nightmares before, in the *Commedia* or in *The Rape of the Lock*, but this one is distinctly modern. More savage than Pope's, more narrowly psychological than Dante's, this fantasy is twin to the cases reported in Freud's *The Interpretation of Dreams* or to George Grosz's drawings of Berlin. Reason can stumble through this queer pastiche but is sent spinning when we find that all this fantasy is simple fact. The blowtorch-man is a fire-eater in a side show, the stripper just that, the condemned train a roller-coaster, and the crowded scene, Lakewood Midway at carnival time. With some care Dickey has led us into his poem, forcing us to see both the literal and the figurative dimensions of its sense, refusing to let us simplify.

In the second stanza Dickey quickly reasserts the figurativeness of the carnival setting. Just in case his realistic explanation of the hallucinatory first stanza may have been too surprising and too distracting, he makes another ride, the dodgem cars, explicitly figurative by using them as one term of a simile: "each in his vehicle half/In control, half-helplessly power-mad/As was in the traffic that brought him." After this reminder, the poem need not be so explicit with its images; Dickey has prepared us for the symbols that he must use. In the literal scene, the poet is walking quietly and alone in the carnival crowd when he sees with surprise that his mother and father are there, "he leaning/On a dog-chewed cane, she wrapped to the nose/In the fur of exhausted weasels." Age and sexuality are finely caught here as the phallic symbols of cane and wrap are modified by their worn, literal substance. More than anything else, it is precisely this shadow of sexual energy in his parents that surprises the poet. They are so old. What can they celebrate? "I believed them buried [that verb is no accident] miles back/In the country, in the faint sleep/Of the old, and had not thought to be/On this of all nights compelled/To follow where they led. . . ."

In the stanza which follows, similar details reinforce this effect of tired fact scarcely covering powerful fancy. His mother carries a teddy bear that is as insistently symbolic as a weasel wrap and dog-chewed cane; she holds it as if it were a child, and it was won for her "on the waning whip" of his father's right arm. The "crippled Stetson" which his father wears may not be so suggestive, except in its bobbing movement, but even here one could cite a section of Freud's dream book headed simply "A Hat as a Symbol of a Man (or of Male Genitals)." The poem's central image, of the old couple riding on a ferris wheel, needs no such footnoting:

They laughed;
She clung to him; then suddenly
The Wheel of wheels was turning
The colored night around.
They climbed aboard. My God, they rose
Above me, stopped themselves, and swayed
Fifty feet up; he pointed
With his toothed cane, and took in
The whole Midway till they dropped,
Came down, went from me, came and went
Faster and faster, going up backward,
Cresting, out-topping, falling roundly.

"The Wheel of wheels" is a perfectly apt description of a ferris wheel, but here it is also an intensive and a symbol. The cane, too, has become ambiguous with a new-old strength, for "toothed" may still mean "dog-chewed" but it suggests "possessing teeth." And all of the verbs that move these lines carry into them a phallic significance that nearly obliterates their letter. The whole passage is rich with a sense that scarcely requires glossing, even though it is this large image that elicits from the poet those attempts at direct statement our analysis began with.

But working our way up to these statements as the poem meant us to, we find that the lesson read is something more than a moral tag at its close. Recognition sparks within and without this poem, for "The Celebration" is peculiarly reflexive. Its images know themselves as they would be known, and the "whirling impulse" this poet sees, he teaches us to see, with all the fervent pragmatism of a revivalist. "Believers, I have seen/The wheel in the middle of the air. . . ." Though such language is borrowed from an old faith and testament, with some wit it calls a new generation of dreamers back to the constant task of prophecy: in omens find a responsible joy, and let it find you.

Believers, I have seen
The wheel in the middle of the air
Where old age rises and laughs,

The 1966 National Book Award winners–Arthur M. Schlesinger, Jr., Janet Flanner, Katherine Anne Porter, and James Dickey–with New York Mayor John V. Lindsay (third from left), who gave the welcoming speech at the awards dinner

And on Lakewood Midway became
In five strides a kind of loving,
A mortal, a dutiful son.

With this poem and others like it, Dickey seems to be saying to his contemporaries, "Look, I can do it too," and also "Look, how narrow this thing that we have done." "The Celebration" is a first-rate product of our time's craft of dreams, but it is also ours in ways that are not so admirable: in the passivity and in the privacy of its vision. Dreams happen to a person, and if you live in and for them, you wait and are paid for your waiting in coin of no man's realm. Clearly, a balanced art demands visions that one chooses as well as those that one is chosen by, and visions *of more than one's self.* Poetry, at least, should be dreams that one can trade in. Concern with the trap of solipsism, that Wordsworth and Sartre both know so well, and concern for a poetry that is performance as well as visitation run throughout *Buckdancer's Choice.* One finds it in certain implications of "The Celebration" 's moral close: in seeing others oblivious of me, I see myself and my responsibilities, my "duty." One finds it in the way that this small book is crammed with the full reality of other persons: generations of family, friends, an old teacher with a bad heart, a truck driver drowning in tenderness, a voyeur, a slaveowner, enemies from an old war, and victims. One finds it in Dickey's appetite for

those things that, once
Established, cannot be changed by angels,
Devils, lightning, ice, or indifference:
Identities! Identities!

in a context where these "Identities" are both the mathematics that Mangham teaches and the man that he is as the poet's remembering "establishes" him. One finds it, conversely, in Dickey's reaction to "an angel's too-realized/Unbearable memoryless face." One finds it, particularly, in his sense of memory as counter-weight to dream, public and willed, and in such poems as "Buckdancer's Choice."

Intended or not, the use of this poem as title piece flaunts such a book as John Berryman's *Seventy-Seven Dream Songs,* for "Buckdancer's Choice" is a song, too, but not a dream song. It is an old song that minstrels once danced to, shuffling and flapping their arms like stunted wings, and the poem remembers it as it was performed. The poem begins by recalling the poet's mother, "dying of breathless angina" but finding breath and life of a sort in whistling to herself "the thousand variations" of this one song. It also remembers the poet as a boy who "crept close to the wall/Sock-footed, to hear the sounds alter,/ Her tongue like a mockingbird's beak/Through stratum after stratum of a tone. . . ." Behind this spot of time lies another evoked by it: the house in which the boy listens is "barnlike, theatrelike," he is "sock-footed," and his mother's whistle calls up in him "a sight like a one-man band,/Freed black, with cymbals at heel,/An ex-slave who thrivingly danced/To the ring of his own clashing light. . . ." Together, these two moments of time past form a metaphor of sorts whose point is most immediately that time does pass. "For years, they have all been dying/Out, the classic buck-and-wing men/Of traveling minstrel shows;/With them also an old woman/Was dying of breathless angina. . . ."

But there are three faces to this metaphor–the minstrel's, the mother's, and the boy's–and only the first two are stained by death. The song speaks for each of them in different ways proclaiming

what choices there are
For the last dancers of their kind,
For ill women and for all slaves
Of death, and children enchanted at walls
With a brass-beating glow underfoot,
Not dancing but nearly risen
Through barnlike, theatrelike houses
On the wings of the buck and wing.

Choices and *risen* are the most difficult terms in this last and fullest statement of the metaphor. Clearly, they are meant to give the image its final shape by opposing the dying mother and the last dancer to the boy who does not die and, apparently, to the poet who remembers him with this poem. The alignment is clear, if not its sense. Why *choices*?

To choose is to be free, and the buckdancer is a freed slave who celebrates his freedom by dancing out "The thousand variations of one song," thriving all the while in the choices of his dance. His dying art remembered frees the woman who is slave to the nearness of her death, for his song is both a literal artifact making it possible for her to partake of a joy her dying body denies her and a kind of emblematic definition of its own use. Joy is the one song, but she simply cannot identify with it; rather, she must achieve her own identity as a kind of thousand-and-first variation of it. Art's long memory has saved for her the fact of joy, but she must join with it, finding herself in her own performance of this joy as a dancer finds identity in the strict measure of his dance or as variations find themselves in a sounding theme.

The boy and the poet who remembers him complete the literal scene by making something nearly heroic out of the invalid's ultimate lyricism. In listening to his mother "warbling all day to herself," the boy reverses the movement from minstrel show to muffled sickroom by transforming the house into a kind of theatre, while the poet remembering this three-personed song in his poem restores it entirely to the public domain so that we, too, may use it. Perhaps this is one justification for the poem's claim that the vanishing dancer and the dying woman are countered by a "risen" boy: the song she appropriates–and what could be more private than the "prone music" of an invalid's whistle–he takes back for himself and in time performs, that others may for the moment find themselves, and company, in "Buckdancer's Choice."

But "risen" makes figurative sense as well as literal, as it must when it involves even such mimic wings as the buckdancer's elbows suggest. At first glance, "risen" looks like more of that southern evangelical baroque that is such an engaging quality of Dickey's imagination, but here I think the religious implications are more precise and more serious. "Risen" is but the end of something that has been building from the first lines of the poem. For example, why should his mother's whistle have split the air into just "nine levels"? Is the number meant to remind us of the nine muses, or of the nine heavens through which Dante rose as the blessed were manifest to him under the conditions of space and time? When this same fracted air, in *terza senza rima,* is offered as proving "some gift of tongues of the whistler," the reference is more certainly religious and more illuminating.

Speaking in tongues is described several times in the *New Testament.* In *Acts* St. Peter defends the authenticity of the experience in terms which could suggest Dickey's poem: "your sons and daughters shall prophesy,/And your young men shall see visions,/And your old men shall dream dreams" (2:17). However, St. Paul's discussion of the gift of tongues seems more relevant to a reading of Dickey's poem. In *I Corinthians 14,* he develops at some length the distinction between tongues and prophecy that St. Peter hints at with his young prophets and aged dreamers. According to St. Paul, the man with the gift of tongues speaks in mysteries to his God; his spirit prays, but his understanding is not fruitful unless his words are interpreted for him and for others. To the unbelievers, speaking in tongues will seem testimony only of madness in the speaker. (In this context, the address "Believers, I have seen. . ." at the close of "The Celebration" acquires further ironic bite.) Describing his mother's whistle as a gift of tongues, Dickey draws heavily upon St. Paul's conception and even language, for St. Paul calls this a "speaking into the air" and expands his claim with a series of musical metaphors. More important, Dickey's reference seems to involve St. Paul's valuation of the experience: speaking in tongues is a valid gift of the spirit, but the gift of prophecy is much greater. The prophet is a tuned pipe and harp, a certain trumpet; he speaks to all for the sake of all. He is a bearer of public visions. If the old woman has received the gift of tongues, her son hopes for the gift of tuned speech, for the gift of prophecy; and in time he receives it, as this poem testifies most powerfully.

No wonder, then, that Dickey chooses "Buckdancer's Choice" as the title piece for this collection: it is a perfect emblem of the art he would achieve. Modern poetry has been content too long with an invalid's private song. Dickey is reaching once more for the time that was and the time that is to be. He is reaching for prophecy.

Dickey's verbal skills were always considerable; they have grown more sure. In his earlier books the fluent movement of his verse was overwhelmed at times by a surge of anapests, and diction was marred by conventional insincerities. Those poems had a brother dying "ablaze with the meaning of typhoid" and fell too often into the cadence of "O grasses and fence wire of glory/ That have been burned like a coral with depth. . . ." Now, such cadences are modulated by carefully indicated pauses within the line: "He has only to pass by a tree moodily walking head down. . . ." and his familiar elegiac and meditative vocabulary includes new tones, like the impeccable gaucherie of "Homeowners unite./All families lie together, though some are burned alive./The others try to feel/For them. Some can, it is often said." Still, these are not the clearest measure of Dickey's growth or of his achievement in this new book. Poems of real substance may be recognized by what they do to our commonplaces about poetry, not cancelling them out but making them more true than they were before. We have known for a long time that the modern poet seeks in "la plénitude du grand songe" for "memorable speech." The virtue of *Buckdancer's Choice* is to insist that the deepest dreams belong to languages not to men and that the best poetry is speech remembering.

PRESS CONFERENCE:
"James Dickey on Poetry and Teaching," *Publishers Weekly*, 189 (28 March 1966): 34.

Dickey received a National Book Award for his fourth book of poetry, Buckdancer's Choice *(1965). The Tuesday, 15 March 1966, presentation of the awards highlighted a week-long series of social and literary events. The awards ceremony was preceded by a press conference moderated by W. G. Rogers. The winners' remarks were excerpted in* Publishers Weekly.

James Dickey, winner of the 17th National Book Award in poetry for "Buckdancer's Choice" (*Wesleyan University Press*), is a tall Southerner, who will be consultant in poetry in English to the Library of Congress in 1966-67. During World War II and the Korean War he flew some 100 missions for the Air Force, for which he was decorated several times. Most of what Mr. Dickey had to say dealt with his role as a poet and teacher, but the mark of his military experience was on him, too, in his closing remarks.

On Teaching: "I like to teach very much under the right conditions (I'll just let that be a little mysterious)," Mr. Dickey said. "You can always learn from anybody you meet. The more you can get to know students, the more you can get them to open up. I don't know what the ideal life is for a poet or anybody else. I tremble to think of such a thing. But being paid for teaching will help a poet to survive as well as anything else. I hit the teaching profession like a thief and run."

A Poet's Social Responsibility: Asked to comment on the social responsibility of the poet today, Mr. Dickey, who is probably six feet four, said, "I begin to shake when people ask me questions of this sort." Mr. Dickey went on to say that he thought poets would do well not to approach poetry "from that angle." He suggested that instead of trying to bring about reform, poets should try to "express their vision of seeing." Much poetry of social reform, "written with the best intent, is so awful," he said. The poet should not allow too much "good will" to interfere with what he, himself, feels and believes. The whole business of what he does feel may shift, but the poet "has to go with the vision of a thing which he knows he had at the time he was writing about it."

On the Craft of Writing: "It has always seemed to me that language has something magical about it," James Dickey said. "Every time I sit down to write I have the most marvelous feeling of expectancy about what might happen. It has never seemed anything but a very great privilege to me to be able to write poetry. I was in the wars for so many years I've come to look at the rest of my life from the viewpoint of a survivor. To make the confrontation with a blank piece of paper is something of a personal miracle to me."

SPEECH:
"James Dickey's NBA Remarks," *Publishers Weekly,* 189 (28 March 1966): 35.

Dickey's acceptance speech at the National Book Awards dinner was briefly summarized in Publishers Weekly.

Mr. Dickey spoke with an engaging diffidence, remarking at the outset, "Most of you have never seen me before, and very likely you will never see me again," he remarked at the beginning. Discussing his poetry, he observed, in part, "I find that I write poetry because I want to know something–to come to know it, even if I have to invent what I know–by living with it on as many levels as I can, by being intimate with it, severe with it, angry with, baffled by it, in love with it. But what always emerges is the sense of its *importance,* or at least its importance to me, being quite literally all that I have."

ARTICLE:
From H. L. Weatherby, "The Way of Exchange in James Dickey's Poetry," *Sewanee Review,* 74 (July-September 1966): 669-680.

Weatherby's early essay is the single most important analysis of Dickey's central thematic method. Weatherby's study has provided the basis for later studies, which use his commentary as a point of departure or development. Weatherby recognized early in Dickey's career that the poet's vision involved a mystical exchange of identity between the Self and the Other–with humans, with animals, with inanimate objects–to gain a renewed perspective on his world.

At least one way of judging the quality of a poet's work is to decide how close he comes to realizing what he set out to do. In the case of James Dickey the intention is fairly clear–to find some light which is not "too feeble to show/my world as I knew it must be." The complexity arises when we try to show how, and how well, he achieves this.

The passage I have just quoted is from "The Owl King," which appears in the [1962] volume, *Drowning with Others.* It is neither so good a poem nor so good a collection as the subsequent ones, *Helmets* [1964] and *Buckdancer's Choice* [1965], which are our present concern; but in several of these earlier poems we find Dickey developing the images through which in the later poetry he is to go about seeing his world. A poem from the earlier collection which will serve our purposes very well is "A Dog Sleeping on my Feet." Here the situation is a simple one, but one which provides a vehicle for most of Dickey's recurrent themes. A fox hound is asleep on a man's leg, and the man is a poet, writing while the hound sleeps and writing about what is being transmitted from the dog's life into his own. "For now, with my feet beneath him/dying like embers,/the poem is beginning to move/up through my pine-prickling legs/out of the night wood,/taking hold of the pen by my fingers."

The result of this transmission is, we imply, the sort of poem Dickey wants to write, one in which the light is sufficiently strong to see the world as it *really* is. Moreover the poem makes it clear how the poet goes about getting this light, and, in seeing how, we get to the heart of all Dickey's poetry, early and late. The light seems to come from some rather mysterious process of exchange between a man and his opposites. In this poem and a great many others the opposition and exchange is between men and animals, but, as we shall see later, it may also occur between men who are opposed to each other by nationality, between the living and the dead, between men and trees, and even between men and wrecked machinery. However, in each of these instances, the same thing happens which occurs here between a man and a dog. Therefore this poem can be used as a key to what I would regard as the central pattern in all Dickey's poetry. By entering into the dog the poet participates in the dog's experience of the chase. . . .

However, as one can see immediately, there is more to the exchange than that. This experience is by no means a simple matter of a man's projecting himself into the beast for the purpose of understanding. The poem which is the product of the exchange presents not simply a dog's perception but a composite vision which is both human and animal at once. In other words the exchange is literally that–an entrance not only of man into dog, but also of dog into man. Dickey is careful never to let this fact out of our sight; the

This Week

1. Do two more drafts of May Day

2. Write two two-minute talks

   a. The American Family vs. the Husband's Job

   b. The Fantasy Life

(American husband: why is he so milked of himself, so denatured, so done in and negative) and so on. One mildly is surprised that he has a home, that he lives anywhere. Montherlant's "Strangeness" — But is this not a kind of poison?

Fantasy life: T E Lawrence quote. Reisman's "the enrichment of fantasy" Miniver Cheevy, Walter Mitty, the comic characters. This is why the secret life of Walter Mitty is one of the funniest stories every written, and also one of the saddest. Difference between fact and fantasy. How the self acts in fantasy, and how in fact. How would we be if we were really our own fantasy-selves? The few moments in our lives when this happens are the ones we remember. The personal and Platonic ontos on that serves us as model. The egotistical sublime, and so on. Some of the entries of Ned Rorem: the main feeling one gets is one of misery, despite the fact that the author is apparently pretty well-off, he is surely very handsome and young, and talented, sought after by the rich, recognized by his peers, and the rest. Life of Frost quote from. Drugs? — Dreams Huxley Arrival quote - Elder Olson -

3. Get Collected Poems ready from Wesleyan cut-outs. Send this and script of Falling to Lockwood for comment, meanwhile holding out May Day to finish.

4. Catch up with all important correspondence. —

whether or not a sustained kind of fantasy — with no worries and only excitement, meaning and value, interest — might not be better than what we have: "reality." We have brains that are capable of being influenced in this way. What about a complete surrender of the will, and an acceptance of the fantasy world as — if not "reality" — at least as preferable? —

the "new," the other self, the preferable, non-limited self. —

Dickey's work schedule, probably for late 1966. The poem "Falling" appeared in the 11 February 1967 New Yorker, *and "May Day Sermon" appeared in the April 1967* Atlantic *(Author's private papers).*

dog's immediate participation in violent scent and movement is fixed and stilled by his participation in the man's intellect. Notice, for instance, that the streams are "stock-still with the pressure of moonlight." In fact all the movement of the poem is motionless; the rushing in the dark ends in absolute, white stillness "on the brightness of paper." Moreover, the dog's running legs are the poet's "killed legs," asleep where the dog is sleeping on them; and this joint participation in sleep is itself important. For the exchange to become possible the opposites, the man and the dog, must die to each other. The dog must give up his immediate perception to the man and the man must give up his power of reflection, his power to fix and see, to the dog, so that in the giving and taking, the mutual surrender, a new and otherwise impossible point of view can be created.

What this new point of view sees is by no means new; in fact the paradox of motionless motion, the still point of the turning world, the perfect union of man and his opposites, the *me* and the *not me*, is what poetry always tries to express. Even Dickey's images, in this poem at least, are not very original. The still stream reminds one of Wordsworth's stationary blasts of waterfalls in Simplon Pass; the chase motionless on white is reminiscent of Keats's urn; and the terms in which Dickey presents the paradoxical relationship between animal life and rational death suggest Yeats's Byzantium poems. But the effort to resolve these paradoxes through the process of exchange which we have just examined may very well be unique with Dickey. If that is true it may be safe to say that he has achieved a new way of doing what all poets do or try to do in one way or another, for Simplon Pass, the urn, and Byzantium are all efforts to throw a light on the world which will show it as the poet knows it must be. . . .

Buckdancer's Choice contains the best poetry in the three collections. One reason for the improvement is simply Dickey's growing ability to make language do what it is supposed to do. However, in addition to this there is also in this later poetry a new sense of the consequences of the exchange. The dog wakes up and so do the man's legs; at that point the poet returns to human speech. The hunter in "Springer Mountain" gets back finally into his clothes. But to take the exchange seriously is to risk staying under, and the best poems in *Buckdancer's Choice* show an awareness of this risk.

Among the finest of these is "Pursuit from Under," in which the poet, through "the journal of Arctic explorers," is able to experience, in August on his father's farm, "the cold of a personal ice age," the terror of the killer whale who follows always "under the frozen pane,/turning as you do, zigzagging," until he finally shatters through and confronts both the explorers and the poet in their exchange of understanding with "an image/of how the downed dead pursue us." The explorers have had the vision of the snow, the poet the vision of the family field, but in the new landscape of the exchange the explorers know

> That not only in the snow
> But in the family field
>
> The small shadow moves,
> And under bare feet in the summer:
> That somewhere turf will heave,
> And the outraged breath of the dead,
> So long held, will form
>
> Unbreathably around the living.

And the poet knows that instead of walking barefoot "so that nothing on earth can have changed/ on the ground where I was raised" he will now have to "pitch a tent in the pasture, and starve."

Another sign that Dickey is aware of the danger is the presence in this last volume of a number of poems in which, as in "The Driver," the cost of the exchange makes it impossible. "The Firebombing" is one of these. The poet has dropped napalm on a Japanese village from cold blue heights of "aesthetic contemplation," and isolated in those heights he finds that he cannot enter "the *heart* of the fire." Even at the end of twenty years in his own suburban residence he is still unable "to get down there or see/what really happened." The reason?–that he has never been able to take upon himself the suffering of the Japanese as he could take upon himself the dreams of a dog or the head of a boar. He cannot imagine at his own "unfired door" a person burning, "with its ears crackling off/like powdery leaves" or "with children of ashes." In fact he can imagine nothing at his door that he hasn't lived with twenty years, and in that fact alone we see the failure of the exchange which is always between opposites–dead men and live men, the suffering and the secure. . . .

I suggested at the outset that at least one way to measure a poet is by how well he has realized his intentions. I suppose at this point it will be perfectly obvious that I think James Dickey is a very fine poet who has attempted to see his world in a remarkable way and has had considerable success in doing so. However, I hold one reservation which seems to me worth stating. The way of exchange is as dangerous a thing aesthetically as it is spiritually, and whereas Dickey's later poems show that he is fully aware of the spiritual danger, I am by no means sure that he has guarded himself sufficiently against the aesthetic. There is always something a little bit staged, exotic, preposterous, and consequently affected about Dickey's situations. All of them lend themselves to parody except those like "The Shark's Parlor" which parody themselves, and if a reader is tempted to giggle when he shouldn't it always means that the poet has fallen short of complete success. I am deeply moved by a poem like "Springer Mountain," but I cannot help being slightly amused at the same time by the softening, middle-aged man's running naked with the buck. In the same way there is something mildly preposterous about putting on cock's spurs and a boar's head in order to pray. As the language in the later poetry grows stronger there is less and less opportunity for the ludicrous, but even here there is sometimes a hint of it–something a little bit silly about pitching a tent in the field and starving with cattle all around.

The reason for this weakness in the poetry is that the kind of vision which Dickey attempts, and in part achieves, requires a great deal of the reader's imagination. By staring intently in a certain light you may eventually see your world as you know it must be, but you may also break under the strain of the staring. According to Christian doctrine, when Nature is redeemed through our Lord's exchange with the dead, men and sharks, lions and lambs, Japanese and Americans, the hunters and the hunted, will all lie down together in a new landscape under a light strong enough and constant enough to show us our world as we have all known always that it must be–and without any strain of staring. Short of that, poetry can, as we know, give us some anticipation of those "other worlds and other seas," but it has been only the very greatest poets–Dante, Spenser, Shakespeare, and possibly Yeats–who have managed it with complete success. Obviously any effort toward this vision that does not take into consideration the aesthetic equivalent of the passion and death is going to wind up sounding fixed and dishonest. For the poet as poet there can be no last-minute leap to the surface for air, no hesitation to undergo his sea change or enter into the heart of the fire. Short of that sacrifice a poetry which attempts such a vision will prove in the last analysis to be affected. That is why most great poetry is tragic, dealing only with the impossibility of the vision.

In his volume of criticism *The Suspect in Poetry*, which was published in 1964 but which contains reviews of contemporary poets published over a period of several years, Dickey sets up a standard of absolute honesty by which poetry is to be judged and according to which he finds most contemporary poetry lacking. Those elements which are "suspect" in poetry are those which readers cannot "believe in as 'reality' "–a "series of unbelievable contrivances, none of which has the power of bringing forth a genuine response." Exactly how unbelievable contrivance can become is amply illustrated by Dickey's examination of people like Allen Ginsberg, Thom Gunn, or Harold Witt, and I think it is indisputable that Dickey himself is considerably above them. On the other hand he has attempted something very difficult, and it seems to me that in doing so he does risk the very contrivance that he warns against. However, I feel sure that he must be aware of the danger himself.

BOOK REVIEW:

"Robert Frost, Man and Myth," *Atlantic Monthly*, 218 (November 1966): 53-57; collected as "Robert Frost," in *Babel to Byzantium*, pp. 200-209.

Dickey's first published commentary on Robert Frost was a review of Robert Frost: The Early Years, *the first volume of Lawrance Thompson's biography of Frost.*

"Belovèd" is a term that must always be mistrusted when applied to artists, and particularly to poets. Poets are likely to be belovèd for only a few of the right reasons, and for almost all the wrong ones: for saying things we want to hear, for furnishing us with an image of ourselves that we enjoy believing in, even for living for a long time in the public eye and pronouncing sagely on current affairs. Robert Frost has been long admired for all these things, and is consequently one of the most misread writers in the whole of American literature.

In Frost's case the reputation has come, at least to some extent, from the powerful additive of the Robert Frost Story, a secular myth of surprising power and tenacity: an image that has eaten into the rock of the American psyche and engraved Frost's very engravable face as in a kind of Mount Rushmore of the nation's consciousness. The "Frost Story" would, in fact, make quite an acceptable film script, even allowing for the notorious difficulty Hollywood has in dealing with writers. We enjoy wandering off, mentally, into a scenario of this sort, partly because we know that the main facts of the Frost Story, leaving aside the interpretation that has been put upon them, *are* facts, and also because the Story is and has long been something we believe in with the conviction accorded only to people and events in which we want to believe and will have no other way. Frost is unassailable, a national treasure, a remnant of the frontier and the Thoreauistic virtues of shrewd Yankeedom, the hero of the dozing American daydream of self-reliance and experience-won wisdom we feel guilty about betraying every time we eat a TV dinner or punch a computer. The Frost Story stands over against all that we have become, and hints with mysterious and canny authority that it all might have been otherwise–even that it might yet be so.

It is a dream, of course. To us a dream, surely, but also a kind of dream to Frost, and despite the authenticity of whatever settings the film might choose for its backgrounds, despite the rugged physical presence of Frost himself, any film made of such elements would have to partake of nostalgic visions. It might open, for example, with a sequence showing Frost moving among his Properties–apple trees, birch trees, stone fences, dark woods with snow falling into them, ax handles, shovels, woodpiles, ladders, New England brooks, taciturn neighbors–and then modulate into a conversation with Frost for that cryptic, homely, devious, *delightful* way of making sense out of life–any aspect of it–that the public so loved him for: his way of reducing all generalities to local fact so that they become not only understandable but controllable.

If one wanted to include chronology one might have a little difficulty in making Frost's life in England interesting, for aside from showing some of the places he lived in and visited and photographs of some of the people he knew, like Ezra Pound, Edward Thomas, and Lascelles Abercrombie, it would be hard to do much more than suggest his experiences there. Most of this part would probably have to be carried by voice-over narration, and might deal with Frost manfully being his Own Man, resisting being exploited and misinterpreted by Ezra Pound ("that great intellect abloom in hair"), and with his being a kind of literary Ben Franklin in Georgian England, uncorrupted and wary, delighting the jaded and oversophisticated with, well, his authenticity.

One might then work forward by easy stages into what everybody knows is coming: the great Recognitions of the final years, the readings, the lectures and interviews, the conferences with students and the press–thus affording more time for the Frost Talk–the voyage to Russia and the meeting with Khrushchev, and so on, all culminating in the Ultimate Reading, the Kennedy Inaugural and its little drama of the sunlight, Vice President Johnson's top hat, and the details familiar to those who watch great as well as small events on television. Another poet, Galway Kinnell, has written of this occasion:

> And as the Presidents
> Also on the platform
> Began flashing nervously
> Their Presidential smiles
> For the harmless old guy,
> And poets watching on the TV
> Started thinking, Well that's
> The end of *that* tradition,
>
> And the managers of the event
> Said, Boys this is it,
> This sonofabitch poet
> Is gonna croak,
> Putting the paper aside
> You drew forth
> From your great faithful heart
> The poem.

That drawing forth of the poem from "the great faithful heart" would be the end–how could you top it?–and everyone could leave the theater surer than ever that he had inherited something, some way of responding and speaking as an American, that matters.

To move from this drama of public appearances to Lawrance Thompson's *Robert Frost: The Early Years* is to move, if not wholly out of the myth–for Thompson is very much in its thrall, despite all that he knows of Frost's actual life and personality–then rather into the area of its making, and the reasons for its making. One cannot inhabit Dr. Thompson's book, even under the influence of the Story (or the film, for legends are probably all films of one kind or another), without ceasing to be comfortable in one's prior assumptions. As partial as it is, Dr. Thompson's account is yet the fully documented record of what Frost was like when he was not belovèd: when he was, in fact, a fanatically selfish, egocentric, and at times dangerous man; was, from the evidence, one of the least lovable figures in American literature. What we get from Dr. Thompson is the much less cinematic narrative (and yet, what if someone tried to film *this* Frost Story?) of the construction of a complex mask, a *persona,* an invented personality that the world, following the man, was pleased, was overjoyed, finally, to take as an authentic identity, and whose main interest, biographically and humanly, comes from the fact that the mask is almost the diametrical opposite of the personality that lived in and motivated the man all his life. Most of *Robert Frost: The Early Years,* which takes Frost up through his period in England, is concerned with the twined alternatives of fear and *hubris:* with Frost's desperate efforts to establish and maintain his self-image in the face of every conceivable discouragement, the period when he would quit any job–he quit a good many–go back on any commitment, throw over any trust or personal relationship which did not accord him the deference he persuaded himself he deserved. Dr. Thompson talks persuasively–though not, I think, conclusively–of Frost's need to protect his sensibility from crasser natures and desensitizing work, but one never really believes that this justified Frost's arrogance and callousness on the many occasions when they were the most observable things about him. These were the years of Frost's hating and turning on anyone who helped or cared for him, from his friends like Carl Burrell, who worked his poultry farm for him while he nursed his ego, to his grandfather, whose generous legacy Frost insisted on interpreting as a way of "writing off" the poet and "sending him out to die" on a farm that the grandfather actually purchased to give Frost a livelihood and a profession.

The fact that this is the "official" biography keeps coming back to one as one reads, and with this a recognition of the burden that must surely have been on Dr. Thompson's shoulders in writing it: the difficulty in dovetailing the author's bias in favor of his subject–for it is abundantly apparent that Thompson really does deeply care for Frost's work and also for Frost himself–and the necessity to tell what did in reality occur on various occasions. Dr. Thompson has large numbers of facts, and the first task of the biographer is to make facts *seem* facts, stand up as facts before any interpretation is made from them. One of the ways to do this is to be pedestrian, for the world's facts are pedestrian, and most of the time simply sit there saying over and over again, I am here, I am true, I happened, without any particular emphasis. Consequently there is a good deal of material like "at this stage the Frosts had an unexpected visitor, none other than Edmund J. Harwood, from whom Frost's grandfather had bought the Derry farm" and "another acquaintance was made that evening, a burly red-faced country squire named John C. Chase, the modestly well-to-do owner of a local wood-working factory, which turned out a variety of products including tongue-depressors and similarly shaped tags for marking trees and shrubs in nurseries." This makes for a certain monotony, but one is inclined to go along with it partly because it is the truth–the man's name *was* John C. Chase, and he *did* make tongue depressors–but mainly because it is a necessary background for the second and far more important of the biographer's tasks, that of interpretation. That part is primarily psychological, and if the protagonist has not chosen to tell either the biographer or someone else why he said or did something on a given occasion–and one must be constantly wary of taking him at his word–one must surmise. Dr. Thompson is very good at this, most of the time, but also at some points unconsciously funny.

> During her sophomore year, Jeanie [Frost's sister] suffered through moods of depression much like those which had beset her, intermittently, since her childhood days in San Francisco. Her spells of tears, hysteria, ravings, which caused her to miss more and more days of school, puzzled her mother increasingly. In the midst of one spell Jeanie was making so much noise that Mrs. Frost turned desperately to her son for help. Enraged, he stormed into Jeanie's bedroom, found her lying face down on the bed, turned her over, and slapped her across the face with the flat of his hand. Just for a moment the one blow had the desired effect: Jeanie grew silent, stopped crying completely, and sat up. She stared at her brother and then said, scornfully, "You cad, you coward." That was not Rob's only use of violence when trying to help his sister.

When other incidents indicate clearly that brother and sister absolutely detested each other, one has a certain hesitation in identifying "Rob's" motive as helpfulness. Yet it seems to me that Dr. Thompson's deductions are right a great deal more than they are wrong, and that is really all we can ask of a mortal biographer.

Frost was born in San Francisco in 1874. We watch him live through the decline and death of his alcoholic, ambitious father, follow him as he is shunted around New England as a poor relation, supported by his gentle, mystical mother's pathetically inept attempts to be a teacher. We see him develop, as compensation, a fanatical and paranoiac self-esteem with its attendant devils of humiliation, jealousy, and frustration. He considers suicide, tries poultry farming, loses a child, settles on poetry as a way of salvation–something, at last, that he *can* do, at least to some extent–borrows money and fails to pay it back, perseveres with a great deal of tenacity and courage but also with a sullen self-righteousness with which one can have but very little sympathy.

He wanted, and from his early days–Dr. Thompson makes much of his "idealism," learned from his mother–to be "great," distinctive, different, a law unto himself, admired but not restricted by those who admired him. He did well in high school when he found that good marks earned him a distinction he had never had before, but he was continually hampered by his arrogance and his jealousy of others, and after graduation seems to have been able to do little else but insult the people who tried to help him and accept and quit one humiliating job after another with as bad grace as possible.

During all this time, however, his writing developed, and in a remarkably straight line. He had, almost from the beginning, a flair for straightforward, uncomplicated versification of the traditional kind, and a stubborn belief that poetry should sound "like talk." He also apparently fastened very early on the notion that to hint is better than to say, and the idea that there are ways of saying, of seeming to say, both more and less than one seems to be saying.

Determining all questions of technique was his conception of the imaginative faculty as being essentially *protection,* self-protection, armor for the self-image. Looking back on Frost through the lens of Dr. Thompson's book, one finds it obvious that the mode, the manner in which a man lies, and what he lies about–these things, and the *form* of his lies–are the main things to investigate in a poet's life and work. The events of Frost's life, events similar to those experienced by a great many people, are not nearly so important as the interpretation he put upon them. The *persona* of the Frost Story was made year by year, poem by poem, of elements of the actual life Frost lived, reinterpreted by the exigencies of the *persona.* He had, for example, some knowledge of farming, though he was never a farmer by anything but default. Physically he was a lazy man, which is perhaps why images of work figure so strongly in his poems. Through these figures in his most famous pieces, probably his best poems–haying, apple-picking, mowing, cleaning springs, and mending walls–he indulged in what with him was the only effective mode of self-defense he had been able to devise: the capacity to claim competence at the menial tasks he habitually shirked, and to assert, from that claim, authority, "earned truth," and a wisdom elusive, personal, and yet final.

At his simplest, his most rhythmical and cryptic, Frost is a remarkable poet. In deceptively "straight" syntax and in rhymes that are like the first rhymes one thinks of when one thinks of rhymes, Frost found his particular way of making mysteries and moral judgments start up from the ground under the reader's feet, come out of the work one did in order to survive and the environment in which both the work and the survival prolonged themselves, leap into the mind from a tuft of flowers, an ax handle suddenly become sin itself, as when "the snake stood up for evil in the garden." This individualizing and localizing way of getting generalities to reveal themselves–original sin, universal Design, love, death, fate, large meanings of all kinds–is a major factor in Frost's approach, and is his most original and valuable contribution to poetry. Like most procedures, it has both its triumphs and its self-belittlements, and there are both good Frost poems and awful ones, not as dissimilar as one might think, to bear this out.

The trouble, of course, is that Frost had but little idea of when he was in a position to make an effective ("earned") judgment and when he was not. In the beginning he was cautious about this, but when the public spurred him on, he was perfectly willing to pronounce on anything and everything, in poems or out of them. This resulted in the odd mixture of buffoonery and common sense (but hardly ever more than that) of his last years.

And yet at his best, which we must do him the service of identifying as his most characteristic, he is perfectly amazing. We have all harbored at odd times a suspicion that the key to large Significances lay close at hand, could we but find it. Frost understood how this feeling could be made to serve as the backbone of a kind of poetry that was not only profound but humanly convincing as well, as most poetry, panting and sweating to be linguistically interesting, is not. One *believes* the Frost voice. That itself is a technical triumph, and of the highest kind. It enables the poems to come without being challenged into places in the consciousness of the "average" reader that have been very little visited before, and almost never by poems.

Yet it is well to remember, for all the uplifting force that it has legitimately, and illegitimately, been in so many lives, for all the conclusion-drawing and generalizing that the public has esteemed and rewarded it for, that the emotions of pain, fear, and confusion are the roots of Frost's poetry. Lionel Trilling, with his usual perceptiveness, has seen this, and seen it better than anyone else, perhaps even including Frost, ever saw it. Trilling's Frost of darkness and terror is more nearly the real Frost, the Frost permanently valuable as a poet, than any other, and it is in poems where these emotions fuse with his methods–poems like "Design"–that he moves us most.

What he accomplished, in the end, was what he became. Not what he became as a public figure, forgotten as quickly as other public figures are, but what he became as a poet. He survives in what he made his own invented being say. His main achievement, it seems to me, is the creation of a particular kind of poetry-speaking voice. He, as much as any American poet, brought convincingness of tone into poetry, and made of it a gauge against which all poetry would inevitably have to be tried. This voice endures in a few powerful and utterly original poems: "After Apple-Picking," "Provide, Provide," "To Earthward."

Dr. Thompson's authoritative and loving book makes clear that Frost's way was the only one open to him, and also the fact that, among other things, his poems were a tremendous *physical* feat, a lifelong muscular striving after survival. Though tragically hard on the people who loved him, put up with him, and suffered because of him, Frost's courage and stubbornness are plain, and they are impressive. But no one who reads this book will ever again believe in the Frost Story, the Frost myth, which includes the premises that Frost the man was kindly, forebearing, energetic, hardworking, good-neighborly, or anything but the small-minded, vindictive, ill-tempered, egotistic, cruel, and unforgiving man he was until the world deigned to accept at face value his estimate of himself. What price art, indeed? Dr. Thompson's biography has, or should have, the effect of leading us all into a private place–the grave of judgment, or the beginning of it–where we ponder long and long the nature "of life and art," their connections and interconnections, and the appalling risk, the cost in lives and minds not only of putting rhythmical symbols of ink on a white page, but of encountering, of reading them as well.

BOOK REVIEW:

Michael Goldman, "Inventing the American Heart," *Nation,* 204 (24 April 1967): 529-530.

Goldman's review of Poems 1957-1967 *(1967) provides an overview of Dickey's first five books of poetry, sections of which are reprinted in this volume along with new poems. In his review Goldman assesses the poet's maturing themes and techniques, concentrating on Dickey's increasingly dark, highly imaginative vision, which produces "terrifying poetry."*

One of the things we should mean when we call a poet "good" is that his work returns us to the world and not merely to the poet. We do not assimilate good poetry; we become included in its imagination. James Dickey is a good poet, very good. The appearance of this volume, containing most of his four previous books and a substantial amount of new work, makes it clear that by a continuing act of the imagination Dickey has penetrated a large and unfamiliar portion of the world. The life he establishes is fearful, often inhuman, but it is necessary because in it we recognize ourselves. He lifts something out of our experience that our mind has not yet been able to play upon, and frees us to encounter it.

Dickey's poems are remarkable for imagination, in the most literal sense, for their power of grasping and making images. But these are not the "images" the tradition of poetry has taught us to expect. They are neither minute visual notations nor elaborately constructed symbols. Here is the beginning of "A Screened Porch in the Country":

All of them are sitting
Inside a lamp of coarse wire
And being in all directions
Shed upon darkness

This is more than a type of high wit, more than a strikingly accurate piece of description. Dickey gives the moment a natural energy, not the energy of the poet's insistence upon his own personality but the energy of a vast life outside the poet which moves all things through one another and through him.

For many poets the image is a form of self-projection, a personal signature that they inscribe upon experience. For others it is a kind of affectionate clarity, a loving selective focus. But Dickey incorporates everything he sees into an image that is in motion, a momentarily complete environment flexing and warm like living tissue, within which he moves. It is as if the world about him became an animal, and he entered its body.

In "Cherrylog Road," the poet remembers how as a young man he made his way to a rendezvous through the abandoned hulks of an automobile graveyard. He goes from a Ford to an Essex to a Chevrolet:

None had the same body heat
I changed with them inward, toward
The weedy heart of the junkyard

His images are bodies within which he changes, moving toward a heart which is not his heart but a heart of experience–an animal center, usually dangerous. He moves mainly by water in the earliest poems, which are somewhat diffuse and "romantic" in aura, and in the very latest poems he seems increasingly concerned with movement through the air, but the movement is always into a realm where animal powers lurk, foxes or snakes or enemies, where the explorer becomes his exploration and the hunter puts on his victim's skin. Dickey returns again and again to the figure of a man putting on someone else's body, a hollowed-out boar's head, a suit of armor, a dead man's helmet. Even the spurs of the "Power and Light" man are like a gamecock's spurs; and of course the hero of this poem takes on power from the wires to which he climbs:

flung up on towers
walking
Over mountains   my charged hair
standing on end   crossing
The sickled, slaughtered alleys of timber
Where the lines loop and crackle on
their gallows.

And when the power and light man comes home and shuts himself in his basement to drink he feels a similar energy coming at him through the ground:

. . . in the deep sway of under-
ground among the roots
That bend like branches   all things
connect   and stream
Toward light and speech   tingle   rock
like a powerline in wind,
Like a man working, drunk on
pine-moves   the sun in the socket
Of his shoulder . . .
Far under the grass of my grave, I drink
like a man

The night before
Resurrection Day.

For Dickey, an image is like a special kind of clothing, a charged shape of the outside world that he puts on, in order to connect himself to the world's monstrous power.

The last section of the book is devoted to poems written since *Buckdancer's Choice* (which a year ago won the National Book Award), and here Dickey seems to confront the monstrous even more directly. There are a number of magnificent poems (particularly "Sustainment," "The Head-Aim," as well as "Power and Light"), and in most of them, some inhuman power possesses the human body. "The Head-Aim" discusses how to be an animal:

You must throw your arms
Like broken sticks into the alder creek
And lean to aim the head.
. . . This is the whole secret of being
Inhuman.

"The Sheep-Child" is about the legendary offspring of a farm boy and a sheep; the bulk of the poem is devoted to a speech by this "woolly baby" supposedly "pickled in alcohol" in a museum in Atlanta. Like many of the poems it is also concerned with the values that may rise out of our experience of the inhuman. The sheep-child says of the farm boys:

Dreaming of me,
They groan   they wait   they suffer
Themselves, they marry they raise their
kind.

Dickey attempts a more encouraging conclusion, with less success, in "Falling,"a poem about a stewardess who falls to her death from an air-

Dickey with University of South Carolina President Thomas Jones on the day of the May 1968 graduation ceremonies, at which Dickey delivered the commencement address, "Computerized Rape and the Vale of Soul-Making." The speech was first published in the Winter 1968 issue of the University of South Carolina Magazine *and later collected in* Night Hurdling *(1983)*

liner. It seizes the subject brilliantly and characteristically:

As though she blew

The door down with a silent blast from
her lungs . . .
. . . falling   living   beginning to be
something
That no one has ever been and lived
through

But at the end as the girl lies with a broken back in a Kansas field, Dickey tries to assert a positive value for the experience. She

Feels herself go   go toward   go
outward   breathes at last fully
Not   and tries   less   once   tries
tries AH, GOD–

By and large, Dickey is more convincing at terror than exaltation, but terror–as opposed to the nervous irritation for which so much of our poetry settles–is a rare thing in poetry, and it clears the heart.

A special quality in these poems–at least for another poet–is Dickey's surrender to his scenes. Today, poets frequently write about their surrenders–to pain, madness, drugs, anger, sex, nirvana–but their surrenders so often turn out to be seizures, spasms of the nerves and of the will. Dickey, "self-possessed in self-surrender," allows himself to register fully the terrible life that flows between the self and the world. He knows the world is the bigger of the two and that the self grows by exposure to it. It is his sense of the threat and alluring power of the world, which is also the threat and alluring power of the self, that governs his imagination and gives it a fearful energy. When he writes about a girl hideously scarred by windshield glass in an automobile accident he begins:

All glass may yet be whole
She thinks, it may be put together
From the deep inner flashing of her
face.

And in the opening lines of "The Ice Skin," he seems to be describing the very process of tragedy:

All things that go deep enough
Into rain and cold
Take on, before they break down
A shining in every part.
The necks of slender trees
Reel under it, too much crowned,
Like princes dressing as kings.

And the redwoods let sink their branches
Like arms that try to hold buckets
Filling slowly with diamonds
Until a cannon goes off
Somewhere inside the still trunk
And a limb breaks, just before
midnight,
Plunging houses into the darkness
And hands into cupboards, all seeking
Candles, and finding each other.
There is this skin

Always waiting in cold-enough air.

This succeeds not because the poet has tried to come up with an arresting string of symbols for tragedy, but because through his imagination he has included himself in tragic life.

In Dickey's poems there is very little of that secret dialogue among words, the sense of "words talking among themselves" that Auden refers to, which is the usual source of root vitality in poetry. His secret dialogue is among images–they flow into and transform one another, breaking out of the literal pattern and insisting on their own visionary, contrapuntal life.

Verbally, Dickey has all the breath he needs; his language is never exhausted and seldom inexact. Yet it remains true that what I have called the secret dialogue among words is a characteristic of the greatest poetry: every word infects every other word, impregnates every other word, bites every other word, makes a flesh with every other word–and it is this verbal power which, till now, has not been markedly present in Dickey's work. Now this is an *ultimate* power, very rare in its true form. It should not be confused with the mere appearance of verbal power, which may be contrived by any poet who is willing to devote his career to never taking risks. It has nothing to do with what reviewers call "the distinctive voice." We praise a poet for having a distinctive voice only when there is nothing else distinctive about him. Some poets may give us a svelte stuffed animal, but Dickey gives us the living mouth and lung and claw. And when his language takes on its own animal life, while still remaining transparent to the life of its images, we have a poetry that no active poet has bettered:

and wandered the lane of water

Upstream and home,
His bridle dragging, his saddle
Maniacally wrenched, stopping often to
drink
Entirely, his eyes receiving bright
pebbles,
His head in his own image where it
flowed.

Dickey's strangeness is peculiarly American (though I suspect that in the next few years it will prove very successful with foreign audiences). The "natural world" of America is very different from the natural world of, say, England, and yet when American poets come to write about nature, they write poems that are finally no different in method from English nature poetry. That is, they give us a *paysage moralisé,* more or less precisely noted, a landscape which reflects the human image. There may be disorder in it; we may even observe "nature red in tooth and claw," but even the chaotic is placed in a frame of civilized observation. Nature is observed by man, who seems always firmly anchored in the human world. This is the method of Herbert and Gray, of Keats and Yeats; it is also the method of Williams and Frost. The "nature" Frost observes often seems to lie at the edge of the inhuman American wilderness, but Frost deals only with what is at the edge, and always includes what he sees in a firmly moralized landscape. Whitman, too, sees nature in a human setting; it is a projection of his own inclusive self. But just as Dickey's typical use of the image is different from that of Whitman, Williams or Frost, so the poetry he produces is, at its most distinctive, like no other "nature poetry."

In Dickey's work, the inhuman is no longer contained in the human arena. He has created a poetry of American nature, a nature we recognize in Melville, in the documents of American his-

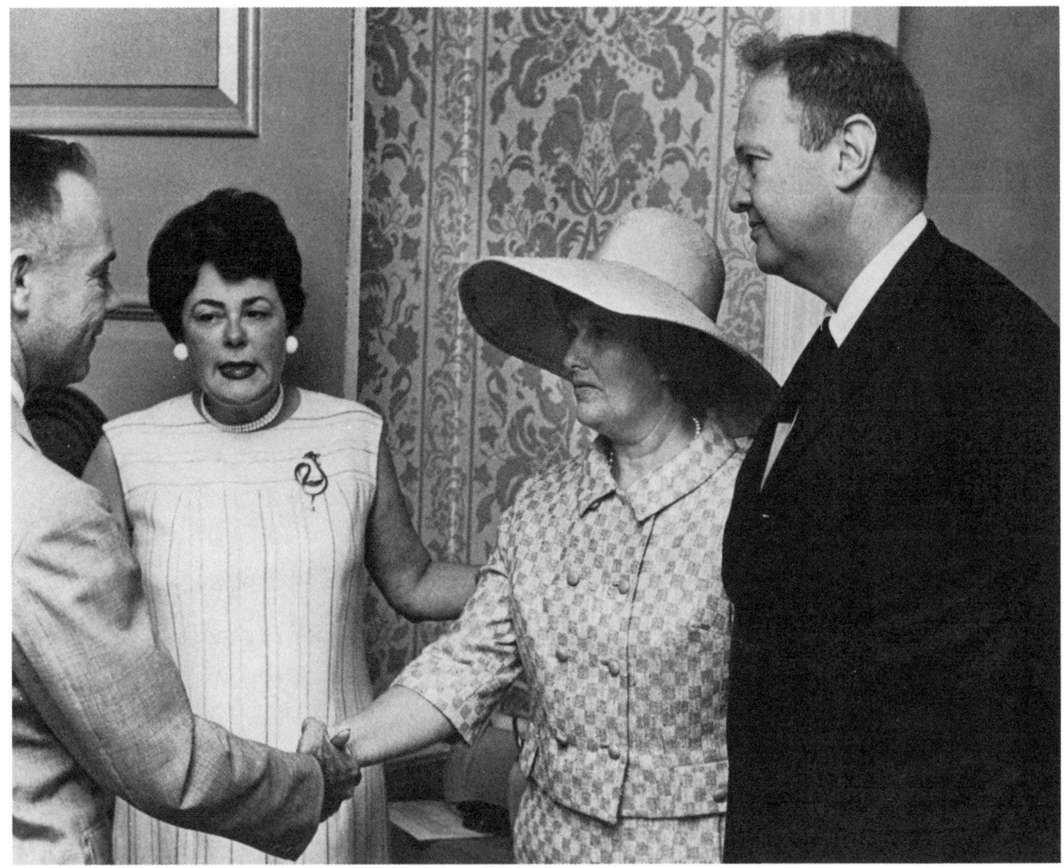

James and Maxine Dickey, with Mrs. Thomas Jones, greeting a guest at the reception following the May 1968 University of South Carolina commencement

tory, and in the daily papers. Its subject is the wilderness that was raped by the first settlers and has taken its revenge by continuing to dominate and excite our hearts. Dickey moves out into the wilderness, is contained in it, and runs with the animals. It is a terrible risk he takes, and it produces, at its best, a terrifying poetry.

ARTICLE:
Phil Casey, " 'Dazzlingly Simple' Poetry Is Predicted for the Future," *Washington Post,* 25 April 1967, p. A9.

Dickey was appointed the Poetry Consultant for the Library of Congress for 1966-1968. While in that position he delivered two lectures, "Spinning the Crystal Ball" (1967) and "Metaphor as Pure Adventure" (1968), and arranged for readings and lectures by many other poets. This article on Dickey's 1967 lecture reports his views about the demise of confessional poetry and the rise of an involving, affirmative poetry.

The poetry in our future will be simpler, said poet James Dickey, no doubt striking a spark of hope in every heart at Coolidge Auditorium last night.

But then he cooled it, confessing that his happy prediction was based largely on prejudice, guess and hope: in short, the way he'd like things to be.

"And if the speech turns out to be clairvoyant," said the tall, robust consultant in poetry to the Library of Congress, "I will be more surprised than any of you."

Clear-seeing or not, the 43-year-old poet conjured up a lovely sight:

"I think that the new poetry will be a poetry of the dazzlingly simple statement . . . a stark, warm simplicity of vision: the simplicity that opens out deeper into the world and carries us with it . . . We need that worse than we need anything else–not sensation, but feeling; mainly the feeling of ourselves. And any poetry that I want to read in the future will find its own way of conveying this basic, this irreducible sense of being."

Dickey, last year's winner of the National Book Award for Poetry, was lecturing in the Library's auditorium on "Spinning the Crystal Ball; Some Guesses at the Future of American Poetry."

It has been argued for years," he said, "that ours is a complex age, and that a complex age . . . demands a complex poetry. This seems to me to display what logicians call the analogical error. I think that the poetry of the future is going to go back the other way, back toward basic-sounding statements about them . . . aware all the time that certain constants must be affirmed, or not much of life will be worth anything. . .

"The great thing about poetry has always been that it can speak to people deeply about things of genuine concern . . .(but) the poem has become a kind of high-cult objet d'art, a 'superior amusement' as Eliot once termed it. I believe that the true poets of the future will repudiate that notion absolutely."

The new and important poetry will have, Dickey said, "a sense of the absolute basics of life, and for these the language of Eliot and Empson is not right. For this kind of poetry needs nothing more or less than the simple language of necessity . . . 'multiplicity of references' and 'richness of ambiguity' are no longer going to be the criteria by which the value of poetry is measured.

Dickey sees the possibility of a "tribal" or "folk" poetry, "something naive and utterly convincing, immediately accessible, animistic, communal, dance-like."

"Allen Tate once remarked that he thought of his poems as comments on those human situations from which there is no escape." Dickey said, "Well, there is no escape from the toothbrush and the rug that is wearing thin, or from the mirror in the hall and the dripping faucet."

BOOK REVIEW:

Paul Carroll, "James Dickey as Critic" *Chicago Review,* 20 (November 1968): 82-87.

Carroll's important review of Babel to Byzantium: Poets and Poetry Now *(1968) identifies Dickey's strengths as a critic and defends him against what Carroll regards as unjustified attacks, particularly on political or moral grounds, by other writers.*

After I talk about this collection of book reviews and essays on modern poets–which seems to me the sanest, most invigorating and most fun to read since Randall Jarrell's *Poetry and the Age* (1953)–I want to try and put into perspective a nasty attempt at poetic fratricide in which James Dickey has been the target. Why I bother with such dirty literary linen is simple: I want everybody to read and enjoy Mr. Dickey without the distraction encouraged by the scuttlebutt resulting from the attempt at fratricide, which was manufactured, for the most part, by envy, it would seem. Not only has James Dickey shown the unmistakable "blue sign of god on the forehead," as St.-John Perse describes the true poet, which holds the promise that we may have a major poet in our midst (indeed, why his collected *Poems: 1957-67* failed to win the 1968 Pulitzer Prize remains, to my mind, more baffling than the intricacies displayed in most of the theories regarding John F. Kennedy's assassination) but he also writes the kind of criticism I admire–namely, direct, personal talk about this poet or that poem in his or its own skin, as it were.

What commends the prose in *Babel to Byzantium* is similar to what makes the best of Mr. Dickey's poems memorable: the honesty and authority of the insight, unburdened by literary fashion or even by the critic's previous judgment; and the originality and power of the imagination at work on material that counts.

When I suggest that the insight is honest and has authority I mean that it is the last thing from that type of tidy, judicious opinion one reads (only during Lent, hopefully) in so many reviews and essays. One learns to trust Dickey to say only what he feels. What he feels can compel you, in turn, to reread a writer whom you may have dismissed as an adolescent infatuation or to open yourself to one whom you've never read. Of Kenneth Patchen for instance, Dickey says: "It is wrong of us to wish Patchen would 'pull himself together.' He has never been together. He cannot write poems, as this present book (*When We Were Here Together*) heartlessly demonstrates. But his authentic and terrible hallucinations infrequently come to great good among the words which they must use. We should leave it at that," he concludes, "and take what we can from him." Or of John Logan and the lack of wider recognition his work merits but hasn't received: "His strange kind of innocence, walking in and out of his ecclesiastical and literary knowledgeableness, is not an easy thing to talk about, though anyone who reads Mr. Logan cannot fail to be excited and uplifted by it." Then the insight blazes: "(Logan) is far beyond the Idols of the Marketplace and works where the work itself is done out of regard for the world he lives in and the people he lives among because he is helplessly and joyously what he is."

Fluctuating quotations on the literary stock market obviously do not interest Dickey. He refuses to take on faith alone, for example, the veneration afforded Charles Olson and his poetics of "composition by field" by some of the poets associated with the old Black Mountain College and by some of the Beat poets, as well as by some of the younger poets, longing, it would seem, for apostolic succession. Examining Olson's theory and its practice in *The Maximus Poems,* Dickey finds both second-hand and not too interesting news. But he is not out to hatchet another poet, granting that Olson's mind "seems to me quite a capable one, and at all points working hard to say what it has been given it. That is enough, because it has to be." On the other hand, J. V. Cunningham, John Frederick Nims, Elder Olson, and Reed Whittemore are treated as poets and not as "minor voices from the '40s." Nims, for one, is often dismissed by fellow poets and critics as a virtuoso. Not by Dickey: "Mr. Nims has worked hard for a good many years to achieve his style of unremitting brilliance, and it behooves us to look closely at what he is doing"–which he does, with care and energy.

And the originality and power of the imagination seem without equal, in my opinion, among practicing critics. "Opening a book by Robert Penn Warren is like putting out the light of the sun," Dickey observes, "or like plunging into the labyrinth and feeling the thread break after the first corner is passed." His is an imagination which leaps beyond mere critical insight: "One will never come out the same Self as that in which one entered. When he is good, and often when he is bad, you had as soon read Warren as live." Truths such as this, arrived at only through the imagination, occur again and again throughout this book.

In addition, Dickey almost always exhibits that rare gift: he is able to transcend a fundamental antipathy to some poet's work–which he describes, however, clearly and forcefully–and to discover what he feels is genuine in the poems. After arguing that Robert Duncan, for instance, is "certainly one of the most unpityingly pretentious poets I have ever come across," he also praises Duncan's "ingenuousness," the originality of his intellect, and several "marvelous" Duncan poems. Richard Wilbur, James Merrill, Allen Ginsberg, and Gene Derwood are other poets whom Dickey dislikes. In each, however, he finds nuggets of genuine poetry.

In brief, these book reviews of some 65 American and British poets are free of that myopia, parochialism and occasional smugness or patronizing tone found in much criticism. Instead, Dickey's reviews are clear-sighted, catholic in taste, and exuberantly respectful as only one poet can be towards the effort of one of his fellows. Best of all, Dickey ignores what he calls the critic's expected "System of Evaluation," which he is supposed to defend not only on its practical and local instances but in its broader theoretical and philosophical implications as well. On the contrary, Dickey explores only his immediate, existential experience of this poet or that poem. And he does so in clear, masculine prose. (His lack of a critical system is the only possible fault I can find in this book. As far as I'm concerned, however, such lack is a virtue).

In addition to the book reviews, there are longer essays on Edwin Arlington Robinson–a valuable discussion which I know will send me back to Robinson soon–and on Robert Frost–an analysis so accurate in defining both Frost's genius and his spiteful, egocentric personality that one feels like laughing and weeping at once. Then there are five good shorter essays on individual poems, ranging from Smart's "A Song of David" to Francis Thompson's "The Hound of Heaven" to Williams' "The Yachts." (An entire book on individual poems he loves would be a happy event, I think, from which everybody would benefit.)

Finally, three essays are grouped under the umbrella, "The Poet Turns on Himself." "Barnstorming for Poetry" delineates what it feels like for a middleaged man suddenly to find himself a literary lion overnight as he sings, staggers, and suffers from college to college during an exhausting, exhilarating reading tour. Every poet who has ever run such a curious gauntlet will read this piece with (what Melville called in a far different context, I'm afraid) "that shock of recognition." "Notes on the Decline of Outrage" should be read, and read carefully, by anyone who likes to think of James Dickey as a Georgia redneck. He isn't. What we come to know instead is a man, who was born white and raised in the Georgia of 40 years ago, trying to explore, as much in touch with his feelings as he can get, what it means *to him* to think about abandoning inherited, familial attitudes towards Negroes. What that man decides, as well as how he reaches the de-

Dickey, Carolina Professor of English and Poet-in-Residence, teaching a class at the University of South Carolina, fall 1969

cision, will not satisfy those addicted to easy abstract slogans; but I suspect the essay will be admired by those who care more about individuals than abstractions or clichés or finding a mirror which will reflect their opinions and prejudices. I know I admire the essay almost as much as James Baldwin's masterpiece, "Down at the Cross: Letter from a Region in My Mind," and for the same reason: both offer one man, feeling and thinking with his own heart, memories, and brains.

Now, I'd like to turn to the attempt at poetic fratricide mentioned at the beginning of this review.

"The Hunting of the Dickey" has become a popular, if vulgar, sport among a growing number of poets and poetasters. A few weeks ago, for example, I heard one of the younger poets, who is bright and well-read, dismiss Dickey as being the David Ogilvy of American verse. When asked if he'd read such magnificent Dickey poems as "The Sheep Child," "Slave Quarters" or "The Heaven of Animals," he admitted, rather sheepishly, he had not; even more depressing, the poet confessed that, due to bad-mouthing against Dickey he'd heard along the literary grapevine, he'd decided not to bother with the criticism collected in *Babel to Byzantium.*

Exactly what *are* Dickey's crimes or sins? I thought, after this melancholy encounter. Most of the charges I've heard poets make against Dickey seem to have been brought into melodramatic focus by Robert Bly in his well-read essay, "The Collapse of James Dickey" (*The Sixties,* Spring, 1967). In that piece, Mr. (I almost said Captain) Bly tries to secure Dickey to the yardarm and flog him because some of the poems in *Buckdancer's Choice* (National Book Award, 1966) exhibit "a gloating about power over others." According to Bly, this gloating manifests itself most clearly in such poems as "Slave Quarters"–that almost classic work depicting the sensibility of a contemporary white Southerner enmeshed in the cunning bondage of memory and fantasy of what an antebellum plantation owner might have felt–and in "Firebombing"–a long, often tedious poem which, with considerable honesty and power, embodies an attempt by a middleaged suburbanite to relive in memory the excitement and youthful virility felt when he was a bomber pilot flying missions over Japan in World War II. Both are poems of "memory and desire": haunting, masculine, poignant. Clearly the first is not the apologia pro rednecks Mr. Bly discovers, nor is the latter a paean to "the American habit of firebombing Asians." But Bly shows little interest in reading them as poems: instead, he chooses to bully poems into being flagrantly "repulsive" examples of what he claims is their author's moral leprosy.

The Bly essay concludes, then, with a libel against Mr. Dickey. The poet is branded as "a sort of Georgia cracker Kipling," presumably because he earns an annual $25,000 from activities resulting from his being a poet, publishes some of his verse in *The New Yorker,* allegedly supports the Vietnam war, and reveals himself in general as "a toady to the government, supporting all movement toward Empire."

Frankly, the Bly essay appalled me. How could a critic with his sensibility and extremely wide reading, I wondered, allow his argument to be grounded on the silly assumption that since the Dickey poems espouse few of the virtues cherished by white Northern liberals, the poems were "repulsive" and their author an Establishment stooge and moral pariah? Mr. Bly's essay is so shrill and wrong-headed that it almost seems unnecessary to recall that Ezra Pound and T. S. Eliot despised equalitarian democracy and, by implication, most, if not all, liberal goals; or that Apollinaire adored the war on the Western Front; or that Dante firmly believed that unless one were a baptized believer in the One, Holy, Roman, Catholic, and Apostolic Church one was destined for eternal misery in either hell or limbo.

Here, then, are the crimes for which Mr. Dickey stands accused by Mr. Bly and other devotees of "The Hunting of the Dickey" clan. In his poems, he explores feelings and memories of one man existing in his own flesh and bone, instead of using poetry to elicit attention by mouthing this or that current liberal or Far Left attitude about the Negro revolution or the Vietnam conflict. In addition, he earns a decent living for his family by doing what he can do with consummate skill: write poetry, read it in public, and teach it in the classroom. In other words, his crimes or sins are the ancient ones: talent, independence of attitude, and recognition and reward. Worst of all, he is only 45. Ten years ago, he was unpublished and unknown. Today, he stands as the first of his generation to have published a collected poems and a volume of criticism on modern and contemporary poets. Success is, as Ambrose Bierce reminds us, "the one unpardonable sin against one's fellows."

(Regarding Mr. Dickey's views on Vietnam, I know only that when we talked about that wretched war one afternoon in September, 1967, the poet said that, after a lot of hard thought, he hadn't made up his mind as yet. In my opinion, our involvement in Vietnam is murder–barbarous, immoral, infectious–and I told Dickey as much. But I also remembered that Camus refused to join the supporters of the Algerian rebels in 1957, stating that he hadn't made up his mind, thereby provoking vicious denunciations from intellectuals of the Left, including Sartre. Moreover, Dickey mentioned the possibility that he might become a speech writer for Senator Eugene McCarthy. What began as a casual acquaintanceship in 1966, when the poet assumed his responsibilities as poet to the Library of Congress, had matured into what Dickey implied was a closer relationship. At that time, he clearly was a McCarthy man; I don't know how he feels today, and it doesn't matter, of course, in so far as the irresponsible smear that he's a toady of the Pentagon and White House is concerned.)

I've spent time in describing this inept attempt at poetic fratricide by Mr. Bly–most of whose criticism and work as editor, translator and gadfly-at-large to the literary community, and whose exemplary public stands against the Vietnam war I admire without reservation–in order to say to him and to other members of "The Hunting of the Dickey" society, including that young poet: If you allow such popular but false images of James Dickey as "redneck" or "war-lover" or "careerist" to keep you from reading *Babel to Byzantium,* or from reading it with an unclouded eye, you'll be depriving yourself of criticism as it should be written. The man who wrote this book clearly loves and serves the god of poetry and the god's faithful disciples with (as the Baltimore Catechism prescribes with regard to another deity) his whole heart, and his whole soul, and whole mind, and whole strength.

NEWS RELEASE:
University of South Carolina, Department of Public Relations Office, 22 September 1968.

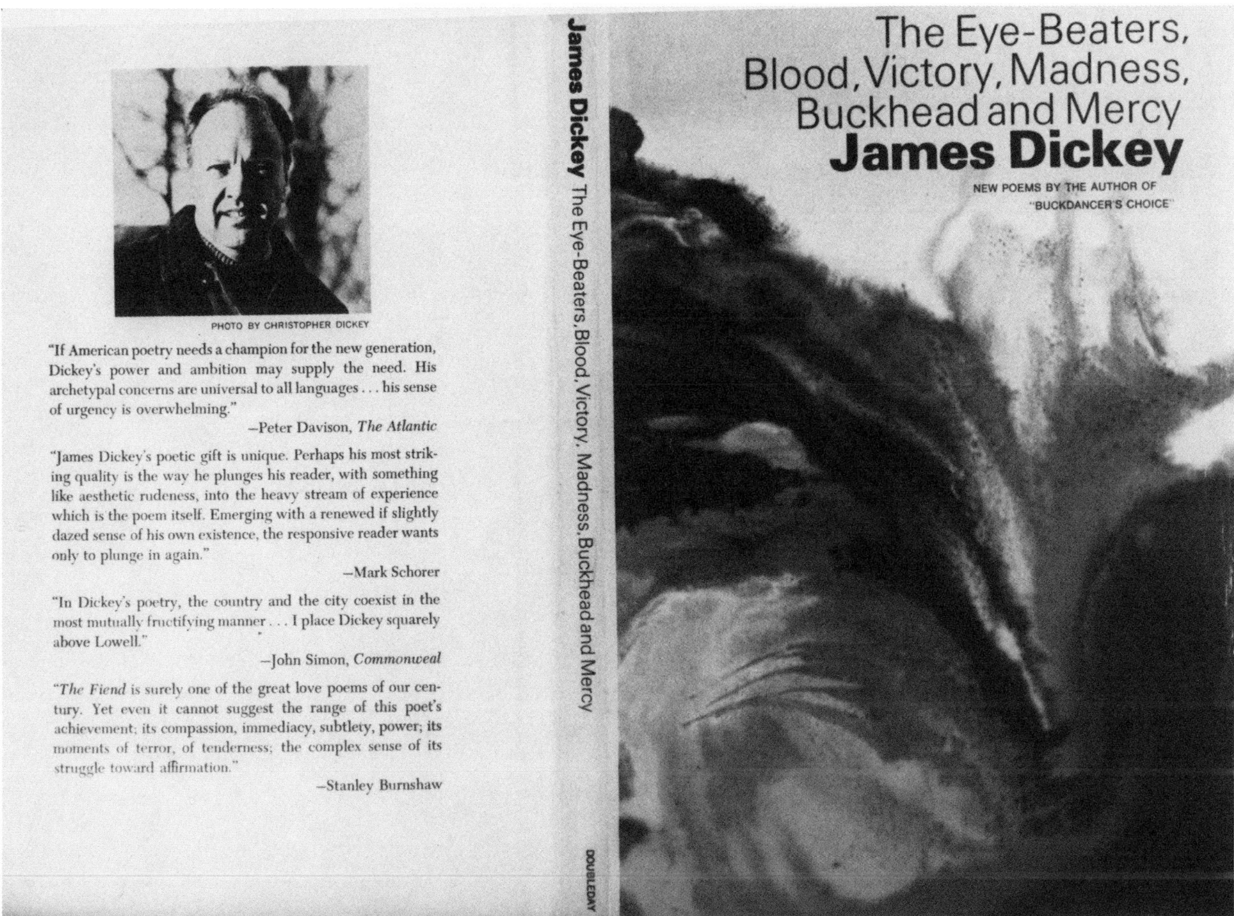

PHOTO BY CHRISTOPHER DICKEY
"If American poetry needs a champion for the new generation, Dickey's power and ambition may supply the need. His archetypal concerns are universal to all languages . . . his sense of urgency is overwhelming."
—Peter Davison, The Atlantic
"James Dickey's poetic gift is unique. Perhaps his most striking quality is the way he plunges his reader, with something like aesthetic rudeness, into the heavy stream of experience which is the poem itself. Emerging with a renewed if slightly dazed sense of his own existence, the responsive reader wants only to plunge in again."
—Mark Schorer
"In Dickey's poetry, the country and the city coexist in the most mutually fructifying manner . . . I place Dickey squarely above Lowell."
—John Simon, Commonweal
"The Fiend is surely one of the great love poems of our century. Yet even it cannot suggest the range of this poet's achievement: its compassion, immediacy, subtlety, power; its moments of terror, of tenderness; the complex sense of its struggle toward affirmation."
—Stanley Burnshaw
James Dickey The Eye-Beaters, Blood, Victory, Madness, Buckhead and Mercy
DOUBLEDAY
The Eye-Beaters, Blood, Victory, Madness, Buckhead and Mercy
James Dickey
NEW POEMS BY THE AUTHOR OF "BUCKDANCER'S CHOICE"

Dust jacket, with a design Dickey suggested, for his sixth collection of poetry (1970). The book includes such major poems as "Looking for the Buckhead Boys," "Messages," "Victory," and "Turning Away."

In 1968 Dickey was appointed to a chaired professorship in the English department at the University of South Carolina. The news release was accompanied by a statement from university President Thomas F. Jones. The Dickey family's permanent move to Columbia in 1969 was an important event for the writer for whom the concept of home had always been a significant subject. His essay "Why I Live in South Carolina," published in the April 1981 issue of Esquire *and reprinted in* Night Hurdling *as "The Starry Place Between the Antlers," develops the meaning to him of his South Carolina home.*

COLUMBIA, S. C.–James Dickey, one of America's most widely published poets, "has found a home"–the University of South Carolina and Columbia.

He and his family moved here Aug. 26 where he will be poet-in-residence and professor of English at USC, holding the Chair of Literature supported by the University's Educational Foundation.

Mrs. Dickey says their move to a permanent home in a pleasant Southern setting is a "culmination of a lifelong dream" for them. Dickey's latest position as consultant in poetry to the Library of Congress and his previous work have had the family "racketing around all over the globe" for 20 years, according to Mrs. Dickey.

Having just settled in Columbia, Dickey must go on the road again for at least another four months. He will fulfill obligations for the Franklin Foundation lectures at the Georgia Institute of Technology in Atlanta Sept. 26-Dec. 5. succeeding such guests as former University of Chicago Chancellor Robert M. Hutchins, poet Mark Van Doren and novelist Robert Penn Warren.

He will spend two weeks after that at Washington University in St. Louis, Mo., where many of his writings are "libraried." Then, it's back home, Columbia.

Turning Away

If you have said the thing
You must have said, to make
Another's face fall like a shadow,
Then you must turn away,

Turn away to a window or wall,
Or turn straight into the sun
Which burns like a vision of judgment,
Or turn to the depth of a wood.

Whatever is there is bright,
And will be saved from time;
~~As long as you both shall live.~~
The framed wind flowing

Onto your plaster features,
The blank stone looking
Through you and finding nothing,
The still wood finally stirring

All through itself with your breath,
As though the breath were held,
Were held, but could not be.
Now, with your head coming back

Around the room, and back
From the trees, the wild
Eternal stone, and the sun
Of judgment, you dread to find

Nothing where everything fled
The hurt you need not have given.
And it may be that on turning
Back from turning away,

You learn what love can endure
As a face displaces the wood,
The light of the sun, the wall,
The world that pain holds bright

And timeless as its best work
Of art, as great and as empty,
And that one you believed
Slain by a word, is standing

Harmed, but the same, the same.

Two early drafts of the final poem in The Eye-Beaters *(Author's private papers)*

Turning Away

I

(warm)

If you have said the thing
You must have said to make another's face
Fall like a shadow,

Then you must turn away,
Turn away to a window or a wall
Or turn straight into the sun.

Whatever is there is bright,
Too bright, like a final judgment:
The framed wind flowing

Onto your calm, disowned features,
The blank stone looking upon you
As though creating you wrongly,

The still wood distantly stirring
For lack of words.

What have I said in this light
Your face like a shadow fall
And I must turn away
Turn away to a window or a wall

What have you said, or not said
One after the other, the darkest
Expressions like shadows fall
And you must turn away
Turn away to a window or a wall,
Or turn straight into the sun.

II

Now, with any gaze coming back
From the trees, the frantic
Intelligent stone, from the sun

Whose light came through your eyes and left
No image, you dread to find
Nothing where tenderness fled

(visible appropriate)

The hurt you need not have given:
Turning back from turning away
You may learn what love can endure

As a visage displaces the wood,
The wall, the light of the sun,
The pain that makes the world bright

(intense)

And strange as a lived work of art,
As great, and as empty,
And that one whom I had believed

Slain by a word, is standing
Harmed, but the same, the same.

Dickey is writing again, too. After some break, he is working on some poetry, as well as completing a novel, while enjoying a few weeks "at home."

Several of his poems will appear soon in The Atlantic and in Harper's. Houghton-Mifflin will publish his book.

Dickey, not altogether new to the state, as he played freshman football at Clemson University in 1941, brings his family–wife Maxine and two sons–to Columbia from a 150-year-old federal brick house in Leesburg, Va. . . .

STATEMENT BY PRESIDENT THOMAS F. JONES
ON APPOINTMENT OF MR. JAMES DICKEY

It is a high compliment to our University and the fine people of our State that our nation's leading poet has chosen to make his home with us.

James Dickey is both a great poet and an outstanding personage. He radiates an infectious enthusiasm for the true values which make life in our society meaningful and really worthwhile. He can be counted on to be a strong and positive influence on campus life and life throughout our State.

The University is deeply grateful to the Educational Foundation of the University for its assistance in making possible a suitable Chair of Literature for Professor Dickey.

BOOK REVIEW:
Richard Howard, "Resurrection for a Little While," *Nation,* 210 (23 March 1970): 341-342.

One of Dickey's earliest advocates, Howard has commented on the poet's development through the years. In "On James Dickey," which appeared in the Summer 1966 Partisan Review, *Howard identified Dickey as "the telluric Maker Wallace Stevens had called for in prophesying that the great poems of heaven and hell have been written and the great poem of the earth remains to be written." Howard's review of Dickey's sixth volume of poetry,* The Eye-Beaters, Blood, Victory, Madness, Buckhead and Mercy *(1970), extends his view of Dickey as a poet of the earth, a figure caught between the hell of death in its various guises and the heaven of winning a qualified triumph over despair. Nineteen-seventy proved to be one of Dickey's most productive years, for in addition to* The Eye-Beaters, *he also publishd his first novel,* Deliverance, *and his nonfiction* Self-Interviews, *and he saw the release of the Encyclopaedia Britannica film about him,* Lord, Let Me Die, but Not Die Out.

Those who come cold to this new collection–a dozen extended texts playing fast and loose with a handful of intended emblems–will not, at first sight, be warmed. The look of these poems on the page is disconcerting: forms are sundered, wrenched apart rather than wrought together; rhythms are an inference from the speaking voice rather than a condition of it; lines are spread or sprung between margin and gutter to produce luminous, layered walls of print, a Rothko of language, often aerated by great white holes; or else the rifted phrases, cunningly enjambed, are centered, one over the other, to erect a column of symmetrical deformities, a kind of shaped prose. *Long lines in the air,* Dickey calls them, and like Blake's prophecies, their mere aspect intimidates–willed to the end, spacious enough to accommodate death-defying leaps of revolution, spare enough to collapse upon a single word.

As a poet of five incandescent volumes amassed within a decade into a monument (*Poems 1957-1967*), as a critic whose appetite and opinions range, indeed, *From Babel to Byzantium,* as a winner of the National Book Award, as a Consultant in Poetry to the Library of Congress, and preeminently as an athlete of the *personal appearance* (what other kind? what less? as he would ask)–James Dickey has seen to it that not many of us will approach his work cold. The very persistence of such solicitude as his may have chilled some readers, may have caused them to come, by now, cool to the ebullient career. But whatever the temperature readings among Mr. Dickey's readers, I should like to hover briefly over the situation of his poetry as it was so handsomely packaged three years ago, before having a look at recent manifestations, further developments.

Renewal, transcendence, ecstasy–he has sought these things in his own person, and by any means, at all costs. At all costs to the art as well as to the artist's life, Dickey seeks and speaks for a triumph over death, a transformation within the merely mortal body, praying somehow to live, convulsively, explosively, beyond the norms of utterance. It cannot be socialized, this vision, it cannot even be shared–it can only be given, given away, given over. Abjuring myth and even narrative, foreswearing ritual and even recurrence, the poet has recast the entire process of poetry as he himself has practiced and proved it into an ecstasy without fixtures, an awakening without constants, a sublimity without negation.

Sleeping off the light/of the world . . . what could I do but make the graveyards soar? James Dickey now asks–though there is a charged assertion in the "question" as the poet puts it, *like a king starting out on a journey/away from all things that he knows.* This new book is clamorous with unknowns, with quittances, with relegations: *How the body works/how hard it works/is not everything: everything is how/much glory in it. . . .* And though there are recapitulations, too, inferences from the old imperial phenomenology: *I thirsted like a prince/ then like a king/then like an empire like a world/on fire*– though there are echoes, contaminations of the mineral litanies of moon and stone which had led to the wrong ecstasy (wrong because unchanging, unrenewed): *On magic ground/of the dead new world . . . in the universal playground/of stones . . . we walk, our glass heads shimmering with absolute heat/and cold . . . We will take back the very stones/ of Time, and build it where we live*– though there are rueful and middle-aged invocations to sport, punning imageries of physical prowess: *out over water and back/to earth . . . that is all, but like all joy/ on earth and water,/in bones and in wings and in light/ it is a gamble. It is play*– there is in this latest, glancingly titled volume a gaining emphasis on release, on regeneration and renewal out of suffering and failure itself, out of the flagging and the painful and the hindered, which makes against any sustained performance, any consistency of practice in the art: *we are this world: we are/the only men. What hope is there at home/in the azure of breath, or here with the stone dead secret?*

From a fallen life, an aging body, a disgraceful age, Dickey craves not identity nor even delectation but *Deliverance,* as his new novel is called, and his impatience with the procedures of tradition (*tell me what I need to know about my time/in the world . . . light me a torch with what we have preserved/ of lightning*), his fury with the delations of biography (*the mad weeping Keeper who can't keep/a God-damned thing who knows he can't keep everything/or anything alive: none of his rooms, his people,/his past, his youth, himself,/but cannot let them die*), explore the meaning of his search even as they no longer exploit but merely explode the means.

No poetry of our time is so determined upon exaltation, no poetry of our time is so exposed to debasement. The wonder of it, and the reward, is the success in submission (*so have you changed to this*), the assent which turns to ascent: *Companion, if we climb our mortal bodies/high . . . we shall find ourselves/flying with the life/of the birds of death;* the assumption of mortality, darkness, torment (*pure triumph, pure acceptance*) which positively "enables" transfiguration: *the words written after the end/of every marriage manual, back/to the beginning, saying/Change; form again; flee.*

When it is said that a man has fallen, as I have said it of Dickey and as he so often says it of himself, though he says that he is falling, our latest Lucifer, *falling back/back to the body-raising fire . . . back from the dark side/of the mind*–when this world is called a fallen world, what is meant is that our soul, our aspirations, our hungers have collapsed into our present body, our present landscape, and that the instruments of our transcendence are at the same time the tools of our undoing; *resurrection for a little while,* as Dickey laments and exults.

Visiting a home for blind children and inventing a fiction of archetypal reversion to save his reason, in the most exorbitant, and inevitably the most intimate of all his title poems, "The Eye-Beaters," Dickey affords a clue if not a key to his extravagant, his excessive creations; what we merely see is not enough, yet the fictions–the poems–by which we might beguile our blindness are not the case (*Indeed I know it is not so/I am trying to make it/make something/make them make me/ reinvent the vision of the race/knowing the blind must see/by magic or nothing*).

These contradictions between life as we know it to be and life as we make it up for ourselves (*I have put history out*), these terrible reversals of what is given and what is taken, generate for Dickey–he tells us straight out: *I pass beyond in secret/in perversity and the sheer/despair of invention*–a transcendental poetics of the fallen world, a phenomenology of light and darkness, rising and falling, burning, turning and submitting (to list his five favorite gerunds) which can accommodate any experience, even the most trivial, the most degrading, or the most grandiose–such as being the Luce Publications laureate on the occasion of the moonshot.

I. A. Richards once said that poems have been written on mountaintops during thunderstorms, but not good poems; nor is Dickey's "Apollo," addressed to us from the mind of an astronaut on the moon, a "good poem." But addressed to us from the mind of James Dickey it is a great poem, a hymn of recuperation, a reiteration in the original sense of the word, a going-over, from the merciless perfections of death to

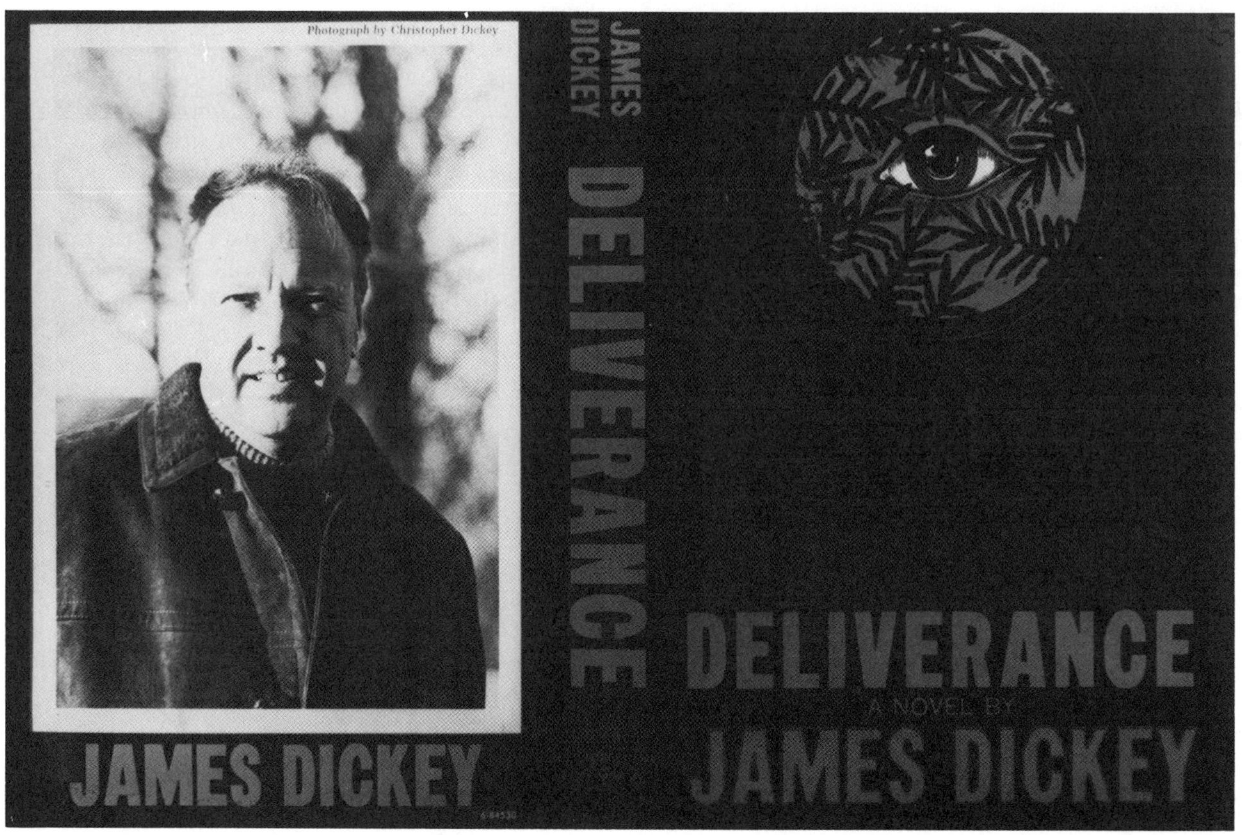

Dust jacket for the first edition of Dickey's 1970 novel, which was a best-seller and a critical success.

all the chronicles of diminution which star this book: "Diabetes," "The Cancer Match," "Madness," "Venom," "Variations on Estrangement."

It is not the Pentagon-primed scapegoat who speaks thus, but the poet of natural consummation, traveling *back through the last dark/of the moon, past the dim ritual/random stones of oblivion, and through the blinding edge/of moonlight into the sun/ beholding the blue planet* [earth] *steeped in its dream of reality, its calculated vision shaking with/the only love.* Consummation, the burning of the world and the fulfillment of a sacred marriage–that is the analogy of all Dickey's poetry; that is what he makes of the moon, or of the return from the moon: *a final form/and color at last comes out/of you alone putting it all/together like nothing/here like almighty / glory.*

In the unfallen world, which is to say in the risen world, the world where there is no contrast between a man's desire and his power, in what Blake calls Eden, there are two fundamental processes of the imagination, warfare and hunting. In the fallen world from which Dickey seeks deliverance, these processes are perverted into different kinds of murder; though as far back as "The Heaven of Animals" Dickey had articulated the intuition of a transfigured being: *at the cycle's center/ they fall, they are torn,/they rise, they walk again.*

My references to Blake, in characterizing the look of Dickey's new poems as well as their license, are merely a response to Dickey's own lead. In a glorious new poem of hunting, "The Lord in the Air," Dickey quotes Blake, who tells us *to make a friend and companion of these Images of wonder.* Dickey ends "The Eye-Beaters," moreover, with the line *bring me my spear.* And it is in Blake's spirit that Dickey celebrates his son's hunting in this poem, gloating when the boy blows a wood whistle that will lure the crows to *meet the Lord/of their stolen voice in the air,* exulting that a man has the power *in a sound like warning, like marriage . . . to call out the black birds, but not for betrayal, or to call/up death or desire, but only to give give what was never.*

In the unfallen world to which these poems always allude, to which they sometimes approach, and which they even, at appalling moments, create; in the risen world, then, hunting and warfare become struggle and search, as Blake saw in his Titanic vision of Orc piercing into *the elemen-*

tal Planets and the orbs of eccentric fire, of the Creator God twisting the sinews of the Tyger's heart. That is the consummation of these texts which insist upon anguish and madness, which in their very presentment on the page rehearse mortality. It is James Dickey's achievement, a great achievement even for him, to see the risen world "through" the other one, through an *enormous green bright growing No/that frees forever.*

The cost to his poetry is tremendous, for it has cost him the poems themselves–there are not poems here, I mean to say, there is only–only!–poetry; the cost to himself he reckons up in a terrible litany of losses: an *everyday–a livable death at last.* What is gained is that giant utterance, the expression of a state wherein *the earth's whole history blazes/to become this light/for you are released to all others,/all places and times of all . . . dead, immortal, or coming.*

BOOK REVIEW:

Donald W. Markos, "Art and Immediacy: James Dickey's *Deliverance,*" *Southern Review,* new series, 7 (Summer 1971): 947-953.

Dickey's first novel, Deliverance *(1970), achieved a widespread popularity among readers. The novel remained on the best-seller list for months, and two years after its appearance the Warner Brothers movie–for which Dickey wrote the screenplay, suggested the musical theme "Duellin' Banjos," and acted the role of Sheriff Bullard–proved equally appealing. The movie received an Oscar nomination for the year's best picture. The novel's popularity, however, caused some difficulty in literary circles, since an assumption exists that a popular work is probably not a "serious" one. Yet, just as one of Dickey's avowed purposes has been to restore the narrative to poetry, so too did he employ the dynamic narrative of his novel to explore significant themes. Markos's comments about* Deliverance *suggest not only how the novel achieves its power and depth but also the critical shortsightedness of some reviewers. At present,* Deliverance *is widely acclaimed by both general and scholarly readers. The novel has also achieved an international audience, having been translated into more than twenty-five languages and having won France's Prix Medicis (1971).*

I must waive at the outset the critic's usual tone of detachment and state that few books have emotionally gripped me the way James Dickey's *Deliverance* has. I hesitate to call it a great book because the scope of its experience is too narrow, its characterizations too thin; but it is a remarkable book, an intense book. It is a book that can make your hands cold; and the book should be spoken of in this way, for intensity of experience is what the book is about. Dickey is a master at describing unusual sensations and actions. But he is a redskin with paleface perspectives. His novel is not without literary sophistication in its conscious handling of theme and point of view. In fact, Dickey has performed the unusual feat of turning a formula for a popular novel into a serious work of fiction.

Benjamin DeMott, reviewing the novel for *Saturday Review* (March 28, 1970), considers it "an emptily rhetorical horse opera played in canoes," "the experience as a whole . . . weightless, silly, soft." True, the elements of mindless popular fiction are there–adventure, violence, brutality, homosexuality–but these elements are an integral part of the book's meaning. DeMott places Dickey in what he calls the "more life" school, including writers like Norman Mailer whose romanticism takes the form of a pursuit of intensity at all cost–the same mindless craving, according to DeMott, that afflicts society at large. Indeed, the novel shares with our times a fascination with intensified and distorted states of mind. The canoe trip is in some ways a "psychedelic trip," with visions of a lone chicken head floating in a river of feathers (near a poultry-processing plant), of grotesque attackers, of an owl's claw thrust through the top of the tent, of the moonlit river seen from the dangerous height of a scaled cliff. But what DeMott fails to see is that the novel itself qualifies the search for sensation; it is aware of the limitations of the "more life" attitude of its would-be superman, Lewis Medlock, although it is certainly more sympathetic to the "more life" craving than to the "no life" stagnation of suburbia.

There is some truth in DeMott's objection that the weakness in Dickey's poetry is the "poet's inclination to regard a poem as a contrivance for the display of one particular attitude–that for living into the edge of force present in any given moment of being"; yet I believe his review of the novel is misleading and unfair. Not only is the novel more freshly and intensely alive than most of Dickey's poems; it is more wise. The poems are usually about sensational subjects–snake poisonings, rapists, bombings, accidents–heightened by fantasy and surreal imagery. Always present is a self-conscious reminder–explicit or implicit–that the experience is not routinely normal. The poems are not without reflection, but the emphasis is clearly on immediacy, on closeup identifica-

11.

September 14th

I woke up Friday strangely excited, coming forward slowly in the weak chill darkness of the room with Martha beside me, her head wrapped in a towel against sinusitis. I had no wish to touch her warm, comfortably overweight body, but thought instead of the girl we had photographed, and of the mote in her eye, a more penetrating fragment of herself because she was almost naked. She was the figure standing in the center of impossibility, and that made her important, mythical. She was better this way than in the flesh, and I touched her shoulder again in memory, this time feeling the sexual charge she hadn't carried before. Yet independently of that image, and leaving it, as it were, in bed with Martha's heavy form, I got up and walked into the living room. It was half-lit dark; the moon was gone from the floor and windows, and the soft shining around the house did not seem to come from any source, especially any source in the sky, but from the world itself, going into the pine trees in the back yard and becoming more and more exactly their shape, glowing neither inward nor outward, but standing and holding that light. I stood looking at one of the few dawns I had seen in the last ten years, and Martha came out of the bedroom in a frilled lumpy gown, frowned questionin at me, and continued on into the kitchen. I dressed in the living room in a nylon flying suit I had bought at Army surplus: nylon dried out quick, I had been told. What gear I had was piled on the sofa. I had an old sleeping bag, also bought at Army surplus, which my little boy usually kept in his room, a Japanese-made air mattress and hand-pump. I had also bought seventy-five feet of nylon (dacron) rope because someone had once told me never to be in the woods without rope. On top of all this lay the bow. It was a good one, though the laminations were beginning to tire a little, letting a few fibreglass splinters rise off the edges of the upper limb. I had four reconditioned aluminum target arrows in a bow-quiver taped to the bow, for I wanted to be able to carry everything in one hand, and I had no back-quiver anyway. I had tried to camouflage the arrows with black and green house-paint, making long random slashes up and down the shafts, and had sharpened the four-bladed heads on my next-door neighbor's emery wheel. That was one thing I had done well, for they were nearly as sh sharp as new razor-blades, and I had put a slight burring roughness, very good for deep cutting, on them with a file. I had the file and a smal

Pages from a revised draft for Deliverance *(Author's private papers)*

110.

(house) where he is a guest, careful to get his head near or into the toilet bowl. I put my head back down, and went away again.

(SPACE BREAK)

The hardness of the rock against my breath woke me; it was too difficult to get air. I rose up and the man was gone. I would have lain there forever but for that, but I knew I ~~must~~ [had to] do something. I propped up and looked at myself. The arrow had gone through about an inch of flesh, and I would either have to cut through it ~~[illegible]~~ or pull ~~[illegible]~~ [the shaft] through. As carefully as I could, but with the pain of every movement touching my soul, I stripped the feathers off the arrow, and then set my teeth [and started to] work it through and out. It came slowly, and I quailed when I thought of the bad camouflage paint I was leaving inside the wound, but there was no ~~place~~ [[illegible]] to quail away from it. I licked my hand and put the saliva on the shaft, hoping that ~~it would~~ [it would help] lubricate ~~it~~, but there was no difference in the pain, and I bent over the arrow and ~~worked it each~~ [moved it through me] inch by inch. ~~until it was free.~~ The wound changed; [it was freed;] the ~~arrow~~ [shaft] came away in my hand. Holding it, I straightened and slid to the ground off the rock.

Walking was odd and one-sided but not impossible. I went to where the man had been. The ground was no longer red, but it was wet. I looked at the woods, and remembered what little I knew about deer-hunting: after hitting the deer with the arrow, you are supposed to wait a half hour and then follow ~~his~~ [its] blood trail. I had no idea how long[, too,] it had been, but I believed ~~he~~ [the man] could not be far away. I got down on my hands and knees and began to look for moist spots in the ground.

Wherever I could find stones and pebbles I felt lucky, for there was blood on [some of] them; they held it better than sand. He had moved toward the woods, [and at the edge of them I found the ~~[illegible]~~ rifle, at the place where [illegible]) tion with the action from the actor's point of view. The novel, however, attempts to assess the value of immediacy in man's life. Part of DeMott's error is his too easy identification of the narrator with the author, which DeMott explains as Dickey's desire to experience vicariously the Exciting Role, to identify with the narrator as he takes charge of survival operations and becomes the "new Mr. Vibrancy," replacing the injured Lewis Medlock as the foreground character: "Perhaps the very act of self-indulgently cutting himself into the action should be seen as a bit of evidence confirming the charge of mad appetition leveled against the present culture." But all of these charges, cogently and brilliantly stated, are based on an inadequate awareness of the author's controlling presence in the novel and of the larger perspective in which the novel frames the sensational action.

First of all, instead of identifying Dickey with the narrator, it is more plausible to speculate that all four of the men are projections of some part of the author. Lewis Medlock reflects Dickey's enthusiasm for archery and woodsmanship, but he is also the kind of masculine hero that Dickey, or any man for that matter, might sometime dream of being. Drew, the quiet, good-natured guitarist, is, perhaps, Dickey the guitarist, lover of simple folk music, untempted by the attractions of madness. Bobby, the most effeminate and ineffectual member of the group, might represent any man's fears about himself. The narrator, I imagine, does come closest to being like the author, though it is quite a mistake to describe this overweight, exhausted, battered skeptic as a "new Mr. Vibrancy." He succeeds not because he becomes another Medlock, but because he remains during the wilderness crisis what he was in civilian life–methodical, cautious, down-to-earth. During the escape, Medlock tells the narrator, "you're doing it better than I could do" (p. 229). The remark is not mere flattery. The book has established from the beginning that Medlock, although incredibly fit and skilled, is too much of a dreamer. As a symbol, he represents a romantic ideal that cannot survive in actuality. This is especially indicated by his accident-proneness. The man who can both enter the world of dream sensation and yet survive needs to be someone with the capacity for realistic judgment like the narrator. Bobby is totally unsympathetic towards the experience to begin with and he derives nothing from the trip except humiliation. Drew is too gentle and decent to survive. Medlock's broken leg is the symbolic culmination of a tendency toward accident which betrays his out-of-touchness with reality. Only the narrator has the capacity to immerse himself temporarily in the transcendent and to survive permanently enriched by the experience, which takes on for him the solidity and realness of an object, a possession. But even he does not derive the full meaning and enrichment possible from such an experience. There is a hint of a faint artistic awakening in the narrator, a graphics layout man for an advertising agency. But I have a strong feeling that Dickey is alluding in this novel to the nature of his own artistic awakening, something fuller and richer than the mild and incomplete change in the narrator. The novel seems to be a veiled statement about the awakening of the artist through the experience of beauty and terror, an experience similar to that described in Whitman's "Out of the Cradle" or in Wordsworth's *The Prelude.*

Indeed, nature mysticism is an essential part of the novel, relevant to the narrator's partial artistic awakening. The narrator's perceptions are refreshed by his exposure to new and extreme conditions. His awareness of the natural world is intensified by fear, pain, and exhaustion. The narrator's perilous effort, for example, to scale the cliff is described in terms of a sexual embrace. The climb brings him to an extreme vantage point physically and psychically, from which the river appears "blank and mindless with beauty. It was the most glorious thing I have ever seen. But it was not seeing, really. For once it was not just seeing. It was beholding. I *beheld* the river in its icy pit of brightness, in its far-below sound and indifference, in its large coil and tiny points and flashes of the moon, in its long sinuous form, in its uncomprehending consequence" (p. 171). The experience is reminiscent of Dickey's poem about the falling stewardess beholding the world with a final intensity. It also brings to mind Wordsworth's recollection of plundering a raven's nest:

> While on the perilous ridge I hung alone,
> With what strange utterance did the loud dry wind
> Blow through my ear! the sky seemed not a sky
> Of earth–and with what motion moved the clouds!

Dickey rightly belongs with what DeMott loosely terms the "more life" school, but more specifically Dickey is one of those nature mystics, including Whitman, Lawrence, and Roethke, who em-

Dickey, dressed for his role as Sheriff Bullard in the film version of his novel Deliverance, *on location in Georgia with his son Christopher*

phasize the importance of *touch* as a way of merging with nature.

Frost, too, knew this impulse toward abandonment, as in poems like "Stopping by Woods," but kept a much tighter rein over it than Dickey does, although ultimately Dickey's narrator also pulls back from total immersion because he, too, has "promises to keep." That the narrator is an incipient romantic is evident in the beginning of the book. Describing his sleep habits, he says, "Something in the world had to pull me back, for every night I went down deep, and if I had any sensation during sleep, it was of going deeper and deeper, trying to reach a point, a line or border" (p. 25). A canoe trip down a fast, powerful river is one of the best ways to indulge the desire to be carried along for forces greater than oneself. On the first night of the trip, the penetration of the wilderness into human consciousness is strikingly accomplished as the claw of an owl breaks through the canvas roof of the tent just above the narrator's head. Next morning he steps out into an eerie fog which seems to absorb him and to claim him as a part of nature: "I looked at my legs and they were gone, and my hands at my sides also; I stood with the fog eating me alive" (p. 94). The temptation to succumb to the river, after the canoe capsizes, is especially great: "I felt myself fading out into the unbelievable violence and brutality of the river, joining it. This is not such a bad way to go, I thought" (p. 144).

That the novel proposes a theme–the necessary freshening of perception by risking extreme conditions–is evidence that Dickey at least was after something more serious than a "horse opera played in canoes." The bad guys in this horse opera are not merely bad guys but a personification of mindless, random evil. Dickey has dealt with questions that certainly, from time to time, must haunt modern urban man, faced with increasing loss of self-sufficiency: "What could I do if I were physically attacked? How can I get out of the rut of approaching middle age? How could I survive after a nuclear holocaust?" The novel is, in an obvious sense, a celebration of an anachronistic concept of manhood, a glorification of physical fitness, daring, cool-headedness, technical skill; but it does not propose that all men embark on canoe trips or undergo a regimen of

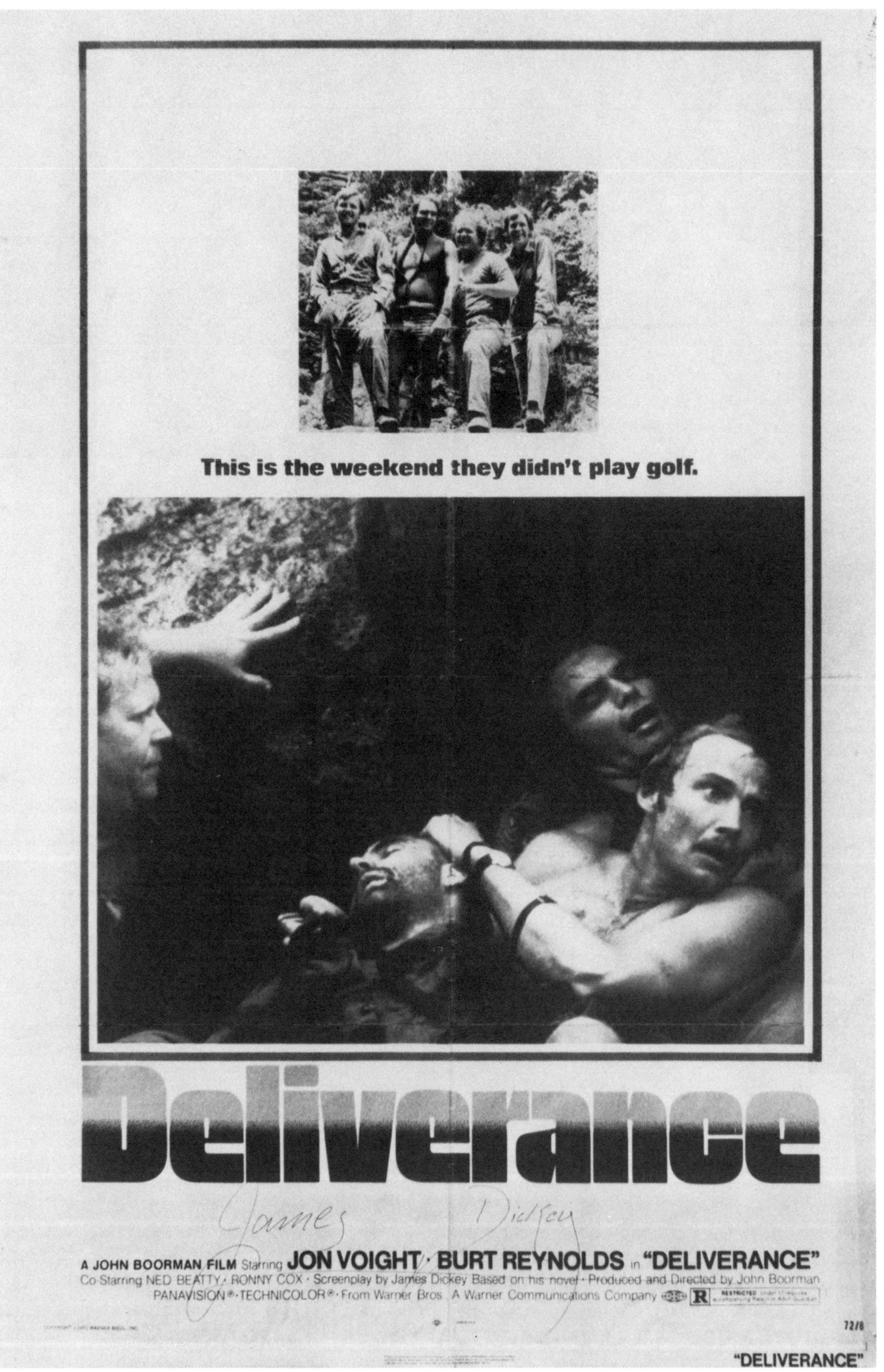

Lobby poster for the 1972 Warner Brothers movie version of Dickey's first novel. Dickey wrote the screenplay, suggested the musical theme "Duellin' Banjos," and acted the role of Sheriff Bullard. The movie, which like the novel was a popular and critical success, was nominated for an Academy Award as the best film of the year.

Dickey, circa 1970, at his Lake Katherine home, on his Pawley's Island hammock

weight lifting and archery in order to salvage their manhood. An interesting conversation between Medlock and the narrator prior to the outing reveals that masculine prowess is not the primary norm of the book. In response to the narrator's accusation, "What you've got is a fantasy life," Medlock replies:

> That's all anybody's got. It depends on how strong your fantasy is, and whether you really–*really*–in your own mind, fit into your own fantasy, whether you measure up to what you've fantasized. I don't know what yours is, but I'll bet you don't come up to it. (p. 49)

Medlock admits that his fantasy of primitive survival in the woods is an improbable one, but in one important sense it is a plausible fantasy, one that energizes Lewis to discipline himself, gives him a sense of identity which "delivers" him from the routine expectations of society. It is a fantasy because the circumstances in which he envisions his survival are only remotely possible; but it is plausible because, were the improbable circumstances to occur, Lewis would be prepared to act with at least a fair chance of success. The important thing is that he *has* a fantasy which he can live up to and which he actively invests in–regardless of whether the fantasy involves survival, sex, racing, ice-skating, travel, painting, skin-diving, radical politics, or whatever can genuinely involve the imagination.

There is a note of sadness, even of elegy, in the ending of the novel. There is the suggestion that the narrator's vivid experience can never be repeated, that all vivid experiences can be retained only in memory or art. Medlock recovers from his leg injury, but walks with a limp: "He can die now; he knows that dying is better than immortality" (p. 277). He finds himself becoming a Zen archer, able to relax his relentless and untiring will. Medlock can relinquish his dream of self-sufficiency because he has at least partially experienced his fantasy. The narrator's own fantasies, which involved the model with a "gold-glowing mote" in her eye, have also lost their force: "I still loved the way she looked, but her gold-halved eye had lost its fascination. Its place was with the night river, in the land of impossibility" (p. 277).

While nothing in his life now rivals, nor probably ever will rival, the dream-intensity of his wilderness experience, he is not left with a sense of forlornness, as a Poe hero might have been, upon the return from the land of dreams or the loss of imaginative power. Instead, the experience has quietly, though partially, revitalized him and reconciled him to reality. He gets on better with people and is better at his work. He does not, like his author, become "a full time poet at the age of 38" as the book jacket tells us; but he does experience some kind of artistic awakening. Before the trip he had felt great relief when his agency fired George Holley, a frustrated artist. Now the narrator rehires Holley and comes to regard him as his best friend, next to Medlock. They do much serious talking about art and the narrator has even tried a few collages himself. In contrast to its intensity and brevity, the wilderness adventure has produced long-lasting beneficial effects on the narrator: "In me it still is, and will be until I die, green, rocky, deep, fast, slow, and beautiful beyond reality" (p. 275).

The note of sadness comes in the fact that his rebirth is incomplete, that the experience is unrepeatable (unless one *is* an artist) both for the individual and also maybe for a whole generation. The last paragraph places the experience in a symbolic-historical perspective. The Cahulawassee River has been inundated by the new lake formed by the dam. Even the river's name has been diminished to Cahula ("Lake Cahula"). Few people will ever realize that a wild river once ran beneath the lake, that an incredibly beautiful and painful adventure took place on that river. The last sentence is significant:

> One big marina is already built on the south end of the lake, and my wife's younger brother says that the area is just beginning to catch on, especially with the new generation, the one just getting out of high school. (p. 278)

The new generation will regard the lake as a resort area. Whatever thrills they seek will not require the old wilderness-survival disciplines of body, mind, and craftsmanship. They, too, may share with the author a fascination with unusual sensations and states of mind, but their "trips" will characteristically be drug-induced inward journeys where the only discipline involved is the willingness and courage to submit to the drug.

TELEVISION PROFILE:
From *Profile: James Dickey,* South Carolina Educational Television, video-taped 11 February 1974.

After the popular success of both the novel and the movie version of Deliverance, *Dickey was often asked to comment on a variety of subjects related to the novel, to writing, and to his nonliterary interests.*

I think any writer is essentially a bookman, or a bibliophile in some way. . . . I was book poor for so many years that it is hard for me to get rid of a book. . . . I like books. I read hours after hours, and the world of words as words intersecting with experience is really my domain. I can't think of anything else I would rather do; there is not any momentary pleasure . . . that I would prefer to reading.

I love anything to do with the human imagination, especially as it expresses itself in words. I am a compulsive writer which I suppose is a good thing for a writer to be. . . . I don't have enough time for poetry, not nearly enough. But since that is the center of the creative wheel for me, everything else comes out of poetry. Novels, screen writing, essays–everything comes out of that. That's got to hold firm. So, no matter what happens, I do some poetry every day, even if it's changing a semi-colon in a line. . . . In order to be a poet at all you have to find ways of intensifying your own personal perception so that your perception passes into you, even into your blood stream. . . .

The hunters like to feel that there are still a few years when we can enter into nature on a life- and- death basis, in the old, ancient, ritualistic function of hunting and being with the animal in his own environment. I don't like guns myself for this purpose . . . but I do like the bow and arrow because the environment of the animal is entered into by having to get into such a proximity with him in order to have any prospect at all of success in the hunt . . . and because the odds are all on the animal's side. But not completely–you might get lucky, in a place like Bull Island with its eerie, unearthly kind of beauty. It's such a setting to do *this* sort of thing in. It's such that a man would never forget it and would want to remember it on his death bed–that he really did do that, and that he did it under those circumstances.

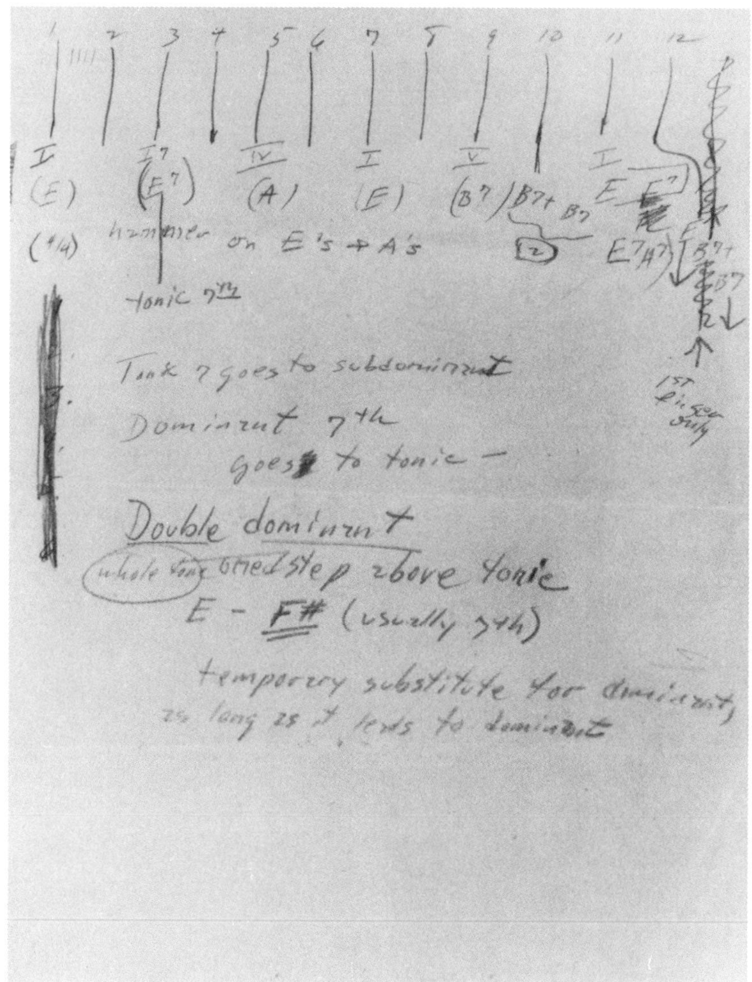

Dickey's notes on playing the guitar (Author's private papers)

BOOK REVIEW:

David Herbert Donald, "Promised Land or Paradise Lost: The South Beheld," *Georgia Review,* 29 (Spring 1975): 184-187.

In this review of Jericho: The South Beheld *(1977), Donald comments on the artistic vision of the South achieved in Hubert Shuptrine's paintings and Dickey's narrative.* Jericho: The South Beheld *was the first large-format book on which Dickey collaborated with a visual artist.*

The most beautiful book ever published about the South, *Jericho* is the work of two Southern artists, Herbert Shuptrine, the painter, and James Dickey, the poet and novelist. In 1972 Shuptrine, who had previously won recognition as an abstract painter in oils but who had recently shifted to a Wyeth-type realism and to transparent watercolors, was commissioned by Oxmoor House of Birmingham and its magazine affiliate, *Southern Living,* to record Southern scenes and Southern faces. Traveling for two years and for more than 15,000 miles, Shuptrine explored the back roads of the South that lead to the isolated mountain fastnesses of Appalachia, to the remote rural counties of the Piedmont, and to the overgrown estuaries of the Sea Islands. He visited places where the old-fashioned ways of the South–picking cotton by hand, making lye soap in a black iron pot, drying coonskins on the barn door–have not been forgotten. Believing that Shuptrine was painting a kind of pictorial atlas of the South, the publishers then invited Dickey to provide an accompanying text. *Jericho,* the lavishly produced result of this collaboration, contains 101 of Shuptrine's paintings and drawings, mostly in color, and a narrative by Dickey of about 12,000 words.

"Collaboration" is not perhaps precisely the word for the Shuptrine-Dickey partnership in

Key of ___ 3/4 time

DANVILLE GIRL

1. My pocket book was empty, my heart was full of pain,

Ten thousand miles away from home, bummin' ~~xxx~~ a railroad train.

I was standin' on the station, smokin' a cheap cigar,

Waitin' for the next freight train to carry an empty car.

2. When I got off at Danville, got stuck on a Danville girl.
You can bet your life she was out of sight, she wore those Danville curls,
She took me into her kitchen, she treated me nice and fine,
She got me in the notion of bummin' all the time.

3. She wore her hat on the back of her head, like high-tone people do.
But the very next train came down the line, I bid that girl adieu.
I pulled my cap down over myeyes, walked down to the railroad tracks;
There I caught the next freight train, nevver to come back.

* *

Key of ___ 4/4 time

CRAWDAD SONG

1. You get a line and I'll get a pole, Honey

You get a line and I'll get a pole, Babe,

You get a line and I'll get a pole,

We'll go down to the crawdad hole,

Honey, sugar baby mine.

2. Yonder is a man with a pack on his back, Honey, etc. etc.
Totin' all the crawdads he can pack. etc..

3. Hurry up babe you slept too late Honey, etc..
The crawdad man just past your gate. etc.

4. What you gonna do when the lake runs dry, Honey, etc...
Sit on the bank and watch the crawdads die. etc...

* *

Key of ___ 3/4 time

MICHAEL ROW THE BOAT ASHORE

1. Michael row the boat ashore, Halleluia

Michael row the boeat ashore, Halleluia

2. Michael's boat is a music boat, etc...

3. Sister help to trim the sails, etc...

4. Jordan's river is chilly and cold Halleluia
Chills the body but not the soul, Halleluia

5. Jordan's river is deep and wide, Halleluia
Milk and honey on the other side, Halleluia.

Dickey annotated this folk song with chord changes while he was learning to play the guitar (Author's private papers) this book. Each man traveled his own way through the South, recording in watercolors or in words vignettes that seemed to him significant. Shuptrine sent Dickey his paintings, and Dickey "put them on the floors, on the walls, on the ceilings of innumerable cinder-block Southern motel rooms, where, cramped between a Home of the Whopper and a tire-iron-changing Shell station, [he] went to sleep" while still thinking of them. But, as Dickey says, "we have made no attempt in this book to have paintings and words coincide."

Indeed, there are considerable variations between these two versions of the South, one visual, the other verbal. For Shuptrine the heart of the South is the mountain country, especially in North Carolina. One-third of his paintings are of North Carolina scenes. Another third are from the adjacent states of Virginia, Tennessee, Georgia, and South Carolina. Dickey, on the other hand, takes the South to encompass "fourteen or so states," and he invites his readers to travel in "a gigantic spiral, going . . . first along the Gulf Coast, through the bayous and over the Delta and the Great River, then into the huge and bewildering and heartening blue of West Texas, then north to Arkansas, through Kentucky and West Virginia and Virginia, briefly down the South Carolina coast . . . through Appalachia into Atlanta." Shuptrine is an artist of the countryside and of country folk; not one of his paintings depicts life in any Southern city or town. Dickey, on the other hand, is fascinated by the oddities of small-town life in the South, with its juke-joints, horse races, and revival meetings. Shuptrine, as Dickey remarks, is an artist "struck by *things*"; he is a superb draftsman of trees, coon dogs, and country churns but frequently fails when he tries to capture faces. Dickey, who writes of the Southern landscape in a blur of rhetoric, is at his best in portraying people: the faith-healer who puts the head of a rattlesnake into his mouth; the North Carolina boy who robs a bank; the mill girl from Ellijay, Georgia, who at her loom "concentrates meanly" on the next softball game.

Yet, for all their differences, Shuptrine and Dickey share a vision of the South. For both it is Jericho, that fabulous first city the Israelites saw in the Promised Land, that foretaste of comfort and permanence to which they were entitled after forty years in the wilderness. For both Shuptrine and Dickey the South is a place where the spirit can be at ease. "Be whole here," they urge their readers. Both men think of the region as, fundamentally, land, for in the South, Dickey writes, "the land . . . is part of the mind." The love for the land they share shines through every page of *Jericho,* whether in Dickey's prose-poem about West Texas, that "kind of land-ocean, constant but quivering with late morning," which makes your scalp dance "with vastness, and the colors," or in Shuptrine's "Hemlock Summit" of Pisgah forest, North Carolina, where every tree is the object of his careful, loving attention. Since the land is central, both artists see countryfolk as the true Southerners. Shuptrine, as has been mentioned, ignores all town and city people. Dickey includes townsmen, but mostly as eccentrics; the "main roads of Jericho," he firmly asserts, are the "red dirt and infinitely complicated back roads."

Since the South of isolated hill folk, of dusty back roads, of cluttered country stores is gradually disappearing, transformed by what C. Vann Woodward has called "the bulldozer revolution," Dickey and Shuptrine portray a way of life that is dying, or that has already disappeared. A recognition of this fact unconsciously permeates the work of both artists. Though Dickey's prose includes some robust country humor and a few nourishing country recipes, his language is elegaic; even while celebrating the South, his rhetoric has a dying fall. In a garden of azaleas–perhaps in Mobile–he shows us the owner, who "stands with both hands in the time-shade, bowed down with his money, exhausted with the income and upkeep of ancient Jericho, with the expense, the overhead of flowers, of old ladies fainting with vegetative rapture." Or, more explicitly, he writes: "This is a land of ghosts, and we feel nowhere come-truer than in a cemetery."

Less explicitly Shuptrine's paintings express the same mood. The gravestones in his cemeteries are tilted, through age and neglect; his Sunday buggy, the cushions long ago destroyed, stands surrounded by weeds; his rice mill is unpainted and windowless, a home for bats and bad dreams. Even Shuptrine's trees are gnarled, twisted, and ancient, the healthiest branches long since pruned away. The omnipresent brown-ochre coloring of Shuptrine's paintings further reenforces the sense of a world in its final autumn. Perhaps the feeling of impending doom is responsible for the vague focus, the want of sharp outline, in so many of his paintings. Nowhere does he show the sharp light that gives tangible mass to Edward Hopper's buildings; nowhere does he exhibit the precision of Wyeth's drawing. For Shuptrine, as for Dickey, the South is an ancient and decaying lady, to be portrayed with tender-

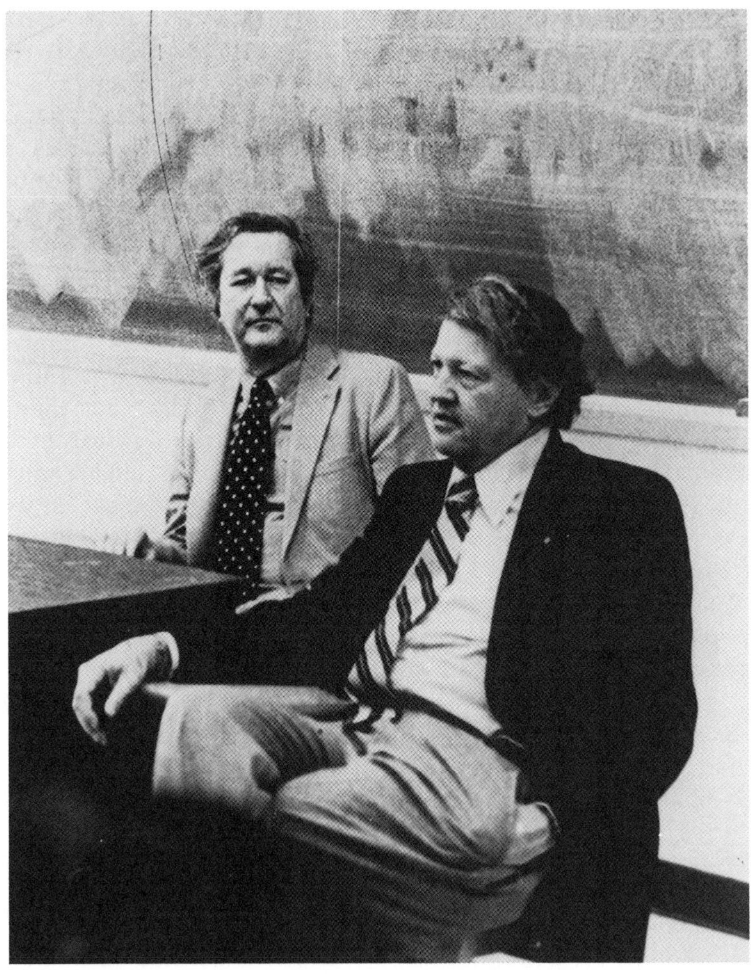

Dickey with his friend novelist William Styron, during a January 1974 classroom session at the University of South Carolina

ness and affection and with a proper reticence about the wrinkles and furrows wrought by age.

Jericho is, then, a book as curious and ambivalent as it is beautiful. Though both Dickey and Shuptrine think of the South as a land flowing with milk and honey, their book reveals that both artists on a deeper level are aware that they are depicting a way of life that is almost gone. "Jericho was ours first," Dickey admits. "It was lost." What their superb book is, then, is not so much a preview of the Promised Land but a nostalgic glance at Paradise Lost.

LETTER:

To Jimmy Carter (carbon), unpublished; author's private papers.

When his fellow Georgian Jimmy Carter became the Democratic candidate for President of the United States, Dickey sent him the following letter. On 25 August 1976 Carter replied with a letter praising cultural and regional diversity as a source of strength for the nation. He also admired Dickey's quotation from Santayana.

When Carter was elected President, Dickey was invited to read his poem "The Strength of Fields" at the televised Inauguration celebration held at the Kennedy Center in January 1977. Soon afterward Dickey acted as Carter's personal representative while opening the Franklin-Jefferson exhibit in Mexico City in March 1977.

August 4, 1976

Dear Jimmy Carter,

It has been a couple of years since we have got together. As I recollect, it was at some kind of ceremony where I received an award in Atlanta. There is a picture of you wearing my pheasant-banded hat, which picture can be forthcoming on receipt of a tape-recording of "Hail to the Chief." Since you subsequently asked me to become Poet Laureate of Georgia–which I did not feel it prudent to do since I now reside in South

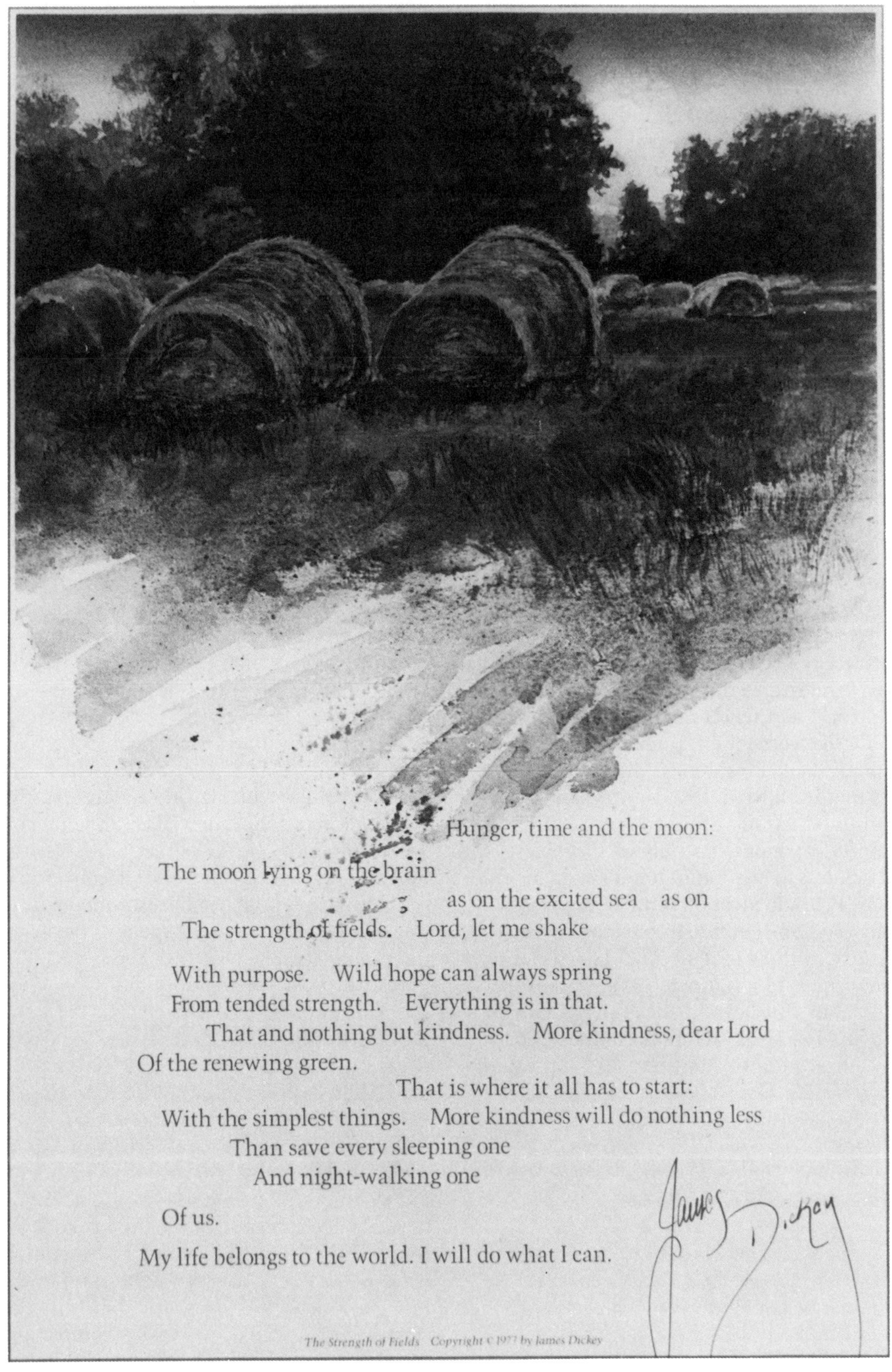

Hunger, time and the moon:
The moon lying on the brain
as on the excited sea as on
The strength of fields. Lord, let me shake
With purpose. Wild hope can always spring
From tended strength. Everything is in that.
That and nothing but kindness. More kindness, dear Lord
Of the renewing green.
That is where it all has to start:
With the simplest things. More kindness will do nothing less
Than save every sleeping one
And night-walking one
Of us.
My life belongs to the world. I will do what I can.

James Dickey

Broadside printing (1984) of an excerpt from "The Strength of Fields," which Dickey read during the celebrations for President Jimmy Carter's inauguration, 20 January 1977

Carolina–I yet offer some free advice about your candidacy. I understand full well that unsolicited advice is almost never welcome, although at odd times it may be advantageous.

The clue to our national and international salvation lies not in a futile yearning for a nebulous "unity," but in an emphasis on diversity, or the right–and eventual glory, given the right government–of differences. The South is not the East and the East is not the Pacific Northwest, nor is any one of these Alaska or Hawaii. What we should seek, as a political organ, is a reaffirmation of the principle of difference, both local and individual. As President–which you certainly shall become–you would do well to affirm cultural pluralism among the various ethnic and political groups of our nation. Men need, above all, pride: pride in themselves and pride in their heritage. I once did a film on this matter for USIA, narrated by Ben Gazzara. You could see this any time you wished to do so. It is called *Celebration,* loosely based on John Kennedy's book, *A Nation of Immigrants,* and it stresses the fact that in America ethnic groups do not lose their identity, and can celebrate these roots while still remaining a part of the American ethos. This is at the same time paradoxical and true.

I would like very much, Jimmy, to see an emphasis, under your Presidency, on the diversity of peoples that we have in this country, and a fertile cross-pollenization of different kinds of groups, mores, fashions, and all of the diversity that gives richness to life. Let us not insist on an impossible and Platonic ideal of "unity," but emphasize the majestic and endlessly fascinating *fact* of the variegated country that we are. There can be various ways open to a national organization that could effect this. But beyond these suggestions, I could not go. I am, as the philosopher George Santayana once said of himself, "An ignorant man; almost a poet."

BOOK REVIEW:
Stanley Burnshaw, "James Dickey," *Agenda,* 14-15 (Winter-Spring 1977): 120-124.

Burnshaw's review of The Zodiac *(1976) was one of the few appraisals that presented Dickey's long poem as a successful venture into a new form and voice.*

Who is Hendrik Marsman, 1899-1940? The name was unknown in America till seven years after his death, when "The Zodiac," rendered by Adriaan Barnouw from Dutch into English, appeared in *The Sewanee Review.* Measured in terms of public response, the poem made no impact at all, but within at least one reader it sent down roots. And whether he knew it or not, for more than twenty years the poem-and-poet kept living and growing within their host till they came to demand nothing less than another birth. Perhaps if Marsman had lived–he was killed by a torpedo in the North Atlantic early in World War II–"their" book might not have been born. "I have never been able to disassociate the poem from the poet," said Dickey in *Self-Interviews* about Malcolm Lowry's journey to Norway "just to meet" a man whose work had profoundly moved him. *The Zodiac* is a kindred act of homage.

"This poem is based on another of the same title by Hendrik Marsman," Dickey explains, and "with the exception of a few lines, is completely my own." "Based" is the warranted word. Part I of Dickey's poem is almost as long (414 lines) as the whole of Marsman's (422), Parts II-XII even longer. But the telling difference grows out of the two conceptions of the hero: "A drunken Dutch poet who returns to his home in Amsterdam after years of travel and tries desperately to relate himself, by means of stars, to the universe" (p. vii).

Assuming Barnouw's text to be faithful to Marsman's, we face two works which are fairly close in story but in other ways vastly apart. Marsman's narrator describes and interprets the hero's thoughts, feelings, acts; he philosophizes, he exclaims–and all in verse of conventional patterns: spare, condensed, restrained. In Dickey's poem the hero himself speaks, moans, shouts, questions, streams with visions, spits out four-letter words, curses his soul and God. Dickey disposes the words on the page as a prosody music-score, the margins and spaces reflecting the twists, turns, leaps of a man half-drunk, half-mad, half-supersane: a more-than-lifesize creature torn between whisky and stars.

How can one trace the drift of a poem with such shifts in mood and scene? "The man I'm telling you about," it begins, "brought himself back alive . . . He's here/. . . over the broker's peaceful/ open-bay office at the corner of two canals." The window proffers the city-sights but nothing below can attract his eyes, for "He moves among stars . . . star-crazed, mad with connecting things . . . that lay their meanings/Over billions of light years." "The secret," he knows, can be found in the Zodiac. He has only to "solve it . . . believe it . . . learn to read it . . . as poetry."

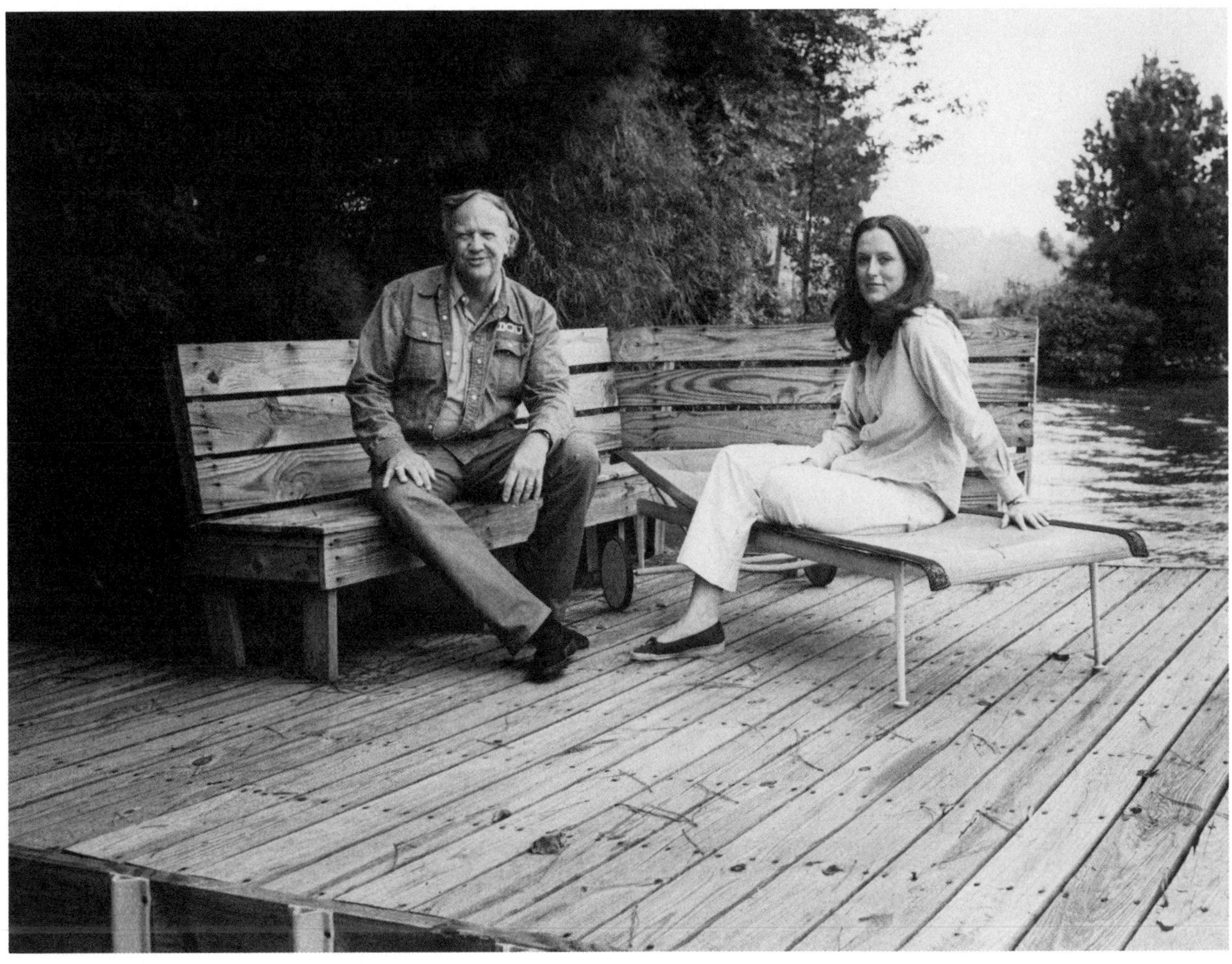

Dickey and his second wife, Deborah Dodson Dickey, on the dock of their Lake Katherine home. They were married in 1976.

"Light," he says to his lamp, "you're a strange creature." Flicking the rods, he sends them spinning through the Zodiac: "the white walls stagger . . . By God, those designs are saying *some*thing"–the vision fades. "Look, stupid, get your nose out of the sky." He begins to write, "the paper runs with signs." They stop, but by dawn "Something" has come through: "It's staring you right in the face. The *secret*/Is whiteness . . . on whiteness you can release/The blackness . . . Whiteness is death is dying/For human words to raise it from purity." Mad with defiant joy, he cries:

> Where God once stood in the stadium
> Of European history, and battled mankind in the blue air
> Of manmade curses . . .
>
> I'd put something overhead something new: a new beast
> For the Zodiac. I'd say to myself like a man
> Bartending for God, . . .
> What'll it *be*? What new creature
>
> Would you *like* up there?
>
> . . . You've *got* a Crab . . .
>
> My head is smashed with *aquavit,*
>
> And I've a damn good Lobster in it . . .
>
> His eye his eye
>
> I'll make blue-white, so that the thing
> Will cut and go deep and *heal* . . .

The vision fails. "Why not die/And breathe Heaven" instead?–"He turns his eyes down/Into trees, into human life./Into the human hair-gray/Thicket of twilight."

If the words above give a paltry account of lines 1-414, blame the dazzling ranges and riches of thought that flail at the world-wearied man

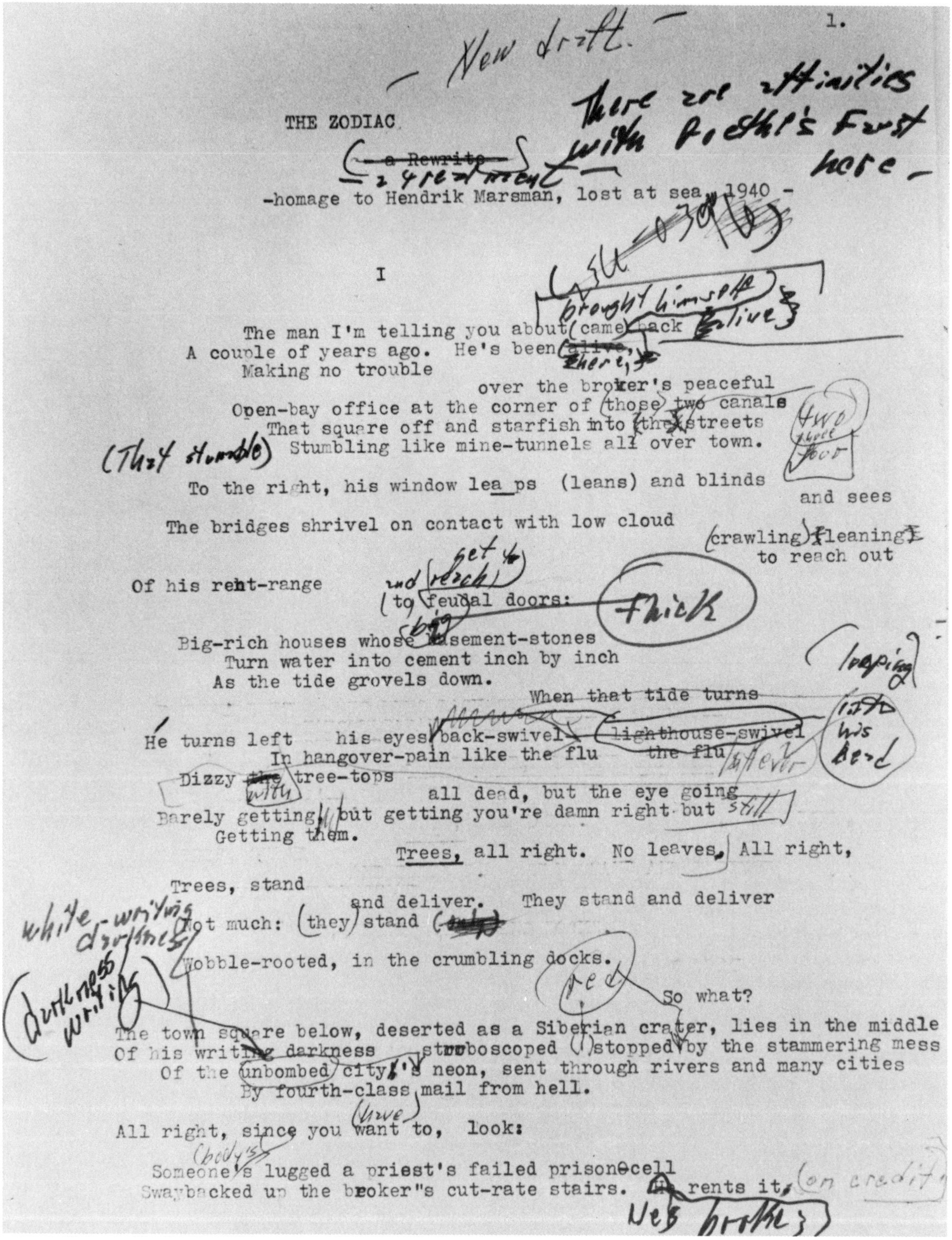

1.

— New draft. —

There are affinities with Goethe's Faust here —

THE ZODIAC

(~~a Rewrite~~ / a treatment)

-homage to Hendrik Marsman, lost at sea, 1940 -

I

The man I'm telling you about came back
A couple of years ago. He's been alive,
Making no trouble
over the broker's peaceful
Open-bay office at the corner of those two canals
That square off and starfish into the streets
Stumbling like mine-tunnels all over town.

To the right, his window leaps (leans) and blinds
and sees
The bridges shrivel on contact with low cloud
crawling leaning
to reach out
Of his rent-range
to feudal doors:

Big-rich houses whose basement-stones
Turn water into cement inch by inch
As the tide grovels down.
~~When that tide turns~~

He turns left ~~his eyes~~ back-swivel ~~lighthouse-swivel~~
In ~~hangover-pain like the flu~~ ~~the flu~~
Dizzy ~~the~~ tree-tops
all dead, but the eye going
Barely getting, but getting you're damn right but
Getting them.
Trees, all right. No leaves. All right,

Trees, stand
and deliver. They stand and deliver
Not much: they stand
Wobble-rooted, in the crumbling docks.

So what?

The town square below, deserted as a Siberian crater, lies in the middle
Of his writing darkness stroboscoped stopped by the stammering mess
Of the unbombed city's neon, sent through rivers and many cities
By fourth-class mail from hell.

All right, since you want to, look:

Someone's lugged a priest's failed prison cell
Swaybacked up the broker's cut-rate stairs. He rents it,

The Zodiac *(1976), Dickey's rewriting of a poem by Hendrik Marsman, was first published in an edition of 61 copies–each with a leaf from his working draft (Author's private papers)*

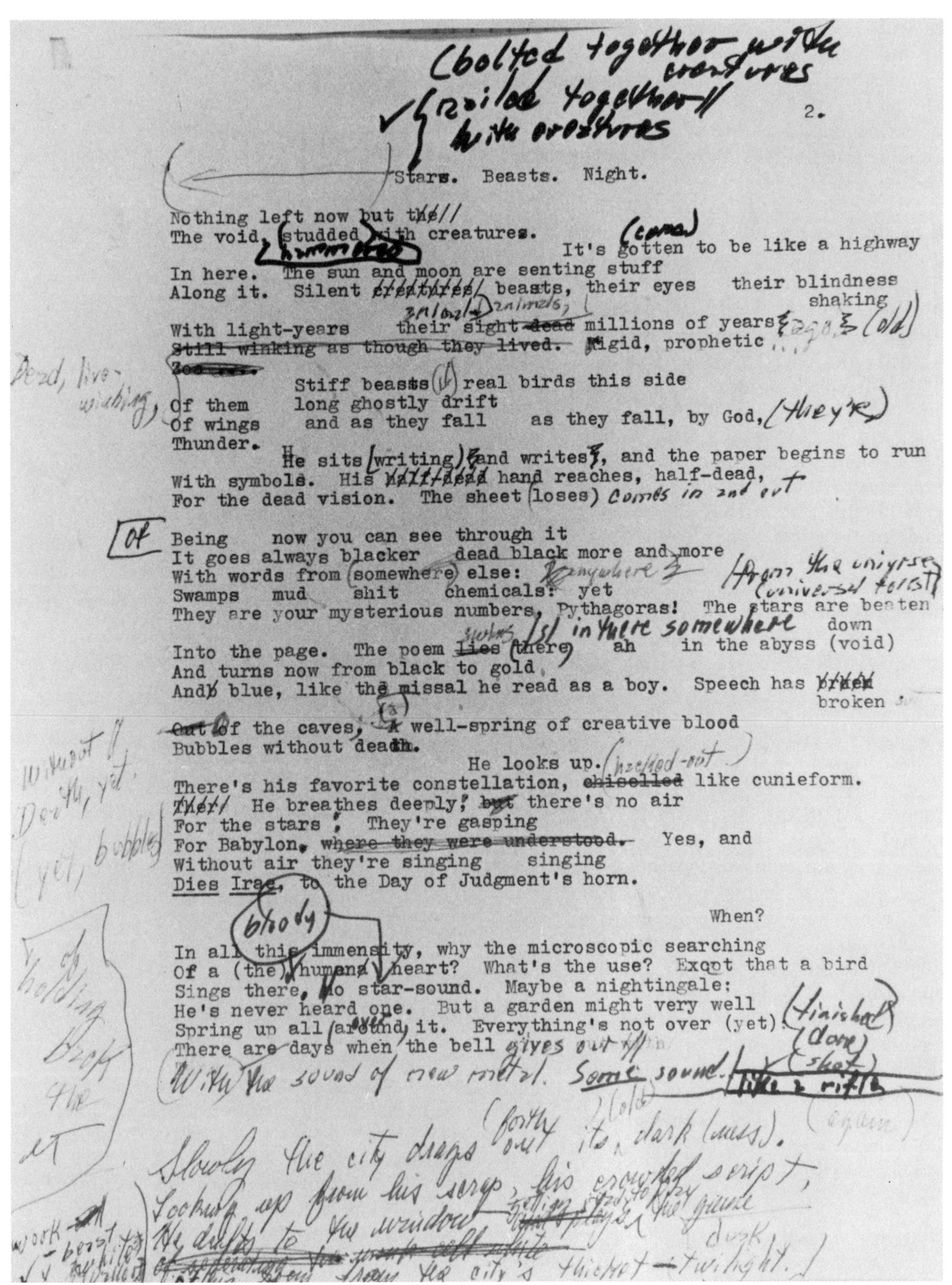
2.

Stars. Beasts. Night.

Nothing left now but the
The void, studded with creatures.
It's gotten to be like a highway
In here. The sun and moon are senting stuff
Along it. Silent beasts, their eyes their blindness
shaking
With light-years their sight millions of years
Rigid, prophetic
Stiff beasts real birds this side
Of them long ghostly drift
Of wings and as they fall as they fall, by God,
Thunder.
He sits and writes, and the paper begins to run
With symbols. His hand reaches, half-dead,
For the dead vision. The sheet loses

Being now you can see through it
It goes always blacker dead black more and more
With words from somewhere else:
Swamps mud shit chemicals: yet
They are your mysterious numbers, Pythagoras! The stars are beaten
down
Into the page. The poem there ah in the abyss (void)
And turns now from black to gold
And blue, like the missal he read as a boy. Speech has
broken
of the caves, well-spring of creative blood
Bubbles without death.
He looks up.
There's his favorite constellation, like cunieform.
He breathes deeply; there's no air
For the stars. They're gasping
For Babylon. Yes, and
Without air they're singing singing
Dies Irae, to the Day of Judgment's horn.

When?

In all this immensity, why the microscopic searching
Of a (the) human heart? What's the use? Exept that a bird
Sings there, no star-sound. Maybe a nightingale:
He's never heard one. But a garden might very well
Spring up all around it. Everything's not over (yet).
There are days when the bell

who is drunk as much with his search as with aquavit. "Words. How?" Part I ends. Parts II-XII seek "the answer," as he leaves his cell for the streets, on a quasi-mystical quest for the certain, the ultimate, meanings of his own existence, and, by extension, mankind's. No prose account could provide more than flashing hints as he makes his Via Dolorosa:

(II) "A clock smash-bongs" from the tower.–Time? But Time is like Cancer: "the thing that eats." Reasoning leaps: "If Cancer dies overhead/ It dies everywhere!"–and again he tries to replace the killing Crab with his healing Lobster, and fails. (III) Scenes from his travels soothe and entrance him, but "forgetting keeps moving in." Confusions finally calm at the thought of his grave as home. (IV) Walking the dark, he comes on a strange "all-mighty stone" lifted from earth's beginning into the night. Without "that hugely mortal beast": nothing of man or of God. As the thought fades from his mind, light from Venus, the love-star, wakes his desire. (V) "Bed-dark" half-asleep in his room, he asks: do my nightmares rise and fall "in reprisal fear of God"? (VI) Dreams, monsters of stars–and then "idea of love." (VII) Don't couple with "the intellect or a cold womb," he warns himself. Even your poems are doomed. Only above in the sky is "the world original": "the Zodiac shines anew" each night. (VIII) Sun: "time to city-drift": by the dead canals where autumn trees "help their leaves hold back . . . life-death-breath." (IX) Strangely led to his father's house, scene of a youthful embittered love, he hears his mother's words grind out of the rock "Never come back here . . Go for the empty road!" (X) Alone again in his room: a woman climbing the stairs . . . does it matter," "even love," "when the world's dying"? (XI) But now–at the house of a friend: "talk rushes over" cheese, gin, women, politics. Everything changed and the same! "He polar-bears through the room." An accordion's sounds quicken his heart–and he's "home." (XII) "A day like that. But afterwards the fire/Comes straight down through the roof, white-lightning nightfall . . ./on the white sheet of paper/. . . He's making a black horizon".

Oh my own soul, put me in a solar boat.
  Come into one of these hands
  Bringing quietness and the rare belief
That I can steer this strange craft to the morning
Land that sleeps in the universe on all horizons . . .

Mallarmé sought "the secret's answer" on earth ("Things already exist . . . we have simply to see their relationships"); the Dutch poet reads it in the sky. But for both, humanity's salvaging power is the same: the "creative" answer. Mallarmé calls for "composing the Book, the Orphic explanation of the earth . . . attempted by every writer." Dickey's speaker goes further, affirming that man will not fail himself so long as he is able to conceive the world imaginatively–

So long as the hand can hold its island
  Of blazing paper, and bleed for its images:
  Make what it can of what is:
    So long as the spirit hurls on space
The star-beasts of intellect and madness.

The avowal is no useless fancy. Poetry's "reenactment of unification" (as *The Seamless Web* sought to make clear) overcomes the divisiveness within ourselves, among ourselves, and between ourselves and the universe. Poetry thus can no longer be viewed as a cultural ornament. Rather by providing as it does the fulfillment of a need of our nature, poetry serves as an instrument for human survival.

In *Sorties*, a book which I urged on my fellow-judges for a National Book Award, Dickey declared "I want my poem to devour the reader, so that he cannot possibly put it down as he reads it, or forget about it." *The Zodiac* sets a new height in this writer's achievement. It is surely the most disturbingly remarkable booklength poem in decades, charged as it is with the "raw vitalism," "the convincing speech," the insights, the visions, the unflagging intensity that Dickey attains in the finest works of his art. Let the reader make himself ready to roll with this poem as it draws him into its vortex of search and light.

PROFILE:

R. V. Cassill, "The Most Dangerous Game of the Poet James Dickey," *South Carolina Review*, 10 (April 1978): 7-11.

In a special Dickey issue of the South Carolina Review, *fiction writer Cassill provides a witty, perceptive assessment of Dickey, the man and the writer.*

I have, as Emerson put it, the habit of tacking together the old and the new, a slick story called "The Most Dangerous Game" (about the hunting of one man by another) with my reading of the *Poems*. I am a great reader only in the common, folk, sense of that term. We mean, us folk,

Dickey at the age of fifty-six.

that we read a *lot*, when we claim for ourselves that we are "great readers." I read the faces, dispositions, destinies and quirks of poets I have known, as well as what is committed to print. And when I can not elegantly tack it together, I let it tack itself together, the way it wants to be together, the way the Poet has intended it to come together in the imagination of great readers.

To be sure, in his printed *Poems*, Dickey has said all that needs to be said (for the great reader) about himself as poet.

> I swore to myself I would see
> When all but my seeing had failed.
> Every light was too feeble to show
> My world as I knew it must be. . . .
>
> from *The Owl King*

After reading that, all commentators and explicators might have the grace to be silent–were they not committed to the most dangerous game of hunting the bowman, hid in the thicket of his poem, holding the great bow at full draw.

To keep the fatal bargain of the hunt, the pursuing reader may imagine

THE INVENTION OF THE POET

"Art is the path of the creator to his work." The way to write a poem is to make yourself a poet. The first stroke of genius is to see that the poet worthy of These States is blind as an owl. To see that you are a Southern boy environed by a host of talented Southron epigones twitching to go "North toward home" and be praised by the Ruling Circles for the perfection of their verse.

To know that you in turn would be welcomed on the stage of the YMHA by the RC's if you went up there to speak smartly about Miss Eudora and Mr. Ransom and were reverent about Traveler (while you helped them snicker down Whitman and the Midwesterners and made the South into a commodity package). While you helped the Artificial Sodomites misread and package the Catholicism of Flannery O'Connor so she could become a favorite in Good Schools. You see the rules of the Poetry Game as the fool-killing darkness. You see that you can not beat them at their own game, that if they catch you trying they will attack you as an upstart Southern catbird from the advertising world trying to beautify himself with their expensively dyed feathers.

You must transform the game while you play it (the only game in town). You ignite the darkness, show the "dark burn" and push your sight out slowly–"Inch by inch, as into stone."

You invent a persona that will pass–if the motion is swift and furious enough–as another pseudo-Sartoris making the Poetry Circuit, casting artificial Snopeses before the real Chillingworths of the RCE (Ruling Circle Establishment).

You play the guitar, like Certified Youth. You read at the YMHA. You have come North toward home. But you never quite fool those who made the rules of the game. They have your number. It is a no-win game. Game? Which game are we talking about? Bow? Who has the bow? Isn't this supposed to be a slick story? Why do the Suitors have the Great Bow and the first turn at stringing it? So, push your sight inch by inch into the stone, if you can. The Bow is only your metaphor, the arrows are noodles to tickle the ribs of the Suitors, and No One is shining beside you in the fabulous darkness.

An Anecdote To Change The Tone And The Imagery

I am told (by Dickey-watchers) that when a committee was considering whether to invite the poet to Vanderbilt for a literary festival, an aging Fugitive advised: "Do not bring Dickey to the campus. He will ravish your women."

Someone, somehow, is calling out of the darkness; the women no longer listen to wise Pentheus recite the Law of the Golden Mean!

Anecdotes Not So Fancy

Peter Taylor and I spent some summer days with Jim at the University of Utah in (I believe) 1967. We were housed in a women's dorm with an overview of green lawns where the sprinklers swept back and forth all day with generous monotony to keep the campus from reverting to its natural condition. From dormitory windows we could look across Salt Lake City to some awful, distant mountains where there were said to be copper mines. I think it safe to say that, sober and not sober, Peter, Jim and I enjoyed each other's company, talked with that peculiar ecstasy of middle-aged men who love language and lore, mindful that the stories they exchange are always conditioned by the dormitory walls, the dumb and ceaseless artificial fountains and the brutal desert that environs them.

Since that time I have seen Jim less frequently than I have seen Peter. When Peter and I have got together, we try (impossibly) to keep up on Jim. Not as outsiders to his story or his stories or the stories about him.

Peter says, "Do you know what I hear Jim is telling about Utah?" His eyes (mid many wrinkles), his ancient, glittering eyes, are gay, and we are both afloat on the kind of laughter that comes last.

"I heard that Jim was telling how Cassill was shacked up with a gorgeous coed . . ."

"Who had no soul at all . . ."

". . . who had no soul at all. This Cassill . . ."

"This low-born Cassill."

Nods. ". . . was causing Brewster Ghiselin fits because, though Brewster is personally very tolerant we were in a strait-laced Mormon community, where such goings-on are bound to have repercussions and to reflect badly on the summer school writing program.

And there we abide, Peter and I, storytellers caught up in an everlasting fiction we share with Jim. Safer than we will ever be amid the untrustworthy specifications of biographical data.

The Poet Among The Animals

"The deepest mysteries of human existence are sleep, language, dreams, madness, beasts, and sex"–said the New Englander, who really had, after all, seen the silhouette of Sweeney straddled in the sun–just hadn't been taken in by that spectacle, as the epigones always are.

Those critical biographers who dangerously hunt the man in his work, the possessor of the eyes behind the eyes, might have their best luck with "The Sheep Child." Here (again) with daz-

1.

Three Poems of Flight-Sleep

I

Camden Town

- Army Air Corps, 1943 -

With this you trim it. (You do it right and (it'll) fly
(By) Itself. Now get up there and get those lazy-
eights down. A check-ride's coming at you
Next week. [I took off] Yes, and I got in the Stearman like stealing two hundred and twenty horses
I had learned just enough of this.
Of escape from the Air Corps.
The cold was purple with the open
Cockpit, and the water behind me (,) being
The East, dimmed out. I put the nose on the white sun
And trimmed the ship. The altimeter (chose) (stopped) skewered
Six thousand (feet). We were all stable: myself, the plane,
The earth everywhere
Small in its things with cold
But vast beneath, (All) the needles on the panel
Locked together, and a banner like World War One
Tore at my head, streaming from my helmet in the wind.
I drew it down down under the instruments
Down where the rudder pedals made small corrections
Better than my feet down where I could ride on faith
And trim, the aircraft slightly cocked
But holding the West by a needle. I pulled down my helmet-flaps and droned
With flight-sleep. Near death
My watch stopped. I knew it, for I felt the Cadet
Barracks of Camden die like time, and "There's a war on"
Die, and no one could groan in the dark of the bottom
Bunk to his haggard instructor I tried
I tried to do what you said I tried tried
No; never. No one ever said no one would ever believe someone saw
An aircraft with no pilot showing: I would have to become
A legend, curled up on the floor with all the Western World
Coming at me under the floor-mat, minute after minute,
cold purples,
Small trains and warbound highways,
All (beneath) flight-sleep. Nothing mattered but to rest in the winter
Sun beginning to go
Down early. My hands in my armpits, I lay with my flapped head
Next to the small air-moves
Of the rudder-pedals, dreaming of letting go letting go
The cold the war the Cadet Program and my peanut-faced
Instructor and his maps. No maps no world no love
But this. Nothing can fail when you go below
The instruments. Wait till the moon. Then. Then.

But no. When the waters at Camden town died, then so
Did I, for good. I got up bitterly, bitter to be

[Handwritten marginalia: "I was in / Death's baby / machine, that led / to the fighters / and / bombers but / training, here / in the lone purple, / For something else."; "All"; "out of sight"; "(held in) entering"; "irony"]

Revised draft for a poem based on Dickey's U.S. Army Air Corps experience. "Camden Town" was published in the Spring 1970 issue of the Virginia Quarterly Review *and was collected as part one of "Two Poems of Flight-Sleep" in his 1979 book* The Strength of Fields *(Author's private papers).*

zling frankness the poet tells us who he is. He is the one who dies "staring" (the owl's eyes again, by which we recognize him through his disguises of Professor and Successful Reader). Jim Dickey is the one whose hoof and hand clasp each other, who frightens the farm boys into suffering themselves, marrying, and raising their kind. What prudent boy would choose to imitate the destiny of the poet?

HOW THE POET ACQUIRED THE GREAT BOW

I delight to imagine that he bought it in the sporting goods section of some outlet store, at the price a boy can afford. I have to imagine that there was a neural, intuitive recognition of what he had taken into his hand when he first lifted the bow from the display shelf where it was offered for sale. It had to be what they call a real bow with an economic value and definable physical properties before it could be handled as a real bow with metaphoric properties. Nerves and intuition had to assent before language shaped to an affirmation. If the bow does not say "Kill" to the hand, then the reading is off to a false start that can never be retrieved by talent, study, imitation or earnest effort.

When the bow says "Kill" the boys asks, "Who?"

"The False Suitors," says the bow.

"Sure a lot of them," says the boy.

"You will be helped."

That is the way I imagine it started. So James Dickey became an avid archer, as it says on the dust jacket of one of his books. The book is *Deliverance* and, as we know, it contains a passage in which the archer kills someone with a broadhead arrow. It's not a passage I mean to examine for its "literary value" nor comb for its "psychological revelations" but rather to cite for its general coincidence with the pattern of action in Richard Connell's slick story "The Most Dangerous Game," mentioned earlier. (Jim, there are High-minded Suitors all around us who think all novels are slick stories, just as they think all bows are recreational appliances, which is why they will never kill anyone with either of them.) The Hunted becomes the Hunter, maybe that's all there is to it, except that in *Deliverace* the implications are spelled out a little bit more. After the first killing Gentry draws a bead on his companion Bobby. *Might have* killed him too.

BUT IS THE NOVEL UP TO THE STANDARD OF THE POET?

Hell's bells, I'm not going to get into the question of the ranking of *Deliverance,* because that would lead right on to increasingly foolish questions about Dickey's rank as a poet on the national, international, and eternal scale.

It would lead right on, in the circumstantial world, to the question of whether Jim Dickey is "the Muhammed Ali of poetry."

That is a game we don't play, men, women and poets.

We know (and live by) the right answer to that foolish and journalistic-academic question: "Muhammed Ali is the Muhammed Ali of poetry." Jim Dickey is the Jim Dickey of poetry (as William Dickey is the William Dickey of poetry). Men and women are all in the most dangerous game one and by one. We follow the man or the woman by the track of the verse, and, in the kingdom, each will live and die with his and her own name. (Another poet whom I know has named his son Patrice. I know him as poet by the naming of his son. Poets do not name their sons–or their friends–except as poets.) Poets do not write novels except as poets. Or go on the circuit. Beat the guitar.

My encounter with Jim Dickey will be in the Cage Country. We meet each other when the sunglasses have been pushed back. And he will say–and I will quote–"your moves were exactly right for a few things in this world: we know you when you come." Head-aim, Jim. Fuck the liars and the cowards. We speak, we hear, we answer.

CADENZA: IF YOU HAVE CAUGHT A LIVING EYE, JUST WINK AS YOU DEPART.

Nothing we have said is new. The Word is common. The word is common as our circumstances. The Poet is all of us, not Man Reading at The YMHA. We advance, we retire. If you have pushed your sight into the stone–with your "grim techniques"–the stone is still the stone.

However, if, after sleepless nights, you have got the Great Bow strung, She who is shining beside you is, as always, Athena. The False Suitors, though they change their names, are still the same False Suitors. Our women die and change and deny their name, but have, always, the same name. Which we utter.

BOOK REVIEW:

From Laurence Lieberman, "Exchanges: Inventions in Two Voices," *Sewanee Review,* 88 (Summer 1980): lxv-lxvi.

(For) The Death of Lombardi

I never played for you. You'd have thrown
Me off the team on my best day--
No guts, maybe not enough speed,
Yet running in my mind
As Paul Hornung, I made it here
With the others, sprinting down railroad tracks,
Hurdling bushes and backyard Cyclone
Fences, through city after city, to stand, at last, around you,
Exhausted, exalted, pale
As a hospital. You are holding us
Millions together: those who played for you, and those who entered the bodi
Of Bart Starr, Donny Anderson, Ray Nitchke, Jerry Kramer
Through the snowing tube, playing painlessly
In the snows of Green Bay Stadium, some of us drunk
On much-advertised beer some old, some in other
Hospitals, most (of us) middle-aged
And at home. Here you summon us, lying under
The surgical snows and hold us hold us
Like cancer.
The Crab has you, and to him
And to us you whisper Drive, Drive. In dying in death
You give us no choice
Either. Jerry Kramer's face hovers, real, pale,
We others dream ourselves there, and no one speaks
But you. Far away in the mountains, driving hard
Through the snows, Marshall of the Vikings, driving burning
Twenty dollar bills to stay alive, says, still
Alive, sa "I wouldn't beh here
If it weren't for the lessons of football." Vince, when the surgeons
cut loose
Two feet of your intestine, the Crab whirled up whirled out
Of the lost gut and caught you again
Higher up. Around your bed the knocked-out teeth like hail(stones)
Stream down miles of adhesive tape from ankles and hands
Writhe like vines in the room gallons of sweat blaze in buckets
In the corners the blue and yellow of bruises
Make one vast sunset around you. No one understands you.
What holds us here? You are dying by the code
You made us by. Yes, coach, it is true: love-hate is stronger
Than either love or hate. Into the weekly, inescapable dance
Of spedd and pain you led us, and brought us here, weeping,
But as men. Or, you who made us, did you discover
The worst of us: brutality aggression deception the cause of
Inflicted on others for money? Did you make of us, indeed,
Figments over-specialized, brutal ghosts
Who could have been real
Men in a better sense? Too late. There's nothing elsexxxxxx
For us: we've got to believe we're still
Xxxxxxxxxxxxxxxxxxxxxxxxxxxx
Winning we're winning all the time
You lie there forever, Vince.

Revised draft for Dickey's tribute to football coach Vince Lombardi. The poem was first published in the September 1971 Esquire *and collected in 1979 in* The Strength of Fields *(Author's private papers).*

Lieberman was one of the first poet-critics to recognize mystical, visionary characteristics in Dickey's poetry. In his review of The Strength of Fields *(1979) Lieberman also preserved James Wright's assessment of Dickey's works.*

James Dickey's *Deliverance* broke new ground in the art of fiction. His first translations, which comprise roughly a third of his remarkable new collection and are no less radical and innovatory, break new ground in the art of transcribing the poetry of foreign tongues ("unEnglish") into his native tongue. As Dickey moves across the sound barrier between the inscrutable *other* language and his own, we sense a wizardry of infinitesimal shifts and adjustments not unlike the atomic transmutations of one metal slowly alchemizing into another. Whatever the line and stanzaic pattern of the original poem, Dickey employs a characteristic spacing device to suggest the nuances of magical interlocking of two voices, two languages. . . . Bewitched by the sorceries of dual authorship in "Mexican Valley," after Octavio Paz, a reader catches glimmerings of a profound cohabitation of two human spirits in the one verse-skin.

In other new modes of Dickey's ventriloquist art ("Exchanges," "Reunioning Dialogue," etc.), the author–via two alternating speakers–achieves the illusion that he *exchanges,* or barters, larynxes with a succession of kindred humans, as if organs of speech can be transplanted from one man's throat to another's. Dickey groans, sighs, "mumbles" lofty utterance with the vocal chords of "a dead poet" (Trumbull Stickney), the newly-inaugurated U.S. president (Jimmy Carter), a classical hall-of-fame football coach (Vince Lombardi), astronauts, New York City marathon runners, peace-time fighter pilots drugged in "flight-sleep," as well as the many supreme living poets of other languages (Paz, Montale, Yevtushenko, etc.).

"The one authentic genius writing poetry in America today is James Dickey," chanted James Wright to a class of my creative writing students a few years ago. Now that Wright is dead, Dickey and Robert Penn Warren are the only surviving visionaries of our language who belong to that elect few: master prosodists balancing on the knife-edge of supernal Being, whose genius for outstripping the supposed limits of available experience is wedded to matchless artistry.

BOOK REVIEW:
Susan Ludvigson, "A Radical Departure for James Dickey," *Columbia* [South Carolina] *State,* 31 October 1982, p. G6.

A former student in Dickey's verse composition class at the University of South Carolina and a published poet, Ludvigson focuses on Dickey's ability to express the female world "male-imagined" in Puella *(1982), while noting Dickey's technical innovations as he shifts from his familiar narrative approach to a new lyric mode in this volume.*

Think of the towering, broad shouldered huntsman in the photographs: wide-brimmed Stetson shading the tanned face, bow and arrows gripped in one steady hand, "American Manhood" the invisible caption.

Think of the novel *Deliverance,* and the WW II poems, such as "The Firebombing," from the National Book Award-winning *Buckdancer's Choice,* or the much-anthologized "The Performance." Now here is *Puella,* his 11th collection of poems–a radical departure for James Dickey, whose image as a "man's man" is suddenly admirably enlarged. In *Puella* Dickey assumes the persona of his young wife Deborah, and in that role he explores and imagines a girl's growth toward maturity.

This isn't the first time James Dickey has written from a female perspective, of course. Who could forget his stunning long poem "Falling," in which a stewardess plunges from an airplane to her death. But here Dickey creates a sustained, book-length journey into, through, and beyond female adolescence. The choice of the Latin word "puella" (girl) suggests the mythic significance the poet intends for the life he conjures partly from fact, partly from romantic vision. The result? A surprisingly androgynous experience as real–and as idealized–as that of any male or female passage from child to adult.

Male writers who convincingly enter a woman's consciousness are relatively rare. Flaubert and James and a handful of others come to mind. Among contemporary poets, perhaps the most notable is Randall Jarrell, whose "Woman at the Washington Zoo" and several other poems are wonderful examples of the male writer transcending the limits of his own sex.

In *Self Interviews,* published a dozen years ago, Dickey acknowledges his affinity with Jarrell: "Randall Jarrell seemed so much like me. He had sort of the same background . . . there seemed to be something in the temperament of

The Rain Guitar

The water-grass under had never waved
But one way. It showed me that flow is forever
Sealed from rain in a weir. For some reason having
To do with Winchester, I was sitting on my guitar case
Watching nothing but eelgrass trying to go downstream
with all the right motions
But one. I had on a sweater whose threads were opening
Like mouths with rain. A bridge ~~cobbled over~~ with a man
~~With a man,~~ who came near and cast a fish- cobbled over; he —
thread into the weir. I had no line and no feeling.
I had nothing to do with fish
But my eyes on the grass they hid in, and only a little
With rain. What could I do, with what I had?
I got out my guitar, that's supposed to improve
With moisture, and hit the lowest
And loudest chord. The drops that were falling
Just then, rang out with G. The man fishing
Turned around. Play it, he said through his pipe. with cold fingers
There I went, fast as I could. The strings shook
With drops. North Georgia reeled in a buck dance
Over the weir. Where was the town
Cathedral, in all this? Out of sight, but present. around, somewhere
Play some more of that,
He said, and cast. The Music-wood shone,
Getting better faster than it liked;
Improvement ~~That is~~ supposed to take years
~~Came on it like rain.~~ It darkened (2nd rang)
And rang like chimes. I kept it simple ~~for my cold~~
~~fingers,~~ and loud as I could. My sweater collapsed and the rain
reached
My underwear. I picked, the guitar showered
Off itself as though it were the one
~~Raining~~. He cast to the mountain
Music. His wood leg tapped
On the cobbles. Memories of many men
Hung, rain-faced, improving, sealed-off
In the weir. I started playing Australian
Versions of British marching songs. His ~~leg tapped~~ legs and marched
Like ~~many men~~ companions. I was Air Force,
I said. So was I; I picked
This up in Burma, he said, tapping his gone leg (lost)
With his fly-rod, as Burma and North Georgia reeled,
Rapped, cast, chimed, darkened, ~~and~~ improved and drew
down
Cathedral water, buck
Dancing like many men.

Cathedral water, ~~the right rain.~~

2nd improved.

Revised draft for one of Dickey's most frequently reprinted poems. It first appeared in the 8 January 1972 issue of the New Yorker *and was collected in* The Strength of Fields *(Author's private papers).*

the writer–I hadn't met him at that time–very much like the part of myself that I wanted most to set down on paper. There was a humanistic feeling of compassion and gentleness about him." Jarrell, a master of the persona poem in the female voice, suggests the difficulty of the task Dickey recently completed. In his poem "Cinderella" Jarrell writes: " 'What men want . . .' said the godmother softly–/How she went on it is hard for man to say."

Hard as it is, the effort to imagine the inner life not just of another person, but of the opposite sex, is worth the trouble. In *Puella,* Dickey does what many of us are trying to do–in poems and in living: to put ourselves so entirely into the minds and hearts and bodies of those unlike ourselves that we can truly empathize, truly know, through our own imaginative capacities, the joys and fears and failures of our fellow humans. To escape the limits of sex is to make possible a similar erasing of the boundaries of race, nationality, age–all those demarcations that separate us from each other. We can only applaud Dickey's emergence, in the fifth decade of his life, as a poet who speaks for a more encompassing humanity than one rooted primarily in male experience.

The voice in these poems remains, nonetheless, the distinctive voice of the James Dickey we know: here are the driving, recognizable rhythms of the loosely dactylic line (not real meter, but the dactyl and its mirror twin, the anapest, recur often enough to feel dominant). Here too is the romantic vision typical of many of Dickey's past poems (the subtitle for one poem is "Deborah as Winged Seed, Descending with Others," and for another "Imagining Herself as the Environment, She Speaks to James Wright at Sundown").

In "Deborah as Scion," the speaker explores her relationship with the female members of her own family: "As I stand here going back/And back, from mother to mother: I am totally them in the eyebrows,/Breasts, breaths and butt:/You, never met Grandmother of the fields/Of death, who laid this frail dress/Most freshly down, I stand now in your closed bones,/Sucked-in, in your magic tackle, taking whatever . . ."

We sense the authentic in this mythic search for identity, for one's place in the family, in the universe. At the end of the poem the persona speaks of the merging of these women: "And we can hold, woman on woman,/This dusk if no other/and we will now, all of us combining,/Open one hand./Blood into light Is possible: lamp, lace and tackle paired bones of the deep Rapture/surviving reviving, and wearing well/For this sundown, and not any other,/In the one depth/Without levels, deepening for us."

The reader is drawn into the depth, into the sense of life deepening with understanding, with the prospect of wisdom.

And when, in "Deborah in Ancient Lingerie, in Thin Oak Over Creek," the speaker discovers her power to achieve, to be competent in boylike gymnastics as well as at anything else she envisions for herself, we share her triumph. Her insistent "I can do," echoed throughout the poem, is the affirmation too of the poet, who can make language the means to a breakthrough in perception, a risk not unlike Deborah's balancing on the oak limb.

Dickey once said, "You enter into the experience that you have imagined and try to realize it. And that entering and committing-to is what makes writing poetry so damned exciting." The successful imagining of another life, and of other lives, is equally exciting for the reader who asks Dickey's central question in *Puella:* "Who can tell who was born of what?"

EULOGY:

James Dickey, "For Richard Hugo," *Corona,* 3 (1983): 16-17.

Dickey's longtime friend and fellow poet Richard Hugo died of cancer 22 October 1982.

In the late fifties I was introduced to Richard Hugo in a letter from James Wright, who had been in one of Theodore Roethke's poetry workshops with Dick a few years earlier. Immediately a good many connections showed themselves. Poetry, of course, was one, but I had not up to that time known a poet who had as much of an interest in the outdoors as I did, and in the human mystiques that can have meaning only there. His mania was fishing and mine was bowhunting; we planned trip after trip together–letters filled with the wilderness–on which we would do both, somewhere either in the Cascades or the Great Smokies. Dick was a good organizer of such epistolary expeditions; he always envisioned them as being into the remotest possible places–some, I now think, imaginary–and as I came to know him better I gradually understood that this was because he looked on them essentially as escape; I understood this to be the case because I did also; Dick was working as a writer of training manuals at the Boeing Aircraft Com-

Remnant Water, Drained Lake

Here in the thrust-green ~~alive~~ alive timing
~~His~~ Grass wind and thin surface almost touching withholding
~~(Touching) withholding~~
Three times four five each other
Hairlined backwater barely there and it
Utterly: left left
comes what is left
Of the gone depth arriving
Into the weeds belly-up,
One carp now knowing how
Grass and also
Thorn-shucks and seeds can outstay him :

Next to (out of) the dead lake the inlet
Trembles seine-presence (pressure) in something of the last
Rippling grass in the brown slow dance
Learned from green a hundred acres of escaped water come down (coming)
To death-mud shaking
(In) Its only pool holding the dead one diving up,
Bursting his stomach in weeds in the gruel
Of scum and around him all grass in a bristling sail
Takes off and comes back. Here in the dry hood I am watching
Alone (,) in my tribal sweat my people gone my fish spinning
Beneath me and I die
Waiting will wait out
The blank judgment given only
In ruination's sucking acre wait and make the no-sound
Praise and a shocked fire like scales
an open-gut flash
An open eye with thumb-pressure
Brain ~~Strike~~ my winter-wool head
Waiting for nothing
To be proved and will wait
For nothing for good.

(through) ripples of wire-touched water (chain-linked)
what used to be chain-linked water
deep-blowing water,
Tiny waves flat-moving fence of wire-touched water

Working draft for poem that first appeared in the 10 March 1973 issue of the New Yorker *and was collected in* The Strength of Fields *(Author's private papers)*

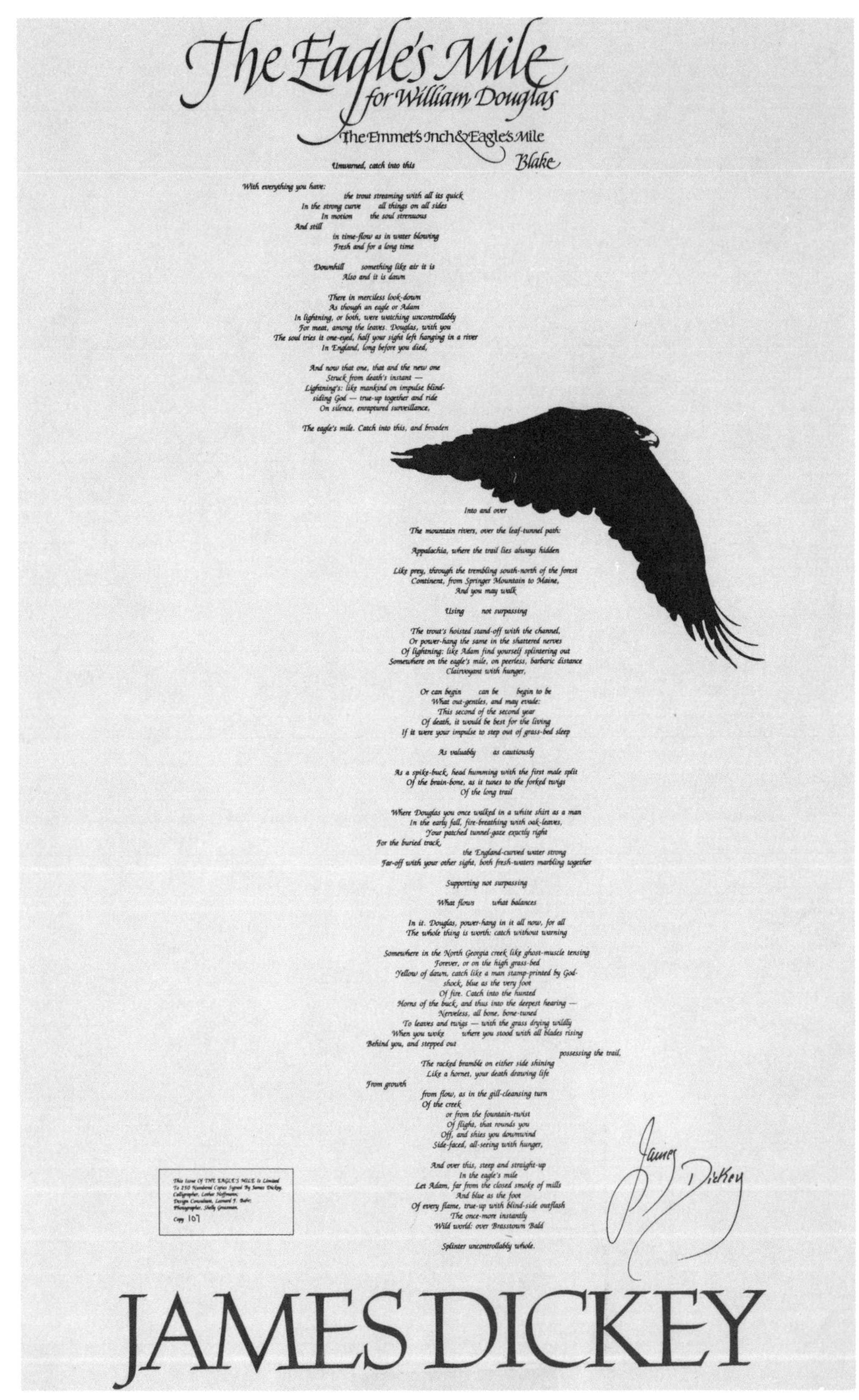

The Eagle's Mile
for William Douglas

The Emmet's Inch & Eagle's Mile
Blake

Unwarned, catch into this

With everything you have:
the trout streaming with all its quick
In the strong curve all things on all sides
In motion the soul strenuous
And still
in time-flow as in water blowing
Fresh and for a long time

Downhill something like air it is
Also and it is dawn

There in merciless look-down
As though an eagle or Adam
In lightning, or both, were watching uncontrollably
For meat, among the leaves. Douglas, with you
The soul tries it one-eyed, half your sight left hanging in a river
In England, long before you died,

And now that one, that and the new one
Struck from death's instant —
Lightning's: like mankind on impulse blind-
siding God — true-up together and ride
On silence, enraptured surveillance,

The eagle's mile. Catch into this, and broaden

Into and over

The mountain rivers, over the leaf-tunnel path:

Appalachia, where the trail lies always hidden

Like prey, through the trembling south-north of the forest
Continent, from Springer Mountain to Maine,
And you may walk

Using not surpassing

The trout's hoisted stand-off with the channel,
Or power-hang the same in the shattered nerves
Of lightning: like Adam find yourself splintering out
Somewhere on the eagle's mile, on peerless, barbaric distance
Clairvoyant with hunger,

Or can begin can be begin to be
What out-gentles, and may evade:
This second of the second year
Of death, it would be best for the living
If it were your impulse to step out of grass-bed sleep

As valuably as cautiously

As a spike-buck, head humming with the first male split
Of the brain-bone, as it tunes to the forked twigs
Of the long trail

Where Douglas you once walked in a white shirt as a man
In the early fall, fire-breathing with oak-leaves,
Your patched tunnel-gaze exactly right
For the buried track,
the England-curved water strong
Far-off with your other sight, both fresh-waters marbling together

Supporting not surpassing

What flows what balances

In it. Douglas, power-hang in it all now, for all
The whole thing is worth: catch without warning

Somewhere in the North Georgia creek like ghost-muscle tensing
Forever, or on the high grass-bed
Yellow of dawn, catch like a man stamp-printed by God-
shock, blue as the very foot
Of fire. Catch into the hunted
Horns of the buck, and thus into the deepest hearing —
Nerveless, all bone, bone-tuned
To leaves and twigs — with the grass drying wildly
When you woke where you stood with all blades rising
Behind you, and stepped out
possessing the trail,
The racked bramble on either side shining
Like a hornet, your death drawing life
From growth
from flow, as in the gill-cleansing turn
Of the creek
or from the fountain-twist
Of flight, that rounds you
Off, and shies you downwind
Side-faced, all-seeing with hunger,

And over this, steep and straight-up
In the eagle's mile
Let Adam, far from the closed smoke of mills
And blue as the foot
Of every flame, true-up with blind-side outflash
The once-more instantly
Wild world: over Brasstown Bald

Splinter uncontrollably whole.

This Issue Of THE EAGLE'S MILE Is Limited To 250 Numbered Copies Signed By James Dickey.
Calligrapher, Lothar Hoffmann;
Design Consultant, Leonard J. Bahr;
Photographer, Shelly Grossman.
Copy 107

James Dickey

JAMES DICKEY

Broadside (1981). The poem, an example of Dickey's "open" verse, pays tribute to United States Supreme Court Justice William O. Douglas. It was collected in Night Hurdling.

pany in Seattle and I was turning out advertising copy for Coca-Cola in Atlanta. What saved us, I am sure, from despair and sterility was the extraordinary purity and promise of the forests and rivers, the trout, the deer and the elk, that we sent through the air back and forth. Dick Hugo always had, for me, the privileged aspect of the co-conspirator, the Secret Brother, and I rejoiced in his liberation from American industry as much as I did in my own from American commerce. The bond between us was very strong, based on poetry and on a wild, physical and vanishing world, and it also had elements of what might have been fate. When I lay in the Mason Clinic in Seattle after major surgery three years ago, Dick Hugo's was the first voice I heard over the phone, after I came out from under the anesthetic. He proposed to drive from his home in Missoula to Seattle to render what support he could, including blood–if the bloods matched, and he was sure they would–and if I had not discouraged him, would have driven there through the stone snows of Mt. St. Helens, which at that time were hovering and jamming between us. Two years after that, I heard his voice again calling long distance. "I'm out here in Mason Clinic, Jim," he said. "I've got lung cancer." For a moment I could think of nothing to reply. What could there have been? Then he added, "I'm in your old room. Maybe that'll be worth something." I told him that I hoped it would, but that no matter what he must get out, for we had not yet packed in to the Cascades, not yet escaped.

From his first book, called initially *Triangle for Green Men* and sent to me in manuscript, I followed Dick's work closely, and I was delighted but not surprised to see his true idiom appear with more and more authority and power in successive volumes. The colloquial tone, at the same time sardonic and schoolboy earnest, is just right for him, and can take on, and take in, an astonishing variety of subjects, all memorable, all domains of the same perplexed, dogged and humorous personality. I am glad there is so much of Dick's work, especially of the later poetry, because the large numbers of good poems will make his place among us and our children–and theirs–more secure, and that will be a good thing for the human sensibilities of the future, particularly for those who need or want their beliefs in the wilderness renewed.

Hold on out there, Dick Hugo. I am sixty, myself. We beat the American system, got our work done and got out into poetry, teaching, and the love of the people who loved us.

And on the upper Snoqualmie, somewhere, we will pack in yet.

ROUND-TABLE DISCUSSION:
From "James Dickey Symposium: A Celebration," University of South Carolina, 1-4 February 1983.

On 5 February 1983, the Saturday morning after the formal events of the symposium held to commemorate Dickey's sixtieth birthday, this previously unpublished discussion was recorded. Participants included such well-known men of letters as John Simon, Richard Howard, Harold Bloom, and Monroe Spears. Also involved in the discussion were University of South Carolina English professor George Geckle, Clemson University professor Robert Hill; poet Susan Ludvigson; and Dickey.

Geckle: When I first met Jim Dickey over a kitchen sink in 1968, he discovered with delight that I taught Renaissance drama and began quoting obscure lines from Webster and Middleton and Jonson and Marlowe. I knew the lines, and like a good academic I could have given act, scene, and line, but I could not have quoted them. I was stunned because while I had heard something about Jim Dickey it certainly had not been this. Over the years I have not lost the surprise and wonder at the breadth and sheer amount of knowledge the man has.

Howard: I don't think that it's so startling that Jim has read everything. I think that he's supposed to have read everything. Quite simply, the training of a poet in the English language is to have read what has preceded him. As it turns out, every poet of some strength and individual characteristics has done this. I marvel at it and delight in it, but in a different way. I remember in 1965, when I first encountered Jim, I was a bit surprised by his familiarity with what I thought of as somewhat obscure French writers. This surprise was because that sort of knowledge seemed to be outside the realm of a person I thought of as a powerfully regional poet who had even then spoken with a strong sense of place and climate. As far as his relation to English writing, it didn't surprise me that he knew most of it and had strong feelings about most of it. It seems to me to be what he should have had. You are mistaken if you think that it is wonderful to have read every-

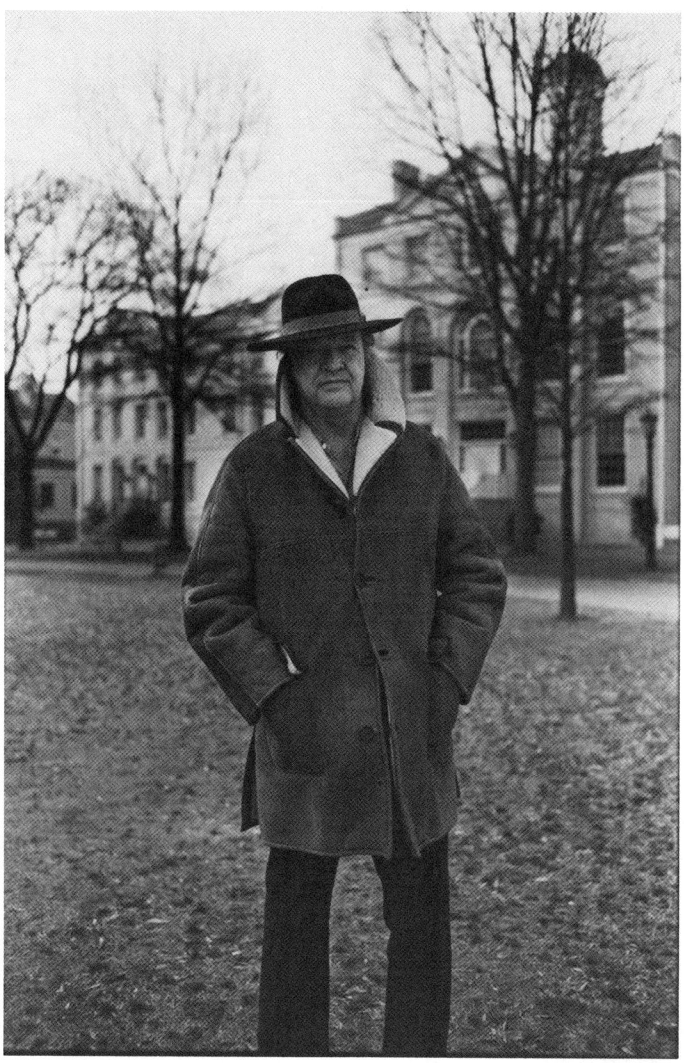

Dickey on the Horseshoe, the original grounds of the University of South Carolina, circa 1981

thing. It is merely what you have to do to be a poet.

Simon: But let me add something to this. It is one thing to read about Patrice de la Tour du Pin in a volume by some urbane academic critic; however, to be walking through the north Georgia woods (I assume there are woods in north Georgia) and to find among the–whatever they are–the palmettos, suddenly, a French pine tree, and a French tower too, for de la Tour du Pin is both, built in this particular locale, in this ambience, gives both de la Tour du Pin and the northern Georgia woods a new life. And it is a kind of third, a tertium quid, emerging, which is particularly astonishing, and that combination is what is so exciting in Dickey's thought and work.

Spears: I would like to differ with Richard in his assertion that all poets do this. I have known an awful lot who didn't. Although I am reaching the age when one fears to be thought a "viewer with alarm," one of the things I can't help viewing with alarm is how many would-be poets nowadays don't want to read anything, especially any other poet and especially in any other language. Jim is a fine example of the diametrical opposite.

Bloom: I think that would be true of what one would call the strong poet. That doesn't mean, by the way, that the opinions are necessarily those that the critical tradition is going to accept. Some of Jim's critical opinions, it seems to me, are justified and justifiable and will probably be confirmed by the canon-making choice of tradition, some possibly not as he would be the first,

Dickey with his daughter, Bronwen, born 1981

himself, to tell you. You have but to compare *Babel to Byzantium* with *The Suspect in Poetry* to see that he is a man who has passionately changed his mind. He passionately salutes certain poets and later passionately renounces them.

I think of a poet whose letters Jim has quoted so often, Hart Crane, who is a powerful reader of other poets and a man with enormous, deep erudition in English and American Poetry. As Jim found, he was also a man whose passionate critical judgment has, more often than not, been borne out. There are, and I hope I do not disfigure the occasion by saying so, some of Jim's most recent judgments, as in the epiloque to *Babel to Byzantium,* in which . . .

Dickey: I repudiate all my previous opinions . . .

Bloom: Well, not all, but certain . . .

Simon: Very few, not really enough for my taste.

Bloom: I can think of one instance. I have always shared with Jim, I thought, a passionate admiration for the poetry of Edwin Arlington Robinson. I was dismayed to see, in what I hope was simply a fit of splendid fury, a withdrawal of his admiration.

Dickey: I may come back to that.

Simon: But, you see, this is wonderful. For Jim to write his introduction to Robinson he obviously had to read all that claptrap from one end to the other. What comes out of it is one great line. He is able to zero in on that one nugget: in this case "Lingard with his eerie joy." He brings us back this one wonderful nugget out of an absolute pile of I won't tell you what.

Bloom: There I must differ although you have been eloquent as always. Jim's is a passionate mode of criticism. It is like Swinburne's; that is a precise analogue. It has the same rush of language as the poetry.

Simon: May I add one thing? I remember being very impressed, as I still am, by my former boss and mentor, Harry Levin. He was the first man I ever met who, if you called up on the phone before noon, would say things to you like, "How do you think Raskolnikov slept last night?" Or he would say, "I think Emma Bovary had a wonderful day yesterday, don't you?" This is a man who really lived in those inventions. Those creations were more alive to him than anything else. And in Dickey's enormous, voracious erudition there is that same kind of hunger to know everything, to digest everything. But what you could not do with Harry Levin would be to discuss him or your neighbor or fellow teacher or whatever. With Dickey there's always life; there's always existence; there's always reality; there's always what happened to you and to him and to your common friend. And that's wonderful. That is his definition of poetry, too: that it is a total possession of reality and a total possession of the imagination and fusing them together and somehow creating the ultimate artifact that transcends artifact.

Spears: That's a fine statement, and I'd like to add to it. I'm always amused and pleased by what Jim says in interviews: "When it comes to choosing between art and life, I'll take life anytime. Keep the thing thoroughly alive."

Howard: One of the things which interests me about Jim's poetry as an exemplification of the American lyric is the distinction between what I will call intellectual hardware–names, dates, places–and an abluting impulse in American poetry, an emptying-out quality. The poetry always empties out. The prose, both the fiction and the criticism, is full of exactitudes and nailings down. Occasionally the lyric impulse will attach itself to a place. While there are lyrics titled with exactitude as to where we are, the lyric itself usually refuses what one might call local attachments, whereas the kind of man that Dickey is–and the kind of expression that his prose insists on–is one of great veracity and connection to feelings, objects, time. I'm amazed by the abstraction and withdrawal, the ablution, let's call it–there is probably a critical term for this.

Bloom: I am about to apply one of my own devising, taken from St. Paul. It is gnosis, and though Richard and I haven't discussed this aspect of the poetry, I think that we are on the same track. This quality is, I think, the characteristic trope of all of Jim's poetry of the early motion. What we have neglected is the middle motion–that is, where the work has been from 1966 down to the present moment. Even in those poems of what look like violent possession of personality and situation, such as "Mayday Sermon," "Falling," and "Slave Quarters," and which reach the grandest scale in *The Zodiac,* the most characteristic stance that the language of the poem takes on is that of a rather systematic emptying out of sense. I do not mean sense as meaning but rather as the apprehension of particulars. It is a *defensive* movement, a type of gnosis.

In St. Paul's letters gnosis is the process voluntarily undergone by Christ when he empties himself of the divinity and accepts being purely a man, being purely a human who can then be crucified and die a human death on the cross. For Jim this is not in a religious sense but in a more technical or poetic sense–a characteristic undoing, what rhetoricians might call a metonymizing. Freud discusses three types of movement of this sort: regression, which I think is not operative in this aspect of Jim's work; a repetition compulsion, which I also think is not applicable in this case; and undoing. The undoing mechanism is ritualistic and has to do with the fear of violating a taboo, which is a kind of lustration in which you perpetually seek to wash off the stain, yet you cannot wash it off. So it is related to some mood of guilt which cannot be eradicated. This seems to be a striking technical characteristic of Dickey's poetic language, even in a poem which is as abundant in its imagery as *The Zodiac.* When you examine the individual images you find that they are not images of presence; they are images of absence. They are images of something which has not quite departed but which is in the act of departing. It is in that sense that I believe the early and middle works are very much involved in each other.

The kind of tribute that we have been paying Jim as teacher and passionate critic of poetry is equally applicable to his poetry, but you have to change the terminology because it is a solitary poetry, not gregarious. It is as much as Whitman's a hermetic kind of poetry and has the courage to see that this is the case. There is a split between the man and poet, and I think that in a dualist that would be inevitable. There is a split between art and life, however strongly one stands on the side of life.

One of the stigmata which marks this is an extraordinary sense that something within, I think in Jim's case the poet qua poet, does not feel free unless he is totally alone. The other, and perhaps even more alienated and alienating stigmata, is a sense that what matters most in one (and matters overwhelmingly in this poet as poet) is something which does not belong to the creation at all, which seems to be earliest, seems to go back before the creation.

It is difficult to reconcile this to Jim's public persona, but I think that in the end he is profoundly a dualist. His yearnings may be monistic but he reminds me of Emerson in that regard. Emerson has a powerful passage in his notebooks in which with some anguish he cries out, "seer of unity, believer in unity, I yet behold two." I think this is one reason Jim's middle poetry is so much more problematic than the earlier motion was. It is hard not to love the earlier poetry. It makes populist gestures but is more difficult and hermetic than it appears to be. The middle poetry, of which *The Zodiac* is the most distinguished and certainly the most ambitious single representative, is a more difficult poetry to come to terms with because in spite of its vitalistic gestures, vitalistic realities and intensities, it is no longer easily accessible on the surface. *The Zodiac* is not an easy poem for any reader.

Hill: By way of trying to explore this question, and not exactly disagreeing with you, I am troubled a bit about the omission particularly of the later works. I admire *The Zodiac* as well and find it problematic in certain ways, but it seems to me that part of the problem you've expressed has to do with the preconception of the isolated Dickey, this propensity to empty out. I'm thinking that the middle period–and particularly in poems like "May Day Sermon," "The Eye-Beaters," *The Zodiac,* and the poems in *Strength of Fields*–there is more reaching out to the other world in the sense of the social world. I'm not sure that it is enough to say that it's just problematic because it doesn't fit the earlier, ritualistic Dickey. It seems to me that one of his impulses in the middle works is an inclusiveness that is itself a kind of satisfaction and, indeed, joy.

Bloom: I can also recognize those currents of an almost desperate reaching out after not that kind of divine otherness of the early reaching, but toward a man speaking to man, to use a Wordsworthian phrase. What I find as a single reader who has pondered these poems is strongest in *The Zodiac.* What was certainly strongest to me in "May Day Sermon," "Slave Quarters," and "Falling" are not the gestures of human community. They are the gestures of a kind of vertigo, of an increasingly solitary consciousness in a world which, in spite of itself, is almost systematically emptying of objects. That is what seems to me to be imagistically and poetically most impressive. It comes at a very high human cost, and then it is very moving. There is a kind of attempt on the part of the poet and the poetry to modify this, to qualify this, to reach out and make gestures toward community. But these gestures seem to me imagistically and rhetorically weaker than that bleaker and more uncanny quality of solitary consciousness. By any mode of criticism, there are some three dozen or more poems in the first three volumes which are not problematical: which really have made for themselves a place in the canon of American poetry, and indeed the poetry of the English language.

There is something which *is* problematical, as well as ambitious, about most of the major poems from the middle period down to the present. I don't see how any critic of any persuasion or judgment could simply dismiss them. At the same time there are elements of disunity, most certainly, which have to do with the split that we're talking about: the increasing dualism. As the years pass and I come to know them better, I will value them more highly than I do now. But I quote that Emersonian version of what he calls the New England law of compensation: "Nothing is got for nothing." There is a very high price, including a high poetic price, which is at times being paid in Dickey's work of his middle period.

Hill: Is it a high poetic price, or is it our critical categories that have to pay the price when a poet does something that's important?

1.

DELIGHTS OF THE EDGE

Henry de Montherlant, the fine, fiery novelist and essayist of the muscles, guts and sexual organs, of pride and chance-taking, once said, "If your life ever bores you, then risk it." Montherlant is probably, even more than Hemingway, our philosopher of actions, of the delights of the edge.

I thought of this a couple of years ago in North Georgia, sitting a couple of hundred feet above a dammed river, on pinestraw and with my feet at a very real edge. My wife and I were looking down onto a section of the Tallulah River where a film of mine called Deliverance was being made. Both our sons were below us, far out of the range of our voices, my oldest boy working on the shooting crew, my youngest, thirteen, just visiting. The state-run dam was closed, which meant that the great rocky fall-offs had no water to fall off them. But they had my boys. We lay at the edge, hoping they would do nothing foolish, but also io ntensely interested in what they would do. The filming was taking place on both sides of the river, and, at the edge of a ninety-foot drop, there was a primitive kind of set-up where you could walk across the river holding a rope. There was also a place where you had to jump over a kind of trickling gap, still holding to the rope. Or not holding to the rope. Below you (my son) for ninety feet --I kept going up and down the rock-cruelties with field-glasses --was nothing but a set of stones designed by the universe ages ago to demonstrate the utter indifference of wild nature to the body of human beings. Any rock in your descent was certain to be deadly death--dealing. My wife and I said, almost at the same time, "I hope Kevin doesn. t try it."

But then of course he did. The high-perched parents could do nothing to prevent it: could do nothing, in fact, but watch like strange

Revised typescript page from Dickey's essay on the attractions of danger, published in the June 1974 Mademoiselle *and collected in his 1983 book,* Night Hurdling *(Author's private papers)*

Bloom: There are many critical categories, and I am, myself, horribly eclectic. I don't think I have any single category. I began by writing long commentaries on Blake, and all my life I have worked with poems that might have been considered extreme. I think that I am the kind of reader that by temperament and training is naturally inclined to *The Zodiac,* and I voted for it in my review in the *New Republic.* But I don't think that Jim's poetry is served by *not* seeing that there is something much more difficult and unsettled about the poetry of the middle period as compared to other poems we have talked about.

Hill: How do you see the *Puella* poems, following this line?

Bloom: I haven't really digested them. I began to read them only six or eight months ago. There are, I think, different kinds of problems there. It's hard to say–the diction, at times, cannot quite support the intensity of the poet's love. It is too close, perhaps.

The issue of dualism is somewhat muted. I see your point implicitly. You could say that he is either veiling the dualism or blinding himself to it as much as possible. It would be tactless of him and he's always had superb decorum and poetic tact.

Hill: Is there not the possibility that there's a genuine resolution happening in these later poems?

Bloom: I see no sign of it as yet. After all, we are talking about the middle period. The gentleman is sixty, and we trust that he will still be writing in twenty years.

Howard: There seems to be a kind of split among the people here between the idea of what Yeats calls "the smiling public man" and the thunderous private one whom we all know. I hear from those of you who are with Jim a great deal and who want rather quickly to close the lid and say, "Yes, it's all one. We've seen it all." And it seems to me that you are sitting rather tightly on the lid. You want to leave him in there–you've got your Jim Dickey and you've got him home–almost. You have no exceptions, no false leads, no ways which lead nowhere, no parts of the labyrinth that lead against a dead wall. You have resolved him into an almost transparent honeycomb. It sounds to me like you really want to cut off access.

Hill: That's not a fair statement. That's not what I'm saying at all. I've see Jim Dickey's work in an almost constant evolution, constant reworking, constant experimentation. And I think that there are some dead ends. For instance, I think that "Looking for the Buckhead Boys," amusing as it is, is a dead end as a kind of public, chatty poem. And it seems to me that there are a lot of poems like that. As an intelligent critic of his own poetry, he recognizes this in his own work. My feeling is that it's the people outside here who feel they have Dickey nailed down. We see him day to day, as the poems come out.

Dickey: All this learning is certainly impressive to the transfixed bard. In listening to all these learned commentaries, hearing Emerson referred to, I'm reminded of the only anecdote I ever heard about Emerson. Emerson lent a Concord farmer a copy of Plato. He saw the farmer in a couple of months, and the farmer sort of silently handed him back the book. Emerson asked him what he thought of it, and the farmer said, "It's all right. . . . He's got a lot of my ideas in that book." I think that Richard Howard and Harold Bloom and John Simon and Monroe Spears and Bob Hill all have a lot of my ideas. Everybody's right: especially the ones that are favorable.

Bloom: I am much interested in the issue of influence and how the influence process works. As I said last night, I cannot think of a poem by Jim that is as free of genre distinction as "Approaching Prayer." If I were to try to set his mode, I think that there are always precursor figures. There always is an internalized contest with those figures. There is a debt to Roethke and Yeats more than any other. There is a lesser debt to Dylan Thomas in diction, though in nothing else. I think that Jim is more of a phenomenon as a poet than Thomas. Jim is a poet comparable to Roethke whom he has many times proclaimed the greatest American poet–a judgment difficult to accept since we have had Walt Whitman, Emily Dickinson, Wallace Stevens, and Hart Crane. Other critics would name Pound and Frost, and I would speak of E. A. Robinson.

Roethke is more of an assimilator of poems. Roethke's two best books are the two middle books, *The Lost Son* and *Praise to the End.* He is most himself in these books. The curious thing about *The Far Field,* which has always disappointed me, is a kind of return of the dead in their own voices rather than in Roethke's voice. There are poems in *The Far Field* that are astonishingly Whitman's, Eliot's, Yeats's, and in other places, Stevens's. It's the sort of phenomenon you find in Howard Nemerov, for instance, who is an exemplary poet and man of letters; but I don't enjoy his poetry because those same poets and Auden are on every page. For some reason Roethke's precursors take that kind of complex revenge on him in the final phase. If I compare Roethke's early poems to Jim's early poems, there is no doubt that Jim's are light years ahead of Roethke's achievements in the early work. Then if one takes *The Lost Son* and *Praise to the End* and compared them to Jim's middle phase, from about 1966 to 1982, it would be hard for me to judge. Jim is more ambitious and as original. And Jim's is on a larger scale and more cosmological.

Howard: One of the things about Dickey's criticism of Roethke is that it has been needed. Roethke has become unfashionable and has vanished from the scene, except for Jim's admiration of him. I've been most grateful to Jim for his insistence that Roethke will be a presence among us. There is in the literary world a virtual reluctance to do more than pay a kind of stiff upper lip service to this figure.

Bloom: It just seems to me that Dickey's first phase is more important than Roethke's. At this point I think that I have to award the palm to Roethke in terms of the middle poems as in *The Lost Son,* but then I somehow have every mystical apprehension and expectation that we are not in for *The Far Field* from Jim. I hope that his shrewdness about his own poetry has been gathering for us.

Dickey: I'd like to say a couple of things about Roethke. To an astounding degree he can involve the reader in the situation of the poem. But there is one thing wrong with him, one besetting trouble. His subject matter is so narrow, and he keeps saying the same thing over and over in different ways. I don't mean to turn against my own figures of adulation, but he seems not to involve himself with other people very much. He doesn't write well about people, and he has little or no dramatic sense.

Bloom: And Wallace Stevens is also a great poet who doesn't write well about people and also has no dramatic sense.

Geckle: One of the striking characteristics of Dickey's poetry is his ability to constantly surprise the reader. What is it about his poetry that can still surprise you?

Bloom: The recklessness. He takes enormous aesthetic chances at every point. One should not deceive oneself: no one could take such extraordinary chances and succeed all the time. It would be impossible.

Dickey: That pleases me as much as anything that's ever been said about me. That is just what I want to do. I have lots of faults as a writer, but I do try to stay on the edge and not do the same thing again. The latest battle I am trying to fight is a battle of diction. I made an address at the South Atlantic Modern Language Association a couple of months ago on different aspects of this, and I took off from a journal entry by Winfield Townley Scott. He talked about the differences in poetic approach and cited one famous line from Hart Crane as an example of the purely verbal approach: "The seal's wide spindrift gaze toward paradise." Here, everything is a marvelous, insightful flash of language, and the emphasis is on the language itself. *Spindrift* is a nice nautical term but it has nothing to do with real seals.

Another line he quoted was Robinson's, "And he was all alone there when he died," which has to do with an actual situation. This is a life situation, and the emphasis is on the situation that the poem depicts rather than on the linguistic way in which it is couched. It seemed to me, as I read through my earlier work, most all I could stand of it, that I was too much on the side of the experiential, unnecessarily so for several books. So many of my things seemed like versified anecdotes. I tried to make them come through with power and tried to make the scene have a certain visionary aspect to it. But it seemed to me that there was still too much of that experience and not enough emphasis on the linguistic component of the poem. In *Puella* I tried to go over to the side of the linguist. I don't know how successful *Puella* is, but I wouldn't have missed doing it. I enjoyed it, and it opened up a whole dimension of language that I had shamefully neglected before. One of the lines that I remember from *Puella* is an attempt to give a kind of linguistic rendition of distance, which would have been out of place with any of my other work: "The near hills thinning with overreach." That kind of line would not have been a part of anything in an earlier poem because it would have taken away from the narrative or the anecdotal force of the kind of poem I previously tried to write. The kind exemplified in *Puella* was right for that sort of thing. It's a whole new ball game.

Ludvigson: One thing I would like to talk about, since I'm the only woman on the program, is Mr. Dickey's relationship to women in his poems. I was very impressed in *Puella* with the willingness of the poet to take on the persona of a woman, especially a poet who has been known primarily for his male view of the world. I think, Mr. Dickey, that you've been giving yourself too little credit for the other kinds of linguistic inventiveness in the early poems and maybe not putting enough emphasis on how much you do with characters in *Puella.* I think that you have a lot of success in speaking through the sensibility of a woman in those poems and arriving at a kind of androgynous vision of what it is like to approach puberty and go through the process of becoming a woman. I was surprised to find some of this same willingness to identify with women in the older poetry, like in one called "Chenille." I've liked that poem for a long time. In "Chenille" an old woman who is fairly crazy makes these wonderful bedspreads with fantasy animal figures, not like the peacocks that are turned out by machines in what seems to be a male-dominated world. This woman who becomes almost a Godlike figure is the nurturing one. There is a Garden of Eden kind of scene, but instead of the woman's being the traditional vehicle for everyone being thrown out of the garden, she is the one who nurtures the speaker. Even the snake is nurturing in this poem. Even in this early poem Dickey's view of the role of women is fascinating and complex.

Simon: As someone who is by vocation a theater critic–and a poetry critic, if at all, only by avocation–I think I'm allowed to say simplistic, laymanish things that no one of you others is permitted to utter. As a theater and film critic I have to take taxis from one theater to another. New York is full of potholes, and the ride is sometimes bumpy. I think there are basically two kinds of Dickey poems: *with* potholes and *without* potholes. I like the ones without potholes much better. I could ride those anapests from here to eternity, but those others give me an awfully bumpy ride.

TELEVISION INTERVIEW:
From *Nature and Violence,* South Carolina Educational Television, recorded 18 March 1983.

In this passage from a videotaped interview, Dickey comments on his reasons for returning to live in the South and on the appeal the South holds for him.

I have lived many different places, but I chose to come back to the South to live because when one is born in a place it is more or less in the blood, or in the bone marrow, or in the tone of the voice and in the way you see things and react to things and to people. . . . The Southerner's relation to nature is somewhat different from what it is in other parts of the country. Part of it depends on the climate and part depends on the geography, on the topography of the South. We have a great deal of Appalachia in the South. We have a tremendous scan of birds and trees and animals in the South. . . . I think that one of the things that a Southerner has going into his particular makeup . . . from the beginning is that the Southerner has been involved with the hunt. . . . A Southerner loves the outdoors. . . . I would say the essence of the South resides in certain attitudes toward one's own people, toward kinship. We have a stronger sense of the family here than they have anywhere else in the country. . . . Sometimes I count whatever blessings I have. . . . For my particular mentality and constitution and preoccupations, one of the luckiest things that ever happened to me, or may be the luckiest, was that I was born a Southerner. It's right for me.

BOOK REVIEW:
Paul Rice, Review of *Night Hurdling: Poems, Essays, Conversations, Commencements, and Afterwords, Georgia Review,* 38 (Fall 1984): 647-650.

Rice's review emphasizes how this multigenre collection demonstrates Dickey's willingness to take risks.

More than any poet in America since Pound, James Dickey has been on the bloody end of *argumentum ad hominem* (only the Englishman Ted Hughes has been equally abused in recent

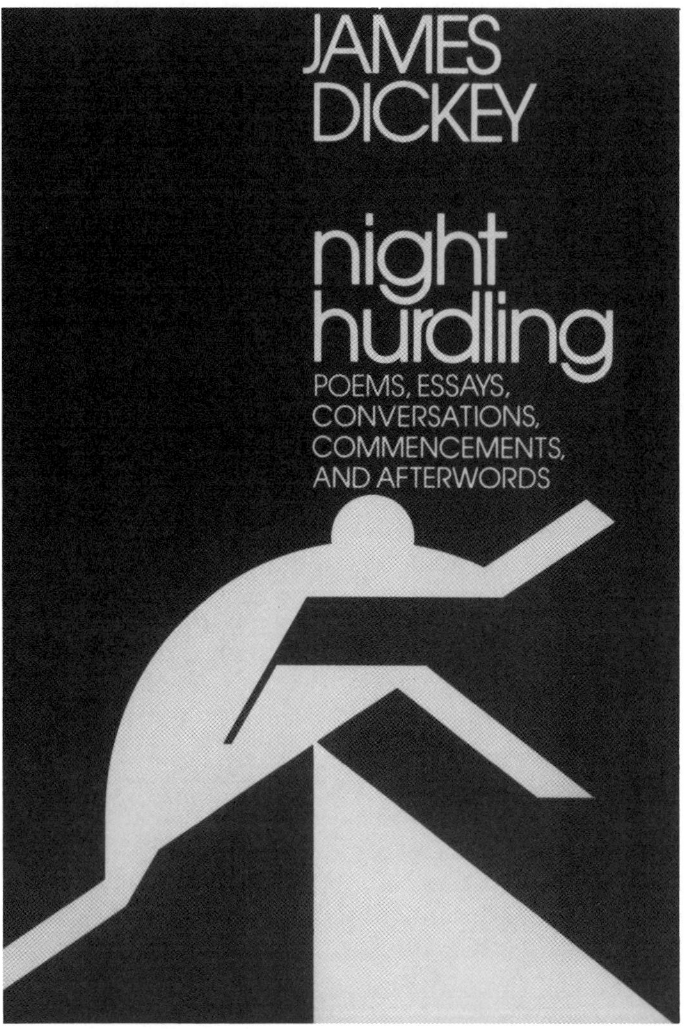

Dust jacket for Dickey's 1983 collection of four poems, nine interviews, and thirty-four essays and addresses

times), so that his attempt to assemble a collection of writings specifically calculated to assert identity may seem a dangerous baring of the underbelly to critical darts. But the Dickey we know from *Poems 1957-1967* and his 1970 novel *Deliverance* has never hesitated in the face of risk, so the move is perfectly in character. In the introduction to *Night Hurdling,* a group of self-chosen prose pieces ranging over the last two decades of his career in letters, Dickey says:

> The question of identity . . . continued to preoccupy me with the topics and forms of this book. I have decided, after making whatever "tests" I could on the material, that such identity as these pieces have comes at odd, instinctive moments, in flickers of meaning, metaphors, chains of words, assumptions, assertions–some of them contradictory–and in places that not everyone would think likely.

Indeed, there is a "come-and-get-me" quality about the provocative opener, *Night Hurdling*'s Genesis, "The Enemy from Eden." In this piece, a narrative persona ("the One") fashions a blowgun from aluminum tubing. He makes darts of coat-hanger wire, files them to a point on his concrete driveway, provides them with an aerodynamic cone made from rolled-up typing paper, fits them to the blowgun with his wife's sewing scissors, and sets out to hunt the Eastern diamondback, whose sound comes from "the Bible, from God in His endless malevolence, from out of the depths of the universal abyss. . . ." This is "the Enemy," and "the One" stalks it, confronts it, and blows a dart into its brain: "You are trying to kill, with the breath of life. . . . The needle is in the brain. Universal Evil does not know what to do with it." Later, in an autobiographical essay entitled "The Starry Place Between the Antlers,"

Dickey admits that one reason he likes living in South Carolina is that there are plenty of snakes to pursue "with a long, dusty aluminum pipe and darts made of coat-hangers and typing paper, and whatever weapon my breath is."

Given this kind of juggling with fiction and nonfiction, how can we find the identity of James Dickey in his fight with a serpent–a fight in which "the One" becomes even more God-like than his Edenic progenitor and actually wins? Can we find *the* James Dickey in any of the pieces in *Night Hurdling,* a book which seems at first glance to present a self-caricatured poseur? Probably not. But there are more important things to find. Dickey makes a much better seeker among Mysteries than a Mystery himself, however much he inflates his diction, so "The Enemy from Eden" is a proper beginning for this collection: it defines the limits of the field, and it speaks symbolically of the two matters which have always formed the basis for Dickey's unique vision. One of these, as seen in "Eden," is the quest for an ideal manhood. (That this quest, and this essay, will send feminist and Freudian critics out for blowguns of their own is, for Dickey, just a sharpening of the point.) Even more important, however, is his search for value in *poesis.*

Dickey has always had a strong sense of what is and is not good poetry and good *for* poetry, and he has been willing to defend the art against those he sees as less-than-honest or incomplete in their practice. An early statement of this position came in a 1959 essay on the poetry of James Merrill, published in *Babel to Byzantium:*

> James Merrill is the most graceful, attractive, and accomplished of the "elegants": . . . the rootless, well-mannered, multilingual young men . . . who have done everything perfectly according to quite acceptable standards, and have . . . stopped short of real significance, real engagement, of the daring and self-forgetfulness that might have made the Word come alive, preferring as they did to settle for décor, decorum, and the approval of a body of like-minded critics who affirmed the assumptions of this approach, and pointed out little tricks of rhyme and phrasing as if these were permanently valuable additions to the spirit.

Up against these elegants, Dickey has placed committed, significant, language-centered making. *Night Hurdling* energetically records the last twenty years of his devotion. He has not changed his mind about Merrill.

Those looking for poetic self-assessments among the writings in this collection may be disappointed until they learn how to catch Dickey talking about his own poetry and the values he considers important in the art. Readers need to look for Dickey's most vocal and animated affirmation of the virtues of other poets he discusses; in most of these cases Dickey is worshiping his own reflection. In "The Water-Bug's Mittens" for instance, he says of Pound: "I like the maker (the *fabbro*) of the clean phrase and the hard-edged imaginative image. . . ," and he talks more completely of art and value in "The Weathered Hand and Silent Space," a piece on Robert Penn Warren:

> The source of Warren's stunning power is *angst,* a kind of radiant metaphysical terror, projected outward into the natural world, particularly into its waiting waste expanses. . . . He is direct, scathingly honest, and totally serious about what he feels. . . . He plunges as though compulsively into the largest of subjects: those that seem to cry out for capitalization and afflatus. . . . The odd tone . . . is compounded of southern dialect, Elizabethanisms overstaying into country speech . . . and always present in rural areas where mountains have gathered to preserve them. . . .

Dickey is from the mountains of North Georgia. He knows all about this desire to fly off the edge, mastering the grand gesture, declaiming like Sidney and Shakespeare.

In one of his best essays here, "The G.I. Can of Beets, The Fox in the Wave, and The Hammers Over Open Ground," he openly commits himself to a category–something he has always seemed loath to do before. He establishes a dichotomy between poets of the "Commentary-On-Life party, the Human-Conditioners" (including Frost, Robinson, Masters, and Hardy) and the "Magic-Language exemplars" (among whom are Hopkins, Crane, and Stevens). The distinction is to be found in the poetic locus of control: "For the Magicians, language itself must be paramount." Dickey confirms, in case we need it, that while he is "not of the party of the magic-language practitioners," he has always "tried to work out with the magical side of the language." Teamed with his dedication to value and language, and his often vituperative opposition to what he once called "the closed, marmoreal, to-be-contemplated kind of poetry," there is in *Night Hurdling* a belief in the Poetry of Behavior wherein commitment forces action, and wherein the language of poetry reflects (and perhaps causes) doing-in-the-world.

Dickey's second main concern, the search for a perfect manhood, proceeds naturally from this belief. In fact, the chief value of *Night Hurdling* lies in the evidence it presents about the search of an intelligent and talented man for a definition of Male Good, for a positive image of masculine action. Robert Bly, in a 1982 *New Age* interview, addresses considerations which clarify the nature of Dickey's grappling with the image and tradition of masculinity. The proper search for the male Ideal, Bly suggests, can come only after the male has first acknowledged and embraced the feminine side of himself, and then looked beyond his feminine side into the "deep pool." "The deep nourishing and spiritually radiant energy," according to Bly, "lies not in the feminine side, but in the deep masculine," which is not "the macho masculine, the snowmobile masculine," but "forceful action undertaken, not without compassion, but with resolve. The ability of the male to shout and be fierce is not the same as treating people like objects, demanding land or empire. . . ." Bly's statements characterize much of James Dickey's obviously male-concerned writing and thinking.

The title essay in *Night Hurdling* recounts a high-school sports experience, a night race between the underdog narrator and "a fine hurdler from Canton, Georgia." It is the story of "fierce rivalry," of "new friendship" between enemies. The young Dickey/persona wins the race, but with an effort that injures him: "I hit [the last hurdle] with the inner ankle of my left foot, tearing the flesh to the bone." Then, crossing the finish line, he "smashed into the spectators and bowled over a little boy, hitting straight into his nose with my knee." The victor received congratulations yet took time to pick up the boy, wipe the blood from his nose, comfort him, and kiss him. The comparison between the victorious hurdler and Bly's notions of the ideal male is complete: the Greek concept of "Zeus energy" which encompasses intelligence, robust health, compassionate authority, good will and leadership as the "sum positive power accepted by the male in the service of the community" is epitomized by the winner in "Night Hurdling." The narrator confirms the worth of his costly victory, calling it "the best moment I ever had out of sports."

Throughout Dickey's poetry and prose we see a concern with man the hunter/fisher. In "A Hand-Line: In Pursuit of the Grey Soul," a well-honed fishing essay, he explores the "day-glow excitement" that "involves every iota of the body and . . . imagination." Concerned also with the nature/nurture question and its implications for male behavior–with the fight-or-flight response and the emotional and chemical implications of facing opposition or running–Dickey recalls these conflicts over and over again, centering them in his ubiquitous theme of predation ("I have always liked rituals involving animals, especially predators . . ."). Casting out for value in each manly activity, Dickey sings the joy of the "Heaven-through-the-guts" adrenaline rush that occurs when his narrator (in "Delights of the Edge") falls asleep while bow-hunting for deer and awakes to see what he thinks is a puma: "Here was one of the edges, and I was there. . . . What I had seen was deathless, even if it had not been there. Adrenaline hit solid. Mine. I rose like the wild king of forever." This vision places the narrator for a moment near his ideal male, who combines the ghost muscles of the puma with the eye of the deer to "begin to be what out-gentles and can evade."

Much of what is available in *Night Hurdling* is like this. And though the book contains plenty of what we have known all along about Dickey's powerful language, it also offers hitherto uncollected "flickers of meaning" which might help readers to change not only their minds but their behavior as well. If some of what Dickey says here seems like posturing, we need to remember the nature of the beasts he hunts, and that there are few models in literature to help him. When we remember also that the Indian put on the face of his prey in order to overpower it with its own spirit, we will forgive the self-indulgence in the *Night Hurdling* methodology.

TELEVISION INTERVIEW:
From *Carolina Journal,* South Carolina Educational Television, videotaped 19 December 1986.

Dickey has always displayed an imaginative capability to enter into the world of play, fear, and innocence of children. He has written poems for and about his children throughout his career, manifesting his unabashed engagement with and affection for them. For a segment of Carolina Journal, *Dickey talked about writing poetry, story telling, and* Bronwen, the Traw, and the Shape Shifter *(1986), the children's book he wrote for his daughter, Bronwen.*

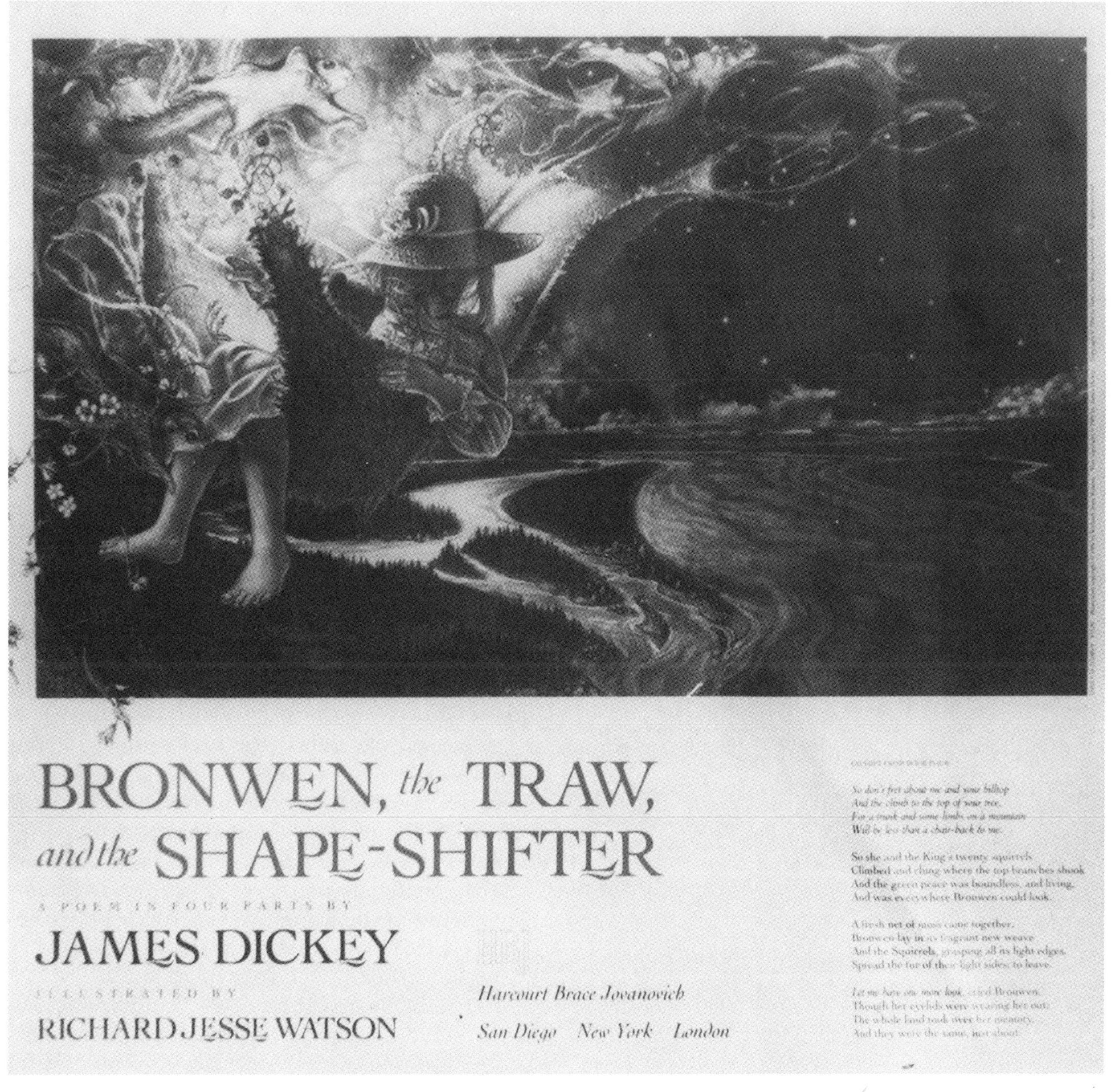

Poster for Dickey's second children's book (1986), inspired by his daughter, Bronwen

I like to tell stories and telling stories is a wonderful way to get children to get to sleep. If you ever want to hold a child's attention, develop some kind of narrative with the child himself or herself as the hero or heroine. That makes it fun for them. 'Cause then they get their imagination and their ego together and if you help them do that they're enthralled with their own new life that you're telling them about, and then they go to sleep.

But if you're a writer, if the storyteller is a writer, he gets interested in his own story. And he thinks maybe other children will like it, too. Almost any writer has a good deal of childhood left in him, innocence, and that's the best part of anybody; if you can preserve that you will have a good life . . . It's not the night that children are afraid of, but the images that the night makes possible and the fears that the dark give rise to–in other words, the coming of the Shape-Shifter. The dark can make the shapes, can enable or maybe even force the child to imagine the most frightening thing that its mind can conceive and they don't know that they are *not* there. Because the All-Dark is making it impossible to see what is there. So what they see is what they imagine. And the Shape-Shifter can take any shape that is frightening. Any.

And so when Bronwen goes with her magical garden tool to fight against the All-Dark and the Shape-Shifter and the Lair of the All-Dark–each of the forms is what she has to defeat. But when she's got them beat, she got them *all* beat. And the result of Bronwen's victory over the All-Dark and the Shape-Shifter and the Flying Squirrels is that no child will ever be frightened by the dark again.

* * *

The excitement of writing as you go on with it is that more opens up to you. I don't see how anybody could ever have writer's block or be stuck with a subject matter or anything like that. . . . This business of people choked up and not being able to write is something I don't understand. My problem is having too much stuff.

I believe that a great deal of anything I do is intuitive. I try to bring as much of rationality and the play of reasoning faculties as I can, but I will throw out something reasonable in favor of something that I feel every time. Maybe that makes me a romantic rather than a classic poet, but I have long ceased to ponder those kinds of differentiations.

BOOK REVIEW:

John Calvin Batchelor, "James Dickey's Odyssey of Death and Deception," *Washington Post Book World*, 24 May 1987, pp. 1-2.

Published seventeen years after the popularly and critically successful Deliverance, Alnilam *was Dickey's attempt to break new ground in his fiction. A more massive, less obviously dramatic and accessible novel than* Deliverance, Alnilam *explores the nature of human knowledge and power against the background of the World War II air war. Employing an intriguing but also disconcerting blind protagonist, the bold innovation of the split-page narrative, and a highly meditative tone, the novel tended to confuse readers and reviewers alike, who expected the page-turning qualities of* Deliverance. *Batchelor, himself a novelist, was among those reviewers who recognized the central purpose of Dickey's thematic and technical effects in* Alnilam.

James Dickey has commented that there is a tradition in the South that what a blind person tells you is true–that "a blind person can feel your face and tell you not only what you look like but what your character is like."

Alnilam is the mythical and sinister second novel of an internationally prominent poet, appearing 17 years after his folkloric *Deliverance.* It combines James Dickey's curious opinion of the relationship between blindness and truth with his gift for evoking the tall-tale Southland, where language stalks with the ferocity of a hunter. The novel is also possessed by the mystical motion of flying like a predatory bird. For James Dickey was a World War II combat pilot, and he has never entirely landed his mind's eye throughout his busy, happy and, truth to tell, muscularly Southron career.

There is a spooky strangeness to *Alnilam,* however, that may discomfit readers accustomed to Dickey's rough-hewn, regional voice. Set on a world-scale canvas during World War II, the novel pursues the ambitious art of myth-making. And what Dickey has to say, slowly and angrily, amounts to a vertiginous decrying of the 20th century's military cults, from imperialism to communism to fascism to, just perhaps, American jingoism.

The novel's title is the initial oddity; it derives from the central star in the belt of the constellation Orion, the warrior-hunter. Alnilam is Arabic for "a belt of pearls," quite properly because, along with its two companions (Mintaka and Alnitak), it forms the waist of the most prominent figure in the winter sky: as Tennyson wrote, "Those three stars of the airy Giant's zone/That glitter burnished by the frosty dark . . ."

The title is not just poetry, though; it is also the name of a secret boy's club among the cadets at an inconsequential Air Corps training base. The time is the middle of World War II; the place is the make-believe Peckover, N.C., somewhere between the Cape Fear River and the Piedmont plateau.

In the manner of a Greek yarn, Dickey's story begins simply. Frank Cahill, a 54-year-old Atlanta amusement park owner, receives a telegram informing him that his only child, Joel, has perished in a training accident at Peckover. Cahill is a brawny, unapologetic, vain, self-confident man whose pregnant wife left him 19 years earlier. Therefore he has never seen his now dead son, and his fate is doubly dark, for Frank Cahill has recently been blinded by diabetes. For the simplest of reasons then, idle whim, he sets out by bus to bury his son's remains, taking along with him the

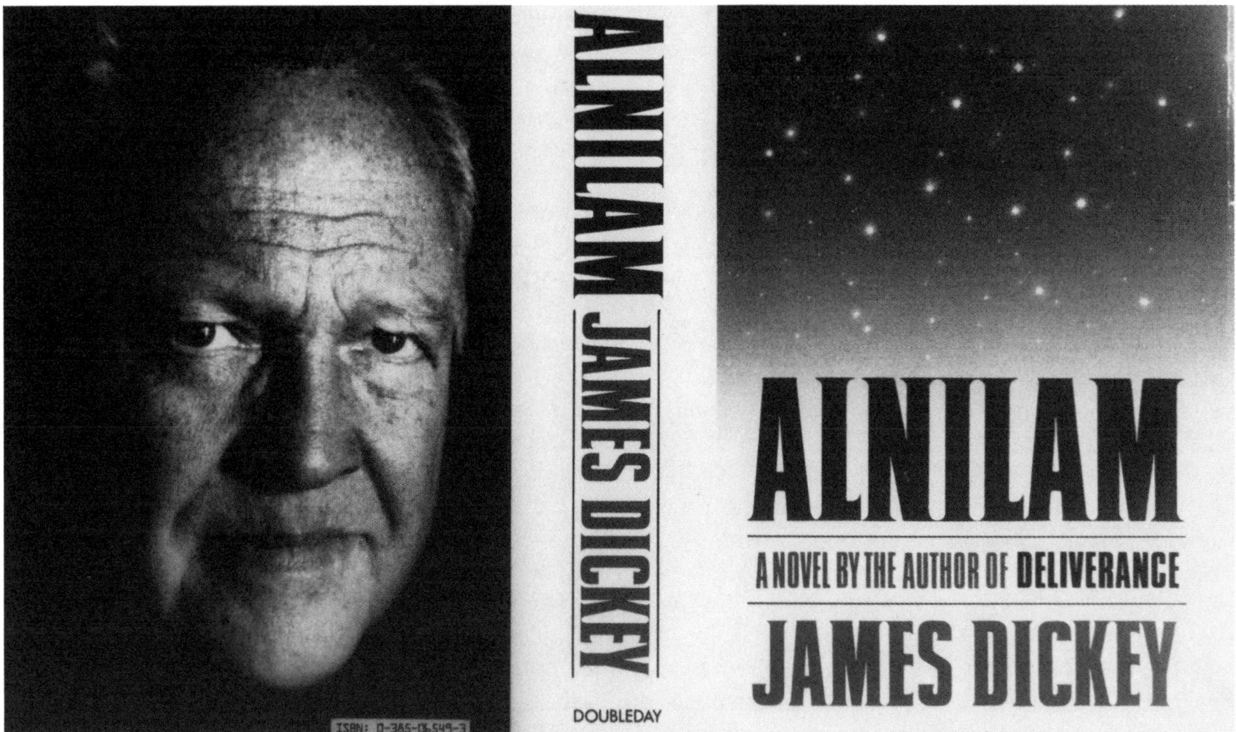

Dust jacket for Dickey's 1987 novel. The title refers to the middle star in the belt of the constellation Orion, the Hunter. Dickey translates the Arabic word Alnilam *as "string of pearls."*

sentinel Zack, a murderous black wolflike dog who provides eyes and security.

The mystery spirals when Frank Cahill learns from the camp commandant that they have not been able to find Joel's body. Joel is said to have been a gifted cadet-pilot, yet inexplicably he swooped over a brush fire, was pulled down by a downdraft, was rescued in bad shape by a farmer, then escaped the farmer to flee first back into the fire and then into the nearby river, where he finally disappeared after what one notes was an ancient progression: air, earth, fire and water.

Cahill hears the explanation and is neither aggrieved nor repelled; he is merely curious. Why is everyone being so solicitous, from the colonel to the fellow cadets and flight instructors? He is invited to stay on until graduation Sunday, when Joel would have gained his wings. He is offered the run of the camp, out of pity but also out of respect. Frank Cahill shrugs. It does not come to him, as it does to a suspicious reader, that he is caught up in the Oedipal drama, except topsy-turvy: Laius is blind and alive, Oedipus is missing-in-action. Ineluctably, Frank Cahill begins an exploration of the quintessential truth: Who was this boy Joel Cahill to die like that?

It is important to note that Frank Cahill is a truth teller as well as seeker. And Dickey emphasizes his insights with a stylistic innovation. Now and again, the text page is divided into two columns. The left hand in bold face is what the blind Frank Cahill senses and thinks even as the right-hand column is what the narrator describes, the actions of everyone else. The effect is difficult on the eye and often disorienting. One soon learns to read the right side the way one uses a fast forward button, and then to review Cahill's brooding thoughts for more clues.

Frank Cahill enlists several apparently reliable confederates in his quest, two of them combat veterans, one Joe's former flight instructor, another the flight surgeon, and, most elusively of all, a "wild mountain girl of the cotton mills." Each of them describes something not only of Joel but also of the nature of flying. Accordingly, in what must be a hard-won memory of his own ordeals, Dickey lavishes some excellent prose on combat-flying:

"I see those aircraft strung out," (reports a Pacific war navigator) "holding visual contact as long as they could, holding to my figures . . . It's not brotherhood, it's not teamwork, it's not *esprit de corps*. It's just eighty-five men in big airplanes up there in the dark, more than half lost, and it's one guy with a few instruments and a set of tables, up there with them . . . We went out to kill people, and we must have killed a good bunch of them. We're lucky in the Air Corps, come to think of it; we never have to see what we do . . . Maybe that's one reason you don't think about death when you're on a mission, except your own, and the main feeling when you're on the way back is life; it's a life feeling."

Episodically, Frank Cahill assembles a recon photograph of his son: flush-faced, psoriatic, adolescently defiant, mathematically adept, sexually sadistic, what one man calls someone "who doesn't question himself," another calls unmilitary, and another calls a "demon from the pit." Frank recovers a broken front tooth from the crash and confronts Joel's comrades, the Alnilam echelon. What he learns in the end is pathetic for so brief a life; it is also creepy.

It would be bad manners to reveal more of the puzzle except to say that the narrative explodes with a climax revealing the depravity of a world of boys at war, European, Asian or American. As far-fetched as it sounds, Frank Cahill unearths a conspiracy that resembles, in its wacky brutality, the same sort of totemic cabal that originally launched Lenin, Mussolini and Hitler, and that may have collected around more up-to-date militants.

Yet questions worry a measure of *Alnilam.* How far does Dickey want us to interpret all of this? He writes splendidly of flying yet opines that "the airplane is a mutilation machine." He speaks convincingly for the magic of the sky yet warns against windy cranks creating starry-eyed cults, even back-handing Christianity. And he offers the strangest assurance that those who plot for ultimate power will ultimately fail because of the inevitable Judas and because they always go too far. Betrayal and mass murder? If that is our common defense against military cults, then justice is not simply blind; it is tardy.

ARTICLE:

Monroe Spears, "James Dickey as Southern Visionary," *Virginia Quarterly Review,* 63 (Winter 1987): 110-123.

Dickey often credits Monroe Spears, one of the poet's instructors at Vanderbilt University, with teaching him to see that a writer need not be restricted to what literally happened, that he may dramatize instead an invented reality. In turn Spears has remained one of Dickey's most perceptive critics. In this essay, a version of which was first presented on 4 February 1983 at the James Dickey Symposium at the University of South Carolina, Spears identifies Dickey's particular visionary perspective.

Some years ago James Dickey, who will be 64 next month, responded to an interviewer's question about the sense in which he was a Southern writer with the ringing declaration that "the best thing that ever happened to me was to have been born a Southerner. First as a man and then as a writer." He would not want to feel that he was limited in any way by being a Southerner or was expected to "indulge in the kind of regional chauvinism that has sometimes been indulged in by Southern writers," he said, but the tragic history of the South gave him a set of values "some of which are deplorable, obviously, but also some of which are the best things that I have ever had as a human being." Southerners, he suggested, let their ancestors help: "I have only run-of-the-mill ancestors but they knew that one was supposed to do certain things. Even the sense of evil, which is very strong with me, would not exist if I had no sense of what evil was."

Dickey is convinced, then, that being Southern is central to the way he thinks and feels, but doesn't want to be thought of as *merely* regional; he suggests that the most valuable Southern quality is a special awareness of the personal past in the sense of inheriting traditions and codes of values from one's ancestors, and a special awareness of the regional past in its full tragic meaning, including the sense of evil. But rather than continue to depend on Dickey's own statements, now that I have used him to run interference for me, let me try to define more specifically just what kind of Southern writer he is and how he is related to other Southern writers.

The obvious starting-point is his relation to the Fugitive-Agrarian groups. Except for Donald Davidson, all the Fugitives and most of the Agrarians had left Vanderbilt long before Dickey arrived; so there was no possibility of personal influence. But Ransom, Tate, and Warren had become major figures in the literary world, and Brooks, Jarrell, and others were establishing high reputations. Vanderbilt students and faculty–most of them–were proud of the connection, and the campus was alive with legends of the days when giants had walked that very earth. In this context, creative writing seemed exciting and important to a good many students, and so did being a Southerner. It seems plain enough that

Dickey's commitment to poetry and his awareness of his identity as Southerner owed much both to his reading of the Fugitive-Agrarian writers and to the Vanderbilt tradition of respect for serious writing. R. V. Cassill is amusing but, I think, quite wrong when he portrays Dickey as a rebellious Young Turk who refused to conform to the Southern ruling circles by speaking "smartly about Miss Eudora and Mr. Ransom" and being "reverent about Traveler" while snickering down Whitman and the Midwesterners. In the first place, the Southern literary establishment, insofar as there ever was one, was not reverential about Traveler; Tate abandoned his biography of Lee because he had ceased to believe in him, and *The Fugitive* announced early that it fled nothing so much as the genteel pieties of the Old South. In the second place, Dickey was recognized early by the Southerners and usually given whatever awards they had to offer. While he never had the rare good luck the Fugitives did of close association with a group of like-minded peers, the fact that the tradition of serious writing was still alive at Vanderbilt kept him from the near-total isolation of a writer like Faulkner. A few years ago Tate went on record with the opinion that Dickey is the best poet the South has produced since the heyday of the Fugitives, and Warren has said in the *South Carolina Review* that he is "among Jim's greatest admirers" and in the *New York Times Book Review* that *The Zodiac* is a major achievement, worthy of comparison to Hart Crane's *The Bridge.*

In recent years some nostalgic epigones of the Fugitive-Agrarians at Vanderbilt have written requiems for the Southern Literary Renascence, maintaining that it has suffered death by melancholy. Their thesis is that Southern literature has been dying since World War II, when modernism triumphed over the South; and any hope is illusory. I have never quite believed in the Southern Renascence, suspecting that it was created artificially, like Frankenstein's monster, in the laboratories of academic critics; and reports of the loss of such artificial life need not disturb us. At any rate, Dickey, thank God, like Madison Jones and others of his contemporaries at Vanderbilt, and like such older Southern writers as Robert Penn Warren, Walker Percy, and Eudora Welty, doesn't know he's dead and refuses to lie down. As stubbornly as the astronomical phenomena that Galileo saw through his telescope in spite of the irrefutable arguments of his learned opponents that they couldn't possibly be there, the works of these writers continue to exist and to grow, unquestionably alive. Most of us, however we may feel about the modern world, would rather have the poems and novels than have a thesis about it demonstrated; and our own Poe has taught us to beware of premature burial. So we will be grateful that some of our writers flourish, and we will refuse to abandon hope.

II

While Dickey seems to have no interest in Agrarianism as a political or economic program, he shares with the Agrarians a deep concern about man's relation to nature and the distortions produced in this relation by the increasing urbanism and commercialism of our society. Dickey's true subject, however, is neither rural nor urban, but *suburban.* Since Southern cities are smaller, their suburbs are not wholly distinct from nearby small towns, and both maintain more connection with the country than their Northern counterparts. Compare, in this respect, those Dickey represents with John Cheever's dormitory suburbs around New York, with swimming pools linked in one giant fantasy. But both writers describe the modern nuclear family—nuclear both in being small and without the connections families used to have and in being under the threat of nuclear war. In these respects there is little difference between North and South, though the South may be slightly less nuclear simply because it is less urban.

Dickey's remarkable achievement is that he has taken his subject seriously and redeemed the word *suburban* from its comic or pejorative overtones. Instead of describing bored wives at the country club, adulteries in Commuterdom, hysteria and desperation breaking out from the pressures of enforced uniformity, or the absurdities of Little League baseball, he shows us a suburban world that is still in touch with a nature that remains wild, not tamed or prettified. Dickey's suburbs have no cute ceramic animals, no dear little Bambis or gnomes on the lawns, but the call of the real wild, an inner nature answering to outer. *Deliverance* is the most extended example, with its gradual revelation that the wilderness has always been present in the suburbs, whose security is an illusion. On the other hand, "The Firebombing" treats the homeowner's longing for security sympathetically because of his vivid awareness of its precariousness in view of what he did to his Japanese counterparts. "Dark Ones" transmutes into

1.

(Note to Jeannette: As far as the pagination of this section is concerened, I'll just number the pages "1, 2, 3, and so on," to keep track. Actually, this section begins just after the Cahill is Blind material, so, here, we are going back a ways from the Knives portion we've just been working on. You'll see how the whole thing comes together as we go along. I plan to write the book in sequence from now on, so there won't be any more jumping around from one section to another.)

A gentle wood-stopped thudding came through the cold cover. Zack's head rose, and his ears part-way.

"What is it?" Cahill said, (finding himself already) more awake than not in the last of his sleep.

"Time to go," a boy's voice said. "Let me in and I'll help you."

"No thanks, Tim," Cahill said. "I can get myself together all right. But come in, anyway. What the hell would I be locking up?"

Zack propped on his forelegs, preparing the first tone of his full animal thunder, as Pfc. Sistrunk entered. He was a pale, good-natured twenty-year old Armored Force draftee from Allentown, Pennsylvania returning to Fort Bragg from a three-day pass to Atlanta, where he had gone to visit a girl met on another bus. That was all Cahill knew about him: all that the northern remnants of Georgia had given them in the late afternoon and twilight, and more than the western half of South Carolina and the beginning of the mountains of North Carolina until the bus had broken down.

"Lie back boy," Cahill said to the dog. On down, now. Down. This is a good 'un here. You know a good 'un when you see him. He don't mean nothing. He ain't bothering nobody. Down, Zack. Keep it down."

As Cahill inventoried his few effects and dressed with slow, quickly-touching matter-of-factness, Tim stood uncertainly just inside the door, watching how things were done in a situation he had never before considered. Cahill worked on the small, intense details of his operation with a certain grim pride; his lips made a faint resemblance to silent words as he armed himself into his shirt and buttoned it, looped and knotted his tie with a fastidious skill that Sistrunk would more likely have associated with a musician, sat on the side of the bed and pulled on his trousers, then tied his shoes with his [illegible] turned alternately in Zack's direction and toward the door.

"They tell me they've got us a new bus coming," Tim said.

"That so? About what time?"

"Supposed to be pretty soon. Might already be here."

"One more thing," Cahill said. "Part of the show."

"Take your time. The driver counted heads. They can't leave without us."

Revised typescript pages for Alnilam. *Cahill, the protagonist of Dickey's second novel, is blind; the author developed a split-page technique to present sighted and sightless perspectives (Author's private papers).*

2.

Cahill reached under the pillow and took out the syringe-case. ~~Tim~~ Tim's eyes narrowed and he became aware of the deliberateness of his breath as Cahill sterilized the needle, fumbled out a matchbox, and, working the syringe from one hand to the other with ritual deftness, passed the needle through the flame as the match died. "No doctor ever told me

"This is just extra," Cahill said. ~~//////////~~ to do it this way. It's just something I like, though. Can't hurt none."

He hiked up his shirt, pinched up some of the flab of his stomach, and injected himself. "That's an all-day run," he said. "If its too much juice, I got sugar." He held out two wrapped sugar-cubes on the flat of his hand. "Balance. Blood-balance. That's what the little man said."

Tim for a moment did not reply, then said, "We might as well go on down."

Along what was now for him night's creaking and weight-fearing North Carolina country hall they went to the stairs whose number Cahill stubbornly remembered. With no word or touch from Tim they came correctly to the clock, and hesitated.

"What time is it?" Cahill asked.

"Quarter to seven."

"You ain't got the guts to say 'first light' have you? How're you ~~ever~~ going to kill anybody? Ain't you ever seen a blind man before?"

"Yes, I have. And I don't know how I'm going to kill anybody. I hope ~~nobody~~ I don't get ~~asks me~~ asked to. I'm a mechanic, or I will be in six weeks. That's all I know."

DARK

The porch opened him, and he sensed it as solid with invisible landscape. Though small, the wind must carry distance(s), and concentrated these into the bitterness of penetration. No stars now, or the last ones. He was supposed to be among hills ~~now~~; he willed the sensation of being surrounded and placed by risings of land and irregularities of height, and concluded that the air in his nostrils like piano-wire Had come down far slopes and lifted to him from the near ground, still full of trees and bushes, bearing to the porch the snow that they held in an ~~unwatched~~ disregarded indifference, ~~blown~~ as they hovered motionless in ~~clear~~ alien dissolving light.

LIGHT

A step below Cahill and Zack, Tim steadied his eyes on the low forms of the hills close about them, patchily covered with snow in inept and flawless forms. Two silver-and-blue commercial buses were pulled up on the near side of the highway, and their sack-bodied drivers appeared to be arguing with different aspects of steam; their heads were barely visible amongst the clamor of their breath.

poetry the evening ritual of the arrival home of the commuters.

To say that Dickey is a visionary poet is a paralyzingly obvious assertion: almost every poem he writes describes a vision of one kind or another, and in recent years he has dealt explicitly with the loss of physical vision in works such as the unfinished novel *Cahill is Blind*. Perhaps he will become the patron or mascot of the ophthalmologists, as Wallace Stevens was adopted by the ice-cream manufacturers after writing "The Emperor of Ice-Cream." Yet the truism is worth repeating, for it says something about his relation to Southern literature. Dickey belongs to the line of visionaries running from Blake through Rimbaud and Whitman to such modern exemplars as Hart Crane, George Barker, Dylan Thomas, and Theodore Roethke. It is noteworthy that there are no Southern names on this list, since as far as I know there are few Southern poets who could be called visionary. Tate and Warren, for example, are in their different ways primarily concerned with history, with attempting to relate the past to the present. Perhaps one reason good Southern poets have shied away from the visionary mode is that they remember how much older Southern poetry was emasculated by the necessity of avoiding politics and hence driven from reality into fake vision. The old Southern tradition of escapism and sentimentality–of high gutless swooning, to borrow a phrase from Faulkner–was certainly one thing the Fugitives were fleeing. South Carolinian Henry Timrod often exemplified this tradition, and Tate surely intended a contrast with Timrod's "Ode Sung at the Decoration of the Graves of the Confederate Dead at Magnolia Cemetery" when he wrote his own ironic "Ode to the Confederate Dead." Timrod's "Ethnogenesis" is a kind of vision, it is true, but appallingly detached from any sense of reality: in it the new Confederacy, with its economy based on cotton and slavery, is seen as bringing wealth, moral improvement, and a better climate to the whole world.

Before Dickey, the only Southern poet who was a true visionary was Poe; and his visions, as every schoolchild knows, were very peculiar indeed. Though one might argue that Dickey's poetic rhythms are often incantatory, and intended to put the reader into a kind of trance state, they are far more subtle than Poe's blatantly hypnagogic music; and though both poets are most interested in states of consciousness beyond normal waking life, they are not interested in the same states. Much as I would like to, I don't see how I can make a case for any resemblance beyond the fact that they are both visionaries. Dickey has none of Poe's morbid preoccupation with death, his concern being rather with new and different modes of life; you can't imagine his saying that the ideal poetic subject is the *death* of a beautiful woman. Poe strives obsessively to make the reader feel the horror of being a living soul in a dead body, of an irreparable crack or split in the edifice of the mind, of long-ago irremediable losses. Dickey, in contrast, produces in the reader a new awareness of nonhuman forms of life, from dogs on the feet to owls in the woods and panthers in the zoo; the poems seek new forms of union, wider possibilities of consciousness. Mind and body are not separated as they are in Poe, but totally fused. Finally, Dickey gets into his poems a solid feeling of everyday reality and normal experience before moving to transcend them. It is this feeling or rendering that distinguishes him not only from Poe but from the kind of fantasy that is now so enormously popular in movies and cheap fiction. Dickey's visions have nothing in common with these self-indulgent daydreams unrelated to any kind of reality.

III

Dickey's most ambitious visionary poem is certainly *The Zodiac*, which deals with nothing less than the meaning of the visible universe. Since it is based on a work by the Dutch poet Hendrik Marsman, whom Dickey retains as speaker and protagonist of the poem, it has nothing whatever to do with the South; the point of view is distinctively European when it is not cosmic. Why would Dickey choose to adopt a persona so different from his usual one? Partly, I would guess, because the difference was liberating: writing as Marsman, Dickey has a different mask of the self and different memories. Instead of the South or the wartime Pacific, he writes as a man of an earlier European generation about Amsterdam; instead of writing as a survivor, he is now one who will die early in the same war. Even the name *Marsman* may have reinforced this appeal: an author with a message from outer space. But on a deeper level, Marsman's poem expresses concerns and beliefs that Dickey shares. Dickey has always been moved by astronomy and by the religious sense of "how wild, inexplicable, marvelous, and endless creation is." His religion "involves myself and the universe, and it does not admit of any kind of intermediary, such as Jesus or the Bible." He would like to be reincarnated as a migratory sea bird like a tern or wandering albatross. The themes of the aging wanderer returning home and so finding his own identity and of the poet's reexamination and reaffirmation of his poetic faith and vocation–we might call them the *Ulysses* and *Lycidas* archetypes–must have appealed to Dickey with peculiar force in the Dutch poem. Imitating Marsman, then, frees Dickey from his usual self and gives him a fresh start at the same time that it provides him with a way of expressing some of his most deeply felt concerns and beliefs from a different perspective. By transforming the language, he makes Marsman's poem his own. Giving it a tone quite different from Marsman's and with far more dramatic power and variety, he makes it emphatically contemporary and personal. Through this process of expansion and dramatization, Dickey's poem becomes about twice as long as Marsman's.

The central fact about the protagonist is that he is a poet dedicated to the belief that poetry reveals ultimate truth and that it comes from sources above or beyond the rational intellect. Under the pressure of impending catastrophe–for he feels that he has wasted and misused his life, and he sees his world moving swiftly to destruction in World War II–he reexamines this visionary faith. The drama consists in his struggle to clarify and reaffirm it. Like all poets who conceive of their art as lamp rather than mirror, he worries that the light will die with the guttering lamp and vacillates about the reality of what it reveals; but he has the additional problems of distinguishing the hallucinations produced by delirium tremens from reality and of reconciling a knowledge of modern astronomy with belief in the significance of the zodiac. The zodiac may seem a curiously archaic and implausible locus of poetic faith; but it is its age and mythological richness that make it the supreme test case of the relation between man's imagination and God's. To believe in its significance is to believe that the universe is not meaningless, that there is a connection between the little world of man and the great world of the stars, between inside and outside.

To show the difference between Marsman's poem and Dickey's, let me quote the conclusion, in which the main themes are recapitulated. Here is Marsman (no doubt rather flatly translated):

O spirit, grant to this small hand
The calm and quiet resolution
To steer the ship on to the morning land
That slumbering waits and each horizon's bar.
And give that he who listens to the swish
That sweeps along the waving of the planets
And through the whirling of the emerald sea
May tune the instruments upon the fork
Which at the touch reveals the structural form
Of the immemorial European song
That sounded at the dawn of cultured life,
Whose course began upon the azure sea
And shall still undulate through the west world
As long as the afflatus spans around space
A firmament of intellect and dream.

And here is Dickey's version, a triumph of what Lowell called imitation:

Oh my own soul, put me in a solar boat.
Come into one of these hands
Bringing quietness and the rare belief
That I can steer this strange craft to the morning

Land that sleeps   in the universe on all horizons
And give this home-come man who listens in his room

To the rush and flare of his father
Drawn at the speed of light to Heaven
Through the wrong end of his telescope, expanding the universe,
The instrument   the tuning-fork–
He'll flick it with his bandless wedding-finger–
Which at a touch reveals the form
Of the time-loaded European music
That poetry has never really found,
Undecipherable as God's bad, Heavenly sketches,
Involving fortress and flower, vine and wine and bone,
And shall vibrate through the western world
So long as the hand can hold its island
Of blazing paper, and bleed for its images:
Make what it can of what is:

So long as the spirit hurls on space
The star-beasts of intellect and madness.

Poets of other persuasions do not seek meaning in the stars. Auden could say cheerfully, "Looking up at the stars, I know quite well/That for all they care, I can go to hell," and Warren that the stars "are only a backdrop for/The human condition" and the sky "has murder in the eye, and I/Have murder in the heart, for I/Am only human. We look at each other, the sky and I./We understand each other. . . ." Visionary poets, however, affirm that there is a relation, that the stars are saying something to man. Just what they say is, naturally, impossible to state in cool discursive prose. But Dickey's essential affirmation would seem to be essentially the same as that made by his visionary predecessors, from Blake through Hart Crane and the Dylan Thomas of *Altarwise by Owllight:* the analogy, or identity, of the poetic imagination and the divine power that created the stars. For this symbolic affirmation, the zodiac works better than Brooklyn bridge.

IV

To say that visionary poets do not age well is an academic understatement or litotes. Rimbaud gave up poetry for gun-running at the age of 19, and Hart Crane leaped into the sea at 30; Dylan Thomas drank himself to death at 39, and Roethke, after increasingly harrowing bouts of mania and depression, in his fifties. Blake and Smart, under cover of madness, made it into their fifties. But except for Whitman, who was only in one sense a visionary poet, it is hard to think of any who attained the age of 60. Dickey's achievement in surviving not only two wars but the special hazards that beset his kind of poet is, then, a notable one: like Faulkner's Dilsey, he has endured.

Dickey has not only remained very much active, but he has continued to grow and develop. His latest volume, *Puella,* seems to me to mark his entrance into a distinctive new stage. In *Puella* there is a shift from the cosmic vision of *The Zodiac* to a very different kind of vision that might be called domestic. The poet is not tamed but gentled as he lovingly describes what Hopkins called the *mundus muliebris,* the woman's world inhabited by the daughter-wife figure whose girlhood he relives. At the risk of embarrassing Dickey, I might suggest a large and vague parallel with the change in Shakespeare's career from tragedies like *Lear* to romances like *Cymbeline, The Winter's Tale,* and *The Tempest,* with their themes of reconciliation, fulfillment, the joy of recovering what was thought to be lost forever. Deborah in these poems has something in common with Marina, Perdita, Miranda, and other such young girls in these plays; with Yeats' Dancers and the daughter for whom he wrote the great prayer; and with the young girls in Hopkins–in "Margaret, are you grieving" and the "Echo" poems, for example. (I am beginning to sound like those 19th-century studies of the girlhood of Shakespeare's heroines; but that is the mood of the book, with its charming epigraph from T. Sturge Moore: "I lived in thee, and dreamed, and waked/Twice what I had been." If the word *mellow* had not been preempted by Doonesbury's Californians, it would be hard to avoid using it here. This is also the first time the word *charming* has been conceivable as a description of Dickey's poetry.)

The girl in the poems is intensely herself, yet she is also representative of all young girls, as the title *Puella* suggests. She is pictured in scenes that are archetypal, sometimes *rites de passage,* sometimes with mythical or historical contexts; sometimes heraldic as if in medieval tapestry, sometimes playfully absurd as if in a modern folk-naïve painting. While the poems are obviously very personal, they exhibit a new kind of formality, both in the speaker's attitude toward his subject–affection tinged with gentle humor, folk ceremoniousness, a degree of detachment making possible fresh appreciation of physical beauty–and in the verse itself. Dickey has always treasured the "wildness" aspect of Hopkins, as did Roethke–"Long live the weeds and the wildness yet!"–but these poems show a new sense of the beauty of formal sound-patterns that is often reminiscent of that poet. There is a tenderness, a delicacy, a fresh appreciation of the beauty of the visible universe that seem to owe something to Hopkins while being also strongly individual.

The beginning of "Heraldic: Deborah and Horse in Morning Forest," has an epigraph from Hopkins and is a kind of homage to that poet:

> It could be that nothing you could do
> Could keep you from stepping out and blooding-in
> An all-out blinding heraldry for this:
> A blurred momentum-flag
>
> That must be seen sleep-weathered and six-legged,
> Brindling and throwing off limbo-light
>
> Of barns. . . .

In another, Hopkins' verse-techniques are used to describe Deborah's piano-playing:

> With a fresh, gangling resonance
> Truing handsomely, I draw on left-handed space
> For a brave ballast shelving and bracing, and from it,
> then, the light
> Prowling lift-off, the treble's strewn search and wide-angle glitter.

As for playful folk-ceremony poems–a world apart from what some critic calls the "country surrealism" of "May Day Sermon"–there are "Deborah and Deirdre as Drunk Bridesmaids Foot-Racing at Daybreak" and "Veer-Voices: Two Sisters under Crows," in both of which the titles are enough for present purposes. But I cannot resist quoting the end of my favorite poem in the book, "Deborah in Ancient Lingerie, in Thin Oak over Creek." This is both a vision, at once tender and absurd, of Deborah in her "album bloomers" diving into the creek, and a ritual acted out in the poem itself:

> . . . snake-screaming,
> Withering, foster-parenting for animals
> I can do
> very gently from just about
> Right over you, I can do
> at no great height I can do
> and bear
> And counter-balance and do
> and half-sway and do
> and sway
> and outsway and
> do.

The poems move from the realism of "Deborah as Scion," where she is seen "In Lace and Whalebone" thinking of the kind of looks she has inherited–"Bull-headed, big-busted . . . I am totally them in the/eyebrows,/Breasts, breath and butt"–to the visionary heights of "The Lyric Beasts," where she speaks as "Dancer to Audience" and becomes a kind of goddess challenging the audience to "Rise and on faith/Follow." In a sense, I suppose the book is Dickey's reply to the radical feminists, for Deborah in it is both herself and Dickey's ideal modern woman, enacting her archetypal feminine role in full mythic resonance, but not enslaved or swallowed up by it. If so, Kate Millett and Adrienne Rich may eat their hearts out!

I have not mentioned many qualities in Dickey that might be called distinctively Southern, on the ground that they are large, vague, and obvious–more obvious in the novel *Deliverance* and the two books about the South, *Jericho* and *God's Images,* than in the poetry–but perhaps they should be summed up briefly. A strong sense of place is the first, as in the poems about Cherrylog Road, kudzu, chenille, the Buckhead boys, the woman preacher, and the lawyer's daughter whose dive from the Eugene Talmadge Bridge brought revelation from the burning bush. Love of story-telling, and hence of communal myth, is important, and from this it is a short step to love of ceremony and ritual both within the family and with other life-forms, from the Owl King to *Puella.* Dickey's humor is more frequently present than most people seem to realize, but its most characteristic form is the preposterous lie or grotesquely implausible vision which outrages the reader but then turns out to be, in a deeper sense, true. Like most Southerners, he has a strong religious sense: his poems are often sermons or prayers or invocations. But his creed might be called natural supernaturalism, or fundamentalism so fundamental that it concerns man's relation to all other life forms.

As we have seen, Dickey has little significant relation to earlier Southern writing; it would take a truly ingenious academic to show how he was influenced by Sidney Lanier! Poe seems to be his only Southern predecessor in being a genuine visionary; but he was a very different kind: whereas Poe's visions are of horror and death-in-life, Dickey's are of larger modes of life. Dickey is, in fact, so far from being a regionalist in any exclusive sense that the spiritual ancestors most prominent in his recent poetry are that New Englander of the New Englanders, Joseph Trumbull Stickney, who lies behind the wonderful poem "Exchanges"; the Dutch poet and sailor Hendrik Marsman, who lies behind *The Zodiac;* and the English Jesuit G. M. Hopkins, who lies behind *Puella.*

In contrast to more recent Southern poets like Tate and Warren, Dickey has not been interested in communion with other humans through acceptance of the human condition but in getting beyond ordinary humanity to participate in the life of nonhuman creatures and in more-than-human forces. His essential subject has been exchange or metamorphosis or *participation mystique* between man and wild animals, fish, or birds; or, in *Zodiac,* stars and the mysterious universe in general. Since the rational mind is a hindrance, or at best irrelevant, to this quest, his poems represent extreme states of consciousness: intoxication, terror, rage, lust, hallucination, somnambulism or mystical exaltation. His concern is not the limitations but the possibilities of human and nonhuman nature, not history but vision.

As I have tried to suggest, his latest book, *Puella,* constitutes a new kind of vision, back from the cosmic extremities of *The Zodiac* to the human and domestic world. The figure of the daughter-wife is suffused with a new tenderness,

SEATING PLAN ON STAGE

1 Hortense Calisher
2 John Updike
3 Milton Babbitt
4 William Styron
5 John Hollander
6 Mario Vargas Llosa
7 James Thomas Flexner
8 James Dickey
9 Alfred Kazin
10 Richard Meier
11 Francis Thorne
12 Arata Isozaki
13 Wolf Kahn
14 Elmer Bischoff
15 Irving Howe
16 Giorgio Cavallon
17 Mario Davidovsky
18 Alex Katz
19 Cynthia Ozick
20 Raymond Carver
21 Christopher Brown
22 David Cope
23 James DeMartino
24 David Bottoms
25 Susan Hauptman
26 Rosellen Brown
27 Richard Argosh
28 Timothy Geller
29 Saul Steinberg
30 Barbara W. Tuchman
31 May Swenson
32 William Schuman
33 Louise Talma
34 Arthur Schlesinger, Jr.
35 Wayne Thiebaud
36 John McPhee
37 George Tooker
38 Leslie Fiedler
39 C. Vann Woodward
40 Evan S. Connell
41 Charles Wuorinen
42 Chaim Gross
43 Daisy Youngblood
44 John McCormick
45 Hale Smith
46 James Seay
47 Chinary Ung
48 Norman Williams
49 Jacob Druckman
50 Fred Lerdahl
51 Elizabeth Spencer
52 Howard Nemerov
53 William Jay Smith
54 Robert Motherwell
55 Ned Rorem
56 Jacob Lawrence
57 Philip Pearlstein
58 Stanley Kunitz
59 Joseph Mitchell
60 George F. Kennan
61 John Johansen
62 Kenneth Burke
63 Gary Snyder
64 Lukas Foss
65 Gerald H. Plain
66 Kaye Gibbons
67 Martin Boykan
68 David Koblitz
69 Andrew Hudgins
70 Anthony Korf
71 Gregg Smith
72 Frank Lobdell
73 William Meredith
74 Russell Baker
75 William Maxwell
76 John Barth
77 Richard Lippold
78 John Malcolm Brinnin
79 R.W.B. Lewis
80 Paul Cadmus
81 Ibram Lassaw
82 Amy Clampitt
83 Edward Hoagland
84 David Del Tredici
85 Ross Lee Finney
86 Peter Taylor
87 Edward Hirsch
88 Clement Greenberg
89 Thomas McMahon
90 Diane Johnson
91 Susan Lichtman
92 Robert Stone
93 Mark Kilstofte
94 Behzad Ranjbaran
95 Anne Poor
96 Joan Didion
97 Anthony Hecht
98 William Gaddis
99 Emily Hahn
100 Marisol Escobar
101 William Bailey
102 Dimitri Hadzi
103 Arthur Berger
104 Miriam Gideon
105 William Bergsma
106 John Hawkes
107 David Diamond
108 Ulysses Kay
109 David A. Scott
110 David J. Vayo
111 William Barrett
112 Jack Beeson
113 Lennart Anderson
114 Edward Albee
115 Hugo Weisgall
116 E. L. Doctorow
117 George Perle
118 Allen Ginsberg
119 Richard Eberhart
120 Jonathan Maslow
121 John Ashbery
122 Eleanor Clark
124 Cleanth Brooks

SEATED IN THE ORCHESTRA:

Andre Dubus
Helen Frankenthaler
James Merrill
Reynolds Price

On 18 May 1988 Dickey was inducted into the prestigious fifty-member American Academy of Arts and Letters. On stage with Dickey were some of America's most important writers, composers, painters, and literary critics.

gentleness, and humor, and the verse takes on a new formal musicality. A Jungian would say that the girl in these poems is an *anima*-figure; but whether the sense of fulfillment and joy in these poems comes from integration of the personality or from some deeper cause, I will not attempt to decide. Nor will I comment on the fact that Deborah is not only Southern but South Carolinian; Southern chivalry toward ladies who have the misfortune to be born elsewhere forbids it. But I will risk the charge of Southern chauvinism by saying that the book is a most notable contribution to Southern letters.

ARTICLE:
Ronald Baughman, "James Dickey Induction–Academy of Arts and Letters," *James Dickey Newsletter*, 4 (Fall 1988): 2-3.

Dickey's induction into the fifty-member academy of painters, musicians, critics, and writers is one of the crowning honors of his career.

On Wednesday, May 18, 1988, James Dickey was officially inducted into the American Academy of Arts and Letters, and thus received one of America's highest awards for artistic accomplishment. Also inducted into the Academy were novelist William Styron and, posthumously, scholar Joseph Campbell.

Inside the Academy's headquarters at West 155th and Broadway in New York City, an audience of more than 500 watched as the new members were honored. On stage with Dickey and Styron sat 126 distinguished fellows of the Academy or its parent organization, the National Institute of Arts and Letters. . . . The National Institute was established in 1898 as part of the American Social Science Association. In 1904, founding members of the Institute created the American Academy of Arts and Letters to honor those men and women who had achieved highest distinction in literature, music, and visual arts. Writers William Dean Howells, Henry James, and Mark Twain were among the first Academy inductees. Today, the Academy is limited to 50 lifetime members. Since 1923, each of the 50 members has been assigned a chair on the back of which is a brass plaque listing the names and dates of occupancy of its holder. Dickey's Chair number 15 was previously occupied by scholar Wilbur Cross, painter Raphael Soyer, and novelist John Steinbeck.

Fiction writer and Academy President Hortense Calisher gave the opening address. Novelist John Updike, the Academy's Chancellor, next noted that since 1983 the Academy had expanded to include honorary members from the international community of the arts such as Peruvian writer Mario Vargas Llosa, the keynote speaker. Then, poet John Hollander, Secretary of the Institute, read the citations admitting Dickey, Campbell, and Styron to the Academy.

Following further announcements of awards and honors, the platform party and the audience met for a reception on the Academy's terrace.

BOOK REVIEW:
Gordon Van Ness, "Review: *Wayfarer: A Voice from the Southern Mountains*," *James Dickey Newsletter*, 5 (Spring 1989): 31-33.

In his third collaboration with a visual artist–the previous two works being Jericho: The South Beheld *(1974) with Hubert Shuptrine and* God's Images *(1977) with Marvin Hayes–Dickey worked with photographer William A. Bake to create* Wayfarer. *Van Ness's review of* Wayfarer *emphasizes the ways in which Dickey's text is a much more fully realized exploration of characters and of a region than is usually found in so-called coffee-table books.*

"I seen you in the last light, and I come on down." So declares the unnamed narrator to a wayfarer he encounters at the opening of James Dickey's most recent work. Having lived his life in the Appalachians, the speaker is both superstitious and wise. When the unidentified traveler falls ill, the narrator uses mountain remedies to restore his health. His commentary, in a voice honestly given and humanly real, takes the wayfarer–and the reader–on a journey into the Southern mountains, talking about the food, geography, customs, handiwork, folklore, and music. As the speaker quietly asserts: "We ain't got everything, but we got somethin'." When the book concludes, we have touched something powerful, something mysterious at blood level, tied to and held by the land and, like the wayfarer, we are "bound to the hills."

Certain statements need immediately to be made about *Wayfarer*. First, though earlier reviews have labeled it only a coffee-table book, it is not, or at least not only or even principally, that. Nor does it fit easily into other identifiable categories or genres. Fiction, non-fiction prose, and poetic prose all seem inadequate descriptive terms. It is not simply a question of the book's mingling of words and photographs, a sort of double vision seen previously in *Intervisions.* William Bake's photography offers an emotional immediacy that not so much adheres as coheres to the story. Rather the power of the book derives from Dickey's understated language that speaks of truth not in its lesser, verifiable aspects but as an imaginative connection. The words, the created tone, carry one closer to what the Southern Appalachians are in and of themselves. When the speaker, commenting on what the land offers to eat, says, "The food up here's got life in it. It comes out of a real place, a place that's like it's supposed to be," the reader senses emotionally, feels swarm upon him, the mysterious and more fundamental reality of what Dickey presents.

This effort to approach the Appalachians, to confront their spatial and metaphoric fullness, leads to another observation about *Wayfarer:* the reader is being guided on nothing less than an heroic journey to uncover, or perhaps recover, something now lost to modern man. In the "Healing" section, the speaker asserts, "I'll go get you some of this-here old stoney water from the well. It'll reach down in you, I can guarantee." What Dickey presents in this section of his story does just that–reaches down–such that in "Departure" the narrator states of the mountain folks, "They got ways of knowin'." Having been guided and instructed about "Hands," "Wood," "Beasts," "Strings and Voices," and "Kin" (among other lessons), the reader intuitively knows at the conclusion that, like the Cherokee Indians who named the Chattooga, "We have crossed here."

Dickey's belief in the individual voice, in the figure whose words narrate life's essential wonder, reverberates throughout his writing. Both his fiction and his poetry celebrate the speaker who courageously starts over again, who returns to first things, to primal sources, and who then must relate what he has learned. It is a voice, too, suddenly, amazingly there, capable of coming from the most unexpected places as the poet follows his own personae. And as Dickey states in his essay, "The Poet Turns on Himself," that voice is latent in everyone: "there is a poet–or a kind of poet–buried in every human being like Ariel in his tree. . . . [and] the people whom we are pleased to call poets are only those who have felt the need and contrived the means to release the spirit from its prison." Some chance occurrence–the fall of an airline stewardess from a plane, the three-day quest of a drunken Dutch poet to achieve "triangular eyesight," or a young girl's burning of her doll made from house wood–such events have begun for Dickey a poetic exploration not only of the processes that govern life, but also of man's awful responsibility to drive toward self-discovery and self-determination. The encounter between the narrator and the wayfarer, then, offers a familiar Dickey interest–the confrontation between an individual and something, or someone, whose knowledge is beyond him, but which is undeniably real and vital and life-enhancing.

That something, of course, is the Southern mountains, whose paths, peaks, and hollows Dickey claims as his beginnings and whose "ways" he believes in. He has treated various of these traditions, or rituals, earlier in his poetry. Foxhunting and quilting, for example, about which the narrator in *Wayfarer* speaks, appear in "Listening to Foxhounds" and "Chenille." But the narrative framework of the new book permits a greater expansiveness, a breadth of treatment that enables Dickey to suggest a larger natural inclusiveness in the world. When the narrator states, "It don't matter why it comes, but it does; it comes on through, and it's done been put into both of us, don't you see," he moves beyond a simple discussion of family relationships or blood lines. For Dickey's concern is with something more basic, more primitive–the lines of connection that link all men to the land and the natural impulse, the human need, to create and re-create what one sees and hears in the world.

What makes *Wayfarer* different from, say, *The Zodiac* or *Puella,* aside from its attempt to have the visual and poetic mediums co-exist or interact, is not their subjects: at their heart, all depict a figure who seeks either an exchange, or a confrontation, or what might best be termed simply a nearing. Rather these works differ in the nature of the nearing itself, of the shared experience. The speaker in *Wayfarer,* whatever else he is, acts as an intermediary, a gatekeeper or spirit of a place. Unlike the Dutch poet or Deborah in the other works, he neither unites himself with "God's scrambled zoo" nor personifies primal forces to say with quiet and assertive truth, "I am/ The surround." He is what Joseph Campbell in *The Hero with a Thousand Faces* calls simply "a protective figure" or guide, who provides the adventurer with protective amulets, as evidenced by his giving the wayfarer a fairy stone, which is "like a cross" and which brings "good luck."

At the end of the book, the wayfarer finally speaks as he prepares to leave and continue his journey. He has learned of mountain customs and mountain people and become an initiate into larger knowledge, keener mysteries. Asked by the narrator to remember all he has seen and heard "because we're losin' it; we're gonna lose it all," he quotes from John Crowe Ransom's "Antique Harvesters." The moment is strangely dramatic, in part because these are the first words in the wayfarer's transformed life and in part because we wonder what he could possibly say–whether he will attempt to notate the inexpressible:

> But see, if you peep shrewdly, she hath not stooped;
> Take no thought of her servitors that have dropped,
> For we are nothing; and if one talk of death–
> Why, the ribs of the earth subsist frail as a breath
> If but God wearieth.

Here is the new priest, a man who has been both outside and in, who has crossed a threshold and penetrated to forgotten truths, and who gives back the words of a poet, an offering of sorts to the one who has guided him but who has doubts. The wayfarer must return from where he came, now more knowing because of his passage. He has seen and heard and is forever changed.

For the reader, *Wayfarer* provides Ransom's "shrewd peep"; it is a book that resonates with Dickey's firm belief in the continuance of the Southern mountains, in their quiet strength and life-enhancing possibilities. "All the edges done come off 'em," the speaker says of these mountains; "That's what makes 'em a place you can live in, more like a home place." Dickey never questions what the Appalachians offer, but he recognizes their human value: "It's natural; it stands to reason." And he recognizes, too, their special magic, their abiding mystery, whose foundations are under attack by careless tourists and by men who go "tappin' the rocks" to mine coal. But as a Southerner, Dickey knows where he himself is standing and where he has stood, and the reader, if he has followed right along, will see and know some things for himself. Let him take what he can and give thanks for the crossing.

INTERVIEW:

This previously unpublished interview was conducted by Ronald Baughman on 17 September 1989 in Columbia, South Carolina. The interviewer attempted to explore aspects of Dickey's life and career that have not been well documented elsewhere.

DLB: Let's start with reference to an upcoming event: the twenty-third of March 1990 marks the twentieth anniversary of the publication of *Deliverance*. How has the novel and the later movie affected your writing career?

Dickey: There's a lot of attention paid to it, but it hasn't affected my writing career in any special way, except that it spurred me on to write another novel. I felt that since I had *Deliverance* under my belt, so to speak, I might chance another one, and I wrote *Alnilam,* which is a much better book. In that regard it had an influence because if I hadn't been satisfied with *Deliverance* I never would have tried to write another novel.

DLB: At last count *Deliverance* has been translated into at least twenty-five languages.

Dickey: Well, I've lost track, but a good many. I keep getting sent editions of it in various languages–Finnish and Japanese, Serbo-Croatian, and so on. I always like to look at the covers. There's little I can do about reading them in their languages, except the three I can make a stab at–French, German, and Spanish. The French version won the Prix Medicis as the best foreign-language novel of the year. I had a good translator, and I was very pleased with the reception in France, and in Germany as well. We just renewed the contracts for various reprints and so on. Sure, it's very gratifying. An author is sort of between two stools on these things. He feels, on one hand, or on one stool, that it's very well deserved, that other people all over the world should be paying attention to what he says. And on the other hand he thinks that maybe it's not so good because he doesn't want to go on and do anything else. You know, he figures he's got it made. But I don't feel that way because the *act* of writing itself is for me the main thing; it's not what happens to the writing that I've already completed, though that's kind of interesting, in a way. Incidentally, I was looking at the Miss America Pageant last night, and the girl who won third place played the music from the film version of *Deliverance* on the flute. My goodness, when she didn't become Miss America, I thought we'd been robbed. I demand a recount.

DLB: Along those same lines, this does make you very much an international novelist with a worldwide audience, doesn't it?

Dickey: Well, yes, I suppose. The poems have been translated into a good many languages, too–maybe ten or twelve. And the reaction to those is more gratifying to me than the reaction to *Deliverance* really, because part of the appeal of *Deliverance* is that it's a page-turner, and consequently gets lumped into the category with lots of other page-turners, when there's more to it than that by a very long shot. The popularity of it, the mass popularity, definitely has something to do, maybe a lot to do, with the thriller aspect of it, especially since that was so much emphasized in the movie.

DLB: As you've said before, you didn't want *Alnilam* to be a *Deliverance II*.

Dickey: No, I did not. You can read both novels and you wouldn't believe the same person wrote them. That's exactly what I wanted.

DLB: *Alnilam* is a much more demanding novel.

Dickey: Sure it is, and you're not going to get thousands of people all over the world who are willing to struggle with what I was trying to do in *Alnilam,* but that's all right with me. It will find the readers that are the right ones for it. It has done that and will continue to do so.

DLB: I agree with Pat Conroy, who said in an interview that *Alnilam* is a novel readers will come back to later. The more thoughtful, perhaps more meditative, hardworking reader will discover this novel.

Dickey: Yes. The analogy really is with poetry in that I don't think any true poet wants his poem to be exhausted in one reading; but in this plasticized culture that we live in, a very great deal that we buy is designed to be thrown away after being used once. I eat at fast food restaurants with the rest of the American public, with plastic spoons and plastic plates and so on: eat with them and throw them in the trash. Too much of the culture is based on that sort of an attitude, not only in foodstuffs and various other items, but in literary works as well, novels and so on. Television programs would be quite a good example. You're not expected to remember anything you see on television. It's just to kill time with, and it flushes right out, and better it should. I've been watching television, I suppose, as long as most people my age–I'm in my mid-sixties now–and I can't think of but maybe eight or ten images from television that stayed with me. A few that you just happen up on every now and then are good, but for me they are mainly from documentaries, a crew up on some glacier in northern Alaska, or somebody in Africa or South America in the jungle or something like that, will tend to stay with me more than these insipid daytime dramas and these awful movies that you see one after the other.

DLB: The movie *Deliverance* was as rewarding as the novel, although in a different sense. You have written a screenplay for *Alnilam?*

Dickey: Yes, I've done the screenplay, but what's going to be done with that by director John Guillermin is unknown to me. I don't have the kind of control over the material that somebody like Fellini has. I wouldn't know what to do with it if I did have. I don't know anything about directing movies, and I have to leave that to John Boorman who did *Deliverance,* or John Guillermin, who's going to do this one if he ever gets around to it. But my part of it is finished.

DLB: I have high hopes for that movie.

Dickey: Well, I don't know if it will ever even be done. A lot of film projects are shelved and so on. Guillermin came here to Columbia several times, and we got on well, and we shunted the screenplay back and forth until we got something that satisfied both of us. But what's going to happen, I really don't know.

DLB: In 1954-1955 you and your family were in Europe, primarily in France, after having received the *Sewanee Review* Fellowship. Going through your private papers I came across the names and addresses and phone numbers of a long list of French writers and the titles of their works you wished to read. Did you get to know a lot of these writers?

Dickey: A few I did, but I was more ambitious then than my means or my energies could command, I suppose. But I did meet several French writers.

DLB: What kind of experience did you have in France?

Dickey: We went there in late summer of '54 and rented an old place on the Cap d'Antibes between Cannes and Nice up on a hill. There was a lighthouse right over our house. We had wonderful weather there too. We went down swimming every day on the beach that Scott Fitzgerald's friend Gerald Murphy had raked all the seaweed off and made into a beach. It's a good pleasant place to swim, and they had pedalos, those things you get in and pedal through the water. I had a little three-year-old boy, Chris, and I tried to work out some new poems. But when the mistral began to blow and it began to get cold, I had to spend most of the day trying to keep the house warm, and I couldn't write quite as much as I wanted to. So, we had Christmas there, and after that, in February, we threw everything in the car and went down to Florence, where we moved into a heated pensione. We'd been trying to keep from freezing for such a long time! Florence itself is cold, and the central heat was mightly welcome.

DLB: And then you returned to Italy–

Dickey: Yes, in '62 I went back on a Guggenheim Fellowship, and we went way on down south of there. Florence is in Tuscany, up in the hills of north-central Italy. But this time we went down on the coast, south of Naples, between Sorrento and Amalfi. There was a little fishing village where we lived, part working village and part tourist village during the season. They had a small American colony there with very pleasant people, and I wrote most of the third book, *Helmets,* there.

DLB: And you said at one time that you lived fairly close to where John Steinbeck was?

Dickey: John Steinbeck came there, but he was just visiting. I met him, and we sat around and had a couple of drinks. The first time I saw him he was sitting at a cafe near the ocean by himself with a martini, rather self-consciously trying to look like Hemingway.

DLB: And not doing it too well?

Dickey: No, and Steinbeck couldn't write like Hemingway either.

DLB: Any Italian writers that you met?

Dickey: I had one afternoon with Alberto Moravia, who is very, very good, but I don't remember meeting any other Italian writers, no.

DLB: Did you not seek them out?

Dickey: No, I didn't. I'm not someone like Stephen Spender who usually goes and finds the writers in the area of any language or any country that he wants to. I mean, I envy that because he has a long, long list of people that he knows, or at least whose acquaintance he's made. But I'm not really like that. The encounter has to be thrown in, sort of. I don't believe I've ever hunted anybody out.

DLB: Did you purposely try to follow your own direction, to focus primarily on home rather than foreign locales, in your writing?

Dickey: I don't know. I would sit down and write about anything that came to me and took my imagination strongly.

DLB: You wrote a poem about an ancient Italian city, "In the Lupanar at Pompeii."

Dickey: Yes, that's an extraordinary place. The guide–we had a wonderful guide, who spoke very good broken English–said that the Pompeiian whorehouse was the only building in the city that still had its roof. I don't know what that signifies. Maybe everything, maybe nothing.

DLB: You've mentioned at times that for some reason the English don't seem to respond to your work as well as do the Europeans.

Dickey: Some of them do. I have some good friends there. But I never went over and cultivated the British reviewers like Robert Lowell did, for example. That never really mattered to me. They could take it or leave it.

DLB: The French and the Italians–

Dickey: And the Germans, especially, yes. I have some very strong supporters in England, but I've never, as they say, set the Thames on fire. I would be a bit suspicious of myself if I had.

DLB: The British are known for their sense of reserve, whereas the romance-language countries, France and Italy, seem to be, generally speaking, of a temperament that would suit yours.

Dickey: Maybe so, but again, when you sit down to write something, you don't really speculate on matters of that kind. That comes after the fact. It may be the case, but it doesn't have any way of entering into the writing, or shouldn't. The main thing that you should be concerned with is putting one word next to another word.

DLB: You have a strong following in Japan, too, do you not?

Dickey: Well, I don't know how strong, but, yes, I suppose I do have readers there. Again, some writers follow the sales of their books and tote up all those figures. I couldn't have any less interest in that if I tried. Some of such an outcome is gratifying, but it can be fatally misleading. And if you are too successful, then you want to do it again, and if you don't do it again, you're devastated. I don't care, truly. I came from the back pages of obscure poetry magazines, and that's where I'll go back to; that's where I belong. I don't belong on an international stage or hobnobbing with movie actors and directors, and raking in all the big money. That world is full of hype and vacuousness, and I don't have any interest in it. I like the writing itself and the people that it brings me into contact with by accident. Rather, some I like, some I don't.

DLB: While we are talking a bit about the Far East, you've made only a few comments about your experiences in Korea.

Dickey: Well, in the Korean War I was mainly in the training command, and I look on that time as a complete limbo for me. The only good thing about it was that I kept on writing, and I began to publish a little bit at that time; but I was not young enough to be excited about flying any more or about teaching anybody else to do what I did. I did what I could; I did the best I could to keep people out of trouble, to keep them from getting hurt or killed. But it was strictly a going-through-the-motions sort of thing with me because writing had taken hold of me, and so flying and night fighter work and the training command was a waste of time for me. As soon as I got out of the service the second time I immediately resigned my commission. I would never risk getting recalled back into the service. It was just a complete waste, the second time.

DLB: You had had quite enough military service before.

Dickey: Yes, I was there when the big doings were going on, and I was quite content to be left with that. I didn't want any more of it. One thing that the United States military learned from the business of the Korean War was not to recall people into the service when they don't want to come. They had all those holdouts down at Lackland; pilots who were called back refused to fly. I never did any of those things. I went on and did what I was asked to do, but I could certainly understand their sentiments. Because those guys held out and because they were mavericks and risked going to Leavenworth because they wouldn't go up any more (they figured they'd already earned their keep), the United States won't call guys back in against their will as they did me and the whole rest of the bunch that went back in '50-'51. They won't do that again.

DLB: Do you think you and your pals in Korea taught the military a lesson?

Dickey: Well, I didn't teach anybody any lessons. I was just, as I said, mainly in the training command and I just flew with the guys who were coming in, the young guys that we were trying to train to do the night fighter work. But, as I say, when I got out of that, there wasn't going to be any more of it for me, ever!

DLB: Before Korea you had started teaching at Rice Institute?

Dickey: Yes, but I had only *just* started. I think I taught through Christmas and had maybe started the second semester when I was recalled. Then when I went back to Rice after Korea, I returned to the lowest of all possible positions in college teaching, teaching freshman composition. The course was called Composition and Report Writing for Engineering Students. But I was writing all the time and was very frustrated that I had published only a few things. I taught two years there after I got back from the service, and at the end of the second year I was asked by the editors and the judges for the second *Sewanee Review* Fellowship to apply for it. I sent in what I had written, and I got the fellowship, and then I walked away from freshman teaching forever, or so I thought. That's when we went to Europe in '54, to France and then to Florence. Then I came briefly to the University of Florida, teaching freshmen again, but I was also the assistant to Andrew Lytle, who was, except for me, the whole creative-writing program. I had one section of my own, and I attended his night session in the library once a week. He taught only about an hour a week, and he got all the money and I got only the wages of a freshman teacher in a horrendous program called C-3, which was monitored by spies who sat in the classroom to see whether or not you deviated one jot from the syllabus. I didn't stay there very long. I had published some poetry in magazines by then, but not enough for a book. And a guy in the advertising business, Thad Horton, had read some things of mine and said that if I ever wanted to go into the ad business to come and see him. So I did go to see him, went to New York and interviewed with his agency, McCann-Erickson, which had just taken over the Coca-Cola account from the Darcy Agency out of St. Louis, which had had it for thirty-some-odd years. And the agency, McCann-Erickson, was opening up on a lot of fronts–Coca-Cola was one of them–and I was taken on as a copywriter for them.

DLB: Let's talk a little bit about *Voiced Connections*. How do you feel about the book?

Dickey: I think it's a good book. If the reader wants the truth about one person's opinions and his preoccupations, I think it's as good a place to get mine as there is. I've had a good many interviews, and sometimes I say the same things over and over again because the questions are the same and my opinions and responses are consequently the same. But *Voiced Connections* has material not covered in other places, so I think people who are interested in my work or what I think I'm trying to do would be interested in this one for that reason, as well as for a good many others.

DLB: The interviews extend from 1965 to 1987 and for me it was fascinating to see how your ideas have evolved.

Dickey: Well, I change a lot. I think holding fixedly to a position, say, an opinion of a writer or of a literary work, is a sign of a sort of decadence. I mean, suppose you have written a book that is greatly in favor of Stephen Crane, and you're on record as saying that you are much in his favor. Suppose that later on, for reasons of your own or because you yourself have changed, you don't have that opinion any more. If you repudiate your own opinions, people think you shilly-shally, you don't have any fixed base of opinion or even any integrity. I think this is a terrible mistake. There are some writers that I've loved previously but that I don't care for at all any more; some that I previously didn't like very much that I now do like. I think you ought to be allowed to say this.

DLB: Does *Wayfarer* manifest an evolving attitude or–?

Dickey: Not evolving really. *Change* would be my word, or a shift in interest. *Wayfarer* is about the country people of Appalachia. I took a good deal of flak from some quarters because of the way in *Deliverance* I portrayed the two depraved rapists on the river bank, mountain men. Some people thought that was my opinion of all mountain people–hillbillies, crackers, or whatever you want to call them–but it isn't. *Wayfarer* is not exactly an atonement. I don't really feel that I need to atone for anything. But it's an attempt to show the likable and the good, enduring, sturdy, interesting part of the Appalachian people. And I think we did that; at least I did it in the way that I wanted.

DLB: *Wayfarer* has such a warm tone.

Dickey: Well, the old man: you should love him! He doesn't condescend to the city man, to the wayfarer, at all. The old man takes in the wayfarer, this guy who's getting sick, and nurses him back to health with the mountain remedies, rat's vein and the lard-filled shirt and all that. The biggest show of faith that the old man can give to the stranger is to tell him about the ways of the people there, and as the stranger gets better he wants to know about these things; he wants to listen to the music, and so on. The old man has only these things to offer, but he doesn't feel like he needs to offer the wayfarer any more. And the wayfarer certainly doesn't want anything but exactly what the old man has as a representative of his culture–and also as a human being that the wayfarer has come to have a very great deal of affection for.

DLB: Is the old man in *Wayfarer* an artistic homage to your father in some way?

Dickey: More to the kind of people that grouped around my father than to him actually. He had an affinity with people up in the hills, some of whom were my relatives. He understood those people, and they understood him. There is a meld which comes from the kind of community that we tried to depict in *Wayfarer,* where certain things are understood, you know, and my father had that. My father was a first-generation city man. His family came down out of the hills, mainly by working for the railroad. My grandfather worked for the Central Georgia Railroad, and that was his way out of the mountains to get into the city of Atlanta during the Reconstruction period. My father was born in 1888. I don't remember exactly where he was born, but I think he was born up in the country. The main thrust was to get the family down out of the mountains and established in Atlanta because they were all, except my father, ambitious to make it in the city, to make money and that sort of thing. My father had no real interest in that. His roots were in the hills, and any time he could get back up there, he took it. His main interest in life was in cockfighting, but I never heard him in my life call it cockfighting; to him it was always "chicken fighting." And I think during his later years it was a source of joy and pride to my father that I came to work at a university whose mascot was the fighting gamecock! Paul Deitzel, the then USC football coach, lived right across the street from us, and my father offered to donate a gamecock out of one of his own strain; he was a good breeder of gamecocks. We met briefly with Paul Deitzel on one occasion when promises were made, but somehow or another I don't think it ever came to anything. Maybe we would have had a better football team if my father's chicken had been the mascot!

DLB: He taught you a lot of the ways of the gamecock?

Dickey: Well, not a lot of them, but what I know about it I know from him. He subscribed and also was a contributor to the two main clandestine gamecock publications, *Grit and Steel* and *The Feathered Warrior.* I think that's very good, *The Feathered Warrior.* The imagination is always working! I don't know who got up the name of that little jake-legged rag of a gamecock magazine *The Feathered Warrior,* but the human imagination is at work full time, twenty-four hours a day, and you can't tell where you are going to encounter it, you know. Whoever thought up *The Feathered Warrior* was all right. This is not the highest reach of the imagination, but imagination it is. And I welcome that, as they say, wherever she may be found.

DLB: Are the magazines still in circulation?

Dickey: I haven't seen a copy since I was in high school. With my father *The Feathered Warrior* and *Grit and Steel* disappeared from my particular attention.

DLB: I'm taken with *Wayfarer* because of the extensive knowledge you have of mountain manners and lore and crafts.

Dickey: In a work as personal as that one is, I hate to use the word *research,* but some few things about geographical locations and so on I looked up. But I am anti-research, basically. I just re-read a book that meant a great deal to me when I was a much younger guy, by Frederic Prokosch, a writer who just died a couple of months ago. He was a poet of some ability, and he wrote a sort of excessively romantic prose. He's sort of like a Berlioz of prose fiction. I don't know if you like Berlioz. He's a sort of going-to-the-limit type of romantic composer. I love Berlioz's stuff, myself. Prokosch is kind of like that. He wrote a book called *The Asiatics* about a young guy who's twenty-two, twenty-three years old and who for some reason or other at the beginning of the novel finds himself in Beirut. This is much before the contemporary agony, maybe fifty, sixty years ago. You don't know what the young man is doing in Beirut, but he has a vague idea that he wants to go and see, to connect up with an uncle of his who lives in Japan. So he starts to beat his way across Asia by any means he can. The novel is called *The Asiatics.* You must read *The Asiatics.* It's so good! I mean, it's pure escapism by a tremendously imaginative escaper.

DLB: That's the best kind.

Dickey: Yes, I think so. But, anyway, I was pleased to find that Frederic Prokosch, the author, had never set foot in Asia. He just made it all up. But if Asia is not like that really, then it ought to be. Again, think about Stephen Crane's writing about the Civil War, which took place when he couldn't possibly have been a participant. I'm against the kind of research-oriented writer who researches the automobile industry or the hotel business and then writes a novel about it. That *can* be done, but it's mechanical. My orientation is that of the poet. Henry James is in some ways one of the great poets. He said that he was thinking about writing a novel about the Coldstream Guards, and somebody said, "Well, you have to go and live with them." But then James said, "Not at all. I can write the novel by looking into the window of the officers' mess for thirty seconds. That's all I need; that's all I want." I work from some sort of principle, or anti-principle, such as that.

DLB: In *Alnilam* you were able, I think, very correctly to get away from a too technical discussion.

Dickey: Well, I read through everybody I could find who wrote on flying. I went through all my old technical manuals, and that sort of thing. Pilots of military aircraft, indeed, any aircraft, are like the astronauts because they won't live unless they pay attention to every technical detail that concerns their flight. But if you get into the technical part of it too much, then you lose the basic *sensation* of flight, which above all I wanted to convey in *Alnilam* by any means: the sensation of the fragile human body up in that alien element, air, which is alien but is also the same element that one breathes. I wanted to get that, to get the precariousness and also the excitement, the very feel of flight. Cylinder-head temperatures or fuel-consumption range and all of those other technical things are important; they contribute to flight; they make it possible. But they are not flight. This is where Joel Cahill comes in. He himself is the essence of flight; he goes beyond the engine. One of the cadets tells the blind man, Joel's father, "What we are learning to do is to fly without the airplane."

DLB: Does this distinction perhaps suggest the difference between verse making and writing poetry?

Dickey: Again, this is something that comes up in the classes that I teach. Karl Shapiro wrote probably the best manual on prosody: *A Prosody Handbook*. It's out of print now, but I urge my students to get it from secondhand shops. And he also has a prose poem about writing the manual on prosody, and he says it's like a blueprint. You can show students the various verse forms, the kinds of rhyme schemes and so on. Some of them are incredibly complicated. Shapiro says they are like blueprints, but blueprints are all right; they have their dreams. The dream of the blueprint is that it shall become the thing that the blueprint is of–the structure, the house, the engine part, or whatever it may be. The dream of the prosodist, the expert in meter, is that from the prosody, from the blueprint, from the rules, shall rise the poem, the real poem. Blueprints–they have their dreams. I teach from that basis.

DLB: In *Alnilam* there is a wonderful passage where Whitehall is describing going on a bombing mission and losing his navigational bearings.

Dickey: Yes, he's talking from the navigator's standpoint, and it weathers in, and he can't get any visuals. He can't see any stars, anything to use his navigational know-how on, and the drama of that part of the book comes from his telling what happened to him, and how he felt when he couldn't see. The only thing that would justify his being up there on a mission, and also the only thing that will ever save his aircraft and the other eighteen is for the stars to come out. He knows what to do if the essential, which in this case is the stars, would just give him a shot at it. But it doesn't happen until right at the end, and then he just gets fragmentary shots of three stars. He triangulates them and sets the alternate course, and it gets them back.

DLB: It's a powerful scene, I think. Did anything like that happen to you?

Dickey: No, I wasn't in the real navigators much; I was in fighters. But I used to see those guys looking out with their sextants and calibrating them. I thought they were on to a superior secret. If you do survive the war and you get to be a middle-aged novelist, you go back to it and you try to solve the secret. Then you write about it.

DLB: The blueprint came through?

Dickey: The blueprint, yes, and the stars came through, the crews got back to New Guinea, and I wrote the novel.

DLB: Is there anything you'd like to say about Robert Penn Warren?

Dickey: He was my best friend among the writers of that generation. He was a remarkably responsible person dedicated entirely to literature and his version of poetry, and a good literary critic, a good novelist. His main characteristic, the one that I esteem the most, is a kind of primitivism, a sort of raw, jagged, unintellectual quality wedded to a very great analytical ability, running somewhat to rhetoric on some occasions, which some critics didn't care for, but I do. He liked to philosophize in verse and in novels as well, and I could take a lot of the philosophizing that Red Warren does. In his narratives he's a great master of the action line; he can really catch you up in a sequence of events. The main thing to me is the poetry that has the ability to *disturb* you. He has not exactly a fixation but a fascination with caves; for example, there's one poem in which he goes down into a cave and lies in the darkness of the underground. And he says, "Is this all?" Then he asks himself a question that is even more unanswerable, "What *is* all?" Warren's friend, Allen Tate, said about his own work, "I think of my poetry as having to do with those human situations from which there is no escape." That statement could certainly characterize Robert Penn Warren's work.

DLB: More than Tate's?

Dickey: Much more, or more than the work of anybody else at all.

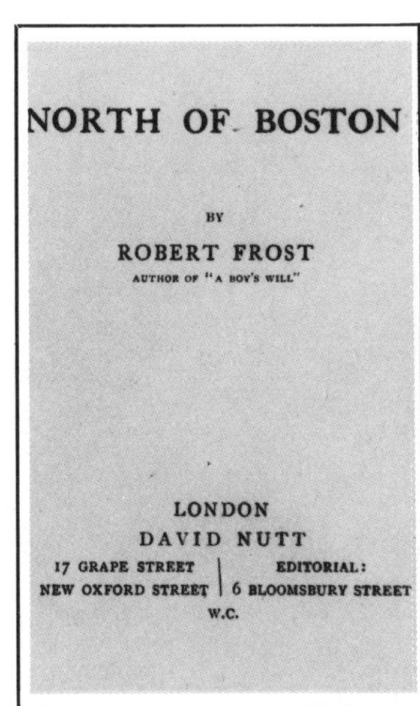
NORTH OF BOSTON

BY

ROBERT FROST

AUTHOR OF "A BOY'S WILL"

LONDON

DAVID NUTT

17 GRAPE STREET | EDITORIAL:

NEW OXFORD STREET | 6 BLOOMSBURY STREET

W.C.

A

WITNESS

TREE

BY

ROBERT

FROST

HENRY HOLT AND COMPANY

NEW YORK

ROBERT FROST

(26 March 1874-29 January 1963)

Karen L. Rood

See the Robert Frost entry in Dictionary of Literary Biography, *volume 54,* American Poets, 1880-1945, Third Series.

MAJOR BOOKS:

Twilight (Lawrence, Mass.: American Printing House?, 1894; facsimile, Charlottesville: Clifton Waller Barrett Library, University of Virginia, 1966);

A Boy's Will (London: David Nutt, 1913; New York: Holt, 1915);

North of Boston (London: David Nutt, 1914; New York: Holt, 1914);

Mountain Interval (New York: Holt, 1916);

Selected Poems (New York: Holt, 1923; London: Heinemann/New York: Holt, 1923);

New Hampshire: A Poem with Notes and Grace Notes (New York: Holt, 1923; London: Grant Richards, 1924);

Selected Poems (New York: Holt, 1928);

West-Running Brook (New York: Holt, 1928);

A Way Out: A One Act Play (New York: Harbor Press, 1929);

The Lovely Shall Be Choosers (New York: Random House, 1929);

The Cow's in the Corn: A One-Act Irish Play in Rhyme (Gaylordsville, Conn.: Slide Mountain Press, 1929);

Collected Poems of Robert Frost (New York: Holt, 1930; London: Longmans, Green, 1930);

The Augustan Books of Poetry: Robert Frost (London: Benn, 1932);

The Lone Striker (New York: Knopf, 1933);

Selected Poems: Third Edition (New York: Holt, 1934);

Three Poems (Hanover, N.H.: Baker Library, 1935);

The Gold Hesperidee (Cortland, N.Y.: Bibliophile Press, 1935);

From Snow to Snow (New York: Holt, 1936);

A Further Range (New York: Holt, 1936; London: Cape, 1937);

Selected Poems (London: Cape, 1936);

Collected Poems of Robert Frost (New York: Holt, 1939; London: Longmans, Green, 1939);

William Prescott Frost, Jr. (1872) and Isabelle Moodie (circa 1872). The two met in autumn 1872 while teaching at a small private academy in Lewistown, Pennsylvania, and were married on 18 March 1873. In July William Frost found employment as a journalist in San Francisco, where Isabelle Frost joined him in November.

Robert Frost, circa 1879, with his sister, Jeanie Florence Frost, born 25 June 1876

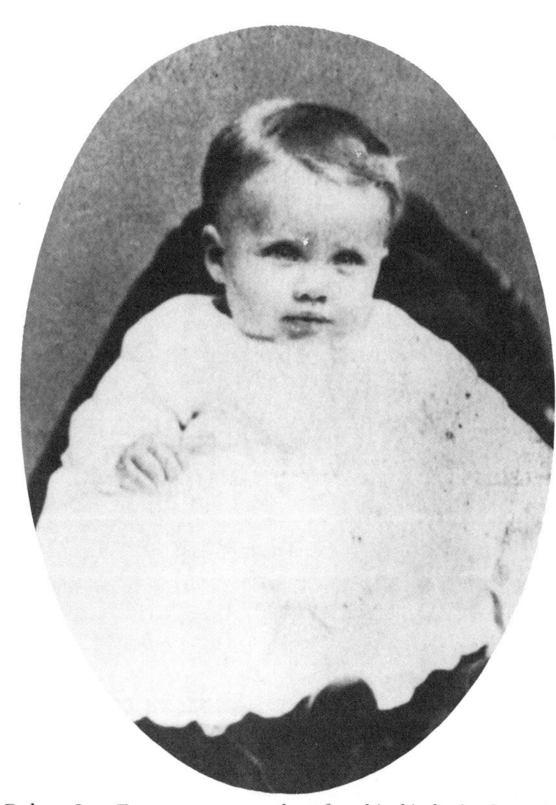

Robert Lee Frost seven months after his birth, in San Francisco on 26 March 1874

A Witness Tree (New York: Holt, 1942; London: Cape, 1943);

Come In and Other Poems, edited by Louis Untermeyer (New York: Holt, 1943; London: Cape, 1944); enlarged as *The Road Not Taken* (New York: Holt, 1951);

A Masque of Reason (New York: Holt, 1945);

The Pocket Book of Robert Frost's Poems, edited by Untermeyer (New York: Pocket Books, 1946);

The Poems of Robert Frost, With an Introductory Essay, "THE CONSTANT SYMBOL" (New York: Modern Library, 1946);

Steeple Bush (New York: Holt, 1947);

A Masque of Mercy (New York: Holt, 1947);

A Sermon (New York: Spiral Press, 1947);

A Masque of Reason by Robert Frost, containing A Masque of Reason, A Masque of Mercy (Two New England Biblicals) together with Steeple Bush and other Poems (London: Cape, 1948);

Complete Poems of Robert Frost, 1949 (New York: Holt, 1949; London: Cape, 1951);

Hard Not To Be King (New York: House of Books, 1951);

Aforesaid (New York: Holt, 1954);

Robert Frost: Selected Poems (Harmondsworth, U.K.: Penguin, 1955);

A Remembrance Collection of New Poems (New York: Holt, 1959);

You Come Too (New York: Holt, 1959; London: Bodley Head, 1964);

Dedication/The Gift Outright/The Inaugural Address (New York: Holt, Rinehart & Winston, 1961);

In the Clearing (New York: Holt, Rinehart & Winston, 1962; London: Holt, Rinehart & Winston, 1962);

Robert Frost: His 'American Send-Off'–1915, edited by Edward Connery Lathem (Lunenburg, Vt.: Stinehour, 1963);

Selected Poems of Robert Frost (New York, Chicago, San Francisco & Toronto: Holt, Rinehart & Winston, 1963);

Robert Frost: Farm-Poultryman, edited by Lathem and Lawrance Thompson (Hanover, N.H.: Dartmouth Publications, 1963);

Robert Frost and the Lawrence, Massachusetts, 'High School Bulletin': The Beginning of a Literary Career, edited by Lathem and Thompson (New York: Grolier Club, 1966);

Selected Prose of Robert Frost, edited by Hyde Cox and Lathem (New York, Chicago & San Francisco: Holt, Rinehart & Winston, 1966);

The Poetry of Robert Frost, edited by Lathem (New York, Chicago & San Francisco: Holt, Rinehart & Winston, 1969);

Robert Frost on Writing, edited by Elaine Barry (New Brunswick: Rutgers University Press, 1972);

Robert Frost: Poetry and Prose, edited by Lathem and Thompson (New York, Chicago & San Francisco: Holt, Rinehart & Winston, 1972);

Stories for Lesley, edited by Roger D. Sell (Charlottesville: Published for the Bibliographical Society of the University of Virginia by the University Press of Virginia, 1984).

OTHER:

Reginald Cook, *Robert Frost: A Living Voice*, includes speeches by Frost (Amherst: University of Massachusetts Press, 1974), pp. 36-195;

"Two Unpublished Plays: *IN AN ART FACTORY, THE GUARDEEN*," edited by Roger D. Sell, *Massachusetts Review*, 26 (Summer-Autumn 1985): 265-340.

BIOGRAPHIES:

Sidney Cox, *A Swinger of Birches: A Portrait of Robert Frost* (New York: New York University Press, 1957);

Elizabeth Shepley Sergeant, *Robert Frost: The Trial by Existence* (New York: Holt, Rinehart & Winston, 1960);

F. D. Reeve, *Robert Frost in Russia* (Boston: Little, Brown, 1964);

Louis Mertins, *Robert Frost: Life and Talks-Walking* (Norman: Univ. of Oklahoma Press, 1965);

Lawrance Thompson, *Robert Frost: The Early Years, 1874-1915* (New York, Chicago & San Francisco: Holt, Rinehart & Winston, 1966); *Robert Frost: The Years of Triumph, 1915-1938* (New York, Chicago & San Francisco: Holt, Rinehart & Winston, 1970); Thompson and R. H. Winnick, *Robert Frost: The Later Years, 1938-1963* (New York: Holt, Rinehart & Winston, 1976); these three volumes abridged by Edward Connery Lathem, with Winnick, as *Robert Frost: A Biography* (New York: Holt, Rinehart & Winston, 1982);

Robert Francis, *Frost: A Time to Talk* (Amherst: University of Massachusetts Press, 1972);

Kathleen Morrison, *Robert Frost: A Pictorial Chronicle* (New York: Holt, Rinehart & Winston, 1974);

Biographical and genealogical account (on this and next two pages) written by William Prescott Frost, Jr., on 24 June 1872, two days before his graduation with honors from Harvard College (Barrett Library, University of Virginia Library)

Please return to Robert Frost Franconia N.H.

I was born at Kingston, N. H., 27 December, 1850. My father, William Prescott Frost, resides at Lawrence, Mass, and is an overseer in the Pacific Mills, in that city. My mother's maiden name was Judith Colcord. She is the daughter of Daniel Colcord and Mary (Woodman) Colcord, who resided at Kingston, N. H.

The first of the Frost family of whom I find any (1) record lived in Devonshire, England. Nicholas Frost was born at Tiverton, Devonshire, about 1595, and came to this country in 1635 or 1636. He settled at what is now Kittery, Me., where he died in 1663. His occupation was farming. His eldest son, (2) Charles, was born at Tiverton, Devonshire, about 1630, and emigrated with his father. He appears to have attained to some distinction in this country, both in civil and in military capacities. He was a "Major" in the forces organized by the settlers against the Indians, and took an active part in the Indian wars in Me. and N. H. He was killed by the Indians at Kittery, where he had settled, in 1697. (3) John, the second son of Charles Frost, was born about 1670. He married the sister of Sir William Pepperell, who was knighted for distinguished service in the Indian war,— being the only American colonist who ever received that honor. John at one time commanded a British man-of-war, and subsequently followed the business of a merchant, at New Castle, N. H. He was at one time a member of the Governor's Council. He died in 1732. (4) William, Gt-Grandfather the second son of John Frost, was born at New Castle, N. H., in 1710, and succeeded his father in mercantile business, dying in 1778. His brother John had a son, Col. John Frost, of the army of the Revolution. George Frost, another brother of William, was a judge of the Court of Common Pleas, in N. H., and also a delegate to one of the Continental Congresses. (5) William, Grandfather the second son of William Frost, was born at New Castle, N. H., in 1755. He was a farmer of that place, and died at Andover, Mass., in 1840. (6) Samuel Abbott Frost, the son of (5) William, was born at Andover, Mass., in 1795. He resided at Andover and at Brentwood, N. H., and followed various avocations, main ly that of farming. He died at Brentwood, N. H., in 1848. He served in the war of 1812. He married Mary Blunt, of Portsmouth, N. H. His eldest son, William Prescott Frost, my father, was born at Eden, Me, in 1823.

William Blunt, the father of Mary Blunt, (wife of S. A. Frost,) was a Revolutionary soldier. He was subsequently a sea-captain, and during the Napoleonic wars his vessel was once captured by the French for having on board goods contraband of war. The Blunts came from England, about 1740.

My maternal grandfather, (3) Daniel Colcord, was born at Kingston, N. H., in 1781, where he died in 1857. He lived his whole life at that place, and followed the trade of plough-making. He served in the war of 1812, and was stationed at Portsmouth, N. H. (2) Daniel, the father of (3) Daniel Colcord, was born at Kingston, N. H., about 1750. He lived and died at Kingston, where he followed the calling of a farmer. (1) Samuel, the father of (2) Daniel Colcord, was probably born at Kingston, N. H., date unknown. He was a farmer of that village, where he died, date unknown. The Colcords without doubt originated in England, but from what part, or at what date, they came to this country, I am unable to learn.

My maternal grandmother, Mary Woodman, was a direct descendant of Edward Woodman, who came to this country from the parish of Christian Malford, Wiltshire, England, in 1635, and who settled at Newbury, Mass. Joshua Woodman, her grandfather, settled at Kingston, N. H., about 1736.

The only ones of my ancestors or relatives whom I know to have received a "liberal education" are of the Woodman family, and are as follows: — Rev. Joseph Woodman, Nassau Hall, 1766: Hon. Jeremiah H. Woodman, Dart. Coll., 1794: Rev. Jabez Woodman, Dart. Coll., 1803: Hon. Charles Woodman, Dart. Coll., 1813: Jabez C. Woodman, Dart. Coll., 1822: Moses E. Woodman, ~~Dart.~~ Bowd. Coll., 1826: Hon. Charles W. Woodman, Dart. Coll., 1829: Theodore C. Woodman, ~~Dart.~~ Bowd. Coll., 1835: Cyrus Woodman, ~~Dart.~~ Bowd. Coll., 1836: Jabez H. Woodman, Bowd. Coll., 1836: Prof. John S. Woodman, Dart. Coll., 1842.

I resided at Kingston, N. H., from Dec. 1850 to Aug. 1852; at Milton, N. H., from Aug. 1852 to Oct. 1853; at Manchester, N. H., from Oct. 1853 to Jan. 1855; at Nashua, N. H., from Jan. 1855 to Nov. 1855; at Lawrence, Mass., from Nov. 1855 to Nov. 1858; at Southbridge, Mass., from Nov. 1858 to Oct., 1860; and at Lawrence, Mass., from Oct. 1860 to June, 1872. During my former residence at Lawrence I attended primary, intermediate, and grammar schools from Mar. 1856 to Nov. 1858. While residing at Southbridge I attended a grammar school from the spring of 1859 to the autumn of 1860. I attended the "Oliver Grammar School," at Lawrence, of which George A. Walton was the principal, from the spring of 1861 to May 1864, at which latter date I was graduated. I attended the "Lawrence High School" from May, 1864 to June 1868, receiving an "English" diploma in 1867, and a "Classical" diploma in 1868. Albert C. Perkins was the Principal of this school. My studies took the character of preparation for a college course in May, 1864, at the "Lawrence High School," although this school makes no pretensions to give boys a college—especially a Harvard College—fit; and though at that time I had no intention of entering college. I have been engaged in no occupation or business other than studying, except that I have reported for the Boston "Saturday Evening Gazette" since 1 July, 1871.

I was led first seriously to think of going to college, in May 1868, by my failure to obtain an appointment to West Point, for which I had made considerable effort, and in which I was thwarted by political influence. I entered in ~~June~~ July, 1868, at the age of 17 yrs., 6 mths., with two and a half conditions. I received a detur in my Sophomore year, and a first "Bowdoin" prize in my Junior year for an essay on "The Hohenstaufens". I am a member of the Phi Beta Kappa society. During my Freshman year I chummed with Edward Stearns Sheldon, at 4 Hollis Hall. During my Sophomore year I roomed alone, at 16 College House. During my Junior year I chummed with Charles Roberts Brickett, at 15 College House, in which room I remained during my Senior year, alone.

My maternal uncle, Daniel Colcord, served through the War of the Rebellion in the 1st. Mass. Heavy Artillery. My cousin Samuel Chandler served during a part of the war in a Wisconsin regiment of Infantry, and was honorably discharged on account of disease contracted while in the service.

I have a considerable fondness for the study of history,—especially political history,—and take much interest in Political Economy. My plans in life are as yet unshaped, though I shall probably go into either journalism or law. At present I am quite undecided as to which of the two to choose.

William Prescott Frost, Jr.

24 June, 1872.

Robert S. Newdick, *Newdick's Season of Frost: An Interrupted Biography of Robert Frost,* edited by William A. Sutton (Albany: State University of New York Press, 1976);

William H. Pritchard, *Frost: A Literary Life Reconsidered* (New York: Oxford University Press, 1984);

Stanley Burnshaw, *Robert Frost Himself* (New York: Braziller, 1986);

John Evangelist Walsh, *Into My Own: The English Years of Robert Frost, 1912-1915* (New York: Grove, 1988).

BIBLIOGRAPHIES:

Lawrance Thompson, *Robert Frost: A Chronological Survey* (Middleton, Conn.: Olin Memorial Library, 1936);

W. B. Shubrick Clymer and Charles R. Green, *Robert Frost: A Bibliography* (Amherst: Jones Library, 1937);

Ray Nash, ed., *Fifty Years of Robert Frost: A Catalogue of the Exhibition Held in Baker Library in the Autumn of 1943* (Hanover: Dartmouth College Library, 1944);

Louis and Esther Mertins, *The Intervals of Robert Frost: A Critical Bibliography* (Berkeley: University of California Press, 1947);

Louis Untermeyer, "Untermeyer-Frost Collection: Partial Contents," in his *Robert Frost: A Backward Look* (Washington, D.C.: Library of Congress, 1964), pp. 27-40;

Uma Paramesuaran, "Robert Frost: A Bibliography of Articles and Books," *Bulletin of Bibliography,* 25 (1967): 46-48, 58, 69, 72;

Donald J. Greiner, *Checklist of Robert Frost* (Columbus, Ohio: Merrill, 1969);

Greiner, "Robert Frost, The Poet as Critic: An Analysis and a Checklist," *South Carolina Review,* 7 (November 1974): 48-60;

Joan St. C. Crane, *Robert Frost: A Descriptive Catalogue of Books and Manuscripts in the Clifton Waller Barrett Library, University of Virginia* (Charlottesville: University Press of Virginia, 1974);

Marlan G. M. Clarke, *The Robert Frost Collection in the Watkinson Library* (Hartford: Watkinson Library, Trinity College, 1974);

Edward Connery Lathem, *Robert Frost 100* (Boston: Godine, 1974);

Peter Van Egmond, *The Critical Reception of Robert Frost* (Boston: G. K. Hall, 1974);

Frank and Melissa Lentricchia, *Robert Frost: A Bibliography, 1913-1974* (Metuchen, N.J.: Scarecrow Press, 1976).

LETTERS:

The Letters of Robert Frost to Louis Untermeyer, edited by Louis Untermeyer (New York: Holt, Rinehart & Winston, 1963; London: Cape, 1964);

Robert Frost and John Bartlett: The Record of a Friendship, edited by Margaret Bartlett Anderson (New York: Holt, Rinehart & Winston, 1963);

Selected Letters of Robert Frost, edited by Lawrance Thompson (New York, Chicago & San Francisco: Holt, Rinehart & Winston, 1964);

Family Letters of Robert and Elinor Frost, edited by Arnold Grade (Albany: State University of New York Press, 1972);

Robert Frost and Sidney Cox: Forty Years of Friendship, edited by William R. Evans (Hanover, N.H. & London: University Press of New England, 1981).

INTERVIEWS:

Interviews with Robert Frost, edited by Edward Connery Lathem (New York, Chicago & San Francisco: Holt, Rinehart & Winston, 1966; London: Cape, 1967).

NOTEBOOKS:

Prose Jottings of Robert Frost: Selections from His Notebooks and Miscellaneous Manuscripts, edited by Edward Connery Lathem and Hyde Cox (Lunenburg, Vt.: Northeast-Kingdom Publishers, 1982).

LOCATION OF ARCHIVES:

The major collections of Frost's papers are in the Clifton Waller Barrett Library, University of Virginia Library; the Dartmouth College Library; the Henry E. Huntington Library, San Marino, California; and the Jones Library, Amherst, Massachusetts.

ARTICLE:

From Robert S. Newdick, "How a Columbus Mother Inspired Her Son to Become the Dean of America's Living Poets," *Columbus Sunday Dispatch,* 17 May 1936, Graphic Section, p. 5.

Newdick, an English professor at Ohio State University whose death in 1939 prevented his completing a biography of Robert Frost, wrote this article about the poet's mother shortly before Frost gave a reading at Ohio State. As an adult, Frost–whose official birth record was destroyed during the San Francisco earthquake and

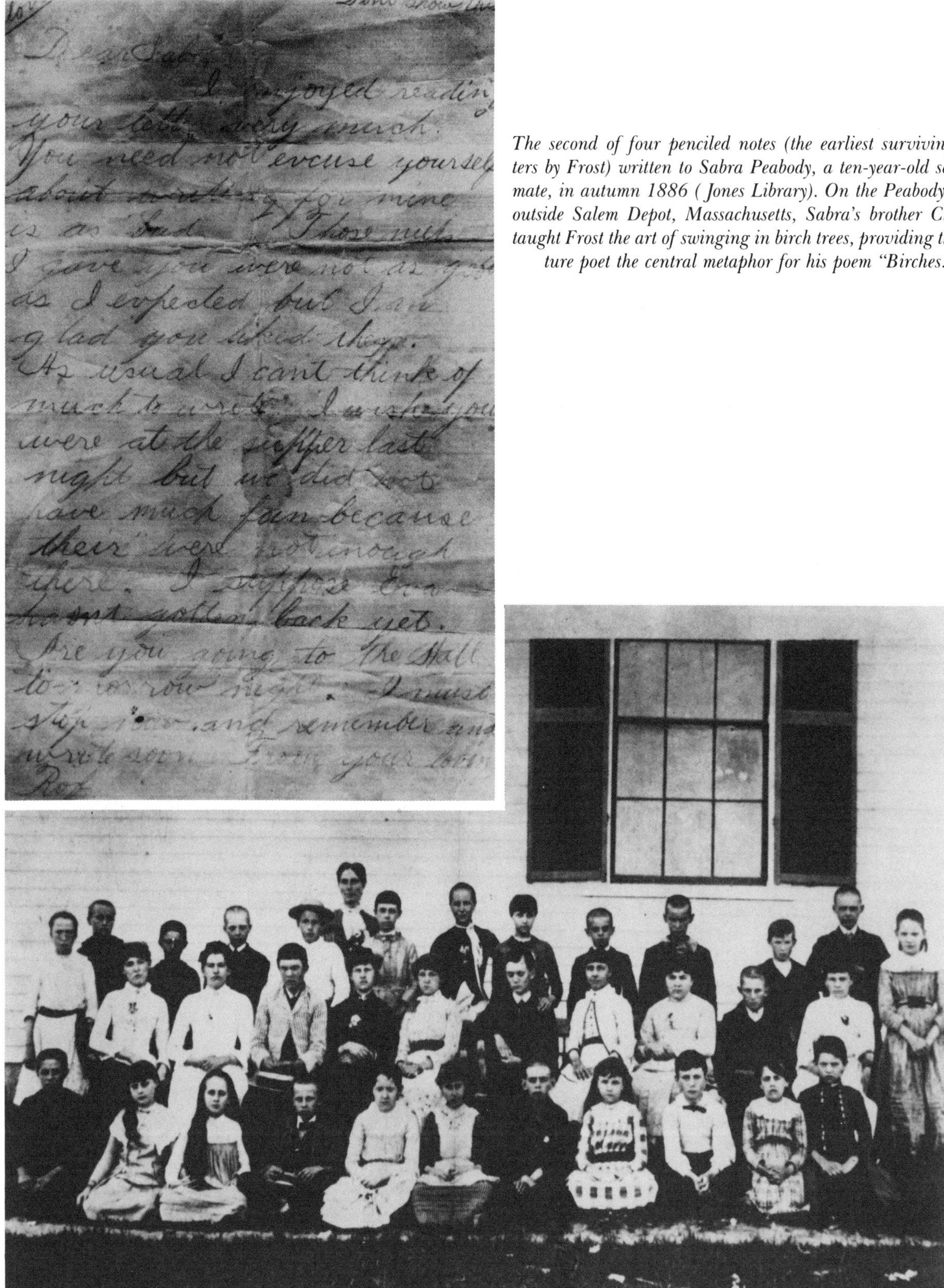

Dont show [illegible]

Dear Sabe,
I enjoyed reading your letter very much. You need not excuse yourself about writing for mine is as bad. Those nuts I gave you were not as good as I expected but I am glad you liked them. As usual I cant think of much to write. I wish you were at the supper last night but we did not have much fun because their were not enough there. I suppose [illegible] hasnt gotten back yet. Are you going to the Hall to-morrow night. I must stop now and remember and write soon. From your [illegible]
Rob

The second of four penciled notes (the earliest surviving letters by Frost) written to Sabra Peabody, a ten-year-old schoolmate, in autumn 1886 (Jones Library). On the Peabody farm outside Salem Depot, Massachusetts, Sabra's brother Charlie taught Frost the art of swinging in birch trees, providing the future poet the central metaphor for his poem "Birches."

Isabelle Moodie Frost with her class at Salem District School Number Six, 1887. Robert Frost (wearing a hat) is standing in front of his mother. Jeanie Frost is third from left in the front row. Sabra Peabody is sixth from left in the same row.

fire of 1906–was uncertain about the year of his birth and settled on 1875, the date he gave Newdick. In the late 1940s or early 1950s Lawrance Thompson, who had succeeded Newdick as Frost's official biographer, discovered conclusive evidence that the poet was born in 1874.

Columbus can rightfully claim some share in the rich and varied background of Robert Frost, dean of America's living poets, and when he steps up to the lectern to begin his reading and talk on poetry, Thurday evening, May 21, in the chapel at Ohio State University there will be in the audience a number of local residents who are blood relatives of his through kinship with his mother.

From lowland Scotland, in the 1830's, there came to America and on out to Ohio, Thomas Moodie, a young barrister newly graduated from the University of Edinburgh. Not long thereafter he sent to the homeland for his affianced bride, and soon they were settled permanently in Columbus.

In the years that followed, he became a prosperous banker, an elder in the First Presbyterian church, and the father of seven daughters and one son. The old Moodie home was on the southwest corner of State and Sixth streets. . . .

Back in lowland Scotland the Moodies were a seafaring family, and the sea had taken its toll of them. It had already taken Thomas Moodie's nephew and namesake; now it took his sea-captain brother, leaving his niece, Isabelle Moodie, an orphan. So, late in the 50's, accompanied by her grandmother who returned at once, rosy-cheeked, dark-haired immigrant Belle Moodie, about 13 years old, came to America, and on to Columbus, to spend the remaining years of her youth with her uncle and his family. . . .

Here she resumed her education, graduating with the class of 1864 from Columbus high school, more recently known as the old Central high school, formerly at Sixth and Broad streets. Her part in the graduation exercises, an essay on Gas, was "received with great favor by the audience," according to an account in the press, and was "unsurpassed by any other effort of the evening." Her graduation picture shows her to have been a strikingly beautiful girl.

Then from 1864 to 1872, save for one year, Miss Moodie taught in the public schools of the city, rising from primary teacher to intermediate teacher, high school teacher, and finally assistant principal of District No. 3. . . .

It was in the 70's, while teaching school in Lewiston, Pa., that Miss Moodie met and married a fellow teacher, William Prescott Frost, jr., the radical scion of a conservative old New England family. He shortly went on to San Francisco; she followed soon afterwards; and their first child was born there on March 26, 1875.

The boy was christened Robert Lee Frost, in token of his father's sympathies with the south. The father, engaged in journalistic work on the Bulletin, was a staunch Democrat. So also, today, is his son, but emphatically a Carter Glass Democrat, not a Rooseveltian.

Frost's biographers have hitherto stressed chiefly the influence on him of New England, not only because of his long residence in that region, but also through his dynamic father and otherwise ancestrally.

There is no lack of evidence, however, for maintaining the stronger influence of his Scot and partially Columbus-bred mother. She invariably understood him when he was a boy, while his father, engrossed in politics, rarely did; she was something of a professional writer and poet herself, and she quietly encouraged her son in his efforts along similar lines; her later Swedenborgian religious convictions were for a while shared by her son and did much to develop the rich vein of mysticism and symbolism in his poetry; and her staunch loyalty was a bulwark to him during many of the long years of his obscurity as an artist.

On the death of the elder Frost in 1885 Mrs. Frost crossed the continent with her two children to her husband's former home in Lawrence, Mass. Robert, hitherto more absorbed in games and play than in study, now set himself seriously to books, and in 1892 was graduated from Lawrence High school at the head of his class, winning the Hood prize "for general excellence" and delivering the valedictory address, "A Monument to Afterthought Unveiled."

EDITORIAL:
Lawrence High School Bulletin, 13 (May 1892): 4; *Robert Frost and the Lawrence, Massachusetts, 'High School Bulletin.'*

The class of 1892 elected Frost chief editor of the Bulletin *for their senior year, but Frost resigned in January 1892 after the failure of his staff to provide their share of the copy forced him to write virtually all of the Decem-*

HIGH SCHOOL BULLETIN.

"HONESTAS ET PERSEVERANTIA."

VOL. XI. LAWRENCE, MASS., APRIL, 1890. NO. 8.

THE SHEPHERD'S SONG.

'Tis the quiet evening,
When the sun sinks low,
And the birds and flowers
To their slumber go;
As the shadows deepen,
And the shades grow long,
Then the sturdy shepherd
Sings his evening song.

"In life's day so varied
All is for the best,
All day we may labour
But at last comes rest;
Though this world may trouble,
And its cares annoy,
In the land we hope for,
Comes eternal joy.

Never be discouraged,
Be both brave and strong
Till you rest in heaven—
It will not be long.
Let your work be joyful,
Hard though it may seem,
And through clouds of darkness
Light once more will gleam."

Then the moon arising
Spreads its mantle gray,
And the shepherd, singing,
Homeward hies his way.
And he sees the valley,
Calm and pure and white,
Glist'ning in the moonlight
Like a mirror bright.

C. J. C. '90.

LA NOCHE TRISTE.

TENOCHTITLAN.

Changed is the scene: the peace
And regal splendor which
Once that city knew are gone,
And war now reigns upon
That throng, who but
A week ago were all
Intent on joy supreme.
Cries of the wounded break
The stillness of the night,
Or challenge of the guard.
The Spaniard many days
Beseiged within the place,
Where kings did rule of old,
Now pressed by hunger by
The all-relentless foe,
Looks for some channel of
Escape. The night is dark;
Black clouds obscure the sky—
A dead calm lies o'er all.
The heart of one is firm,
His mind is constant still,
To all, his word is law.
Cortes his plan hath made,
The time hath come. Each one
His chosen place now takes,
There waits the signal, that
Will start the long retreat.

THE FLIGHT.

Anon the cry comes down the line,
The portals wide are swung,
A long dark line moves out the gate,
And now the flight's begun.

Aye, cautiously it moves at first,
As ship steered o'er the reef,
Looking for danger all unseen,
But which may bring to grief.

Straight for the causeway now they make,
The bridge is borne before,
'Tis ta'en and placed across the flood,
And all go trooping o'er.

Yet e'er the other side is reached,
Wafted along the wind,
The rolling of the snake-skin drum
Comes floating from behind.

And scarcely has its rolling ceased,
Than out upon the lake,
Where all was silence just before,
A conch the calm doth break.

What terror to each heart it bears,
That sound of ill portent,
Each gunner to escape now looks,
On safety all are bent.

Forward they press in wild despair,
On to the next canal,
Held on all sides by foe and sea,
Like deer within corral.

Now surging this way, now in that,
The mass sways to and fro,
The infidel around it sweeps—
Slowly the night doth go.

A war cry soundeth through the night,
The 'tzin! the 'tzin! is there,
His plume nods wildly o'er the scene,
Oh, Spaniard, now beware!

With gaping jaws the cannon stands,
Points it among the horde;
The valiant Leon waits beside,
Ready with match and sword.

The 'tzin quick springeth to his side,
His mace he hurls on high,
It crasheth through the Spanish steel,
And Leon prone doth lie.

Falling, he died beneath his gun,—
He died at duty's call,
And many falling on that night,
Dying, so died they all.

The faithful guarders at the bridge,
Have worked with might and main,
Nor can they move it from its place,
Swollen by damp of rain.

On through the darkness comes the cry,
The cry that all is lost;
Then e'en Cortes takes up the shout,
And o'er the host 'tis tossed.

Some place their safety in the stream,
But sink beneath the tide,
E'en others crossing on the dead,
Thus reach the other side.

Surrounded and alone he sits,
Upon his faithful steed;
Here Alvarado clears a space,
But none might share the deed—

For darkness of that murky night
Hides deeds of brightest fame,
Which in the ages yet to come,
Would light the hero's name.

His faithful charger now hath fall'n,
Pierced to the very heart.
Quick steps he back, his war cry shouts,
Then onward doth he dart.

Runs he, and leaping high in air,
Fixed does he seem a space,
One instant and the deed is done,
He standeth face to face—

With those who on the other side
Their safety now have found.
The thirst for vengeance satisfied,
The Aztec wheels around.

So, as the sun climbs up the sky,
And shoots his dawning rays,
The foe, as parted by his dart,
Each go their sep'rate ways.

Upon the ground the dead men lie,
Trampled midst gold and gore,
The Aztec toward his temple goes,

Frost's first poem, inspired by William Hickling Prescott's History of the Conquest of Mexico *(1843) and written in March 1890, during Frost's sophomore year at Lawrence High School, was "La Noche Triste," published in the April issue of the school magazine, on pages one (above) and two.*

ber 1891 issue in one day. He helped his successor, however, by writing three editorials for the May 1892 issue. In one he expressed ideas that suggested his later thinking about traditional form in poetry.

QUESTION: Can we review an author's thought, retell his story? Yes, if you praise while so doing. Can we review a narrative of travel! No, because that would be a re-review–the traveller reviews God's thoughts (nature) and praises them. Twice told is new–thrice told is old. Herein is a definition of originality (school criterion). We have, nevertheless, found some difficulty in persuading ourselves to this. If we agree on a definition for imagination, evidently, we can still find praise for nature beyond the first writer's. The only true praise is thought. The only thing that can back-bone an essay is thought. We then have one way of getting an essay. The trouble in the school is that in the dim past essays were entirely statistical. It came about that such were confused with those re-reviews spoken of above. And now when we criticize we always think the following paragraph over to ourselves, fearful of the second class:

A custom has its unquestioning followers, its radical enemies, and a class who have generally gone through both these to return to the first in a limited sense,–to follow custom,–not without question, but where it does not conflict with the broader habits of life gained by wanderers among ideas. The second class makes one of the first and third. This is best exemplified in religious thought and controversy. It is the second class that would have "an inquisition to compel liberality."

R. FROST

VALEDICTORY ADDRESS:
"A Monument to After-Thought Unveiled," *Lawrence High School Bulletin,* 13 (June 1892): 10; *Robert Frost and the Lawrence, Massachusetts, 'High School Bulletin.'*

Frost and his future wife, Elinor Miriam White, were co-valedictorians of the Lawrence High School class of 1892. His valedictory address reflects his reading in Wordsworth and Shelley, presenting his defense of the poet's vocation, which he had already chosen for himself.

A tribute to the living? We are away beneath the sombre pines, amid a solitude that dreams to the ceaseless monotone of the west wind, the blue sky looking sleepily between the slowly bending boughs, and to, its veil of morning mist, uplifted by the morning breeze, white as pure thought, the monument of monuments.

From sun-beat dizzy marts, from grassy lawns, from surging summer trees, rise countless marble columns, wrought as noisily as if from snow, and all by the one hand here honored alone in loneliness.

Well might this marble be a shrine, this grove, a temple whence devotees might seek the world again, and fame!

The God–but wait, that carven silence kneeling at its base, whence it tapers away into the boughs above, writes, and this is what she writes:–

There are men–that poet who has left us uniting the battered harp the sea storm cast for him upon the shore, was one of these–who go to death with such grey grandeur that we look back upon their past for some strange sorrow, such as does not fall to others, even though we know sorrow to be the same through all time. They seem like Merlins looking ages from their deep calm eyes. With what awe we stand before the mystery of their persons. Such lives are the growth of the afterthought of the soul–the serene rest after toil, in questioning and answering whence and why misfortune is.

This nobility distinguishes personality only in the degree of its development, and the broader future, will give to every soul the opportunity to come into the possession of this, its divine right. Then, when no man's life is a strife from day to day, from year to year, with poverty, will it be an attribute commonality of the world.

Aggressive life is two-fold: theory, practice; thought, action: and concretely, poetry, statesmanship; philosophy, socialism–infinitely.

Not in the strife of action, is the leader made, nor in the face of crisis, but when all is over, when the mind is swift with keen regret, in the long after-thought. The after-thought of one action is the forethought of the next.

It is when alone, in converse with their own thoughts so much that they live their conventionalities, forgetful of the world's, that men form those habits called the heroism of genius, and lead the progress of the race. This, the supreme rise of the individual–not a conflict of consciousness, an effort to oppose, but bland forgetfulness, a life from self for the world–is the aim of existence.

Lawrence High School in Lawrence, Massachusetts. During his attendance there, from September 1888 through June 1892, Frost wrote for the school magazine, took an active part in the debating society, and–first trying out in his senior year–started at right end on the football team.

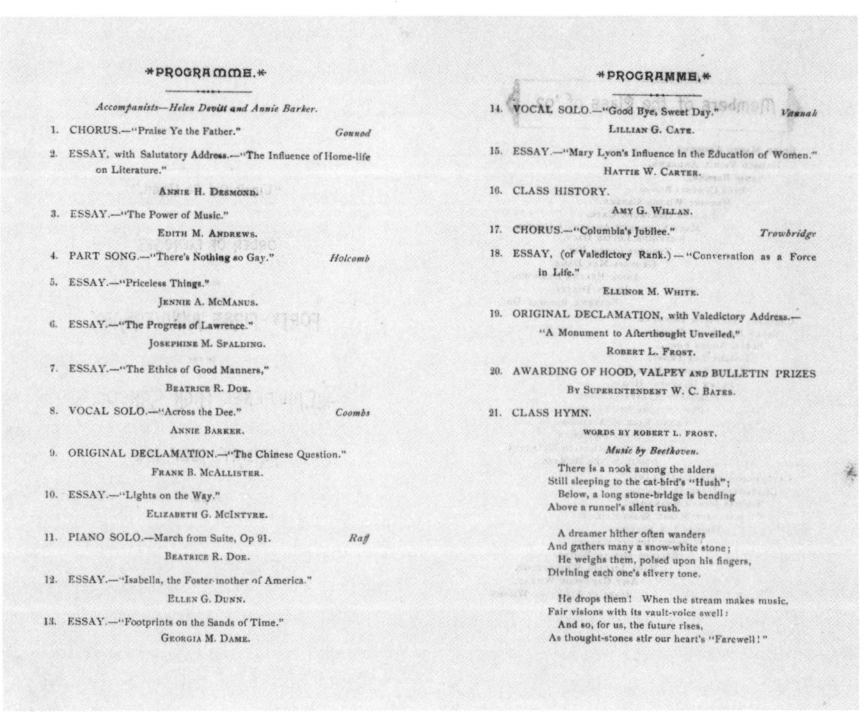

PROGRAMME.

Accompanists—Helen Devitt and Annie Barker.

1. CHORUS.—"Praise Ye the Father." *Gounod*
2. ESSAY, with Salutatory Address.—"The Influence of Home-life on Literature."
   ANNIE H. DESMOND.
3. ESSAY.—"The Power of Music."
   EDITH M. ANDREWS.
4. PART SONG.—"There's Nothing so Gay." *Holcomb*
5. ESSAY.—"Priceless Things."
   JENNIE A. MCMANUS.
6. ESSAY.—"The Progress of Lawrence."
   JOSEPHINE M. SPALDING.
7. ESSAY.—"The Ethics of Good Manners,"
   BEATRICE R. DOE.
8. VOCAL SOLO.—"Across the Dee." *Coombs*
   ANNIE BARKER.
9. ORIGINAL DECLAMATION.—"The Chinese Question."
   FRANK B. MCALLISTER.
10. ESSAY.—"Lights on the Way."
    ELIZABETH G. MCINTYRE.
11. PIANO SOLO.—March from Suite, Op 91. *Raff*
    BEATRICE R. DOE.
12. ESSAY.—"Isabella, the Foster-mother of America."
    ELLEN G. DUNN.
13. ESSAY.—"Footprints on the Sands of Time."
    GEORGIA M. DAME.

PROGRAMME.

14. VOCAL SOLO.—"Good Bye, Sweet Day." *Vannah*
    LILLIAN G. CATE.
15. ESSAY.—"Mary Lyon's Influence in the Education of Women."
    HATTIE W. CARTER.
16. CLASS HISTORY.
    AMY G. WILLAN.
17. CHORUS.—"Columbia's Jubilee." *Trowbridge*
18. ESSAY, (of Valedictory Rank.)—"Conversation as a Force in Life."
    ELLINOR M. WHITE.
19. ORIGINAL DECLAMATION, with Valedictory Address.—"A Monument to Afterthought Unveiled,"
    ROBERT L. FROST.
20. AWARDING OF HOOD, VALPEY AND BULLETIN PRIZES
    BY SUPERINTENDENT W. C. BATES.
21. CLASS HYMN.

WORDS BY ROBERT L. FROST.

Music by Beethoven.

There is a nook among the alders
Still sleeping to the cat-bird's "Hush";
Below, a long stone-bridge is bending
Above a runnel's silent rush.

A dreamer hither often wanders
And gathers many a snow-white stone;
He weighs them, poised upon his fingers,
Divining each one's silvery tone.

He drops them! When the stream makes music,
Fair visions with its vault-voice swell:
And so, for us, the future rises,
As thought-stones stir our heart's "Farewell!"

Program for the 30 June 1892 commencement ceremonies at Lawrence High School. In addition to delivering the valedictory speech, Frost, who was elected class poet, wrote the class hymn and was awarded the Hood Prize, a gold medal for "general excellence and deportment," which he sold the next day as an expression of scorn for the conventional assessment of scholarship that it represented.

Frost in 1892

All this is doubly so of the theoretical. In it the after-thought of long nights beneath the universe, of soul stirrings, of the act of thought itself, is more clearly a part of the next action–its expression. Events influence the first class, the limits of language alone the second.

The poet's insight is his after-thought. It is of varied heart-beats and converse with nature. And the grandest of his ideas come when the last line is written.

Life is an after-thought: how wonderful shall be the world? that is the after-thought of life.

But look again, all this is mere shadow sheen upon the white marble. The one word there is: After-thought.

Now this dark pool beneath the trees is still. There is a white finger on its lips. Let ripples whisper here no more.

And now a last afterthought.

To those who fix today a point through which from earlier years they draw a line of life projected far into the future, this hour is of a deep significance. But there is no change here, and he who thinks to rest will rest as in a winter storm, to die.

Unbounded full ambition for the greatest heights yet unattained is not too noble for one human mind. Who or what can bound our aspirations? Will courage fail before a thousand unfavorable comparisons? There is a space of time when meteor and rain drop falling side by side may touch the yielding earth with equal force. The lighter outspeeding weight may see in a space to strike with greater force. But who at last can tell which has the greater influence [on] the world, the one that bore, as scientist[s] have said, plant life or that which makes it live.

Strength and all the personality that we can crowd upon the world are ours to give in obligation. Let hope be limitless for all and let each follow hope as best he may.

To all old school associations here we show our purposed way in one bell-toned Farewell!

INTERVIEW:

From Edward Connery Lathem, "Freshman Days . . . Robert Frost '96, whose 85th birthday is observed this month, recalls some incidents of his undergraduate period at Dartmouth," *Dartmouth Alumni Magazine*, 51 (March 1959): 16-22.

Frost entered Dartmouth College in autumn 1892 but left before the end of his first semester. Years later he reminisced about his few months at the school.

During the morning we had driven down together from Hanover, and that night in Cambridge, as we sat in the living room of Mr. Frost's home on Brewster Street, we began to talk of his recollections of the period that he had spent as a Dartmouth freshman over sixty-six years ago.

"I had already taken part of my examinations for Harvard, where my father went to college," Mr. Frost recalled in explaining how it was he happened to enter Dartmouth that fall of 1892. "But my grandmother was a little against my going to Harvard. And one of my teachers in the high school took a notion to my writing that he noticed around. (He was hardly my teacher. He was a chemistry man and physics . . . , a Dartmouth man teaching in our Lawrence High School.) And he took a notion to see my grandparents and talk over my going up there."

He could, he remembered, be admitted "just on my record in the high school. I'd been the head of my class, valedictorian."

Undoubtedly, there were a number of things that influenced his favoring the idea of entering Dartmouth, and among them, apparently, was some thought of Richard Hovey, who had been graduated from the College just seven years before: Richard Hovey, *a poet.* "That interested me. . . . I had heard of him. I don't know the date of his books and things, but I must have heard of him before I went up there."

Then, too, the friendly Dartmouth alumnus in discussing the College with him had given him "expectations of literary things" in Hanover, talking of Arthur Sherburne Hardy and the famous "Clothespin" Richardson, members of the faculty with reputations in the world of literature, Professor Hardy as a writer and Charles Francis Richardson as teacher, literary historian, and critic.

"There wasn't much of that, except that he could see the kind I was, sort of. I hadn't set any heart on being a literary person, but I was interested, you could see, in writing. . . ."

Indeed, he had already had a few poems published in the school periodical, the *Bulletin.* "I wrote the first one the second year in the high school. And then I had one in the third year–one or two–and one probably or two in the last year, and one for the commencement, and that's all. I hadn't had any fury of writing, you know. Nothing like that."

A Dartmouth scholarship was, at any rate, arranged for, and Robert Frost, about to become a member of the incoming Class of 1896, "set off for up there with little money to spend and little need of it."

He still remembers with amusement one incident connected with his departure for Hanover. Having two or three hours to wait at Manchester, where he was to take the northbound train, he "went over to the library and got out a book by Hardy that I thought was this Arthur Sherburne Hardy." He knew Professor Hardy had written a novel or two (notably *The Wind of Destiny*, and *But Yet a Woman*), and, of course, the talk of his literary accomplishments had placed the professor prominently in his mind. But, he smiles in reporting, "I guess I hadn't noticed first names enough." The book he chose was, he thinks, either *Two on a Tower* or *A Pair of Blue Eyes*, early works of *Thomas* Hardy. "And maybe I got both of them out," he said with a grin. "And I read at them a little–thought I was going to see the man that wrote them up at Dartmouth."

His train ride northward ended at Norwich, just across the river from Hanover, and he can still visualize "the looks of the station and the wagon that went up," ascending the long, steep hill that leads to the College plain, and carrying him to the beginnings of his brief but memorable collegiate career.

"They gave me a room in the top story of Wentworth Hall on the side toward Dartmouth Hall . . . the back corner room, toward Dartmouth," Mr. Frost related.

"The room was a fair-sized room. I had to furnish it with a few things . . . , all secondhand. And then I had a little bedroom with a cot in it. As I remember that was a homemade cot–boards, as I remember it.

"I don't know what I did the first night. I couldn't have had this secondhand furniture the first night. Where," he puzzled, "do you think I lived? I don't know, somewhere; somebody took me in. No, I don't think so; I think I went right to that room, some way. That's my memory of it.

"Well," he continued, referring to his Wentworth quarters, "the first night I was in there, somebody opened my door and threw something in and upset my lantern; and then I was in the dark for awhile. And then I heard strange noises: not hammering at all, but it turned out that somebody had driven screws into the door so you couldn't open it. And there I was. . . .

"I thought this was all fun. It didn't worry me any. I thought that was what you came to college for," he chuckled. "The door was all abused with having been broken open and everything. . . . You could see this had been going on plenty. Nobody had any real privacy.

"I don't know how I straightened that out that night. I remember . . . some professor came up the stairs, the top stairs. There must have been a lot of noise going on. They must have been making a big row there. I don't remember that too well, but I heard him say, 'Boys, boys, be easy on them.' "

Afterward he was told that it was "Tute" Worthen, then the College's Associate Professor of Mathematics, who had come to quiet the sophomores.

But how did he finally succeed in gaining his freedom from the cell they had created for him?

"Well, I don't know who got me out. . . . I pounded on the door, but I don't remember anybody's coming." Apparently, however, he was eventually able to force it open himself from within.

Then, at the very beginning, he made friends with another freshman there in Wentworth Hall, Preston Shirley of Andover, New Hampshire, and the two became fast friends.

"We held the fort together sometimes," he remembers of that period when night after night marauding sophomores laid siege to the stronghold they garrisoned in Shirley's room. "We decided there was more room down in his place: bigger I guess it must have been. He had a bigger bedroom or something.

"What brought that out was his mother sending him a box of fruit. His door opened inwards; and he couldn't eat the fruit, he knew they'd take it all away from us, unless we barricaded. So I came down there, and we took the closet door off the coal closet. (Each room had a big coal closet. We had to bring in our own coal, and some of us were forced to bring in other people's coal. I didn't get subjugated to doing that, but some did.) We tore off that door and took a slat off of his bed and nailed the slat into the floor and then braced the closet door against the outside door. And nobody could come in there, you see. That was very strong. We really fortified.

"But, of course," Mr. Frost added, "only one could go to class at a time, and we had to cut classes alternately. . . ."

In a different vein, Mr. Frost called to mind that it was while in Hanover, "I bought my first copy of Palgrave's *Golden Treasury*, I think"–a book that was to mean a great deal to him over the years. "I bought that at the book store there." It was an edition in paper covers, and, he revealed, "I've got that still . . . somewhere; I don't know just where."

"We'll go on," he suggested, "and talk about the literary part of it. It couldn't have been long after that that I read Hovey's poem on the death of T. W. Parsons in the old library that's now the museum. I always hope they won't tear that down, because under that arch I went into my idea of publishing something."

It was in Wilson Hall that fall of '92 that the young freshman discovered on the display racks of the library a copy of the November 17th issue of *The Independent*, bearing on its first page Richard Hovey's poem, "Seaward." As he described the experience, ". . . here was a magazine that I had never heard of, but it had a whole front page of poetry–all the page, three columns. . . . And then over on the next page some, I think. And then I leafed over, and there was an editorial on the poem.

"That made a big impression on me. I didn't think that minute that I'll send something there, but that was where it grew on me I'd send a poem there sometime. I don't know whether it came until I'd written the poem. Really, I can't remember that, but when I had the poem that I thought was a poem, I sent it there.

"I only remember," he said, referring to Hovey's poem, "one line of it, one new way of taking the Trinity: 'Trine within trine, inextricably One.' "

But he could still distinctly recall the appearance of that number of the magazine, there in the old library building.

"It was a big sheet. You know what it looks like. It was spread out like a newspaper on one of those open things. And I saw that poem there. As if I could see it today. That's why I must have had, more than you'd know, more interest in such a thing: What is that meaning? What does a big serious poem mean? And then I turned over, found talk about [it] in an editorial. So it meant that I was beginning to think of being a writer, I suppose. I can't remember that. I didn't know whether that was a thing to be or one ought to be or whether I wanted to be or what. I wouldn't know anything about that. I don't know what I thought I wanted to be. I don't know as I thought of anything. I was a good deal lost without minding being lost, you see. . . .

"That arch there, I always think," Mr. Frost reflected, "that that's sort of a beginning for me of something that was going to happen that year. . . .

"Somebody talks about rededication and dedication, and nobody really dedicates himself till long afterward. He doesn't dedicate himself, he get dedicated. He finds himself deep in something and long before he's aware of committing himself. And he's never aware of his taking his life in his hands to go forward to do something or do or die, you know, unless it's to battle or something.

"I didn't think anything like that. I just had it coming on me. I can't tell how it came, this wish to have something: write things and get them printed."

(It was in 1894 that Mr. Frost's poem "My Butterfly" appeared in *The Independent*, his first to be included in a publication of national circulation. It was written the spring after he left college and published the following year. He remembers that the editors "made quite a fuss over it," adding musingly, "sort of a premature fuss." And they were cross with him for having left Dartmouth. "They blamed me for that and reminded me of Milton, who was a very learned man.")

He smiled as he turned to the subject of the "literary society" that he joined. It was the Dartmouth chapter of Theta Delta Chi, and one of the more wealthy brothers was so anxious to have him pledged that he went so far as to pay his entrance fee. "You see," Mr. Frost explained, "I didn't have any money."

He recalls, too, that he made the "opening speech" at the fraternity. "And I wonder," he pondered, "where that went, whether I wrote it out. Probably in those days I would write out something."

"They were very good to me, those fellows were. They'd been told by this man from Lawrence . . . that I was literary I guess, though I didn't know that myself in any definite way. I wasn't thinking of it that way, but he thought I was. . . .

"They didn't bother me except once that I've joked about. I've told about how they came to me, some of them, to know what I was walking in the woods for. And I told them that I was gnawing bark!

"It sounds like American interference with freedom, you know, and independence. Nothing to that. They didn't want freshmen to be too fresh, doing things that others weren't doing."

He was at that time, as he has been throughout life, a great walker, but then, as now, he preferred to walk alone. He and Shirley might spend hours together talking, but they never walked with one another: the one caring nothing for this form of recreation, while the other disliked to talk as he walked.

"I walked all around there many miles. There used to be one, a seven-mile walkaround. . . . I did that quite a lot.

"I didn't have very good health. I was strong in playing games and rushing and all that, but I don't know what was the matter. I think I was dyspeptic and not sleeping well and all that. I had some special arrangement at the dining room not to have supper but just to have a couple of biscuits to take home in the evening. I didn't eat much at night. . . . I wasn't seeing any doctors or anything, [but] I hadn't been very well all my young days."

All the studies of that first term were prescribed, as was the case throughout the freshman year. Beginning the classical course, he took Greek, reading Plato with Prof. George Lord ("That was very nice. I always seemed to like that kind of thing."), algebra with "Tute" Worthen ("He was a great favorite, and somebody that had an interest in the boys."), and Latin. The Latin course, concerned with Livy and Latin composition, was, unfortunately, something of a failure. The young tutor didn't have good discipline and the students treated him rudely:

"If he'd say, 'Take this for tomorrow,' and tomorrow was Monday instead of this week . . . , they'd think that was time to 'wood up,' you know, and stomp the dust out of the floor. They'd do it over any little excuse they could make in that class. Some places they wouldn't do that at all; they wouldn't have thought of doing any such thing. . . .

"The Livy was no success that way. There was something disorderly about the class, I don't know why. The others were all right. There was no funny business with Worthen; and none with George Lord.

"I saw Richardson only once. He spoke to us," Mr. Frost quipped, "to arouse literature in us. And I remember his making a lot of two lines of Shelley about poetry being 'where music and moonlight and feeling are one.' "

He did not get to know any of the members of the faculty during this time in College. "I never spoke to any of them, really. At that age I never got acquainted with teachers. . . . I had people that I might have liked to speak to, but it wouldn't occur to me to do it, you know. I didn't know that was done."

And did he see anything of Prof. Arthur Sherburne Hardy?

"Not a once. He had a delicate wife, and he was much aloof; there was no chance, you see. He wasn't the kind of person. . . . and then I heard his subject was quaternions, way in advanced mathematics where I wouldn't be for quite awhile. . . ."

And Mr. Frost remembers, too, his own departure from College:

"Shirley thought it was awful that I should leave, but I didn't seem to have any sense of what I was doing. I didn't seem to think it was serious at all. I had no notion of being too poor to go on and get learning. Nothing like that. I sort of lost my interest.

"I had a kind of an appetite for a school awhile. (I had avoided school when I was young.) I got it first with love of recess and the noon hour. I couldn't miss what was going on there. So I went to school, an the first thing I knew I was fascinated with arithmetic and geography and history. And they couldn't interest me in grammar, I wouldn't go near the classes. I watched them diagramming a little on the board, but I wouldn't let on that I was learning grammar. I don't know why.

"Then I liked high school. They got me there. I liked it three years, and I got interested in the A's I was getting on top of everything. Then I got sick of that. In the last half I was sick of having teachers pulling my leg . . . just by marks. You see," he laughed, "I began to rebel. But nobody knew that. I hadn't missed a day for three years and a half, and then something came over me; and I resented this strain of being talked about as leading the class with so many persons right up behind me and who was my runner-up and all that. . . . It began to make me nervous, and as I say, I never had very good health in those days. Somebody might say I was nervous–delicate person.

"Up there at College I showed the same symptoms of not wanting to talk about marks. I'd had enough talk about marks. It got to be almost a disease to me.

"And when I went out I just went easily, felt relieved. And Shirley couldn't get it through his head for awhile, but we sat up and celebrated all night the night before I went away. And we celebrated on Turkish fig-paste (Bought a whole lot of that. It's awful stuff!), and sang and carried on and hollered out our windows. And the next day I went down with my little trunk . . . down to Norwich station and decamped."

Just when it was he left Mr. Frost is not sure, although, he says, "I think I had got past Christmas.

"I remember, I think it was at Christmas, that my mother sent a friend of mine up to see how I was keeping house in my room; and the ashes extended from the stove clear into the middle of the room."

Mr. Frost returned to Methuen, the next town to Lawrence, where his mother was having difficulty with some big and unruly boys in her class in the grade school. And this was some part of the son's reason for leaving College. He went to the chairman of the school board and asked to take over her job. . . .

LETTER:
To William Hayes Ward; *Selected Letters of Robert Frost*, p. 19.

Between leaving Dartmouth and his marriage in December 1895, Frost held various jobs in and around Lawrence, Massachusetts, including teacher, mill worker, and newspaper reporter. Early in 1894 he wrote "My Butterfly" and submitted it to the magazine that he had discovered at Dartmouth. When William Hayes Ward, the editor of the Independent, *sent fifteen dollars for the poem and asked for some information about its author, Frost's response revealed his excitement.*

28 March [1894]
Lawrence, Mass.

Editor of the Independant,
Dear Sir:–

The memory of your note will be a fresh pleasure to me when I awaken for a good many mornings to come; which may as well confirm you in the belief that I am still young. I am. The poem you have is the first of mine that any publica-

R. L. Frost, Tremont St, Lawrence, Mass. 1

My Butterfly.
An Elegy.
By R. L. Frost.

Thine emulous fond flowers are dead too,
And the daft sun-assaulter, he
That frighted thee so oft, is fled or dead:
Save only me
Nor is it sad to thee
Save only me.
There is no one to mourn thee in the fields.
The grey grass is scarce dappled with the snow;
Its two banks have not shut upon the river,
But it is long ago,
It seems forever,
Since first I saw thee glance
With all the dazzling other ones,
In airy dalliance,
Precipitate in love,
Tossed up, tossed up and tangling above,
Like a limp rose-wreath in a fairy dance.

2

When that was, the soft mist
Of my two tears hung not on all the fields:
And I was glad for thee,
And glad for me,
I wist.
And didst thou think who tottered wandering on high
Fate had not made ~~you~~ thee for the pleasure of the wind,
With those great careless wings?
'Twas happier to die
And let the days blow by,—
These were the unlearned things.
It seemed God let thee flutter from his gentle clasp,
Then fearful he had let thee win
Too far beyond him to be gathered in,
Snatched thee, o'er-eager, with ungentle grasp,
Jealous of immortality
(In one so fair, forsooth)

The copy of "My Butterfly" that Frost sent to the Independent *(Huntington Library) and the poem as it appeared on page one of the 8 November 1894 issue, with minor revisions made at the request of the editor's sister Susan Hayes Ward, who served as the in-house poetry editor. Frost made further revisions before including the poem in* A Boy's Will *(1913).*

3

O I remember me
How once conspiracy was rife
Against my life,
(The languor of it) and
Surging, the grasses dizzied me of thought,
The breeze three odors brought,
And a gem-flower waved in a wand.
Then when I was distraught
And could not speak,
Sidelong, full on my cheek,
What should that reckless zephyr fling
But the wild touch of your dye-dusty wing.
I found that wing withered today,
For you are dead, I said,
And the strange birds say-
I found it with the withered leaves
Under the eaves.
[illegible] R. F.

MY BUTTERFLY.

AN ELEGY.

BY ROBERT LEE FROST.

THINE emulous, fond flowers are dead too,
And the daft sun-assaulter, he
That frighted thee so oft, is fled or dead;
Save only me
(Nor is it sad to thee),
Save only me
There is none left to mourn thee in the fields.
The gray grass is scarce dappled with the snow;
Its two banks have not shut upon the river;
But it is long ago,
It seems forever,
Since first I saw thee glance,
With all the dazzling other ones,
In airy dalliance,
Precipitate in love,
Tossed, tangled, whirled and whirled above,
Like a limp rose-wreath in a fairy dance.
When that was, the soft mist
Of my two tears hung not on all the fields,
And I was glad for thee,
And glad for me, I wist.

And didst thou think, who tottered wandering on high,
Fate had not made thee for the pleasure of the wind,
With those great, careless wings?
'Twas happier to die
And let the days blow by.
These were the unlearned things.
It seemed God let thee flutter from his gentle clasp,
Then, fearful he had let thee win
Too far beyond him to be gathered in,
Snatched thee, o'er-eager, with ungentle grasp,
Jealous of immortality.

Ah, I remember me
How once conspiracy was rife
Against my life
(The languor of it!), and
Surging, the grasses dizzied me of thought,
The breeze three odors brought,
And a gem flower waved in a wand.
Then, when I was distraught
And could not speak,
Sidelong, full on my cheek,
What should that reckless zephyr fling
But the wild touch of your dye-dusty wing!

I found that wing withered to-day;
For you are dead, I said,
And the strange birds say.
I found it with the withered leaves
Under the eaves.

LAWRENCE, MASS.

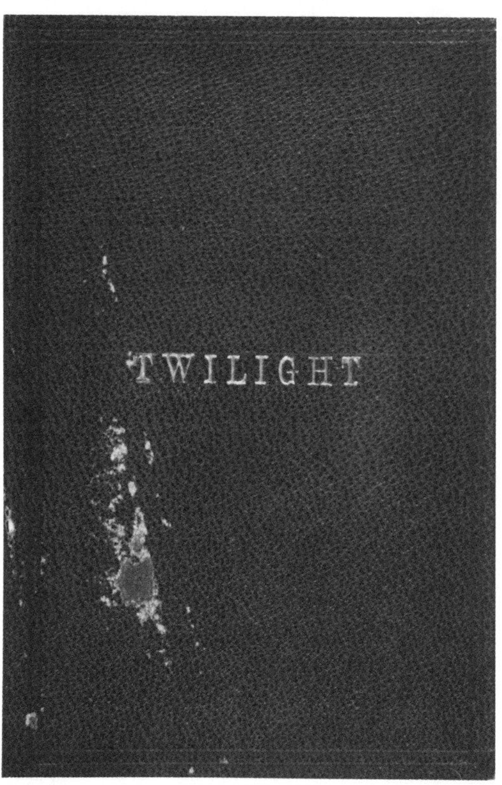

I had two copies of Twilight printed and bound by a job printer in Lawrence Mass in 1894 probably out of pride in what Bliss Carman and Maurice Thompson had said about the poem in it called My Butterfly. One copy I kept for myself and afterward destroyed. The other I gave away to a girl in St Lawrence University to show to her friends. It had no success and deserved none. But it unaccountably survived and has lately leaped into prominence as my first first. A few scattered lines in it [illegible] as much mine [illegible] as any I was ever to write. I deliver it into your care my dear Bernheimer with the last request that you be not too fondly selfish with it, but consent to lend it once in a long long time to some important exhibition of my works as at the Jones Library in Amherst or the Baker at Dartmouth.

Robert Frost

Boston February 1 1940

Cover for the unique copy of Frost's first book and the inscription Frost wrote when he sold it to book collector Earle J. Bernheimer (Barrett Library, University of Virginia Library). The "girl in St. Lawrence University" was the poet's future wife, Elinor White. The small book comprises five poems: "Twilight," "My Butterfly," "Summering," "The Falls," and "An Unhistoric Spot." Only "My Butterfly" was included in any of Frost's full-length books.

tion has accepted. At about the same time however that I sent you this, I disposed of three others in a similar way in other quarters. As yet they are not returned. As for submitting more of my work, you may imagine I shall be only too glad to avail myself of your kindly interest. Nevertheless since I have but recently discovered my powers, I have, of course, no great amount of verses in store and furthermore, being still inexperienced of myself, I cannot easily tell when I will have. But I shall not forget my obligations.

If you mean what might be called the legitimate education I have received when you speak of "training" and "line of study," I hope that the quality of my poem would seem to account for far more of this than I have really had. I am only graduated of a public high school. Besides this, a while ago, I was at Dartmouth College for a few months until recalled by necessity. But this inflexible ambition trains us best, and to love poetry is to study it. Specifically speaking, the few rules I know in this art are my own afterthoughts, or else directly formulated from the masterpieces I reread.

I sincerely hope I have done nothing to make you overestimate me. It cannot be, though, for rather than equal what I have written and be satisfied, I will idle away an age accumulating a greater inspiration.

There is no objection to using my name with the poem.

Yours
Robert Lee Frost.
Tremont St.,
Lawrence, Mass.

* * *

The magazine was called the New York Independent, *and after they bought the poem they asked that when I sent them more would I please spell the name of the magazine correctly.*

* * *

Frost, quoted in Roger Kahn, "A Visit with Robert Frost," Saturday Evening Post *(16 November 1960)*

LETTER:
Maurice Thompson to William Hayes Ward; *Selected Letters of Robert Frost*, pp. 23-24.

When asked by William Hayes Ward to comment on "My Butterfly," Hoosier poet Maurice Thompson responded with praise and a warning.

10 November 1894
Crawfordsville, Indiana

Dear Dr Ward

You asked me to look at the poem, *My Butterfly*, in this week's paper, by Mr. Frost.

I am a trifle dizzy over the election, feel as if a hogshead of salt had rolled over me; but I am not stupid enough yet to fail to see the extreme beauty of that little ode. It gives me a pang to know that its author is poor. To be a poet and be poor is a terrible lot. What hope is there? I have felt the gag in my teeth whenever I wanted to sing–and I'm not much of a poet–a gag that can speak and say to me: "No! go grind for bread! Let the rich men like Tennyson and Swinburne and Lowell and Browning and Holmes do the singing; what right has a poor man to waste his time and breath with song?" But all the same were I a rich man that young Frost should not leave school "for financial reasons." Going back to the poem *My Butterfly*, it has some secret of genius between the lines, an appeal to sympathy lying deep in one's sources of tenderness; and moreover its art is singular and biting, even where the faulty places are almost obtruded. My wife read it aloud to me the other evening when my eyes ached after too hard a day's work; and it made me ashamed that I could feel discouraged when I thought of the probable disappointment in store for young Frost all his life long. If I had a chance to say my say to him I should tell him to forget that he ever read a poem and to never pen another rhyme. I told my brother that years ago and now he is a great lawyer instead of a disappointed poet with a gag in his mouth! I was a better lawyer than he when I was lured away by the Muses. If Frost has good health tell him to learn a trade or profession and carry a sling-shot in his pocket for [the Muse] Aoede.

Always sincerely yours
Maurice Thompson

LETTER:
To LeBaron Russell Briggs; *Selected Letters of Robert Frost*, pp. 29-30.

In autumn 1897 Frost applied for admission to Harvard, hoping to prepare himself for teaching high-school Latin and Greek. The poem he mentions in this let-

Elinor White and Robert Frost at about the time of their marriage, on 19 December 1895. Their first child, Elliott, was born on 25 September 1896.

ter to Briggs, dean of Harvard College, is "Warning," in the 9 September 1897 issue of the Independent. *It was the fourth poem by Frost to be published in that magazine.*

11 September 1897
Lawrence

Dear Sir:

You are the one it seems for me to submit by case to if you will be so kindly as to consider it. You will discover the propriety as I proceed.

I desire to enter Harvard this fall if possible as a candidate for a degree from the outset. It came to me as a surprise only the other day that I might reasonably hope to do so consequently I find myself somewhat unprepared for examination. This is the great difficulty. I graduated from the Lawrence High School as many as five years ago (having in 1891 passed examinations for admission to Harvard occupying seven hours for which I hold a certificate.) It is true that since that time I have been teaching school and tutoring more or less in Latin Algebra and Geometry. Still my studies are all at loose ends. In particular I have neglected my Greek. If proficiency in English were any consideration, I make no doubt I could pass an examination in that. You will find verses of my inditing in the current number of the Independent and others better in back numbers. I might possibly pass in French also and in Physics and Astronomy for that matter but in Greek I fear not. You'll say it doesn't sound very encouraging.

Another embarrassing circumstance is the fact that once upon a time I left Dartmouth without having applied to the proper authorities of that paternalism for an honerable dismissal. I stood not upon the order of my going but went incontinently–for reasons I am free to explain. I assure you the matter will bear looking into.

This is the whole case not very clearly or succinctly stated. The question is what will you advise me to do. Let me say that if I enter college it must be this year or never. It will be hard if a fellow of my age and general intelligence (!) must be debarred from an education for want of technical knowledge representing less than two months work. All I ask is to be admitted. I don't care how many conditions you encumber me with. I will take the examinations if you say so, or I will enter as a special. I am anxious to hear from you soon. Rev. John Hayes of Salem or Rev. W.

Wolcott of this city will answer questions with regard to me.

Respectfully Robert L Frost

LETTER:

LeBaron Russell Briggs to Robert Frost; *Selected Letters of Robert Frost*, p. 30.

Frost was admitted to Harvard as a degree candidate and was awarded a $200 scholarship for his sophomore year in recognition of the "marked excellence" of his academic achievement during his first year, but before the end of the spring 1899 term he withdrew from college for financial and health reasons. Briggs wrote a letter for Frost to use in seeking future employment.

Harvard College,
Cambridge,
March 31st 1899

My dear Mr. Frost:

I am glad to testify that your dismissal from College is honorable; that you have had excellent rank here, winning a Detur as a result of your first year's work; and that I am sorry for the loss of so good a student. I shall gladly have you refer to me for your College record.

Sincerely Yours
L. B. R. Briggs,
Dean

ARTICLE:

"A Typical Small Breeder," from "Three Phases of the Poultry Industry," *Farm-Poultry Semi-Monthly*, 14 (December 1903); *Robert Frost: Farm-Poultryman*, pp. 81-83.

Not long after Frost left Harvard, Elinor Frost gave birth to their first daughter, Lesley, on 28 April 1899. The family doctor, unable to determine whether Frost was suffering from tuberculosis or nervous exhaustion, suggested outdoor employment, and Frost went into the poultry business at a rented farm in Lawrence. Whatever pleasure the Frosts took in the initial success of the new venture was destroyed by the deaths of three-year-old Elliott Frost, from cholera infantum, *on 8 July 1900 and of the poet's mother, from cancer, on 2 November 1900. In early October the Frosts had moved to a farm bought by Frost's grandfather just across the state line in Derry, New Hampshire. Though the people and landscape of Derry figure in many of Frost's finest poems, he wrote little poetry during his first few years there. Instead he wrote prose, mostly local-color sketches about poultry breeders, published in the* Eastern Poultryman *and the* Farm-Poultry Semi-Monthly *during 1903-1905. The subject of the following section of a nonfiction article about three poultry farmers is Frost's neighbor John A. Hall, whose domestic situation was the inspiration for "The Housekeeper," one of Frost's earliest dramatic narrative poems.*

Mr. John A. Hall, of Atkinson, N. H., is a good type of the small breeder. He makes up in the care and real affection he lavishes on his stock for any lack of the business ability that distinguishes so many of our mere middlemen in the fancy. He is always heels over head in pets of one kind or another. In addition to White Wyandottes he indulges a taste for several varieties of ducks and geese, not to mention Runt pigeons and Angora cats on the side. All these creatures share the place of honor about the dooryard and everywhere under foot.

Mr. Hall has bred fancy fowl since he was "big enough to carry a dough dish." He has bred Rocks, Langshans, Cochins, Brahmas; and ribbons and trophies testify as to how he had bred them.

He has never faced the public as an advertiser. He might be regarded as a sort of breeders' breeder. That is to say, it is chiefly other breeders whose acquaintance he has made at the shows that find their way to him to buy. Still he says he has always been able to dispose of all the very good birds he could spare, and sometimes some that he could not spare.

But though he is a fancier first, he has never been so situated that he could afford to disregard the claims of the practical. He owns to having adopted the White Wyandotte for the most practical of reasons, to meet the requirements of his market for dressed poultry.

Mr. Hall has something like a hundred youngsters this year, all sired by one superannuated cock, and the family, though not over numerous, does the old bird credit. Not that they are all show birds, but there is a general freedom from disqualifications. There seems to be no feathered or willow legs. Eyes are good, plumage white to promising white. It is too early yet to judge of finer points of shape and style, but one thing is certain, the youngsters are all that they should be in weight, and that as White Wyandottes go in these parts is saying a great deal.

If houses are more to you than the inmates, you will go elsewhere than Mr. Hall's. The old timer wills sometimes forget surroundings and accessories in the superior interest of the birds themselves. In the matter of housing Mr. Hall carries

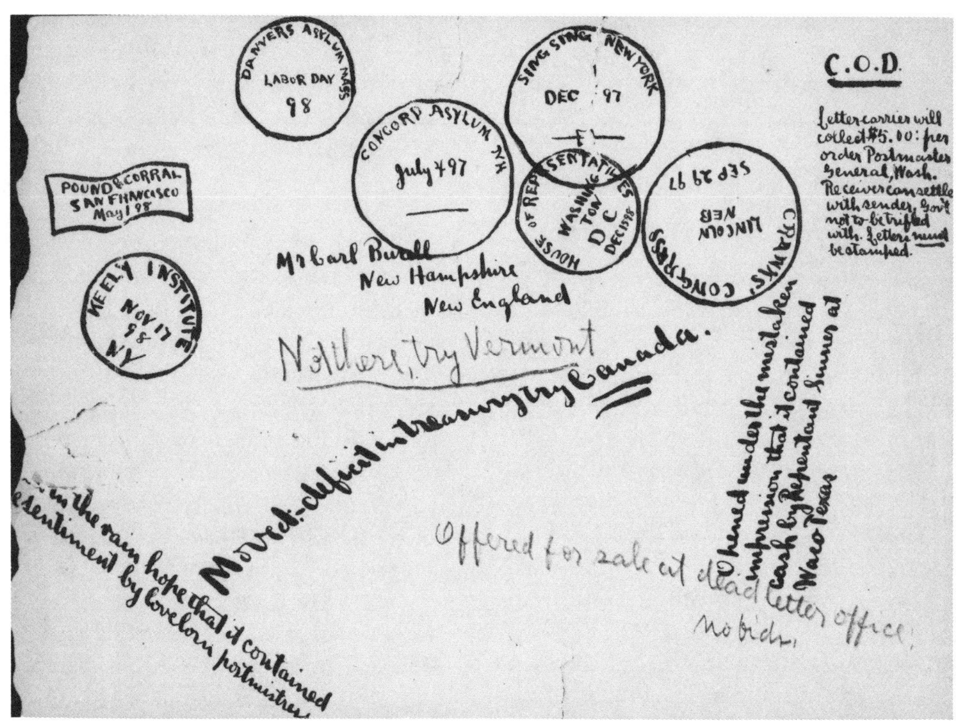

The Parachute

June 13 1897

The Seer Seen

Heels Uppermost in the Waters of the Suncook

Consider the Lilies How They Grow

Clothes Dry

Suncook June 12.– The river here is waist-high and still rising. The people of the valley have all taken to the hills. This afternoon I waded and swam as far as East Pembroke but saw no one. Burell the theosophist is said to be picking flowers in the neighborhood but I saw nothing of him. The explanation is he was probably under water for the time being. No alarm need be felt for his safety as his feet have been seen repeatedly by violently agitated above the placid surface of the flood. The way he keeps his clothes dry

(Continued on Last Page)

Keno

Great Soul in a Little Dog

Bow Legs

An Argument in Favor of Being Good

Lawrence June 12.– The famous yellow dog Keno said to contain the soul of Confucius died at his home on Haverhill St early this morning after many years of suffering on the part of everyone but himself. He had a particularly loud and clear bark an indomitable will and a courage equal to anything. He died holding his master's foot (in his teeth) from a blow of the bread-board as well as of the mop the dish-pan several chairs and the kitchen table. A funeral will not be accorded him.

☞ Send two cent stamp and receive by return mail rejected manuscript.

High Potency vs. High Frequency

Rev. John Hayes Takes a Pill

Attendance 10,000

Salem June 12. ~~John~~ Rev John Hayes took his weekly homeopathic pill at the Opera House last night before a large and appreciative audience. It was evident from his seedy and unkempt appearance that the demonstrator was not yet recovered from his last weeks dose of pulsatilla though he seemed in the best of spirits and with characteristic dispatch produced and swallowed one infinitesimal pill saturated with alchohol the effects of which he no sooner announced than they became apparent. The exibition had been well advertised and all knew what to expect else many must have fainted. The demonstrator reeled like a very Silenus carolled brokenly and sat down so vigorously that his hair stood up. In short he played his part to perfection much to the amusement of the children present and not a few of their less seriously minded elders.

Obituary.

No good republican is prepared to admit that John Brown is dead politically even after all these years. His soul is marching on. If anyone is dead politically it is Grover Cleveland and he has been so pronounced after having been sat upon by the coroner and everyone else. As in the case of the Incas the funeral has been postponed indefinitely that is all.

Notice

Jerry O Sullivan was found half way out of gaol the other day caught between the iron bars of his cell window. He was put back at his own request.

The first of several booklets Frost made for friend and fellow poet Carl Burrell (Dartmouth College Library). Burrell, who shared Frost's love of botany and astronomy and whose atheism had stimulated Frost's thinking about religion, had left Lawrence High School without graduating and gone to work in a box factory, where he was seriously injured in summer 1896. This accident and an insurance agent's visit to the crippled man's bedside was the inspiration for Frost's poem "The Self-Seeker," written in 1913. Ernest Jewell, the subject of "Jewell Gets a Job," was another high-school friend, who had just graduated from Harvard and taken a teaching position at Lawrence High School.

the public cannot fail to be with us in this matter

We understand that the name Noble in the story How Noble Got Away veils a well known character in New England society. Just who would answer to this description we are at a loss to know unless it is Frost former editor of this publication. It has been suggested that it might be Burell but for various reasons we think not.

The Seer Seen

(Continued from First Page)

is by not wearing them. His actions are a sore perplexity to the good folk of the country side as well they may be

Jewell Gets a Job.

Jewell walked from Broadway to Union St and back
Jewell smiled at everyone as Jewell has the knack
He bore himself superbly his hat was in his hand
His clothes were new his face was clean
He
Looked
Just
Grand

The rain had laid the dust but the clouds were rolled away
And everyone was happy but Jewell he was gay
We saw him grow in stature and monsently expand
All seemed to recognize a friend
He
Looked
That
Grand.

Editorial

The Parachute lets everybody down easy. We trust everybody will take our word (parachute) for it.

The feature of our next number will be a scurrilous attack on some famous personage not living. The feature of this number is a full page drawing of the cross-section of the cosmic egg. Among other things we hope to deserve the patronage of all good theosophists. These constitute a large and growing wing of the Populist party and it would be tempting fate to try to reckon without them. We should be pleased to hear from any of them who have been helped to a higher life by our conception of the cosmic egg.

Theosophy as we understand it is not politics neither is it science nor yet religion. It is rather an harmonious mixture of all three with a modicum of opium and no worse in this respect than many of our patent medicines. Theosophy reminds one of the crescent moon: it is the sign of the East appearing in the West. It is characteristic of it that it conflicts with evolution. Assuming that the world is supported by an elephant and the elephant by a turtle it proves beyond a reasonable doubt that Madam Blavatsky had her faults like everyone else. Such is the religion of the future no less than of the past.

We are in receipt of the following communication:-

Sir,

You're a damn liar. I wasn't two weeks old at the time referred to.

H.F.

We feel that there must be some mistake. Who said H.F. was two weeks old at the time referred to. We are not aware of having done so. We do no know who H.F. is. The sympathies of

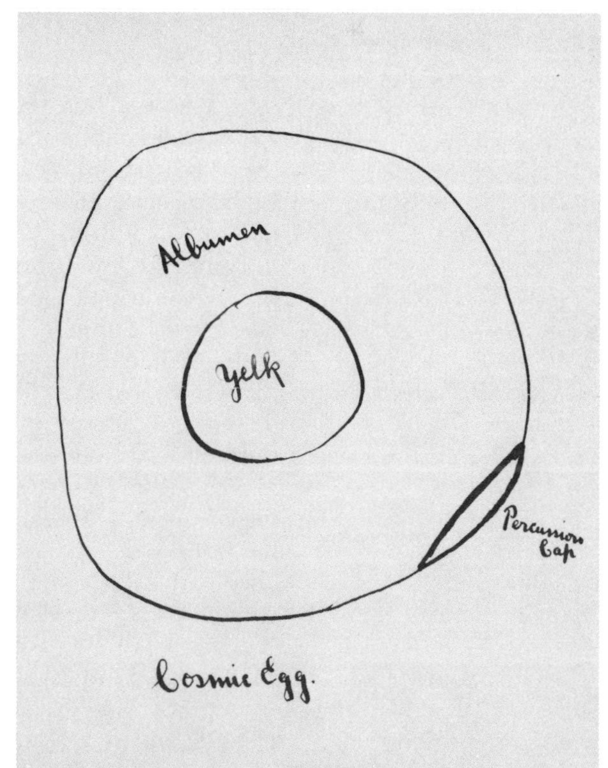

opposition to the sheltered life idea to an extreme. His houses have value to the observer only as illustrating what a hen will roost in and still live. They are airy to say the least. Mr. Hall apologizes for them, but I believe retains them on principle. He says the hens take no more harm from them than an occasional frozen wattle in winter, and on the whole are benefited by them.

Two things in breeding he makes of first importance–size and vigor. It is his experience that weight tends constantly to decline. It is a simple matter to keep it up, only it cannot be left to take care of itself. As for vigor, it is easier to get this right than not. What the stock need is a little judicious neglect. Mr. Hall's geese roost in the trees even in winter. Such a toughening process would be too drastic for hens, but these have to take it according to their strength.

As might be expected, Mr. Hall gives everything free range the year round. He fences in instead of out, finding that two and a half feet will keep hens out where it takes five to keep them in.

Almost any year you may see specimens of Mr. Hall's land or water fowl at some one of the shows, and he lives rather out of the world, perhaps the easiest way to form an opinion of him as a breeder is there. It is worth a little trouble, however, to view his stock as a whole at home, especially his Wyandottes, because it is not everywhere in these days that you will see a lot as uniformly good.

LETTER:
To the Editor, *Farm-Poultry*, 15 (15 February 1904); *Selected Letters to Robert Frost*, p. 34.

Frost's mistaken assertion in "A Typical Small Breeder" that Hall's geese roosted in trees prompted a tongue-in-cheek letter to the editor from Massachusetts farmer H. R. White, who asked what sort of geese Hall raised because "if I could get a breed of that kind I could dispense with coops." Frost's explanation of his error jokingly claimed a sort of poetic license.

Editor *Farm-Poultry:*

In reply to Mr. White's (and yours) of recent date in regard to the error in the article on Mr. Hall's place, there is this to say:-

Geese would sleep out, or float out, let us say, where hens would roost in the trees. To be sure. But what more natural, in speaking of geese in close connection with hens, than to speak of them as if they *were* hens? "Roosts in the trees," has here simply suffered what the grammarians would call attraction from the subject with which it should be in agreement to the one uppermost in the mind. That is all. But the idea will have to stand, viz., that Mr. Hall's geese winter out,–and that is the essential thing. Mr. White is not after the geese that roost in the trees, but geese that don't need coops. Well, Mr. Hall has them that prefer not to use coops, whether they need them or not. My impression is that he has them in several varieties, and I'll risk my impression. But Mr. Hall is a good fellow and will be glad to tell Mr. White about his geese himself–doubtless, also, to do business with him.

R. L. F.

LETTER:
John A. Hall to the Editor, *Farm-Poultry*, 15 (1 March 1904); *Selected Letters of Robert Frost*, pp. 34-35.

Frost's attempt to make light of his error about geese in trees contained a second error, pointed out by an editor's note explaining that "Mr. Frost seems not to be aware of the fact that geese generally remain out of doors by choice practically all the time." The next issue of Farm-Poultry *published a letter to the editor from John Hall, whose response to the goose controversy was written largely or wholly by Frost.*

Editor *Farm-Poultry:*

I noticed Mr. H. R. White's letter in your paper asking about the kind of geese I keep that sleep out in the winter. They are Toulouse, Embden, and Buff. They don't roost in trees. I don't know how Mr. Frost made that mistake, for of course he knows better.

We have often talked about the way they take to the water at night, a favorite place for them to hang up being on a stone just under water. A good many nights in winter, as well as in summer, I have no idea where they are; and I think they are better every way out doors as long as there is any water not frozen over. But speaking of geese in trees, I don't suppose Mr. White has ever seen a duck in a tree. I have. And I once had a duck that laid her eggs in a tree high enough to be out of reach from the ground, and brought off twenty-two ducklings. These were Brazilians, and I don't know what they won't do.

It has always seemed strange to me how people succeed in keeping geese shut up. If I shut mine up they begin to be restless right away, and go off in looks, especially plumage. Mr. White

The Frost children outside their Derry farmhouse, 1908: Marjorie (born 29 March 1905), Lesely (born 28 April 1899), Irma (born 27 June 1903), and Carol (born 27 May 1902). The Frosts' sixth child, Elinor Bettina, was born on 18 June 1907 and died three days later.

Robert and Elinor Frost with their children–Marjorie (on the pony), Lesley, Irma, and Carol–at the farm of John and Mary Lynch in Bethlehem, New Hampshire, summer 1908. During hay-fever season in 1907, 1908, and 1910, Frost who suffered from allergies, took his family to stay as paying guests at the Lynches' farm in the White Mountains. Mary Lynch's stories inspired The Cow's in the Corn *(1927), Frost's one-act "Celtic Drama," and "The Fear" (1913), one of the dramatic narratives in* North of Boston *(1914).*

The poems sent were uncommonly good

West Derry N.H. Feb. 24, '06

Dear Dr Ward:

I trust I do not presume too much on former kindness in addressing these verses to you personally. Sending MS to the Independent can never be quite like sending it anywhere else for me.

I often think of you and your sister in my work. I believe Miss Ward left the staff of the Independent some years ago to write books. Please remember me to her either formally or by showing her any of my verses — whether you can use them or not.

Sincerely yours,

Robert Frost

The Trial By Existance

Even the bravest that are slain
Shall not dissemble their surprise
On waking to find valor reign
Even as on earth in paradise:
And where they sought without the sword
Wide fields of asphodel fore'er,
To find that the utmost reward
Of daring should be still to dare.

2.

The light of heaven falls whole and white
And is not shattered into dyes,
The light forever is morning light;
The hills are verdured pasturewise;
The angel hosts with freshness go
And seek with laughter what to brave;
And binding all is the hushed snow
Of the far-distant breaking wave.

After five years of not submitting poems for publication, Frost sent some manuscripts to William Hayes Ward at the Independent *in early 1906. The note at the top of Frost's cover letter is in Ward's hand. One of the manuscripts enclosed with the letter was probably "The Trial by Existance," which appeared in the 11 October 1906 issue of the* Independent *with "Existence" spelled correctly (Huntington Library).*

3.

And from a cliff top is proclaimed
The gathering of the souls for birth,
The Trial by Existence named,
The obscuration upon earth.
And the slant spirits trooping by
In streams and cross- and counter-streams
Can but give ear to that sweet cry
For its suggestion of what dreams.

4.

And the more loitering are turned
To view once more the sacrifice
Of those who for some good discerned
Will gladly give up paradise.
And a white shimmering concourse rolls
Toward the throne to witness there
The speeding of devoted souls
Which God makes his especial care.

5

And none are taken but who will
Having first heard the life read out
That opens earthward, good and ill
Beyond the shadows of a doubt.
And very beautifully God limns,
And tenderly, life's little dream,
But naught extenuates or dims,
Setting the thing that is supreme

6

Nor is there wanting in the press
Some spirit to stand simply forth
Heroic in its nakedness
Against the uttermost of earth.
The tale of earth's unhonored things
Sounds nobler there than 'neath the sun;
And the mind whirls and the heart sings
And a shout greets the daring one.

7

But always God speaks at the end:
"One thought in agony of life
The bravest would have by for friend,
The memory that he chose the life;
But the pure fate to which you go
Admits no memory of choice,
Or the woe were not earthly woe
To which you give the assenting voice."

8

And so the choice must be again,
But the last choice is still the same.
And the awe passes wonder then
And a hush falls for all acclaim.
And God has ta'en a flower of gold
And broken it, and used therefrom
The mystic link to bind and hold
Spirit to matter till death come.

9

'Tis of the essence of life here,
Though we choose greatly, still to lack
The lasting memory at all clear
That life has for us on the wrack
Nothing but what we somehow chose:
Thus are we wholly stripped of pride
In the pain that has but one close,
Bearing it crushed and mystified.

Robert Frost

West Derry N.H.

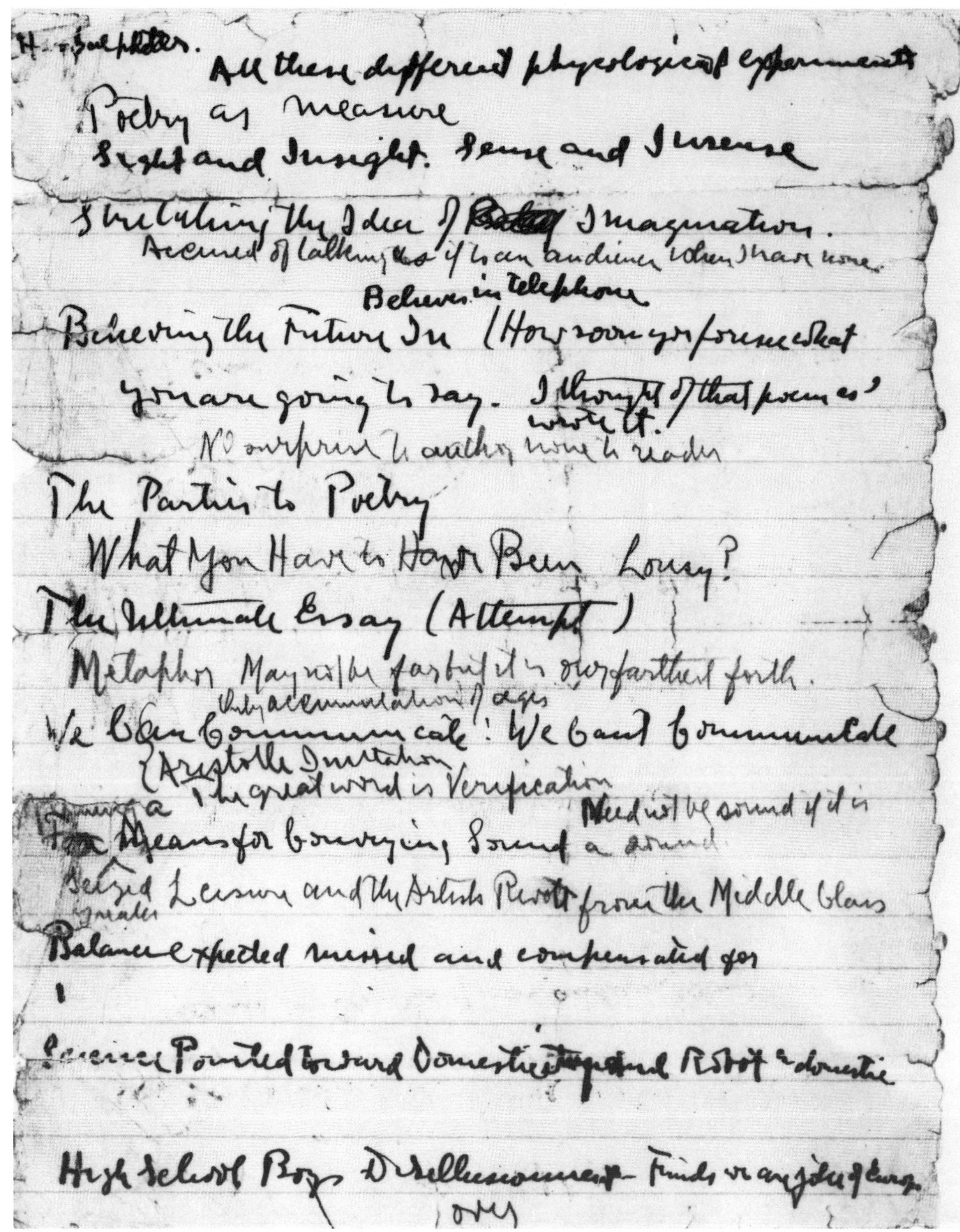
H [illegible]
All these different physiological experiments
Poetry as measure
Sight and Insight. Sense and Insense
Stimulating the Idea of ~~[illegible]~~ Imagination.
Accused of talking as if to an audience when I have none.
Believes in telephone
Believing the Future In (How soon you foresee what
you are going to say. I thought of that poem as I
wrote it.
No surprise to author none to reader
The Parties to Poetry
What You Have to Have Been Lonely?
The Ultimate Essay (Attempt)
Metaphor May not be farthest it is our farthest forth.
Only accumulation of ages
We Can Communicate: We Can't Communicate
{Aristotle Imitation
The great word is Verification
Need not be sound if it is
[illegible] a Means for Conveying Sound a sound
Seized Leisure and the Artist's Revolt from the Middle Class
greater
Balance expected missed and compensated for
Science Pointed toward Domestic [illegible] and Robot domestic
High School Boys Disillusionment Finds in anything of [illegible]
[illegible]

Pages from the notebook Frost kept at Derry, circa 1906-1907 (Barrett Library, University of Virginia Library). In addition to these notes the notebook includes a draft for a verse letter to Carl Burrell, an early version of "The Last Word of a Bluebird" (1930), and the children's stories published as Stories for Lesley (1984).

This is as old as to every day
you can see from it where our idea started
R.F. 1951

I hate most the fellow who makes common stories
of the ~~a~~ flight of man.

He came out of the having mist and contemplated
the terms and accepted them. They were then
as they are now: A little more pleasure than pain,
pain greater in length and breadth but exceeded
by pleasure in height, one more pleasure than pain
~~[illegible]~~ by actual count, ~~or~~ the pleasure of being
alive.

The Fan. (Baseball)

The Tramp Worshipper (A Boy [illegible] the Roadside.

Milton spoke in terms of the studies of his youth ~~of the~~ about the great
events that ~~had drawn~~ were drawing him away from those studies. In Comus

"Love Virtue; she alone is free." The only free man is
the abject slave of virtue. Not so says —. The free man
will use virtue as he will vice to the ends of his own free spirit

The three unities are of Reality Design (Decoration, Form) and Significance:

Architecture may be pure Design — Design only in stone

Thought advances like spilled water along dry ground. Stopping
gathering breaking out and running again.

"Dont write unless you have something to say." ~~Until~~ you have something
to say. Go and get something to say

W. Derry NH Aug 6 '07

A Dream Pang.

I had withdrawn in forest and my song
Was swallowed up in leaves that blew alway;
And to the forest-edge you came one day
(This was my dream) and looked and pondered long
But did not enter tho the wish was strong,
But shook your pensive head as who would say:-
"I dare not – too far in his footsteps stray –
He must seek me, would he undo the wrong."

Not far, but near, I stood and saw it all,
Behind low boughs the trees let down outside,
And the sweet pang it cost me not to call
And tell you that I saw does still abide.–
But 'twas not true that thus you dwelt aloof,
For the woods wake and you are here for proof.

R.F.

Comment: I shall master the sonnet form in time.

HM 7656

Dear Miss Ward:-

I must add my word to urge the visit Mrs Frost proposes in her letter. It would be so very pleasant to see you again and there would be so many things to talk about, that here we are accustomed to keep locked in the bosom of the family from one year's end to another. I sent the inoffensive poem to the unoffending editor and soon, I expect, I shall be enough richer to buy a few more books – Meredith, Dobell, Yeats, and one or two others I shall have to think up. (Have you anything to suggest?) So that you would find us right in the middle of five or six new enthusiasms. That would not bore you too much, I hope. But of course if you are going to plead poverty and stay at home, I have nothing to say. We too have tasted poverty (and all but death) – at the hands of the general practitioner if not of the specialist. It is too bad that we are not where we could see you more easily. Sometime we intend to be nearer New York than we are, if it can come about in the right way. But that is one of the dreams. Poetry, I am afraid, will be less likely to bring us there than prose.

Sincerely

Robert Frost

Choice of Society

Tired of the trees sometimes I crave my kind.
Then I know where to hie me in the dawn –
To a slope where the cattle keep the lawn.
There amid junipers all day reclined,
I view, where far the valley waters wind,
Men in their clustered homes, and further on,
In graves on the hill opposite, men gone,
Living or dead whichever good I find.

But if too soon I tire of both of these,
I have but to turn on my arm and lo,
The sunburnt hillside sets my cheek aglow,
My breathing shakes the bluet like a breeze,
I smell the earth, I smell the bruised plant,
I look into the crater of the ant.

R.F.

Comment: Not quite honest.

[Another infliction on the next page.]

Letter to Susan Hayes Ward, with two sonnets Frost later included in his first book, where "Choice of Society" was revised as "The Vantage Point" (Huntington Library)

Frost raking hay at his Derry farm, 1908. In March 1906 he had begun teaching at Pinkerton Academy, a private school in Derry, and by summer 1909, when he moved his family to rented quarters near the school, he had given up farming.

Robert and Elinor Frost (left) and their children (right)–Lesley, Carol, Irma, and Marjorie– in 1911 at Plymouth, New Hampshire, where Frost had taken a teaching position at Plymouth Normal School. He had sold the Derry farm, which had been left to him by his grandfather.

Frost (standing at far right) as umpire for a Pinkerton Academy baseball game, 1911

The Later Minstrel

Robert L. Frost

Tune Cooling 339

Remember some departed day,
    When bathed in autumn gold,
You wished for some sweet song, and sighed
    For minstrel days of old.

And that same golden autumn day,
    Perhaps the fates would bring
At eve, one knocking at your heart,
    With perfect songs to sing.

You knew that never bard on earth,
    Did wander wide as he—
Who sang the long, long thoughts of Youth,
    The Secret of the Sea.

You knew not when he might not come,
    But while he made delays,
You wronged the wisdom that you had,
    And sighed for vanished days.

Song's times and seasons are its own,
    Its ways past finding out,
But more and more it fills the earth,
    And triumphs over doubt.

Frost at Pinkerton Academy, 1910, and broadside printing of a poem Frost wrote to be sung at a Pinkerton Academy chapel service commemorating the centennial of Henry Wadsworth Longfellow's birth, 27 February 1907 (Jones Library).

needn't think because I let my geese run wild I think any less of them than other folks. They are good ones,–as they ought to be with the advantages I give them. They win, too, where they are shown.

The records in your paper ought to show what they did in Lawrence this year; but I notice they don't. So Mr. Frost was pretty near right about my geese; and if Mr. White wants some good ones that a little rather than not sleep out, I've got them.

John A. Hall

* * *

I wrote up one or two poultrymen . . . filling in the gaps in my knowledge with dream material. I think I managed fairly well except for the time I spoke of John Hall's geese roosting in the trees. I should have let geese severely alone. It took an artistic letter from John Hall himself (I wrote it for the douce man) to save me from the scandal that started. I had a little right on my side. As a matter of fact John Hall had among others a few Brazilians that sometimes roosted on a pollared willow and even on the chimney and he could honestly say so (if some one would write the letter for him, for he was without clerkly learning).

* * *

Frost to John Bartlett, circa 18 March 1913

BOOK REVIEW:
Ezra Pound, Review of *A Boy's Will, Poetry: A Magazine of Verse,* 2 (May 1913): 72-74.

Late in the summer of 1912, the Frosts sailed for England, where Frost intended to devote all his time to writing. Soon after the family had settled in The Bungalow, a small house in Beaconsfield, north of London, Frost gathered some of the manuscripts he had brought to England into a collection he called A Boy's Will *and submitted it to a publisher. It was accepted the book a few days later. Frost met Pound early in March 1913, shortly before the publication of* A Boy's Will, *and helped him to obtain a review copy. Pound's enthusiastic review was the first notice of the book to appear in the United States. Frost was embarrassed to discover in the review twisted elements of an overdramatized autobiography that he had told Pound without intending it for publication.*

I had withdrawn in forest, and my song
Was swallowed up in leaves.

There is another personality in the realm of verse, another American, found, as usual, on this side of the water, by an English publisher long known as a lover of good letters. David Nutt publishes at his own expense *A Boy's Will,* by Robert Frost, the latter having been long scorned by the "great American editors." It is the old story.

Mr. Frost's book is a little raw, and has in it a number of infelicities; underneath them it has the tang of the New Hampshire woods, and it has just this utter sincerity. It is not post-Miltonic or post-Swinburnian or post-Kiplonian. This man has the good sense to speak naturally and to paint the thing, the thing as he sees it. And to do this is a very different matter from gunning about for the circumplectious polysyllable.

It is almost on this account that it is a difficult book to quote from.

She's glad her simple worsted gray
Is silver now with clinging mist–

does not catch your attention. The lady is praising the autumn rain, and he ends the poem, letting her talk.

Not yesterday I learned to know
 The love of bare November days,
Before the coming of the snow;
 But it were vain to tell her so,
And they are better for her praise.

Or again:

 There was never a sound beside the wood but one,
And that was my long scythe whispering to the ground.
....
My long scythe whispered and left the hay to make.

I remember that I was once canoeing and thirsty and I put in to a shanty for water and found a man there who had no water and gave me cold coffee instead. And he didn't understand it, he was from a minor city and he "just set there watchin' the river" and didn't "seem to want to go back," and he didn't much care for anything else. And so I presume he entered into Anunda. And I remember Joseph Campbell telling me of meeting a man on a desolate waste of bogs, and he said to him, "It's rather dull here"; and the man said, "Faith, ye can sit on a middan and dream stars."

Marjorie, Carol, Lesley, and Irma Frost in front of The Bungalow, Beaconsfield, spring 1913. The cottage was so crowded that Frost was soon calling it "The Bung Hole."

And that is the essence of folk poetry with distinction between America and Ireland. And Frost's book reminded me of these things.

There is perhaps as much of Frost's personal tone in the following little catch, which is short enough to quote, as in anything else. It is to his wife, written when his grandfather and his uncle had disinherited him of a comfortable fortune and left him in poverty because he was a useless poet instead of a money-getter.

IN NEGLECT

They leave us so to the way we took,
  As two in whom they were proved mistaken,
That we sit sometimes in a wayside nook,
With mischievous, vagrant, seraphic look,
  And *try* if we cannot feel forsaken.

There are graver things, but they suffer too much by making excerpts. One reads the book for the "tone," which is homely, by intent, and pleasing, never doubting that it comes direct from his own life, and that no two lives are the same.

He has now and then such a swift and bold expression as

The whimper of hawks beside the sun.

He has now and then a beautiful simile, well used, but he is for the most part as simple as the lines I have quoted in opening or as in the poem of mowing. He is without sham and without affectation.

BOOK REVIEW:
[Norman Douglas], Review of *A Boy's Will,* from "Poetry," *English Review,* 14 (June 1913): 505.

Douglas, editor of the English Review, *included his comments on Frost's book in a notice where he also reviewed Patrick MacGill's* Songs of the Dead End, *Rabindranath Tagore's* Gitanjali (Song Offerings), *and* Perse Playbooks, No. 3.

After the subtle refinements of *Gitanjali,* it does one good to glance awhile into the simple woodland philosophy of Mr. Frost. Nowhere on earth, we fancy, is there more outrageous nonsense printed under the name of poetry than in America; and our author, we are told, is an American. All the more credit to him for breaking away from this tradition–if such it can be called–and giving us not derivative, hypersensuous drivel, but an image of things really heard and seen. There is a wild, racy flavour in his poems; they sound that *inevitable* response to nature which is the hall-mark of true lyric feeling.

BOOK REVIEW:
F. S. Flint, Review of *A Boy's Will, Poetry and Drama,* 1 (June 1913): 250.

Frost had met Imagist poet Frank S. Flint at the opening of Harold Monro's Poetry Bookshop, in Kensington, on 8 January 1913. Flint arranged for Frost to meet his fellow American Ezra Pound, who in turn introduced Frost to William Butler Yeats.

Mr Robert Frost's poetry is so much a part of his life that to tell his life would be to explain his poetry. I wish I were authorised to tell it, because the one is as moving as the other–a constant struggle against circumambient stupidity for the right of expression. Be it said, however, that Mr Frost has escaped from America, and that his first book, *A Boy's Will,* has found an English publisher. So much information, extrinsic to the poems, is necessary. Their intrinsic merits are great, despite faults of diction here and there, occasional inversions, and lapses, where he has not been strong enough to bear his own simplicity of utterance. It is this simplicity which is the great charm of his book; and it is a simplicity that proceeds from a candid heart:

MY NOVEMBER GUEST

My Sorrow, when she's here with me,
  Thinks these dark days of autumn rain
Are beautiful as days can be;
She loves the bare, the withered tree;
  She walks the sodden pasture lane.

Her pleasure will not let me stay.
  She talks, and I am fain to list:
She's glad the birds are gone away,
She's glad her simple worsted grey
  Is silver now with clinging mist.

The desolate, deserted trees,
  The faded earth, the heavy sky,
The beauties she so truly sees,
She thinks I have no eye for these,
  And vexes me for reason why.

Not yesterday I learned to know
  The love of bare November days
Before the coming of the snow;
But it were vain to tell her so,
  And they are better for her praise.

Other poems almost or quite as perfect as the one above are: "A Late Walk," "To the Thawing Wind," "Mowing," "Going for Water," "Reluctance." Each poem is the complete expression of one mood, one emotion, one idea. I have tried to find in these poems what is most characteristic of Mr Frost's poetry, and I think it is this: direct observation of the object and immediate correlation with the emotion–spontaneity, subtlety in the evocation of moods, humour, an ear for silences. But behind all is the heart and life of a man, and the more you ponder his poems the more convinced you become that the heart is pure and the life not lived in vain.

LETTER:
To John T. Bartlett; *Selected Letters of Robert Frost,* pp. 75-77.

Frost sent Bartlett, a favorite Pinkerton Academy pupil who had become a reporter in Vancouver, copies of the reivews by Pound, Douglas, and Flint and suggested that he use them in an article for the Derry paper. Bartlett's article, largely a series of quotations from the three reviews, appeared in the Derry News *on 7 November 1913. The forthcoming* Bookman *notice, to which Frost refers hopefully in this letter, turned out to be brief.*

[*c.* 16 June 1913]
Bucks

Dear John:

What do you say if we cook up something to bother the enemies we left behind in Derry? It won't take much cooking, but what it does will come on you. You have two of my reviews now. If you haven't I will see that you have others to take their place. One is good for one reason; the other for another. Pound's [*Poetry: A Magazine of Verse,* May 1913] is a little too personal. I don't mind his calling me raw. He is reckoned raw himself and at the same time perhaps the most prominent of the younger poets here. I object chiefly to what he says about the great American editors. Not that I have any love for the two or three he has in mind. But they are better ignored–at any rate they are better not offended. We may want to use them some time. The other I value chiefly for its source, The English Review, the magazine that found Masefield and Conrad. The editor himself [Norman Douglas] wrote that particular notice.

To Waller Barrett
since he would have it all
in my hand
Robert Frost

A Few Remarks and Acknowledgments

Exact dates are getting harder to be sure of. My Butterfly was printed by 1894. I used to say it was the tenth I ever wrote. That must be about right. Now Close the Windows and Revelation were not written for English A (Har) because offered them in place of themes in 1897-8. I tried to write out the idea of Trial by Existence while still in High School but failed with it. The repetition of a line in Mowing and The Tuft of Flowers shows how far apart they two poems must be. The whole book was pretty evenly spread over twenty years.

I am never to forget the least notice any poem gets from a friend. Susan Hayes Ward of The N.Y. Independent began it all in 93 with My Butterfly. She made Bliss Carman see it And Maurice Thompson. There is a letter from Thompson in existence urging her to stop me before it was too late and save me from the cruel life of a poet. Pound was first caught by In Neglect. Ghost House was published in The Youth's Companion by Mark Howe who didn't disclose himself till years afterward. Mrs David Nutt was the first to "see" the whole book. Then later William Heinemann in England. He objected to my quotations without quotation marks in Love and a Question and Into My Own. Charles Lowell Young said long ago the whole thing began with the second stanza or paragraph of My Butterfly, in the first two lines of that stanza to be exact. Thomas Bird Mosher said Reluctance was all he had ever written and all I needed to have written. Wind and Window Flower pleased ~~Stuart Sherman~~ A Tuft of Flowers read aloud by someone else, Charles Merriam, got me my position (toehold) in Pinkerton Academy in 1905. In America this book as a whole got no notice till after Alfred Harcourt took up North of Boston for Henry Holt in 1915. The Holts have been my sole publishers in this country ever since.

Inscription, with composition dates for poems, in a fair copy of poems in A Boy's Will *that Frost made for book collector Clifton Waller Barrett in 1948 (Barrett Library, University of Virginia Library)*

Photograph of Frost taken for publication in the August 1913 number of the Bookman, *which also included a brief review of* A Boy's Will

I am sending you one more review which you can hold on to for a while. One more still and we shall have the ingredients of our Bouillabais[s]e (sp.) assembled. If nothing slips up we will get that in the August number of The Bookman (English). The editor has asked me for my photograph and a personal note to accompany the review. I suppose everything depends on whether I look young enough in my photograph to grace the ballet. Why did you wear me out teaching you things you knew already?

Well then in August, say, as soon as you get The Bookman you can begin a little article for Morse-back of The News and Enterprise like this:

Former pupils of R. F. at Pink may be interested to learn of the success of his first book published in London. A recent number of The Bookman (Eng.) contains etc.– You are not to get the least bit enthusiastic–I know you my child. Keep strictly to the manner of the disinterested reporter. Make the article out of the reviews almost entirely. In mentioning The English Review you might mention the fact that it is a leading literary monthly here.

All this is if you have time and inclination. It will necessitate some typewriting. I would copy Ezra Pound's article so as to get rid of the break about the editors. Leave in any derogatory remarks. We like those. I fancy I should leave out the quotation from "My November Guest" which mangles a poem that needs to be taken as a whole and they quote it as a whole in the Poetry and Drama review I am enclosing. You see the scheme is to make The Bookman affair the occasion for your article and then drag the rest in by

ROBERT BRIDGES

FLYCATCHERS

SWEET pretty fledgelings, perched on the rail arow, 1
Expectantly happy, where ye can watch below 2
Your parents a-hunting i' the meadow grasses 0
All the gay morning to feed you with flies;

Ye recall me a time sixty summers ago, 3
When, a young chubby chap, I sat just so 4
With others on a school-form rank'd in a row, 5
Not less eager and hungry than you, I trow, 6
With intelligences agape and eyes aglow, 7
While an authoritative old ~~wise-acre~~ acre-wise
Stood over us and from a desk fed us with flies.

Dead flies—such as litter the library south-window, 8
That buzzed at the panes until they fell stiff-baked on the sill,
Or are roll'd up asleep i' the blinds at sunrise,
Or wafer'd flat in a shrunken folio.

A dry biped he was, nurtured likewise
On skins and skeletons, stale from top to toe 9
With all manner of rubbish and all manner of lies.

I heard this great man in a brave theory of rhythm at lunch at the Vienna Café not long since. He holds that our syllables are to be treated in verse as having quantity of many shades. That is to say they are quarter third and fifth notes, as the case may be. Who knows not that no acts upon it is no poet. Well here we have him acting upon it, we are to presume. Poor old man. He is past seventy. It is the fashion to play up to him. He still seems capable of the emotion of disgust. Mind you he has done good things.

THOMAS HARDY

"MY SPIRIT WILL NOT HAUNT THE MOUND"

MY spirit will not haunt the mound
Wherein I rest,
But travel, memory-possessed,
To where my tremulous being found
Life largest, best.

395

Hardy is almost never in a public place. When he is not heard. They say like a little old stone-mason. [illegible] is not the best poem he ever [illegible]. He is an excellent poet and the greatest living novelist here. And I saw a terrible little curtain raiser (hair raiser would be better) the Three Travellers that he made. One traveller after another comes in out of a storm to a feast in a cottage. The first is a convicted sheep stealer escaped from jail where he was to have been hanged next morning. The second is the hangman on his way to the jail to hang him. He sits with the convict on the same bench and sings him a hanging song. He gets his rope out of a bag — But I believe it is all in a short story somewhere. You may have read it.

Pages, with Frost's annotations, from a copy of the December 1913 issue of Poetry and Drama, *which Frost sent to John Bartlett (Barrett Library, University of Virginia Library). This issue also includes "The Fear" and "A Hundred Collars," two of the dramatic narrative poems collected in Frost's next book,* North of Boston, *(1914).*

This is what makes it impossible that I should live long under a criss-cross flag. Me for the three colors the bluebird wears.

AMERICAN POETRY

THIS is not a Chronicle. One cannot write a Chronicle with only a dozen books published during the last eighteen months for data. Nor does an examination of these books, combined with more or less casual acquaintance with American literary journals, suggest that a periodic Chronicle would be of particular interest or value. Nevertheless, this very miscellaneous collection is not devoid of matter for consideration. Consisting of a comprehensive anthology of American Poetry from the time of the Settlement to the end of the last century, two dramatic poems and nine or ten volumes of lyric and narrative verse, it provides some opportunity for discovering what, if any, are the particular characteristics which distinguish American poetry from English poetry and the poetry of other nations.

Now, it is just as well to state at the beginning that I can find no support to a belief that there is any such thing as American poetry; just as an examination of the Metropolitan Museum of New York finally destroyed my idea that there was any such thing as American art. American architecture indisputably exists, but that is obviously less due to a distinctive æsthetic sensibility than to the economic conditions of the nation and its cities. These will obviously not affect its poetry in the same direct way, and poetry therefore provides an excellent test for the real artistic feeling of the nation. Let me, in the first place, hasten to congratulate Professor Bronson on the patriotic labour which he has expended on his anthology; "patriotic," because it is difficult to conceive any other motive for undertaking so extensive and tedious a labour. No blame rests on him that the result is a monument of mediocrity. Though much space has been devoted to the earlier writers, the history of poetry in America begins with Poe and ends, so far as the nineteenth century is concerned, with Whitman. This is not only historically but comprehensively true. The actual poetry of Holmes, Emerson, Whittier, Longfellow, and Lowell combined, when compared with these two, could be put into half a dozen pages. Nevertheless, being representative American poets, they will have to be taken into consideration. No argument can claim this distinction for Poe. His was an exotic genius, of no race or age; his affinities, as has been frequently pointed out, being more Celtic than anything else. This fact does not, of course, disentitle him to the

485

This cuss doesn't know how to find his way around among American writers. No one he mentions is thought anything of on this side — no one of recent date.

Emerson is so American, so original, especially in form, I'll bet you five he couldn't read him if he tried.

Whitman and Poe ad stomachache.

the ears. Say simply "The following is taken from–" Or if you see some other way to go about it, all right. You might do it in the form of a letter to the News, beginning, "I thought former pupils of R F at Pink etc" and sign yourself J. T. B. Anything to make Mrs Superior Sheppard and Lil' Art' Reynolds unhappy. (You put these people into my head.) But I suppose I care less about teasing my out-and-out enemies than my half friends like John C. Chase. I told you how I charged John C. forty dollars for the catalogue and when he winced told him that I didn't get it often but when I did I got about that much for my poetry. He never quite got over that. He clipped a cheap joke on poets one day and sent it to me by Miss Bartley so that she would share in my discomfiture. I only stood it tolerably well. I didn't mind it at first as much. I got tired of it.

Affectionately, mes enfants R. F.

From Poetry and Drama 2s. 6d. (Quarterly) June 1913 London Devonshire St, Theobalds Road.

"x x x x Be it said, however, that Mr. Frost has escaped from America and his first book has found an English publisher. So much information extrinsic to the poems is necessary. Their intrinsic merits are great, despite faults of diction here and there, occasional inversions, and lapses where he has not been strong enough to bear his own simplicity of utterance. It is this simplicity which is the great charm of the book and it is simplicity that proceeds from a candid heart:

My November Guest
(Quoted in full)

Other poems almost or quite as perfect as the one above are: A Late Walk, To the Thawing Wind, Mowing, Going for Water, Reluctance. Each poem is the complete expression of one mood, one emotion, one idea. I have tried to find in these poems what is most characteristic of Mr. Frost's poetry; and I think it is this: direct observation of the object and immediate correlation with the emotion–spontaneity, subtlety evocation of moods, humor, and ear for silences. But, behind in the all is the heart and life of a man x x x x"

The first and last sentences are too personal for my taste. I am not bothered so much by the faultfinding. A little of that won't hurt me.

There was a favorable but unimportant review in T. P.'s Weekly a month or so ago. I have lost track of it. I think it quoted the first poem in the book and mentioned In a Vale. Maybe you have seen it.

You might say that A Late Walk was published in The Pinkerton Critic [October 1910].

I have become acquainted with the author of this [F. S. Flint].

LETTER:
To John T. Bartlett; *Selected Letters of Robert Frost*, pp. 79-80.

Conversations with T. E. Hulme, Imagist and translator of Henri Bergson, helped Frost to refine and articulate his theory of the relationship between natural speech rhythms ("the sound of sense") and poetic meter. This letter to Bartlett appears to be Frost's first attempt to put his ideas into writing.

Fourth of July [1913]
Beaconsfield

Dear John:-

Those initials you quote from T. P.'s belong to a fellow named Buckley and the explanation of Buckley is this that he has recently issued a book with David Nutt, but at his own expense, whereas in my case David Nutt assumed the risks. *And* those other people Buckley reviewed are his personal friends or friends of his friends or if not that simply examples of the kind of wrong horse most fools put their money on. You will be sorry to hear me say so but they are not even craftsmen. Of course there are two ways of using that word the good and the bad one. To be on the safe side it is best to call such dubs mechanics. To be perfectly frank with you I am one of the most notable craftsmen of my time. That will transpire presently. I am possibly the only person going who works on any but a worn out theory (principle I had better say) of versification. You see the great successes in recent poetry have been made on the assumption that the music of words was a matter of harmonised vowels and consonants. Both Swinburne and Tennyson arrived largely at effects in assonation. But they were on the wrong track or at any rate on a short track. They went the length of it. Any one else who goes that way must go after them. And that's where most are going. I alone of English writers have consciously set myself to make music out of what I may call the sound of sense. Now it is possible to have sense without the sound of sense (as in much prose that is supposed to pass muster but makes very dull reading) and the sound of sense without sense (as in Alice in Wonderland which makes anything but dull reading). The best place to get the abstract sound of sense is from voices behind a door that cuts off the words. Ask yourself how these sentences would sound without the words in which they are embodied:

You mean to tell me you can't read?
I said no such thing.
Well read then.
You're not my teacher.

—

He says it's too late.
Oh, say!
Damn an Ingersoll watch anyway.

—

One-two-three–go!
No good! Come back–come back.
Haslam go down there and make those kids get out of the track.

—

Those sounds are summoned by the audile [audial] imagination and they must be positive, strong, and definitely and unmistakeably indicated by the context. The reader must be at no loss to give his voice the posture proper to the sentence. The simple declarative sentence used in making a plain statement is one sound. But Lord love ye it mustn't be worked to death. It is against the law of nature that whole poems should be written in it. If they are written they won't be read. The sound of sense, then. You get that. It is the abstract vitality of our speech. It is pure sound–pure form. One who concerns himself with it more than the subject is an artist. But remember we are still talking merely of the raw material of poetry. An ear and an appetite for these sounds of sense is the first qualification of a writer, be it of prose or verse. But if one is to be a poet he must learn to get cadences by skillfully breaking the sounds of sense with all their irregularity of accent across the regular beat of the metre. Verse in which there is nothing but the beat of the metre furnished by the accents of the pollysyllabic words we call doggerel. Verse is not that. Neither is it the sound of sense alone. It is a resultant from those two. There are only two or three metres that are worth anything. We depend for variety on the infinite play of accents in the sound of sense. The high possibility of emotional expression all lets in this mingling of sense-sound and word-accent. A curious thing. And all this has its bearing on your prose me boy. Never if you can help it write down a sentence in which the voice will not know how to posture *specially*.

That letter head shows how far we have come since we left Pink. Editorial correspondent of the Montreal Star sounds to me. Gad, we get little mail from you.

Affectionately R. F.

Maybe you'll keep this discourse on the sound of sense till I can say more on it.

BOOK REVIEW:
Ezra Pound, Review of *A Boy's Will,* from "In Metre," *New Freewoman,* 1 (1 September 1913): 113.

Pound's second review of A Boy's Will *was published with his assessments of D. H. Lawrence's* Love Poems and Others *and Walter De la Mare's* Peacock Pie. *His comment about the table of contents refers to the prose glosses Frost had placed under each title.*

Mr. Frost comes speaking as simply as does Mr. De la Mare and more soberly, without the wanton vagrancy of fancy, without the balladeering flourish, yet I am not sure that one could not slip some of his verse into Peacock book without anyone being the wiser.

"I dwell in a lonely house I know
That vanished many a summer ago,
And left no trace but the cellar walls."

Mr. Frost has sought the natural cadences of the speech. Many of his opening lines are the lines of common conversation. His language is for the most part natural and simple. The wind working against him in the dark, the noise of his scythe in the grass are very real to him, and it is with little surprise that we learn that his knowledge is actual and not theoretic. He has written life as he has lived it. His very table of contents is not a scheme written into, as the stupidest of his reviewers has said, but simply a statement of his own discovery that some continuity underlies all of the lyrics. In fact what one gets from the book is not any pleasure in pyrotechnics but a conviction of poetic personality, the feel of some sober local wood god, innocent for the most part of

Little Iddens, the Gloucestershire cottage that the Frosts rented in April 1914. Before returning to the United States in February 1915 the Frosts also spent several months living with the Abercrombies at their larger cottage, The Gallows.

our language, half indifferent to, and half dismayed at our customs.

POEM:

Wilfrid Gibson, "The Golden Room," *Atlantic Monthly*, 137 (February 1926): 204-205.

In April 1914, at the suggestion of Lascelles Abercrombie and Wilfrid Gibson, two of the Georgian poets, the Frosts went to live at Little Iddens, a cottage in the Dymock region of Gloucestershire near the Abercrombie family's cottage, The Gallows, and the Gibsons' quarters, the Old Nailshop. John Drinkwater and Rupert Brooke were among the visitors to their fellow poets, as was essayist-critic Edward Thomas, whom Frost had met in October 1913 and with whom he had formed one of his most important friendships. Years later, after Thomas and Brooke had been killed in World War I, Gibson wrote a poetic memoir of an evening spent at the Old Nailshop.

Do you remember the still summer evening
When in the cosy cream-washed living-room
Of the Old Nailshop we all talked and laughed–
Our neighbors from the Gallows, Catherine
And Lascelles Abercrombie; Rupert Brooke;
Eleanor and Robert Frost, living awhile
At Little Iddens, who'd brought over with them
Helen and Edward Thomas? In the lamplight
We talked and laughed, but for the most part listened
While Robert Frost kept on and on and on
In his slow New England fashion for our delight,
Holding us with shrewd turns and racy quips,
And the rare twinkle of his grave blue eyes.

We sat there in the lamplight while the day
Died from rose-latticed casements, and the plovers
Called over the low meadows till the owls
Answered them from the elms; we sat and talked–
Now a quick flash from Abercrombie, now
A murmured dry half-heard aside from Thomas,
Now a clear laughing word from Brooke, and then
Again Frost's rich and ripe philosophy
That had the body and tang of good draught-cider
And poured as clear a stream.

'T was in July
Of nineteen-fourteen that we sat and talked;
Then August brought the war, and scattered us

Now on the crest of an Ægean Isle
Brooke sleeps and dreams of England. Thomas lies

'Neath Vimy Ridge where he among his fellows
Died just as life had touched his lips to song.

And nigh as ruthlessly has life divided
Us who survive, for Abercrombie toils
In a black Northern town beneath the glower
Of hanging smoke, and in America
Frost farms once more, and far from the Old Nailshop
We sojourn by the Western sea.

And yet
Was it for nothing that the little room
All golden in the lamplight thrilled with golden
Laughter from hearts of friends that summer night?
Darkness has fallen on it, and the shadow
May never more be lifted from the hearts
That went through those black years of death, and live.

And still, whenever men and women gather
For talk and laughter on a summer night,
Shall not that lamp rekindle, and the room
Glow once again alive with light and laughter,
And like a singing star in time's abyss
Burn golden-hearted through oblivion?

BOOK REVIEW:
[Lascelles Abercrombie], "A New Voice," *Nation* (London), 15 (13 June 1914): 423-424.

Frost's revolutionary second book, North of Boston, *published on 15 May 1914, displayed the poetic principles that he had been explaining in his letters to Bartlett and to his friends in England, several of whom wrote reviews. Parts of Abercrombie's review were quoted in "The Listener" column of the* Boston Evening Transcript *on 8 July 1914, the first American notice of Frost's book.*

Poetry *per se* is one of the most troublesome things in the world to discuss exactly. Like Goodness and Personal Identity, it is a thing which everyone is aware of, but a thing which, when you try to lay hold of it, proves a ghost that will scarcely be cornered. For, like those famous apparitions in philosophy again, poetry does not come into actual experience as the spectre of its own essence; we know it as the spirit that selects for its embodiment, informs and impregnates, a mass of things derived from racial environment, habits of language, and personal peculiarities. The temptation therefore is to discuss all this material embodiment, these accidents that hold the essence, in the hope that the discussion will turn out to be, by implication, a discussion of the poetry itself–a hope that does not always succeed. But, in the case of Mr. Robert Frost, the temptation is peculiarly irresistible, not only because the enclosing substance of idiosyncrasy, linguistic manners, and circumstantial traits and characteristics, is very interesting and attractive, but perhaps still more because the poetic spirit inhabiting all this is exceptionally shy and elusive; so much so that the most analytically disposed reader must often be wondering whether even a notional existence can be contrived here for poetic impulse apart from expressive substance. That, of course, may be a great compliment; it may mean that poetic impulse has made the exactly appropriate selection of expressive material, and has fused itself into this so completely as to be inextricable. On the contrary, it may also mean that notional existence of poetry, apart from material, cannot be alleged for the same reason that you cannot conceive the notional existence of the heat of a bar of iron when the bar is not perceptibly hot. In the case of Mr. Frost, it seems to us that the explanation is sometimes the one and sometimes the other. His method–we cannot quarrel with it, because in its final result it nearly always accomplishes something remarkable–is to invite us to assist, first, at his careful and deliberate laying of the material for a poetic bonfire; the skill is interesting, and the stuff is evidently combustible; and suddenly, we do not quite know when, while we were intent on these structural preliminaries, we find that a match has been put to the pile. It burns out, as a rule, rather quickly; but while it is burning, substance and fire are completely at one, and at the end we are not left with embers, but with the sense of a swift and memorable experience.

First, however, for the stuff which the fire lays hold of–the personal and circumstantial characteristics of Mr. Frost's poetry. To start with, Mr. Frost is an American poet who noticeably stands out against tradition. That is what one might expect of an American poet; notoriously, it is just what American poetry proves most incapable of doing. In consequence, American poetry has not often been concerned with America; and the first and most obvious novelty in Mr. Frost's poems is their determination to deal unequivocally with everyday life in New England–"North of Boston." It is not, perhaps, quite what one might have anticipated, this New England life

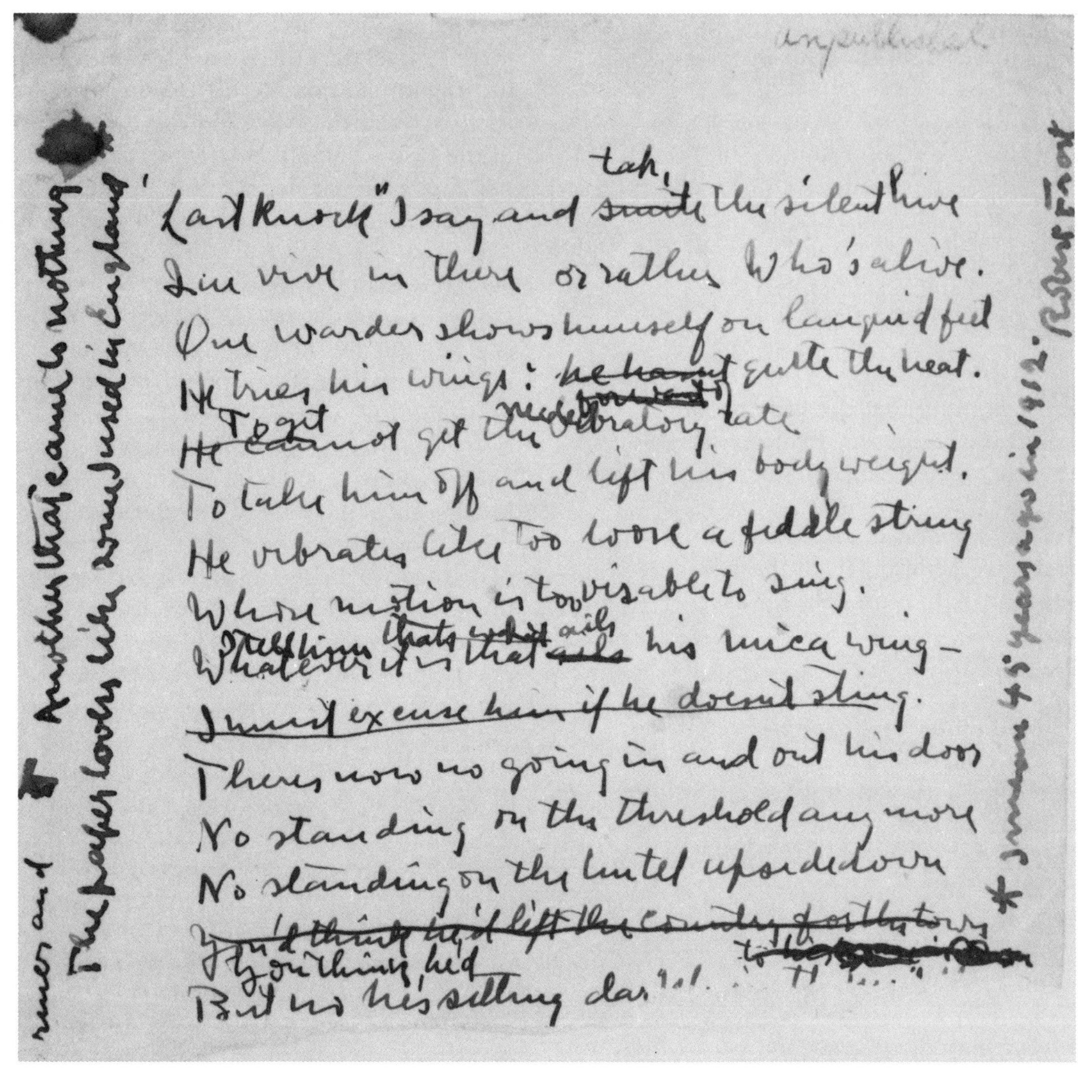
"Last Knock" I say and tak the silent hive
Or rather Who's alive.
One warder shows himself on languid feet
He tries his wings: he hasn't quite the heat.
He cannot get the vibratory rate
To take him off and lift his body weight.
He vibrates like too loose a fiddle string
Whose motion is too visible to sing.
Whatever it is that ails his mica wing—
I must excuse him if he doesn't sting.
There's now no going in and out his door
No standing on the threshold any more
No standing on the lintel upside down
You'd think he'd lift the country for the town
But no he's sitting

Another that came to nothing
The paper looks like some I used in England

*some 45 years ago in 1912. Robert Frost

Draft for an unpublished poem, dating from Frost's 1912-1915 stay in England (Lilly Library, Indiana University)

that Mr. Frost takes as his beloved material; certainly, not what we have come to think of as typical of the United States. Most of Mr. Frost's subjects are in some way connected with farming; the few that touch anything urban have the atmosphere of country towns–nothing in the book, at any rate, suggests in the least a nation of dwellers in vast, roaring, hurly-burlying cities. These specimens of New England life are not greatly different from the corresponding life of the old England; yet there *is* an unmistakable difference, on which it would not be easy to lay one's finger. American democracy contributes to the difference, but is certainly not the most important element in it. The life seems harder and lonelier, and it also seems, oddly enough, more reflective and philosophic. Here, for instance, is a man who has been injured in a saw-mill, talking with his friend:–

> Everything goes the same without me there.
> You can hear the small buzz saws whine, the big saw
> Caterwaul to the hills around the village
> As they both bite the wood. It's all our music.
> One ought as a good villager to like it.
> No doubt it has a sort of prosperous sound,
> And it's our life."
> "Yes, when it's not our death."
> "You make that sound as if it wasn't so
> With everything. What we live by we die by."

The sentiment is not extraordinary, but it seems deeply characteristic. The same sort of reflectiveness sounds through most of these dialogues and soliloquies. It is life that has, on the whole, a pretty hard time of it, though a queer, dry, yet cordial, humor seldom fails it; but it is life that has time to look at itself as well as to look about itself. How much of this is due to Mr. Frost's interpretation of New England we, on this side of the Atlantic, can hardly say; but, if internal evidence goes for anything, life has seldom been made into literature with as little manipulation as in this book.

To say that a poet stands out against tradition is not to accuse him of being a rebel. He may be, as Mr. Frost certainly is, one of those in whom the continual re-adjustment of poetry to life is taking place. When that re-adjustment of poetry to life is taking place. When that re-adjustment comes, manner must inevitably be obedient to matter. And so we find very little of the traditional manner of poetry in Mr. Frost's work; scarcely anything, indeed, save a peculiar adaptation, as his usual form, of the pattern of blank verse. It is poetry which is not much more careful than good prose is to stress and extract the inmost values and suggestive force of words; it elaborates simile and metaphor scarcely more than good conversation does. But it is apt to treat the familiar images and acts of ordinary life much as poetry is usually inclined to treat words–to put them, that is to say, into such positions of relationship that some unexpected virtue comes out of them; it is, in fact, poetry composed, as far as possible, in a language of *things*. The similes, when they do appear, are usually striking, because of the concrete familiarity of the experiences they employ. Thus, a man's recollection of his own boyhood is a vision of

"a little, little boy,
As pale and dim as a match flame in the sun."

The same sort of simile occurs in the following passage, which is quoted, however, as a more general type of Mr. Frost's habit of composing in things:–

"A lantern light from deeper in the barn
Shone on a man and woman in the door,
And threw their lurching shadows on a house
Near by, all dark in every glossy window.
A horse's hoof pawed once the hollow floor,
And the back of the gig they stood beside
Moved in a little. The man grasped a wheel,
The woman spoke out sharply, 'Whoa, stand still!'
'I saw it just as plain as a white plate,'
She said, 'as the light of the dashboard ran
Along the bushes at the roadside–a man's face.' "

Language *quâ* language does very little here; the selection and arrangement of the substance do practically everything. So, at least, it seems at first. But poetry, after all, is an affair of specialized language; and if Mr. Frost's verse be read with some attention, it will soon appear that his verses are built with language specialized for a purpose beyond close, faithful service to concrete imagery. We have heard a good deal lately of the desirability of getting poetry back again into touch with the living vigors of speech. This usually means matters of vocabulary and idiom; and Mr. Frost certainly makes a racy use of New England vernacular. But he goes further; he seems trying to capture and hold within metrical patterns the very tones of speech–the rise and fall, the stressed pauses and little hurries, of spoken language. The kind of metrical modulation to which we are most accustomed–the modulations intended for decoration or purely æsthetic expressiveness–will scarcely be found in his verses. But, instead, we have some novel inflections of metre which can only be designed to reproduce in verse form the actual shape of the sound of whole sentences. As a matter of technique, the attempt is extraordinarily interesting. Sometimes the metrical form goes to pieces; at other times the verse is, however much we try to hear a voice in it, a little monotonous, which may be due to the fact that it is extremely hard to indicate by a verse-movement such an elusive thing as the intonation of speech–supposing that intonation is as constant as accent. But often enough the intention is clear, and the result decidedly exciting. The intention itself is not a new thing in poetry; but such complete reliance on it as the chief element of technique, though it holds Mr. Frost's expression rather tight, is rewarded by some new and very suggestive effects.

Naturally, this technical preoccupation bears strongly on the general form of Mr. Frost's poetry. He uses almost entirely dialogue or soliloquy; he must have somebody talking. We might call these poems psychological idylls. Within their downright knowledge, their vivid observation, and (more important) their rich enjoyment of all kinds of practical life, within their careful rendering into metre of customary speech, the impulse is always psychological–to set up, in some significant attitude, a character or a conflict of characters. The ability to do this can turn a situation which is not very interesting at first into something attractive, as when a rather protracted discourse of two distant relations on genealogy gradually merges into a shy, charming conversation of lovers; or, in a more striking instance, when the rambling speech of an over-tasked farmer's wife works up into a dreadful suggestion of inherited lunacy. If, as we have said, we cannot quarrel with this deliberate method of exposition, it can scarcely be questioned that Mr. Frost is at his best when he can dispense with these structural preliminaries, as in the admirable soliloquy of the old philosopher of a farmer mending his wall, or in the exquisite comedy of the professor sharing a bedroom with the talkative newspaper-agent, or in the stark, formidable tragedy called "Home Burial." Though it is difficult to state absolutely the essential quality of Mr. Frost's poetry, it is not difficult to suggest a comparison. When poetry changes by development rather than by rebellion, it is likely to return on itself. Poetry in Mr. Frost exhibits almost the identical desires and impulses we see in the "bucolic" poems of Theocritus. Nothing so futile as a comparison of personal talents is meant by this; but for general motives, the comparison is true and very suggestive. Poetry, in this book, seems determined, once more, just as it was in Alexandria, to invigorate itself by utilizing the traits and necessities of common life, the habits of common speech, the minds and hearts of common folk. And the impulse of Mr. Frost's poetry is not an isolated phenomenon to-day–therein is its significance; he is doing for New England life, in his own unique and entirely original way, what Mr. Wilfrid Gibson is so splendidly doing for the life of modern England.

BOOK REVIEW:
Wilfrid Gibson, "Simplicity and Sophistication," *Bookman* (London), 46 (July 1914): 183.

Another of the friends with whom Frost had been discussing his ideas about "the sound of sense," Gibson devoted nearly all of a review that was supposed to evaluate four books–Thomas Bouch's Will o' the Wisp and Wandering Voices, *W. H. Abbott's* Vision, *and Griffith Fairfax's* The Horns of Taurus, *as well as* North of Boston–*to Frost's book.*

In its quiet and unsensational way, Mr. Robert Frost's "North of Boston" is the most challenging book of verse that has been published for some time. To the unsophisticated reader it may seem to be an unsophisticated production, the work of a naive and ingenuous mind. Even the innocent reviewer may be beguiled by Mr. Frost's apparent simplicity into forgetting the reviewer's own pet tag about the art which conceals art, mistaking Mr. Frost's assured art for artlessness. Yet, of the four poets now under consideration, Mr. Frost is certainly the most sophisticated. Mr. Bouch and Mr. Abbott have just sufficient sophistication to write pleasant, derivative verse; and even Mr. Fairfax, who has more accomplishment than either, and whose work seldom lacks a scholarly distinction, is not sophisticated enough to conceal his sophistication. He has merely the sophistication of the connoisseur, while Mr. Frost has the sophistication of the artist. Mr. Fairfax has collected poetical phrases in the library; but Mr. Frost has turned the living speech of men and women into poetry. Mr. Fairfax's comparative artlessness is betrayed by his use of artifice, while Mr. Frost's art is revealed by his avoidance of all merely poetical tricks.

> "Crimson, silver, and vair,
> Over the edge of the earth,
> Shifting, shining and rare
> Comes Beauty to birth.
>
> Green is her mantle afloat,
> White the star in her hair,
> The rose red at her throat,
> Crimson, silver and vair."

Thus sings Mr. Fairfax of "Spring," and thus, doubtless, Mr. Frost could sing, if he chose; but I cannot imagine him using words so loosely as to leave even a suspicion in the reader's mind that the poet thought that "vair" was the name of a colour, and that colour green! Nor can I imagine him singling out the rose as a characteristically spring flower.

Hitherto, all the modern American poetry I have come across has been distinguished only by its un-American quality. Indeed, I had come to think there were only two schools of American poets, the Cosmic and the Cosmopolitan. The Cosmic poets, for the main part, still reside in America, where they fill the magazines with poems about "peaks whose floors are shod with rainbows laughing up to God"; while the Cosmopolitan poets live in London, or Paris, and write imitat ion-English, imitation-French, imitation-Latin, imitation-Greek, imitation-Chinese, imitation-Japa nese, and imitation-anything, rather than genuine American poems; though there is hope that, having got as far as Japan, they may go on until they rediscover their native land! But, when they do, they will find that Mr. Frost has been there be-

Edward Thomas, 1913. Until Frost encouraged him to write poetry, Thomas wrote only nonfiction prose.

fore them, making poetry out of the lives of his friends and neighbours in New England. Mr. Frost's poems are American, and they are his own. They are not written according to any arbitrary and exotic formula, though they are in the true tradition of English poetry, which is as much an American inheritance as it is ours. He is individual, without being eccentric. He has become so absorbed in the characters he delineates that he has neither time nor inclination to put on frills, or in any way attract attention to his own originality. The challenge of his work lies in its starkness, in its nakedness of all poetical fripperies. The blank verse in which the tales are written is entirely made up of ordinary speech-phrases, through the medium of which Mr. Frost manages to convey not only the sense of the speakers, but the very tone of their voices. While appreciating the careful and deliberate art which alone could produce this convincing effect of actuality, and all with such a quiet and almost casual air, I am inclined to wonder at times if, in his determination to avoid artifice, Mr. Frost has not discarded too much. There are legitimate excitements, as well as illegitimate, in the enjoyment of verse; and in reading some of these poems I have missed the exhilaration of an impelling and controlling rhythm. And yet there is not a poem in the book that I have not returned to over and over again! To me it seems that "Home Burial" and "The Fear" are the most absolute achievements in the book; but that may only be because they come nearest to the kind of thing I wish to see done in poetry; and the other pieces in the book all contain notable qualities, and qualities which have been too long absent from English verse. Mr. Frost has a keen, humorous sense of character. His characters always make the story, and not the story the characters. Tales that might be mere anecdotes in the hands of another poet take on a universal significance, because of their native veracity and truth to local character. Only by writing about the people he knows personally can a man tell us anything about ourselves or the other people he doesn't know personally.

BOOK REVIEW:
Edward Thomas, Review of *North of Boston, Daily News* (London), 22 July 1914; *A language not to be betrayed: Selected prose of Edward Thomas,* edited by Edna Longley (New York: Persea Books, 1981), pp. 125-127.

Thomas, who supported his wife and three children through free-lance writing, wrote three reviews of North of Boston. *His evaluations were by far the most perceptive of the early assessments of Frost's achievement.*

This is one of the most revolutionary books of modern times, but one of the quietest and least aggressive. It speaks, and it is poetry. It consists of fifteen poems, from fifty to three hundred lines long, depicting scenes from life, chiefly in the country, in New Hampshire. Two neighbour farmers go along the opposite sides of their boundary wall, mending it and speaking of walls and of boundaries. A husband and wife discuss an old vagabond farm servant who has come home to them, as it falls out, to die. Two travellers sit outside a deserted cottage, talking of those who once lived in it, talking until bees in the wall boards drive them away. A man who has lost his feet in a saw-mill talks with a friend, a child, and the lawyer comes from Boston about compensation. The poet himself describes the dreams of his eyes after a long day on a ladder picking apples, and the impression left on him by a neglected woodpile in the snow on an evening walk. All but these last two are dialogue mainly; nearly all are in blank verse.

These poems are revolutionary because they lack the exaggeration of rhetoric, and even at first sight appear to lack the poetic intensity of which rhetoric is an imitation. Their language is free from the poetical words and forms that are the chief material of secondary poets. The metre avoids not only the old-fashioned pomp and sweetness, but the later fashion also of discord and fuss. In fact, the medium is common speech and common decasyllables, and Mr Frost is at no pains to exclude blank verse lines resembling those employed, I think, by Andrew Lang in a leading article printed as prose. Yet almost all these poems are beautiful. They depend not at all on objects commonly admitted to be beautiful; neither have they merely a homely beauty, but are often grand, sometimes magical. Many, if not most, of the separate lines and separate sentences are plain and, in themselves, nothing. But they are bound together and made elements of beauty by a calm eagerness of emotion.

What the poet might have done, could he have permitted himself egoistic rhetoric, we have a glimpse of once or twice where one of his characters tastes a fanciful mood to the full: as where one of the men by the deserted cottage, who has been describing an old-style inhabitant, says:

As I sit here, and often times, I wish
I could be monarch of a desert land
I could devote and dedicate for ever
To the truths we keep coming back and back to.
So desert it would have to be, so walled
By mountain ranges half in summer snow,
No one would covet it or think it worth
The pains of conquering to force change on.
Scattered oases where men dwelt, but mostly
Sand dunes held loosely in tamarisk
Blown over and over themselves in idleness.
Sand grains should sugar in the natal dew
The babe born to the desert, the sand storm
Retard mid-waste my cowering caravans–

There are bees in this wall.' He struck the clapboards,
Fierce heads looked out; small bodies pivoted.
We rose to go. Sunset blazed on the windows.

This passage stands alone. But it is a solitary emotion also that gives him another which I feel obliged to quote in order to hint at the poetry elsewhere spread evenly over whole poems. It is the end of 'The Wood Pile':

I thought that only
Someone who lived in turning to fresh tasks
Could so forget his handiwork on which
He spent himself, the labour of his axe,
And leave it there far from a useful fireplace
To warm the frozen swamp as best it could
With the slow smokeless burning of decay.

The more dramatic pieces have the same beauty in solution, the beauty of life seen by one in whom mystery and tenderness together just outstrip humour and curiosity. This beauty grows like grass over the whole, and blossoms with simple flowers which the reader gradually sets a greater and greater value on, in lines such as these about the dying labourer:

> She put out her hand
> Among the harp-like morning-glory strings
> Taut with the dew from garden bed to eaves,
> As if she played unheard the tenderness
> That wrought on him beside her in the night.
> 'Warren,' she said, 'he has come home to die:
> You needn't be afraid he'll leave you this time.'
> 'Home,' he mocked gently.
> 'Yes, what else but home?
> It all depends on what you mean by home.
> Of course, he's nothing to us, any more
> Than was the hound that came a stranger to us
> Out of the woods, worn out upon the trail.'
> 'Home is the place where, when you have to go there,
> They have to take you in.'
> 'I should have called it
> Something you somehow haven't to deserve.'

The book is not without failures. Mystery falls into obscurity. In some lines I cannot hit upon the required accents. But his successes, like 'The Death of the Hired Man,' put Mr Frost above all other writers of verse in America. He will be accused of keeping monotonously at a low level, because his characters are quiet people, and he has chosen the unresisting medium of blank verse. I will only remark that he would lose far less than most modern writers by being printed as prose. If his work were so printed, it would have little in common with the kind of prose that runs to blank verse: in fact, it would turn out to be closer knit and more intimate than the finest prose is except in its finest passages. It is poetry because it is better than prose.

BOOK REVIEW:
Edward Thomas, Review of *North of Boston, English Review,* 18 (August 1914): 142-143.

This is a collection of dramatic narratives in verse. Some are almost entirely written in dialogue: in only three is the poet a chief character, telling a story, for the most part, in his own words. Thus he has got free from the habit of personal lyric as was, perhaps, foretold by his first book, "A Boy's Will." Already there he had refused the "glory of words" which is the modern poet's embarrassing heritage, yet succeeded in being plain though not mean, in reminding us of poetry without being "poetical." The new volume marks more than the beginning of an experiment like Wordsworth's, but with this difference, that Mr. Frost knows the life of which he writes rather as Dorothy Wordsworth did. That is to say, he sympathises where Wordsworth contemplates. The result is a unique type of eclogue, homely, racy, and touched by a spirit that might, under other circumstances, have made pure lyric on the one hand or drama on the other. Within the space of a hundred lines or so of blank verse it would be hard to compress more rural character and relevant scenery; impossible, perhaps, to do so with less sense of compression and more lightness, unity, and breadth. The language ranges from a never vulgar colloquialism to brief moments of heightened and intense simplicity. There are moments when the plain language and lack of violence make the unaffected verses look like prose, except that the sentences, if spoken aloud, are most felicitously true in rhythm to the emotion. Only at the end of the best pieces, such as "The Death of the Hired Man," "Home Burial," "The Black Cottage," and "The Wood Pile," do we realise that they are masterpieces of deep and mysterious tenderness.

BOOK REVIEW:
Edward Thomas, Review of *North of Boston, New Weekly,* 8 August 1914; *A language not to be betrayed,* pp. 128-130.

This is an original book which will raise the thrilling question, What is poetry? and will be read and re-read for pleasure as well as curiosity, even by those who decide that, at any rate, it is not poetry. At first sight, some will pronounce simply that anyone can write this kind of blank verse, with all its tame common words, straightforward constructions, and innumerable perfectly normal lines. Few that read it through will have been as much astonished by any American since Whitman. Mr Frost owes nothing to Whitman, though had Whitman not helped to sanctify plain labour and ordinary men, Mr Frost might have been different. The colloquialisms, the predominance of conversation (though not one out of fifteen pieces has been printed in dramatic style), and the phrase 'by your leave' (which is an excrescence), may hint at Browning. But I have not met a living poet with a less obvious or more complicated ancestry. Nor is there any brag or challenge about this.

Mr Frost has, in fact, gone back, as Whitman and as Wordsworth went back, through the paraphernalia of poetry into poetry again. With a confidence like genius, he has trusted his conviction that a man will not easily write better than he speaks when some matter has touched him deeply, and he has turned it over until he has no

The Black Cottage

The long grass that flowed in from o'er
The fields all day to her closed door
And lisped about the very sill
Lies dew-drenched, and the elms on high
That rolled all day and tossed and flung
An unseen oriole that sung,
Are with the oriole now still;
And day has passed the cottage by.

And if by guidepost sent astray,
At eventide one passed that way
And paused for sadness, would he guess,
I wonder, by one outward token
The solitary inmate there
Who bows her head with snowy hair
The bread of loneliness to bless
With lips that shape the words unspoken.

Perchance not loveless were she all
Would she but heed the distant call
Of sons who give account of her
Where life and strength and effort stream;
But no, the silence with the rest
The place of memories likes her best,

Manuscript for a lyric version of a dramatic narrative poem published in North of Boston *(Huntington Library). Frost later said that he wrote this lyric, sent to Susan Hayes Ward during his Derry years, and a narrative version of the poem circa 1905. Only three other poems in* North of Boston*–"The Death of the Hired Man," "The Housekeeper," and "Good Hours"–are known to have been written before Frost arrived in England.*

The Black Cottage

Where one was dear before they were
And love made life of girlhood's dream.

No further from the grave is she
Than from those graves her dim eyes see
Across the way beside the wood,
Where all the headstones are of slate
Save only one of marble stone,
And all the names repeat her own
With kindness not to be withstood
And give her but an hour to wait.

Bestarred with fainting fireflies
The pallid meadow mists arise
Tree-high o'er all and with their damp
Release the fragrance of sweet flowers,
And make the weathered cottage old
As black as oozy meadow mould—
The cottage ~~that~~ ~~[illegible]~~ without a lamp
Sinks darkly upon darker hours.

Robert Frost

doubt what it means to him, when he has no purpose to serve beyond expressing it, when he has no audience to be bullied or flattered, when he is free, and speech takes one form and no other. Whatever discipline further was necessary, he has got from the use of the good old English medium of blank verse.

Mr Frost, the reader should be reminded, writes of what he or some country neighbour in New Hampshire has seen or done. Extraordinary things have not been sought for. There is but one death, one case of a man coming home to find the woman flown. There is a story of a doctor who has to share an inn bedroom with a stranger, and enters scared, and is at last terrified almost out of his wits, though the stranger is merely a talkative traveller offering him a hundred collars which he has grown out of. Two farmers talk as they repair the boundary wall between them. A husband and wife talk on the staircase about the child lying buried over there in sight of the house. An old woman discusses her daughter's running away from the man they kept house for. Here is no 'Lucy Grey,' no 'Thorn,' no 'Idiot Boy.' Yet it might be said that Mr Frost sometimes combines an effect resembling Wordsworth's, while he shows us directly less of his own feelings, and more of other people's, than Wordsworth did.

It is drama with a lyric intensity which often borders on magic. A line now and then can be quoted to prove Mr Frost capable of doing what other poets do, as in this description: 'Part of a moon was falling down the west,/Dragging the whole sky with it to the hills . . . ,' or:

> 'There are bees in this wall.' He struck the clapboards,
> Fierce heads looked out; small bodies pivoted.
> We rose to go. Sunset blazed on the windows.

or: 'Cottages in a row/Up to their shining eyes in snow.'

The pieces without dialogue rise up more than once to passages like this about a deserted woodpile in the snow of a swamp:

> No runner tracks in this year's snow looped near it.
> And it was older sure than this year's cutting,
> Or even last year's or the year's before.
> The wood was grey and the bark warping off it,
> And the pile somewhat sunken. Clematis
> Had wound strings round and round it like a bundle.
> What held it though on one side was a tree
> Still growing, and on one a stake and prop,
> These latter about to fall. I thought that only
> Someone who lived in turning to fresh tasks
> Could so forget his handiwork on which
> He spent himself, the labour of his axe,
> And leave it there far from a useful fireplace
> To warm the frozen swamp as best it could
> With the slow smokeless burning of decay.

But the effect of each poem is one and indivisible. You can hardly pick out a single line more than a single word. There are no show words or lines. The concentration has been upon the whole, not the parts. Decoration has been forgotten, perhaps for lack of the right kind of vanity and obsession.

In his first book, *A Boy's Will,* when he was still a comparatively isolated, egotistic poet, eagerly considering his own sensations more than what produced them, he did things far more easily quotable, and among them this piece, entitled 'Mowing':

> There was never a sound beside the wood but one,
> And that was my long scythe whispering to the ground.
> What was it it whispered? I knew not well myself;
> Perhaps it was something about the heat of the sun,
> Something, perhaps, about the lack of sound–
> And that was why it whispered and did not speak.
> It was no dream of the gift of idle hours,
> Or easy gold at the hand of fay or elf:
> Anything more than the truth would have seemed too weak
> To the earnest love that laid the swale in rows,
> Not without feeble-pointed spikes of flowers
> (Pale orchises), and scared a bright green snake.
> The fact is the sweetest dream that labour knows.
> My long scythe whispered and left the hay to make.

Those last six lines do more to define Mr Frost than anything I can say. He never will have 'easy gold at the hand of fay or elf ': he can make fact 'the sweetest dream.'

Naturally, then, when his writing crystallizes, it is often in a terse, plain phrase, such as the proverb, 'Good fences make good neighbours,' or 'Three foggy mornings and one rainy day/Will rot the best birch fence a man can build,' or 'From the time when one is sick to death,/ One is alone, and he dies more alone,' or 'Pressed into service means pressed out of shape.'

But even this kind of characteristic detail is very much less important than the main result, which is a richly homely thing beyond the grasp of any power except poetry. It is a beautiful achievement, and I think a unique one, as perfectly Mr Frost's own as his vocabulary, the ordinary English speech of a man accustomed to poetry and philosophy, more colloquial and idiomatic than the ordinary man dares to use even in a letter, almost entirely lacking the emphatic hackneyed forms of journalists and other rhetoricians, and possessing a kind of healthy, natural delicacy like Wordsworth's, or at least Shelley's, rather than that of Keats.

BOOK REVIEW:
Ezra Pound, "Modern Georgics," *Poetry*, 5 (December 1914): 127-130.

Pound used his review of North of Boston *as a platform for an attack on close-minded American editors, disturbing Frost, who feared that such vituperation would prejudice American publishers against him. Frost had not submitted a book-length manuscript to a publisher before his arrival in England. American magazine editors, however, were not always receptive to his poems. The* Atlantic Monthly, *for example, had found "no place" for Frost's "vigorous verse" when he had sent, from Gloucestershire, several of the poems that were about to be published in* North of Boston.

It is a sinister thing that so American, I might even say so parochial, a talent as that of Robert Frost should have to be exported before it can find due encouragement and recognition.

Even Emerson had sufficient elasticity of mind to find something in the "yawp." One doesn't need to like a book or a poem or a picture in order to recognize artistic vigor. But the typical American editor of the last twenty years has resolutely shut his mind against serious American writing. I do not exaggerate, I quote exactly, when I say that these gentlemen deliberately write to authors that such and such a matter is "too unfamiliar to our readers."

There was once an American editor who would even print me, so I showed him Frost's *Death of the Hired Man*. He wouldn't have it; he printed a weak pseudo-Masefieldian poem about a hired man two months before, one written in a stilted pseudo-literary language, with all sorts of floridities and worn-out ornaments.

Mr. Frost is an honest writer, writing from himself, from his own knowledge and emotion; not simply picking up the manner which magazines are accepting at the moment, and applying it to topics in vogue. He is quite consciously and definitely putting New England rural life into verse. He is not using themes that anybody could have cribbed out of Ovid.

There are only two passion in art; there are only love and hate–with endless modifications. Frost has been honestly fond of the New England people, I dare say with spells of irritation. He has given their life honestly and seriously. He has never turned aside to make fun of it. He has taken their tragedy as tragedy, their stubbornness as stubbornness. I know more of farm life than I did before I had read his poems. That means I know more of "Life."

Mr. Frost has dared to write, and for the most part with success, in the natural speech of New England; in natural spoken speech, which is very different from the "natural" speech of the newspapers, and of many professors. His poetry is a bit slow, but you aren't held up every five minutes by the feeling that you are listening to a fool; so perhaps you read it just as easily and quickly as you might read the verse of some of the sillier and more "vivacious" writers.

A sane man knows that a prose short story can't be much better than the short stories of De Maupassant or of "Steve" Crane. Frost's work is interesting, incidentally, because there has been during the last few years an effort to proceed from the prose short story to the short story in verse. Francis Jammes has done a successful novel in verse, in a third of the space a prose novel would have taken–*Existences* in *La Triomphe de la Vie*. Vildrac and D. H. Lawrence have employed verse successfully for short stories. Masefield is not part of this movement. He has avoided all the difficulties of the immeasurably difficult art of good prose by using a slap-dash, flabby verse which has been accepted in New Zealand. Jammes, Vildrac and Lawrence have lived up to the exigencies of prose and have gained by brevity. This counts with serious artists.

Very well, then, Mr. Frost holds up a mirror to nature, not an oleograph. It is natural and proper that I should have to come abroad to get printed, or that "H. D."–with her clear-cut derivations and her revivifications of Greece–should have to come abroad; or that Fletcher–with his *tic* and his discords and his contrariety and extended knowledge of everything–should have to come abroad. One need not censure the country; it is easier for us to emigrate than for America to change her civilization fast enough to please us. But why, IF there are serious people in America, desiring literature of America, literature accepting present conditions, rendering American life with sober fidelity–why, in heaven's name, is this book of New England eclogues given us under a foreign imprint?

Professors to the contrary notwithstanding, no one expects Jane Austen to be as interesting as Stendhal. A book about a dull, stupid, hemmed-in sort of life, by a person who has lived it, will never be as interesting as the work of some author who has comprehended many men's manners and seen many grades and conditions of existence. But Mr. Frost's people are distinctly real. Their speech is real; he has known them. I don't want much to meet them, but I know that they exist, and what is more, that they exist as he has portrayed them.

Mr. Frost has humor, but he is not its victim. *The Code* has a pervasive humor, the humor of things as they are, not that of an author trying to be funny, or trying to "bring out" the ludicrous phase of some incident or character because he dares not rely on sheer presentation. There is nothing more nauseating to the developed mind than that sort of local buffoonery which the advertisements call "racy"–the village wit presenting some village joke which is worn out everywhere else. It is a great comfort to find someone who tries to give life, the life of the rural district, as a whole, evenly, and not merely as a hook to hang jokes on. The easiest thing to see about a man is an eccentric or worn-out garment, and one is godforsakenly tired of the post-Bret-Hartian, post-Mark-Twainian humorist.

Mr. Frost's work is not "accomplished," but it is the work of a man who will make neither concessions nor pretences. He will perform no money-tricks. His stuff sticks in your head–not his words, nor his phrases, nor his cadences, but his subject matter. You do not confuse one of his poems with another in your memory. His book is a contribution to American literature, the sort of sound work that will develop into very interesting literature if persevered in.

I don't know that one is called upon to judge between the poems in *North of Boston. The Death of the Hired Man* is perhaps the best, or *The Housekeeper*, though here the construction is a bit straggly. There are moments in *Mending Wall. The Black Cottage* is very clearly stated.

BOOK REVIEW:

Amy Lowell, Review of *North of Boston* (American edition), *New Republic*, 2 (20 February 1915): 81-82.

The American edition of North of Boston *was published on 20 February 1915 by Henry Holt, whose wife, Florence Taber Holt, had discovered the book during the previous summer. On the day he and his family arrived in New York from England, Frost found on a newsstand in Grand Central Station the issue of the* New Republic *including this review by Imagist poet Amy Lowell.*

Some six months ago there appeared in London a modest little green-covered book, entitled "North of Boston." It was by an American living in England, so its publication on the other side of the Atlantic came about quite naturally, and was no reflection on the perspicacity of our publishers at home. To those of us who admire Mr. Frost's book it is no small pleasure to take up this new edition, bearing an American imprint, and feel that the stigma of non-comprehension so often put upon us by expatriated Americans can never be justified in this case.

Indeed, Mr. Frost is only expatriated in a physical sense. Living in England he is, nevertheless, saturated with New England. For not only is his work New England in subject, it is so in technique. No hint of European forms has crept into it. It is certainly the most American volume of poetry which has appeared for some time. I use the word American in the way it is constantly employed by contemporary reviewers, to mean work of a color so local as to be almost photographic. Mr. Frost's book is American in the sense that Whittier is American, and not at all in that subtler sense in which Poe ranks as the greatest American poet.

The thing which makes Mr. Frost's work remarkable is the fact that he has chosen to write it as verse. We have been flooded for twenty years with New England stories in prose. The finest and most discerning are the little masterpieces of Alice Brown. She too is a poet in her descriptions, she too has caught the desolation and "dourness" of lonely New England farms, but unlike Mr. Frost she has a rare sense of humor, and that, too, is of New England, although no hint of it appears in "North of Boston." And just because of the lack of it, just because its place is taken by an irony, sardonic and grim, Mr. Frost's book reveals a disease which is eating into the vitals of our New England life, at least in its rural communities.

What is there in the hard, vigorous climate of these states which plants the seeds of degeneration? Is the violence and ugliness of their reli-

Frost in the parlor of his Franconia, New Hampshire, home, 1915. The Frosts lived in this farmhouse, which they bought soon after their return from England, for at least part of each year until September 1920, when they sold it and bought another farm, in South Shaftsbury, Vermont.

gious belief the cause of these twisted and tortured lives? Have the sane, full-blooded men all been drafted away to the cities, or the West, leaving behind only feeble reminders of a once fine stock? The question again demands an answer after the reading of Mr. Frost's book.

Other countries can rear a sturdy peasantry on the soil, a peasantry which maintains itself for generations, heavy and slow perhaps, but strong and self-replenishing; and this for a length of time beside which our New England civilization is as nothing. We are often told that the telephone has done much to decrease insanity in the farming districts, and doubtless it is true. New England winters are long and isolating. But what about Russian winters, Polish, Swedish, Norwegian? After all, the telephone is a very modern invention, and these countries have been rearing a sturdy peasantry for hundreds of years. It is said that the country people of these nations are less highly organized, less well educated, than are New Englanders, and so better able to stand the loneliness of long winters. But this does not explain the great numbers of people, sprung from old New England stock, but not themselves living in remote country places, who go insane.

It is a question for the psychiatrist to answer, and it would be interesting to ask it with "North of Boston" as a text-book to go by. Mr. Frost has reproduced both people and scenery with a vividness which is extraordinary. Here are the huge hills, undraped by any sympathetic legend, felt as things hard and unyielding, almost sinister, not exactly feared, but regarded as in some sort influences nevertheless. Here are great stretches of blueberry pasture lying in the sun; and again, autumn orchards cracking with fruit which it is almost too much trouble to gather. Heavy thunderstorms drench the lonely roads and spatter on the walls of farm-houses rotting in abandonment; and the modern New England town, with narrow frame houses, visited by drummers alone, is painted in all its ugliness. For Mr. Frost's is not the kindly New England of Whittier, nor the humorous and sensible one of Lowell; it is a latter-day New England, where a civilization is decaying to give place to another and very different one.

Mr. Frost does not deal with the changed population, with the Canadians and Finns who are taking up the deserted farms. His people are left-overs of the old stock, morbid, pursued by phantoms, slowly sinking to insanity. In "The Black Cottage" we have the pathos of the abandoned house, after the death of the stern, narrow woman who had lived in it. In "A Servant to Servants" we have a woman already insane once and drifting there again, with the consciousness that her drab, monotonous life is bringing it upon her. "Home Burial" gives the morbidness of death in these remote places; a woman unable to take up her life again when her only child had died. The charming idyll, "After Apple-picking," is dusted over with something uncanny, and "The Fear" is a horrible revelation of those undercurrents which go on as much in the country as in the city, and with remorse eating away whatever satisfaction the following of desire might have brought. That is also the theme of "The Housekeeper," while "The Generations of Men" shows that foolish pride in a useless race which is so strange a characteristic of these people. It is all here–the book is the epitome of a decaying New England.

And how deftly it is done! Take this picture:

We chanced in passing by that afternoon
To catch it in a sort of mental picture
Among tar-banded ancient cherry trees,
Set well back from the road in rank lodged grass,
The little cottage we were speaking of.
A front with just a door between two windows,
Fresh painted by the shower a velvet black.

Or this, of blueberries:

It must be on charcoal they fatten their fruit.
I taste in them sometimes the flavor of soot.
And after all really they're ebony skinned:
The blue's but a mist from the breath of the wind,
A tarnish that goes at a touch of the hand,
And less than the tan with which pickers are tanned.

"The Fear" begins with these lines, and we get not only the picture, but the accompanying noises;

A lantern light from deeper in the barn
Shone on a man and woman in the door
And threw their lurching shadows on a house
Near by, all dark in every glossy window.
A horse's hoof pawed once the hollow floor,
And the back of the gig they stood beside
Moved in a little.

The creak and shift of the wheels is quite plain, although it is not mentioned.

I have said that Mr. Frost's work is almost photographic. The qualification was unnecessary, it is photographic. The pictures, the characters, are reproduced directly from life, they are burnt into his mind as though it were a sensitive plate. He gives out what has been put in, unchanged by any personal mental process. His imagination is bounded by what he has seen, he is confined within the limits of his experience (or at least what might have been his experience) and bent all one way like the windblown trees of New England hillsides.

In America we are always a little late in following artistic leads. "Les Soirées de Médun," and all Zola's long influence, are passing away in Europe. In England, even such a would-be realist as Masefield lights his stories with bursts of a very rare imagination. No such bursts flame over Mr. Frost's work. He tells you what he has seen *exactly* as he has seen it. And in the word *exactly* lies the half of his talent. The other half is a great and beautiful simplicity of phrase, the inheritance of a race brought up on the English Bible. Mr. Frost's work is not in the least objective. He is not writing of people whom he has met in summer vacations, who strike him as interesting, and whose life he thinks worthy of perpetuation. Mr. Frost writes as a man under the spell of a fixed idea. He is as racial as his own puppets. One of the great interests of the book is the uncompromising New Englander it reveals. That he could have written half so valuable a book had such not been the case I very much doubt. Art is rooted in the soil, and only the very greatest men can be both cosmopolitan and great. Mr. Frost is as New England as Burns is Scotch, Synge Irish, or Mistral Provençal.

And Mr. Frost has chosen his medium with an unerring sense of fitness. As there is no rare and vivid imaginative force playing over his subjects, so there is no exotic music pulsing through his verse. He has not been seduced into subtleties of expression which would be painfully out of place. His words are simple, straightforward, direct, manly, and there is an elemental quality in all he does which would surely be lost if he chose to pursue niceties of phrase. He writes in classic metres in a way to set the teeth of all the poets of the older schools on edge; and he writes in classic metres, and uses inversions and *clichés* whenever he pleases, those devices so abhorred by the newest generation. He goes his own way, regardless of anyone else's rules, and the result is a book of unusual power and sincerity.

The poems are written for the most part in blank verse, blank verse which does not hesitate to leave out a syllable or put one in, whenever it feels like it. To the classicist such liberties would be unendurable. But the method has its advantages. It suggests the hardness and roughness of New England granite. It is halting and maimed, like the life it portrays, unyielding in substance, and broken in effect.

Mr. Frost has done that remarkable thing, caught a fleeting epoch and stamped it into print. He might have done it as well in prose, but I do not think so, and if the book is not great poetry, it is nevertheless a remarkable achievement.

MEMOIR:
From Bygones: The Recollections of Louis Untermeyer (New York: Harcourt, Brace & World, 1965), pp. 46-49.

One of Frost's most enduring friendships was with poet Louis Untermeyer, whose memoir Bygones *includes a description of his first meeting with Frost, in May 1915.*

I had discovered Robert Frost when I was twenty-eight. I discovered him on the wrong continent. Thanks to a close friendship with William Rose Benét, at that time a junior editor on the *Century Magazine*, the Century Company had published–and paid for–my first professional volume of poetry, *Challenge*, which lived up to its title by being composed chiefly of high-pitched poems of protest. I sent copies abroad. I had extended my geographical range by corresponding with J. M. Synge and such English poets as Thomas Hardy, Harold Monro, W. W. Gibson, and Lascelles Abercrombie.

It was in the December, 1913, issue of Monro's quarterly, *Poetry and Drama*, that I encountered the name of Robert Frost. It was signed to two poems, "The Fear" and "A Hundred Collars." Seeing them in what seemed an exclusively British Magazine, I assumed that they were written by an Englishman, and expressed my surprise that any "foreigner" could so graphically communicate the air and idiom of New England. Lascelles Abercrombie soon disabused me; he told me how Frost had come from New Hampshire to become his and Gibson's neighbor near the Gloucestershire border. He had come for two reasons: because he could not make a living either at farming or at writing, in the United States, and because his wife wanted to live for a while "under thatch."

Frost had heard my name long before I knew his. "I was already feeling a good deal acquainted with you," he said after we became friends, "from having heard your name so often mentioned under a certain thatch roof in Ryton, Dymock, Gloucestershire, England," which happened to be the cottage Lascelles Abercrombie had grimly called, as "a last resort," The Gallows. "Your critique of my *Emblems of Love* is not only the most gratifying review the book has had, but it is also the first notice it has received in America," Abercrombie had written. "As an insufficient quid pro quo let me thank you for you own book of poems and let me answer your inquiry about Robert Frost. He is my friend and neighbor, but he does not belong to us. On the contrary, he belongs to you, for he is an American, a New Englander by way of California, where he was born by a freak of circumstance. It is odd that he should be in England at all, although he seems at home here, odder that his first book should be issued by the French widow of an English publisher in London, so far from his native habitat . . . . "

Frost's first book, *A Boy's Will*–the title taken from a line of one of Frost's favorite poems, Longfellow's "My Lost Youth"–was the second to be published in the United States. It appeared after the success of *North of Boston*, also published in England, had convinced Henry Holt and Company that Frost was a safe commercial risk. The publisher's faith (or gambling instinct) was justified. Between 1914 and 1961 *North of Boston*, separately and as part of the *Collected Poems*, sold well over nine hundred thousand copies, and Frost's eighth book of poems, the slender *In the Clearing*, became an immediate best seller; eighty thousand copies were sold within six months.

My review of *North of Boston*, in which I aped Emerson's salute to Whitman by hailing Frost at the beginning of a great career, was one of the first things to greet the poet upon his return to America in February, 1915. We met a few weeks later. I was twenty-nine; he was forty-one.

The character of Frost's background was in his features. In his old age it was a chiseled stone face, but even in youth the bones seemed made of New Hampshire granite or Vermont marble; the skin had the look of alabaster. It was, how-

The Frost family visiting in Bridgewater, New Hampshire, 1915. Lesley and Irma are kneeling with Marjorie and Carol seated in front of them

ever, anything but a cold face. The eyes, deep-set and the palest possible blue, were quizzically alert; the mouth, with its bee-stung lower lip, was frankly sensuous. He was inordinately shy. Recognition of the poet had been belated; as a result, he was unusually vulnerable, fearful of even a private appearance.

The first time I heard any of Frost's poems read aloud was when he read them at a small social gathering in Malden, Massachusetts. He read them badly. He was, he said, "too exposed," too conscious of being exhibited, too unused to the role of the poet in public. Half a century has gone by and much has been mercifully or happily forgotten, but I remember that evening with the greatest clarity: the proper Bostonians, fashionably dressed, listening with a mixture of curiosity, skepticism, and tolerance to a "rustic" from the Northeast Corner who had teased the imagination of the metropolis; Frost, declining to comment on his work, reciting or, as he called it, "saying" a couple of lyrics and a few of the monologues from *North of Boston*, refusing to be quaint (he was deeply offended when someone introduced him as "our farmer-poet"), and underplaying, actually throwing away, line after line. His readings, like his poems, were the essence of understatement.

It was an incredible contrast to his later appearances when, again and again, he would charm packed audiences not only with poems his listeners knew by heart but also with roaming commentaries, lightly profound and seriously playful, full of unexpected twists of thought, a verbal legerdemain which he manipulated with the skill and glee of a virtuoso actor who enjoyed acting.

We became friends at once. The almost four-hundred-page volume *The Letters of Robert Frost to Louis Untermeyer*, published in 1963, not quite a year after his death, is both the record of a long friendship and the portrait of a man and his mind. It is also, though it was never intended to be, a gradually unfolding and completely unguarded autobiography. The many faces of Frost (the sly teaser, the tormented man, the farmer who had failed, the poet who had been denied an audience) and the many facets of the person (the large aims and the small irritations, the torturing sensitivities, the malicious hurts and the grim stoicism) were already there at forty.

At forty Robert was sure of his poetry but unsure of himself. After years of neglect–publishers had found his talk-flavored poetry too plain, too "unpoetic" for poetry–he was not put at ease by sudden success. On the contrary. The countless honors that came later could never compensate for the long, lonely times when he had to suffer the humiliation of being a failure. He was afraid that he might be only a temporary fashion; he hated being regarded as a peculiar phenomenon, a rural idiosyncrasy with an odd idiom. He remembered how such bucolic poets as Burns and Clare had become a season's vogue, and he dreaded being dropped for some other "novelty." These were not unnatural fears, suspicions, jealousies. Assurance came slowly. After rejecting some of his early poems–"we regret that the *Atlantic* has no place for your vigorous verse"–the same magazine printed the same poems as soon as the poet's importance had been acknowledged. Honorary degrees were to descend upon him. The "drop-out" who had been unwilling to graduate from two universities would be invited to be "poet in residence" at a dozen institutions of learning. The awards, honors, and prizes were to pile up, but even at forty he was writing to me with that combination of wry badinage and bitter wisdom which characterize his later work.

BOOK REVIEW:

Louis Untermeyer, Review of *North of Boston, Chicago Evening Post,* 23 April 1915, p. 11.

Though Untermeyer's review of North of Boston *was published before he met Frost, it did not appear as early as Untermeyer recalled in his memoir. Next to his review in the* Chicago Evening Post *was an article about Frost by the newspaper's literary editor, Llewellyn Jones, who discussed* A Boy's Will, *which was published in the United States by Holt in late April 1915.*

With or without all technical and esthetic considerations, this book of Robert Frost's stirs me tremendously. It stirs me from such a bald statement to even balder superlatives. I have little respect–literary respect–for anyone who can read the shortest of these poems without feeling the skill and power in them. But I have far more respect for the man who can see nothing at all in this volume than for him who, discovering many other things in it, cannot see the poetry in it. For that attitude represents a theory of poetry as false as it is doctrinaire. And also as common. Even some of Mr. Frost's most ardent adherents begin and end their praises by saying, with a more or less deprecatory gesture, "Whether this is poetry or not" . . . or, even more frequently, "While this may not be poetry in the strict sense. . . ." And so on, to less cautious stammerings.

Waiving that nebulous and glib phrase concerning "the strict sense" which screens nothing behind its pomposity, it is the very misapprehension of an art that misleads the well-meaning and wary. For poetry has more than one function, one manifestation and one standard. The touchstone test applied to poetry is about as satisfactory as measuring a twisting river with an inflexible yardstick. So when one comes with his inched-off and ruled notions of let us say, "glamour," he is very likely to find none of it here. But if he throws away his measuring rod he is apt to find something else in its place; something which I think is a sterner but even more genuine sort of "glamour."

There is, for instance, a lack of "poetic" figures and phrases in this volume; a lack of regard for the outlines and fragility of the medium; a lack of finesse, of nicely rounded rhetoric or raptures. But altho these are all the property and perquisites of even the greatest poets, Mr. Frost neglects them–and still writes poetry. I cannot recall a single obviously "poetic" line in "A Hundred Collars" or "The Self-Seeker"–to take two dissimilar poems–and yet the sum total of these two is undeniably poetic. In no particular thing that has been said, but rather in the retrospect, the afterglow, is it most apparent. The effect rather than the statement is poetry; the air is almost electric with it.

Not that Mr. Frost cannot write colorful and sharp images. He can and does. But only when the mood rises to demand them: they are not dragged in by the hair or used as a peg to hang a passage on. Here, for instance, in the midst of "The Death of the Hired Man" (possibly the roundest and most poignant thing in the book) is this bit:

> Part of a moon was falling down the west,
> Dragging the whole sky with it to the hills.
> Its light poured softly in her lap. She saw
> And spread her apron to it. She put out her hand
> Among the harplike morning-glory strings,
> Taut with the dew from garden bed to eaves,
> As if she played unheard the tenderness
> That wrought on him beside her in the night.

There is another thing that poetry can do and that Mr. Frost's work does. And that is to crystallize. Poetry is removed from prose not only because it tells a thing more nobly but more quickly. A disciple of Dr. Jung could never have summed up the force of psycho-analysis in less than a quarto volume; James Oppenheim prophetically synthesizes and reflects it all in eight pages of "The Unborn." You will find most of Professor Whicher's imposing "Faery Myths" in Keats' "Belle Dame sans Merci." The Japanese have some of their most vivid tragedies told in poems of seventeen syllables. . . . . And so when Robert Frost tells a story or sketches a character, the use of the poetic line gives it a clarity that is made sharper by its brevity.

This all, as a consideration from the lesser and more craftsmanlike standpoint. Apart from its poetic content, these fifteen poems glow with their honest, first-hand apprehension of life. It is New England life that is here: the atmosphere and idiom of it. The color, and for that matter the absence of color, is as faithfully reproduced as is that of the Arran Islands in the plays of Synge and the racy Paris slang in the ballades of Villon. Behind the persons in these poems one can feel a people. Often this sense of character is keenest when the person is suggested rather than drawn. Now that I think of it, it occurs to me that some of Mr. Frost's finest characterizations do not speak; they do not even appear. The high-hearted adventurer, for instance, in "The Wood-pile" (a lesser poet would have bungled the theme; or, more likely, would never have seen it); that unknown, careless rover, continually turning to fresh tasks. Or the tired, incompetent hired man, a mediocrity typical enough to be tragic. Or that positive, tight-lipped old lady in "The Black Cottage."

On the other hand, take, as an example of pure delineative power, the first brief poem. In "Mending Wall" you have, in two pages, the gait, the impress, the very souls of two people. The poem is in the first person and in the alternate whimsy and a something like natural anarchy one gets a full-length portrait of one. The other person has just one line–repeated: but the portrait is no less full. He is drawn as completely as tho the artist had put in every wrinkle and trouser-crease. . . . And it is after one has put the volume down that the power of these people persists–and becomes something bigger. One feels that one has perceived beneath the opposition of two men, the struggle of two forces as primal as Order and Revolution.

All of which is neither as fanciful or as rhetorical as it sounds, and Mr. Frost would be the first to disclaim any vatic intentions. At least I hope he would for his power lies not alone in his directness, but in his avoidance of making his figures and landscapes metaphysical, symbolic or in any way larger than they are. For sheer dramatic feeling I know few scenes tenser than "The Fear," with its vague, suggestive background. Nor do I know many novels disclosing the brooding insanity that springs from the stark and lonely rigors of farm life, as well as "A Servant to Servants." There's humor in Frost, too. "The Code" has a big-shouldered kind of it. And "Blueberries" has a lesser tho more genial shade. It is impossible to quote scraps of these poems; it is, owing to the proverbial exigencies of space, equally impossible to quote an entire poem. Besides, these poems should be read in batches and out loud. Most poems should, for that matter, but these, particularly, because of their colloquial flow and their conversational give-and-take, call for the tongue. And, incidentally, the nasal twang, if one can manage it.

As the last-paragraph kind of climax it should be insisted that Mr. Frost's work is indigenous and as American as Whitman's. And, outside of the fact that he is much more local and much less rhapsodic than Whitman, there is, it is true, a decided bond between them. There is the same clear sight, honesty of expression, freedom from pose and old patterns (patterns either of speech or thought) and fidelity to his times.

ARTICLE:

William Stanley Braithwaite, "A Poet of New England: Robert Frost a New Exponent of

Life," *Boston Evening Transcript*, 28 April 1915, III:4.

Early in March 1915 Frost went to Boston, where he visited Amy Lowell and found himself lionized by the local literati, among them Atlantic Monthly *editor Ellery Sedgwick, whose magazine had rejected some of the poems he was now praising. One of the literary critics Frost met was William Stanley Braithwaite, poetry editor for the* Boston Evening Transcript *and editor of an annual* Anthology of Magazine Verse, *who subsequently wrote two enthusiastic articles about Frost and included Frost poems in his anthologies. The first of his articles is reprinted here.*

Under the surface of New England art is New England life, and this life has been adumbrated in the best poetry wherever it has been created throughout the country during the last forty years. A localized New England art, I am speaking now of verse, really ceased more than a generation ago. Half a century of the famous New England poets never did more than scratch the surface of this life. Emerson went a little deeper than his contemporaries, but he brought up water instead of soil; Whittier went wider in all directions from the centre but he never fertilized the ground for anything better than a staple poetic crop. In all matters of expression these poets kept pretty closely to the traditional methods of the English poets, and achieving the ordinary they let the best of the unique material which lay about them go by without getting into their verse. It took the generation of novelists and storytellers succeeding them to show what New England life and character really was like. Hawthorne in their midst really saw and knew New England life and character, but he took it in its invisible and not visible aspects and left us with a sense of light rather than substance. But Howells and James, Sarah Orne Jewett, Mary E. Wilkins and Alice Brown gave us the fabric of New England, with all its qualities of inner and outer existence, moral and social, individually and collectively.

The natural expression of New England, however, is a poetic expression. And poetry is coming back to New England as its natural voice. Since 1870 there can be no doubt that Aldrich was the most considerable poet with the New England substance in his work. But he was a perfect craftsman rather than an illuminating perceptor of life. One came after him much later, who is today our foremost poet in whom the very fundamental substance of New England life burns with extraordinary intensity. This poet is Edwin Arlington Robinson, who has localized the New England environment in the mythical Tilbury Town of his poems, and the essence of the New England spirit in those strange characters that make up the masculine gallery of his work. There comes now another poet to help Robinson uphold the poetic supremacy of New England: one in whose veins as in Robinson's flows generations of New England blood, and who like him has evoked from the New England tradition an art that is once native and new, and through whose individual expression we get an entirely new value of the homely dramatic, psychologic and simply human sense of this life. This poet is Robert Frost.

Mr. Frost's first book, "A Boy's Will," appeared in England in 1913. Last year his second book, "North of Boston," was also brought out in England, and was immediately acclaimed by all the authoritative English critics as an achievement "much finer, much more near the ground and much more national, in the true sense, than anything that Whitman gave the world." It must be remembered that Mr. Frost had no influence to attract this critical attention except what the work itself commanded. He has accomplished what no other American poet of this generation has accomplished, and that is, unheralded, unintroduced, untrumpeted, he has won the acceptance of an English publisher on his own terms, and the unqualified approbation of a voluntary English criticism. These two volumes have been recently reprinted in America, almost simultaneously with Mr. Frost's return to his home in New Hampshire after several years' absence in England.

Though Mr. Frost's two books were published in two consecutive years, they represent a more divergent period of development. The earlier book expresses an individuality, the later interprets a community. Completely as "A Boy's Will" performs its nature in the lyrical demonstration of an individual who attempts to account for himself and emotional experiences in a social scheme he tries to understand and define, its greatest spiritual and human value is a preparation for the more wonderful analysis of the objective experiences of life which the poet limns in "North of Boston." As is shown, the two books really represent two points of view, and between the two there is a very startling contrast in both method and substance. What the first essentially represents is shown in the first book in a piece called "Mowing":

> There was never a sound beside the wood but one,
> And that was my long scythe whispering to the ground.
> What was it it whispered? I knew not well myself;
> Perhaps it was something about the heat of the sun,
> Something, perhaps, about the lack of sound–
> And that was why it whispered and did not speak.
> It was no dream of the gift of idle hours,
> Or easy gold at the hand of fay or elf:
> Anything more than truth would have seemed too weak
> To the earnest love that laid the swale in rows,
> Not without feeble–pointed spikes of flowers
> (Pale orchises), and scared a bright green snake.
> The fact is the sweetest dream that labor knows.
> My long scythe whispered and left the hay to make.

But he had come to realize a different philosophy which is indicated in the opening poem called "Mending Wall," in "North of Boston." It was a philosophy rather of art than of substance; the substance would include too many terms that make up the quality of life as it touched the rural community and farm life of New England to be reduced to a word.

Now on its technical side the blank verse poems, with nearly always a story of New England farm life, in "North of Boston," is clearly against the tradition of blank verse. In the first place it is not literary. That is, the language of these poems is not the language of literature, but the speech of life and a very particular quality of life and its special influences. It has, nevertheless, been common for poets to strive and achieve this effect of vernacular speech, but both the beauty and the vitality of Mr. Frost's accomplishment in molding this veracious utterance of his types into a significant and new form of verse is that the meaning has the same absolute actually and intimacy with life as the tones of words have with the voice. The result of this thoroughly sincere and artistic effort to enhance a more closely knit idiomatic speech into art, by giving heat and force to its substance, I should say, will at first be a little puzzling to the reader until he has caught the perfect rhythm of its undermeaning. The reader must recognize the fact, as an English critic truthfully remarked, it is poetry that is changed by development rather than by rebellion. And in so doing it has lost nothing, in spite of having lost the decorative modulations in metrical effect to which we have been accustomed in verse, of the patterned texture in which all the qualities of the emotions are reproduced. These blank verse narratives of New England farm life are naturally of course, set in the very emphasis of natural features: the landscape with its woods, rocks, meadows and hills, flowers and berries, rain and clouds and sunlight, the presence of these familiarly known and passionately loved things, show how Mr. Frost so nearly completely preoccupied with the greyness of his human environment can weave out of this same vigorous actuality of speech and meaning vivid and picturesque moods full of mystery and beauty.

For all his hard substance of human circumstance in these narratives Mr. Frost is an idyllist. The poems are always in the form of dialogue or soliloquy, and the rendering in its significance is always psychological. The very spirit of Theocritus for the first time pervades through Mr. Frost our New England farms and meadows. The atmosphere of the bucolic life has never been so delicately transported into literature by an American poet before. In spite of all the other qualities which make Mr. Frost's poems remarkable, it is this natural delicacy of vision which gives a tone to the atmosphere which envelops the undertone of his subjects. Take the passage from "The Generations of Men," that delightful idyl of the gathering of the descendants of the Stark families in reunion at the home of the original Stark, when two members hithero unknown to each other fall in love. The day of the celebration it rained and only two, a young man and a young girl, ventured out and met upon the road in a secluded spot. They had introduced themselves as possessing Stark blood, and the intimacy progressed along lines of a common interest until the young man worked up under the feminine spell of his companion plays with fantasy, and says:

> From the sense of our having been together–
> But why take time for what I'm like to hear?
> I'll tell you what the voices really say.
> You will do very well right where you are
> A little longer. I mustn't feel too hurried,
> Or I can't give myself to hear the voices.
> Is this some trance you are withdrawing into?
> You must be very still; you mustn't talk.
> I'll hardly breathe.
> The voices seem to say–
> I'm waiting.
> Don't! The voices seem to say:
> Call her Nausicaas, the unafraid
> Of an acquaintance made adventurously.
> I let you say that–on consideration.

The Franconia, New Hampshire, farm house that the Frosts bought after their return to the United States in 1915

> I don't see very well how you can help it.
> You want the truth. I speak but by the voices.
> You see they know I haven't had your name.
> Though what a name should matter between us–
> I shall suspect–
> Be good. The voices say:
> Call her Nausicaas, and take a timber
> That you shall find lies in the cellar charred
> Among the raspberries and hew and shape it
> For a door-sill or other corner piece
> In a new cottage on the ancient spot.
> The life is not yet all gone out of it.
> And come and make your summer dwelling here,
> And perhaps she will come, still unafraid,
> And sit before you in the open door
> With flowers in her lap until they fade,
> But not come in across the sacred sill–

And the young girl realizing, no doubt around her heart as showing in the catch of her voice, the significance of his words, replies in the beginning of her speech,

> I wonder where your oracle is tending.
> You can see that there's something wrong with it,
> Or it would speak in dialect. . . .

Though this poem is a favorite of mine, it is only a lighter and fairer toned idyl among the others of this book. Such a one as "The Death of the Hired Man," grimly realistic as it is, has been highly praised, but "A Hundred Dollars," in which the humor of a man of learning sharing the same bedroom with a garrulous newspaper agent makes a delightful comedy, "Home Burial," in which the callousness of a father burying his only child brings out the poignant difference in the sensibility of the father and mother and the feeling of bitter antagonism killing the love of the wife for the husband, "Blueberries," an exquisitely rhymed pastoral of a family living on the foraged bounty of the fields, "A Servant to Servant," in which an overburdened farmer's wife talks until she suggests to the reader that her life is lived under the shadow of inherited lunacy, and other such poems as "The Housekeeper," "The Bear," "The Self-Seeker," all prove that not only is there still an inexhaustible store of material in New England life, but that Mr. Frost is the first poet for half a century to express it completely with a fresh, original and appealing way of his own. By it he places himself with almost a single achievement in the very front rank of contemporary American poets.

COLUMN:
From William Dean Howells, "Editor's Easy Chair," *Harper's Magazine*, 131 (September 1915): 634-637.

While some critics wondered why Frost did not write his dramatic narratives in free verse or even prose, the Dean of American Letters praised Frost's use of blank verse while criticizing the vers libre of his contemporaries, including that of Edgar Lee Masters, with whom less perceptive critics frequently linked Frost.

If we could believe the publishers (and we are far from wishing to dispute them) we are in the presence of such a poetic sunburst as has not flashed upon the world within something like a geological period. They assure the reader of the fact from the covers of a good third of the sixteen or seventeen volumes of recent verse at hand, and if not from all it may be because all publishers cannot give way to their feelings in equal measure. Or, one may not have so many feelings as another, though he may be of the same emotional make; and it is to be considered that perhaps these avowals on the book covers are less the expression of passionate admiration than of an ardor for publicity. What is to be said in favor of them is that the purposing purchaser cannot complain in any instance that he does not know what he is getting. Our own case is a little different, and as an habitually appreciative critic, we have to lament that our praise has been taken out of our mouths; our friendly phrases come to our pens tarnished with use from the publisher's glowing hands, and we are at loss what to say of poets and poetry already so sung, so sounded, so, as it were, dinned into us. Not that we blame the authors any more than the publishers. The poets could not help being so wonderful, and the publishers could not help wondering at them, but quite the same we find ourselves a little disabled by the situation, and we have to arm ourselves for something more than our customary justice in dealing with these young poets, though they have been already so bountifully recognized at their great worth, they must not have one of our carefully chosen, hand-painted adjectives the less. The time was when their praise would not have been lavish, so confident, so authoritative, from the trade; but now all is new. New outside as well as inside their books, and the Easy Chair must not grumble, as Easy Chair are apt to do, with or without reason, merely from getting on in years.

But *is* all so new inside these books, which came to us, rustling in this tinsel of compliment, this machine-lace of professional glorification? We say no; there is a good deal of the eternal beautiful which cannot put on even a new form, however it would come masking in novel phase. The best things in the new poets are of the oldest form, and where some of the second-best brave it in the fashions which are supposed new, after all it is only a reversion to the novelties of an earlier day. There is much straining in several of the books for the mechanical emancipation of *vers libre*; but Walt Whitman broke loose sixty years ago, and before him the Proverbial Philosophy of Martin Farquhar Tupper danced in the rhythm of David's psalmody. Until now, in fact, *vers libre* has been rhythmical, and it had remained only for what we may call the shredded prose of the new poets to attest their newness in that at least. But, no, are they new even in that? We have not forgotten the *Black Riders* of Stephen Crane, very powerful things in the beat of their short lines, rhymeless, meterless. Yet were they quite shredded prose, like Miss Amy Lowell's *vers libre*, in her *Sword Blades and Poppy Seeds*, or the epitaphs of Mr. Edgar Lee Master's *Spoon River Anthology?* Not quite, however, for though the *Black Riders* did not prance or curvet, they did somehow march; they did keep time as prose never does at it best.

It is when Miss Lowell permits herself to rhyme and to measure her verse that we are most aware of her being indeed a poet with something to say, something to make us feel. It is when the strong thinking of Mr. Masters makes us forget the formlessness of his shredded prose that we realize the extraordinary worth of his work. It is really something extraordinary, that truth about themselves which his dead folk speak from their village graveyard; for it is the truth about the human nature of us, if not the whole truth about our respective lives. We should say that we were some of us better than those dead folk, though some of us are as much worse as can be. Yet as to the form of their record, it is shredded prose without even a slow, inscriptional pulse in it, and we doubt if it will last, for a witness of the civic and ethical quality of our time, as a long as the rhymes of Uncle Walt Mason, beaten merrily out on his typewriter, and day by day testifying to our nature, by no means altogether fallen. His rhymes wear the mask of prose, just as the poetry of Mr. Masters wears the mask of verse; but neither of them has the sound of the spiritual verity which the exalted phrase of the great Emily Dickinson bore to the reader's soul, with its proud unheed of whether it was prose or verse.

Frost with Lesley (top left), Marjorie (center), Carol (top right), and two unidentified friends on Mount Lafayette, in the Franconia Mountains of New Hampshire, circa 1916

Freak for freak, we prefer compressed verse to shredded prose, but because both of these are freak things we will not decide whether Uncle Walt will be more enduring than Mr. Masters. We merely speak here of their respective truth to our human nature and our American mood of it. Prophecy is not our job, or not our present job, but we have a fancy that when it comes to any next book of shredded prose it will not be so eagerly welcomed as some next book of Mr. Robert Frost's or Mr. Dana Burnet's. Mr. Frost's volumes, *A Boy's Will* and *North of Boston*, have already made their public on both sides of the Atlantic, and they merit the favor they have won. They are very genuinely and unaffectedly expressive of rustic New England, and of its deeps as well as it shallows. We should say the earlier book sings rather the most, but youth is apt to sing most, and there is strong, sweet music in them both. Here is no *vers libre*, no shredded prose, but very sweet rhyme and pleasant rhythm, though it does not always keep step (wilfully breaks step at times, we should say), but always remains faithful to the lineage of poetry that danced before it walked. When we say Mr. Frost's work is unaffectedly expressive of New England life, we do not mean that it is unconsciously expressive; we do not much believe in unconscious art, and we rather think that his fine intelligence tingles with a sense of that life and beautifully knows what it is at in dealing with it. If we may imagine the quality of Sarah Orne Jewett and Miss Mary Wilkins and Miss Alice Brown finding metrical utterance, we shall have such pleasure in characterizing Mr. Frost's poetry as comes to us from knowing what things are by knowing what they are like; but this knowledge by no means unlocks the secret of his charm, and it does not adequately suggest the range of his very distinctive power. His manly power is manliest in penetrating to the heart of the womanhood in that womanliest phase of it, the New England phase. Dirge, or idyl, or tragedy, or comedy, or burlesque, it is always the skill of the artist born and artist trained which is at play, or call it work, for our delight. Amidst the often striving and straining of the new poetry, here is the old poetry as young as ever; and new only in extending the bounds of sympathy through the recorded to the unrecorded knowledge of humanity. One might have thought there was not much left to say of New England humanity, but here it is as freshly and keenly sensed as if it had been felt before, and imparted in study and story with a touch as sure and a courage as loyal as if the poet dealt with it merely for the joy of it.

But of course he does not do that. He deals with it because he must master it, must impart it just as he must possess it. . . .

INTERVIEW:
"Poetry of Axe Handles," *Philadelphia Public Ledger,* 4 April 1916, p. 11; *Interviews with Robert Frost,* pp. 18-21.

After a shaky start at reading his poems in public, Frost gradually became more at ease in front of audiences, and in early 1916 he went on the first of many reading tours. In Philadelphia during April of that year he talked about a poem-in-progress, "The Ax-Helve," which was first published a year and a half later, in the September 1917 issue of the Atlantic Monthly.

Rule number one for poets who hope some day to duplicate the success Robert Frost, poet of the granite-hilled farms of the White Mountains, has achieved in his *North of Boston* is "Never larrup an emotion. Set yourself against the moon. Resist the moon. If the moon's going to do anything to you, it's up to the moon."

Mr. Frost has wind-blown cheeks and clear blue eyes. He's a Yankee of Yankees and glad of it, even though eminent critics of the stamp of Edward Garnett haven't hesitated to rank him with Theocritus and Wordsworth as a delineator of pastoral life in such of his poignant poems as "The Death of the Hired Man" and "Home Burial."

Fresh from his farm on Sugar Hill, Franconia, New Hampshire, where Mt. Lafayette towers and the Old Man of the Mountains frowns, Mr. Frost is paying his first visit to Philadelphia. Quite recently he's been skiing over rugged country, tapping maple trees, and shaping up new poems.

Mr. Frost lolled back in a comfortable chair at the Art Club yesterday and talked of one of these new poems–not because he's writing it, for he's very shy in speaking of his work, but because it illustrates his grip on humanity the world over. It's a poem that concerns an axe-handle.

"The thing you hate in poetry is segregated stuff–like love, the moon, and murder," he said.

He lighted a cigarette, commenting that he had learned cigarette smoking in England, where one of his cronies was Rupert Brooke, most promising of young English poets, who lost his life at the front.

"Love, the moon, and murder have poetry in them by common consent. But it's in other places. It's in the axe-handle of a French Canadian woodchopper, and it's in 'poultry-stricken ground' (quoting John Masefield).

"You know the Canadian woodchoppers whittle their axe-handles, following the curve of the grain, and they're strong and beautiful. Art should follow lines in nature, like the grain of an axe-handle. False art puts curves on things that haven't any curves.

"We think the word 'provincial' is a shameful word here in America. But it is [the] Englishman's pride. You can't be universal without being provincial, can you? It's like trying to embrace the wind."

It wasn't so very many months ago that Mr. Frost "arrived." He is a man of about forty-five years and has a wife and four children living in his little farmhouse on Sugar Hill. Near him are the White Mountain homes of Prof. Cornelius Weygandt of the University of Pennsylvania and Justice Robert von Moschzisker.

The poet is staying here with Dr. Weygandt. He was entertained at luncheon at the Art Club yesterday by the Justice. He spoke last night in Germantown and reads at four o'clock this afternoon before the Arts Association of the University.

The recognition that has come to him as a successful and powerful poet is perhaps best indicated by the fact that he has been selected as this year's Phi Beta Kappa poet at Harvard. The magazines are clamoring for his work, and the colleges and universities want him as much–even more, since he is an American–as they wanted John Masefield or Alfred Noyes.

Mr. Frost is simplicity itself, a strong man, a direct man–a man who believes, as he says, that America needs poets who "get tight-up to things." He detests what he calls "guide-book poetry." He admits that he is a poor farmer. He believes, strange as it may sound, that Puritanism "hasn't yet had its day, and it might be fun to set it up as an artistic doctrine."

Speaking of Puritanism, Mr. Frost has no use for "easy criers and weepers."

"Which is the more terrible," he asks, "a man or a woman weeping? The men, of course. That's Puritanism."

He intends to be "more of a farmer" than he is, but never a "kid-glove or gentleman farmer."

"My country," he says, "is a milk and sugar country. We get what runs from the trees and what runs from the cows. You can't do much real farming, for we have frost every month in the year. You know, the White Mountain farmers say they have nine months of winter and three months of late-in-the-fall!" He laughed as he recalled his struggles with the granite soil.

If anything more than a reading of Mr. Frost's poem "Home Burial" (in which a rugged father buries his child in the yard of his farmhouse) is needed to convince everyone that he's a Yankee to the backbone, he will admit that his ancestors found New Hampshire back in 1630.

"One of them was an Indian fighter, and a cunning one," he says. "He invited the Indians to a barbecue. They stacked their arms, and he promptly killed them. Unfortunately for that ancestor, he didn't kill all of them. A few who were left came back after him on a Sunday morning after he'd finished praying, and got even." [. . .]

Mr. Frost had a very bad grudge against "guide-book poetry" yesterday. It was so bad that he gave a couple of very bad examples of it, dictating them with a Yankee twang, softened somewhat into a drawl by his life in England.

"This is ridiculous, of course," he said, "but it's guide-book poetry–certainly vers libre; you know the White Mountains goes in for vers libre!–and it shows what's the matter with American poets who lay poetry on things. I don't remember who wrote it!

> One of the most deplorable facts about the White
> Mountains
> Is the lack of legends.
> Imagination, therefore, must be requisitioned
> To supply the story
> That gave a name to this beautiful spot."

He chuckled. Then:

"The point I'm making lies in that line, 'Imagination . . . must be requisitioned.' The curse of our poetry is that we lay it on things. Pocketsful of poetic adjectives like pocketsful of peanuts carried into a park for the gray squirrels! You can take it as gospel, that's not what we want.

"But people say to me: 'The facts themselves aren't enough. You've got to do something to them, haven't you? They can't be poetical unless a poet handles them.'

"To that I have a very simple answer. It's this: Anything you do to the facts falsifies them, but anything the facts do to you–yes, even against your will; yes, resist them with all your strength–transforms them into poetry."

Which, as any one who reads him or talks with him will soon discover, is the secret of Robert Frost's success. He is a Puritan who has fought the soil for sustenance and has fought the world for recognition as a poet. He has won success because he has fought his own emotions, digging into them and behind them, the better to strike the universal note that makes poetry out of axe-handles.

LETTER:
To Louis Untermeyer; *The Letters of Robert Frost to Louis Untermeyer*, pp. 28-31.

Frost's "barding around," as he called his frequent reading tours, enhanced his popularity as a poet and helped him to support his family, but his travels seriously depleted the time and energy he was able to devote to writing. At least twelve of the thirty-two poems in his third book, Mountain Interval *(published 1 December 1916), had been written (or begun) early enough to have been included in* A Boy's Will *in 1913. As*

The Little Things of War 16

The battle rent a cobweb diamond-strung,
And cut a flower stalk by a groundbird's nest
Before it stained a single human breast.
The stricken flower bent double and so hung.
And still the bird revisited her young.
A butterfly the flower's fall dispossessed
A moment sought in air her place of rest,
Then lightly stooped to it and fluttering clung.

On the bare upland pasture there had spread
O'er night 'twixt mullein stalks a wheel of thread
And straining cables wet with silver dew.
A sudden passing bullet shook it dry;
The expectant spider ran to greet the fly,
But finding nothing, sullenly withdrew.

A poem in the manuscript booklet Frost sent to Susan Hayes Ward for Christmas in 1912 (Huntington Library). The poem was slightly revised and retitled "Range-Finding" before it was published in Mountain Interval.

many as seven others were written in England. In this letter Frost expressed the fear that he was losing his poetic powers. As he warmed to his subject, however, Frost began to exaggerate and slipped into pure fabrication, knowing that he could count on Untermeyer to recognize his "fooling" and to understand that the fourth and fifth books mentioned here did not exist.

[Franconia, N.H.
4 May 1916]

Dear Old Louis

When I have borne in memory what has tamed Great Poets, hey? Am I be blamed etc? No you ain't. Or as Browning (masc.) has it:

> That was I that died last night
> When there shone no moon at all
> Nor to pierce the strained and tight
> Tent of heaven one planet small.
> Might was dead and so was Right.

Not to be any more obvious than I have to be to set at rest your brotherly fears for my future which I have no doubt you assume to be somehow or other wrapped up in me, I am going to tell you something I never but once let out of the bag before and that was just after I reached London and before I had begun to value myself for what I was worth.* It is a very damaging secret and you may not thank me for taking you into it when I tell you that I have often wished I could be sure that the other sharer of it had perished in the war. It is this: The poet in me died nearly ten years ago. Fortunately he had run through several phases, four to be exact, all well-defined, before he went. The calf I was in the nineties I merely take to market. I am become my own salesman. Two of my phases you have been so–what shall I say–as to like. Take care that you don't get your mouth set to declare the other two (as I release them) a falling-off of power, for that is

*(Toop.)

what they can't be whatever else they may be, since they were almost inextricably mixed with the first two in the writing and only my sagacity has separated or sorted them in the afterthought for putting on the market. Did you ever hear of quite such a case of Scotch-Yankee calculation? You should have seen the look on the face of the Englishman I first confessed this to! I won't name him lest it should bring you two together. While he has never actually betrayed me, he has made himself an enemy of me and all my works. He regards me as a little heinous. As you look back don't you see how a lot of things I have said begin to take meaning from this? Well . . .

But anyway you are freed from anxiety about my running all to philosophy. It makes no difference what I run to now. I needn't be the least bit tender of myself. Of course I'm glad it's all up with Masters, my hated rival. He wasn't foresighted enough, I'll bet, to provide against the evil day that is come to him. He failed to take warning from the example of Shelley who philosophized and died young. But me, the day I did The Trial by Existence (*Boy's Will*) says I to myself, this is the way of all flesh. I was not much over twenty, but I was wise for my years. I knew then that it was a race between me the poet and that in me that would be flirting with the entelechies or the coming on of that in me. I must get as much done as possible before thirty. I tell you, Louis, it's all over at thirty. People expect us to keep right on and it is as well to have something to show for our time on earth. Anyway that was the way I thought I might feel. And I took measures accordingly. And now my time is my own. I have myself all in a strong box where I can unfold as a personality at discretion. Someone asks with a teasing eye, "Have you done that Phi Beta Kappa poem yet?" "No, I don't know that I have, as you may say." "You seem not to be particularly uneasy about it." "Oh, that's because I know where it's coming from, don't you know." Great effect of strength and mastery!

Now you know more about me than anyone else knows except that Londoner we won't count because he may be dead of a lachrymous.

And don't think mention of the war is anything to go by. I could give you proof that twenty years ago in a small book I did on Boeme and the Technique of Sincerity I was saying "The heroic emotions, like all the rest of the emotions, never know when they ought to be felt after the first time. Either they will be felt too soon or too late from fear of being felt too soon."

Ever thine

R. F.

I must give you a sample from the fourth book, "Pitchblende." As a matter of fact and to be perfectly honest with you there is a fifth unnamed as yet, the only one unnamed (the third has been long known as "Mountain Interval") and I think the most surprising of the lot (circa 1903). But none of that now.

OLD AGE

My old uncle is long and narrow.
And when he starts to rise
After his after-dinner nap
I think to myself
He may do it this once more
But this is the last time.
He lets one leg slip off the lounge
And fall to the floor.
But still he lies
And looks to God through the ceiling.
The next thing is to get to his outside elbow
And so to a sitting posture
And so to his feet.
I avert my eyes for him till he does it.
Once I said from the heart,
"What is it, Uncle?–
Pain or just weakness?
Can't we do anything for it?"
He said "It's Specific Gravity"
"Do you mean by that that it's grave?"
"No, not as bad as that yet, child,
But it's the Grave coming on."
Then I knew he didn't mean Seriousness
When he said Gravity.
Old age may not be kittenish
But it is not necessarily serious.

R.F.

Someone writes to tell me that the Poetry Society had one of my poems to abuse in manuscript the other night. Absolutely without my knowledge and consent. I don't mind their abuse, but I do mind their trying to make it look as if I was fool enough to come before them for judgment except with something I had cooked up for their limitations. Protest for me, will you? I wonder how in the world they got the manuscript.

BOOK REVIEW:

Harriet Monroe, "Frost and Masters," *Poetry: A Magazine of Verse,* 9 (January 1917): 202-207.

Though it includes a dozen or so strong poems–among them "Birches" and "The Road Not Taken"– Mountain Interval *was greeted with much less enthusiasm than* North of Boston, *which had been a bestseller. In this review of* Mountain Interval *and Edgar Lee Masters's* The Great Valley *Monroe expresses views about the two poets' literary kinship that were common early in their careers.*

By the time this review was published Frost had begun teaching at Amherst College. With the exception of three academic years at the University of Michigan (1921-1923 and 1925-1926) and time away from academe in 1920 and 1921, Frost's affiliation with Amherst continued until soon after the death of Elinor Frost in March 1938. As his reputation as a poet grew, his teaching responsibilities decreased.

In Kipling's story of primitive men the bard becomes a thing of awe because he can "tell the tale of the tribe," can save the tribe from engulfing oblivion by "making words run up and down in men's hearts"–words that move too grandly to be forgotten. In the final accounting perhaps this is the first function of the bard, even more his office than the setting of dreams to magic measures.

These two poets, Frost and Masters, are telling the tale of the tribe, the varying tales of their separate tribes; and the simultaneous appearance of their latest books tempts one to comparison and contrast. Reading the two books as a whole, without stopping for details, one gets an overpowering impression, not only of two different individuals but of two different crowds. In Frost Puritan New England speaks with a voice as absolute as New Hampshire's granite hills. Whittier wandered there once, singing a few songs, and Emerson from those slopes looked inward and outward for truth. But neither of these felt New England as Frost feels it.

In the same way Masters tells the tale of his tribe. We have had–we have now–other poets of the Middle West. Whitman of course included this vast pioneer-peopled plain in his sublimated vision of These States as a cosmic democracy. Riley and Eugene Field–both town-lovers hardly aware of Mother Earth–delighted in, and to a certain extent individualized, the traditional rural types of this region, types handed down from Mark Twain, Bill Nye and other great humorists. Vachel Lindsay loves the Middle West like a big brother, pleads with it, sings of and to it, glorifies it with troubadour poems, making it picturesque, weaving a glamour around it. And Carl Sandburg loves Chicago and its sea-hearted lake, knows it intimately, as a cosmopolis. But perhaps none of these has got this particular region into his blood and bones so deeply as Mr. Masters, who was "raised" in one of its typical villages and who lives in its typical great city.

"Yankees are what they always were," sings Mr. Frost. His New England is the same old New England of the pilgrim fathers–a harsh, austere, velvet-coated-granite earth, bringing forth rigid, narrow, heroic men and women, hard but with unexpected softnesses. Their religion has been modified since Cotton Mather, but not their character, at least not the character of those who stay on their farms, resisting the call of the West and the lure of towns. To present this earth, these people, the poet employs usually a blank verse as massive as they, as stript of all apologies and adornments. His poetry is sparing, austere, even a bit crabbèd at times; but now and then it lights up with a sudden and intimate beauty, a beauty springing from life-long love and intuition, as in these images of trees from two different poems:

> A resurrected tree,
> A tree that had been down and raised again,
> A barkless spectre–he had halted too,
> As if for fear of treading upon me.
> ....
>
> She had no saying dark enough
> For the dark pine that kept
> Forever trying the window-latch
> Of the room where they slept.

Nature is always thus an integral part of Mr. Frost's human dramas–not a mere background but one of the cast. It is wonderful how he builds up the terrific winter tempest in *Snow,* for example, and does it, not by mere statement, but through the talk of those delicately contrasted characters, the dry skeptical wife, the slower matter-of-fact husband, and the deep-breathing, deep-dreaming evangelist, lover of life and the storm. And "a springtime passion for the earth," with human life–yes, and brute life–as a part of it, burns in such poems as *In the Home Stretch, Putting in the Seed, Birches,* and *The Cow in Apple Time.*

It is appropriate, no doubt, that Masters should be less selective than Frost–the West is less reserved than New England. Against Frost's one hundred pages we have nearly three hundred from Masters, and *The Great Valley* is his second book of this year. The watchful critic must regret much of it; especially he must wonder, to the extreme of amazement, why the poet should have reverted to *Marsyas* and *Apollo at Pherae,* which are in the mood of those early books whose academic unexpressiveness will always be one of the curiosities of literature. But one must take a poet as he is, and this poet has to pour out whatever is in his heart, and leave his readers, or Father Time, to do the sifting. He has to do this, moreover in a spirit of careless abundance which throws off magic lines in a mass of coarser texture–flowers, grasses and weeds together under a brilliant and generous procreative sun.

But this is the prairie's exuberant way–one must look at this poet, not in close detail, but in the mass. Thus one may get from him, as from the prairies themselves, a sense of space and richness. One feels in him too the idealistic vision of a man accustomed to far horizons–that impatience with things near, things more or less faithless to the imminent beauty, and that relief in the contemplation of things remote, beauty's survivals or prophecies.

This chaotic half-baked civilization, growing up out of these broad and fruitful plains into dull little towns and mad great cities, all fitfully, inadequately spiritualized–this one feels in Mr. Masters' books. One feels also a deep and tragic love of it, a thwarted but rooted faith in it, which cannot be destroyed by all the messy materialism, the soul-wasting "efficiency," which he sees around him. His "great valley" is dominated by the gigantic sombre figure of Lincoln, the Autochthon of his dream–Lincoln, who ever renews his power in the imagination of the people, growing greater, like the elder Titans, through the mists of time.

How much of all this Mr. Masters presents with adequate poetic magic no critic can define as yet. We, his neighbors and contemporaries, find–most of us–the very essence of it in *Spoon River,* which will surely tell something of the tale of our tribe to those who come after us. We find something of its atmosphere also, its light and shade and space, in the longer monologues of the later books, though here the theme is more consciously and as a rule less creatively presented. But in all one is carried along by a wave of power–the cumulative effect, like a geometrical progression, seems out of proportion to the separate steps that make it. This is the reader's tribute, no doubt, to the poet's rich and generous personality–that of a deeply informed man of the modern world, something between Chaucer and Rabelais, but burning darkly in his heart a little secret candle to some mediaeval saint.

One can not leave Mr. Masters without protesting against the new edition of *Spoon River,* now unfortunately the only one on sale. The so-called "illustrations" by Oliver Herford are pitiful beyond words. So embellished, the book looks like the typical ornamental volume on Reuben's parlor table.

To return to our parallel–it is important that two rich districts of this country, each an individual and powerful personality, are finding modern interpreters. Who will speak as well for the South, and for the Far West between sea and mountains?

LETTER:
To Edward Garnett, *Selected Letters of Robert Frost,* p. 217.

Edward Thomas died in battle on 9 April 1917. Another of Thomas's friends, Edward Garrett, had written an extremely positive article about Frost for the Atlantic Monthly *(August 1915), but he considered* Mountain Interval *disappointing in comparison to* North of Boston.

29 April 1917
Amherst

Dear Mr Garnett:

Edward Thomas was the only brother I ever had. I fail to see how we can have been so much to each other, he an Englishman and I an American and our first meeting put off till we were both in middle life. I hadn't a plan for the future that didn't include him.

You must like his poetry as well as I do and do everything you can for it. His last word to me, his "pen ultimate word," as he called it, was that what he cared most for was the name of poet. His poetry is so very brave–so unconsciously brave. He didn't think of it for a moment as war poetry, though that is what it is. It ought to be called Roads to France. "Now all roads lead to France, and heavy is the tread of the living, but the dead, returning, lightly dance," he says. He was so impurturbably the poet through everything to the end. If there is any merit in self-possession, I can say I never saw anyone less put off himself by unaccustomed danger, less put off his game. His concern to the last was what it had always been, to touch earthly things and come as near them in words as words would come.

South Shaftsbury Vt
June 28 1921

My dear Mrs Conkling:

I should like to scatter a dozen or two of your circulars over the country if I don't have to promise results to obtain them of you. And you needn't thank me. I'll be doing it for myself and the cause as much as for you.

Don't ask me too confidingly about what you ought to expect of publishers. I don't feel that I am very much on the inside with that gentry. You wouldn't look to me as an authority on them if you knew the story of my mix-up with David Nutt in England. I might be a better and a truer poet if I were a business man too. But I'm not a business man too. All I can tell you about royalties is that fifteen per cent seems good to me. It is what I get on everything, common editions and preferred. I'm glad Hilda is going to have the honor of a special edition. You ought to be touched by this mark of her publisher's good friendship.

I am grateful that you should have thought to link Edward Thomas' name with mine in one of your lectures. You will be careful, I know, not to say anything to exalt either of us at the expense of the other. There's a story going round that might lead you to exaggerate our debt to each other. Anything we may be thought to have in common we had before we met. When Hodgson introduced us at a coffee house in London in 1913 I had written two and a half of my three books he had written all but two or three of his thirty. The most our congeniality could do was confirm us both in what we were. There was never a moment's thought about who may have been influencing whom. The least rivalry of that kind would have taken something from our friendship. We were greater friends than almost any two ever were practising the same art. I don't mean that we did nothing for each other. As I have said we encouraged each other in our adventurous ways. Beyond that anything we did was very practical. He gave me standing as a poet – he more than anyone else, though of course I have to thank Abercrombie, Hueffer, Pound and some others for help too. I dragged him out from under the heap of his own work in prose he was buried alive under. He was throwing to his big perfunctory histories of Marlborough and the like written to order such poetry as would make him a name if he were but given credit for it. I made him see that he owed it to himself and the poetry to have it

Letter to Grace Hazard Conkling, head of the English department at Smith College, in which Frost discusses Edward Thomas (Barrett Library, University of Virginia Library). At least three of Frost's poems were inspired by his friendship with Thomas: "The Road Not Taken" (sent to Thomas in 1915), "To E. T." (a memorial written 1917-1920), and "Iris by Night" (first published in 1936).

out by itself in poetic form where it must suffer itself to be admired. It took me some time. I bantered, teased and bullied ~~him~~ all the summer we were together at Leddington and Ryton. All he had to do was put his poetry in a form that declared itself. The theme must be the same, the accent exactly the same. He saw it and he was tempted. It was plain that he had wanted to be a poet all the years he had been writing about poets not worth his little finger. But he was afeared (though a soldier). His timidity was funny and fascinating. I had about given him up, he had turned his thoughts to enlistment and I mine to sailing for ~~there~~ home when he wrote his first poem. The decision

he made in going into the army helped him make the other decision to be a poet in form. And a very fine poet. And a poet all in his own right. The accent is absolutely his own. You can hear it everywhere in his prose, where if he had left it, however, it would have been lost.

You won't quote me in any of this please. It is much too personal. I simply wanted you to know before you went ahead. The point is that what we had in common we had from before we were born. Make as much of that as you will but dont tell anyone we gave each other anything but a boost.

With our best wishes to you and the children. We shall look forward to seeing you at Middlebury.

Sincerely yours
Robert Frost

~~The steaming horses think it queer~~
~~To~~
The ~~horse~~ ~~horses~~ [little horse must] think it queer
~~We~~ [To] stop without a farm house near
Between a ~~forest and a~~ [the woods and frozen] lake
The darkest evening of the year

~~He~~ [She] gives [her] harness bells a shake
To ask if there is some mistake
The only other sound's [the] sweep
Of easy wind and ~~fall~~ [downy] flake.

The woods are lovely dark and deep
But I have promises to keep
~~[illegible]~~
And miles to go before I sleep
And miles to go before I sleep

Page from the first draft for "Stopping by Woods on a Snowy Evening" (Jones Library). If Frost had kept the line he crossed out in the last stanza, his interlocking rhyme scheme–in which the third line of one stanza establishes the rhyme used in the first, second, and fourth lines of the next–would have committed him to writing another stanza.

Do what you can for him and never mind me for the present. I sent you a copy of Mountain Interval, but perhaps it is as well you didnt get it for your review if you were not going to be pleased with it. I can hear Edward Thomas saying in defense of In the Home Stretch that it would cut just as it is into a dozen or more of your Chinese impressionistic poems and perhaps gain something by the cutting for the reader whose taste had been formed on the kiln-dried tabule poetry of your Pounds and Masterses. I look on theirs as synthetical chemical products put together after a formula. It's too long a story to go into with anyone I'm not sure it wouldn't bore. There's something in the living sentence (in the shape of it) that is more important than any phrasing or chosen word. And it's something you can only achieve when going free. The Hill Wife ought to be some sort of answer to you. It is just as much one poem as the other but more articulated so to speak. It shows its parts and it shows that they may be taken by themselves as poems of fashionable length. . . .

Sincerely yours Robert Frost

LETTER:

To Sylvester Baxter, March 1923; from R. C. Townsend, "In Defense of Form: A Letter from Robert Frost to Sylvester Baxter, 1923," *New England Quarterly*, 36 (June 1963): 241-249.

Frost wrote the first draft for "Stopping by Woods on a Snowy Evening" early one morning in June 1922, having stayed up all night to work on the title poem for his next book, New Hampshire. *After "Stopping by Woods" appeared in the 7 March 1923 issue of the* New Republic, *Boston literary critic Sylvester Baxter asked Frost why he ended the poem as he did. In his response Frost also commented on William Rose Benét's poem "Moon Rider" and Winifred Welles's poem "Cloth-of-Gold," both published in the same issue of the* New Republic. *Connick is artist Charles Jay Connick.*

Dear Sylvester:

I'm surprised at you that you should be the one of all my poetical friends to miss the reason for the repetend in Stopping by Woods. There should be two reasons one of meaning and one of form. You get the first and fail of the second. What the repetend does internally you come very near: what it does externally is save me from a third line promising another stanza. If the third line had been dead in all the other stanzas your judgement would be correct. A dead line in the last stanza alone would have been a flaw. I considered for a moment four of a kind in the last stanza but that would have made five including the third in the stanza before it. I considered for a moment winding up with a three line stanza. The repetend was the only logical way to end such a poem. I am afraid you have hurt your nice sense of form by writing too much free verse lately. Why don't you do your outcast Christmas tree in tight tight regular verse?–And let me see it.

Bill Benét's is a terrible example of really first rate poetical words and lines that come to nothing in the aggregate. In detail he is a little like De la Mare (in this particular poem). But with De la Mare the whole poem is always the thing. He is never just a texture.

Winnifred Wells' poem is good.

You and Connick will be welcome. I was reminded of Connick by some beautiful windows of his I saw in Columbia Missouri early in the winter. Can you give me his address? I'd like to write him a line.

Take my word for it you wont often look on as flawless a piece of work as Stopping by Woods. It seems to me you show little faith not to believe that I could have wound up the poem in any way I thought best. But I forgive you.

Ever Yours
Robert Frost

I stood the Texax [*sic*] trip and twelve lectures rotten and have been sick as a result of it all winter. I've had flu on flu. Hope you are flourishing.

BOOK REVIEW:

Louis Untermeyer, "Robert Frost's 'New Hampshire,'" *Bookman* (New York), 58 (January 1924): 578-580.

Frost was awarded the first of his four Pulitzer Prizes for New Hampshire, *published on 15 November 1923. Though he had written to Untermeyer in 1916 that "the poet in me died nearly ten years ago," Frost wrote most of the poems in this book during the three years prior to its publication.*

It is somewhat more than seven years since Frost, following "North of Boston" with an equally characteristic though less integrated volume, published "Mountain Interval." The latter work never succeeded to the popularity of its famous forerunner, and for no other reason but its very lack of unity. "North of Boston" presented a pattern–to many a dark and terrible pattern–in its interknit New England monologues; "Mountain Interval" scattered its effects, introduced new inflections, puzzled the admirers of Frost's "grey monotones" by an infusion of bright colors. Yet some of this poet's finest moments are in the lesser known book. Nothing from the more popular collection will last longer than the dramatically suspended "Snow," the idyllic "Birches," or the intensity of the "Hill Wife" lyrics; even "The Death of the Hired Man" scarcely surpasses the charged pathos of "An Old Man's Winter Night."

And now, after seven years, we have "New Hampshire" which, structurally, is a cross between both its predecessors. With an almost equal division of narratives and lyrics, it seems to recall "Mountain Interval," but the unity of "North of Boston" is achieved by a peculiar and simple device. "New Hampshire" pretends to be nothing but a long poem with notes and grace notes, and the title poem (some fourteen pages long) purports merely to celebrate Frost's favorite state. Very gravely, the rambling tribute to the state that "hasn't much of anything to sell" is starred and dotted with scientific numerals in the manner of the most profound treatise, the references being to poems that look at first as if they were only inserted to reenforce the text. In reality, these explanatory "notes" are some of the richest poems of our time, poems steeped in that extraordinary blend of intellect and emotion which is Frost's particular magic. Thus the tiny numeral after the line:

She has one witch–old style[1]

refers us to [1] "The Witch of Coös," one of the most singularly related ghost stories in poetry. Thus, another strange narrative is introduced in this way:

I met a Californian who would
Talk California–a state so blessed,
He said, in climate none had ever died there
A natural death, and Vigilance Committees
Had had to organize to stock the graveyards?[2]
And vindicate the state's humanity.
"Just the way Stefansson runs on," I murmured,
"About the British Arctic. That's what comes
Of being in the market with a climate."

[2] Cf. page 51, "Place for a Third."

But is it a different poet that breaks silence after seven years with so unusual an arrangement? Will the admirers of the earlier Frost fail to find him in this strange composition? Frost himself might answer with the words of the first poem in his first book:

They would not find me changed from him they knew–
Only more sure of all I thought was true.

Nothing, really, has changed. The idiom is clearer, the convictions have deepened–the essential things, the point of view, the tone of voice, remain the same. The following imaginative lyric is typical of the later Frost. It would be easy to point to it as a proof of Frost's maturer warmth and show how with the increase of years his style has grown more genial–were it not for the fact that this poem was written at the age of twenty and published in "The Youth's Companion" in 1896. As readers of "New Hampshire" will look for it in vain, I take the liberty of quoting it in full:

THE FLOWER-BOAT

The fisherman's swapping a yarn for a yarn
Under the hand of the village barber;
And here in the angle of house and barn
His deep-sea dory has found a harbor.

At anchor she rides the sunny sod
As full to the gunnel of flowers growing
As ever she turned her home with cod
From George's Bank when winds were blowing.

And I judge from that Elysian freight
That all they ask is rougher weather,
And dory and master will sail by fate
To seek for the Happy Isles together.

And here, in "New Hampshire"–in exactly the same half playful, half pathetic accents, in precisely the same curious pitch–is an exquisite and similar fantasy:

A BOUNDLESS MOMENT

He halted in the wind, and–what was that
Far in the maples, pale, but not a ghost?
He stood there bringing March against his thought,
And yet too ready to believe the most.

"Oh, that's the Paradise-in-bloom," I said;
And truly it was fair enough for flowers
Had we but in us to assume in March
Such white luxuriance of May for ours.

We stood a moment so in a strange world,

Myself as one his own pretense deceives;
And then I said the truth (and we moved on):
A young beech clinging to its last year's leaves.

It is this colloquially colored extravagance, this deceptive conversational tone, which is so full of spiritual implications. It is the picture first ("The fact is the sweetest dream that labor knows") but it never remains a purely pictorial representation. Beneath the light touch of such a poem, one is conscious of suggested depths, of a quiet but compelling affirmation, of a faith great enough to dare to believe too much. "Two Look at Two" repeats this confidence with a more personal emotion–again in the framework of a picture–drenched in the trembling colors and quivering tenderness of twilight.

What change there is, is one of emphasis. It seems incredible that most of the appraisers of Frost's previous work spoke chiefly of its grimness, whereas its whimsicality, though less obvious, was equally pronounced. In "Mountain Interval," the occasional quizzical raillery of "North of Boston" was more apparent, the momentary descent of the eyelash was perceptibly prolonged; in "New Hampshire" it declares itself on every page. The very form of the new book is an extended piece of badinage; the long title poem is a broad smile from beginning to end; the most serious of the narratives sparkle with a slily intimate banter. This increase in humor, so rich in its varying timbres, will irritate the literal minded almost as much as it will delight those to whom fact and fantasy are not inimical opposites but continually shifting facets of the same many sided thing. The orthodox Cambridgian (Mass.), for example, will boil over at such an outrageous heresy as:

Her husband was worth millions.
I think he owned some shares in Harvard College.

The critics who concluded that Frost was too overburdened with his lonely farms and isolated cottages, who maintained that he could never be "whimsical or quaint," will scarcely know what to make of this volume in which practically every poem proceeds from a magnified whimsicality. There will be those who, granting the charm of this elfin imagination, may question its use in such serious themes. Yet what is poetry but metaphor–what is it but the establishing of a congruity between apparently unrelated things? What then is metaphor but the child of whimsy?

So much has been made of Frost's factual realism that at the risk of being redundant I insist that, beneath the surface naturalism, his work is distinguished–even impelled–by a rare and fantastic mind. This side of Frost's genius has been so underemphasized that I may be allowed to overstress it by directing attention to the fundamental quaintness of conception of "Paul's Wife," the extraordinarily adroit "An Empty Threat," "A Star in a Stone-Boat," that lovely chain of tercets, and "Wild Grapes," which is a feminine complement to "Birches."

But it is in the lyrics that Frost's warmth is most apparent. There are few circumlocutory asides, few *sotto voce* murmurs, in these direct communications–only a firm intensity. A great love of the New England countryside, of earth itself, surges from such poems as "Stopping By Woods on a Snowy Evening," "Gathering Leaves," "In a Disused Graveyard," and the brightly ironic "The Need of Being Versed in Country Things." A less physical and almost unearthly passion speaks in the beautiful though troubled lines of "To Earthward," the mystical sonority of "I Will Sing You One-O," and the condensed wisdom of "Fire and Ice." I consider the last, one of the greatest epigrammatic poems in the English language; every line–and there are only nine altogether–seems to have been carved in crystal. Similarly concentrated, though in far lighter accents, is this perfectly balanced composition. It seems so spontaneous and integrated a song that it is interesting to note that the first six lines were composed a score of years ago, Frost having waited twenty years for the last two.

Nature's first green is gold,
Her hardest hue to hold.
Her early leaf's a flower;
But only so an hour.
Then leaf subsides to leaf.
So Eden sank to grief,
So dawn goes down to day.
Nothing gold can stay.

In the very simplicity of these lines we have the unaffected originality of Frost. With absolute freedom from contemporary fashions, technical trickery, or the latest erudite slang, Frost has created a poetry which is at one time full of heat and humor, a poetry that belongs not only to the America of our own day but to the richest records of English verse.

LETTER:
To Louis Untermeyer [excerpt]; *The Letters of Robert Frost to Louis Untermeyer*, pp. 165-168.

In this letter to Untermeyer Frost expanded on some ideas about style that he developed while teaching an English course called "Readings" at Amherst.

[Amherst, Mass.
March 10, 1924]

Dear Old Louis:

Since last I saw you I have come to the conclusion that style in prose or verse is that which indicates how the writer takes himself and what he is saying. Let the sound of Stevenson go through your mind empty and you will realize that he never took himself other than as an amusement. Do the same with Swinburne and you will see that he took himself as a wonder. Many sensitive natures have plainly shown by their style that they took themselves lightly in self-defense. They are the ironists. Some fair to good writers have no style and so leave us ignorant of how they take themselves. But that is the one important thing to know: because on it depends our likes and dislikes. A novelist seems to be the only kind of writer who can make a name without a style: which is only one more reason for not bothering with the novel. I am not satisfied to let it go with the aphorism that the style is the man. The man's ideas would be some element then of his style. So would his deeds. But I would narrow the definition. His deeds are his deeds; his ideas are his ideas. His style is the way he carries himself toward his ideas and deeds. Mind you if he is down-spirited it will be all he can do to have the ideas without the carriage. The style is out of his superfluity. It is the mind skating circles round itself as it moves forward. Emerson had one of the noblest least egotistical of styles. By comparison with it Thoreau's was conceited, Whitman's bumptious. Carlyle's way of taking himself simply infuriates me. Longfellow took himself with the gentlest twinkle. I don't suppose you know his miracle play in The Golden Legend, or Birds of Killingworth, Simon Danz, or Othere.

I own any form of humor shows fear and inferiority. Irony is simply a kind of guardedness. So is a twinkle. It keeps the reader from criticism. Whittier, when he shows any style at all, is probably a greater person than Longfellow as he is lifted priestlike above consideration of the scornful. Belief is better than anything else, and it is best when rapt, above paying its respects to anybody's doubt whatsoever. At bottom the world isn't a joke. We only joke about it to avoid an issue with someone to let someone know that we know he's there with his questions: to disarm him by seeming to have heard and done justice to his side of the standing argument. Humor is the most engaging cowardice. With it myself I have been able to hold some of my enemy in play far out of gunshot.

LETTER:
To Lesley Frost; *Family Letters of Robert and Elinor Frost*, pp. 123-125.

On 4 August 1928 Robert and Elinor Frost sailed for France with their daughter Marjorie, who stayed with a French family while her parents went on to England, where they visited old friends, including J. C. Squire, editor of the London Mercury, *barrister-poet John W. Haines, and poets John Freeman, Wilfrid Gibson, Lascelles Abercrombie, Walter De la Mare, W. H. Davies, Frank S. Flint, and Harold Monro, owner of the Poetry Bookshop, who introduced Frost to T. S. Eliot during this visit. Marion Dodd was the owner of a bookstore in Northampton, Massachusetts, where Lesley Frost had worked. The book by Helen Thomas mentioned at the end of this letter is* As It Was *(1926), an autobiography that revealed much about her difficult marriage to Frost's friend the late Edward Thomas.*

Midhurst, Hucclecote,
Gloucester
[11 September 1928]

Dear Leslie:

We dont seem to have had evidence that you have had any letter from us. If the stream keeps on flowing, most of it may sink into the ground and be lost, but some at least must come through sometime to the sea. Be sure to let us know when you are reached.

I've seen a few of the English, J.C. Squier, John Freeman, and the Hainses – not to mention the not least mentionable Badnee or Mrs Hyatt of Ryton Dymmock Gloucestershire. She's all sole alone there now (rent free I suppose by the kindness of the farmer her husband was shepherd for.) The people at the Gallows are at enmity with the neighborhood and drove us off when we tried to look the old place over. Probably they were ashamed of the rundown condition of the property–everything overgrown and the thatch rotted and fallen in. The people at Little Iddens were glad to show us in. That place is better than we left it. The Woods have moved away from the big house.

Passport photograph of Elinor and Robert Frost, 1928

The Gibsons live at Letchworth where the children can have the advantages of the Quaker schools. Gibson's stock as a poet is quoted very low right now. How he lives is a puzzle to his friends. His third of the income from Rupert Brook's books may still be a big help.

De la Mare is not yet well from an operation that nearly killed him. He is the most prominent one of them all, getting out with both prose and verse to even the unliterary reader. W. H. Davies suffers his worst pangs of jealousy over de la Mare. Davies spends a good deal of his time talking about his own relative deserts. Everybody agrees or concedes that he still writes his best. He has married a very young wild thing of no definable class, but partly gypsy [.]

John Freeman, a well to do head of an insurance firm, has climbed into some poetic prominence. He is so dull that I am tempted again to say my poetry to please me must be sensational. Freeman asked me with too obvious eagerness what I should say Hugh Walpoles article in "Books" on him rating him among the first six was likely to do for him in America. I told him almost anything. Which is no more or less than the truth. He wrote the article about me in The Mercury and I ought to be grateful.

There's nobody new to take our place as the younger poets: or so I heard them lamenting with a false note in the Mercury office. The Sitwells and T. S. Elliott were pointedly left out of count.

Laselles has been too busy and recently too ill to write poetry. Theres a play of his that raised a howl a year or two ago for its immorality. The beginning raised my gorge at its stilted vernacular. I got no further. He has several more children than when we last heard.

Flint is I dont know where. [Harold] Monro has moved his book shop [.] I happened to see on his desk a letter signed by Marion Dodd. He is just getting asked to America by Fekins. About

Nature's Neglect

As vain to raise a voice as a sigh
In the tumult of free leaves on high!
What are you in the shadow of trees
Engaged up there with the light and breeze?

Less than the coral-root, you know,
That is content with the daylight low,
And has no leaves at all of its own:
Whose spotted flowers hang meanly down.

You linger your little hour and are gone,
And still the wood sweeps leafily on;
And you would not have it otherwise
In this one place beneath the skies.

You cannot carry away a flower
From the merest passing whim of the hour,
But there are those that wait afar
To make it tell them what you are.

They choose to forget in the thought of you
The love of the thing you bid them to:
And this is a weariness of the soul,
Which nothing but nature can make whole.

Robert Frost

Above: a manuscript Frost sent to Susan Hayes Ward some time between 1901 and 1912 (Huntington Library); at right: manuscript for Frost's revised version, which was published as "Unnoticed" in the Saturday Review of Literature *(28 March 1925) and collected as "On Going Unnoticed" in* West-Running Brook *(Barrett Library, University of Virginia Library)*

On Going Unnoticed

~~Natures Neglect~~

As vain to raise a voice as a sigh
In the tumult of free leaves so high.
What are you in the shadow of trees
Engaged up there with the light and breeze?

Less than the coral-root you know
That is content with the daylight low,
And has no leaves at all of its own;
Whose spotted flowers hang meanly down.

You grasp the bark by a rugged pleat,
And look up small from the forest's feet.
The only leaf it drops goes wide,
Your name not written on either side.

You linger your little hour and are gone,
And still the woods sweep leafily on;
Not even missing the coral-root flower
You took as a trophy of the hour.

published

published.

time, he says. He has wondered at not having been asked long since. He treated me very shabily. He always resented my being.

Haines knows and entertains them all now. He may be as much remembered as any. He is full of them all and rich in all their books. He is his whole law firm now and works hard but finds time for correspondence in all directions.

Mrs. Helen Thomas hasnt been heard from yet. She has entirely new friends. She plans more books about Edward. Nobody blames her to[o] hard for that first one[.]

Affectionately R. F.

BOOK REVIEW:
From Babette Deutsch, "Poets and Poetasters," *Bookman* (New York), 68 (December 1928): 471-473.

West-Running Brook *was published on 19 November 1928, just as the Frosts were returning from England. In reviewing Frost's book–with books of poetry by William Butler Yeats, Thomas Hardy, Sylvia Townsend Warner, William Ellery Leonard, Genevieve Taggard, Allen Tate, and others–Deutsch began with a discussion of Yeats and continued with a favorable comparison between him and Frost; but, like several other reviewers, she found the poems in* West-Running Brook *uneven.*

The one other poet who has achieved a similar unity of vision–though how different a one!–is Robert Frost. His latest volume, *West-Running Brook* (Holt, $2.50), is slight, physically speaking, and contains several pieces that are unworthy of inclusion. Such, for example, are several quatrains, and the piece called "Rose Family," which might have been written by Austin Dobson in his sleep. These flaws notwithstanding, the book as a whole has the seriousness and acuteness which marks all of Frost's work, and while it shows no impressive advance upon his previous achievement, that is high enough to make any new collection of his important. There are no narrative pieces. The lyrics are compact of pity and sly humor and hardihood, all expressed in an easy conversational tone, and all characterized by that familiarity with, and devotion to, the–shall we say, domesticated?–natural scene, to which Frost has accustomed us. It is seldom that a line strikes one as particularly fine, a phrase as peculiarly fitting, a whole poem as singularly lyrical, yet almost every piece is wrought of the true gold of poetry. As for the animating spirit of the volume, one finds it clearest, perhaps, in the title-poem, a dialogue in which one fancies the poet to have the final word, when in these terms he speaks of existence:

It flows beside us in this water brook,
But it flows over us. It flows between us
To separate us for a panic moment.
It flows between us, over us, and *with* us.
And it is time, strength, tone, light, life and love–
And even substance lapsing unsubstantial;
The universal cataract of death
That spends to nothingness–and unresisted,
Save by some strange resistance in itself,
Not just a swerving, but a throwing back,
As if regret were in it and were sacred.
It has this throwing backward on itself
So that the fall of most of it is always
Raising a little, sending up a little. . . .
It is this backward motion toward the source,
Against the stream, that most we see ourselves in,
The tribute of the current to the source.
It is from this in nature we are from.
It is most us.

Among the poems that wear charm like a flower or burn with a special vitality are "Birthplace," "The Bear," "Sand Dunes," "On Looking Up By Chance At The Constellations," "Riders," "Bereft," "Canis Major" and "Once By The Pacific."

LETTER:
To Lesley Frost; *Family Letters of Robert and Elinor Frost*, pp. 160-164.

When Lesley Frost was invited to deliver a lecture on poetry, Frost sent her this assessment of some of his contemporaries. "Reed" is probably Herbert Read, author of Form in Modern Poetry *(1932); "Yates" or "Yeates" is William Butler Yeats. The postscript refers to enclosures that are no longer with the letter.*

[n.p., 1934]

Dear Lesley:

The difficulty of a job like that is to keep it from getting out of your mind for a single instant that you are speaking for Us the Frost Family and not just for yourself. In the last year or two owing to a nasty slap I got from an American follower of Eliots, I confess I have several times forgotten my dignity in speaking in public of Eliot. I mean I have shown a hostility I should like to think in my pride unworthy of my position. I could wish you would do better for us. For the most part describe rather than judge, or seem to judge only in a occasional ironical shading or lightly and unvenomously toward the end.

Frost (center) at a meeting to organize the California Writers' Guild, 1932. Novelist Louis Dodge is on Frost's right while Louis Mertins, a poet and author of books about Frost, is on his left. Remsen Bird, president of Occidental College, and columnist Lee Shippey are standing behind them.

Present them nearly as they would present themselves. Remember you are my daughter you are speaking in Cambridge and Eliots sister Mrs Sheffield the wife of my instructor in English at Harvard may very well be in your audience. Show no animus. Be judicial. Don't take anybody *alive* too seriously.

Let me tell you a few things about the new Movement you may or may not have taken in amid all the talk you have had to listen to.

Ezra Pound was the Prime Mover in the Movement and must always have the credit for whats in it. He was just branching off from the regular poets when we arrived in England. His Δiópia (Doria) had won second prize in a contest where Rupert Brooke's Dust had won first. Δiópia was a more or less conscious departure. The coming in second made it very conscious.

One of the first things Pound thought of was that rhyme and meter made you use too many words and even subsidiary ideas for the sake of coming out even. He and his friends Flint H. D. and Aldington used to play a game of rewriting each others poems to see if they couldnt reduce the number of words. Pound once wrote to me that John Gould Fletcher failed as a free verse writer because he failed to understand the purpose of free verse, which was, namely, to be less free not more free, with the verbiage.

Pound began to talk very early about rhythm alone without meter.

I assume you'll find in Reed his latest descendant a full statement of the doctrine of Inner Form, that is to say the form the subject itself takes if left to itself without any considerations of outer form. Everything else is to have two compulsions, an inner and an outer, a spiritual and a social, an individual and a racial. I want to be good, but that is not enough the state says I have got to be good. Every thing has not only formity but conformity. Everything but poetry according to the Pound-Eliot-Richards-Reed school of art.

For my part I should be as satisfied to play tennis with the net down as to write verse with no verse form set to stay me. I suppose I could display my energy agility and intense nature as well in either case. That's me. Remember you are speaking for them and do them justice. But whatever you do, do Pound justice as the great original.

He was the first Imagist too–although I believe our friend T. E. Hulme coined the name. An Imagist is simply one who insists on clearer sharper less muddled half realized images (chiefly eye images) than the common run of small poets. Thats certainly good as far as it goes. Strange with all their modernity and psychology they didnt have more to say about ear images and other images–even kinesthetic.

Pounds tightness naturally tended to stripping poetry of connective tissue. Never mind connections–they'll take care of themselves–if only you make your poetic points. The method gives a very ancient Old-Testament flavor to expression.

The same aspiration toward brevity and undersaying rather than oversaying has led to the poetry of intimation implication insinuation and innuendo as an object in itself. All poetry has always said something and implied the rest. Well then why have it say anything? Why not have it imply everything? Harte Crane has gone to great lengths here. There's some excuse for their extravagances. It is true much poetry is simply flat from being said too fully outright. I suppose Gertrude Stein has come in confluently to encourage the intimators or innuendots. A little of her is fun, but goes a long way. I read that negroes were chosen to sing her opera because they have less need than white men to know what they are talking about. That is a thing that can be reported without malice. "The bailey beareth away the bell" poem is taken by as justification of poetry by elipsis hiatus and hint. It's a fine poem beyond cavil. I wish somebody could write more like it. Gerard Manley Hopkins' obscurities and awkwardnesses are some more of their Bible. Hopkins is well enough. His friend Robert Bridges judged his limitations very fairly. His poem about All Pied Things good as it is disappoints me by not keeping, short as it is, wholly to pied things. I'm sending you this long poem by Perse as a further instance. I read the Proem in Chapel one morning with success. I had to practice up a way to perform it. Most of the boys laughed but some there were who pretended to be subconscious of what it was about. On the same principle a child of two three and four gets legitimate pleasure out of hearing Miltons Paradise Lost read aloud. If the child's legitimate he does. We've got to keep control of our mysteries. Above all things no vindictiveness.

From Pound down to Eliot they have striven for distinctions by a show of learning, Pound in old French Eliot in forty languages. They quote and you try to see if you can place the quotation. Pound really has great though inaccurate learning. Eliot has even greater. Maurice Hewlett leaned on Pound for medieval facts. Yates has leaned on him for facts and more than facts. Pound has taught Yates his later style of expression. Not many realize this. There's a significant reference to Pound in the preface to Yeates last book.

Last we come to who means the most, Pound or Eliot. Eliot has written in the throes of getting religion and foreswearing a world gone bad with war. That seems deep. But I dont know. Waste Lands–your great grand mother on the grand mother on your mothers side! I doubt if anything was laid waste by war that was not laid waste by peace before.

Claim everything for America. Pound Eliot and Stein are all American though expatriate.

Affectionately PAPA

You'll notice Eliot translates this
 This Song is what I read the boys
 Auden is their latest recruit

Notice in Eliots Ash Wednesday how he misquotes Shakespeare's

"Desiring this mans art and that man's scope"

Why does he do it if on purpose? Is he improving on Shakespeare or merely giving him an interesting twist up to date? Ash Wednesday is supposed to be deeply religious–last phase before going to Rome.

Send it back

LETTER:
To Louis Untermeyer; *The Letters of Robert Frost to Louis Untermeyer,* pp. 241-242.

Marjorie Frost Fraser, the Frosts' youngest child, died of puerperal fever on 2 May 1934, after having given birth to a daughter on 16 March. At the end of this letter Frost refers to Matthew Arnold's "Cadmus and Harmonia," in which the title characters become so grief-stricken over the misfortunes visited on their children

Robert and Elinor Frost, 1935, in the Old Book Room, Maddox House, at Rockford College in Rockford, Illinois, where their daughter Lesley Frost Francis was working

that they ask to be changed into serpents, a request the gods grant.

[Amherst, Mass.
May 15, 1934]

Dear Louis

I told you by letter or telegram what was hanging over us. So you know what to expect. Well, the blow has fallen. The noblest of us all is dead and has taken our hearts out of the world with her. It was a terrible seven weeks' fight–too indelibly terrible on the imagination. No death in war could more than match it for suffering and heroic endurance. Why all this talk in favor of peace? Peace has her victories over poor mortals no less merciless than war. Marge always said she would rather die in a gutter than in a hospital. But it was in a hospital she was caught to die after more than a hundred serum injections and blood transfusions. We were torn afresh every day between the temptation of letting her go untortured or cruelly trying to save her. The only consolation we have is the memory of her greatness through all. Never out of delirium for the last four weeks her responses were of course incorrect. She got little or nothing of what we said to her. The only way I could reach her was by putting my hand backward and forward between us as in counting out and saying with overemphasis *You*–and–*Me*. The last time I did that, the day before she died, she smiled faintly and answered "All the same," frowned slightly and made it "Always the same." Her temperature was then 110, the highest ever known at the Mayo Clinic where as I told you we took her, but too late. The classical theory was not born out in her case that a fine and innocent nature released by madness from the inhibitions of society will give way to all the indecencies. Everything she said, however quaint and awry, was of an almost straining loftiness. It was as if her ruling passion must have been to be wise and good, or it could not have been so strong in death. But curse all doctors who for a moment let down and neglect in childbirth the scientific precautions they have been taught in school. We thought to move heaven and earth–heaven with prayers and earth with money. We moved nothing. And here we are Cadmus and Harmonia not yet placed safely in changed forms.

R.

LETTER:
To *The Amherst Student,* 25 March 1935; *Selected Letters of Robert Frost,* pp. 417-419.

Frost won his second Pulitzer Prize for his first Collected Poems, *published in autumn 1930, the same year in which he was elected to the American Academy of Arts and Letters. While the majority of the reviews were favorable, one by leftist critic Granville Hicks* (New Republic, *3 December 1920) foreshadowed more attacks on Frost from the literary left during the 1930s. Though he did not respond right away, Frost began to formulate an answer to Hicks's charge that Frost's poems failed to deal with the chaotic elements of modern life, making it impossible for him to "contribute directly to the unification, in imaginative terms, of our culture." When the editors of the Amherst College undergraduate newspaper sent him birthday greetings in March 1935, Frost replied with a letter that constitutes a defense against Hicks's charges.*

[*c.* 21 March 1935]
[Key West]

It is very very kind of the *Student* to be showing sympathy with me for my age. But sixty is only a pretty good age. It is not advanced enough. The great thing is to be advanced. Now ninety would be really well along and something to be given credit for.

But speaking of ages, you will often hear it said that the age of the world we live in is particularly bad. I am impatient of such talk. We have no way of knowing that this age is one of the worst in the world's history. Arnold claimed the honor for the age before this. Wordsworth claimed it for the last but one. And so on back through literature. I say they claimed the honor for their ages. They claimed it rather for themselves. It is immodest of a man to think of himself as going down before the worst forces ever mobilized by God.

All ages of the world are bad–a great deal worse anyway than Heaven. If they weren't the world might just as well be Heaven at once and have it over with. One can safely say after from six to thirty thousand years of experience that the evident design is a situation here in which it will always be about equally hard to save your soul. Whatever progress may be taken to mean, it can't mean making the world any easier a place in which to save your soul–or if you dislike hearing your soul mentioned in open meeting, say your decency, your integrity.

Ages may vary a little. One may be a little worse than another. But it is not possible to get outside the age you are in to judge it exactly. Indeed it is as dangerous to try to get outside of anything as large as an age as it would be to engorge a donkey. Witness the many who in the attempt have suffered a dilation from which the tissues and the muscles of the mind have never been able to recover natural shape. They can't pick up anything delicate or small any more. They can't use a pen. They have to use a typewriter. And they gape in agony. They can write huge shapeless novels, huge gobs of raw sincerity bellowing with pain and that's all that they can write.

Fortunately we don't need to know how bad the age is. There is something we can always be doing without reference to how good or how bad the age is. There is at least so much good in the world that it admits of form and the making of form. And not only admits of it, but calls for it. We people are thrust forward out of the suggestions of form in the rolling clouds of nature. In us nature reaches its height of form and through us exceeds itself. When in doubt there is always form for us to go on with. Anyone who has achieved the least form to be sure of it, is lost to the larger excruciations. I think it must stroke faith the right way. The artist, the poet, might be expected to be the most aware of such assurance, but it is really everybody's sanity to feel it and live by it. Fortunately, too, no forms are more engrossing, gratifying, comforting, staying, than those lesser ones we throw off like vortex rings of smoke, all our individual enterprise and needing nobody's cooperation: a basket, a letter, a garden, a room, an idea, a picture, a poem. For these we haven't to get a team together before we can play.

The background is hugeness and confusion shading away from where we stand into black and utter chaos; and against the background any small man-made figure of order and concentration. What pleasanter than that this should be so? Unless we are novelists or economists we don't

Robert Frost and Wallace Stevens, 1935. Both poets were attacked by the literary left during the 1930s.

worry about this confusion; we look out on it with an instrument or tackle it to reduce it. It is partly because we are afraid it might prove too much for us and our blend of democratic-republican-socialist-communist-anarchist party. But it is more because we like it, we were born to it, born used to it and have practical reasons for wanting it there. To me any little form I assert upon it is velvet, as the saying is, and to be considered for how much more it is than nothing. If I were a Platonist I should have to consider it, I suppose, for how much less it is than everything.

LETTER:
To Louis Untermeyer; *Letters of Robert Frost to Louis Untermeyer*, pp. 261-264.

After Edwin Arlington Robinson died on 6 April 1935 Frost was asked to write a foreword for Robinson's soon-to-be-published narrative poem King Jasper. *Frost compiled with an essay that said little about Robinson but was, he realized, the "nearest I ever came to getting myself down in prose," sending the first draft to Untermeyer. When Robinson's publisher asked Frost to say more about Robinson, Frost added some brief comments about a few poems and some remarks about style that resemble the observations he had made in his 10 March 1924 letter to Untermeyer.*

Dear Louis:

I wanted you to see this before I sent it in to Macmillans but they got after me and I had to send it today. They may not like it. If not it will save me the trouble of deciding what I ought to charge for it. I hope you'll like it a little. There is some high, some low, and some Jack (Frost) in it. Game (by which I choose to mean "evaluation") is purposely left out.

Carol and I had a good visit. I came away still feeling full of things I had to say.

Ever yours
Robert Frost

Franconia New Hampshire
August 21, 1935

FOREWORD TO "KING JASPER"

It may come to the notice of posterity (and then again it may not) that this our age ran wild in the quest of new ways to be new. The one old way to be new no longer served. Science put it into our heads that there must be new ways to be new. Those tried were largely by subtraction—elimination. Poetry for example was tried without punctuation. It was tried without capital letters. It was tried without metric frame on which to measure the rhythm. It was tried without any images but those to the eye, and a loud general intoning had to be kept up to cover the total loss of specific images to the ear, those dramatic tones of voice which had hitherto constituted the better half of poetry. It was tried without content under the trade name of poesie pure. It was tried without phrase, epigram, coherence, logic, and consistency. It was tried without ability. I took the confession of one who had deliberately to unlearn what he knew. He made a back-pedalling movement of his hands to illustrate the process. It was tried premature like the delicacy of unborn calf in Asia. It was tried without feeling or sentiment like murder for small pay in the underworld. These many things was it tried without, and what had we left? Still something. The limits of poetry had been sorely strained, but the hope was that the idea had been somewhat brought out.

Robinson stayed content with the old-fashioned way to be new. I remember bringing the subject up with him. How does a man come on his difference, and how does he feel about it when he first finds it out? At first it may well frighten him, as his difference with the Church frightened Martin Luther. There is such a thing as being too willing to be different. And what shall we say to people who are not willing but anxious? What assurance have they that their difference is not insane, eccentric, abortive, inadmissable? Two fears should follow us through life. There is the fear that we shan't prove worthy in the eyes of someone who knows us at least as well as we know ourselves. That is the fear of God. And there is the fear of Man: the fear that men won't understand us and we shall be cut off from them.

We began in infancy by establishing correspondence of eyes with eyes. We recognized that they were the same features and we could do the same things with them. We went on to the visible motion of the lips—smile answered smile; then cautiously, by trial and error, to compare the invisible muscles of the mouth and throat. They were the same and could make the same sounds. We were still together. So far, so good. From here on the wonder grows. It has been said that recognition in art is all. Better say correspondence is all. Mind must convince mind that it can uncurl and wave the same filaments of subtlety, soul convince soul that it can give off the same shimmers of eternity. At no point would anyone but a brute fool want to break off this correspondence. It is all there is to satisfaction; and it is salutary to live in the fear of its being broken off.

The latest proposed experiment of the experimentalists is to use poetry as a vehicle of grievances against the un-Utopian state. As I say, most of their experiments have been by subtraction. This would be by addition of an ingredient that latter day poetry has lacked. A distinction must be made between griefs and grievances. Grievances are probably more useful than griefs. I read in a sort of Sunday School leaflet from Moscow that the grievances of Chekov against the sordidness and dullness of his home-town society have done away with the sordidness and dullness of home-town society all over Russia. They were celebrating the event. The grievances of the great Russians of the last century have given Russia a revolution. The grievances of their great imitators in America may well give us if not a revolution, at least some palliative pensions. We must suffer them to put life at its ugliest and forbid them not, as we value our reputation for liberality.

I had it from one of the youngest lately: "Whereas we once thought literature should be without content, we now know it should be charged as full of propaganda as a child's stocking is with coal when he boasts of having lost faith in Santa Claus." Wrong twice, I told him. Wrong twice and of theory prepense. But he returned to his position after a moment out for reassembly. "Surely art can be considered good only as it prompts to action." How soon, I asked him.

But there is danger of undue levity in teasing the young. The experiment is evidently started. Grievances are certainly a power and are going to be turned on. We must be very tender of our dreamers. They may seem like picketers or members of the committee on rules for the moment. We shan't mind what they seem if only they produce real poems.

But for me, I don't like grievances. I find I gently let them alone wherever published. What I like is griefs, and I like them Robinsonianly profound. I suppose there is no use in asking, but I should think we might be indulged to the extent of having grievances restricted to prose if prose will accept the imposition, and leaving poetry free to go its way in tears.

Robinson was a prince of heartachers amid countless achers of another part. The sincerity he

The Gully House, on the Frosts' second South Shaftsbury farm, which they bought in late 1928 with the royalties from West-Running Brook. *Frost sold this farm after the death of Elinor Frost in 1938.*

wrought in was all sad. He asserted the sacred right of poetry to lean its breast to a thorn and sing its dolefullest. Let weasels suck eggs. I know better where to look for melancholy.

A few superficial irritable grievances, perhaps, as was only human, but these are forgotten in the depth of griefs to which he was plunged.

Grievances are a form of impatience. Griefs are a form of patience. We may be required by law to throw away patience as we have been required to surrender gold; since by throwing away patience and joining the impatient in one rush on the citadel of evil, the hope is we may end the need of patience. There will be nothing left to be patient about. The day of perfection waits on unanimous social action. Two or three more good national elections should do the business. It has been similarly urged on us to give up courage, make cowardice a virtue, and see if that won't end war and the need of courage. Desert religion for science, clean out the holes and corners of the residual unknown, and there will be no more need of religion. (Religion is merely consolation for what we don't know.) But suppose there was some mistake; and the evil stood siege, the war didn't end, and something remained unknowable. Our having disarmed would make our case worse than it had ever been before. Nothing in the latest advices from Wall Street, the League of Nations, or the Vatican inclines me to give up my holdings in patient grief.

There were Robinson and I, it was years ago, and the place (near Boston Common) was the place, as we liked afterwards to call it, of Bitters, because it was with bitters, though without bitterness, we could sit there and look out on the welter of dissatisfaction and experiment in the world around us. It was too long ago to remember who said what, but the sense of the meeting was, we didn't care how arrant a reformer or experimentalist a man was if he gave us real poems. For ourselves, we would hate to be read for any theory upon which we might be supposed to write. We doubted any poem could persist for any theory upon which it might have been written. Take the theory that poetry in our language could be treated as quantitative, for example. Poems had been written in spite of it. And poems are all that matter. The utmost of ambition is to lodge a few poems where they will be hard to get rid of, to lodge a few irreducible bits, where Robinson lodged more than his share.

R. F.

EDITORIAL:

"Recruit Legislator," *Baltimore Sun,* 27 February 1936; *Interviews with Robert Frost,* pp. 85-86.

During the 1930s Frost, a conservative Democrat, began to express his political views both in public and in his poetry. Stopping in Baltimore in February 1936, he told a reporter that he was "anti-Roosevelt" but "not horribly anti-Roosevelt" and gave the reporter a copy of "To a Thinker," which had recently been published in the Saturday Review *(11 January 1936) as "To a Thinker in Office," explaining that the poem was about Pres. Franklin D. Roosevelt. The interview and poem appeared in the 26 February 1936 issue of the* Baltimore Sun *with the headline "Latest Poem By Robert Frost Versifies New Deal Is Lost." The next day the* Sun *printed the editorial comment reprinted here, and on 28 February an editorial in the* New York Times *summarized the Baltimore interview and concluded that in espousing conservative views when so many literary figures were moving to the left Frost was indeed "a 'politician at odd seasons.'" The last line of "To a Thinker," to which the* Baltimore Sun *editorial alludes, is "But trust my instinct–I'm a bard."*

"Poets" Shelley wrote in "A Defence of Poetry," "are the hierophants of an unapprehended inspiration; the mirrors of the gigantic shadows which futurity casts upon the present. . . ." And in a shorter and even more famous sentence, "Poets are the unacknowledged legislators of the World." Many doubtless have recalled his words with satisfaction at times when they sat in darkness and sang to cheer their own solitude.

Recent years, however, have found the poets using Shelley's dictum for more than solace; construing it in a very literal sense, and thinking of their legislative powers in terms of laws of Congress and Parliament. Certainly they are no longer content to see their legislative proposals pass "unacknowledged." They have been eager enough to declare their political position in their work. And it would be difficult plausibly to argue that by so doing they outran Shelley's meaning, for he was, in part, very much the propagandist poet. Anyway, the reader has no right to object to a writer's concern with politics so long as those "gigantic shadows of futurity" do not utterly obscure the bright mirror of his verse.

The latest poet to turn legislator, it seems, is Mr. Robert Frost, whose "To a Thinker" was quoted in *The Sun* of yesterday. But Mr. Frost's enrollment in the ranks of the lawmakers is unusual in two ways. His verses and his comments upon them make it clear that he has not joined the camp of the poetical Left–easily the larger at present time. And he says with great modesty that he doubts that his poem will have much influence. This uncertainty about the effect of the raising of his voice is one with his eagerness to point out that he is not really "horribly anti-Roosevelt."

Probably really moving poetry, whether it be of the "anti-Jacobin" kind or the somewhat subtler sort that comes now from the younger English poets, can be written only out of strong feeling, never out of a wish to be fair all around, to say just so much and no more and then to temper and explain what has been said. Surely Kipling, whose success Mr. Frost aptly recalls, never wrote in any such spirit. No, it is doubtful that Mr. Frost is a lawmaker after all, however he ranks as poet. But, of course, he will not concede that much. The last line of his "To a Thinker" tells us unqualifiedly that he feels he is in the right as a legislator even if the fact goes unacknowledged.

BOOK REVIEW:
R. P. Blackmur, "The Instincts of a Bard," *Nation* (New York), 142 (24 June 1936): 817-819.

During the spring semester of 1936 Frost was Charles Eliot Norton Professor at Harvard, delivering his six lectures to large and enthusiastic audiences. A Further Range, *published at the end of May 1936, earned him a third Pulitzer Prize and received some extremely positive reviews, but it was attacked by influential leftist critics Newton Arvin, Horace Gregory, Rolfe Humphreys, and R. P. Blackmur. Perhaps the most negative of these reviews was Blackmur's. A few years later in "The Critics and Robert Frost"* (Saturday Review, *1 January 1938) Bernard DeVoto called it "the most idiotic review of our time," adding: "The monkeys would have to tap typewriters throughout eternity to surpass it. . . ." When Theodore Morrison offered to write a more reasoned response than DeVoto's to Frost's critics, Frost suggested that "by lingering over them too long we make those fellows more important than I for my part like to think they are."*

It is a hard thing to say of a man grown old and honored in his trade, that he has not learned it. Yet that is what Mr. Frost's new volume, with its further range into matters of politics and the social dilemma, principally demonstrates. The new subjects, as they show themselves poetic failures, reflect back and mark out an identical weakness in poems on the old subjects. It is a weakness of craft, and it arises from a weakness, or an inadequacy, in the attitude of the poet toward the use and substance of poetry as an objective creation–as something others may use on approximately

Plymouth N.H.
Circa Jan. 15 1912

Dear Miss Ward:-

It wasn't to be expected that I would get back to business the minute my train arrived; and I didn't. And that was not because I can't move as fast as a train when I am on a train, but because it is so much further from the literary to the psychophysical than it is from little New York to Plymouth. I have been a constant sufferer since my visit with you from that Where-was-I-when-I-left-off or What-did-I-say-last feeling as I should have made complaint before if I had felt constrained to write you before I got safely and thoroughly home. I must tell you that one day— I couldnt for the life of me say now afterwards— I actually turned a recitation in the History of Education into a recitation of irrelevant verse. But there's no harm done, perhaps even some good. At any rate Elinor and I think so. It will never be counted against you with us that you have encouraged my poor Muse with interest when you couldnt with praise.

If this doesn't look like a very long letter to be writing to a friend and benefactor (by actual count of words it will prove longer than it looks), please remember who it was that Luther thought the proper target to throw ink at by the bottleful. Not the friend and benefactor of anyone in particular was it?

Sincerely yours
Robert Frost

Sonnet on the next page for my Moth and Butterfly book.

In White

A dented spider like a snowdrop white
On a white Heal-all, holding up a moth
Like a white piece of lifeless satin cloth—
Saw ever curious eye so strange a sight?—
Portent in little, assorted death and blight
Like the ingredients of a witches broth?—
The beady spider, the flower like a froth,
And the moth carried like a paper kite.

What had that flower to do with being white,
The blue Brunella every child's delight?
What brought the kindred spider to that height?
(Make we no thesis of the miller's plight.)
What but design of darkness and of night?
Design, design! Do I use the word aright?

RF.

Letter to Susan Hayes Ward written after Frost visited Miss Ward and her brother at their home in Newark, New Jersey (Huntington Library). While traveling to Newark on the train, Frost began reading a recently published translation of Henri Bergson's Creative Evolution, *and on his arrival expressed his enthusiasm for the book to William Hayes Ward, who dismissed it as thoroughly atheistic. After returning home, Frost wrote "In White" as an answer to Ward's charge. Ten years later Frost revised the poem and published it as "Design" in* American Poetry 1922: A Miscellany. *This revised version was first collected in* A Further Range.

the same level as the poet did. Mr. Frost is proud of his weakness and expresses it in the form of an apothegm at the close of the poem called To a Thinker.

> At least don't use your mind too hard,
> But trust my instinct–I'm a bard.

If we may distinguish, and for more than the purposes of this review, a bard is at heart an easygoing versifier of all that comes to hand, and hence never lacks either a subject or the sense of its mastery; and a poet is in the end, whatever he may be at heart, a maker in words, a true imager, of whatever reality there was in his experience, and every resource of the mind must be brought to bear, not only to express his subject, to transform what Mr. Frost means by instinct into poetry, but also to find his subject, to know it when he sees it among the false host of pseudo-subjects. These are the labors of craft–in relation to which the bard's labors are often no more than those of a pharmacist compounding a prescription by formula. In the old bards we look mostly for history, in the modern for escape. Swinburne is the type of modern bard, Yeats of the modern poet. It may be that by accident a bard is also a poet–as Swinburne was; but a poet who writes with only the discipline of a bard writes unfinished poetry of uncertain level and of unequal value. That is the situation of Mr. Frost; and when, as now, he attempts to make poems of his social reactions without first having submitted them to the full travail of the poetic imagination, the situation becomes very clear.

More precisely, taking the longest and most "serious" poem in the book, Build Soil–A Political Pastoral, which is a blank-verse dialogue between Tityrus the poet and Meliboeus the subsistence farmer, we find not poetry but an indifferent argument for a "one-man revolution" turned into dull verse. As bad religious poetry versifies the duty of an attitude toward God, bad social poetry versifies the need of an attitude toward society. Both the duty and the need may be genuine and deeply felt–it is our stock predicament and the great source of fanaticism and deluded action–but before either attitude can become poetry it must be profoundly experienced not only in intention but in the actuality of words. It is the object of craft, and only craft can secure the performance, to complete and objectify the act of experience. Craft in poetry is not limited to meter and rhyme, cadence and phrasing, gesture and posture, to any of the matters that come under the head of incantation, though it must have all these; for great poetry, craft is the whole act of the rational imagination. It must combine the relish and hysteria of words so as to reveal or illuminate the underlying actuality–I do not say logic–of experience.

Mr. Frost does not resort to the complete act of craft. His instincts as a bard do not drive him to the right labor, the complete labor, except by accident and fragmentarily, in a line here and a passage there. In a sense, his most complete and successful poems, the short landscape images where versification seems almost the only weapon of craft needed, are unfinished fragments. The good lines emphasize the bad, the careless, and the irrelevant, and make them intolerable; which is most often the case in activities which depend at critical points upon instinct. Instinct is only dependable in familiar circumstances, and poetry seldom reveals the familiar. A consideration of Desert Places, which is as good as any poem in the book, will show what I mean.

> Snow falling and night falling fast oh fast
> In a field I looked into going past,
> And the ground almost covered smooth in snow,
> But a few weeds and stubble showing last.
>
> The woods around it have it–it is theirs,
> All animals are smothered in their lairs.
> I am too absent-spirited to count;
> The loneliness includes me unawares.
>
> And lonely as it is that loneliness
> Will be more lonely ere it will be less–
> A blanker whiteness of benighted snow
> With no expression, nothing to express.
>
> They cannot scare me with their empty spaces
> Between stars on stars where no human race is.
> I have it in me so much nearer home
> To scare myself with my own desert places.

The same profound instinct that produced the first two stanzas of observation becoming insight allowed Mr. Frost to end his poem with two stanzas of insight that fails to reach the viable point of becoming observation. It may, practically, be a matter of bad rhyming in the fourth stanza, of metrical shapelessness in the third; but at the bottom, in so ambitious a poet as Mr. Frost, it must have been instinct that made the second pair of stanzas evade the experience forced into them by the first pair.

LETTER:

To Wilbert Snow; from his "The Robert Frost I Knew," *Texas Quarterly,* 11 (Autumn 1968): 9-48.

Frost had been arguing with Wilbert Snow, a professor at Wesleyan University, about what Milton had meant when he wrote in book 3 of Paradise Lost, *"in Mercy and Justice both,/Through Heav'n and Earth, so shall my glorie excel,/but Mercy first and last shall brightest shine." His discussion of mercy versus justice in this letter introduces the major theme of two blank-verse dramas that he finished during the next decade:* A Masque of Reason *(completed in 1943 and published in 1945) and* A Masque of Mercy *(completed and published in 1947). The letter was written from Florida; Frost had been going south for part of each winter since 1934 and would continue to do so for the rest of his life.*

Bill Bill

Use your brains a moment while we brush up your vocabulary. You simply must not quibble in a serious matter like a win-at-any cost public debater. Don't pretend you don't know what Milton meant when he said mercy was always first. You know your Milton and your Puritanism. He used it in the sense of first aid to what? To the deserving? No, to the totally depraved and undeserving. That's what we are and have been since the day Eve ate the rotten apple. I bet it was rotten. Eve wouldn't have known the difference. It was probably her first apple. (There you get a genuine first) And look what a city person will eat for an apple from never having seen one on a tree. "In Adam's fall We sinned all." Mercy ensued. There could be nothing for us but mercy first last and all the time from the point of view of the religious pessimist. Milton's first is only relative. It is very like Adam and Eve's being first and yet finding the daughters of men as wives for Cain and Abel. There is the presupposition of a whole set up of sin, failure, judgment, and condemnation. Mercy comes in rather late to pre-

The Bread Loaf Writers' Conference staff in 1939: (front) Mrs. John Gassner, Mrs. Fletcher Pratt, Kathleen Morrison, Mrs. Herbert Agar, Mrs. Robeson Bailey; (middle) John Gassner, Louis Untermeyer, Frost, Edith Mirrielees, Theodore Morrison; (top) Fletcher Pratt, Gorham Munson, Herbert Agar, Richard L. Brown, Bernard DeVoto, Robeson Bailey, Herschel Brickell. Though he had been to Bread Loaf earlier, Frost did not begin attending its summer sessions regularly until the late 1930s. Kathleen Morrison, wife of Harvard Professor and Bread Loaf director Theodore Morrison, had become Frost's assistant a few months after the death of Elinor Frost in 1938 and Frost had moved to Boston to be closer to the Morrisons.

vent execution–sometimes only to delay it. It is too easy to understand Milton. He faced and liked the harshness of our trial. He was no mere New Testament saphead. (I should like to think Christ was none; but have him your own way for the time being. You'd better have read up on your Deuteronomy before I see you again.) Milton loved Cromwell for his Ironsides and Michael for licking the Devil. He had a human weakness for success; he wanted the right to prevail and was fairly sure he knew what right was. Within certain limits he believed in the rewards of merit. But after all was said for the best of us he was willing to admit that before God our whole enterprise from the day we put on fig leaves and went to work had been no better than pitiful.

I'm like that with a class in school. I see the boys as comparatively good and bad but taken as a job lot in the absolute so really good for nothing that I can bring myself to mark them with nothing but mercy and I give them all A or at worst B. Your sense of justice is shocked. You can hardly credit my claim to godlike illogical kindness. I have always been a prey to it. The office where justice sits with the scales over her eyes has never approved of me. I never go there except to try to get a scholarship or a fellowship for some poor fool you probably would have flunked out; particularly a Rhodes Scholarship because I'd rather sacrifice a bad man than a good to the seductions of Cecil Rhodes. There I go distinguishing between the good and bad but I don't readily see how I can avoid it, do you old Tops? (plural as a praise word)?

Illogical kindness–that is mercy. Only those are likely to act on it who know what it is in all its subordination. It was just and logical that a man's body should be taken in slavery when he went beyond his depth in debt. It was illogical that his creditor couldn't take him in slavery and the state should take him merely as a prisoner. It was another step in illogic when it was decided his person should never again be taken at all. Another when it was decided that he shouldn't be reduced by the sheriff below a certain amount of personal property. At every step there were warnings from the conservative that character would be demoralized by the relaxation of strict logical justice. People would go in debt on purpose it

Frost during a 1940 visit to Washington, D.C.

was feared to abuse the rich and thrifty. We are now in our lifetime seeing a great next step taken in this long story of debt–and it will be something if it is all that comes of your New Deal. It is going to be settled once for all that no man's folly or bad luck can ever reduce him to no income at all. A chicken is hatched with enough yolk in its guts to last it several days. Henceforth not only the rich but everybody born is to be sure of at least a few dollars a week as long as he lives. Never more quite down to the quick. That is in America–and while we can afford it. We are all going to fetch in and make that come true. But don't call that social justice. Keep your words in their places. It is illogical kindness. It is mercy. And you and the Lord have mercy on my argument.

Ever yours
R. F.
743 Bay St. North
Gainesville Florida

January 2, 1938

LETTER:
To Robert P. Tristram Coffin; *Selected Letters of Robert Frost*, pp. 461-463.

While preparing to lecture about Frost at Johns Hopkins University, poet Coffin, who had heard Frost give a talk at a Poetry Society of America dinner on 1 April 1937 in New York, asked Frost for a transcript, eliciting instead one of Frost's most important statements of his philosophy and its relationship to his poetry. The Harvard lectures Frost mentions are his Charles Eliot Norton lectures, which he never preapared for publication although he was asked to do so.

24 February 1938
Gainesville

Dear Coffin,

It is my bad luck I am away off down here where I can't help you help me. I suppose you

12

Death.
In the narrow way,
Where it comes down
One wooded hill
To climb the next,
Under the frown
Of gathering night,
Careless and still
The hunter lurks,
With gun depressed,
Facing alone
The alder swamp's
Ghastly snow-white.
And his hound works,
In the offing there,
Like one possessed,
And yelps delight,
And sings and romps,
Bringing him on
The shadowy hare,
For him to rend
And deal a death
That he, nor it,
(Nor I) have wit
To comprehend

Page from the manuscript booklet Frost sent to Susan Hayes Ward at Christmas 1911 (Huntington Library). Frost later cut the first six lines from this poem and published it as "The Rabbit-Hunter" in A Witness Tree *(1942).*

have nothing to call you even part way in this direction till you come to Baltimore for your lectures. I would venture some way into the cold but I mustn't come so far as to seem inconsistent to those with whom I have used the cold as an excuse to stay away from their platforms and dinner tables. A lot would come out in talk once you got me started with what you happened to remember of that Poetry Society affair. I'm terrible about my lectures. In my anxiety to keep them as long as possible from becoming part of my literary life, I leave them rolling round in my head like clouds rolling round in the sky. Watch them long enough and you'll see one near-form change into another near-form. Though I am sure they are hardly permissable on the platform, I continue to bring them there with no more apology than to a parlor or class room. Their chief value to me is for what I pick up from them when I cut across them with a poem under emotion. They have been my inner world of raw material and my instinct has been to keep them raw. That can't long retain their state however. The day approaches when they will lose their fluidity and in spite of my stirring spoon become crystal. Then one kind of fun will be over and I shall have to find another to take its place (tennis most likely or hoeing). I thought I was about ready to let them set when I accepted the Harvard invitation to deliver them in writing after delivering them by word of mouth. Something in me still fights off the written prose. The nearest I ever came to getting myself down in prose was in the preface to Robinson's *King Jasper*. That is so much me that you might suspect the application to him of being forced. It was really no such thing. We two were close akin up to a certain point of thinking. He would have trusted me to go a good way in speaking for him particularly on the art of poetry. We only parted company over the badness of the world. He was cast in the mold of sadness. I am neither optimist nor pessimist. I never voted either ticket. If there is a universal unfitness and unconformity as of a buttoning so started that every button on the vest is in the wrong button hole and the one empty button hole at the top and the one naked button at the bottom so far apart they have no hope of getting together, I don't care to decide whether God did this for the fun of it or for the devil of it. (The two expressions come to practically the same thing anyway.) Then again I am not the Platonist Robinson was. By Platonist I mean one who believes what we have here is an imperfect copy of what is in heaven. The woman you have is an imperfect copy of some woman in heaven or in someone else's bed. Many of the world's greatest–maybe all of them–have been ranged on that romantic side. I am philosophically opposed to having one Iseult for my vocation and another for my avocation; as you may have inferred from a poem called Two Tramps in Mud Time. You see where that lands me on the subject of Dante's Beatrice. Mea culpa. Let me not sound the least bit smug. I define a difference with proper humility. A truly gallant Plantonist will remain a bachelor as Robinson did from unwillingness to reduce any woman to the condition of being used without being idealized.

But you didn't ask me to distinguish between myself and Robinson. I fell accidentally into a footnote to the *King Jasper* preface in self defence. What you asked for is any recollection I have of my recent talks. I may be able to bring some of them back in detail – give me time. What in the world did I say in New York. Was my subject "Neither or Both." Do you want to show me the notes you made? Is there time? I'm going to hurry this off tonight for a beginning and then if you say so try to tell you a little more. One of my subjects at Harvard was Does Wisdom Matter. I mean in art. Does it matter for instance that I am so temperamentally wrong about Beatrice. You can hear more if it is worth your while. Another subject was The Renewal of Words. Molly Colum had been saying the world was old, people were jaded and the languages worn out. My whole lecture was an answer to her defeatism, though I took good care not to name her–and don't you name her. Poetry is the renewal of words forever and ever. Poetry is that by which we live forever and ever unjaded. Poetry is that by which the world is never old. Even the poetry of trade names gives the lie to the unoriginal who would drag us down in their own powerlessness to originate. Heavy they are but not so heavy that we can't rise under them and throw them off.

Well well well——

Sincerely yours Robert Frost

LETTER:

To Robert P. Tristram Coffin; *Selected Letters of Robert Frost,* pp. 464-467.

After Coffin reminded Frost that the subject of his 1 April 1937 talk was "Crudities," Frost expanded on his remarks in his previous letter. "Education by Poetry," mentioned in the last paragraph of this letter, is a talk delivered at Amherst; first published in the Amherst Graduates' Quarterly *for February 1931 and collected in* Selected Prose of Robert Frost *(1966).*

[*c.* 7 March 1938]
[Gainesville]

Dear Coffin:

Your letter brings back my animus of that April 1st. I was gunning for the kind of Americans who fancied themselves as the only Americans incapable of crudity. I started off with some crudity I knew they could join me in laughing at and I ended up with some they might not be so incapable of themselves. But I protested all the way along my love of crudity. I thank the Lord for crudity which is rawness, which is raw material, which is the part of life not yet worked up into form, or at least not worked all the way up. Meet with the fallacy of the foolish: having had a glimpse of finished art, they forever after pine for a life that shall be nothing but finished art. Why not a world safe for art as well as democracy. A real artist delights in roughness for what he can do to it. He's the brute who can knock the corners off the marble block and drag the unbedded beauty out of bed. The statesman (politician) is no different except that he works in a protean mass of material that hardly holds the shape he gives it long enough for him to point it out and get credit for it. His material is the rolling mob. The poet's material is words that for all we may say and feel against them are more manageable than men. Get a few words alone in a study and with plenty of time on your hands you can make them say any thing you please.

You remember the story of the neighbor who asked me how much I got apiece for my books. Then there was the man who after telling me for hours about his big bold business adventures asked me toward morning what I did with myself. I staved off the confession. I likened myself to him in adventurousness. I was a long-shot man too. I liked not to know beforehand what the day might bring forth. And so till he lost patience with me and cried "Shoot!" Well I write poetry. "Hell," he said unhappily "my wife writes that stuff." And it turned out she did. I came on a book of her verse at the house of the President of Sophie Newcomb in New Orleans where she lived and her husband visited. I must tell you the latest. A forty year old telegraph operatress had drawn her own inference from my telegrams. "You write," she said to me one day. "Yes."–"Poetry?" "Yes." "Just the person I'm looking for then. I lost my father a year or so ago and I'd like to get a poem written about him. I'll tell you what I want said." She took paper and pencil.–But how much better or worse was she than the man [Hermann Hagedorn] out of Harvard, New York, real society and literature who came a long way to ask me to write something American to save America? He was sure I could write something really American if I tried. But I must remember to like crudity even in high places and I must be willing to be crude myself for other people's purposes.

In my book of 1923 [*New Hampshire*] I dealt with the crude importunacy of those who would have you a prude or a puke (mewling and puking in the public arms). Choose you this day to be a puke or be disowned by the intelligensia. Fifteen years have gone by and the almost equally disgusting alternatives offered are collectivist or rugged individualist. (Can you bear it?) Here I have to recall myself as a workman to my duty of liking crudity in however amused a way. In this connection I probably told the story of my getting called a counter-revolutionary for not writing my poetry "tendential." By tendential in politics they mean what is sure to happen. After making sure it is going to happen, they don't trust it to happen of itself: they take hold and make it happen. Just so the horsey bets on a sure thing and then does all that in him lies with dope and counter dope, sponges in the nose, bribery and threat to make the sure thing surer. There is a horrid crudity of morals in our idealistic tendential friends. But I must stick to it that I like crudity.

Hegel saw two people marry and produce a third person. That was enough for Hegel–and Marx too it seems. They jumped at the conclusion that so all truth was born. Out of two truths in collision today sprang the one truth to live by tomorrow. A time succession was the fallacy. Marriage, reproduction and the family with a big F have much to answer for in misleading the analogists. Fire flashes from the flint and steel of metaphor and if caught in lint it may be spread, but that is no reason why it should spread to burn the world. That is monomania or monometaphor.

Take Justice and Mercy (you got my pairs of opposing goods exactly). A mind where there was a mind wouldn't think of them as breeding a third thing to live on after they are dead and gone. Justice and Mercy stand each other off and the present stands up between them. Divine Right and Consent do the same with the same result. They are like the two hands that, by first tightening and then loosening the double string between them, make the tin buzzer buzz like a little buzz saw. You must have played with a tin buzzer on the Kennebeck.

Mind where there was a mind would be ashamed to have been radical when young only to be conservative when old. Life sways perilously at the confluence of opposing forces. Poetry in general plays perilously in the same wild place. In particular it plays perilously between truth and make-believe. It might be extravagant poetry to call it true make believe–or making believe what is so.

Of course use anything you can or will. It's a good idea to leave out people's names.

I thought my Education by Poetry might help. It was taken down without my knowledge.

Ever yours R. F.

LETTER:
To Hervey Allen; *Selected Letters of Robert Frost*, p. 470.

Elinor Frost died on 20 March 1938 in Gainesville, Florida. One of the first friends to reach Gainesville–finding Frost, who had been ill himself, in "a state of complete collapse"–was novelist and poet Hervey Allen, who lived in South Miami. In thanking Allen for his help Frost quoted lines from two poems by Alfred, Lord Tennyson: words spoken by Sir Bedivere to his dying king in "The Passing of Arthur" and a line from the following stanzas of "In Memoriam": "Let Love clasp Grief lest both be drown'd,/Let darkness keep her raven gloss./Ah sweeter to be drunk with loss,/To dance with Death, to beat the ground,//Than that the victor Hours should scorn/The long result of love, and boast,/'Behold the man that loved and lost,/But all he was is overworn.' " Six months earlier Frost had written to Unter-

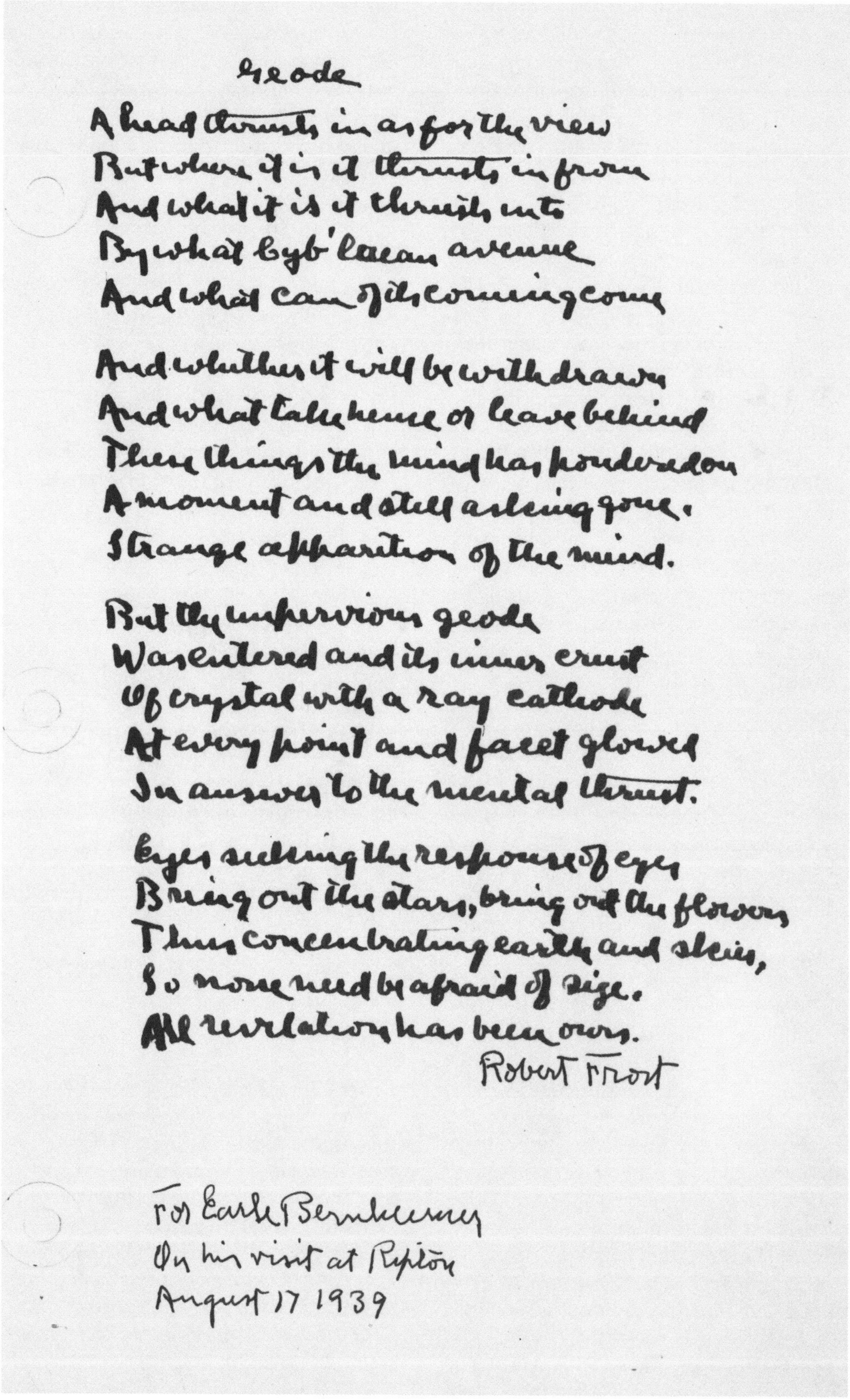

Geode

A head thrusts in as for the view
But where it is it thrusts in from
And what it is it thrusts into
By what Cyb'laean avenue
And what can of its coming come

And whither it will be withdrawn
And what take hence or leave behind
These things the mind has pondered on
A moment and still asking gone.
Strange apparition of the mind.

But the impervious geode
Was entered and its inner crust
Of crystal with a ray cathode
At every point and facet glowed
In answer to the mental thrust.

Eyes seeking the response of eyes
Bring out the stars, bring out the flowers
Thus concentrating earth and skies,
So none need be afraid of size.
All revelation has been ours.

Robert Frost

For Earle Bernheimer
On his visit at Ripton
August 17 1939

Fair copy of a poem first published in the Spring 1938 issue of the Yale Review *(Barrett Library, University of Virginia Library). Frost changed the poem's title to "All Revelation" when he collected it in* A Witness Tree.

meyer that Elinor Frost was "the unspoken half of everything I ever wrote and both halves of many a thing. . . ."

12 April 1938
Gainesville

Dear Hervey:

And I the last go forth companionless
And the days darken round me.
But it is written also by the same hand,
Let darkness keep her raven gloss.
I shall never forget your coming to me with such sympathy.

Ever yours Robert

LETTER:

To William Prescott Frost; *Family Letters of Robert and Elinor Frost,* pp. 218-219.

Frost's son, Carol Frost, who had been suffering from depression, shot and killed himself on 9 October 1940 while his wife, Lillian LaBatt Frost, was in the hospital recovering from surgery. Frost had gone back to Boston after spending several days with his son, and Frost's fifteen-year-old grandson, Prescott, was alone in the house with his father at the time of his suicide. The Hollidays mentioned in this letter, written a few days after Frost had returned home from the funeral, were friends with whom Prescott Frost was staying until his mother could leave the hospital.

Boston
12 October 1940
[Special Delivery]

Dear Prescott

Disaster brought out the heroic in you. You now know you have the courage and nerve for anything you may want or need to be, engineer, inventor or soldier. You would have had plenty of excuse if you had gone to pieces and run out of that house crying for help. From what Lesley reported to me of her talk with Lillian in Pittsfield Friday I judge you were in actual danger there alone with your unhappy father–unhappy to the point of madness. You kept your head and worked your faculties as coolly as a clock on a shelf. You've been tried more than most people are in a whole lifetime. Having said so much, I shan't bring up the subject again (for a long time anyway) either of your bravery or the terrible occasion for it. Let's think forward–I don't mean in big terms all at once, but just taking the days as they come along with a more natural and comfortable interest than I fear you have been permitted for some years past. You are fortunate in the friendship of such splendid people as the Hollidays. I took a great liking to them. They are a great new beginning for you. The spell you and Lillian have been under is broken. You and she can think with some sanity now. So can I with you.

Lillian says Carol thought nobody loved him. Pitiful! His mind was one cloud of suspiciousness. And we cared so much for him that his cloud was our cloud. We tried to enter into his affairs and sympathise with him. We spent hours, you and Lillian of course more hours than I. We could do him no good. Well he has taken his cloud away with him. His difficulty was too hard for us to understand. We never gave it up. He ended it for us. We shall have difficulties of our own ahead, but they will be simple and straightforward I believe. You and I and your mother have the healthy clearness of ordinary plain people. Lesley is that way too. So also is the Kathleen who has set me on my way onward again. We are the tough kind.

You write me and tell me how your mother is and what she's talking about. When she can spare you, come down and we'll see what we can do for amusement. Maybe Kathleen can arrange with Bunty Sage's father for our visiting some laboratories at Technology.

Affectionately Grandpa

BOOK REVIEW:

Wilbert Snow, "Robert Frost, Dean of American Poetry," *New York Herald-Tribune Books,* 10 May 1942, p. 5

Frost was awarded his fourth Pulitzer Prize for A Witness Tree, *published on 23 April 1943. It was a success with the critics and the public, who had bought ten thousand copies by mid June.*

Robert Frost has made such a distinctive contribution to American poetry that almost any reviewer is inclined in advance to say gracious things about his worth when called upon to appraise an additional volume. In the back of the reviewer's mind such poems as "Stopping by Woods on a Snowy Evening," "Birches," "The Road Not Taken" and a dozen more induce him toward partiality. When, therefore, upon opening the new volume, he discovers a number of poems he can whole-heartedly praise as worthy of these old favorites, he feels himself the recipi-

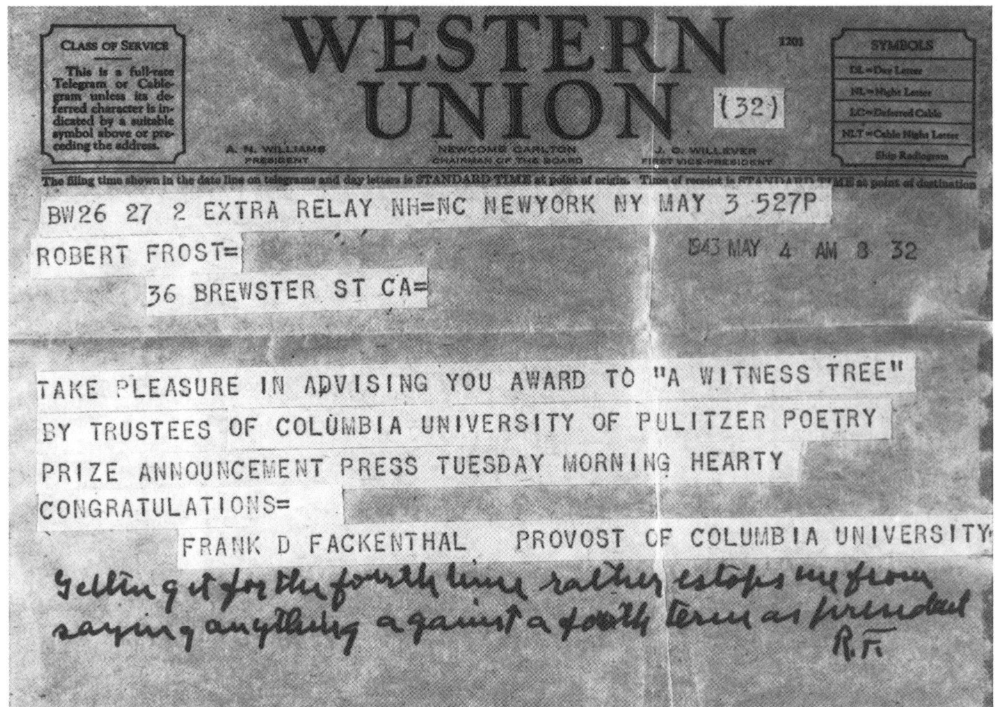

WESTERN UNION

CLASS OF SERVICE
This is a full-rate Telegram or Cablegram unless its deferred character is indicated by a suitable symbol above or preceding the address.

A. N. WILLIAMS PRESIDENT
NEWCOMB CARLTON CHAIRMAN OF THE BOARD
J. C. WILLEVER FIRST VICE-PRESIDENT

1201

SYMBOLS
DL=Day Letter
NL=Night Letter
LC=Deferred Cable
NLT=Cable Night Letter
Ship Radiogram

(32)

The filing time shown in the date line on telegrams and day letters is STANDARD TIME at point of origin. Time of receipt is STANDARD TIME at point of destination

BW26 27 2 EXTRA RELAY NH=NC NEWYORK NY MAY 3 527P

ROBERT FROST=

1943 MAY 4 AM 8 32

36 BREWSTER ST CA=

TAKE PLEASURE IN ADVISING YOU AWARD TO "A WITNESS TREE" BY TRUSTEES OF COLUMBIA UNIVERSITY OF PULITZER POETRY PRIZE ANNOUNCEMENT PRESS TUESDAY MORNING HEARTY CONGRATULATIONS=

FRANK D FACKENTHAL PROVOST OF COLUMBIA UNIVERSITY

Getting it for the fourth time rather estops me from saying anything against a fourth term as president

R.F.

Telegram–with a draft for Frost's reply–informing him that he had won his fourth Pulitzer Prize (Barrett Library, University of Virginia Library

Frost with daughter Lesley Frost Francis, her daughters, Lee and Elinor, and their Airedale, Ricky, in Frost's cabin at the Homer Noble farm in Ripton, Vermont, circa 1945. Frost had bought the farm, near Bread Loaf, in 1939 and spent part of each summer there for the rest of his life, renting the main house to the Morrisons and living in a cabin on the property.

ent of a rich legacy, and wants to impart the good tidings to others.

"A Witness Tree," Frost's latest volume, contains a half dozen poems which have a right to stand with the best things he has written. Of these half dozen, "Come In" is probably destined to be the general favorite. Without departing from the conversational tone which is Frost's especial hall mark, this lyric has color, music, and a triumphant sense of life bubbling through it. "The Silken Tent," a love sonnet, carries through an unusual figure with a sureness of touch which only a master could achieve. "Carpe Diem" is a wise criticism of those who tell us to snatch the present hour. "I Could Give All to Time" is a variation of the same theme, "Time," the last stanza of which reads:

I could give all to Time except—except
What I myself have held. But why declare
The things forbidden that while the Customs slept
I have crossed to Safety with? For I am There,
And what I would not part with I have kept.

"To a Young Wretch" describes the poet's feelings as he ponders what he should do to a youngster who, without asking, has cut a spruce out of his pasture for a Christmas tree. I will venture to call it the finest Christmas poem in American literature. It concludes:

And though in tinsel chain and popcorn rope,
  My tree a captive in your window bay
Has lost its footing on my mountain slope
  And lost the stars of heaven, may, oh, may,
The symbol star it lifts against your ceiling
Help me accept its fate with Christmas feeling.

"The Gift Outright" is a poem which we need to contemplate in our present disturbing crisis. In sixteen blank-verse lines, crowded with overtones, the poem summarizes the story of American culture—our too-long dependence on the Old World and the fatal weakness such dependence brought us.

Something we were withholding made us weak
Until we found it was ourselves
We were withholding from our land of living,
And forthwith found salvation in surrender.

My arbitrary half-dozen mark is already reached and I find I have omitted an unusual poem which originally appeared in one of our magazines under the title "The Geode," and is now called "All Revelation"—a poem which locates everything in heaven and earth in the human mind:

Eyes seeking the response of eyes
  Bring out the stars, bring out the flowers,
Thus concentrating earth and skies
So none need be afraid of size.
  All revelation has been ours.

I find I have omitted also "Happiness Makes Up in Height for What It Lacks in Length," a singing lyric which attributes the lasting sense of warmth and light to the memory of one cloudless day. Nor have I included "The Most of It," with its matchless picture of a buck swimming across a river: "Pushing the crumpled water up ahead." And what could be more Frostian than "A Considerable Speck," a poem in which the author ponders over the presence of a tiny insect on a sheet of white paper, rejoicing to find there what many teachers of English composition have so often failed to discover on sheets of paper, manifestations of life?

No one can know how glad I am to find
On any sheet the least display of mind.

The keynote of Frost is fierce New England individualism; this it is that gives his work an integrated unity. In the new collection he includes a poem written in 1900 "To a Moth Seen in Winter," and its strong individualistic assertion enables it to seem at home here, and yet every book of Frost's seven has some one quality which set it off from the others. In this volume he has left the "lovely, dark and deep" woods of northern New England and turned into the darker and deeper forests of the human mind. Two of the first six poems I have mentioned deal with the concept of time. The fascinating Harvard Phi Beta Kappa poem, "The Lesson for Today," contrasts the dark ages of the past with the encircling gloom of our present-day civilization, and a portion of the poem deals with the effect of the concept of space on human thinking. One whole section of the book is made up of brief gnomic sayings in verse which shows that Frost has been brooding over the wisdom of the East. In other words Frost is turning more and more toward philosophy, although, of course, he has always been more or less of a philosopher in the school of Thoreau and Emerson. Some of the poems here are little more than rhymed fancies; others lack the bullet-like unity of structure to be found in those I have singled out for special praise. The narra-

57

Job. All very splendid. I am flattered proud
To have been in on anything with you.
'Twas a great demonstration, if you say so.
Though incidentally I sometimes wonder
Why it had had to be at my expense.

God It had to be at somebody's expense.
Society can never think things out;
It has to see them acted out by actors,
Devoted actors at a sacrifice—
The ablest actors I can lay my hand on.
~~(Mankind for instance never seems to tire~~
~~Of getting reconvinced in bloody drama~~
~~That Civilization and Utopia~~
~~Are opposites and mutually exclusive,~~
~~So that they cannot both be had at once.)~~
Is that your answer?

Job No, for I have yet
To ask my question. We disparage reason.
But all the time its what were most concerned with.
There's will as motor and there's will as breaks.
Reason is I suppose the steering gear.
The will as breaks cant stop the will as motor
For very long. We're plainly made to go.
We're going anyway and may as well

Page from the manuscript for A Masque of Reason, *lines 217-234 in the published text (Barrett Library, University of Virginia Library)*

21

His favorite reading is seed catalogues
~~And The Rural New Yorker. When we get~~
~~Through here he says he's going to buy a farm.~~
When he gets too agrarian for me
I take to drink—at least I take a drink.
[She has her own glass in a vacant chair.]

Paul — She'll take to drink and see how he likes that.

Keeper — Bel's a solitary social drinker.
She doesn't mind not offering a drink
To anyone around when she is drinking.

Jesse Bel — We're poor—that's why. My man can't earn a living

Keeper — Is it just any city you're against?

Jonah — Yes, but New York will do as an example.

Keeper — Well, you're as good as in New York this minute—
Or bad as in New York.

Jonah — I know I am.
That was where my engagement was to speak
This very night. I had the hall all hired,
The audience assembled. There I was

Page from the manuscript for A Masque of Mercy, *lines 81-96 in the published text (Barrett Library, University of Virginia Library)*

To Russell from R. F.

Directive

Back out of all this now too much for us,
Back in a time made simple by the loss
Of detail, burned, dissolved or broken off
Like graveyard marble ~~with the elements,~~ sculpture in the rain
There is a house that is no more a house.
Upon a farm that is no more a farm
And in a town that is no more a town.
The road there, if you'll let a guide direct you
Who only has at heart your getting lost ~~at least~~,
May seem as if it should have been a quarry —
Great monolithic knees the former town
Long since gave up pretense of keeping covered.
And there's a story in a book about it:
Besides the wear of iron wagon wheels
The ledges show lines ruled southeast northwest
The chisel work of an enormous Glacier
That braced his feet against the Arctic Pole.
You must not mind a certain coolness from him
Still said to haunt this side of Panther Mountain.
Nor need you mind the serial ordeal
Of being watched from forty cellar holes
As if by eye-pairs out of forty firkins.
As for the woods' excitement over you
That sends light rustle rushes to their leaves
Charge that to upstart inexperience.
Where were they all not twenty years ago?
They think too much of having shaded out
A few old pecker-fretted apple trees.
Make up a reassuring song of how
Someone's road home this was once was,
Who may be just ahead of you on foot
Or creaking with a buggy load of grain.

Manuscript inscribed to book collector Russell Alberts, circa 1946 (Barrett Library, University of Virginia Library). "Directive" was first published in the winter 1946 issue of the Virginia Quarterly Review *and collected in* Steeple Bush.

The height of the adventure is the height
Of country where one village culture ended,
Another one began. They both are lost.
And if you're lost enough to find yourself
By now, pull in your ladder road behind you
And put a sign up Closed to all but me.
Then ~~And~~ make yourself at home. The only field
You see's no bigger than a harness gall.
First there's the children's house of make believe,
Some shattered dishes underneath a pine,
The playthings in the playhouse of the children!
Weep for what little things could make them glad.
Then for the house that is no more a house,
But only a belilaced cellar hole,
Now closing slowly like a dent in dough.
This was no playhouse, but a house in earnest.
Your destination and your destiny's
A brook that was the water of this house,
Cold as a spring as yet so near its source,
Too lofty and original to rage.
(We know the valley streams that when aroused
Will leave their tatters hung on barb and thorn.)
I have kept hidden in the instep arch
Of an old cedar at the waterside
A broken ~~goblet like~~ drinking goblet like the Grail
Under a spell so the wrong ones can't find it
So can't get saved as St Mark says they mustn't.
I stole the Goblet from the Children's playhouse.
Here are your waters and your watering place.
Drink and be whole again without confusion.

tive in the book is not equal to the great dramatic narratives to be found in "North of Boston." But he has given us enough first-rate poems here to satisfy the most exacting critic, keep us all in his debt, and leave him secure in his enviable place as the dean of American poetry.

MEMOIR:

From Hewette E. Joyce, "A Few Personal Memories of Robert Frost," *Southern Review*, new series 2 (October 1966): 847-849.

Frost had left academe briefly when Elinor Frost died, but in September 1939 he had begun a two-year term as Ralph Waldo Emerson Fellow at Harvard, followed by another two years there as Fellow in American Civilization. In October 1943 he became George Ticknor Fellow in the Humanities at Dartmouth, remaining there until 1949, when he accepted an appointment as Simpson Lecturer in Literature at Amherst. Joyce, who was on the faculty at Dartmouth, later remembered Frost's approach to Milton's Lycidas.

When Robert Frost was Ticknor Fellow, it was the faculty's privilege to ask him, now and then, to take a class for us. I asked him one day if he would talk to my Seventeenth-Century Literature class. "Yes," he said, "What are they reading?"

"Milton," I replied.

"I'll talk about the short poems, not the long ones."

"We have just come to *Lycidas*," I said. Knowing that *Lycidas* was a favorite of his, I had planned carefully.

That was a really memorable class hour. I had put a text, open at *Lycidas*, on the desk; but he closed it, saying, "If you really like a poem, you remember it. You have your books. If I forget or make mistakes, you tell me." As far as I can remember, he needed no help.

He began reciting, stopping for comments every line or so, one poet talking about another poet's work. He had fun with "Hence with denial vain, and coy excuse . . . " ("Don't be coy now, Muse; you can't back out of this.") I have often wished that I had a tape recording of that brilliant and fascinating hour. When the bell rang he had "covered" perhaps half of the poem. It was Frost as teacher, at his best.

BOOK REVIEW:

Louis Untermeyer, "Still Further Range," *Yale Review*, 37 (September 1947): 138-139.

Reviewers treated Steeple Bush, *published 28 May 1947, with less respect than they had accorded Frost's previous collection. He was particularly stung by a* Time *magazine review (16 June 1947) which suggested that his "Yankee individualism" had "hardened into bitter and often unspired Tory social commentary," adding that* Steeple Bush *did "nothing to enlarge his greatness. . . ." Other reviewers found praiseworthy poems in the book, but even Frost's good friend Untermeyer offered qualified approval.*

This may not be Robert Frost's heaviest or happiest book, but it is one of his shrewdest. It is salted with wit and peppered with satire. Although it is a small book–only sixty-two deeply margined pages–the range is wide: songs, soliloquies, whimsical lyrics, somber speculations, bitter conclusions. The section titles give the key to its variety: "Steeplebush," "Five Nocturnes," "A Spire and Belfry," "Out and Away," "Editorials."

The skeptic note is immediately apparent. Frost is a dogged examiner; he appraises the world without being deceived by its cherished illusions; he doubts both its pretenses and its desperations. Rarely has the poet written so grimly as in "The Broken Drought," "Bursting Rapture," "Why Wait for Science," "No Holy Wars for Them," and particularly "The Ingenuities of Debt," with it pitiless beginning and end:

These I assume were words so deeply meant
They cut themselves in stone for permanent
Like trouble in the brow above the eyes:
"Take Care to Sell Your Horse before He Dies;
The Art of Life Is Passing Losses on." . . .
Sand has been thrusting in the square of door
Across the tessellation of the floor,
And only rests, a serpent on its chin,
Content with contemplating, taking in,
Till it can muster breath inside a hall
To rear against the inscription on the wall.

This is a far and lonely cry from the personal bucolics of "North of Boston," the little lyrics of "A Boy's Will," the appealing pastorals and monologues of "Mountain Interval," "West-Running Brook," and "A Further Range." But the new book is not without some of the old tenderness and the rough half-concealed grace. "A Young Birch" and "Something for Hope" (and especially, "Directive") recall the genius for understatement which is essentially Frost's. Such poems supply added emphasis to that simplicity which is so deceptive and so subtle. Rarely has the sadness of age and the hopelessness of inevitable ruin reached out so tragically as in "Directive." Yet there is no breast-beating, no loud anguish. On the contrary, the tone is detached and seemingly impersonal, lightly if falsely casual:

Back out of all this now too much for us,
Back in a time made simple by the loss
Of detail, burned, dissolved, and broken off
Like graveyard marble sculpture in the weather,
There is a house that is no more a house
Upon a farm that is no more a farm
And in a town that is no more a town.
The road there, if you'll let a guide direct you
Who only has at heart your getting lost,
May seem as if it should have been a quarry–
Great monolithic knees the former town
Long since gave up pretence of keeping covered. . . .
Make yourself up a cheering song of how
Someone's road home from work this once was,
Who may be just ahead of you on foot
Or creaking with a buggy load of grain. . . .

I have implied that this is neither Frost's most commanding nor his most co-ordinated volume. But it is highly characteristic of the man at seventy-three and the poet at any age. It cannot be by-passed. It must be read as part of the still-growing work of America's most considerable contemporary poet.

CRITICAL ESSAY:

Randall Jarrell, "The Other Robert Frost," *Nation*, 165 (25 November 1947): 588, 590-592.

In reviewing Steeple Bush (New York Times Book Review, *1 June 1947), Jarrell had said that most of the poems in the book were the "productions of somebody who once, and somewhere else, was a great poet." A few months later he wrote this far more positive article discussing what he considered Frost's most important poems and presenting an interpretation that challenged the prevailing view of Frost as the uncomplicated, optimistic farmer-poet.*

Besides the Frost that everybody knows there is one whom no one even talks about. Everybody knows what the regular Frost is: the one living poet who has written *good* poems that ordinary readers like without any trouble and understand without any trouble; the conservative editorialist and self-made apothegm-joiner, full of dry wisdom and free, complacent, Yankee enterprise; the Farmer-Poet–this is an imposing private role perfected for public use, a sort of Olympian Will Rogers out of "Tanglewood Tales"; and–last or first of all–Frost is the standing, speaking reproach to any other good modern poet: "If *Frost* can write poetry that's just as easy as Longfellow, you can too–you do too." It's this "easy" side of Frost that is more attractive to academic readers, who are eager to canonize any modern poet who condemns in example the modern poetry which they condemn in precept; and it is this side that has helped to get him neglected or depreciated by intellectuals–the reader of Eliot or Auden usually dismisses Frost as something inconsequentially good that *he* knew all about long ago. Ordinary readers think Frost the greatest poet alive, and love some of his best poems almost as much as they love some of his worst ones. He seems to them a sensible, tender, humorous poet who knows all about trees and farms and folks in New England, and still has managed to get an individualistic, fairly optimistic, thoroughly American philosophy out of what he knows; there's something reassuring about his poetry, they feel–almost like prose. Certainly there's nothing hard or queer or gloomy about it.

These views of Frost, it seems to me, come from not knowing his poems well enough or from knowing the wrong poems too well. Frost's best-known poems, with two or three exceptions, are not his best poems at all: when you read, say, the selections in Untermeyer, you are getting a good synopsis of the ordinary idea of Frost and a bad misrepresentation of the real Frost (my *real*). It would be hard to make a novel list of Eliot's best poems, but my list of ten or twelve of Frost's best poems is likely to seem to anybody too new to be true. This is it: The Witch of Coös, Neither Out Far Nor In Deep, Design, A Servant to Servants, Directive, Provide Provide, Home-Burial, Acquainted with the Night, The Pauper Witch of Grafton, An Old Man's Winter Night, The Gift Outright, Desert Places, and The Fear.

Nothing I say about these poems can make you see what they are like, or what the Frost that matters most is like; if you read them you will see. The Witch of Coös is the best thing of its kind since Chaucer; I've read it to schoolgirls and I've read it to soldiers, and I've never seen an audience that wasn't so amused, scared, and saddened that it shocked them to have to wake up at the end. Home-Burial and A Servant to Servants are two of the most moving and appalling dramatic poems ever written; and how could lyrics be more ingeniously and conclusively merciless than Neither Out Far Nor In Deep, or Design? or more grotesquely and subtly and mercilessly disenchanting than the tender An Old Man's Winter Night? or more unsparingly truthful than Provide Provide? And so far from being obvious, optimistic, orthodox, most of these poems are extraordinarily subtle and strange, poems which express an attitude that, at its most extreme, makes pessimism seem a hopeful evasion; they begin with a flat and terrible reproduction of the evil in the world and end by saying: It's so; and there's nothing you can do about it; and if there were, would *you* ever do it? The limits which existence approaches and falls back from have seldom been stated with such bare composure.

Frost's virtues are extraordinary. No other living poet has written so well about the actions of ordinary men: his wonderful dramatic monologues or dramatic scenes come out of a knowledge of people that few poets have ever had, and they are written in a verse that uses, with absolute mastery, the rhythms of actual speech. Particularly in his blank verse there is a movement so characteristic, so unmistakably and overwhelmingly Frost's that one feels about it almost as the Duchesse de Guermantes felt about the Frans Halses at Haarlem: that even if you caught just a glimpse of them, going by in the street car, you could tell that they were something pretty unusual. It is hard to exaggerate the effect of this exact, spaced-out, prosaic, truthful rhythm, whose objects have the tremendous strength–you find it in Hardy's best poems–of things merely put down and left to speak for themselves. (Though Frost has little of Hardy's self-effacement, his matter-of-fact, lifelong humility; Frost's tenderness, sadness, and humor are adulterated with vanity and a hard complacency.) Frost's seriousness and honesty; the bare sorrow with which things are accepted as they are, neither exaggerated or explained away; the many, many poems in which there are real people with their real speech and real thoughts and real emotions–all this, in conjunction with so much gentleness and subtlety and exactness, such classical understatement and restraint, makes the reader feel that he is not in a book but in a world, and a world that has in common with his own some of the things that are most important in both. I don't need to praise anything so justly famous as Frost's observation of and empathy with everything in Nature from a hornet to a hillside; and he has observed his own nature, one person's random or consequential chains of thoughts and feelings and perceptions, quite as well. (And this person, in the poems, is not the "alienated artist" cut off from everybody who isn't, yum-yum, another alienated artist, but someone like normal people only more so–a normal person in the less common and more important sense of *normal.*) The least crevice of the good poems is saturated with imagination, an imagination that expresses itself in the continuous wit and humor and particularity of what is said, in the hand-hewn or hand-polished texture of its saying. The responsibility and seriousness of Frost's best work are nowhere better manifested than in the organization of these poems–an organization that in its concern for any involution or ramification that really belongs to its subject, and in its severity toward anything else, expresses that absorption into a subject that is prior even to affection.

The organization of Frost's poems is often rather simple or–as people say–"old-fashioned." But, as people ought to know, very complicated organizations are excessively rare in poetry, although in our time a very complicated disorganization has been excessively common; there is more successful organization in Home-Burial or The Witch of Coös than in The Cantos and The Bridge put together. These titles will remind anyone of what is scarcest in Frost: rhetoric and romance, hypnotic verbal excitement, Original Hart Crane–Frost's word-magic is generally of a quiet, sober, bewitching sort, though the contrasts he gets from his grayed or unsaturated shades are often more satisfying to a thoughtful rhetorician than some dazzling arrangements of prismatic colors. Yet there are dazzling passages in Frost:

" . . . So desert it would have to be, so walled
By mountain ranges half in summer snow,
No one would covet it or think it worth
The pains of conquering to force change on.
Scattered oases when men dwelt, but mostly
Sand dunes held loosely in tamarisk
Blown over and over themselves in idleness.
Sand grains should sugar in the natal dew
The babe born to the desert, the sand storm
Retard mid-waste my cowering caravans–
There are bees in this wall." He struck the clapboards,
Fierce heads looked out; small bodies pivoted.
We rose to go. Sunset blazed on the windows.

Frost with Kathleen and Theodore Morrison, 1950

Frost has written, as everybody knows; "I never dared be radical when young/For fear it would make me conservative when old." This is about as truthful as it is metrical. Frost *was* radical when young–he was a very odd and very radical radical, a much more interesting sort than the standard *PM* brand–and now that he's old he's sometimes callously and unimaginatively conservative. Take, for instance, his poems about the atomic bomb in "Steeple Bush"; these amount to a very old and very successful man saying, "I've had my life–why should you worry about yours?" Sometimes it is this public figure, this official role–the Only Genuine Robert Frost in Captivity–that writes the poems, and not the poet himself; and then one gets a self-made man's political editorials, full of cracker-box philosophizing, almanac joke-cracking, of a snake-oil salesman's mysticism; one gets the public figure's relishing consciousness of himself, a surprising constriction of imagination and sympathy; one gets an arch complacency, a complacent archness; and one gets Homely Wisdom till the cows come home. Often the later Frost makes demands on himself that are minimal; he uses a little wit and a little observation and a little sentiment to stuff–not very tight–a little sonnet; and it's not bad, but not good enough to matter, either. The extremely rare, extremely wonderful dramatic and narrative element that is more important than anything else in his early poetry almost disappears from his later work; in it the best poems are usually special-case, rather than all-out, full-scale affairs. The younger Frost is surrounded by his characters, living beings he has known or created; the older Frost is alone. But it is this loneliness that is responsible for the cold finality of poems like Neither out Far Nor in Deep and Provide Provide.

Frost's new books have few of his virtues, most of his vices, and all of his tricks; the heathen who would be converted to Frost by them is hard to construct. "Steeple Bush" (Henry Holt, $2.50) has one wonderful poem, Directive; a fairly good, dazzlingly heartless one, The Ingenuities of Debt; and nothing else that is not better done somewhere else in Frost. "A Masque of Mercy" (Henry Holt, $2.50), though no great shakes–as you see, its style is catching–is a great improvement on the earlier "A Masque of Reason," which is a trivial, frivolous, and bewilderingly corny affair, full of jokes inexplicable except as the contemptuous patter of an old magician perfectly certain that *he* can get away with anything in the world: *What fools these readers be!* Besides, Frost has long ago divorced reason for common sense, and is basking complacently in his bargain; consequently, when common sense has God justify His ways by saying, "I was just showing off to Satan, Job," the performance has all the bleak wisdom of Calvin Coolidge telling you what life comes to at 2 1/2%.

The plot of "A Masque of Mercy" is as simple as that of "Merope," but it is one that is more likely to get Frost recognized as another precursor of surrealism than to get him looked askance at as one of Arnold's Greeks. A bookstore-keeper named My Brother's Keeper has a wife name Jesse Bel; one night Jonah–who, having forgotten both his gourd and what God made of it, is feeling for New York City all that he used to feel for Nineveh–seeks refuge in the bookstore; after a little talk from St. Paul (Jesse Bel's psychiatrist) and a lot from Keeper (a character who develops so much that he finally develops into Robert Frost), Jonah comes to realize that "justice doesn't really matter."

Frost lavishes some care and a lot more self-indulgence on this congenial subject: he has a thorough skepticism about that tame revenge, justice, and a cold certainly that nothing but mercy will do for *us*. What he really warms to is a rejection beyond either justice or mercy, and the most felt and moving part of his poem is the unshaken recognition that

> Our sacrifice, the best we have to offer,
> And not our worst nor second best, our best,
> Our very lives, our lives laid down like Jonah's
> Our lives laid down in war and peace, may not
> Be found acceptable in Heaven' sight. . . .

To feel this Fear of God and to go ahead in spite of it, Frost says, is man's principal virtue, courage. He treats Paul very sympathetically, but gives him speeches that are ineffectual echoes of what he really said; and Frost makes about him that poor old joke which finds that he "theologized Christ almost out of Christianity." *This* is the thanks one gets for discovering Christianity.

SENATE RESOLUTION:

"Seventy-Fifth Anniversary of the Birth of Robert Frost" (S. Res. 244), *Congressional Record,* 96, part 3 (24 March 1950), p. 3997.

Because of the prevailing belief that Frost was born in 1875, the unusual honor of a birthday greeting from the U.S. Senate came on his seventy-sixth birthday. The resolution, introduced by Sen. Robert A. Taft, was adopted by unanimous consent.

Whereas Robert Frost in his books of poetry has given the American people a long series of stories and lyrics which are enjoyed, repeated, and thought about by people of all ages and callings; and

Whereas these poems have helped to guide American thought with humor and wisdom, setting forth to our minds a reliable representation of ourselves and of all men; and

Whereas his work through the past half century has enhanced for many their understanding of the United States and their love of country; and

Whereas Robert Frost has been accorded a secure place in the history of American letters; and

Whereas on March 26 he will celebrate his seventy-fifth birthday: Therefore be it

Resolved, That the Senate of the United States extend him felicitations of the Nation which he has served so well.

REMARKS:

T. S. Eliot, Toast at Books Across the Sea Dinner, 11 June 1957; *Robert Frost: The Later Years, 1938-1963,* pp. 243-244.

Frost spent 20 May-20 June 1957 on a visit to England and Ireland sponsored by the U.S. State Department, receiving many honors, including honorary doctorates from Oxford, Cambridge, and the National University of Ireland. Frost's biographer Lawrance Thompson reported Eliot's remarks as toastmaster at a dinner given in Frost's honor.

Eliot began to speak:

"Mr. Frost," he said, "you have already heard a great number of speeches in your honor in the last few weeks, both in English and in Latin. I wish that I *could* make a speech in your honor in Latin, because it would, perhaps, cover up other imperfections, if my Latin was good enough. But I want to spare you that. I am merely here to propose your health, in my capac-

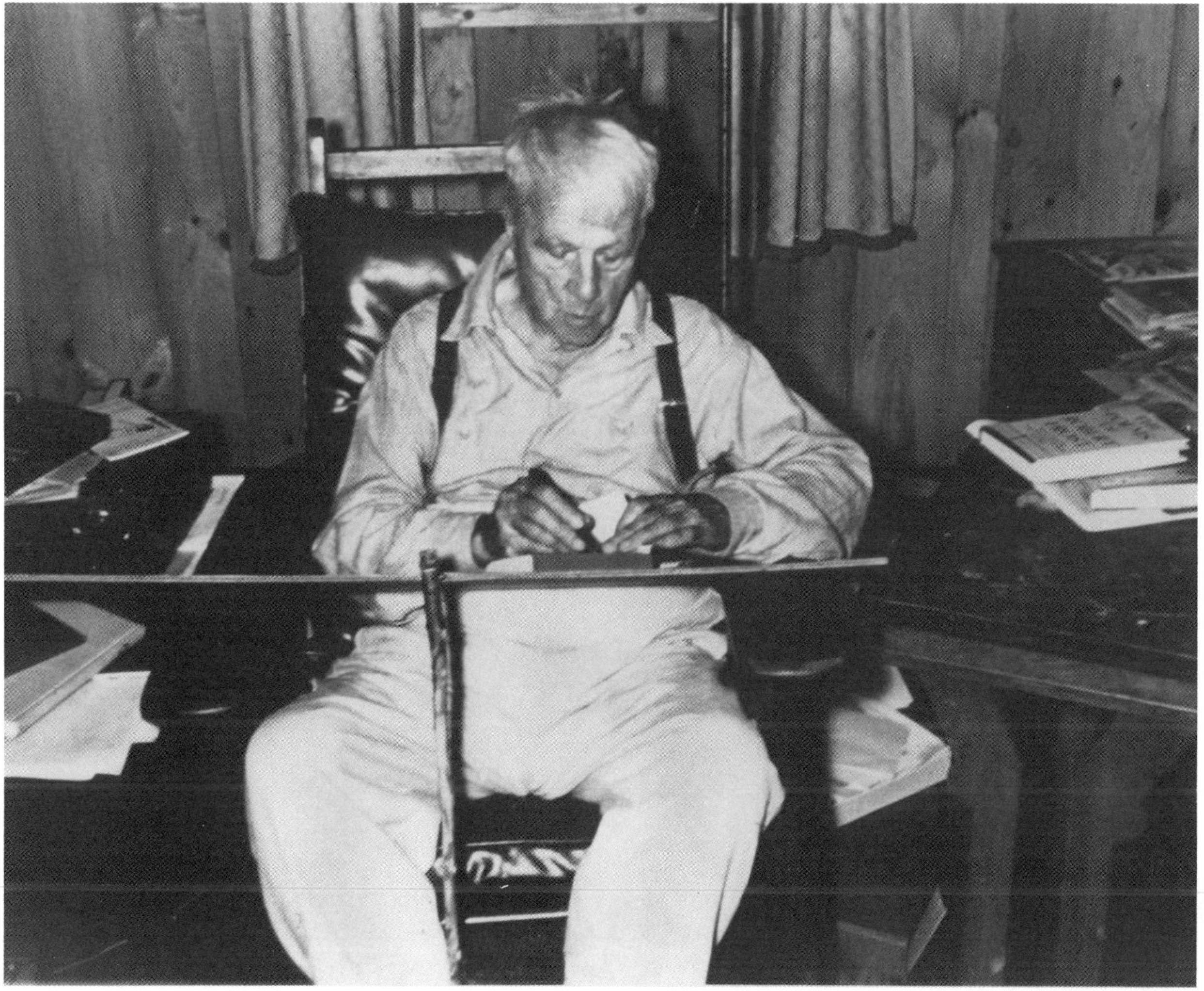

Frost in his cabin at Ripton, Vermont, 16 August 1956. This photograph was taken by a visiting book collector, Howard G. Schmitt, whose aunts had recently made quilts from the academic hoods that had come with the twenty-seven honorary degrees Frost had received by June 1956.

ity as having been a Past-President, during the war, of Books Across the Sea. And it is, I think, appropriate that the first dinner party, I think it is, to be held in this Page Library should be a dinner given by Books Across the Sea to Robert Frost, for Robert Frost's books are very much across the sea, in both directions.

"I would like before proposing a toast merely to drop one or two grains of incense before you.

"Mr. Frost, I never heard your name until I came to this country. I heard it first from Ezra Pound of all people. He told me about you with great enthusiasm. I gathered that you were a protégé of his of whom he expected a good deal. At the same time, I gathered that your work, or what had appeared at that time, was not in Ezra Pound's opinion required reading for *me*. He may have been right, at that time, because I was still in a formative period, and goodness knows what would have happened if you had influenced me at that stage. But, you know, as one gets older, one cares less about movements and tendencies and groups. We all have our own idiom and metric and subject matter, but I have long come to feel that there are only two kinds of poetry–good and bad. And the bad poetry can be very much of one's own type, and the good poetry can be of a very different type.

"Mr. Frost is one of the good poets, and I might say, perhaps, *the* most eminent, the most distinguished, I must call it, Anglo-American poet now living. I have a special weakness, perhaps–no I shouldn't call it a weakness–I have a special understanding of a great deal of his work. Of course, I also have the New England back-

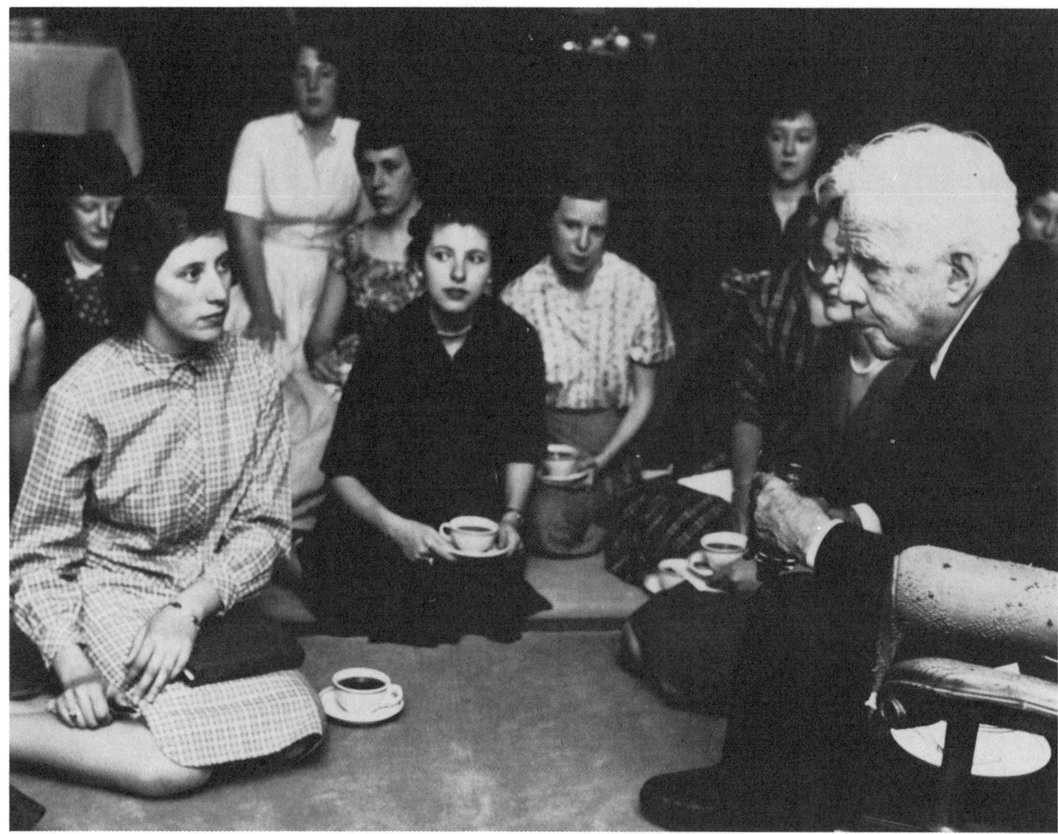

Frost with students at Mount Holyoke, 1956

ground. But I think that there are two kinds of local feeling in poetry. There is one kind which makes that poetry only accessible to people who had the same background, to whom it means a great deal. And there is another kind which can go with universality: the relation of Dante to Florence, of Shakespeare to Warwickshire, of Goethe to the Rhineland, the relation of Robert Frost to New England. He has that universality. And I think that the beginning of his career, and the fact that his first publication and reputation was made in this country, and that he is now hailed in this country universally as the most distinguished American poet, points to that fact.

"Ladies and gentlemen, I give you Robert Frost."

Frost was moved by Eliot's remarks almost to tears. When he rose to acknowledge the tribute, the first thing he said was, "There's nobody living in either country that I'd rather hear that from."

LETTER:
To Archibald MacLeish (first draft); *Selected Letters of Robert Frost,* p. 569.

T. S. Eliot's remarks to Frost and Frost's own talks in England mentioned Ezra Pound's sponsorship of Frost early in his career. Frost and Eliot, along with Ernest Hemingway, had already signed a letter drafted by Archibald MacLeish, which asked the U.S. Attorney General to release Pound from St. Elizabeths Hospital in Washington, D.C. He had been held there for eleven years, after having been found mentally unfit to stand trial on treason charges brought because of pro-Fascist radio broadcasts he had made from Italy during World War II. In this letter, written in response to a request that Frost meet with Assistant Attorney General William P. Rogers to discuss the Pound case, Frost expresses his personal attitude toward Pound. Though Frost wrote letters and made four visits to Washington on Pound's behalf, the major portion of credit for Pound's release, in April 1958, should be assigned to MacLeish, who masterminded the campaign.

24 June 1957
Ripton

Dear Archie

My purpose holds to help you get Ezra let loose though I won't say my misgivings in the whole matter haven't been increased by my talks

Frost, during his 1957 trip to England, visiting the Dymock region of Gloucestershire, where he had lived from April 1914 until early 1916

with Eliot lately, who knows more about Ezra than anybody else and what we can hope to do for his salvation. I should hate to see Ezra die ignominiously in that wretched place where he is for a crime which if proven couldn't have kept him all these years in prison. So you go ahead and make an appointment with the Department of Justice. I suppose we might be prepared to answer for Ezra's relative sanity and ability to get himself taken care of out in the world. Neither you nor I would want to take him into our family or even into our neighborhood. I shall be acting largely on your judgment. I can't bear that anyone's fate should hang too much on mine.

I am tied up here for the moment. I could be in Washington for any time on Wednesday July 17 or Friday the 19th after three o'clock or Saturday. But I should have thought that this time of year wouldn't find people in Washington and the affair might better wait until the Fall.

So much for business–bad business. We mustn't forget the good relations we have promised to have with each other this summer.

Ever yours–on either side of the Atlantic

ARTICLE:
Paul Sampson, "Robert Frost Pays Visit As New 'Poet Laureate,'" *Washington Post,* 22 May 1958, p. C18.

In May 1958 the Library of Congress announced that Frost would be its next Consultant in Poetry. After completion of his term in June 1959, Frost accepted a three-year appointment, beginning in 1960, as Honorary Consultant in the Humanities, a post created for him. The occasion on which Frost was fined $10 for "punchin' someone" was in 1896 after he gave a neighbor a black eye for calling him a coward, and his angry victim brought charges.

Robert Frost, already renowned as America's best-known poet, met the Washington press yesterday and revealed himself as a master of comedy timing as well as an eloquent lyric poet.

Frost reading his poems for a Decca recording released in 1957

Frost held forth wittily and eloquently at a press conference at the Library of Congress called to announce formally his appointment as the Library's Consultant in Poetry in English.

The 84-year-old poet, a four-time winner of the Pulitzer Prize, will assume his duties in October, succeeding Randall Jarrell, who will return to teaching at the University of North Carolina.

Employing subtle changes of expression, effective pauses and straightforward sincerity, Frost fascinated an audience of newspapermen for an hour. He told stories on himself, improvised verse and philosophized on politics and education.

Frost defined the duties of his new job as "making the politicians and stateman more aware of their responsibility to the arts."

He quickly added that he wouldn't have so much confidence in this mission "if I hadn't been so successful in Washington lately." Frost was alluding to his successful efforts in obtaining the release of his fellow poet, Ezra Pound, from St. Elizabeths Hospital.

Frost said the Pound experience was the first "adventure I had with the law." He then paused, memory crept across his face and he added with diffidence: "I never have been in court except for punchin' someone once."

Pressed for details, Frost described his opponent as "just a rival." "He said I hit him," Frost recalled. "The judge looked at me and asked 'Did you hit him.' I said it looks as if I did. I was fined $10, and I thought I'd have to leave town. It was on the front page of the local paper."

He evaded questions about the reasons for the blow by saying it was "too delicate a matter."

Asked the technique he planned for interesting statesmen in the arts, Frost replied: "I guess we'll have to ask them to dinner once in a while . . . You know you can keep giving them your books. Every chance you get inscribe your books to someone."

Frost confided that he has a copy, with "a very nice binding" of the "Complete Works of Robert Frost" ready to inscribe to President Eisenhower.

Frost mentioned he had seen President Eisenhower recently and reporters pressed him for the President's views on poetry and other subjects. Frost looked slyly at his questioners and said, "You see, I told him quite a lot . . . He said he'd be a Jeffersonian Democrat instead of a Jacksonian. Is that important?"

After asking reporters whether he was to amuse them, Frost mentioned that he always thought the phrase "highbrow, middlebrow, lowbrow and no brow" would make a "nice refrain" for a poem. He then improvised a verse about a Carthaginian woman who repulsed the advances of sailors:

"Highbrow, middlebrow, lowbrow and nobrow.
"She had no brow but a
mind of her own.
"She wished the sailors
would let her alone.
"Highbrow, middlebrow, lowbrow, and nobrow."

"I haven't got any further than that," Frost added.

On the serious side, Frost earnestly advocated his plan for "toning up high schools" by making high school teachers more respected members of the community. He suggested setting up special named professorial chairs in high schools "so as to give something to thicken up the place."

SENATE RESOLUTION:
"Tribute to Robert Frost on his 85th Birthday" (S. Res. 95), *Congressional Record*, 105, part 4 (25 March 1959), p. 5162.

Shortly before Frost's birthday in 1954 Lawrance Thompson discovered conclusive proof that Frost was born in 1874, and his eightieth birthday was correctly celebrated on 26 March 1954. Five years later his birthday again brought greetings from the U. S. Senate. The resolution was introduced by Sen. Winston L. Prouty and adopted by unanimous consent.

Whereas in the words of the poet Shelley "Poets are the unacknowledged legislators of the world"; and

Whereas poets have been described as "the movers and the shakers of the world forever"; and

Whereas art, which includes the making of poetry, is said to be "the conscience of mankind"; and

Whereas the Congress, although compelled by the necessities of our time to concentrate its primary attention on things material, nevertheless is fully cognizant of the value and importance to our citizens as long as our Nation shall endure of things of the spirit contained in our national literature, art and culture; and

Whereas Robert Frost, the present Consultant in Poetry in English to the Library of Congress is one of America's and the world's best loved and best known poet-philosophers; and

Whereas throughout his long and distinguished career in the field of letters his poetry and his philosophy have enhanced for many throughout the world their understanding of the United States and its people; and

Whereas for almost half a century Robert Frost has been writing poetry which has brought pleasure, comfort, inspiration, thoughtfulness, keener awareness of nature and greater understanding of fellow human beings to thousands of people in all parts of the civilized world; and

Whereas he has unselfishly devoted many years of his life to teaching and bringing to the youth of our land an appreciation of the finer things of life; and

Where his work has brought him more recognized honors than have come to any other contemporary American poet, including four Pulitzer prizes in poetry, the Helen Haire Levinson Prize, the Russell Loines Memorial Fund Prize, the Mark Twain Medal, the Gold Medal of the National Institute of Arts and Letters, the Silver Medal of the Poetry Society of America, and the Theodore Roosevelt Medal; and

Whereas the Senate of the United States in a resolution on the occasion of his seventy-fifth birthday extended Mr. Frost the "felicitations of this Nation which he has served so well"; and

Whereas on the 26th of March 1959 he will attain the venerable age of 85 years, still enthusiastically carrying forward his writing, his teaching, his philosophizing, his lecturing and his public poetry readings throughout the land: Now, therefore, be it

Resolved, That the Senate of the United States extend to Robert Frost its good wishes on the occasion of his anniversary and salute him as a citizen, as a man, as a poet, and as a representative of our Nation's art and culture, and that the Secretary of the Senate is authorized and directed to transmit to Mr. Frost an engrossed copy of this resolution.

Frost with poet Melvin Tolson

Frost with great-grandchildren Douglas, Marcia, and Katherine Wilber; his granddaughter Elinor; and his daughter Lesley

John F. Kennedy, Frost, and Lyndon B. Johnson at Kennedy's Inauguration, 20 January 1961

ARTICLE:

Richard L. Lyons, "Frost's Poem Wins Hearts at Inaugural," *Washington Post*, 21 January 1961, p. A8.

John F. Kennedy asked Frost to read "The Gift Outright" at the Presidential Inauguration on 20 January 1961. Frost later revised "Dedication," the long poem he wrote to read as a preface to "The Gift Outright," and included it in his 1963 book, In the Clearing, *as "For John F. Kennedy, His Inauguration, Gift outright of 'The Gift Outright' (With some preliminary history in rhyme)."*

Robert Frost in his natural way stole the hearts of the Inaugural crowd yesterday with a poem he recited and another which he couldn't read, because the sun's glare hid the words.

The 86-year-old New England poet, bundled up in heavy overcoat and scarf, recited in his strong voice "The Gift Outright" which he had selected after Mr. Kennedy invited him to take part in the Inaugural program. Frost describes it as the "most national" of his poems. It tells his hopeful thoughts about the destiny of the United States.

But the New England poet had also written specially for the occasion a longer poem expressing his gratification that the arts had been recognized in the ceremony and dedicating his recital to the new President.

Something to Celebrate

"First a dedication," said Frost, as he took his place at the podium. He got through six of the 42 lines, calling the appearance of an artist at such an event "something for us all to celebrate" and then faltered.

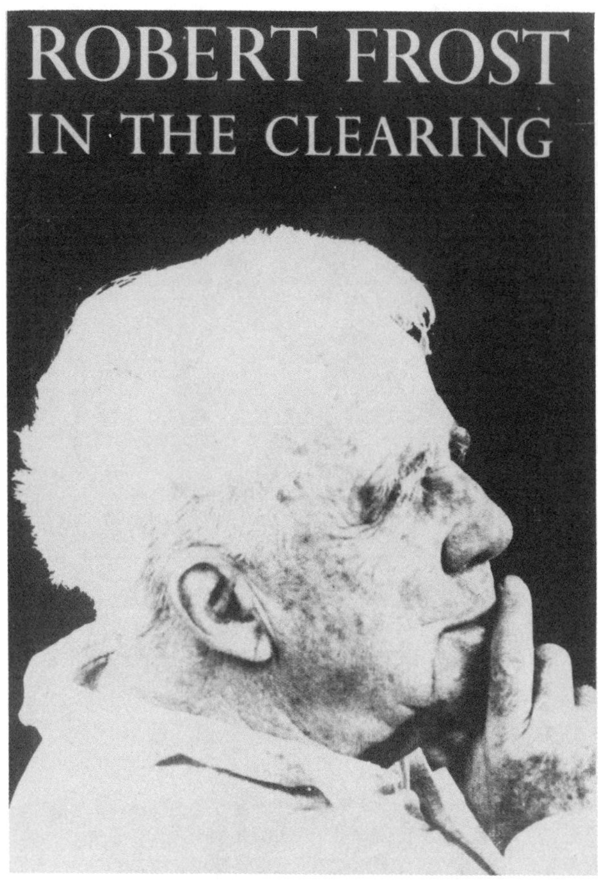

Dust jacket for Frost's last book

"I'm not having a good light here at all," he muttered. "I can't see in this light."

Vice President Lyndon B. Johnson, seated just behind him, leaped forward and tried to shield the sun with his top hat.

"Here, give me that," said Frost. He tried holding Johnson's hat over the typewritten text, but it evidently held out the light as well as the glare. He gave up and "said" the poem he had brought with him in his head.

At Mr. Kennedy's request, Frost changed one word in "The Gift Outright" and announced it as he recited. In the original version written in 1930s, the last line, referring to the United States, said "Such as she was, such as she would become." Yesterday Frost said "would" and then added "and for this occasion let me change to "will."

"What I was leading up to," he then explained of the unread lines, "was to dedicate the poem to the President-elect."

The special poem was titled "Dedication" and said of the first President to think of inviting a poet to participate "this tribute verse to be his own I bring."

It said of the new free nations grown out of Colonialism after the example of the United States:

> "My verse purports to be the guiding chart
> To the o'erturning it was ours to start
> And in it have no unimportant part."

As Frost moved back to his seat, both the new and the old President clasped his hand.

BOOK REVIEW:

Richard Wilbur, "Poems That Soar and Sing and Charm," *New York Herald Tribune Books*, 25 March 1962, p. 3.

On Frost's eighty-eighth birthday Pres. John F. Kennedy presented the poet a special Gold Medal that the U.S. Congress had voted to award him "in recognition of his poetry, which has enriched the culture of the United States and the philosophy of the world." Frost gave the president an inscribed copy of his new book, In the Clearing, *published that day.*

Tomorrow Robert Frost will be 88. This new collection of his poems will be published on his birthday.

"In the Clearing" has an epigraph borrowed from Frost's early poem, "The Pasture"–"and wait to watch the water clear, I may." This illuminates both the old poem and the new book, and it brings to mind something which Frost once said: "All we do in life is a clarification after we stir things up." And then there is a charming poem in the book called "A Cabin in the Clearing." It is a dialogue between the chimney smoke and garden mist, which hover about a house encircled by forest, eavesdropping on the earnest talk of the couple within. The "clearing" of this poem is a little area of human coherence, a bit of the universe become a colony of mind. Frost's title, then, has to do with mind-activity, with clarification with the penetration of nature by human thought and effort.

This is a high-spirited, high-minded book. Despite its Frostian skepticisms and paradoxes, it is sweepingly assertive, and ought to satisfy the sort of critic who values poetry for the philosophy which may be shaken out of it–as some children eat the Cracker Jack for the sake of the prize. A verse "frontispiece," excerpted from the long poem "Kitty Hawk," argues that

With a lantern that wouldnt burn
In too frail a buggy we drove
Behind a great Percheron horse
Through a pitch dark limitless grove

And a man came out of the trees
And took our horse by the head
And reaching back to his ribs
Deliberately stabbed him dead.

The most unquestioning pair
That ever accepted fate
And the least disposed to ascribe
Any more than we had to to hate,

We assumed the man himself
Or someone he had to obey
Wanted us to get down
And walk the rest of the way.

This belongs with The Lockless Door
and was written at about the same time.

One of the poems Frost wrote on the blank endsheets in the copy of Complete Poems of Robert Frost *(1949) that he used during readings in the early 1950s. The poem was first published, with an additional stanza, in Frost's 1962 book* In the Clearing, *but Frost's note at the bottom of the page suggests that it was written circa 1920, with "The Lockless Door"*

"God's own descent
Into flesh was meant
As a demonstration
That the supreme merit
Lay in risking spirit
In substantiation."

Or as Emerson put it in prose, "There seems to be a necessity in spirit to manifest itself in material forms." If men are considerably less than divine in apprehension, if they cannot create "One least germ or coal," nevertheless Frost holds that we, the only creatures who have "thoughts to think," are under divine orders to penetrate matter as far as we can, claiming it for intellect and imagination. The fall from Eden he sees as the "instinctive venture" of a creature designed to enquire, and he makes Jehovah say to Jacob (retracting a few of His recorded injunctions):

"Have no hallowing fears
Anything's forbidden
Just because it's hidden.
Trespass and encroach
On successive spheres
Without self-reproach."

It may surprise some readers that Robert Frost should write a book full of the word "venture," a book whose longest poem celebrates unlimited reaching-out–soaring planes, soaring capsules, soaring thought. These attitudes seem hardly to suit with those, say, that great focal poem "The Mountain," in which an earlier Frost advised a retreat from change, confusion, and "too much" generally into the coherence of local tradition. But after all there has been no fundamental change of mind: first and last, Frost's concern has been for wholeness of life and character, and he is now defending, by a new strategy and on a broader front, the Emersonian values he embraced. In late years, he has become more and more the conscience of his country, and taken upon himself the burden of its confusion: what certain of these poems are directed against is the fear that our society, cowed by its own dangerous powers and potentialities, will go back on those things in man which Frost sees as highest and most human.

"Ours is a Christian adventure into materialism," Frost said not long ago, and the political poems of "In the Clearing" all insist that Americans must see themselves not as ingenious materialists but as riskers of spirit in the realm of matter. "America Is Hard to See" reproaches Columbus with having, in his appetite for Cathayan gold, failed to recognize our continent as "The race's future trial place./A fresh start for the human race." "Our Doom to Bloom" and "The Bad Island–Easter" attack the cynicism of welfare-state thinking while in "How Hard It Is to Keep From Being King," King Darius is counselled to give his people "character and not just food." The lines "For John F. Kennedy His Inauguration" look to the new Administration not for an exacted benevolence but for courage, the pursuit of glory, the bold exercise of power, independence of the mob, and a spirit "answerable to high design." The effect of the whole book, as it bears upon the political poems, is to invest with idealistic vigor a number of ideas which, in earlier embodiments, may have seemed nostalgic, negative and ungenerous. It is a considerable clarification.

But what about the poems as poems? The percentage of "editorials," jokes, aphorisms, and humorous wisdom-verse is high, and of these the present writer prefers the long "Kitty Hawk," which seems to ramble but ends as quite a structure of notions, and two delightful light pieces, "In a Glass of Cider" and "the Objection to Being Stepped On." Still, my reactionary taste is for the lyric and dramatic Frost, who in this volume happily persists. "The Draft Horse" is a sinister yet amusing symbolic poem on Frost's old theme of acceptance, and "Questioning Faces"–a six-line glimpse of an owl just missing a windowpane–is as ponderable as the densest haiku. As for the first four poems in the book, they are rightly placed, and every one a beauty. "Pod of the Milkweed," like Frost's brilliant sonnet "Design," charges some insects and a flower with vast implications: in this case the implications have to do with waste and with the investment of spirit in matter. Of "A Cabin in the Clearing" I have spoken already. "Closed for Good," a version of which appeared in "Complete Poems," is here revised and shortened for the better. And this poem, "Away!," is perhaps the best of all:

Now I out walking
The world desert,
And my shoe and my stocking
Do me no hurt.

I leave behind
Good friends in town.
Let them get well-wined
And go lie down.

Frost with Premier Nikita Khrushchev at Gagra, a resort on the Black Sea, 7 September 1962

Don't think I leave
For the outer dark
Like Adam and Eve
Pull out of the Park.

Forget the myth.
There is no one I
Am put out with
Or put out by.

Unless I'm wrong
I but obey
The urge of a song:
I'm–bound–away!

And I may return
If dissatisfied
With what I learn
From having died.

That is a poem so perfectly dexterous as to seem easy: a gay, venturesome poem to go away by. But stay with us, Mr. Frost. Earth's the right place for happy returns, and may you have many more.

ARTICLE:
"Frost Calls K Generous Ruffian," *Washington Post*, 9 September 1962, p. A10.

In late August 1962, at the request of President Kennedy, Frost left with U. S. Interior Secretary Stewart Udall for ten days in the Soviet Union, as part of a cultural-exchange program.

MOSCOW, Sept. 8 (AP) American poet Robert Frost characterized Soviet Premier Nikita Khrushchev today as "the kind of a ruffian" who is not afraid of a fight or of being magnanimous.

A Soviet woman reporter suggested that Frost meant rough, not ruffian, but the 88-year-old poet, who does not always hear well, went right on talking.

Frost, whose 10-day visit ends tonight, flew down to Gagra on the Black Sea on Friday at Khrushchev's behest and had a talk of an hour or more with the Soviet leader. The interview, judging by Frost's account, rambled all over the lot.

Asked if Khrushchev had given him a message for President Kennedy, Frost said, "Yes, in a way." The poet's associates stopped him from telling what the message was, but Frost said Khrushchev told him to tell the President "not to do this, and to do that, and that he musn't do this and must do that, quite a few things."

All this, he explained, was "not on a low level of partisanship, all high level."

"I knew he was that kind of a ruffian. He's a big fellow. He's all ready for a fight. He's not afraid of us and we're not afraid of him."

Frost said he had hoped to persuade Khrushchev and the Soviets to compete with the United States in "strife and magnanimity," and continued:

"He agrees with strife and with magnanimity. He's no saphead. None of your liberal sapheads for me."

Asked if he and Khrushchev discussed God, the poet replied, "He didn't. But I did. God wants us to contend. The only progress is in conflict."

Frost said he asked Khrushchev if he couldn't do something about the Berlin situation, and Khrushchev replied he was doing all he could.

"I asked him if there was something of ours that he wants, and something of his that we wanted, then we could swap," Frost said, and Khrushchev replied: "That is difficult."

"I did say something against letting a little thing like Berlin decide the fate of nations," Frost said, and Khrushchev "agreed we should take a large look at it."

The poet said he had been criticized at home for admiring Khrushchev's qualities, but "he's our enemy and he's a great man."

Tass, the official news agency, said Frost presented Khrushchev a book of his verses with the inscription: "From a rival in friendship." It quoted him as saying that Khrushchev proved to be "the very hero" he had imagined.

Frost made an appearance on Moscow TV before his departure and recited his old and famous poem, "Mending Wall," with a translator. "He recited it last Wednesday to a literary audience and left his Russian listeners somewhat mystified, for the poem has passages that could fit the Communist Wall in Berlin. One such is the passage, "Before I built a wall, I'd ask to know what I was walling in or walling out, and to whom I was likely to give offense."

OBITUARY TRIBUTES:

From "Kennedy Leads World Eulogies of Poet Robert Frost, Dead at 88," *Washington Post*, 30 January 1963, pp. A1, C6.

BOSTON, Jan. 29–Robert Frost, dean of American poets, died early today at the age of 88.

He was pronounced dead at Peter Bent Brigham Hospital at 1:50 a. m. after two operations, a heart attack and three separate blood clots in his lungs. He was hospitalized Dec. 3.

The four-time Pulitzer Prize winner had been making what doctors called a remarkable recovery until his general condition began deteriorating in the 48 hours preceding his death.

His attending physician, Dr. Roger B. Hickler, said Mr. Frost died shortly after complaining of severe chest pains and a shortness of breath. Cause of death was listed as "probably a pulmonary embolism" (blood clot in the lungs). A team of doctors and several nurses were at his bedside when the end came.

Dr. Hickler said that a few hours before the fatal attack Mr. Frost was "talkative and comfortable."

Operation Dec. 10

The poet underwent his first operation Dec. 10 for removal of a urinary obstruction. Subsequently he had a heart attack and blood clots settled in his lungs. In an attempt to ease the blood clots, doctors tied veins in both legs earlier this month.

Fame came late to the one-time mill worker and New Hampshire farmer, but in his declining years two Presidents of his country honored him signally and at his death men prominent in all walks of national and international life paid him tribute.

President Eisenhower had appointed him consultant in poetry to the Library of Congress. President Kennedy had him as a speaker at his Inaugural and last March gave him a medal voted to him by Congress.

"Poet of Our Time"

President Kennedy noted yesterday that Mr. Frost's death "leaves a vacancy in the American spirit."

Eulogizing the poet as "the great American poet of our time," Mr. Kennedy said in a statement issued by the White House:

"His art and his life summed up the essential qualities of the New England he loved so much; the fresh delight in nature, the plainness in speech, the canny wisdom, and the deep, underlying insight into the human soul.

"His death impoverishes us all; but he has bequeathed his Nation a body of imperishable verse from which Americans will forever gain joy and understanding . . ."

Praise from Khrushchev

From Moscow, Premier Khrushchev wired a message of condolence to Mr. Frost's family. It called him an ardent champion of American-Soviet friendship and noted that his works were "imbued with love for the common man."

The Soviet Writers Union sent a telegram to Mr. Frost's relatives expressing condolences "on the heavy loss suffered by world poetry."

They leave the road to me
To walk in saying naught
Perhaps but to a tree
Inaudibly in thought,
"From you the road receives
A priming coat of leaves."

"And soon for lack of sun,
The chances are, in white
It will be further done
But with a coat so light
The shape of leaves will show
Beneath the brush of snow."

And so on into winter
Till Even I have ceased
To come as a foot printer
And only some slight beast
So mousy or so foxy
Shall print them as my proxy.

How often is the case
I thus owe men a debt
For having left a place
And still do not forget
I owe them some sweet share
For having once been there
R.F.

Manuscript for the version of "Closed for Good" that was published as a Christmas card in 1948 (Lilly Library, Indiana University). Frost revised the poem before it was collected in his last book.

The telegram said that readers in the Soviet Union, which Mr. Frost visited recently, came to love his verses, Tass News Agency reported.

Another telegram of condolence was sent by several Soviet poets who had met Mr. Frost, including Lenin Prize Laureate Eduardes Mezhelaitis, Konstantin Slmonov, Alexei Surkov and Alexander Tvardovsky. The telegram said "we came to love sincerely this great poet and charming man."

Poet and playwright T. S. Eliot and British poet Laureate John Masefield joined the overseas chorus of tribute.

Eliot said he was "very grieved" to hear of the death of Mr. Frost who he said was "a poet of lasting importance."

Masefield, 84, in a message issued through his London publishers said "many in England will hear with grief that Mr. Robert Frost, the very voice of New England, is now no longer living."

Commented Librarian of Congress L. Quincy Mumford:

"For all of us at the Library of Congress, Robert Frost's death is a personal as well as a public sorrow. My staff and I have lost a great and good friend. As a person, he inspired in his associates at the Library a unique affection and respect. As Consultant in Poetry in 1958-59, and then as Honorary Consultant in the Humanities from 1959 to date, he brought to the Library of Congress a wisdom and counsel that cannot be replaced, and he made poetry, as never before, a part of the national consciousness."

Pulitzer prize winning novelist John Hersey expressed sorrow at the news and called it "a pity he never had the Nobel Prize."

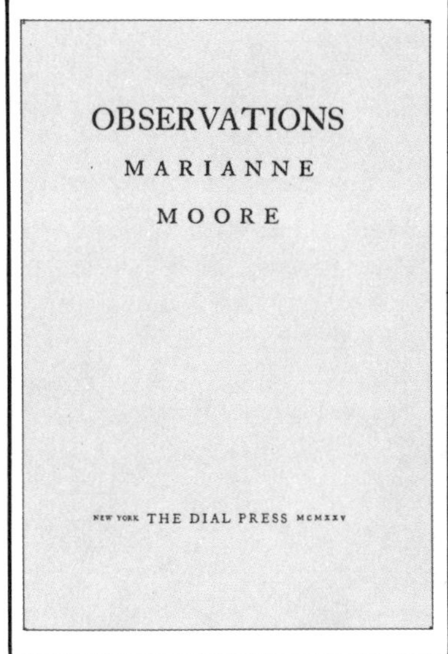

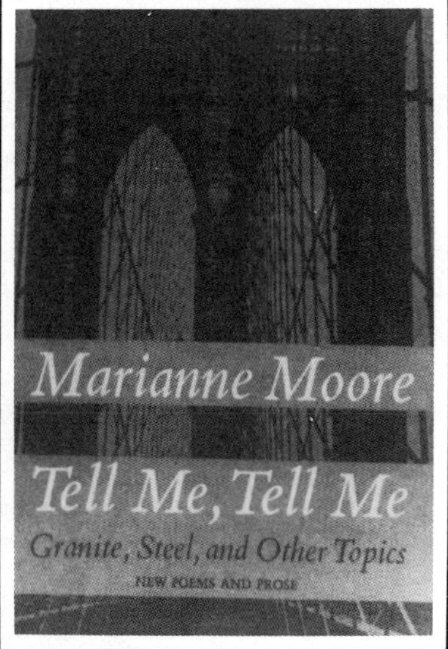

Marianne Moore

(15 November 1887-5 February 1972)

Patricia C. Willis
Beinecke Rare Book and Manuscript Library, Yale University

See the Marianne Moore entry in Dictionary of Literary Biography, *volume 45,* American Poets, 1880-1945: First Series.

MAJOR BOOKS:

Poems (London: Egoist Press, 1921);

Marriage, Manikin, no. 3 (New York: Monroe Wheeler, 1923);

Observations (New York: Dial Press, 1924);

Selected Poems (New York: Macmillan, 1935; London: Faber & Faber, 1935);

What Are Years (New York: Macmillan, 1941);

Nevertheless (New York: Macmillan, 1944);

Collected Poems (London: Faber & Faber, 1951; New York: Macmillan, 1951);

Predilections (New York: Viking, 1955; London: Faber & Faber, 1956);

Like a Bulwark (New York: Viking, 1956; London: Faber & Faber, 1957);

O To Be a Dragon (New York: Viking, 1959);

A Marianne Moore Reader (New York: Viking, 1961);

Tell Me, Tell Me: Granite, Steel, and Other Topics (New York: Viking, 1966);

The Complete Poems of Marianne Moore (New York: Macmillan/Viking, 1967; London: Faber & Faber, 1968; revised and enlarged edition, New York: Macmillan/Viking, 1981);

The Complete Prose of Marianne Moore, edited by Patricia C. Willis (New York: Elisabeth Sifton Books/Viking, 1986; London: Faber & Faber, 1986).

TRANSLATION:

The Fables of La Fontaine (New York: Viking, 1954); abridged as *Selected Fables of La Fontaine* (London: Faber & Faber, 1955).

BIBLIOGRAPHIES:

Eugene P. Sheehy and Kenneth A. Lohf, *The Achievement of Marianne Moore* (New York: New York Public Library, 1958);

Marianne Craig Moore with her mother, Mary Warner Moore, and brother, John Warner Moore, in the library of the manse for the first Presbyterian Church in Kirkwood, Missouri, a suburb of St. Louis, circa 1894. Moore's father suffered a nervous breakdown and was hospitalized before her birth. She was born in the Kirkwood home of her maternal grandfather, the Reverend John R. Warner, who died in 1894. Not long after this photograph was taken, Mary Warner Moore took her two children to live first in Allegheny City (now part of Pittsburgh) and then in Carlisle, Pennsylvania .

Craig S. Abbott, *Marianne Moore: A Descriptive Bibliography* (Pittsburgh: University of Pittsburgh Press, 1977);

Abbott, *Marianne Moore: A Reference Guide* (Boston: G. K. Hall, 1978).

EXHIBITION CATALOGUE:

Patricia C. Willis, *Marianne Moore: Vision into Verse* (Philadelphia: Rosenbach Museum & Library, 1987).

CONCORDANCE:

Gary Lane, ed., *A Concordance to the Poems of Marianne Moore* (New York: Haskell House, 1972).

NEWSLETTER:

The Marianne Moore Newsletter, 1977-1983.

LOCATION OF ARCHIVES:

Marianne Moore's papers, library, living-room furnishings, and personal effects are at the Rosenbach Museum & Library, Philadelphia.

OVERVIEW:

Kathleen Cannell, " 'Durable Poetry in Our Time,' " *Christian Science Monitor*, 11 June 1958, p. 9.

Cannell had known Moore since the 1910s when Moore first met fellow poets in New York. Despite her unusual poetry and her penchant for the minute and the exotic, Moore was known for her quiet life-style. After graduating from Bryn Mawr College in 1909, she taught at the Indian School in Carlisle, Pennsylvania, and then worked at a branch of the New York Public Li-

brary before becoming editor of the Dial *in 1925. In Brooklyn, where she lived from 1929 to 1965, Moore taught tennis to neighborhood children, appeared at local high schools, and attended readings and lectures at the Brooklyn Academy of Music.*

Marianne Moore is valued by many as a unique voice in modern poetry: a singer of the beautiful who believes that "what is good in the world is good because it is useful to life."

The Boston Arts Festival Award for 1958, which Miss Moore will receive on June 15, adds yet another shining leaf to the crowded laurels that have already crowned this American poet: the Pulitzer, the Bollingen, and the National Book Awards (all in the same year); a Guggenheim Fellowship, a Gold Medal and grant from the National Institute of Arts and Letters; the Dial, the Shelley Memorial, the Harriet Monroe, and the Helen Haire Levinson Poetry Prizes.

Miss Moore has been elected member of the American Academy of Arts and Letters, whose membership of 55 includes only 2 women. And the minor awards and Lit. D's bestowed upon her are uncounted.

Reviewing her latest "Collected Poems," one critic called Marianne Moore the most accomplished poet in the English-speaking world today. Her exquisite craftsmanship has been praised by such contemporary poets as William Carlos Williams, Louise Bogan, and e. e. cummings (who won last year's Boston Arts Festival Award).

T. S. Eliot has declared that her poems "form part of the small body of durable poetry written in our time." And the press acclaimed her translation of "The Fables of La Fontaine" as an event in American literary history.

But the recipient of all these honors herself refuses to admit that what she writes is poetry! What then would she call it? "Compositions perhaps," Miss Moore replied to this question. "Didn't Dante say: 'A poem is a composition of words set to music'? Or better still, observations."

Fancy Struck, She Writes

What she really means, one gathers, is that she affects nothing of the poet laureate. She does not improvise command performances. Something strikes her fancy and she finds herself writing about it.

It may be a "swan under the willows . . . with flamingo-colored, maple-leaflike feet," Albrecht Dürer's engraved rhinoceros, a pair of Louis XV Dresden candelabra, or an exotic animal in a documentary film. Most often it is a quotation (for which she has a veritable genius; in her literary critiques her choice of lines from other poets illumines their obscurities in a way some of them confess they never seem able to do for themselves).

Her fancy caught, Marianne Moore uses her subject much as a painter his model or a composer his motif. She develops it in four dimensions, in various scintillating strata, "excavates" its hidden character, amplifies it at infinitely radiating tangents. The final effect may be as beautifully sibylline as a fine abstract painting or a modern symphony.

Even her most ardent admirers are sometimes baffled. One particularly literate critic remarked of "An Octopus," "I don't understand a word." While to her, she says, it is crystal clear that it is the account of a geological expedition to Mt. Rainier!

This American poet, however, who likes to write ". . . not in Greek, not in Latin . . . but in plain American which cats and dogs can read," disapproves of obscurity. She agrees with T. S. Eliot that "poetry must give pleasure."

'Musical . . . Possibilities'

And to aid her readers she appends notes to her published poems (or observations, if you will) giving their origin and their allusions. One is reminded of the series of preliminary drawings Picasso makes for some of his paintings, progressively simplifying the animal or the figure to its ultimate "glyph."

So through Marianne Moore's clues we can track down meanings. Or heeding the author's own advice in "When I Buy Pictures"–"Too stern an intellectual emphasis upon this quality or that detracts from one's enjoyment"–one can take her on faith and enjoy the poems as one does a picture or a piece of music, for the line, the rhythm, the melopoeia.

Plainly she is, like La Fontaine, melomane. W. H. Auden has stressed the "endless musical and structural possibilities of her verse." And she herself says that in spite of literary successes she has never really "adopted" writing in the affectionate way she has painting and music.

Pondering the formidable challenge of translating into English the "Fables," which the French poet Theodore de Banville called "perfection itself and the ultimate expression of genius," Miss Moore decided that it would be "fascinating to try to approximate the felicities of the original

Moore (second from right) as an attendant to the King and Queen of the May at Bryn Mawr College, 1 May 1906

counterpoint and verbal harmonies." It took her 10 years (one year longer than La Fontaine spent in composing the Fables), but she did achieve a poetic, though essentially modern "Mooresque" re-creation, that captured to a phenomenal degree the substance, rhythm, and lilt of the French.

'Real Toads' in Her Gardens

Marianne Moore has almost an obsession for naturalness (a more exact word for which might be authenticity) in writing. This, like her impatience with any striving for eloquence, springs undoubtedly from her own complete integrity. Discussing style she is fond of quoting a pronouncement of Confucius (as translated by Ezra Pound), "The problem of style: When you have effected your meaning, stop!" And she likes rhymes that are "not dogmatic, but that trail away like an echo. For example: 'Its leaps are set to a flageolet.' "

Marianne Moore's poems about animals probably speak the most directly to the general reader. She has an uncanny ability to present for our inspection "imaginary gardens with real toads in them."

She has collected within the covers of her books a menagerie of rare diverting specimens: jerboas, pangolins, mongooses, an albino giraffe, an egret-trimmed porcupine, a famous race horse and a memorable "intellectual cautiously creeping cat." She has observed them with the patience of a zoologist, reproduced them in poetic lapidary form and related them (again like La Fontaine) to the idiosyncrasies of human society.

My friendship with Marianne Moore dates from 1916, shortly after Harriet Monroe had published some of her early works in Poetry maga-

Members of the Bryn Mawr class of 1909: Hilda Doolittle is third from left (partially obscured); Marianne Moore is second from right

zine. We met in New York at a party given by Alfred Kreymborg in her honor, at which Wallace Stevens, Mina Loy, William Carlos Williams, Helen Hoyt, and Maxwell Bodenheim were among poets present.

Marianne and I were drawn together by our delight in unusual animals, and we often went on visits to the zoo, where I am proud to think that I observed the inception of some later poems–notably "The Plumet Basilisk" all about real dragons–which may have sprung from our success in charming the Great Australian Lizard with a flute. I remember standing before the cage of a young elephant, while Marianne admired his fog color, his lacquered hairs like amulets, and reminded me of what Pliny and Herodotus had written about "the Socrates of animals . . . somehow allied to man."

She later wrote about them, in "Elephants" as "Incised with hard wrinkles, embossed with wide ears . . . with hunting-horn curled trunk. . . ."

First Poem Recalled

Marianne Moore was born in St. Louis, but moved with her family at an early age to Carlisle, Pa., where her mother taught English at Metsger Institute for 14 years.

Marianne was not a precocious poet. As a child, though she did nothing but read, she was "suspicious" of poetry, possibly because of forced recitals at grade-school functions. Her first poem was written during her early days at Bryn Mawr and appeared in the college monthly:

> "If you will tell me why the fen
> appears impassible, I then
> will tell you why I think that I
> can get across it if I try."

After graduation from Bryn Mawr, one of Miss Moore's first posts was with the New York Public Library. From 1925 to 1929 she was acting editor of the Dial magazine, which introduced many new writers who have since attained eminence. Of staunch Scottish Presbyterian stock, she brought to bear upon a sophisticated milieu the clarifying influence of her innocent wisdom. Frederick Hoffman in his survey, "The Twenties," hailed her as "the editorial sensibility of the decade."

"Humility, Concentration, and Gusto" (which she considers the necessary qualities for a writer) is the title of a literary essay of the epoch republished in Marianne Moore's prose collection "Predilections." Add to these three an endearing modesty, a delightful sense of humor, a whimsical sense of wonder, extreme scrupulosity, and a touch of punctilio–and you have an image in miniature of the work and character of a poet, whose insistence on moral values makes her a beacon in the pervading literary smog of our time.

'Ivory Lighthouse' Shunned

But far from dwelling in an "ivory lighthouse," Miss Moore is an ardent observer of all the lusty idiosyncrasies of the American Way. She is a baseball fan and has published an ode to the Dodgers. Other hobbies are the theater, documentary films, sailing, and–belying a somewhat fragile appearance–horses and riding.

In Brooklyn, where she now resides, she is known as a good neighbor; and certain trusted tradesmen proudly display autographed copies of her books. With remarkable responsiveness to mood, she looks sometimes tiny, at others stately. She has never cut her hair, which she twines in a snow-feathered coronet around her head. She has strong views on fashion. She dresses with timeless individual smartness and is addicted to tricornes and shiny "Victrola-record" sailors.

Persons conversing with Marianne Moore for the first time have been known to exclaim: "Why, she talks just like her poems!" They are charmed by her unaffected erudition and amazingly original, precise vocabulary.

Probably the young understand Marianne Moore best. The simplicity which appears enigmatic to what Gertrude Stein used to call "the congelation of middle-aged thinking" is to them as transparent as the "Jellyfish," the second poem she remembers writing, which begins:

> "Visible, invisible, a fluctuating charm,
> and amber-colored amethyst inhabits it. . . ."

Adviser to Youth

Miss Moore has been prodigal of her time, talent, and sensibility when it is a question of helping and encouraging (or mercifully discouraging) young poets. Of their work she says: "Some of it is exhilarating and has value, some of it is barefaced depravity." And on the subject of delinquent youth: "What we need is large families, the members of which are affectionate and loyal to the death."

Miss Moore has taught young people–at the Indian School in Carlisle right after her graduation; given a course in contemporary poets at Bryn Mawr; directed a poetry workshop at Wagner College on Staten Island; held seminars, indefatigably sat on juries of poetry contests, criticized literally miles of aspirants' lines, answered thousands of their letters. Each year she shuttles from coast to coast, giving lectures and readings at colleges.

Whenever an appearance by Marianne Moore is announced, a goodly throng of young students turns out. Cicero's "Teach, Stir the Mind, Afford Enjoyment" is her educational ideal. And she balances these elements in readings of her verse interspersed with informal conversational comment.

She reads her poems simply, with no attempt at scientific enunciation or special expressiveness, as though she scrupled to influence audiences in their favor by histrionics. Listeners have to hang on her words to catch the witty sparks she flings at them, with a little laugh at herself and a toss of the head like a playful pony, an invisible mane tracing an effect of gaiety in the air. And everyone laughs with her in delight at her shrewdly brilliant appraisals.

"It's a funny business, isn't it?" she was overheard saying to a poet with a crew cut after a lecture at Harvard.

The opening poem in Marianne Moore's latest published collection is entitled: "Bulwarked Against Fate," (from "Like A Bulwark," Viking Press, New York). It is this American poet's impassioned affirmation of the individual's freedom to choose the good in art and life, and it reads:

> "Affirmed. Pent by power that holds it fast–
> a paradox. Pent. Hard pressed,
> you take the blame and are inviolate.
> Abased at last;
> not the tempest-tossed.
> Compressed: firmed by the thrust of the blast
> till compact, like a bulwark against fate;
> lead-saluted,
> saluted by lead?
> As though flying Old Glory full mast."

INTERVIEW:

Donald Hall, Interview with Marianne Moore, *Paris Review* (Winter 1961); from *A Marianne Moore Reader* (New York: Viking, 1961), pp. 253-273.

This interview promotes two misconceptions: that Moore majored in biology while in college and that she had no interest in a career in literature. On the contrary, al-

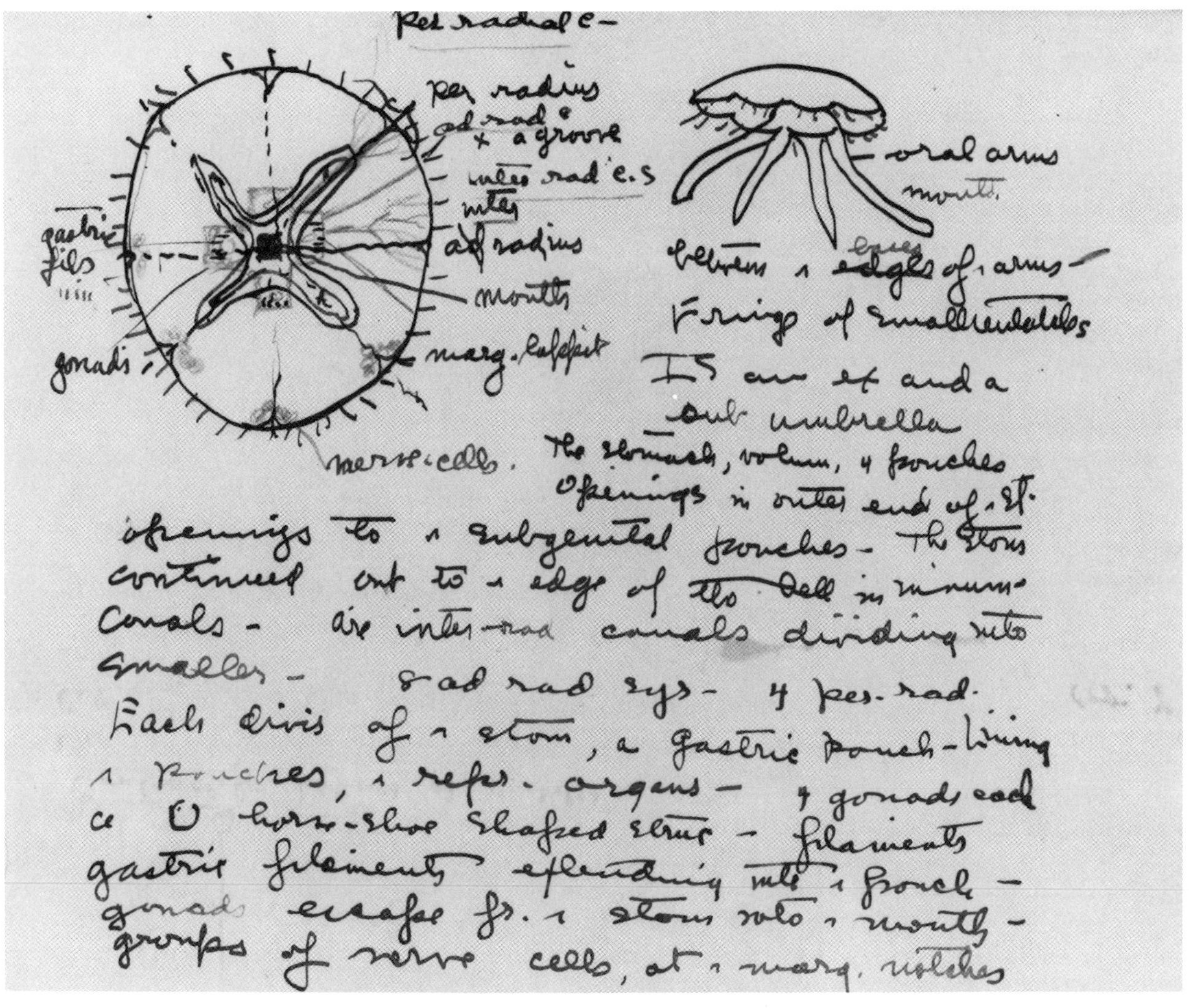

Page from Moore's laboratory notebook for a comparative-anatomy course she took in 1908 (Rosenbach Museum & Library). Her poem "A Jelly-Fish" was first published in the June 1909 issue of the Lantern, *the Bryn Mawr alumnae magazine. The poem was republished in the Spring-Summer 1957 issue of the* Trinity Review *and collected in* O To Be a Dragon *(1959).*

though she studied biology extensively at Bryn Mawr, she majored in history-politics-economics, and her letters to her family make clear that she relished her work on the college literary magazine. Soon after college, she began to write poems and submit them to little magazines, receiving many rejections until both Poetry *and the* Egoist *published her poems in 1915.*

Q: Miss Moore, I understand that you were born in St. Louis only about ten months before T. S. Eliot. Did your families know each other?

A: No, we did not know the Eliots. We lived in Kirkwood, Missouri, where my grandfather was pastor of the First Presbyterian Church. T. S. Eliot's grandfather–Dr. William Eliot–was a Unitarian. We left when I was about seven, my grandfather having died in 1894, February 20th. My grandfather like Dr. Eliot had attended ministerial meetings in St. Louis. Also, at stated intervals, various ministers met for luncheon. After one of these luncheons my grandfather said, "When Dr. William Eliot asks the blessing and says, 'and this we ask in the name of our Lord Jesus Christ,' he is Trinitarian enough for me." The Mary Institute, for girls, was endowed by him as a memorial to his daughter Mary, who had died.

Q: How old were you when you started to write poems?

A: Well, let me see, in Bryn Mawr. I think I was eighteen when I entered Bryn Mawr. I was born in 1887, I entered college in 1906. Now how old would I have been? Can you deduce my probable age?

Q: Eighteen or nineteen.

A: I had no literary plans, but I was interested in the undergraduate monthly magazine, and to my surprise (I wrote one or two little things for it) the editors elected me to the board. It was my sophomore year–I am sure it was–and I stayed on, I believe. And then when I had left college I offered contributions (we weren't paid) to the *Lantern*, the alumnae magazine. But I didn't feel that my product was anything to shake the world.

Q: At what point did poetry become world-shaking for you?

A: Never! I believe I was interested in painting then. At least I said so. I remember Mrs. Otis Skinner asking at Commencement time, the year I was graduated, "What would you like to be?"

"A painter," I said.

"Well, I'm not surprised," Mrs. Skinner answered. I had something on that she liked, some kind of summer dress. She commended it–said, "I'm not at all surprised."

I like stories. I like fiction. And–this sounds rather pathetic, bizarre as well–I think verse perhaps was for me the next best thing to it. Didn't I write something one time, "Part of a Poem, Part of a Novel, Part of a Play"? I think I was all too truthful. I could visualize scenes, and deplored the fact that Henry James had to do it unchallenged.

Now, if I couldn't write fiction, I'd like to write plays. To me the theater is the most pleasant, in fact my favorite form of recreation.

Q: Do you go often?

A: No. Never. Unless someone invites me. Lillian Hellman invited me to *Toys in the Attic*, and I am very happy that she did. I would have had no notion of the vitality of the thing, have lost sight of her skill as a writer if I hadn't seen the play; would like to go again. The accuracy of the vernacular! That's the kind of thing I'm interested in, am always taking down little local expressions and accents. I think I should be in some philological operation or enterprise, am really much interested in dialect and intonations. I scarcely think of any that comes into my so-called poems at all.

Q: I wonder what Bryn Mawr meant for you as a poet. You write that most of your time there was spent in the biological laboratory. Did you like biology better than literature as a subject for study? Did the training possibly affect your poetry?

A: I had hoped to make French and English my major studies, and took the required two-year English course–five hours a week–but was not able to elect a course until my junior year. I did not attain the requisite academic stand of eighty until that year. I then elected seventeenth-century imitative writing–Fuller, Hooker, Bacon, Bishop Andrewes, and others. Lectures in French were in French, and I had had no spoken French.

Did laboratory studies affect my poetry? I am sure they did. I found the biology courses–minor, major, and histology–exhilarating. I thought, in fact, of studying medicine. Precision, economy of statement, logic employed to ends that are disinterested, drawing and identifying, liberate–at least have some bearing on–the imagination, it seems to me.

Q: Whom did you know in the literary world, before you came to New York? Did you know Bryher and H.D.?

A: It's very hard to get these things seriatim. I met Bryher in 1921 in New York. H.D. was my classmate at Bryn Mawr. She was there, I think, only two years. She was a non-resident and I did not realize that she was interested in writing.

Q: Did you know Ezra Pound and William Carlos Williams through her? Didn't she know them at the University of Pennsylvania?

A: Yes. She did. I didn't meet them. I had met no writers until 1916 when I visited New York, when a friend in Carlisle wanted me to accompany her.

Q: So you were isolated really from modern poetry until 1916?

A: Yes.

Marianne Moore at her home in Carlisle, Pennsylvania, about 1911. After graduating from Bryn Mawr in June 1909, she took a one-year secretarial course at the Carlisle Commercial College and then worked for two months on the staff of Melvil Dewey, the devisor of the Dewey Decimal System and a simplified method of spelling, at his resort in Lake Placid, New York. Moore and her mother spent the summer of 1911 in Europe, and when they returned the poet became a teacher of business subjects at the United States Indian School in Carlisle. She remained there until Summer 1914.

Q: Was that your first trip to New York, when you went there for six days and decided that you wanted to live there?

A: Oh, no. Several times my mother had taken my brother and me sightseeing and to shop; on the way to Boston, or Maine, and to Washington and Florida. My senior year in college in 1909, I visited Dr. Charles Spraguesmith's daughter, Hilda, at Christmas time in New York. And Louis Anspacher lectured in a very ornamental way at Cooper Union. There was plenty of music at Carnegie Hall, and I got a sense of what was going on in New York.

Q: And what was going on made you want to come back?

A: It probably did, when Miss Cowdrey in Carlisle invited me to come with her for a week. It was the visit in 1916 that made me want to live there. I don't know what put it into her head to do it, or why she wasn't likely to have a better time without me. She was most skeptical of my venturing forth to bohemian parties. But I was fearless about that. In the first place, I didn't think anyone would try to harm me, but if they did I felt impervious. It never occurred to me that chaperones were important.

Q: Do you suppose that moving to New York, and the stimulation of the writers whom you found there, led you to write more poems than you would otherwise have written?

A: I'm sure it did–seeing what others wrote, liking this or that. With me it's always some fortuity that traps me. I certainly never intended to write poetry. That never came into my head. And now, too, I think each time I write that it may be the last time; then I'm charmed by something and seem to have to say something. Everything I have written is the result of reading or of interest in people, I'm sure of that. I had no ambition to be a writer.

Q: Let me see. You taught at the Carlisle Indian school after Bryn Mawr. Then after you moved to New York in 1918 you taught at a private school and worked in a library. Did these occupations have anything to do with you as a writer?

A: I think they hardened my muscles considerably, my mental approach to things. Working as a librarian was a big help, a tremendous help. Miss Leonard of the Hudson Park branch of the New York Public Library opposite our house came to see me one day. I wasn't in, and she asked my mother did she think I would care to be on the staff, work in the library, because I was so fond of books and liked to talk about them to people. My mother said no, she thought not; the shoemaker's children never have shoes, I probably would feel if I joined the staff that I'd have no time to read. When I came home she told me, and I said, "Why, certainly. Ideal. I'll tell her. Only I couldn't work more than half a day." If I had worked all day and maybe evenings or overtime, like the mechanics, why, it would *not* have been ideal.

As a free service we were assigned books to review and I did like that. We didn't get paid but we had the chance to diagnose. I reveled in it. Somewhere I believe I have carbon copies of those "P-slip" summaries. They were the kind of things that brought the worst-best out. I was always wondering why they didn't honor me with an art book or medical book or even a history, or criticism. But no, it was fiction, silent-movie fiction.

Q: Did you travel at this time? Did you go to Europe at all?

A: In 1911. My mother and I went to England for about two months, July and August probably. We went to Paris and we stayed on the left bank, in a pension in the rue Valette, where Calvin wrote his *Institutes,* I believe. Not far from the Panthéon and the Luxembourg Gardens. I have been much interested in Sylvia Beach's book–reading about Ezra Pound and his Paris days. Where was I and what was I doing? I think, with the objective, an evening stroll–it was one of the hottest summers the world has ever known, 1911–we walked along to 12, rue de L'Odéon, to see Sylvia Beach's shop. It wouldn't occur to me to say, "Here am I, I'm a writer, would you talk to me a while?" I had no feeling at all like that. I wanted to observe things. And we went to every museum in Paris, I think, except two.

Q: Have you been back since?

A: Not to Paris. Only to England in 1935 or 1936. I like England.

Q: You have mostly stayed put in Brooklyn, then, since you moved here in 1929?

A: Except for four trips to the West: Los Angeles, San Francisco, Puget Sound, and British Columbia. My mother and I went through the canal previously, to San Francisco, and by rail to Seattle.

Q: Have you missed the Dodgers here, since *they* went West?

A: Very much, and I am told that they miss us.

Q: I am still interested in those early years in New York. William Carlos Williams, in his *Autobiography,* says that you were "a rafter holding up the superstructure of our uncompleted building," when he talks about the Greenwich Village group of writers. I guess these were people who contributed to *Others.*

A: I never was a rafter holding up anyone! I have his *Autobiography* and took him to task for his misinformed statements about Robert McAlmon and Bryher. In my indignation I missed some things I ought to have seen.

Q: To what extent did the *Others* contributors form a group?

A: We did foregather a little. Alfred Kreymborg was editor, and was married to Gertrude Lord at the time, one of the loveliest persons you could ever meet. And they had a little apartment somewhere in the village. There was considerable unanimity about the group.

Q: Someone called Alfred Kreymborg your American discoverer. Do you suppose this is true?

A: It could be said, perhaps; he did all he could to promote me. Miss Monroe and the Aldingtons had asked me simultaneously to contribute to *Poetry* and the *Egoist* in 1917 at the same time.

Alfred Kreymborg was not inhibited. I was a little different from the others. He thought I might pass as a novelty, I guess.

Q: What was your reaction when H.D. and Bryher brought out your first collection, which they called *Poems*, in 1921 without your knowledge? Why had you delayed to do it yourself?

A: To issue my slight product–conspicuously tentative–seemed to me premature. I disliked the term "poetry" for any but Chaucer's or Shakespeare's or Dante's. I do not now feel quite my original hostility to the word, since it is a convenient almost unavoidable term for the thing (although hardly for me–my observations, experiments in rhythm, or exercises in composition). What I write, as I have said before, could only be called poetry because there is no other category in which to put it.

For the chivalry of the undertaking–issuing my verse for me in 1921, certainly in format choicer than the content–I am intensely grateful. Again, in 1925, it seemed to me not very self-interested of Faber and Faber, and simultaneously of the Macmillan Company, to propose a *Selected Poems* for me. Desultory occasional magazine publications seemed to me sufficient, conspicuous enough.

Q: Had you been sending poems to magazines before the *Egoist* printed your first poem?

A: I must have. I have a little curio, a little wee book about two by three inches, or two and a half by three inches, in which I systematically entered everything sent out, when I got it back, if they took it, and how much I got for it. That lasted about a year, I think. I can't care as much as all that. I don't know that I submitted anything that wasn't extorted from me.

I have at present three onerous tasks, and each interferes with the others, and I don't know how I am going to write anything. If I get a promising idea I set it down, and it stays there. I don't make myself do anything with it. I've had several things in the *New Yorker*. And I said to them, "I might never write again," and not to expect me to. I never knew anyone who had a passion for words who had as much difficulty in saying things as I do and I very seldom say them in a manner I like. If I do it's because I don't know I'm trying. I've written several things for the *New Yorker*–and I did want to write *them.*

Q: When did you last write a poem?

A: It appeared in August. What was it about? Oh . . . Carnegie Hall. You see, anything that really rouses me . . .

Q: How does a poem start for you?

A: A felicitous phrase springs to mind–a word or two, say–simultaneous usually with some thought or object of equal attraction: "Its leaps should be *set* / to the flageo*let*"; "Katydid-wing subdivided by *sun* / till the nettings are *legion.*" I like light rhymes, inconspicuous rhymes and unpompous conspicuous rhymes: Gilbert and Sullivan:

> and yet when someone's near
> we manage to appear
> as impervious to fear
> as anybody here.

I have a passion for rhythm and accent, so blundered into versifying. Considering the stanza the unit, I came to hazard hyphens at the end of the line, but found that readers are distracted from the content by hyphens, so I try not to use them.

My interest in La Fontaine originated entirely independent of content. I then fell a prey to that surgical kind of courtesy of his.

I fear that appearances are worshiped throughout
  France
    Whereas pre-eminence perchance
    Merely means a pushing person.

I like the unaccented syllable and accented near-rhyme:

By love and his blindness
Possibly a service was done,
Let lovers say. A lonely man has no criterion.

Q: What in your reading or your background led you to write the way you do write? Was imagism a help to you?

A: No. I wondered why anyone would adopt the term.

Q: The descriptiveness of your poems has nothing to do with them, you think?

A: No; I really don't. I was rather sorry to be a pariah, or at least that I had no connection with anything. But I *did* feel gratitude to *Others.*

Q: Where do you think your style of writing came from? Was it a gradual accumulation, out of your character? Or does it have literary antecedents?

A: Not so far as I know. Ezra Pound said, "Someone has been reading Laforgue, and French authors." Well, sad to say, I had not read any of them until fairly recently. Retroactively I see that Francis Jammes' titles and treatment are a good deal like my own. I seem almost a plagiarist.

Q: And the extensive use of quotations?

A: I was just trying to be honorable and not to steal things. I've always felt that if a thing had been said in the *best* way, how can you say it better? If I wanted to say something and somebody had said it ideally, then I'd take it but give the person credit for it. That's all there is to it. If you are charmed by an author, I think it's a very strange and invalid imagination that doesn't long to share it. Somebody else should read it, don't you think?

Q: Did any prose stylists help you in finding your poetic style? Elizabeth Bishop mentions Poe's prose, in connection with your writing, and you have always made people think of Henry James.

A: Prose stylists, very much. Doctor Johnson on Richard Savage: "He was in two months illegitimated by the Parliament, and disowned by his mother, doomed to poverty and obscurity, and launched upon the ocean of life only that he might be swallowed by its quicksands, or dashed upon its rocks. . . . it was his peculiar happiness that he scarcely ever found a stranger whom he did not leave a friend; but it must likewise be added that, he had not often a friend long without obliging him to become a stranger." Or Edmund Burke on the colonies: "You can shear a wolf; but will he comply?" Or Sir Thomas Browne: "States are not governed by Ergotisms." He calls a bee "that industrious flie," and his home his "hive." His manner is a kind of erudition-proof sweetness. Or Sir Francis Bacon: "Civil War is like the heat of fever; a foreign war is like the heat of exercise." Or Cellini: "I had by me a dog black as a mulberry. . . . I swelled up in my rage like an asp." Or Caesar's *Commentaries,* and Xenophon's *Cynegeticus:* the gusto and interest in every detail! In Henry James it is the essays and letters especially that affect me. In Ezra Pound, *The Spirit of Romance:* his definiteness, his indigenously unmistakable accent. Charles Norman says in his biography of Ezra Pound that he said to a poet, "Nothing, *nothing,* that you couldn't in some circumstance, under stress of some emotion, *actually say.*" And Ezra said of Shakespeare and Dante, "Here we are with the masters; of neither can we say, 'He is the greater'; of each we must say, 'He is unexcelled.' "

Q: Do you have in your own work any favorites and unfavorites?

A: Indeed, I do. I think the most difficult thing for me is to be satisfactorily lucid, yet have enough implication in it to suit myself. That's a problem. And I don't approve of my "enigmas," or as somebody said, "the not ungreen grass."

I said to my mother one time, "How did you ever permit me to let this be printed?"

And she said, "You didn't ask my advice."

Q: One time I heard you giving a reading, and I think you said that you didn't like "In Distrust of Merits," which is one of your most popular poems.

A: I do like it; it is sincere but I wouldn't call it a poem. It's truthful; it is testimony–to the fact that war is intolerable, and unjust.

Q: How can you call it not a poem, on what basis?

A: Haphazard; as form, what has it? It is just a protest–disjointed, exclamatory. Emotion overpowered me. First this thought and then that.

Q: Your mother said that you hadn't asked her advice. Did you ever? Do you go for criticism to your family or friends?

A: Well, not my friends, but my brother if I get a chance. When my mother said "You didn't ask my advice" must have been years ago, because when I wrote "A Face," I had written something first about "the adder and the child with a bowl of porridge," and she said, "It won't do."

"All right," I said, "but I have to produce something." Cyril Connolly had asked me for something for *Horizon*. So I wrote "A Face." That is one of the few things I ever set down that didn't give me much trouble. She said, "I like it." I remember that.

Then, much before that, I wrote "The Buffalo." I thought it would probably outrage a number of persons because it had to me a kind of pleasing jerky progress. I thought, "Well, if it seems bad my brother will tell me, and if it has a point he'll detect it."

And he said, with considerable gusto, "It takes my fancy." I was happy as could be.

Q: Did you ever suppress anything because of family objections?

A: Yes, "the adder and the child with a bowl of porridge." I never even wanted to improve it.

You know, Mr. Saintsbury said that Andrew Lang wanted him to contribute something on Poe, and he did, and Lang returned it. Mr. Saintsbury said, "Once a thing has been rejected, I would not offer it to the most different of editors." That shocked me. I have offered a thing, submitted it thirty-five times. Not simultaneously, of course.

Q: A poem?

A: Yes. I am very tenacious.

Q: Do people ever ask you to write poems for them?

A: Continually. Everything from on the death of a dog to a little item for an album.

Q: Do you ever write them?

A: Oh, perhaps; usually quote something. Once when I was in the library we gave a party for Miss Leonard, and I wrote a line or two of doggerel about a bouquet of violets we gave her. It has no life or point. It was meant well but didn't amount to anything. Then in college, I had a sonnet as an assignment. The epitome of weakness.

Q: I'm interested in asking about the principles, and the methods, of your way of writing. What is the rationale behind syllabic verse? How does it differ from free verse in which the line length is controlled visually but not arithmetically?

A: It never occurred to me that what I wrote was something to define. I am governed by the pull of the sentence as the pull of a fabric is governed by gravity. I like the end-stopped line and dislike the reversed order of words; like symmetry.

Q: How do you plan the shape of your stanzas? I am thinking of the poems, usually syllabic, which employ a repeated stanza form. Do you ever experiment with shapes before you write, by drawing lines on a page?

A: Never. I never "plan" a stanza. Words cluster like chromosomes, determining the procedure. I may influence an arrangement or thin it, then try to have successive stanzas identical with the first. Spontaneous initial originality–say, impetus–seems difficult to reproduce consciously later. As Stravinsky said about pitch, "If I transpose it for some reason, I am in danger of losing the freshness of first contact and will have difficulty in recapturing its attractiveness."

No, I never "draw lines." I make a rhyme conspicuous, to me at a glance, by underlining with red, blue, or other pencil–as many colors as I have rhymes to differentiate. However, if the phrases recur in too incoherent an architecture–as print–I notice that the words as a tune do not sound right.

I may start a piece, find it obstructive, lack a way out, and not complete the thing for a year, or years, am thrifty. I salvage anything promising and set it down in a small notebook.

Q: I wonder if the act of translating La Fontaine's *Fables* helped you as a writer.

A: Indeed it did. It was the best help I've ever had.

I suffered frustration. I'm, so naïve, so docile, I *tend* to take anybody's word for anything the person says, even in matters of art. The publisher who had commissioned the *Fables* died. I had no publisher. Well, I struggled on for a time and it didn't go very well. I thought, I'd better ask if they don't want to terminate the contract; then I could offer it elsewhere. I thought Macmillan, who took an interest in me, might like it. *Might.* The editor in charge of translations said, "Well, I studied French at Cornell, took a degree in French, I love French, and . . . well, I think you'd better put it away for a while." "How long?" I said. "About ten years; besides, it will hurt your own work. You won't write so well afterward."

"Oh," I said, "that's one reason I was undertaking it; I thought it would train me and give me momentum." Much dejected, I asked, "What is wrong? Have I not a good ear? Are the meanings not sound?"

"Well, there are conflicts," the editor reiterated, as it seemed to me, countless times. I don't know yet what they are or were. (A little "editorial.")

I said, "Don't write me an extenuating letter, please. Just send back the material in the envelope I put with it." I had submitted it in January and this was May. I had had a kind of uneasy hope that all would be well; meanwhile had volumes, hours, and years of work yet to do and might as well go on and do it, I had thought. The ultimatum was devastating.

At the same time Monroe Engel of the Viking Press wrote to me and said that he had supposed I had a committment for my *Fables,* but if I hadn't would I let Viking Press see them? I feel an everlasting gratitude to him.

However, I said, "I can't offer you something which somebody else thinks isn't fit to print. I would have to have someone to stabilize it and guarantee that the meanings are sound."

Mr. Engel said, "Who do you think could do that? Whom would you like?"

I said, "Harry Levin," because he had written a cogent, very shrewd review of Edna St. Vincent Millay's and George Dillon's translation of Baudelaire. I admired its finesse.

Mr. Engel said, "I'll ask him. But you won't hear for a long time. He's very busy. And how much do you think we ought to offer him?"

"Well," I said, "not less that ten dollars a Book; there would be no incentive in undertaking the bother of it, if it weren't twenty."

He said, "that would reduce your royalties too much on an advance."

I said, "I don't want an advance, wouldn't even consider one."

"Well," he said, "that is like you."

And then Harry Levin said, quite soon, that he would be glad to do it as a "refreshment against the chores of the term." It was a very dubious refreshment, let me tell you. (He is precise, and not abusive, and did not "resign.")

Q: I've been asking you about your poems, which is of course what interests me most. But you were editor of *The Dial,* too, and I want to ask you a few things about that. You were editor from 1925 until it ended in 1929, I think. How did you first come to be associated with it?

A: Let me see. I think I took the initiative. I sent the editors a couple of things and they sent them back. And Lola Ridge had a party–she had a large apartment on the ground floor somewhere–and John Reed and Marsden Hartley, who was very confident with the brush, and Scofield Thayer, editor of *The Dial,* were there. And much to my disgust, we were induced each to read something we had written. And Scofield Thayer said of my piece, "Would you send that to us at *The Dial?*"

"I did send it," I said.

And he said, "Well, send it again." That is how it began, I think. Then he said, one time, "I'd like you to meet my partner, Sibley Watson," and invited me to tea at 152 W. 13th St. I was impressed. Doctor Watson is rare. He said nothing, but what he did say was striking and the significance would creep over you because unanticipated. And they asked me to join the staff, at *The Dial.*

Q: I have just been looking at that magazine, the years when you edited it. It's an incredible magazine.

A: *The Dial.* There *were* good things in it, weren't there?

Q: Yes. It combined George Saintsbury and Ezra Pound in the same issue. How do you account for it? What made it so good?

A: Lack of fear, for one thing. We didn't care what other people said. I never knew a magazine which was so self-propulsive. Everybody liked what he was doing, and when we made grievous mistakes we were sorry but we laughed over them.

Q: Louise Bogan said that *The Dial* made clear "the obvious division between American *avant-garde* and American conventional writing." Do you think this kind of division continues or has continued? Was this in any way a deliberate policy?

A: I think that individuality was the great thing. We were not conforming to anything. We certainly didn't have a policy, except I remember hearing the word "intensity" very often. A thing must have "intensity." That seemed to be the criterion.

The thing applied to it, I think, that should apply to your own writing. As George Grosz said, at that last meeting he attended at the National Institute, "How did I come to be an artist? Endless curiosity, observation, research–and a great amount of joy in the thing." It was a matter of taking a liking to things. Things that were in accordance with your taste. I think that was it. And we didn't care how unhomogeneous they might seem. Didn't Aristotle say that it is the mark of the poet to see resemblances between apparently incongruous things? There was any amount of attraction about it.

Q: Do you think there is anything in the change of literary life in America that would make *The Dial* different if it existed today under the same editors? Were there any special conditions in the twenties that made the literary life of America different?

A: I think it is always about the same.

Q: I wonder if it had survived into the thirties if it might have made that rather dry literary decade a little better.

A: I think so. Because we weren't in captivity to anything.

Q: Was it just finances that made it stop?

A: No, it wasn't the depression. Conditions changed. Scofield Thayer had a nervous breakdown, and he didn't come to meetings. Doctor Watson was interested in photography–was studying medicine; is a doctor of medicine, and lived in Rochester. I was alone. I didn't know that Rochester was about a night's journey away, and I would say to Doctor Watson, "Couldn't you come in for a make-up meeting, or send us these manuscripts and say what you think of them?" I may, as usual, have exaggerated my enslavement and my preoccupation with tasks–writing letters and reading manuscripts. Originally I had said I would come if I didn't have to write letters and didn't have to see contributors. And presently I was doing both. I think it was largely chivalry–the decision to discontinue the magazine–because I didn't have time for work of my own.

Q: I wonder how you worked as an editor. Hart Crane complains, in one of his letters, that you rearranged "The Wine Menagerie" and changed the title. Do you feel that you were justified? Did you ask for revisions from many poets?

A: No. We had an inflexible rule: do not ask changes of so much as a comma. Accept it or reject it. But in that instance I felt that in compassion I should disregard the rule.

Hart Crane complains of me? Well, I complain of *him.* He liked *The Dial* and we liked him–friends, and with certain tastes in common. He was in dire need of money. It seemed careless not to so much as ask if he might like to make some changes ("like" in quotations.) His gratitude was ardent and later his repudiation of it commensurate–he perhaps being in both instances under a disability with which I was not familiar. (Penalizing us for compassion?) I say "us," and should say "me." Really I am not used to having people in that bemused state. He was so *anxious* to have us take that thing, and so *delighted.* "Well, if you would modify it a little," I said, "we would like it better." I never attended "their" wild parties, as Lachaise once said. It was lawless of me to suggest changes; I disobeyed.

Q: Have you had editors suggest changes to you? Changes in your own poems, I mean?

A: No, but my ardor to be helped being sincere, I sometimes *induce* assistance: the *Times,* the *Herald Tribune,* the *New Yorker,* have a number of times had to patch and piece me out. If you have a genius of an editor, you are blessed: e.g., T.S. Eliot and Ezra Pound, Harry Levin, and others; Irita Van Doren and Miss Belle Rosenbaum.

Have I found "help" helpful? I certainly have; and in three instances when I was at *The Dial,* I hazarded suggestions the results of which were to me drama. Excoriated by George Haven Schauffler for offering to suggest a verbal change or two in his translation of Thomas Mann's *Disorder and Early Sorrow,* I must have posted the suggestions before I was able to withdraw them. In any case, his joyous subsequent retraction of abuse, and his pleasure in the narrative, were not unwelcome. Gilbert Seldes strongly commended me for excisions proposed by me in his "Jonathan Edwards" (for *The Dial*); and I have not ceased to marvel at the overrating by Mark Van Doren of editorial conscience on my reverting (after an interval) to keeping some final lines I had wished he would omit. (Verse! but not a sonnet.)

We should try to judge the work of others by the most that it is, and our own, if not by the least that it is, take the least into consideration. I feel that I would not be worth a button if not grateful to be preserved from myself, and informed if what I have written is not to the point. I think we should feel free, like La Fontaine's captious critic, to say, if asked, "Your phrases are too long, and the content is not good. Break up the type and put it in the font." As Kenneth Burke says in *Counter-Statement:* "[Great] artists feel as opportunity what others feel as a menace. This ability does not, I believe, derive from exceptional strength, it probably arises purely from professional interest the artist may take in his difficulties."

Lew Sarett says, in the *Poetry Society Bulletin,* we ask of a poet: Does this mean something? Does the poet say what he has to say and in his own manner? Does it stir the reader?

Shouldn't we replace vanity with honesty, as Robert Frost recommends? Annoyances abound. We should not find them lethal–a baffled printer's emendations for instance (my "elephant with frog-colored skin" instead of "fog-colored skin," and "the power of the invisible is the invisible," instead of "the power of the visible is the invisible") sounding like a parody on my meticulousness; a glasshopper instead of a grasshopper.

Q: Editing *The Dial* must have acquainted you with the writers of the day whom you did not know already. Had you known Hart Crane earlier?

A: Yes, I did. You remember *Broom?* Toward at the beginning of that magazine, in 1921, Lola Ridge was very hospitable, and she invited to a party–previous to my work on *The Dial*–Kay Boyle and her husband, a French soldier, and Hart Crane, Elinor Wylie, and some others. I took a great liking to Hart Crane. We talked about French bindings, and he was diffident and modest and seemed to have so much intuition, such a feel for things, for books–really a bibliophile–that I took special interest in him. And Doctor Watson and Scofield Thayer liked him–felt that he was one of our talents, that he couldn't fit himself into an IBM position to find a livelihood; that we ought to, whenever we could, take anything he sent us.

I know a cousin of his, Joe Nowak, who is rather proud of him. He lives here in Brooklyn, and is, at the Dry Dock Savings Bank and used to work in antiques. Joe was very convinced of Hart's sincerity and his innate love of all that I have specified. Anyhow, *The Bridge* is a grand theme. Here and there I think he could have firmed it up. A writer is unfair to himself when he is unable to be hard on himself.

Q: Did Crane have anything to do with *Others?*

A: *Others* antedated *Broom. Others* was Alfred Kreymborg and Skipwith Cannell, William Carlos Williams, Wallace Stevens–odd; I nearly met him a dozen times before I did meet him in 1941 at Mount Holyoke, at the college's *Entretiens de Pontigny* of which Professor Gustav Cohen was chairman. Wallace Stevens was Henry Church's favorite American poet. Mr. Church had published him and some others, and me, in *Mésure,* in Paris. Raymond Queneau translated us.

During the French program at Mount Holyoke one afternoon Wallace Stevens had a discourse, the one about Goethe dancing, on a packet-boat in black wool stockings. My mother and I were there; and I gave a reading with commentary. Henry Church had an astoundingly beautiful Panama hat–a sort of pork-pie with a wide brim, a little like Bernard Berenson's hats. I have never seen as fine a weave, and he had a pepper-and-salt shawl which he draped about himself. This lecture was on the lawn.

Wallace Stevens was extremely friendly. We should have had a tape recorder on that occasion, for at lunch they seated us all at a kind of refectory table and a girl kept asking him questions such as, "Mr. Stevens have you read the–*Four–Quartets?*"

"Of course, but I can't read much of Eliot or I wouldn't have any individuality of my own."

Q: Do you read new poetry now? Do you try to keep up?

A: I am always seeing it–I am sent some every day. Some, good. But it does interfere with my work. I can't get much done. Yet I would be a monster if I tossed everything away without looking at it; I write more notes, letters, cards in an hour than is sane.

Although everyone is penalized by being quoted inexactly, I wonder if there is anybody alive whose remarks are so often paraphrased as mine–printed as verbatim. It is really martyrdom.

In his book *Ezra Pound,* Charles Norman was very scrupulous. He got several things exactly right. The first time I met Ezra Pound, when he came here to see my mother and me, I said that Henry Eliot seemed to me more nearly the artist than anyone I had ever met. "Now, now," said Ezra. "Be careful." Maybe that isn't exact, but he quotes it just the way I said it.

Q: Do you mean Henry Ware Eliot, T.S. Eliot's brother?

A: Yes. After the Henry Eliots moved from Chicago to New York to–is it 68th Street? It's the street on which Hunter College is–to an apartment there, they invited me to dinner, I should think at T.S. Eliot's suggestion, and I took to them immediately. I felt as if I'd known them a great while. It was some time before I felt that way about T.S. Eliot.

About inaccuracies–when I went to see Ezra Pound at St. Elizabeth's, about the third time I went, the official who escorted me to the grounds said, "Good of you to come to see him," and I said, "Good? You have no idea how much he has done for me, and others." This pertains to an early rather than final visit.

I was not in the habit of asking experts or anybody else to help me with things that I was doing, unless it was a librarian or someone whose business it was to help applicants; or a teacher. But I was desperate when Macmillan declined my *Fables.* I had worked about four years on them and sent Ezra Pound several–although I hesitated. I didn't like to bother him. He had enough trouble without that; but finally I said, "Would you have time to tell me if the rhythms grate on you? Is my ear not good?"

Q: He replied?

A: Yes, said, "The least touch of merit upsets these blighters."

Q: When you first read Pound in 1916, did you recognize him as one of the great ones?

A: Surely did. *The Spirit of Romance.* I don't think anybody could read that book and feel that a flounderer was writing.

Q: What about the early poems?

A: Yes. They seemed a little didactic, but I liked them.

Q: I wanted to ask you a few questions about poetry in general. Somewhere you have said that originality is a by-product of sincerity. You often use moral terms in your criticism. Is the necessary morality specifically literary, a moral use of words, or is it larger? In what way must a man be good if he is to write good poems?

A: If emotion is strong enough, the words are unambiguous. Someone asked Robert Frost (is this right?) if he was selective. He said, "Call it passionate preference."

Must a man be good to write good poems? The villains in Shakespeare are not illiterate, are they? But rectitude *has* a ring that is implicative, I would say. And with *no* integrity, a man is not likely to write the kind of book I read.

Q: Eliot, in his introduction to your *Selected Poems,* talks about your function as poet relative to the living language, as he calls it. Do you

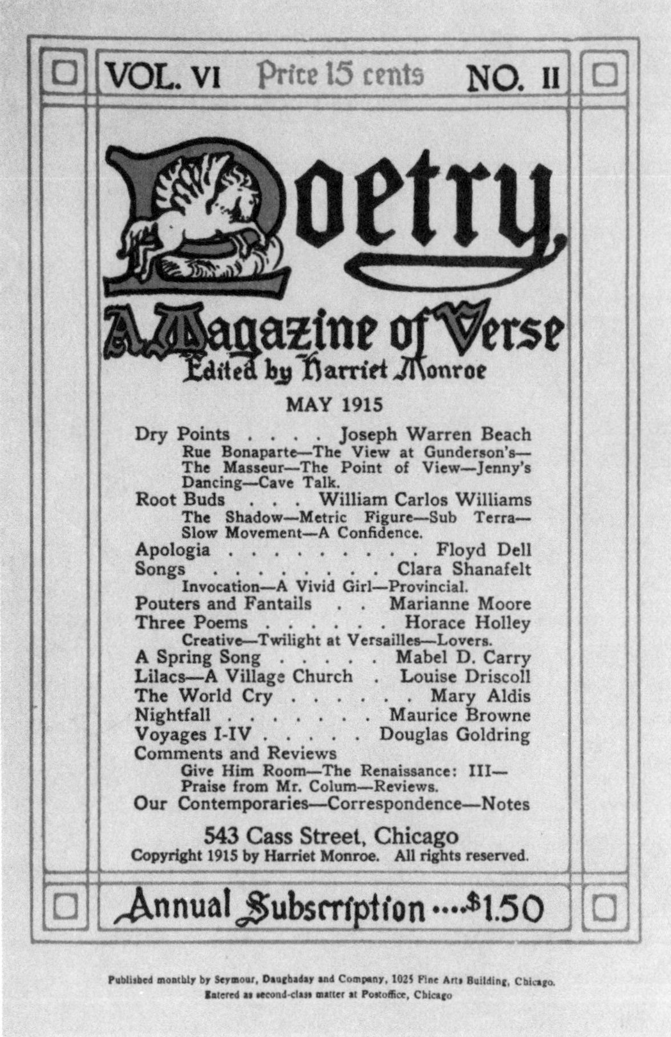

VOL. VI Price 15 cents NO. II

Poetry

A Magazine of Verse

Edited by Harriet Monroe

MAY 1915

Dry Points . . . . Joseph Warren Beach
Rue Bonaparte—The View at Gunderson's—The Masseur—The Point of View—Jenny's Dancing—Cave Talk.
Root Buds . . . William Carlos Williams
The Shadow—Metric Figure—Sub Terra—Slow Movement—A Confidence.
Apologia . . . . Floyd Dell
Songs . . . . Clara Shanafelt
Invocation—A Vivid Girl—Provincial.
Pouters and Fantails . . Marianne Moore
Three Poems . . . . . . Horace Holley
Creative—Twilight at Versailles—Lovers.
A Spring Song . . . . . Mabel D. Carry
Lilacs—A Village Church . Louise Driscoll
The World Cry . . . . . . Mary Aldis
Nightfall . . . . Maurice Browne
Voyages I-IV . . . . . Douglas Goldring
Comments and Reviews
Give Him Room—The Renaissance: III—Praise from Mr. Colum—Reviews.
Our Contemporaries—Correspondence—Notes

543 Cass Street, Chicago

Copyright 1915 by Harriet Monroe. All rights reserved.

Annual Subscription $1.50

Published monthly by Seymour, Daughaday and Company, 1025 Fine Arts Building, Chicago.
Entered as second-class matter at Postoffice, Chicago

Moore's first professionally published poems appeared in the April 1915 issue of the Egoist *and the May 1915 issue of* Poetry *(front cover above). In September 1916 Moore and her mother went to live with her brother, who had graduated from Princeton Theological Seminary and been appointed pastor to Ogdon Memorial Presbyterian Church in Chatham, New Jersey. Two years later he resigned to become a chaplain in the U.S. Navy, and Moore and her mother moved to 14 St. Luke's Place in Greenwich Village.*

agree that this is a function of a poet? How does the poetry have the effect on the living language? What's the mechanics of it?

A: You accept certain modes of saying a thing. Or strongly repudiate things. You do something of your own, you modify, invent a variant or revive a root meaning. Any doubt about that?

Q: I want to ask you a question about your correspondence with the Ford Motor Company, those letters which were printed in the *New Yorker*. They were looking for a name for the car they eventually called the Edsel, and they asked you to think of a name that would make people admire the car–

A: Elegance and grace, they said it would have–

Q: ". . . some visceral feeling of elegance, fleetness, advanced features and design. A name, in short, which flashes a dramatically desirable picture in people's minds."

A: Really?

Q: That's what they said, in their first letter to you. I was thinking about this in connection with my question about language. Do you remember Pound's talk about expression and meaning? He says that when expression and meaning are far apart, the culture is in a bad way. I was wondering if this request doesn't ask you to remove expression a bit further from meaning.

A: No, I don't think so. At least, to exposit the irresistibleness of the car. I got deep in motors and turbines and recessed wheels. No. That seemed to me a very worthy pursuit. I was more interested in the mechanics. I am interested in mechanisms, mechanics in general. And I enjoyed the assignment, for all that it was abortive.

Dr. Pick at Marquette University procured a young demonstrator of the Edsel to call for me in a black one, to convey me to the auditorium. Nothing was wrong with that Edsel! I thought it was a very handsome car. It came out the wrong year.

Q: Another thing: In your criticism you make frequent analogies between the poet and the scientist. Do you think this analogy is helpful to the modern poet? Most people would consider the comparison a paradox, and assume that the poet and the scientist are opposed.

A: Do the poet and scientist not work analogously? Both are willing to waste effort. To be hard on himself is one of the main strengths of each. Each is attentive to clues, each must narrow the choice, must strive for precision. As George Grosz says, "In art there is no place for gossip and but a small place for the satirist." The objective is fertile procedure. Is it not? Jacob Bronowski says in the *Saturday Evening Post* that science is not a mere collection of discoveries, but that science is the process of discovering. In any case it's not established once and for all; it's evolving.

Q: One last question. I was intrigued when you wrote that "America has in Wallace Stevens at least one artist whom professionalism will not demolish." What sort of literary professionalism did you have in mind? And do you find this a feature of America still?

A: Yes. I think that writers sometimes lose verve and pugnacity, and he never would say "frame of reference" or "I wouldn't know."

A question I am often asked is: "What work can I find that will enable me to spend my whole time writing?" Charles Ives, the composer, says, "You cannot set art off in a corner and hope for it to have vitality, reality, and substance. The fabric weaves itself whole. My work in music helped my business and my work in business helped my music." I am like Charles Ives. I guess Lawrence Durrell and Henry Miller would not agree with me.

Q: But how does professionalism make a writer lose his verve and pugnacity?

A: Money may have something to do with it and being regarded as a pundit; Wallace Stevens was really very much annoyed at being catalogued, categorized, and compelled to be scientific about what he was doing–to give satisfaction, to answer the teachers. He wouldn't do that.

I think the same of William Carlos Williams. I think he wouldn't make so much of the great American language if he were plausible; and tractable. That's the beauty of it; he is willing to be reckless; if you can't be that, what's the point of the whole thing?

ARTICLE:

H. D. [Hilda Doolittle], "Marianne Moore," *Egoist*, 3 (August 1916); 118-119.

This article by her Bryn Mawr College classmate, and Imagist poet, brought Moore's poetry to the attention of the avant-garde literary world. The collection to which H. D. refers is probably an unpublished manuscript.

I have before me a collection of poems. They have appeared for the most part in various American periodicals. And readers of THE EGOIST are familiar with certain of these curiously wrought patterns, these quaint turns of thought and concealed, half-playful ironies. They have puzzled over such poems as "To a Steam Roller" or "Diligence is to Magic as Progress is to Flight" and asked–what is this all about–" "scarecrows of aesthetic procedures"–"weight hardened creatures"–"prosaic necessities," etc. etc. They have read Miss Marianne Moore's poems again and again, and puzzle, or does it mean something?

Does it mean something?

"FEED ME, ALSO, RIVER GOD

"Lest by diminished vitality and abated
Vigilance, I become food for crocodiles–for that quicksand
Of gluttony which is legion. It is there–close at hand–
On either side
Of me. You remember the Israelites who said

Moore in 1921. During the previous year, her poems had begun to appear in the Dial, *and she had gone to work at the Hudson Park Branch of the New York Public Library, across the street from her Greenwich Village apartment.*

in pride
"And stoutness of heart: 'The bricks are fallen down,
we will
Build with hewn stone, the sycamores are cut down,
we will change to
Cedars?' I am not ambitious to dress stones,
to renew
Forts, nor to match
My value in action, against their ability to catch

"Up with arrested prosperity. I am not like
Them, indefatigable, but if you are a god you will
Not descriminate against me. Yet–if you may ful-
fill
None but prayers dressed
As gifts in return for your own
gifts–disregard
the request."

I think that it does mean something. And if Miss Moore is laughing at us, it is laughter that catches us, that holds, fascinates and half-paralyses us, as light flashed from a very fine steel blade, wielded playfully, ironically, with all the fine shades of thrust and counter-thrust, with absolute surety and with absolute disdain. Yet with all the assurance of the perfect swordsman, the perfect technician, I like to imagine that there is as well something of the despair of the perfect artist–"see, you cannot know what I mean–exactly what I mean," she seems to say, half-pitying that the adversary is dull–that we are so dull–" and I do not intend that you shall know–my sword is very much keener than your sword, my hand surer than your hand–but you shall not know that I know you are beaten."

Yet we are not always baffled. Miss Moore turns her perfect craft as the perfect craftsman must inevitably do, to some direct presentation of beauty, clear, cut in flowing lines, but so delicately that the very screen she craves seems meant to stand only in that serene palace of her own world of inspiration–frail, yet as all beautiful things are, absolutely hard–and destined to endure longer. Far longer than the toppling sky-scraper, and the world of shrapnel and machine-guns in which we live.

The clear, flawless tones of Miss Moore's poetry come like bell-notes, like notes from some palace-bell carved beneath the sea. Indeed I seem to place this very screen in some mermaid's palace.

"HE MADE THIS SCREEN

"Not of silver nor of coral,
But of weatherbeaten laurel.
"Here, he introduced a sea
Uniform like tapestry;

"Here, a fig-tree;" there, a face ;
There, a dragon circling space–

"Designating here, a bower;
There, a pointed passion-flower."

As I say the rhythm and the tones of her words come as through some "sea-change"–and surely there is "something rich and strange" in this "Talisman"–

"Under a splintered mast,
Torn from the ship and cast
Near her hull,

"A stumbling shepherd found
Embedded in the ground,
A sea-gull

"Of lapis lazuli,
A scarab of the sea,
With wings spread–

"Curling its coral feet,
Parting its beak to greet
Men long dead."

Miss Marianne Moore is an American. And I think in reading Miss Moore's poems we in England should be strengthened. We are torn in our ambitions, our desires are crushed, we hear from all sides that art is destined to a long period of abeyance, and that the reconstruction of Europe must take all the genius of the race. I do not believe that. There are others here in England who do not for one moment believe that beauty will be one whit bruised by all this turmoil and distress.

Miss Moore helps us. She is fighting in her country a battle against squalor and commercialism. We are all fighting the same battle. And we must strengthen each other in this one absolute bond–our devotion to the beautiful English language.

BOOK REVIEW:
Ezra Pound, Review of *Others An Anthology of New Verse (1917)*, edited by Alfred Kreymborg, *Little Review*, 4 (March 1918): 56-58.

Reviewing the Others *anthology for 1917, Ezra Pound set forth his first pronouncements on Moore and Mina Loy. The following year saw the beginning of Moore's lifelong correspondence with Pound which, along with her reviews of his Cantos, contains some of her most polemically charged writing.*

The Cuala Press has issued a volume of Mr. Yeats' latest poems, the quality of which is well known to our readers and needs no further exposition. Among other books received for review is a sequence by Moireen Fox, a new book of short poems by Joseph Campbell, and the "Others" Anthology for 1917. This last gives I think the first adequate presentation of Mina Loy and Marianne Moore, who have, without exaggerated "nationalism," without waving of banners and general phrases about Columbia gem of the ocean, succeeded in, or fallen into, producing something distinctly American in quality, not merely distinguishable as Americans by reason of current national faults.

Their work is neither simple, sensuous nor passionate, but as we are no longer governed by the *North American Review* we need not condemn poems merely because they do not fit some stock phrase of rhetorical criticism.

(For example an infinitely greater artist than Tennyson uses six "six" 'ss and one "z" in a single line. It is one of the most musical lines in Provencal and opens a poem especially commended by Dante. Let us leave the realm of promoted typists who quote the stock phrases of text books.)

In the verse of Marianne Moore I detect traces of emotion; in that of Mina Loy I detect no emotion whatever. Both of these women are, possibly in unconsciousness, among the followers of Jules Laforgue (whose work shows a great deal of emotion). It is possible, as I have written, or intended to write elsewhere, to divide poetry into three sorts: (1.) melopoeia, to wit, poetry which moves by its music, whether it be a music in the words or an aptitude for, or suggestion of, accompanying music; (2.) imagism, or poetry wherein the feelings of painting and sculpture are predominant (certain men move in phantasmagoria; the images of their gods, whole countryside, stretches of hill land and forest, travel with them); and there is, thirdly, logopoeia or poetry that is akin to nothing but language, which is a dance of the intelligence among words and ideas and modification of ideas and characters. Pope and the eighteenth-century writers had in this medium a certain limited range. The intelligence of Laforgue ran through the whole gamut of his time. T. S. Eliot has gone on with it. Browning wrote a condensed form of drama, full of things of the senses, scarcely ever pure logopoeia.

One wonders what the devil anyone will make of this sort of thing who has not in their wit all the clues. It has none of the stupidity beloved of the "lyric" enthusiast and the writer and reader who take refuge in scenery description of nature, because they are unable to cope with the human. These two contributors to the "Others" Anthology write logopoeia. It is, in their case, the utterance of clever people in despair, or hovering upon the brink of that precipice. It is of those who have acceded with Renan "La bêtise humaine est la seule chose qui donne une idée de l'infini." It is a mind cry, more than a heart cry. "Take the world if thou wilt but leave me an asylum for my affection" is not their lamentation but rather "In the midst of this desolation, give me at least one intelligence to converse with."

The arid clarity, not without its own beauty, of le tempérament de l'Americaine, is in the poems of these, I think, graduates or post-graduates. If they have not received B. A.s or M. A.'s or B. Sc-s they do not need them.

The point of my praise, for I intend this as praise, even if I do not burst into the phrases of Victor Hugo, is that without any pretences and without clamours about nationality, these girls have written a distinctly national product, they have written something which would not have come out of any other country, and (while I have before now seen a deal of rubbish by both of them) they are, as selected by Mr. Kreymborg, interesting and readable (by me, that is. I am aware that even the poems before me would drive numerous not wholly unintelligent readers into a fury of rage-out-of-puzzlement.) Both these poets have said a number of things not to be found in the current numbers of *Everybody's*, the *Century* or *McClure's*. "The Effectual Marriage", "French Peacock", "My Apish Cousins" have each in its way given me pleasure. Miss Moore has already prewritten her counterblast to my criticism in her poem "To a Steam Roller".

Kreymborg's anthology contains poems by Eliot; by Cannell, who manages to get still a drop more poetry from that worn subject, the deity (monotheist); and by Carlos Williams who often delights me by his opacity, a distinctly unamerican quality, and not without its own value. Mr. Kreymborg is getting his eye in.

COMMENT:

From W. C. Blum [James Sibley Watson, Jr.], "American Letter," *Dial*, 70 (May 1921): 562-568.

The co-owner of the Dial *offered this notice of Moore in the company of Pound, William Carlos Williams, and E. E. Cummings, shortly before the appearance of Moore's first book,* Poems, *published in England in July 1921 by her friends H. D., Bryher (Winifred Ellerman), and Robert McAlmon at Harriet Shaw Weaver's Egoist Press. Moore had attempted to discourage the publication, feeling that she was not yet ready for a book.*

Traverse City, Mich., April, 1921

The idea of making a survey or inventory of recent American writing has occurred to several persons this winter, and because I found their attempts so very unsatisfactory from the point of view not only of the serious fellow who worries over the United States but of the reader as well, who wants something really new and bang-up to read, I decided to write things down as they appear to one in Traverse City.

Up north here, in this thin air and beside this purified Michigan, one is in a more fortunate position for surveying the country, I believe, than in New York or San Francisco, or Urbana, Ill. Much tiresome nonsense fails to carry over these protecting sand hills.

As one would not care to imitate Prof. Sherman and his extraordinarily awful catalogue of ships, it is to be a question only of the most serious young writers, critics who are serious about ideas or pleasure, and poets who are serious about both. They have all probably detested one another, or will do so when the occasion offers, but to us each one appears as a blessing. It is to their interactions with one another and with a small audience, that we shall look for something in America even more interesting.

First I should like to discuss what seems to me very significant, and what nearly everyone else has minimized or overlooked: we have, or had quite recently, a group of writers, more or less able, whose intentions were sufficiently circumscribed to make them what in France would be called a "school" of literary criticism. I realize that many people consider schools superfluous; tell you that England got on without them, that great men are accidents. But the dispersion or absence of taste and thought here is surely more fatiguing than any concentration of intelligences could possibly be. Besides, this is no longer an Anglo-Saxon country; perhaps the French method would just suit us. At least the momentary association of Van Wyck Brooks, Randolph Bourne, Waldo Frank, James Oppenheim, Paul Rosenfeld, and the rest in the Seven Arts was more stimulating for them and for us than to have had them all over the lot. Their combination produced a "movement" and furnished the "resistance" (so plaintively asked for by The Little Review) which is necessary to a healthy opposition. Only Mencken has the Quixotism to react against nothing at all backed by the police and the professions.

Who first applied psychoanalysis to America I do not know, though I suspect Randolph Bourne. People had been growling about the puritans for centuries, when here in a moment the whole disease and machinery of puritanism was shown up. Psychoanalysis fitted beautifully, more beautifully than ever before or since. America was plainly suppressed, infantile, imitative, inverted; Whitman the only free voice we ever found. Bourne, the genius of the group, outlined the campaign in a few masterly essays, and The Ordeal of Mark Twain and Our America remain to show how admirably an idea can be run into the ground by a patient and an impatient mind.

Apart from Paul Rosenfeld, who has always seen or heard what he criticized as well as dreamed about it, the Seven Arts group was interested too exclusively in the soul. Charlie Chaplin appeared to them not as a series of precise, rectangular gestures, but as the frustrated clown that exists in the heart of every American. This sort of observation is considered by people like Francis Hackett to be very valuable, and is easy to do and, when slickly done, perhaps, easy to read. But it has no more direct bearing on art than any other bi-product of psychoanalysis.

Of course when one wishes to be a literary critic in one's own country, and when that country offers no literature for discussion, one naturally takes to psychology in self-defense; but the Seven Arts group was too ready to disregard and despise as un-American very admirable and very American poets like Ezra Pound, Marianne Moore, and William Carlos Williams for one to have much faith in their affection for art. . . .

When Marianne Moore rhymes she reminds us that the eighteenth century, too, desired lucidity.

> "Despising sham, you used your sword
> To riddle the conventions of excess;
> Nor did the king love you the less."

Separate lines of hers often read like the classical prose to which we are supposed to have become accustomed in school. She borrows or invents long quotations ("interpreting life through the medium of the emotions," "deluded him with loitering formality, doing its duty as if it did it not") which she works into her poems without the slightest inappropriateness. Like Rimbaud she uses the most matter-of-fact constructions, critical rather than poetic phrases, so that extraordinary expansions of mood are uncovered without warning:

> " . . . your dress, a
> magnificent square
> cathedral of uniform
> and at the same time, diverse appearance—a species of
> vertical vineyard rustling in the storm
> of conventional opinion."

> " . . . Gordon

Craig with his 'this is I' and 'this is mine,' with his three
wise men, his 'sad French greens' and his Chinese cherries–
Gordon Craig so

inclinational and unashamed–has carried
the precept of being a good critic, to the last extreme. And
Burke is a
psychologist–of acute, raccoon-
like curiosity."

These penetrating or sensible remarks, spoken so distinctly and as though with the back turned, following one another with such shattering politeness and efficiency, have a broken rhythm–pile up and resolve.

There is no end of other tricks besides.

BOOK REVIEW:
Harriet Monroe, "A Symposium on Marianne Moore," *Poetry,* 19 (January 1922): 208-216.

Harriet Monroe, the first American magazine editor to publish poems by Moore, had had a falling-out with the poet in 1918. In an attempt to be fair, Monroe gathered reviews of Moore's Poems *from supporters–H. D., Bryher, and Yvor Winters–and detractors–Marion Strobel and Pearl Andelson. Moore, like her colleagues Williams, Pound, and Wallace Stevens, would not publish in* Poetry *again until the 1930s, after the demise of the* Dial *in 1929.*

Such contrary opinions of this provocative little pamphlet have reached us that perhaps the most suggestive review will be a more or less questioning rehearsal of them. Miss Moore's steely and recondite art has long been a rallying-point for the radicals. Although her first appearance was in POETRY–in May, 1915, most of the entries in these twenty-four closely printed pages date from *Others* and *The Egoist,* a few from *The Dial* and *Contact.* Rumor has hinted that the selection and publication were made by certain friends of the author without her knowledge.

If one were to accept the challenge of the title, and of the geometrical verse-designs which frame these cryptic observations, one might be led straight to the ancient and rather futile inquiry, What is poetry? Poetry is evidently a matter of individual definition. H. D., surely a critic of authority, calls Miss Moore a poet, and a number of young radicals are eager to pronounce her "a very great poet," as Yvor Winters did in a recent letter. "With the exception of Wallace Stevens," he wrote, "she is about the only person since Rimbaud who has had any very profound or intricate knowledge and command of sound; and I am not sure but I think her about the best poet in this country except for Mr. Stevens."

A more moderate admirer, Miss Winifred Bryher, sends us the following estimate from England:

> This volume is the study of a Marco Polo detained at home. It is the fretting of a wish against wish until the self is drawn, not into a world of air and adventure, but into a narrower self, patient, dutiful and precise. *Those Various Scalpels* is sharper than a diamond. It is as brilliant a poem as any written of late years, and yet it is but a play with the outside of substances and the inside of thoughts too tired to feel emotion. And *Dock Rats* again, or *England,* are wrought as finely as the old Egyptians wrought figures from an inch-high piece of emerald; but they lack the one experience of life for which life was created.
>
> The temperament behind the words is not a passive one, however much environment may have forced meditation upon it as a form of "protective coloration." The spirit is robust, that of a man with facts and countries to discover and not that of a woman sewing at tapestries. But something has come between the free spirit and its desire–a psychological uneasiness that is expressed in these few perfect but static studies of a highly evolved intellect.
>
> Technically it is a triumphant book. There are scenes which are a joy to remember; the shifting color of
>
> wade
> through black jade
> of the crow-blue mussel shells–
>
> And the vivid beauty of *The Talisman:*
>
> Under a splintered mast,
> torn from ship and cast
> near her hull,
>
> a stumbling shepherd found
> embedded in the ground,
> a sea-gull
>
> of lapis lazuli,
> a scarab of the sea,
> with wings spread–
> curling its coral feet,
> parting its beak to greet
> men long dead.

Marianne Moore (third from right) and her brother, John Warner Moore (second from right), with a climbing party on Mount Rainier, summer 1922, during one of two visits to the region that inspired Moore's poem "An Octopus," published in the December 1924 issue of the Dial *and collected later that month in* Observations

Miss Moore has preferred, to date, to express simply the pictorial aspect of the universe, and she has fulfilled perfectly each self-imposed task. Her *Poems* are an important addition to American literature, to the entire literature of the modern world. Only, Marco Polo, your sword is ready and your kingdoms wait. May it soon please you to leave the fireside and ride forth.

But Miss Moore's admirers don't have it all their own way. Here is the point of view of one of POETRY'S associate editors, Marion Strobel:

Even a gymnast should have grace. If we find ourselves one of an audience in a side-show we prefer to see the well-muscled lady in tights stand on her head smilingly, with a certain nonchalance, rather than grit her teeth, perspire, and make us conscious of her neck muscles. Still, we would rather not see her at all.

Just so we would rather not follow the contortions of Miss Moore's well-developed mind–she makes us so conscious of her knowledge! And because we are conscious that she has brains, that she is exceedingly well-informed, we are the more irritated that she has not learned to write with simplicity.

The subject-matter of her poems is inevitably dry; the manner of expression pedantic. She shouts at our stupidity: "Literature is a phase of life"; "Words are constructive when they are true–the opaque allusion, the simulated flight upward, accomplishes nothing." And we yawn back at Miss Moore's omniscience.

And another poet-critic, Pearl Andelson, says:

Marianne Moore has much the Emily Dickinson type of mind, but where Emily Dickinson's not infrequent obscurities arise out of an authentic mysticism, Marianne Moore's are more likely the result of a relentless discipline in the subtler "ologies" and "osophies." She is brilliant at times to the point of gaudiness, although one feels that in her brilliance she is most herself. As to form, the fact that she wavers between prose and poetry is not disguised by the breath-taking line-formation. Indeed, I should say the incongruous effect was heightened, rather than diminished, by occasional rhyming. The same, for the most part, may be said of content as of form. Such poems as *Picking and Choosing* and *Poetry* are hybrids of a flagrantly prose origin.

Well, let us turn to the book—without prejudice one way or the other. In the first place, the lady is delightfully independent; she says in *Black Earth:*

Openly, yes
with the naturalness
of the hippopotamus or the alligator
when it climbs out on the bank to experience the

sun, I do these
things which I do, which please
no one but myself. Now I breathe and now I am sub-
merged; the blemishes stand up and shout when the object

in view was a
renaissance; shall I say
the contrary? The sediment of the river which
encrusts my joints makes me very gray, but I am used

to it, it may
remain there; do away
with it and I am myself done away with, for the
patina of circumstance can but enrich what was

there to begin
with. This elephant skin
which I inhabit; fibred over like the shell of
the cocoanut, this piece of black glass through which no light

can filter—cut
into checkers by rut
upon rut of unpreventable experience—
it is a manual for the peanut-tongued and the
hairy-toed. Black
but beautiful, my back
is full of the history of power, Of power? What
is powerful and what is not? My soul shall never
be cut into
by a wooden spear.

And so on for about forty more lines, which develop and elaborate the elephantine symbol, and then drop it, as it were, in mid-career, with a quizzical trunk-flourish. As *Black Earth* is admirably representative of its author's thought and style, it may serve as the text for a few inquiries.

Meditative self-confession is no novelty in English poetry—we have countless examples in as many different patterns. Hamlet's soliloquies, Gray's *Elegy,* Pope's *Essay on Man,* Byron's *Childe Harold,* Whitman's *Song of Myself,* many sonnets by Milton, Wordsworth, Keats and other supreme sonneteers—these are but a few of the numerous high precedents in English poetry for more or less imaginative and more or less metrical meditation. And one may not deny imaginative power to the mind which can create and round out and energize so effectively the grotesque image which appears when she holds up the mirror to her soul. Neither may one refuse any poet the right to attempt new metrical patterns; since only through such attempts does any achievement become possible—any enrichment of the English prosodic scheme.

So it remains to attempt to estimate the validity of Miss Moore's processes and the degree of her achievement. Unquestionably there is a poet within the hard, deliberately patterned crust of such soliloquies as *Black Earth, Those Various Scalpels, Pedantic Literalist, Reinforcements*—almost any of these titles—though a poet too sternly controlled by a stiffly geometrical intellectuality. Miss Moore is a terror of her Pegasus; she knows of what sentimental excesses that unruly steed is capable, and so her ironic mind harnesses down his wings and her iron hand holds a stiff rein. This mood yields prose oftener than poetry, but it wrings out now and then the reluctant beauty of a grotesque, or even, more rarely, such a lyric as *Talisman.*

No amount of line patterning can make anything but statement and argument out of many of the entries in this book—for example, *Picking and Choosing,* which begins:

Literature is a phase of life: if
one is afraid of it, the situation is irremediable; if
one approaches it familiarly,
what one says of it is worthless. Words are constructive

when they are true; the opaque illusion–the simulated flight

upward–accomplishes nothing. Why cloud the fact
that Shaw is self-conscious in the field of sentiment but is otherwise rewarding? that James
is all that has been
said of him but is not profound? It is not Hardy
the distinguished novelist and Hardy the poet, but one man

"interpreting life through the medium of the emotions."

If the mood instinctively flouts the muse, what of the method? If the mood may rarely yield more than the hard reluctant beauty of a grotesque, is the method inevitable and right, fitting words musically, magically to the motive, as in all the masterpieces of the art? Well, let me confess that I do not find the divine shapeliness and sound-richness which Mr. Winters referred to in his letter. What I do find in certain poems is a brilliant array of subtly discordant harmonies not unlike those of certain ultra-modern composers, set forth in stanza-forms purely empirical even when emphasized by rhyme, forms which impose themselves arbitrarily upon word-structure and sentence-structure instead of accepting happily the limitations of the art's materials, as all art must. When Miss Moore uses the first syllable of *accident* as a whole line to rhyme with *lack,* or the article *a* as a line to rhyme with the end of *Persia;* when she ends a stanza in a split infinitive, or in the middle of the swift word *very*–indeed, anywhere in the middle of words or sentences, she is forcing her pattern upon materials which naturally reject it, she is giving a wry twist even though her aim is a grotesque; and when her aim is more serious, such verbal whimsicalities strike at once the intensely false note of affectation. And as she takes her own way in these details of style, so she gives little heed to the more general laws of shapeliness; each poem begins as it ends and ends as it begins–a coruscating succession of ideas, with little curve of growth or climax.

What I do find throughout this book is wit–wit fundamental and instinctive which expresses itself not only in words, phrases, rhymes, rhythms, but in ideas, emotions. The grim and haughty humor of this lady strikes deep, so deep as to absorb her dreams and possess her soul. She feels immense incongruities, and the incongruity of her little ego among them moves her art not to grandeur but to scorn. As a satirist she is at times almost sublime–what contrary devil balks her even at those moments, tempting her art to its most inscrutable perversities?

Youth is sometimes penetrating in self-diagnosis. I am tempted to recall the first poem Miss Moore ever published–*That Harp You Play So Well,* from the 1915 group in POETRY:

O David, if I had
Your power, I should be glad–
 In harping, with the sling,
 In patient reasoning!

Blake, Homer, Job, and you,
Have made old wine-skins new.
 Your energies have wrought
 Stout continents of thought.

But, David, if the heart
Be brass, what boots the art
 Of exorcising wrong,
 Of harping to a song?

The sceptre and the ring
And every royal thing
 Will fail. Grief's lustiness
 Must cure the harp's distress.

"If the heart be brass . . . every royal thing will fail." It is not this reviewer who says that, or invokes for this poet "grief 's lustiness." May even grief soften a heart of brass? And is a deep resistless humor like Miss Moore's the most subtly corrosive destroyer of greatness?

BOOK REVIEW:

T. S. Eliot, "Marianne Moore," review of *Poems* and *Marriage, Dial,* 75 (December 1923): 594-597.

Eliot had first noticed Moore in print in the Egoist *(1918), the same year Moore reviewed his* Prufrock and Other Observations. *Later, Eliot became Moore's English publisher, and the two continued to respect one another's poetry.*

Two years ago Miss Moore's book of *Poems*–so far as I know her only book–was published in London by The Egoist Press; and I then undertook to review it for THE DIAL. This promise, for one reason after another, I never fulfilled. Now another poem has appeared, Marriage, published by Manikin, printed apparently in Germany, and with a parenthetical introduction by Mr. Glenway Wescott. Meanwhile I have read Miss Moore's poems a good many times, and always with exactly the same pleasure and satisfaction in something quite definite and solid. Because of a promise which, because of the long delay, may be considered as having been broken, and because I can only, at the moment, think of five contemporary poets–English, Irish, American, French, and German–whose work excites me as much as, or more than, Miss Moore's , I find myself compelled to say something about them. Not that there is much that is usefully said about any new work of art–I do not rate criticism so highly; but one ought, in honesty, to publish one's beliefs.

Mr. Wescott has, in fact, written a good introduction; I only think that his distinction between proletariat art and aristocratic art is an artificial and unimportant distinction with dangerous consequences. So far as a proletariat art is art at all, it is the same thing in essence as aristocratic art; but in general, and at the present time, the middle-class art (which is what I believe Mr. Wescott to have in mind when he speaks of proletariat art (the proletariat *is* middle class in America) is much more artificial than anything else; it plays with sham ideas, sham emotions, and even sham sensations. On the other hand a real aristocracy is essentially of the same blood as the people over whom it rules: a real aristocracy is not a Baltenland aristocracy of foreign race. This apparently purely political definition applies to art as well: fine art is the *refinement*, not the antithesis, of popular art. Miss Moore's poetry may not seem to confirm this statement. I agree with Mr. Wescott that it is "aristocratic," in that it can only please a very small number of people. But it is not, or not wholly, aristocratic in the Baltenland sense. I see in it at least three elements: a quite new rhythm, which I think is the most valuable thing; a peculiar and brilliant and rather satirical use of what is not, as material, an "aristocratic" language at all, but simply the curious jargon produced in America by universal university education–that jargon which makes it impossible for Americans to talk for half an hour without using the terms of psychoanalysis, and which has introduced "moron" as more forcible than "idiot"; and finally an almost primitive simplicity of phrase. There may be more. Up to the present time Miss Moore has concerned herself with practising and perfecting a given formation of elements; it will depend, I think, on her ability to *shatter* this formation and painfully reconstruct, whether Miss Moore makes another invention equal in merit to the first.

Rhythm, of course, is a highly personal matter; it is not a verse-form. It is always the real pattern in the carpet, the scheme of organization of thought, feeling, and vocabulary, the way in which everything comes together. It is very uncommon. What is certain is that Miss Moore's poems always read very well aloud. That quality is something which no system of scansion can define. It is not separable from the use of words, in Miss Moore's case the conscious and complete appreciation of every word, and in relation to every other word, as it goes by. I think that Those Various Scalpels is an excellent example for study. Here the rhythm depends partly upon the transformation-changes from one image to another, so that the second image is superimposed before the first has quite faded, and upon the dexterity of change of vocabulary from one image to another. "Snow sown by tearing winds on the cordage of disabled ships:" has that Latin, epigrammatic succinctness, laconic austerity, which leaps out unexpectedly (altogether in Talisman).

"your raised hand
an ambiguous signature:"

is a distinct shift of manner; it is not an image, but the indication of a fulness of meaning which is unnecessary to pursue.

"blood on the stone floors of French chateaux, with
regard to which guides are so affirmative:"

is a satirical (consciously or unconsciously it does not matter) refinement of that pleasantry (not flippancy, which is something with a more definite purpose) of speech which characterizes the American language, that pleasantry, uneasy, solemn, or self-conscious, which inspires both the jargon of the laboratory and the slang of the comic strip. Miss Moore works this uneasy language of stereotype–as of a whole people playing uncomfortably at clenches and clevelandisms–with impeccable skill into her pattern. She uses words like "fractional," "vertical," "infinitesimal," "astringently"; phrases like "excessive popularity," "a liability rather than an asset," "mask of profundity," "vestibule of experience," "diminished vitality," "arrested prosperity." If this were all, Miss Moore would be no different from her imitators.

The merit consists in the combination, in the point of view which Miss Moore possesses at the same time. What her imitators cannot get are the swift dissolving images, like the mussel shell

> "opening and shutting itself like
> an
> injured fan"

and phrases like

> "the sea when it proffers flattery in exchange for hemp rye, flax, horses, platinum, timber and fur."

> "Truth is no Apollo
> Belvedere, no formal thing. The wave may go over it if it likes."

or a magnificence of phrase like

> "I recall their magnificence, now not more magnificent
> than it is dim"

(how like Valery's "*entre les pins palpite, entre les tombes*" or like his "*eternellement, Eternellement le bout mordre*").

And also they cannot imitate her animals and birds–

> "the parrakeet–
> . . . destroying
> bark and portions of the food it could not eat."

Mr. Wescott, if he agrees with all or even with part of what I have written, will probably consider it as an affirmation of his belief in a kind of "aristocratic" art drawing no sustenance from the soil. "An aristocratic art, emulating the condition of ritual." But of course *all* art emulates the condition of ritual. That is what it comes from and to that it must always return for nourishment. And nothing belongs more properly to the people than ritual–or indeed than aristocracy itself, a popular invention to serve popular needs. (I suppose the Ku Klux Klan is a popular ritual–as popular as a ritual can be in a country where there are only variations *within* the middle class.) Miss Moore's relation to the soil is not a simple one, or rather it is to various soils–to that of Latium and to that of Attica I believe (or at least to that of the Aegean litoral) as well as most positively to the soil (well top-dressed) of America. There are several reasons (buried in this essay) why Miss Moore's poetry is almost completely neglected in England, beside the simple reason that it is too good, "in this age of hard striving," to be appreciated anywhere.

And there is one final, and "magnificent" compliment: Miss Moore's poetry is as "feminine" as Christina Rossetti's, one never forgets that it is written by a woman; but with both one never thinks of this particularity as anything but a positive virtue.

ANNOUNCEMENT:

[Scofield Thayer], "Announcement," *Dial,* 78 (January 1925): 89-90.

Thayer, editor and co-owner of the Dial, *in announcing the presentation of the Dial Award to Marianne Moore for* Observations, *published the previous autumn, soars in his appreciation and seats Moore in the chair left vacant by Emily Dickinson.*

> *Ring, for the scant salvation!*
> *Emily Dickinson*

I have the honour to announce that our annual acknowledgement of distinguished service to American letters this year recognizes the unusual literary virtue of Miss Marianne Moore. In thus singling out for the moment one whose already published work will so beyond mortal hap single her out through generations, one who seems to us so incomparably, since the death of Emily Dickinson, America's most distinguished poetess, we esteem that we fulfil in an especial degree our functions of criticism and of propaganda, those twin functions wherefore we exist: the function of discrimination between the one and the so very, very–the so very lamentably–many; and the function of exhibiting–so widely as may lie within our strait means–that single one. We so esteem in this case especially because on the one hand the work of Miss Moore is itself of so inordinate and of so patent a value; and because on the other hand it has hitherto remained, among the unfortunate American public, so meagrely relished and so signally unacclaimed.

We cannot set right the balance; we cannot turn over the whole misinformed continent. Nor can we annihilate the gross and the lax. Nor can we perceptibly diminish the exuberance of the vulgar, dead and–practically–living. We can but light our beacon, and–for a worth-while moment–flare a name worth flaring.

We do so not primarily in tribute to Miss Marianne Moore. I imagine she had chosen, for herself, to rest unflared. (She does not go in for personal flaring.) And anyhow, she has now for some years lived and worked without possibility of evading the knowledge of that esteem in which she is universally held. I write the word "universally" not without attention. The extant universe of those competent to judge in matters of contemporary English and American prosody is not conterminous with the physical universe of Sir Isaac Newton. . . . Mr Thomas Eliot, of London, is one who, notoriously, does not extend credit to any fly-by-night or wild-cat poet or concern: the London banker is a conservative animal. And Mr T. S. Eliot, in ranking Miss Moore among the half-dozen most "exciting" contemporary European and American poets, rightly worded the consensus of opinion of those qualified to judge. He rightly and merely expressed the considered judgement of the informed literary middle-of-the-road.

We flare not in glorification; we flare in practical service. Service not to that Juggernaut, the Reading Public,–that Juggernaut which is well served in being served badly. Service rather to the Imaginative Individual, to him who is in our world always the Marooned Individual. The towns, the villages, the prairies and the sandbars, of this North American Continent support many such. For since neither by the public pictures nor by the family radios are the hungerings of imagination appeased, therefore have these their being for ever in isolation, for ever shut and cut off. Therefore have these sharp eyes, the sharper for long fasting, eyes which, I have been encouraged to believe, are wont to pick out and to follow our own irregular and unchartered sailings. And it is for these important eyes that we run up, as one does a gala pennon, this blithe and gala name, this meadow-lark and white-heeled name, this name of Marianne Moore. . . . And it is to the hearts of these–being neither gross nor lax–that I do hereby commend the admonitory asceticisms of Miss Marianne Moore.

LETTER:

To Casper Harvey, *Marianne Moore Newsletter,* 4 (Spring 1980): 15-16.

A member of the Missouri Writers' Guild, aware that a poet born in his state had won the Dial Award, requested personal information for publication in the Kansas City Journal Post.

14 St. Luke's Place
New York City
January 27, 1925

Casper Harvey, Secretary-Treasurer
Missouri Writers' Guild
Liberty, Missouri

Dear Mr. Harvey:

I thank you for the interest which led you to write to me and I wished very much to reply to your letter at once. I am happy to tell you anything that might be of interest to others living in my state, though I hardly feel free to claim it as mine since I lived in it only seven years. The greater part of my life was spent in Carlisle, Pennsylvania where I was prepared for Bryn Mawr, from which I was graduated in 1909. Returning to Carlisle, I taught stenography at the Carlisle government Indian School for three and a half years. In 1915, a few poems of mine were published by the London EGOIST; a little later several were published in Miss Harriet Monroe's magazine, POETRY. Poems of mine were published also, in Alfred Kreymborg's magazine, OTHERS. Through the exigencies of the war, I came to live in New York where I have been engaged in library work for the past five years. A poem which I wrote in August, 1914, I had sufficient confidence in, to submit to twenty-six magazines before it was accepted a year later; for the most part, however, although writing is my chief interest, it has been an avocation sometimes completely discontinued. In assisting me to succeed–in so far as I have succeeded–I feel that the impetus to produce as good work as I could, has come, first, from reading; from reading authors whose material and method afforded me perfect entertainment–Sir Francis Bacon, Chaucer, Spenser, Defoe, Bunyan, Sir Thomas Browne, Leigh Hunt, Burke, Dr. Johnson, Anthony Trollope, Hardy, Henry James, W. B. Yeats, W. H. Hudson, and Sidney's The Defense of Poesie. I have been entertained and instructed by advertisements and book reviews in PUNCH, in the London SPECTATOR, in THE LONDON TIMES, by reviews in the Fortnightly DIAL, the present DIAL, by reviews published in THE ENGLISH REVIEW during the years 1907-1911; by Gordon Craig's books and other publications, of his. And I have learned I feel, from technical books, which, in addition to being instructive and entertaining, seemed to me, aesthetically accomplished–John McGraw's "How to Play Baseball," Christy Mathewson's "Pitching in a Pinch," Tilden's books on tennis, W. Rhead's "the Earthenware Collector," Harold Baynes's manual on dogs published by The National Geographic Magazine, articles in THE JOURNAL OF NATURAL HISTORY. The exactness and esprit of the work mentioned led me to submit to various publications, critical work which has in no case been declined, though I have never in any case, achieved what entirely satisfied me. It has also been a matter of great interest to me to accurately record the exact phraseology of notable people (educated or uneducated) with whom I have been associated; and in this connection perhaps I may say autobiographic writing by any valued author, interests me more than any other writing by that author.

Since you ask for a photograph, I shall make an effort to send you one, though I cannot think that THE DIAL's phenomenal tribute to my work would be augmented by such a photograph as I am able to send you.

My book "Observations," published recently by The Dial Press (not The Dial Publishing Company), 153 West 13th Street, New York City–is a collection of poems written within the years 1914-1924. Notes appended to the book will show that reading and the conversation of my friends have been the inspiration of my work.

The editors of THE DIAL, could they know of your letter, would be grateful for your accuracy in denominating the Dial award–just that. The slovenliness of the term "prize," is not only misleading but peculiarly objectionable to the editors of THE DIAL as to those who have been honored by its confidence.

COLUMN:
[Thayer], "Comment," *Dial,* 78 (February 1925): 174-180.

Thayer followed his announcement of the Dial Award to Moore with articles about her in three monthly editor's "Comment" columns. He thrust Moore before a wide public, the circulation of the Dial *having climbed to about 18,000. In June 1925 Thayer announced that he would leave the magazine and appoint Moore editor.*

"Compression is the first grace of style."
Democritus

We have decided to endeavour to keep alight, anyhow through these glum winter months, our beacon for Miss Marianne Moore.

I should here like to expose certain literary fragments, torn jaggedly from the hard context, fragments which, being felt out with the hammer of our intellect, return the consistency of rock crystal, fragments which, being thrown upon the hearth of our sympathetic understanding, betray the immense, the salt-veined, the profoundly-premeditated, chromatization of enkindled driftwood.

> "It is a far cry from the 'queen full of jewels'
> and the beau with the muff,
> from the gilt coach shaped like a perfume bottle,
> to the conjunction of the Monongahela and the
> Allegheny,
> and the scholastic philosophy of the wilderness
> to combat which one must stand outside and laugh
> since to go in is to be lost."

Was there ever a sentence so packed? Has any other poet ever given us, in such abundance, examples in "the first grace of style"? And if there be any so thoughtless as to boggle at the word "poet" applied to one who composes sentences of this nature–in the popular mind the poetical flux goes on and off at a tangent of her own sweet own–let him collate these Observations of Miss Moore with the Essays of one who exhibits–in a degree not second to that of Miss Moore–the same "first grace of style": let him weigh the ponderable sentences of Sir Francis Bacon. There also speaks a master: but there speaks, Miss Moore's generous laudation of him notwithstanding,[1] not what I myself should denominate a "poet." Both in the verse of Miss Moore and in the prose of Lord Bacon the intellect is always in the saddle, squarely. But in Lord Bacon this rider has his own way always; it is his dominance we note. He rides like a Roman Emperor: and the horse, like the wife, of Caesar shall be above suspicion. The mount of Caesar may be furnished with blinders; and the saddle and the harness may rightly be of iron: for the life of an imperial mount is neither in the eyes nor in the body; it may legitimately go on only in the head of the imperial rider.

Not so the mount of a poet: not so the mount of Miss Moore. And if sometimes the manoeuvres of her intellect are difficult of comprehension, this is not for any equestrian deficiency in the more than Caesarhood of that erect mind. This is because Pegasus himself is party to each manoeuvre. Those immortal eyes are open to this world; those immortal nostrils flare to every world-born gust; those immortal ears have apprehended the apposite dissonances of wilding stars; that immortal tail plumes on its unemperored own. There are wild oats in that stout belly; and those prepotent wings will not lie meek. A wingèd horse will dart for beauty; a wingèd horse will have his wingèd shy. Intellect in the saddle–yes, squarely–but an intellect

> "incorps'd and demi-natur'd
> With the brave beast."

An intellect which is part and parcel of the body. An intellect which smells the May. An intellect susceptible of seduction.

One may sit a long time in the mullioned and leaded and Tudor embrasures of that Lord Keeper of the Great Seal before one makes out a "beau with the muff" or a "gilt coach shaped like a perfume bottle." Nor, if you do espy such, will you likely espy them in the predicament of a confrontation with "the conjunction of the Monongahela and the Allegheny." . . . In other words, you will not generally uncover in those deeply spaded Essays wild images of the imagination, images that have been culled abroad, and encompassed here for their own sweet-smelling sakes; still less will you find such intricately juxtaposed to one another, with the odd, quizzical, poet's appetition for the showering criss-cross of quite inextricable and quite soul-dissolving overtones. Miss Marianne Moore and Sir Francis Bacon alike possess the analytical mind: Miss Marianne Moore possesses an analytical nose also, and is (as a woman should be) inclined to follow it. And her analyses, inordinately ordinate as they so victoriously are, subserve an end beyond analysis: their admirable elbows admirably *ad hoc*, their high rearings and higher boltings, their altogether porcupinity impeccable,–these are just Miss Moore's private ways of delivering Miss Moore's aesthetic fact. "By their fruits ye shall know them": and by their poetical end are these wanderingly suspended periods constituted a poetical technique as legitimate as the traditionally ordained verbal complication of a Provençal sestina.

> "I remember a swan under the willows in Oxford
> with flamingo colored, maple-
> leaflike feet. It reconnoitered like a battle
> ship. Disbelief and conscious fastidiousness were the
> staple
> ingredients in its
> disinclination to move. Finally its hardihood
> was not proof against its
> proclivity to more fully appraise such bits
> of food as the stream
>
> bore counter to it; it made away with what I gave it
> to eat."

After the consciously articulated analysis of one who exhibits, upon such an occasion of state as this, the consciously beautiful and fastidious assurance wherewith that swan itself aloofly floats, the words "made away with"–Have you seen a swan do it?

> "the lucid movements of the royal yacht upon the
> learned
> scenery of Egypt–"

How that yacht veritably coils! Like the sophisticated and fine-bolted–as white flour has been fine-bolted–cousin to the agility of a conger-eel! And how the pyramid and the sphinx, obedient to the quiet exorcism of Miss Moore, block in the appropriate background! It is all of one piece: it exhibits, in a more defined medium, the solidity of a line from Tacitus.

> "Spectacular and nimble animal the fish,
> Whose scales turn aside the sun's sword with their
> polish."

This of New York harbor:

> "the square-rigged four-rigged four-master, the
> liner,
> the battleship like the two-
> thirds submerged section of an iceberg; the tug
> dipping and pushing, the bell striking as it comes;
> the
> steam yacht, lying
> like a new made arrow on the
>
> stream;"

Has any one ever described an ironclad battleship before? And have you ever observed a tug poke, manifoldly pulsating, up the North River? Have you ever seen a long, slim, low, American-designed steam-yacht stretched and combed and strained by the current whereon and -in she lies? Have you ever seen a new-made arrow on a stream?

> "Springing about with
> froglike ac-
> curacy"

I cite this fraction from an exhaustive discussion of the intramural and the extra-mural activities of a feline gentleman (*nomine Petrus*) because it exhibits, in a startling fashion, what alarming effects Miss Moore can, from her severe and individual literary form, upon occasion draw. We have all observed, perhaps upon a flowered Aubusson, a cat "springing about," but until Miss Moore had developed her individual technique of typography, that technique in accordance with which a word is often run from one line into, or rather *onto,* another, and in some cases, as here, even from one stanza or strophe *onto* another–until this development had been achieved, Miss Moore herself could not have startled us into this proximity almost too immediate to her aroused cat.

"the mouse's limp tail hanging like a shoelace from its
mouth–"

And in the poem entitled To Military Progress the phrase applied to the quick-gathering crows

"Black minute-men."

The Observation To a Steam Roller is, in America, of social interest:

"You crush all the particles down
into close conformity, and then walk back and
forth
on them.

Sparkling chips of rock
are crushed down to the level of the parent block."

Miss Moore is herself a "Sparkling chip," but of too hard a wildness to be ever "crushed down."

"and the fractional magnificence of Florentine
goldwork–"

It has been said that should all records of Greek civilization by some future glacial period be erased, from the significance of one Athenian coin could some Cuvier of the humanities reconstruct the Hellenic world. So from this refined torque of words who could not reconstruct "the fractional magnificence" of that Etruscan culture and civilization of which the refinement of Florence was but the most subtle epigone? And how inevitably the astute, the careful-tempered and careful-eyed, goldsmith of Etruria had, not grudgingly, evinced his professional approbation for the achieved balance of Miss Moore's exhibit!

"and the fractional magnificence of Florentine"

The subtly-incised excellence of these aligned consonants and vowels, the simple and orderly progression from "and the frac" (how fortunate is the short "a" preceding the hard "c") through the mitigated expansion of "tional magnificence [this word mitigated by the short "i's"] of Florentine" to that word which hangs so carefully by itself, so pear-shaped and concave, so packed and pounded of solid weight, that word which hangs like a pear-shaped pendant of solid, hammered gold:

"goldwork–"

I recommend further, for the discolouration of drab nights, the following tried solidities: chunks that are neither logs nor blocks, chunks many-cornered, chunks awkward to get a hold on, and yet more awkward to lift and place, chunks that I have said to be of what is called, not wholly fortunately, "*drift*-wood"–chunks of brine and iron: A Grave; England; Picking and Choosing; When I Buy Pictures; and the whole of Peter; and of that mastery of New York harbor from which I have already carved out a considerable segment, but which had better have been enflamed entire–Dock Rats.

And here is another which is not a chunk of drift-wood at all. It appears to be of a substance to which I find in Nature no parallel. Not even in that Nature which has undergone enrichment by the savingly salt and savingly sterile sea. *It is of stone, and it is premeditatedly molten and moulded.* As neither flint nor rock-crystal, as neither basalt nor jasper, as neither chrysoprase nor jade, can in fire be molten and moulded. And yet it is of harder stone than these.

"Under a splintered mast,
Torn from the ship and cast
Near her hull,

A stumbling shepherd found
Embedded in the ground,
A seagull

Of lapislazuli,

A scarab of the sea,

With wings spread–

Curling its coral feet,
Parting its beak to greet
Men long dead."

One is aware that, for a considerable period, this poem, itself "a scarab of the sea," will come cropping up, will come knocking up, (oddly, to be sure, for what is so mineral, so otherwise than flowerlike) in anthologies. It will greet us "long dead."

Reading a poem like this, reading the poetry of Miss Moore in general, one realizes that also mineral is an organic growth. For this Talisman is indubitably mineral, like a Japanese dwarf-pine. Rooted in, and nourished from, the primal rock, this impersonality exhibits the tortuous precision of an object arithmetically prime.

Note:

[1]Cf. Sir Frances Bacon, by Marianne Moore. THE DIAL, April 1924.

COLUMN:
[Thayer], "Comment," *Dial,* 78 (April 1925): 354-356.

The lion civilly rampant.
MARIANNE MOORE.

I have already found occasion to allude to the less ostentatious (but not for that any the less worthy) department in this orderly volume of Observations. This ancillary department of "Notes" leaves little for the critic to say. In these indeed we witness a phenomenon rare in the Annals of English Poesie,–we witness a poet bringing himself (in this the therefore more surprising instance *her*self) to book. Clearly, this marks an advance; and one hopes that now the ground has been broken, other poets may, in their future ramping, exhibit a parallel civility.

I shall not in this place dwell upon the copious erudition here displayed, an erudition which, taking off, gracefully, from the Grave of Adam, and progressing by a natural sequence through the prophets Amos and Isaiah, does not for that high lineage disdain the less prophetic learning of Greece and Rome; an erudition which cites Herodotus and Pliny, Democritus and the enterprising Xenophon; an erudition which, "treading chasms," embraces at once the knowledgeable Robert of Sorbonne, the inveterate Duns Scotus of Mob Quad, the reprehensible Hegel of Germany, and the Reverends J. W. Darr and Edwin H. Kellogg of our own fortunate land; an erudition which ranges equitably from "At the age of five or six, John Andrews, son of Dr C. M. Andrews," to "An old gentleman during a game of chess"; an erudition which, triumphantly, establishes contact with our more modern interests, an erudition which relies upon The Perfect Host, in Vogue (August 1, 1921); Paper–As Long as a Man, As Thin as a Hair, in The New York Times (June 13, 1921); and Multiple Consciousness or Reflex Action of Unaccustomed Range, in the very reliable Scientific American (January, 1922); an erudition which amazes with the names of Puttick, and of Prodgers, and of the almost equally important Mr W. P. Pycraft.

I confine myself to pointing out a Novelty, a New Thing in Letters. The Reading Public of Dark and Light Ages has been familiar with rich and varied species of that important natural genus, Footnote. I shall not here codify. But in what would generally be held to be the less noble department of a volume, like this one, of inspirational nature–in this humble and serviceable department of "Notes"–there dawns upon the attentive and grateful eye a literary species hitherto unrecorded. It is the literary species, the footnote species, of *further aesthetic unfoldment.* I beg leave to style this, provisionally, the Footnote *aesthétique et noble,* or, in our less precise tongue, the *Footnote of Aesthetic Ennoblement.*

That dependable poet and critic, Mr Eliot of London, made, in The Waste Land, "a contribution to modern literature as important, in its way, as Ulysses itself," I have been told. And the footnotes to that important poem, those footnotes which Mr Eliot and his American publisher, Mr Horace Liveright, rightly incorporated in the book publication of Mr Eliot's poem, were the talk of the town. Yet these now date: they belong to the pre-Moore period: they are content pedestrianly to explain. And in the Demesne of High Poesie explanations, howsoever needful and adroit, are wont to be estimated small beer.

Permit me, in illustration of my point, to cite four lines from Miss Moore's ultimate Observation, and her note thereanent:

And Sir John Hawkins' Florida
"abounding in land unicorns and lions,
since where the one is,
its arch enemy cannot be missing."

Whence the interested reader gathers that Sir John Hawkins, discovering the Floridian flat-spaces to be tawny with lions, naturally deduced there from the presence of the, one imagines, more *farouche* and hardly-come-upon unicorn. But "abounding in land unicorns": Violet A. Wilson; "Hawkins affirmed the existence of land unicorns in the forests of Florida, and from their presence deducted abundance of lions because of the antipathy between the two animals, so that 'where the one is the other cannot be missing.' " Now the Man of Feeling, *l'homme sensible,* will, upon reading this pertinent note, be aesthetically *bouleversé.* It is therefore my desire to establish this note a "trial-piece" as to one's susceptibility to the most refined in art: had Mr Francis T. Palgrave had the anthological advantage of compiling his Golden Treasury a century or two later than he did (to wit, *after* the poetical activity of Miss Marianne Moore) I make no doubt he would have included in that invaluable compendium not only the Observation, Sea Unicorns and Land Unicorns, but also this ancillary note. And not apropros the Loss of the Royal George, but apropos this note (it being taken, of course, in aesthetic conjunction with the poem) he would have written: "This little [note] might be called one of our trial-pieces in regard to taste." And further he would have continued "He who relishes it may assure himself *se valde profecisse* in poetry." And the Royal George would have sunk, and W. Cowper would have sung, in vain. . . . It is nice to deduct from the existence of unicorns the presence of lions–any one of us, properly coached, would have liked to do it. But to deduce from the established presence of unicorns an "abundance of lions"–this is a privilege reserved by Fate to two very definite and restricted classes, to the knighted sea-captains of Elizabethan England and to poetesses who read with their eyes open, to poetesses who have "Ransacked the ages" and "spoiled the climes" that they may tender us a footnote of wildest caressing loveliness, a footnote affording a perverse and counter-natural overtone, a footnote which deducts, by a precise inversion of accepted poetic usage, from out the *metaphysico-mythological* the *natural-historical,* prosaically.

BOOK REVIEW:

Herbert S. Gorman, "Miss Moore's Art Is Not a Democratic One: Poetic 'Observations' of the Winner of The Dial Annual Award," *New York Times Book Review,* 1 February 1925, p. 5.

After Moore's Observations *received the prestigious Dial Award, her first American book of poems received wide attention.*

When the Dial made its annual award of $2,000 to Miss Marianne Moore some weeks ago it gave inordinate pleasure to an audience of readers which had long since overgrown the limitations of a coterie. This audience had read and re-read Miss Moore's poems as they had appeared in The Dial, her earlier book published by the Egoist Press, London, and one or two other odd pieces, notably "Marriage," which had been charmingly printed in Monroe Wheeler's Manikin. Almost simultaneously with The Dial award appeared "Observations," Miss Moore's first book to be issued in the regular trade way and between cloth covers. It is interesting to note that Miss Moore is the first writer to be so honored who has such a small bulk of work behind her. Sherwood Anderson was the author of five or six volumes when he received the award. Van Wyck Brooks could boast as many when he became the lucky recipient. T. S. Eliot's output was more meagre, but besides his poetry he had to his credit "The Sacred Wood," a volume of distinctly stimulating critical excursions. Miss Moore, therefore, is a lesser known personage in point of general circulation, and because this is so it is to be hoped that the award will quite definitely aid her in widening her audience. Certainly no one who possesses a quick interest in contemporary American poetry can afford to remain in ignorance of her sharp, intellectually compact, aristocratic work.

It is difficult to place Miss Moore. "Observations" inevitably becomes a starting point. From what ashes her Phoenix-like talent rises, with its sharp and glittering beak and, withal, gentle eye, becomes a matter of dubious speculation. Of one thing we may rest assured from the start–there is no pose, no dependence on unusual subterfuges, no willful attempts to astonish, here. "Observations" is the sort of a book it is because Miss Moore's mind is the sort of a mind it is. Her work–a sort of condensed intellectuality that sways between a matter-of-factness that is really about as matter-of-fact as a pearl and a symbolism that peers over these observations almost constantly–is compact with the lucidities of unusual mental attacks. What obscurity there may seem to be does not centre itself in her phraseology, broken lines or curious rhythmical effects. It is rather in her peculiar and somehow always pertinent approach toward the subject that is engrossing her for the moment. She observes visible phenomena with a rare and detached precision, and the acute speculations that result therefrom somehow seem to be just the right thing after one has pondered them, followed Miss Moore's progression and comprehended her serene and poised mental agility. After all, the contemporary urge in art is split into two diverse directions. One of them is an attempted return to primitive values, high simplicities and starkness. The other proceeds along more formalized ways and is emphasized by those ritualistic adornments that become the elaborate adumbrations of difficult connotations. Miss Moore's art, possibly, emerges on this second way, although her complexities are no more than the cunning and subtle approximations of complicated and intellectual observation in itself. She is the direct opposite of sentimentality, blatancy, bathos, mere prettiness, fancy verbal adornment and melody for melody's sake. Because of this it is quite possible that her audience will continue to be a small gathering. Her art is not a democratic art in any sense of the word. But this is assuredly no belittlement of her essential value to contemporary American poetry, for she brings to it that fastidiousness and intellectualization that it sadly needs.

Her emotion is an emotion of the mind, an emotion that raised itself at moments in the work of Emily Dickinson, that is more ruddily circumscribed by Mrs. Elinor Wylie at times, that is emphatically lacking in the work of Miss Millay. In some of Miss Moore's shorter pieces (and it is to be suspected that these are earlier work) she displays an epigrammatic savageness that is plainly the reflex of emotion. Such efforts as "To an Intra-Mural Rat," "To a Chameleon," "Nothing Will Cure the Sick Lion But to Eat an Ape," and "To Be Liked by You Would Be a Calamity" reveal this facet of her mind. Even here, however, urbanity, a composure of the senses, cools what might in another poet have been an outcry. Miss Moore never escapes the intellectual observance: her mind instinctively deals with the subject. Her quick penetration and instant recognition of nuances is revealed in the last two lines of the short piece called "To Be Liked by You Would Be a Calamity."

"Attack is more piquant than con-
cord," but when
You tell me frankly that you would
like to feel
My flesh beneath your feet,
I'm all abroad; I can but put
my weapon up, and
Bow you out.
Gesticulation–it is half the language.
Let unsheathed gesticulation be the
steel
Your courtesy must meet,
Since in your hearing words
are mute, which to my senses
Are a shout.

The question of color comes up. Nothing could do Miss Moore more wrong than the tacit espousal of the belittling assertion that her work is all compact of a dry cerebrility. It is true that her palette is primarily her own; not an untidy diffusion of primary hues, but a more selective equipment of subtler pigments. Yet reading through the various efforts in "Observations" one will be halted constantly by pertinent pictures flung out with unquestioned vividness. They are not "set" for display, but are essential links in the progressing chain of thought or observation. One cannot get away from this word "observation," for it is peculiarly applicable to Miss Moore's work and she showed her usual rare judgment in so christening her book. These observations imply pictures as well as intellectual comment, and no one can read "A Talisman," "Black Earth," "Those Various Scalpels," "An Octopus," and "Sea Unicorns and Land Unicorns" without having pictures in the purest colors impinge on his mentality and that imaginary eye before which poetry passes like some sort of a burning pageant. One need but take "Those Various Scalpels."

Those
various sounds consistently indis-
tinct, like intermingled echoes
struck from thin glasses successively
at random–the inflection disguised;
your hair, the tails of two
fighting-cocks head to head in
stone–like sculptured scimitars
re-
peating the curve of your ears in
reverse order: your eyes,
flowers of ice

and
snow sown by tearing winds on the
cordage of disabled ships: your
raised hand
an ambiguous signature: your

cheeks, those rosettes of blood on
the stone floors of French cha-

teaux with regard to which the
guides are so affirmative:
your other hand

a
bundle of lances all alike, partly hid
by emeralds from Persia
and the fractional magnificence
of Florentine goldwork–a collec-
tion of half a dozen little ob-
jects made fine
with enamel in gray, yellow, and
dragon fly blue; a lemon, a
pear
and three bunches of grapes, tied
with silver; your dress, a mag-
nificent square
cathedral of uniform
and at the same time, diverse ap-
pearance–a species of vertical
vineyard rustling in the storm
of conventional opinion. Are
they weapons or scalpels?
Whetted

to
brilliance by the hard majesty of
that sophistication which is su-
perior to opportunity, these
things are rich instruments with
which to experiment but sur-
gery is not tentative. Why dis-
sect destiny with instruments
which
are more highly specialized than
the tissues of destiny itself?

This poem contains within itself practically all the peculiarities of Miss Moore's style. Here are pictures set forth with an undeniable clarity and an intellectualized ending that is both keen and apropos. Here also are those peculiar signatures upon a poem which show it to be Marianne Moore's craftsmanship, namely, the forced rhymes which are sometimes induced by splitting up a word, as in the last verse, where "to" is rhymed with "su." It is here, perhaps, that the professional cavilers will have their bumptious fun. This question of technique is a vexatious one, and the fairest approach to it seems to rest in the assertion that any technique is vindicated that becomes successful in best exploiting the personality and expression of the person who employs it. Miss Moore's technique is a dogmatic one, a conscious bit of mathematics, but it seems to suit her, and after one has read her poems a few times and gotten memories of Alfred, Lord Tennyson, out of one's mind the reader will discover a quaint pleasure in this new form. Rhythms will begin to hit his ear so dulled with the eternally even tomtoms of verse and he will perceive a reason for Miss Moore's particular form.

No particular attempt has been made here to go into the deeper significances of Miss Moore's thought, to expound that admirable poem called "Marriage," for instance, or to enlarge upon "Sea Unicorns and Land Unicorns." But such a proceeding would postulate a more extended treatment, for Miss Moore's thought overbrims her book and warrants time and attention. It is enough to assert that she exhibits a keen, restless yet urbane, scalpel-like intelligence that is quite undismayed in the face of difficulty. Where other poets would turn away or dismiss the mood in a gentle lyric, Miss Moore adjusts her perspicacity, investigates with a cool ardor, observes, comments and dissects. It is truth that she seeks essentially. In "In the Days of Prismatic Color" she ends the poem by exclaiming:

Truth is no Apollo
Belvedere, no formal thing. The
wave may go over it if it likes.
Know that it will be there when it
says:
"I shall be there when the wave
has gone by."

It is that truth that will be there after all sorts of monstrous waves have gone by that Miss Moore is desirous to observe. She undoubtedly possesses an instinctive detestation of prettifications, adornments, veils and false gestures, and with the inspired keenness of the logician who knows that logic is not an end in itself she applies herself to the observation of phenomena, physical and spiritual, and draws her own conclusions.

ARTICLE:
William Carlos Williams, "Marianne Moore," *Dial*, 78 (May 1925): 394-401.

Williams and Moore had first met when Moore lived in Chatham, New Jersey, 1916-1918, and Williams in Rutherford. A champion of her early work, Williams had included her poems when he edited Others *and* Contact. *He had hoped to see this essay, written about 1923, in the* Dial *earlier, but T. S. Eliot and others had temporarily preempted him.*

The best work is always neglected and there is no critic among the older men who has cared to champion the newer names from outside the battle. The established critic will not read. So it is that the present writers must turn interpreters of their own work. Even those who enjoy modern work are not always intelligent, but often seem at a loss to know the white marks from the black. But modernism is distressing to many who would at least tolerate it if they knew how. These individuals who cannot bear the necessary appearance of disorder in all immediacy, could be led to appreciation through critical study.

If one come with Miss Moore's work to some wary friend and say, "Everything is worthless but the best and this is the best," adding, "–only with difficulty discerned," will he see anything, if he be at all well read, but destruction? From my experience he will be shocked and bewildered. He will perceive absolutely nothing except that his whole preconceived scheme of values has been ruined. And this is exactly what he should see, a break *through* all preconceptions of poetic form and mood and pace, a flaw, a crack in the bowl. It is this that one means when he says destruction and creation are simultaneous. But this is not easy to accept. Miss Moore, using the same material as all others before her, comes at it so effectively at a new angle as to throw out of fashion the classical-conventional poetry to which one is used and puts her own and that about her in its place. The old stops are discarded. This must antagonize many. Furthermore there is a multiplication, a quickening, a burrowing through, a blasting aside, a dynamization, a flight over–it is modern, but the critic must show that this is only to reveal an essential poetry through the mass, as always, and with superlative effect in this case.

A course in mathematics would not be wasted on a poet, or a reader of poetry, if he remembered no more from it than the geometrical principle of the intersection of loci: from all angles lines converging and crossing establish points. He might carry it further and say in his imagination, that apprehension perforates, at places, through to understanding–as white is at the intersection of blue and green and yellow and red. It is this white light that is the background of all good work. Aware of this one may read the Greeks or the Elizabethans or Sidney Lanier, even Robert Bridges, and preserve interest, poise, and enjoyment. He may visit Virginia or China, and when friends, eager to please, playfully lead him about for pockets of local colour–he may go. Local colour is not, as the parodists, the localists believe, an object of art. It is merely a variant serving to locate some point of white penetration. The intensification of desire toward this purity is the modern variant. It is that which interests me most and seems most solid among the qualities I witness in my contemporaries; it is a quality present in much or even all that Miss Moore does.

Poems, like painting, can be interesting because of the subject with which they deal. The baby glove of a Pharaoh can be so presented as to bring tears to the eyes. And it need not be bad work because it has to do with a favourite cat dead. Poetry, rare and never willingly recognized, only its accidental colours make it tolerable to most. If it be of a red colouration those who like red will follow and be led restfully astray. So it is with hymns, battle songs, love ditties, elegies. Humanity sees itself in them, sees with delight this, that, and the other quality with which it is familiar, the good placed attractively and the bad thrown into a counter light. This is inevitable. But in any anthology it will be found that men have been hard put to it at all times to tell which is poetry and which the impost. This is hard. The difficult thing to realize is that the thrust must go through to the white, at least somewhere.

Good modern work, far from being the fragmentary, neurotic thing its disunderstanders think it, is nothing more than work compelled by these conditions. It is a multiplication of impulses that by their several flights, crossing at all eccentric angles, *might* enlighten. As a phase, in its slightest beginning, it is not yet nearly complete. And it is not rising as an arc; it is more a disc pierced here and there by light; it is really distressingly broken up. But so does any attack seem at the moment of engagement, multiple units crazy except when viewed as a whole.

Surely there is no poetry so active as that of to-day, so unbound, so dangerous to the mass of mediocrity, if one should understand it, so fleet, hard to capture, so delightful to pursue. It is clarifying in its movements as a wild animal whose walk corrects that of men. Who shall separate the good Whitman from the bad, the dreadful New England maunderers from the others, put air under and around the living and leave the dead to fall dead? Who? None but poems, such as Miss Moore's, their cleanliness, lack of cement, clarity, gentleness. It grows impossible for the eye to rest long upon the object of the drawing.

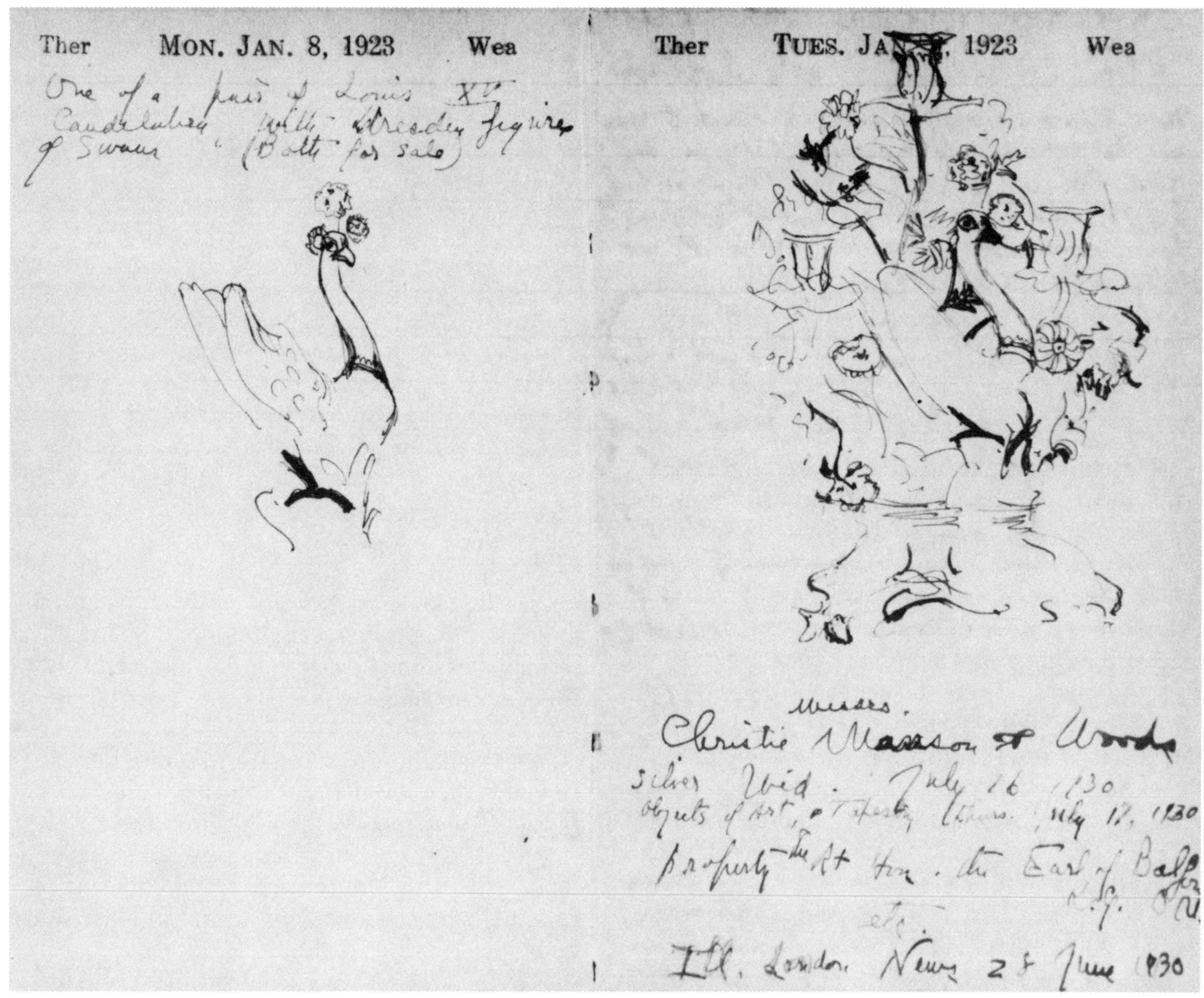

Ther MON. JAN. 8, 1923 Wea
One of a pair of Louis XV Candelabra with Dresden figure of Swans (Both for sale)
Ther TUES. JA 1923 Wea
Messrs.
Christie Manson & Woods
Ill. London News 28 June 1930

Pages from Moore's notebook, with drawings and notes relating to a pair of Louis XV candelabra sold at auction in 1930 (Rosenbach Museum & Library), an inspiration for Moore's poem "No Swan So Fine," first published in the October 1932 issue of Poetry *and collected in her 1935* Selected Poems

Here is an escape from the old dilemma. The unessential is put rapidly aside as the eye searches between for illumination. Miss Moore undertakes in her work to separate the poetry from the subject entirely–like all the moderns. In this she has been rarely successful and this is important.

Unlike the painters the poet has not resorted to distortions or the abstract in form. Miss Moore accomplishes a like result by rapidity of movement. A poem such as Marriage is an anthology of transit. It is a pleasure that can be held firm only by moving rapidly from one thing to the next. It gives the impression of a passage *through.* There is a distaste for lingering, as in Emily Dickinson. As in Emily Dickinson there is too a fastidious precision of thought where unrhymes fill the purpose better than rhymes. There is a swiftness impaling beauty, but no impatience as in so much present-day trouble with verse. It is a rapidity too swift for touch, a seraphic quality, one might have said yesterday. There is, however, no breast that warms the bars of heaven; it is at most a swiftness that passes without repugnance from thing to thing.

The only help I ever got from Miss Moore toward the understanding of her verse was that she despised connectives. Any other assistance would have been an impoliteness, since she has always been sure of herself if not of others. The complete poem is there waiting: all the wit, the colour, the constructive ability (not a particularly strong point that however). And the quality of satisfaction gathered from reading her is that one may seek long in those exciting mazes sure of coming out at the right door in the end. There is nothing missing but the connectives.

The thought is compact, accurate, and accurately planted. In fact the garden, since it is a garden more than a statue, is found to be curiously of porcelain. It is the mythical, indestructible garden of pleasure, perhaps greatly pressed for space to-day, but there and intact, nevertheless.

I don't know where, except in modern poetry, this quality of the brittle, highly set off porcelain garden exists and nowhere in modern work better than with Miss Moore. It is this chief beauty of to-day, this hard crest to nature, that makes the best present work with its "unnatural" appearance seem so thoroughly gratuitous, so difficult to explain, and so doubly a treasure of seclusion. It is the white of a clarity beyond the facts.

There is in the newer work a perfectly definite handling of the materials with a given intention to relate them in a certain way–a handling that is intensely, intentionally selective. There is a definite place where the matters of the day may meet if they choose or not, but it they assemble it must be there. There is no compromise. Miss Moore never falls from the place inhabited by poems. It is hard to give an illustration of this from her work because it is everywhere. One must be careful, though, not to understand this as a mystical support, a danger we are skirting safely, I hope, in our time.

Poe in his most read first essay quotes Nathaniel Willis' poem, The Two Women, admiring in full and one senses at once the reason: there is a quality to the *feeling* there that affected Poe tremendously. This mystical quality that endeared Poe to Father Tabb the poet-priest, still seems to many the essence of poetry itself. It would be idle to name many who have been happily mystical and remained good poets: Poe, Blake, Francis Thompson, et cetera.

But what I wish to point is that there need be no stilled and archaic heaven, no ducking under religiosities to have poetry and to have it stand in its place beyond "nature." Poems have a separate existence uncompelled by nature or the supernatural. There is a "special" place which poems, as all works of art, must occupy, but it is quite definitely the same as that where bricks or coloured threads are handled.

In painting, Ingres realized the essentiality of drawing and each perfect part seemed to float free from his work, by itself. There is much in this that applies beautifully to Miss Moore. It is a perfect drawing that attains to a separate existence which might, if it please, be called mystical, but is in fact no more than the practicability of design.

To Miss Moore an apple remains an apple whether it be in Eden or the fruit bowl where it curls. But that would be hard to prove–

'dazzled by the apple.'

The apple is left there, suspended. One is not made to feel that as an apple it has anything particularly to do with poetry or that as such it needs special treatment; one goes on. Because of this the direct object does seem unaffected. It seems as free from the smears of mystery, as pliant, as "natural" as Venus on the wave. Because of this her work is never indecorous as where nature is itself concerned. These are great virtues.

Without effort Miss Moore encounters the affairs which concern her as one would naturally in reading or upon a walk outdoors. She is not a Swinburne stumbling to music, but one always finds her moving forward ably, in thought, unimpeded by a rhythm. Her own rhythm is particularly revealing. It does not interfere with her progress; it is the movement of the animal, it does not put itself first and ask the other to follow.

Nor is "thought" the thing that she contends with. Miss Moore uses the thought most interestingly and wonderfully to my mind. I don't know but that this technical excellence is one of the greatest pleasures I get from her. She occupies the thought to its end, and goes on–without connectives. To me this is thrilling. The essence is not broken, nothing is injured. It is a kind hand to a merciless mind at home in the thought as in the cruder image. In the best modern verse room has been made for the best of modern thought and Miss Moore thinks straight.

Only the most modern work has attempted to do without *ex machina* props of all sorts, without rhyme, assonance, the feudal master beat, the excuse of "nature," of the spirit, mysticism, religiosity, "love," "humour," "death." Work such as Miss Moore's holds its bloom to-day not by using slang, not by its moral abandon or puritanical steadfastness, but by the aesthetic pleasure engendered where pure craftsmanship joins hard surfaces skilfully.

Poetry has taken many disguises which by cross reading or intense penetration it is possible to go through to the core. Through intersection of loci their multiplicity may become revelatory. The significance of much reading being that this "thing" grow clearer, remain fresh, be more present to the mind. To read more thoroughly than this is idleness: a common classroom absurdity.

One may agree tentatively with Glenway Wescott, that there is a division taking place in America between a proletarian art, full of sincerities, on the one side and an aristocratic and ritualistic art on the other. One may agree, but it is necessary to scrutinize such as statement carefully.

There cannot be two arts of poetry really. There is weight and there is disencumberedness. There can be no schism, except that which has always existed between art and its approaches. There cannot be a proletarian art—even among savages. There is a proletarian taste. To have achieved an organization even of that is to have escaped it.

And to organize into a pattern is also, true enough, to "approach the conditions of ritual." But here I would again go slow. I see only escape from the conditions of ritual in Miss Moore's work: a rush through wind if not toward some patent "end" at least away from pursuit, a pursuit perhaps by ritual. If from such a flight a ritual results it is more the care of those who follow than of the one who leads. "Ritual," too often to suit my ear, connotes a stereotyped mode of procedure from which pleasure has passed, whereas the poetry, to which my attention clings, if it ever knew those conditions, is distinguished only as it leaves them behind.

It is at least amusing, in this connexion, to quote from Others, Volume I, Number 5, November 1915—quoted in turn from J. B. Kerfoot in Life: "Perhaps you are unfamiliar with this 'new poetry' that is called 'revolutionary.' . . . It is the expression of a democracy of feeling rebelling against an aristocracy of form."

> "As if a death mask ever could replace
> Life's faulty excellence!"

There are two elements essential to Miss Moore's scheme of composition: the hard and unaffected concept of the apple itself as an idea, then its edge to edge contact with the things which surround it—the coil of a snake, leaves at various depths, or as it may be; and without connectives unless it be poetry, the inevitable connective, if you will.

Marriage, through which thought does not penetrate, appeared to Miss Moore a legitimate object for art, an art that would not halt from using thought about it, however, as it might want to. Against marriage, "this institution, perhaps one should say enterprise—" Miss Moore launched her thought not to have it appear arsenaled as in a text book on psychology, but to stay among apples and giraffes in a poem. The interstices for the light and not the interstitial web of the thought concerned her, or so it seems to me. Thus the material is as the handling: the thought, the word, the rhythm—all in the style. The effect is in the penetration of the light itself, how much, how little; the appearance of the luminous background.

Of marriage there is no solution in the poem and no attempt at a solution; nor is there an attempt to shirk thought about it, to make marriage beautiful or otherwise by "poetic" treatment. There is beauty and it is thoughtless, as marriage or a cave inhabited by the sounds and colours of waves, as in the time of prismatic colour, as England with its baby rivers, as G. B. Shaw, or chanticleer, or a fish, or an elephant with its strictly practical appendages. All these things are inescapably caught in the beauty of Miss Moore's passage through them; they all have at least edges. This too is a quality that greatly pleases me: definite objects which give a clear contour to her force. Is it a flight, a symphony, a ghost, a mathematic? The usual evasion is to call them poems.

Miss Moore gets great pleasure from wiping soiled words or cutting them clean out, removing the aureoles that have been pasted about them or taking them bodily from greasy contexts. For the compositions which Miss Moore intends, each word should first stand crystal clear with no attachments; not even an aroma. As a cross light upon this Miss Moore's personal dislike for flowers that have both a satisfying appearance *and* an odour of perfume is worth noticing.

With Miss Moore a word is a word most when it is separated out by science, treated with acid to remove the smudges, washed, dried, and placed right side up on a clean surface. Now one may say that this is a word. Now it may be used, and how?

It may be used not to smear it again with thinking (the attachments of thought) but in such a way that it will remain scrupulously itself, clean, perfect, unnicked beside other words in a parade. There must be edges. This casts some light I think on the simplicity of design in much of Miss Moore's work. There must be recognizable edges against the ground which cannot, as she might desire it, be left entirely white. Prose

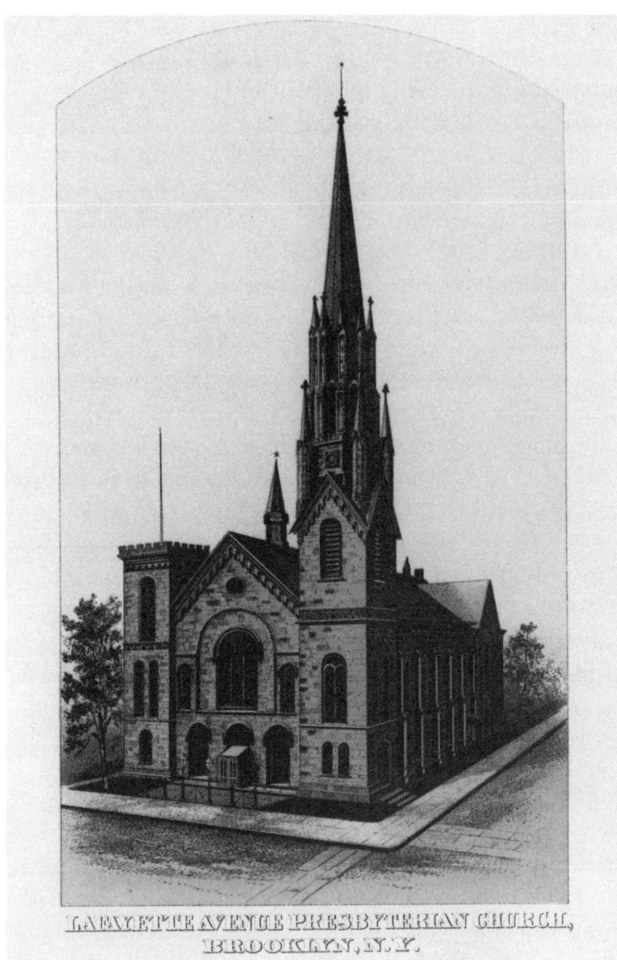

The church Moore attended after she and her mother moved to 260 Cumberland Street, Brooklyn Heights, in 1929. Moore alluded to its steeple in "The Steeple-Jack" first published in the June 1932 issue of Poetry *and collected in Moore's 1935* Selected Poems.

would be all black, a complete block, painted or etched over, but solid.

There is almost no overlaying at all. The effect is of every object sufficiently uncovered to be easily recognizable. This simplicity, with the light coming through from between the perfectly plain masses, is however extremely bewildering to one who has been accustomed to look at the usual "poem," the commonplace opaque board covered with vain curlicues. They forget, those who would read Miss Moore aright, that white circular discs grouped closely edge to edge upon a dark table make black six-pointed stars.

The "useful result" is an accuracy to which this simplicity of design greatly adds. The effect is for the effect to remain "true"; nothing loses its identity because of the composition, but the parts in their assembly remain quite as "natural" as before they were gathered. There is no "sentiment"; the softening effect of word upon word is nil; everything is in the style. To make this ten times evident is Miss Moore's constant care. There seems to be almost too great a wish to be transparent and it is here if anywhere that Miss Moore's later work will show a change, I think.

The general effect is of a rise through the humanities, the sciences, without evading "thought," through anything, if not everything of the best of modern life; taking whatever there is as it comes, using it and leaving it drained of its pleasure, but otherwise undamaged. Miss Moore does not compromise science with poetry. In this again she is ably modern.

And from this clarity, this acid cleansing, this unblinking willingness, her poems result, a true modern crystallization, the fine essence of today which I have spoken of as the porcelain garden.

Or one will think a little of primitive masonry, the units unglued and as in the greatest early constructions unstandardized.

In such work as Critics and Connoisseurs, and Poetry, Miss Moore succeeds in having the "thing" which is her concern move freely, unencumbered by the images or the difficulties of thought. In such work there is no "suggestiveness," no tiresome "subtlety" of trend to be heavily followed, no painstaking refinement of sentiment. There is surely a choice evident in all her work, a very definite quality of choice in her material, a thinness perhaps, but a very welcome and no little surprising absence of moral tone. The choice being entirely natural and completely arbitrary is not in the least offensive, in fact it has been turned curiously to advantage throughout.

From what I have read it was in Critics and Connoisseurs that the successful method used later began first to appear: If a thought presents itself the force moves through it easily and completely: so the thought also has revealed the "thing"–that is all. The thought is used exactly as the apple, it is the same insoluble block. In Miss Moore's work the purely stated idea has an edge exactly like a fruit or a tree or a serpent.

To use anything: rhyme, thought, colour, apple, verb–so as to illumine it, is the modern prerogative; a stintless inclusion. It is Miss Moore's success.

The diction, the phrase construction, is unaffected. To use a "poetic" inversion of language, or even such a special posture of speech, still discernible in Miss Moore's earlier work, is to confess an inability to have penetrated with poetry some crevice of understanding; that special things and special places are reserved for art, that it is unable, that it requires fostering. This is unbearable.

Poetry is not limited in that way. It need not say either

> Bound without.
> Boundless within.

It has as little to do with the soul as with ermine robes or graveyards. It is not noble, sad, funny. It is poetry. It is free. It is escapeless. It goes where it will. It is in danger; escapes if it can.

This is new! The quality is not new, but the freedom is new, the unbridled leap.

The dangers are thereby multiplied–but the clarity is increased. Nothing but the perfect and the clear.

INTRODUCTION:
T. S. Eliot, Introduction to Moore's *Selected Poems* (1935), pp. vii-xiv.

Eliot, an editor at Faber & Faber, London, published this book in England and arranged the poems, placing most-recent work at the beginning.

We know very little about the value of the work of our contemporaries, almost as little as we know about our own. It may have merits which exist only for contemporary sensibility; it may have concealed virtues which will only become apparent with time. How it will rank when we are all dead authors ourselves we cannot say with any precision. If one is to talk about one's contemporaries at all, therefore, it is important to make up our minds as to what we can affirm with confidence, and as to what must be a matter of doubting conjecture. The last thing, certainly, that we are likely to know about them is their 'greatness', or their relative distinction or triviality in relation to the standard of 'greatness'. For in greatness are involved moral and social relations, relations which can only be perceived from a remoter perspective, and which may be said even to be created in the process of history: we cannot tell, in advance, what any poetry is going to do, how it will operate upon later generations. But the *genuineness* of poetry is something which we have some warrant for believing that a small number, but only a small number, of contemporary readers can recognise. I say positively only a small number, because it seems probable that when any poet conquers a really large public in his lifetime, an increasing proportion of his admirers will admire him for extraneous reasons. Not necessarily for bad reasons, but because he becomes known merely as a symbol, in giving a kind of stimulation, or consolation, to his readers, which is a function of his peculiar relation to them in time. Such effect upon contemporary readers may be a legitimate and proper result of some great poetry, but it has been also the result of much ephemeral poetry.

It does not seem to matter much whether one has to struggle with an age which is unconscious and self-satisfied, and therefore hostile to new forms of poetry, or with one like the present which is self-conscious and distrustful of itself, and avid for new forms which will give it status and self-respect. For many modern readers any superficial novelty of form is evidence of, or is as good as, newness of sensibility; and if the sensibility is fundamentally dull and second-hand, so much the better; for there is no quicker way of catching an immediate, if transient, popularity, than to serve stale goods in new packages. One of the tests–though it be only a negative test–of anything really new and genuine, seems to be its capacity for exciting aversion among 'lovers of poetry'.

I am aware that prejudice makes me underrate certain authors: I see them rather as public enemies than as subjects for criticism; and I dare say that a different prejudice makes me uncritically favourable to others. I may even admire the right authors for the wrong reasons. But I am much more confident of my appreciation of the authors whom I admire, than of my depreciation of the authors who leave me cold or who exasperate me. And in asserting that what I call *genuineness* is a more important thing to recognise in a contemporary than *greatness,* I am distinguishing between his function while living and his function when dead. Living, the poet is carrying on that struggle for the maintenance of a living language, for the maintenance of its strength, its subtlety, for the preservation of quality of feeling, which must be kept up in every generation; dead, he provides standards for those who take up the struggle after him. Miss Moore is, I believe, one of those few who have done the language some service in my lifetime.

So far back as my memory extends, which is to the pages of *The Egoist* during the War, and of *The Little Review* and *The Dial* in the years immediately following, Miss Moore has no immediate poetic derivations. I cannot, therefore, fill up my pages with the usual account of influences and development. There is one early poem, *A Talisman,* not reprinted in the text of this volume, which I will quote in full here, because it suggests a slight influence of H. D., certainly of H. D. rather than of any other 'Imagist':

Under a splintered mast
Torn from the ship and cast
  Near her hull,

A stumbling shepherd found
Embedded in the ground
  A sea-gull

Of lapis-lazuli,
A scarab of the sea,
  With wings spread–

Curling its coral feet,
Parting its beak to greet
  Men long dead.

The sentiment is commonplace, and I cannot see what a bird carved of *lapis-lazuli* should be doing with *coral* feet; but even here the cadence, the use of rhyme, and a certain authoritativeness of manner distinguish the poem. Looking at Miss Moore's poems of a slightly later period, I should say that she had taken to heart the repeated reminder of Mr. Pound: that poetry should be as well written as prose. She seems to have saturated her mind in the perfections of prose, in its precision rather than its purple; and to have found her rhythm, her poetry, her appreciation of the individual word, for herself.

The first aspect in which Miss Moore's poetry is likely to strike the reader is that of minute detail rather than that of emotional unity. The gift for detailed observation, for finding the exact words for some experience of the eye, is liable to disperse the attention of the relaxed reader. The minutiae may even irritate the unwary, or arouse in them only the pleasurable astonishment evoked by the carved ivory ball with eleven other balls inside it, the full-rigged ship in a bottle, the skeleton of the crucifix-fish. The bewilderment consequent upon trying to follow so alert an eye, so quick a process of association, may produce the effect of some 'metaphysical' poetry. To the moderately intellectual the poems may appear to be intellectual exercises; only to those whose intellection moves more easily will they immediately appear to have emotional value. But the detail has always its service to perform on the whole. The similes are there for use; as the mussel-shell 'opening and shutting itself like an injured fan' (where *injured* has an ambiguity good enough for M. Empson), the waves 'as formal as the scales on a fish'. They make us see the object more clearly, though we may not understand immediately why our attention has been called to this object, and though we may not immediately grasp its association with a number of other objects. So, in her amused and affectionate attention to animals–from the domestic cat, to 'to popularize the mule', to the most exotic strangers from the tropics, she succeeds at once in startling us into an unusual awareness of visual patterns, with something like the fascination of a high-powered microscope.

Miss Moore's poetry, or most of it, might be classified as 'descriptive' rather than 'lyrical' or 'dramatic'. Descriptive poetry is supposed to be

BIRD, BEAST OR FISH? The rare Plumet Basilisk lizard from Costa Rica, newest arrival in the London Zoo. It is brilliant green, with a plume, or fin, down its back in contrasting color. Underwood

N.Y. Herald Tribune 26 Jan. 1930

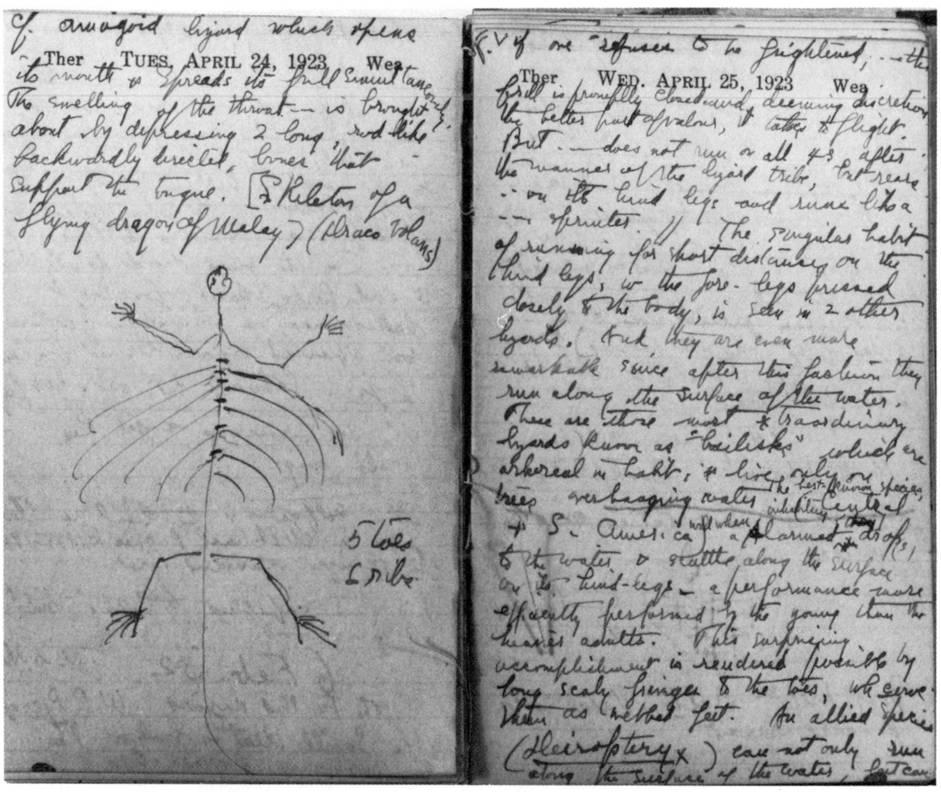

Ther TUES. APRIL 24, 1923 Wea

Ther WED. APRIL 25, 1923 Wea

Sources for Moore's "The Plumet Basilisk": (top) Moore's clipping from the 26 January 1930 issue of the New York Herald Tribune *and (bottom) her notebook drawing of a Malay dragon skeleton, circa 1932 (Rosenbach Museum & Library). The poem was first published in the October-December 1933 issue of* Hound & Horn *and was collected in Moore's 1935* Selected Poems.

dated to a period, and to be condemned thereby; but it is really one of the permanent modes of expression. In the eighteenth-century–or say a period which includes *Cooper's Hill, Windsor Forest,* and Gray's *Elegy*–the scene described is a point of departure for meditations on one thing or another. The poetry of the Romantic Age, from Byron at his worst to Wordsworth at his best, wavers between the reflective and the evocative; but the description, the picture set before you, is always there for the same purpose. The aim of 'imagism', so far as I understand it, or so far as it had any, was to induce a peculiar concentration upon something visual, and to set in motion an expanding succession of concentric feelings. Some of Miss Moore's poems–for instance with animal or bird subjects–have a very wide spread of association. It would be difficult to say what is the 'subject-matter' of *The Jerboa.* For a mind of such agility, and for a sensibility so reticent, the minor subject, such as a pleasant little sand-coloured skipping animal, may be the best release for the major emotions. Only the pedantic literalist could consider the subject-matter to be trivial; the triviality is in himself. We all have to choose whatever subject-matter allows us the most powerful and most secret release; and that is a personal affair.

The result is often something that the majority will call frigid; for the feel things in one's own way, however intensely, is likely to look like frigidity to those who can only feel in accepted ways.

> The deepest feeling always shows itself in silence;
> not in silence, but restraint.

It shows itself in a control which makes possible the fusion of the ironic-conversational and the high-rhetorical, as

> I recall their magnificence, now not more magnificent
> than it is dim. It is difficult to recall the ornament,
> speech, and precise manner of what one might
> call the minor acquaintances twenty
> years back. . . .
> strict with tension, malignant
> in its power over us and deeper
> than the sea when it proffers flattery in exchange
> for hemp,
> rye, flax, horses, platinum, timber and fur.

As one would expect from the kind of activity which I have been trying to indicate, Miss Moore's versification is anything but 'free'. Many of the poems are in exact, and sometimes complicated formal patterns, and move with the elegance of a minuet. ('Elegance', indeed, is one of her certain attributes.) Some of the poems (e.g. *Marriage, An Octopus*) are unrhymed; in others (e.g. *Sea Unicorns and Land Unicorns*) rhyme or assonance is introduced irregularly; in a number of the poems rhyme is part of a regular pattern interwoven with unrhymed endings. Miss Moore's use of rhyme is in itself a definite innovation in metric.

In the conventional forms of rhyme the stress given by the rhyme tends to fall in the same place as the stress given by the sense. The extreme case, at its best, is the pentameter couplet of Pope. Poets before and after Pope have given variety, sometimes at the expense of smoothness, by deliberately separating the stresses, from time to time; but this separation–often effected simply by longer periods or more involved syntax–can hardly be considered as more than a deviation from the norm for the purpose of avoiding monotony. The tendency of some of the best contemporary poetry is of course to dispense with rhyme altogether; but some of those who do use it have used it here and there to make a pattern directly in contrast with the sense and rhythm pattern, to give a greater intricacy. Some of the internal rhyming of Hopkins is to the point. (Genuine or auditory internal rhyme must not be confused with false or visual internal rhyme. If a poem reads just as well when cut up so that all the rhymes fall at the end of lines, then the internal rhyme is false and only a typographical caprice, an in Oscar Wilde's *Sphynx.*) This rhyme, which forms a pattern *against* the metric and sense pattern of the poem, may be either heavy or light–that is to say, either *heavier* or *lighter* than the other pattern. The two kinds, heavy and light, have doubtless different uses which remain to be explored. Of the *light* rhyme Miss Moore is the greatest living master; and indeed she is the first, so far as I know, who has investigated its possibilities. It will be observed that the effect sometimes requires giving a word slightly more analytical pronunciation, or stressing a syllable more than ordinarily:

> al-
> ways has been–at the antipodes from the init-
> ial great truths. 'Part of it was crawling, part of it
> was about to crawl, the rest
> was torpid in its lair.' In the short-legged, fit-
> ful advance. . . .

It is sometimes obtained by the use of articles as rhyme words:

> an
> injured fan.
>   The barnacles which encrust the side
>   of the wave, cannot hide . . .
> the
> turquoise sea
>   of bodies. The water drives a wedge . . .

In a good deal of what is sometimes (with an unconscious theological innuendo) called 'modernist' verse one finds either an excess or a defect of technical attention. The former appears in an emphasis upon words rather than things, and the latter in an emphasis upon things and an indifference to words. In either case, the poem is formless, just as the most accomplished sonnet, if it is an attempt to express matter unsuitable for sonnet form, is formless. But a precise fitness of form and matter mean also a balance between them: thus the form, the pattern movement, has a solemnity of its own (e.g. Shakespeare's songs), however light and gay the human emotion concerned; and a gaiety of its own, however serious or tragic the emotion. The choruses of Sophocles, as well as the songs of Shakespeare, have another concern besides the human action of which they are spectators, and without this other concern there is not poetry. And on the other hand, if you aim only at the poetry in poetry, there is no poetry either.

My conviction, for what it is worth, has remained unchanged for the last fourteen years: that Miss Moore's poems form part of the small body of durable poetry written in our time; of that small body of writings, among what passes for poetry, in which an original sensibility and alert intelligence and deep feeling have been engaged in maintaining the life of the English language.

The original suggestion was that I should make a selection, from both previously published and more recent poems. But Miss Moore exercised her own rights of proscription first, so drastically, that I have been concerned to preserve rather than abate. I have therefore hardly done more than settle the order of the contents. This book contains all that Miss Moore was willing to reprint from the volume *Observations* (The Dial Press, New York, 1924), together with the poems written since that date which she is willing to publish.

BOOK REVIEW:
From I. M. Parsons, "New Verse," *Spectator,* 26 April 1935, p. 704.

Moore's Selected Poems *encouraged perceptive readers to recognize Moore's precision of language and "poetic intensity," which other readers found merely difficult or confusing. In reviewing her* Selected Poems *with books by Edward Roditi, L. L. Wyn Griffith, George Barker, and Dylan Thomas, Parsons praises only Moore, calling on readers to recognize her significance.*

Miss Marianne Moore is a writer less known in this country than many other American poets with smaller claims on our attention. A single volume, in 1921, is all that has been previously published here of her work, and those of us to whom her name is not entirely new are probably familiar with it only through the pages of *The Dial* or, more recently, of Mr. Pound's *Active Anthology.* In that collection, it seemed to me, Miss Moore stood out as the single contributor of importance whose reputation was not already recognized on either side of the Atlantic. And this impression is confirmed by the present volume of *Selected Poems,* which comprises all that Miss Moore is willing to have published, or republished, of her work up to the present time. For whatever else one may think about Miss Moore's poetry, its genuineness, is not to be questioned; and few readers will dispute Mr. Eliot's contention that genuineness, as distinct from greatness, is a quality that may sometimes be recognized during a writer's lifetime. Mr. Eliot himself, in his Introduction, is ready to go considerably further in praise of Miss Moore. He speaks of her as one of the few who have performed some service to the English tongue "by carrying on that struggle for the maintenance of a living language, for the maintenance of its strength, its subtlety, for the preservation of quality of feeling, which must be kept up in every generation." Those who take the trouble to read Miss Moore's poems with attention will surely agree. For the bone of so much contemporary poetry is its diffuseness, its lack of identification between feeling and expression, either through too vague and indeterminate, or, in an effort to avoid the commonplace, too self-conscious and eccentric a use of language. Whereas Miss Moore uses English precisely, with a terse austerity which is the first step toward poetic intensity. And if the majority of readers (of whom I must count myself one) find that their chief pleasure in Miss Moore's work springs from her exact and searching eye, her intricate pattern of observation, rather than from any profound revelation of an internal truth, they will still find her one of the few contemporary writers with a sensibility keen enough and a technique accomplished enough to justify the pleasurable effect of continued reading. . . .

LETTER:
To Dorothea Gray, *Marianne Moore Newsletter*, 2 (Fall 1978): 11.

Moore was asked by Dorothea Gray of the American Association of University Women for a profile, describing her background, reading tastes, techniques and goals in writing, influences, representative poems, and philosophy, as well as what Moore thought to be the task of the poet after World War I.

260 Cumberland Street
Brooklyn, New York
November 5, 1935

Dear Miss Gray:

I was born in 1887 and was graduated from Bryn Mawr in 1908; but if you have access to WHO'S WHO, a little more information than this is given there.

The authors I have cared most for are Chaucer, Spenser, Sir Philip Sidney, Sir Thomas Browne, Dr. Johnson, Anthony Trollope, W. H. Hudson, and Thomas Hardy. [See LIVING AUTHORS; the H. W. Wilson Company–in the reference department of most public libraries.] I have been influenced by the Bible and Bach's* music and point of view I think. Contemporarily I have been influenced by Ezra Pound, T. S. Eliot, Wallace Stevens, W. C. Williams, and E. E. Cummings; and if the word contemporary could be used in this connection, by Gerard Hopkins.

I have not succeeded in expressing what I feel about life and art, but as verse, The Jerboa, The Buffalo, and The Steeple-Jack, please me most. With regard to technique, I have a liking for the unaccented rhyme, and the movement of the poem musically is more important I feel than the conventional look of the lines on the page. Therefore I tend to regard the stanza as the unit of composition rather than the line; and although it is a dangerous principle to follow, because it provokes query and distracts thought from the theme, I sometimes divide a word at the end of a line or end of a stanza; and often use the title of a poem as continuous with the first line of the poem.

My outlook on life appears I think, in a prose article of mine that appeared in THE HOUND & HORN, April-June, 1934: *Henry James as a Characteristic American.*

I do not see how it is possible for one to live without religious faith, or shall I say without capacity for it. War and the reaction from are inescapable in their effect on the mind, I admit, and thus enter into the "task" of the writer; but I would say–for myself at any rate–a person is not under any circumstances doing other than trying to express without affectation, irrepressible conviction that has, in some specific form, taken possession of him.

*J. S. Bach

BOOK REVIEW:
Wallace Stevens, "A Poet that Matters," *Life and Letters To-day*, 13 (December 1935): 61-65.

Stevens was the first critic to connect Moore's work to the "romantic," and thereby to his own. Some years later, following several careful reviews of Stevens's poetry, Moore wrote a poem about him, "Pretiolae."

The tall pages of *Selected Poems* by Marianne Moore are the papers of a scrupulous spirit. The merely fastidious spirit *à la mode* is likely to be on the verge of suffocation from hyperaesthesia. But Miss Moore's is an unaffected, witty, colloquial sort of spirit. In *The Fish,* for instance, the lines move the rhythm of sea-fans waving to and fro under water. They are lines of exquisite propriety. Yet in this poem she uses what appears, aesthetically, to be most inapposite language:

"All
external
  marks of abuse are present on this
  defiant edifice–
    all the physical features of."

Everywhere in the book there is this enhancing diversity. In consequence, one has more often than not a sense of invigoration not usually communicated by the merely fastidious.

That Miss Moore is scrupulous, the lines just quoted demonstrate. *All* and *external* are rhymes enough for anyone who finds full rhymes to be crude. The same thing is true of *this* and *edifice.* Thus, the lines which at first glance appeared to contain no rhymes whatever, have on a second look a more intricate appearance. Moreover, the units of the lines are syllables and not

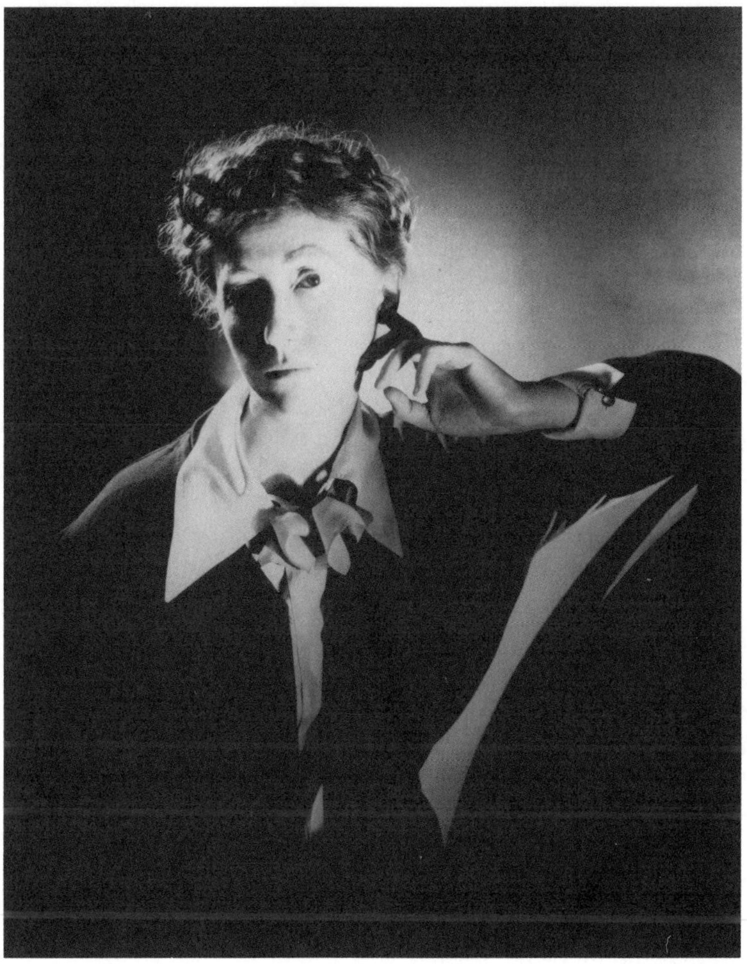

Marianne Moore, 1935

feet; the first line contains one syllable; the second three; the third nine; the fourth six; the last eight. This scheme is repeated with exactness throughout the poem. It is this scheme that requires Miss Moore to end with stanza with *of*, and that occasionally requires her to pass, elsewhere, from one line to the next in the middle of a word. If the verse is not to be free, its alternative is to be rigid. Finally, in printing the lines, the first two have been set well to the left, the next two have been set in a little to the right and the last has been set in still father to the right. Now, all these things contribute to the effect of the stanza. The light rhymes please one unconsciously. The exactness with which the syllables are repeated, the larger recurrences as the stanzas are repeated, the indentations which arrest the eye, even if slightly: all these things assist in creating and in modulating the rhythm. In addition, Miss Moore instinctively relates sounds. There is a relation between the groups of letters *ext, ks, phys*. The *i*'s in *defiant edifice* are related. As these relations change, not only the sounds change, but the colours, the texture, the effects also change.

The poem with which the book opens, *The Steeple-Jack*, is highly characteristic. The lines and stanzas flow innocently. Nevertheless, throughout the dozen stanzas the lines repeat themselves, syllable by syllable, without variation. The stanzas are mechanisms. Yet instead of producing a mechanical effect, they produce an effect of ease. In one of her poems Miss Moore writes of

"... intermingled echoes
struck from thin glasses successively at random–."

In the *Steeple-Jack* she writes of

"a sea the purple of the peacock's neck is
paled to greenish azure as Dürer changed
the pine green of the Tyrol to peacock blue."

The strong sounds of *the purple of the peacock's neck* contrast and intermingle with the lighter sounds of *paled to a greenish azure* and return again to the strong sounds of the last line. The colours of the first and second lines acquire a quality from their association with the word Dürer and the pine green and the peacock blue of the last line owe something to the word Tyrol and the image of the Tyrol. This is not all going too finely into minutiae. For with Miss Moore these things lie on the surface.

The Steeple-Jack serves, too, to illustrate what interests Miss Moore. The point of the poem is a view of the common-place. The view is that of Dürer or of Miss Moore in the mask or mood of Dürer, or, more definitely, perhaps, under the stimulus of Dürer. The common-place is, say, a New England fishing-village. Whatever the poem may do for Dürer or for the village, it does many happy things for Miss Moore and for those who delight in her. Obviously, having in mind the subject-matter of the poem, Miss Moore *donne dans le romanesque.* Consciously, the point of the poem may have been something wholly casual. It may lie in the words

"it is a privilege to see so
much confusion."

Consciously, it may have had no more point than the wish to make note of observations made while in the cloud of a mood. That is Miss Moore's method. Subject, with her, is often incidental. There are in *The Steeple-Jack* the following creatures: eight stranded whales, a fish, sea-gulls, the peacock of the peacock's neck referred to a moment ago, a guinea, a twenty-five pound lobster, an exotic serpent (by allusion), a ring-lizard, a snake (also by allusion), a crocodile, cats, cobras, rats, the diffident little newt and a spider. This is a modest collection. Miss Moore makes the most lavish snake-charmer look like a visitor. The people in the poem are Dürer;

"The college student
named Ambrose sits on the hill-side
with his not-native books and hat
and sees boats
at sea progress white and rigid as if in
a groove";

and C. J. Poole, Steeple-Jack, with one or two references to others. Poole is merely a sign on the sidewalk with his name on it. The last stanza is:–

"It could not be dangerous to be living
in a town like this, of simple people,
who have a steeple-jack placing danger signs by the church
while he is gilding the solid-
pointed star, which on a steeple
stands for hope."

Stendhal in his *Pensées* said:

"Le bel esprit comme on sait fut de tout
temps l'ennemi le plus refide du genie."

Miss Moore's wit, however, does not in the least imperil what she is about. Out of her whales and the college student and Poole and the danger signs she composes a poem simple, radiant with imagination, contemporaneous, displaying everywhere her sensitive handling. The poem leaves one indubitably convinced that she leans to the romantic.

And so she should, with a difference. In *The Steeple-Jack* she observes the fog on the seaside flowers and trees

"so that you have
the tropics at first hand: the trumpet vine . . .
or moon vines trained on fishing-twine.."

She then writes

". . . There are no banyans, frangipani nor
jack-fruit trees; nor an exotic serpent
life."

If she had said in so many words that there were banyans, frangipani, and so on, she would have been romantic in the sense in which the romantic is a relic of the imagination. She hybridises the thing by a negative. That is one way. Equally she hybridizes it by association. Moon-vines are moon-vines and tedious. But moon-vines trained on fishing-twine are something else and they are as perfectly as it is possible for anything to be what interest Miss Moore. They are an intermingling. The imagination grasps at such things and sates itself, instantaneously, in them. Yet clearly they are romantic. At this point one very well might stop for definitions. It is clear enough, without all that, to say that the romantic in the pejorative sense merely connotes obsolescence, but that the word has, or should have, another sense. Thus, when A. E. Powell in *The Romantic Theory of Poetry* writes of the romantic poet,

Marianne Moore, circa 1938

> "He seeks to reproduce for us the feeling as it lives within himself; and for the sake of a feeling which he thinks is interesting or important he will insert passages which contribute nothing to the effect of the work as a whole,"

she is surely not thinking of the romantic in the derogatory sense. True, when Professor Babbitt speaks of the romantic, he means the romantic. Romantic objects are things, like garden furniture or colonial lingerie or, not to burden the imagination, country millinery.

Yes, but the romantic in its other sense, meaning always the living and at the same time the imaginative, the youthful, the delicate and a variety of things which it is not necessary to try to particularise at the moment, constitutes the vital element in poetry. It is absurd to wince at being called a romantic poet. Unless one is that, one is not a poet at all. That, of course, does not mean banyans and frangipani; and it cannot for long mean no banyans and no frangipani. Just what it means, Miss Moore's book discloses. It means, now-a-days, an uncommon intelligence. It means in a time like our own of violent feelings, equally violent feelings and the most skilful expression of the genuine. Miss Moore's lines,

> "the shadows of the Alps
> imprisoning in their folds like flies in amber, the rhythms
> of the skating rink"

might so easily have been pottered over and nullified; and how hilarious, how skilful they are! Only the other day there was a comment on "Samuel Prout's romantic renderings of mediaeval fountains." The commentator was far from meaning mediaeval renderings of romantic fountains. For him Prout's renderings were romantic because the delighted him and since the imagination does not often delight in the same thing twice, it may be assumed that by romantic he meant something that was, for his particular imagination, an indulgence and a satisfaction.

Professor Babbitt says that

> "a thing is romantic when, as Aristotle would say, it is wonderful rather than probable . . . A thing is romantic when it is strange, unexpected, intense, superlative, extreme, unique, etc."

It must also be living. It must always be living. It is in the sense of living intensity, living singularly that it is the vital element in poetry. The most brilliant instance of the romantic in this sense is Mr. Eliot, who incessantly revives the past and creates the future. It is a process of cross-fertilisation, an immense process, all arts considered, of hybridisation. Mr. Eliot's *Prelude* with the smell of steaks in passageways, is an instance, in the sense that the smell of steaks in the Parnassian air is a thing perfectly fulfilling Professor Babbitt's specifications. Hamlet in modern dress is another instance of hybridisation. Any playing of a well-known concerto by an unknown artist is another. Miss Moore's book is a collection of just that. It is not a matter of phrases, nor of odd-looking lines, nor of poems from which one must wholly take, giving anything whatsoever at one's peril. Poetry for her is "a place for the genuine." If the conception of the poet as a creature ferocious with ornamental fury survives anywhere except in the school books, it badly needs a few pungent footnotes. We do not want "high-sounding interpretation." We want to understand. We want, as she says,

> "imaginary gardens with real toads in them."

The very conjunction of imaginary gardens and real toads is one more specimen of the romantic of Miss Moore. Above all things she demands

> "the raw material of poetry in
> all its rawness."

She demands the romantic that is genuine, that is living, the enriching poetic reality.

Miss Moore's form is not the quirk of a self-conscious writer. She is not a writer. She is a woman who has profound needs. In any project for poetry (and one wishes that the world of tailors, plasterers, bar-keepers could bring itself to accept poets in a matter-of-fact way) the first effort should be devoted to establishing that poets are men and women, not writers. Miss Moore may have had more than one reason for adding in the *Notes* appended to her book that in *Peter,* the hero "built for the midnight grass-party," was a

> "Cat owned by Miss Magdalen Heuber and
> Miss Maria Weniger."

But this amusing stroke is, after all, a bit of probity, whatever else it may be. That Miss Moore uses her wit is a bit of probity. The romantic that falsifies is rot and that is true even though the romantic inevitably falsifies: it falsifies but it does not vitiate. It is an association of the true and the false. It is not the true. It is not the false. It is both. The school of poetry that believes in sticking to the facts would be stoned if it was not sticking to the facts in a world in which there are no facts: or some such thing.

This brings one round to a final word. Miss Moore's *emportements* are few. Instead of being intentionally one of the most original of contemporary or modern poets, she is merely one of the most truthful. People with a passion for the truth are always original. She says:

> "Truth is no Apollo."

She has thought much about people and about poetry, and the truth, and she has done this with all the energy of an intense mind and imagination and this book is the significant result. It contains the veritable thing.

ARTICLE:
William Carlos Williams, "Marianne Moore," *Quarterly Review of Literature,* 4 (1948): 125-126.

Williams contrasts Moore's poetry to T. S. Eliot's with references to "The Hollow Men" and The Waste Land. *Despite her friendship with Williams, Moore would disagree with him over his treatment of women in* Paterson.

The magic name, Marianne Moore, has been among my most cherished possessions for nearly forty years, synonymous with much that I hold dearest to my heart. If this invites a definition of love it is something I do not intend to develop in this place. On the contrary I intend to describe, very briefly and indirectly, a talent.

It is a talent which diminishes the tom-toming on the hollow men of a wasteland to an irrelevant pitter-patter. Nothing is hollow or waste to the imagination of Marianne Moore.

The Famous Chilcat Blanket

By S. Hall Young, D. D.

A CHIEFTAIN'S ROBE

No proof of the Japanese origin of the Alaska Thlingets is stronger than that contained in the figures and construction of the Chilcat blanket. The history of weaving by these ingenious people is lost in the midst of antiquity, and even the significance of these strange but artistic figures, woven so deftly, is obscure.

The great white mountain goat of the northwest coast, the oldest animal of the North American Continent in point of origin, the beast of the Pliocene, furnishes the hair. This long, strong, white hair with its substratum of wooly fur, is obtained from the winter coat of this animal; then it is woven by hand. Sometimes a man, sometimes a woman, is the weaver. Various colors are weighted by bladders full of stone, and all the warp is hung upon a pole, and the woof worked in by hand needles. The blankets are very thick and firm. To give body to the warp sometimes bark is twisted in with the coarser yarn, but the cross threads are pure wool, and some of them exceedingly fine. The dyes are three: purplish black obtained from the ink-pot of the cuttle-fish, a delicate light blue from the blueberry, and an exquisite yellow from the root of the yellow cedar. The colors, with the pure white and the undyed hair, are woven into these strange figures.

Masons have professed to see in the Chilcat blanket masonic emblems, and one of their writers went so far as to try to prove by these figures that the Thlingets were descended from the ancient Jews, and practiced Masonic rites.

Thirty-five years ago these splendid blankets, sometimes eight feet across by six feet in depth including the long white fringe, sold for twenty-five or thirty dollars. Now for an inferior blanket tourists have to pay from one hundred and fifty to two hundred dollars, and even at such a price these blankets are very hard to obtain.

The splendid chieftain's robe shown in the picture could not be obtained now for less than three or four hundred dollars. These robes were handed down from uncle to nephew, and were packed in yellow cedar boxes, with great care to protect them from the moths.

The totemic figure on this robe is that of the beaver, proving the chief to belong to the grand Totem of the Crow, and the sub-Totem of the Beaver. There are also whale and crow emblems which the experienced only can detect.

There is little religious significance in these figures, as these totemic images were never objects of worship, but were emblems of the pride and glory of the family.

卐

Moore's clipping from the May 1916 issue of the Home Mission Monthly *(Rosenbach Museum & Library). In February 1942, while writing "The Wood-Weasel," Moore drew on this article for her description of the skunk's "chieftain's coat of Chilcat cloth." The poem was first published in the April 1942 issue of the* Harvard Advocate *and collected in* Nevertheless *(1944)*

How so slight a woman can so roar, like a secret Niagara, and with so gracious an inference, is one with all mysteries where strength masquerading as weakness–a woman, a frail woman–bewilders us. Miss Moore in constant attendance upon her mother the greater part of her life has lived as though she needed just that emphasis to point up the nature of her powers.

Marianne Moore (whom for no adequate reason I always associate in my mind with Marie Laurencin who may be the size of a horse for all I know) once expressed admiration for Mina Loy; that was in 1916, let us say. I think it was because Mina was wearing a leopard-skin coat at the time and Marianne had stood there with her mouth open looking at her.

Marianne had two cords, cables rather, of red hair coiled around her rather small cranium when I first saw her and was straight up and down like the two-by-fours of a building under construction. She would laugh with a gesture of withdrawal after making some able assertion as if you yourself had said it and she were agreeing with you.

A statement she would defend, I think, is that man essentially is very much like the other animals–or a ship coming in from the sea–or an empty snail-shell: but there's not much use saying a thing like that unless you can prove it.

Therefore Miss Moore has taken recourse to the mathematics of art. Picasso does no different: a portrait is a stratagem singularly related to a movement among the means of the craft. By making these operative, relationships become self-apparent–the animal lives with a human certainty. This is strangely worshipful. Nor does one always know against what one is defending oneself.

I saw yesterday what might roughly be referred to as a birthday card–made by some child a hundred or so years ago in, I think, Andover, Massachusetts. It was approximately three inches in its greatest dimension, formally framed in black, the mat inside the frame being of a particularly brilliant crimson velvet, a little on the cerise side and wholly undimmed by age. This enclosed a mounted bouquet of minute paper flowers upon the remnants of what had been several artificial little twigs among greenish blue leaves.

There were in all three identically shaped four-petaled flowers, one a faded blue, one pinkish and one white, perfectly flat as though punched out of tissue paper. At the bottom of the bouquet, placed loosely across the stems under the glass, was a slightly crumpled legend plainly printed on a narrow half-inch strip of white paper:

Walk on roses.

I never saw a more apt expression. Its size had no relation to the merits of its composition or execution.

I don't know what else to say of Marianne Moore–or rather I should like to talk on indefinitely about her, an endless research into those relationships which her poems, her use of the materials of poetry, connote. For I don't think there is a better poet writing in America today or one who touches so deftly so great a range of our thought.

This is the amazing thing about a good writer, he seems to make the world come toward him to brush against the spines of his shrub. So that in looking at some apparently small object one feels the swirl of great events.

What it is that gives us this sensation, this conviction, it is impossible to know but that it is the proof which the poem offers us there can be little doubt.

COMMENTARY:

Edwin Denby, "A Poet on Pavlova Photographs," *New York Herald Tribune*, 18 June 1944, IV 6.

New York's premier dance critic read Moore's article "Anna Pavlova" in Dance Index *and recognized the closeness of spirit connecting the dancer and the poet. In another article for the same magazine, Moore reviewed the "Elephant Ballet," a circus act in which elephants performed a dance choreographed by George Balanchine of the New York City Ballet.*

"An Album of Pavlova Photographs" with "accompanying notes" by Marianne Moore is the very astonishing contents of the latest issue of "Dance Index"–price, one quarter; admirers of Pavlova and admirers of Miss Moore will not want to miss so remarkable an item. There are thirty-one photographs of the great ballerina, who holds the rank of greatest in our century, despite Kshessinska and Egorova, Karsavina, Spessiva and Doubrovska, who were her brilliant peers in the days of her glory. And there are six pages of comment by our great poetess–scholarly, subtle and accurate, in an impeccable prose that has the floating balance, the light pauses and the recurrent soaring instants of classic dancing. The style is a homage to the dancer, precisely delicate and delicately spontaneous.

Miss Moore's article is first of all a collage of quotations from the celebrated appreciators–Svetloff, Levinson, C. W. Beaumont, Oliveroff, Dandre and Stier. They tell very little of Pavlova's craftsmanship, of that technique she worked at so devotedly and which must have been full of discoveries and procedures worth passing on to later dancers and dance lovers. Miss Moore includes what technical hints she has found, but the eyewitnesses describe Pavlova's dancing mostly by the device of spiritual rhapsodies. Miss Moore quotes the most vivid evocation, Levinson's description of the "Dying Swan," and translates it beautifully. From the innumerable other tributes she selects a phrase here, a sentence there and reassembles them with so keen a sense of style that they give you a clearer picture of dancing than in their original context.

Still the quotations keep their bias–a parlorlike spirituality that is unsatisfactory. Miss Moore does not shatter their decorousness; she vivifies it by adding to it herself physical and moral perceptions of real elegance. Like Gautiier she can manage a rapturous moment without losing her balance. "In the photograph of her . . . in the grass . . . the descending line of the propped forearm, of her dress and other hand, of ankle and foot, continues to the grass with the naturalness of a streamer of seaweed–an inevitable and stately serpentine which imparts to the seated figure the ease of a standing one." Or "We see her in the gavotte advancing with the swirling grace of a flag and the decorum of an impalla deer."

But it is by her private moral perceptions, appearing for an instant and at rare intervals, that Miss Moore gives us the sharpest equivalent for the actual fact of classic dancing. She notes on a picture of a twelve-year-old Pavlova: . . . "the erectness of the head, the absolutely horizontal brows, indicating power of self-denial; the eyes dense, with imagination and sombered with solicitude; the hair, severely competent; the dress, dainty more than proud." And after describing a hand pose: "These truthful hands, the most sincere and the least greedy imaginable. . . . "She notes Pavlova's use of the passive voice when the dancer wrote: . . . "I was permitted to style myself Premiere Danseuse . . . later I was granted the title of Ballerina." This classic modesty Miss Moore recurs to: "She had power for a most unusual reason–she did not present as valuable the personality from which she could not escape." And later, suggesting the quality of Pavlova's expression, Miss Moore asks, "Why should one so innocent, so natural, so ardent be sad? If self-control is the essential condition of conveying emotion and giving is giving up, we still cannot feel that renunciation had made Pavlova sad; may it have been that for lives that one loves there are things even love cannot do?" And later Miss Moore herself answers, "That which is able to change the heart proves itself."

Morally speaking, this describes correct classic dancing: it is a poet's metaphor of its final grace. A journalist asked the sprightly Danilova what was the most important quality for a ballerina. "Modesty," she answered quickly.

BIOGRAPHY:

Grace Schulman, "Marianne Moore and E. McKnight Kauffer: Two Characteristic Americans," *Twentieth Century Literature,* 30 (Summer/Fall 1982): 175-180.

Grace Schulman's parents had known Moore for many years and their daughter knew both Moore and Kauffer, a gifted artist who worked for T. S. Eliot at Faber and Faber in London until he returned to the United States at the beginning of World War II.

Early in the nineteen-fifties, Marianne Moore wrote that "a few real artists are alive today," and listed among them E. McKnight Kauffer, the graphic designer, along with Casals, Soledad, Hans Mardersteig, Alec Guinness and the Lippizan horsemen. In a catalogue note for an exhibit of Kauffer's drawings, the poet wrote: "Instinctiveness, imagination, and 'the sense of artistic difficulty' with him, have interacted till we have an objectified logic of sensibility as inescapable as the colors refracted from a prism."

In the preceding decade they had become close friends, supporting one another in personal crises that were also times of spiritual renewal and growth. Moore once wrote to Kauffer of their common belief, despite affliction and suffering, in "anastasis–the going forward," and in what John Fiske, the American philosopher, had called "the reasonableness of God's work." She wrote: "So let not your heart be troubled, neither let it be afraid."

Meeting and corresponding frequently, the two artists found stimulation in each other's thoughts about books, events and mutual friends. Often they expressed deep concern about one another's well-being. For example, Moore was troubled about her slender colleague's tendency, like her own, to neglect meals when he was preoccupied. With characteristically serious, genuine affection, she mailed ten dollars to Kauffer with instructions to go to Miss Hettie Hamper's restaurant "for a meal (say once a day?) and you will like her food." Then, quoting Frances Steloff, of the Gotham Book Mart, Moore told Kauffer: " 'Her chef is the very best in New York. Nothing is greasy. Nothing is overcooked, nothing undercooked.' Everything is tempting."

Nor was their affinity limited to personal matters. In their work, they shared traits that were fundamental to their primary effects. Born in Middle America within three years of one another (Kauffer in Montana, 1890, and Moore in Missouri, 1887), they carried forward an American tradition in their eclecticism of subject matter. Creating art of common lives and of knowledge, both insisted on the artist's freedom to contemplate any information without diminished energy. The two craftsmen extended the scope of art by transmuting material that was banal: "here if nowhere else in the world, 'street art' is art," Moore wrote of Kauffer's drawings, and the statement applies to her versified newspaper quotations and recorded telephone messages as well as to Kauffer's advertising symbols. Furthermore, if they were influenced by foreign models, they shared an American quality of combined adventurousness and reserve. Their work is characterized by restrained passion, resulting from their simultaneous awareness and control of life's terrors.

Both artists depicted living things with exactitude, building their art on a foundation of precise, factual information. In "Poetry," Moore urges the concrete presentation of living things ("Hands that can grasp, eyes/that can dilate"). In

The Mind is an Enchanting Thing;

is an enchanted thing
like the glaze on the katydid-wing
subdivided by sun
till the nettings are legion.
Like Gieseking playing Scarlatti,

. . . . How quickly beauty enters it.

Early draft (top) for a poem that was first published in the 18 December 1943 issue of Nation *and collected in* Nevertheless *and (bottom) Moore's drawing of a kiwi, which inspired the reference to the "kiwi's rain-shawl/of haired feathers" that she later added to the poem (Rosenbach Museum & Library)*

Kauffer's posters, hands are indeed "hands that can grasp": seamen's hands grasping a rope ("Player's Cigarettes") and whittling wood (American Airlines "East Coast"); a hand lifting a telephone receiver ("Come on the Telephone"); a hand arresting traffic, its movement captured by the use of three colors ("Stop 'Em to Sell 'Em"). We find in his paintings "eyes/that can dilate," bells that can ring, ships that can sail.

If precision was their common aim, however, it was counterbalanced by their faith in the imagination's power to transform reality, for they distilled their art from the interaction of the mind with commonplace objects. One of the books Moore borrowed from Kauffer and discussed with him was the New Directions edition of Paul Valéry's *Selected Writings,* containing an essay that Kauffer had marked: "Fragments from 'Introduction to the Method of Leonardo da Vinci.' " In this piece, Valéry wrote that the mind of the artist, seeking exactitude, groups perceptions around an object and projects a structure of multiple properties. This kind of transmutation is at the heart of the work of Kauffer and Moore. "What is more precise than precision? Illusion," the poet wrote, and the paradox illuminates their common tendency to depict real things under the changing, enchanted gaze of the mind's eye: Kauffer portrays "The Tower of London" as a structure that is half real and half allegorical; his country family in "Whitsuntide Holiday" are solid common people and angels.

Another of the artistic bonds between the two artists was their fascination with machines, and their mutual desire to *know* their engines, turbines, motors and recessed wheels. "I am interested in mechanisms, mechanics in general," Moore told Donald Hall, describing her painstaking and aborted attempt to help the Ford Motor Company find a name for the Edsel. With the fastidiousness, and often the tone, of engineers, she and Kauffer explored these mechanisms: the poet investigated such instruments as "Four Quartz Crystal Clocks" ("There are four vibrators, the world's exactest clocks"); the painter caught the essence of machines in designs such as the bale label illustration, "El Progreso," in which he approximates the speed and power of a railway train.

Related to their interest in machines was their concentration on the mathematic regularities in man-made enterprises as well as in nature. Geometric shapes were organizing principles of Kauffer's perceptions, and Moore, who shared this concern, quoted Kauffer's observation about geometry in nature at the outset of "The Icosasphere," a tribute to a twenty-faced structure built by an engineer. The poem opens:

> "In Buckinghamshire hedgerows
> the birds nesting in the merged green destiny
> weave little bits of string and moths and feathers and thistledown
> in parabolic curves."

In her use of this quotation, Moore captured Kauffer's joyful curiosity about geometric harmony in common things. Once he jotted in a notebook: "Designing is order–the cube–the circle–the triangle all parts of equipment–and symbols of order." In a poster of 1933, "You Can Be Sure of Shell," he conveys the certainty of Shell by presenting an unbreakable chain of elongated links. His use of the triangle and the circle serve the precision and naturalness of "The Early Bird" poster for *The Daily Herald* of 1920.

However curious they were about technology, though, their delight in machines had the converse expression of horror. "People's Surroundings," first published in 1922, is Moore's infernal urban vision of a "vast indestructible necropolis," whose residents are similar to Eliot's wretched crowds in *The Waste Land* and to the human automatons in *Paterson,* by William Carlos Williams. Analogous to all of these poems is Kauffer's "Metropolis" (1926), a painting that embodies a "waste land" of skyscrapers and industrial wheels. Partially obscured by the wheels, pitifully subjugated men walk like robots, their heads bowed.

Horror, yes; but if technology repelled Kauffer, why would he depict the metropolis with such care and tough-minded accuracy? There is no simple answer, for it was, I believe, the multiple view of the mind that was central to the achievements of both artists. Besides adhering to the many-sided internal vision, they pursued the truths of their respective crafts rather than propagating any belief or attitude. But Kauffer and Moore criticized mechanical enterprises that employed the distortion of scientific measurement to destroy or diminish living things. Resembling Kauffer's "Metropolis," Moore's poem, "To a Steam Roller," embodies an extended metaphor of a destructive mechanism. In it, the poet addresses a devastating machine that is flattening the landscape: "You crush all the particles down/into close conformity, and then walk back and forth on them." The poet and the poster designer admired geometric precision for its similarity to exactitude in the mind of the artist as it comes to terms with things of the world. Both artists, though, were horrified that science should be abused to enslave people. Both found impact in the accuracy of human perception, but danger in man's misuse of that faculty.

In the best work of both Americans, life's terrifying mysteries are only partially contained by structural devices that hold reality at a remove from perception. The ways in which they achieve this constitute their most powerful effects. In Moore's poem, "A Grave," the poet partially conceals the terror of death by her conversational tone and by her presentation of images that challenge perception. The sea is "beautiful under networks of foam," but it is frightening, for it has "nothing to give but a well-excavated grave." And in "Marriage," she contrasts whimsical, witty phrases with language that captures an irrational current of the mind in passages that convey the destruction of reason by passion.

These contrasts of harmony and chaos are found in Kauffer's greatest work. In "Route 160, Reigate," Kauffer presents a row of black gnarled trees backed by straight trees in a brilliant, unearthly red color. The gnarled and the straight, the black and the red, combine to give an effect that is all the more strange for its partial adherence to naturalness. In his book-jacket illustration for *Winds,* by St.-John Perse, Kauffer employs geometrically neat lettering, but places near the title a jagged line that extends off the page. It is the precision and, conversely, the deceptively unruly view of life, both coexistent in the mind, that the two artists confronted in their greatest achievements. Theirs was a kind of American adventurousness and control that brought curiosity to its farthest reaches and most staggering dangers and risks. It was a quality they shared with their countryman, Henry James, who had, Moore wrote, a "mind 'incapable of the shut door in any direction.' "

BOOK REVIEW:
Edwin Muir, "Thou Art Translated." *The Observer,* 24 April 1955, p. 14.

Moore spent ten years translating The Fables of La Fontaine *(1954), a task which preempted time from her own poetry and had an effect on her writing. Muir is reviewing* Selected Fables of Fontaine, *an abridgement of the American edition, published in London by Faber & Faber in 1955.*

Miss Marianne Moore is a poet of such emphatic individuality that whatever she deals with takes on her unmistakable impress. She has done all she can with La Fontaine, and the result is a volume of fables by Marianne Moore. One could not ask for anything better or anything different. I do not mean by this that she has been unfaithful, by her lights, to her original; clearly she has taken heroic pains to be as faithful as possible; but she suffers from a disadvantage which for her reader is an advantage; she has her own voice.

Writers with no voice at all could have rendered more smoothly the smoothness and wit and natural elegance of La Fontaine. There is elegance in these translations, but it is Miss Moore's kind of elegance, which is not natural in the ordinary sense but full of witty unexpected turns. Puck did not translate Bottom more radically than she has translated the fables, though she has crowned them with something more delicate than an ass's head, something resembling a wise and civilised serpent irrevocably endowed with a modern sensibility.

How directness can be turned into ind irectness–and given a new quality for the speculative mind–is illustrated in almost every page of this fascinating book. A poem begins:–

> A serpent has mobility,

which is simple enough to be almost in the style of La Fontaine, but then it goes on:–

> Which can shatter intrepidity.
> The tail-tip's mental to-and-fro
> And tail-like taper head's quick
>   blow–
> Like Fate's–have the power to appal.
> Each end had thought for years that
>   it had no equal
> And that it alone knew
>   What to do.

One can see Miss Moore thinking herself into the mechanism of the serpent, not only by bringing head and tail into such a lively reciprocal relation, but by the movement of the lines. This is a more complex, intellectual snake than La Fontaine's, and the creation of a poet who, as the dust-cover reminds us, has dealt with "elephants and jerboas, snakes and swans, mongooses and monkeys, pelicans and pangolins," and is now saturated with fabulous experience.

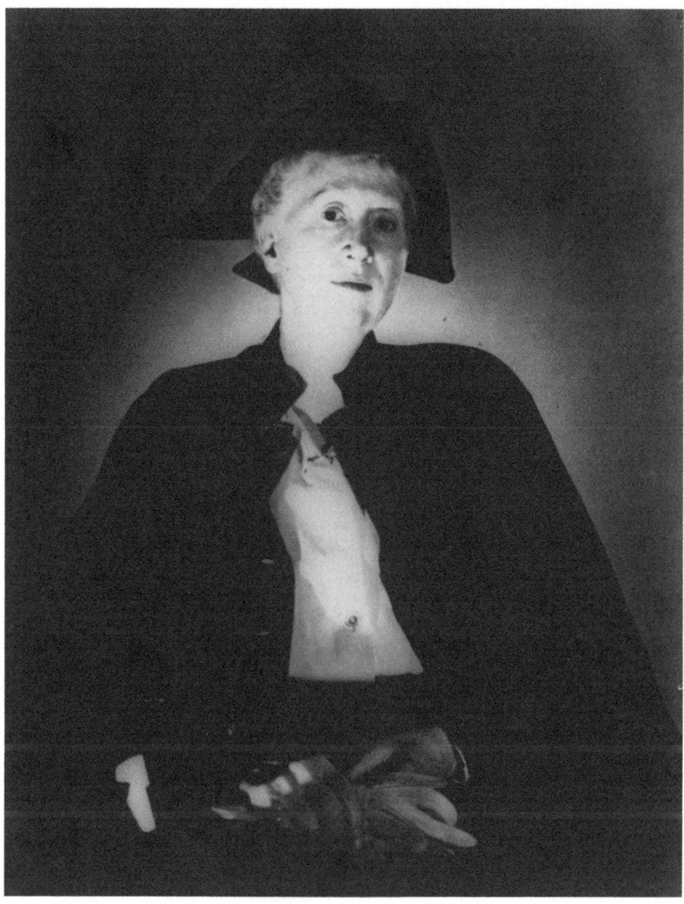

Marianne Moore, 1955

The work of translation must have been made much more difficult by Miss Moore's resolve to "approximate the original rhythms of the fables." She does at times reach an approximation but hardly ever a resemblance; she only gets near enough to point the difference. This is not through any lack of care. She has gone to great trouble to get the exact flow of the French. I quote her own words:–

> In this regard the reading aloud by Wallace Fowlie and Robert Franc, of certain typical fables, obviated purblindness of indecision.

That is Miss Moore's real voice, and it tells us why, in spite of her pains, these poems sound so little like their originals.

That is because La Fontaine is La Fontaine and Miss Marianne Moore is Miss Marianne Moore: the fact that they have both written poems about animals does not matter at all. That the result has fallen out as it has done, and that the flavour of Miss Moore's poetry is so strong in it, is a matter for satisfaction, not for regret. The only regrettable thing is that the difficulty of the task has constricted her powers. This can be seen in an occasional crudity of rhyme, a line contorted unnaturally in order to place the required word at the end: a surprising disfigurement in a poet of such experience.

But the book is fascinating whether it is read as an addition to Miss Moore's poetry, or as an indirect commentary on the poetry of La Fontaine. The rivalry between the original and the rendering issues in high comedy. Those who like Miss Moore's poetry will enjoy this book.

BOOK REVIEW:

Babette Deutsch, "Medley of Marianne Moore," *New York Herald Tribune Book Review,* 27 January 1959, p. 5.

Moore's use of quotations baffled many of her readers, who did not realize how the poet created different voices in counterpoint with her own. Deutsch discusses

Moore's poetic "reticence" in this review of Like a Bulwark.

The collection of new poems by Marianne Moore consists of less than a dozen short pieces and so is a fresh example of her reserve. This is further exemplified in the unobtrusiveness of the metric and the game of hide-and-seek that the sly rhymes play. Another index to her reticence is her willingness to let someone else–it may be Oliver Goldsmith, Ovid, St. Paul, or a writer in "Time" magazine–speak for her. Approximately half of this exiguous volume is given over to bibliographical notes, which are enlivened by a couple of illustrations, one of them a drawing by a six-year-old Spaniard whose people fought, in vain, for the Republic, and by a memorably witty poem from the pen of the Marquise de Boufflers. Source material of this kind is welcome, but Miss Moore's penchant for quotation has its drawbacks. One would prefer more of those phrases in which she herself succinctly defines what her perceptivity discerns. With what accuracy she delineates Dürer's magnificently absurd rhino, the racehorse, Tom Fool, the peculiar charm residing in "the feather touch, the giraffe eyes" of the departed jazzman, Fats Waller, and the not wholly different charm of a sycamore: "Against a gun-metal sky I saw an albino giraffe." The curiosities of the sensible world in which her eye delights, the solving of technical problems which enables her to delight her readers, appear, however, 'to be secondary concerns for her. Whether she considers the creatures and the plants, Mozart's music or the staff of Aesculapius, Miss Moore is always occupied with the way in which they can be used to point a moral. She can summon real toads. The imaginary gardens that they inhabit have now the elegant look of Versailles, and again suggest the strict paths where one might meet a Greek fabulist bowed under his legend.

BOOK REVIEW:
Muriel Rukeyser, "The Rhythm Is the Person," *Saturday Review of Literature,* 42 (19 September 1959): 17-18.

Few critics recognized the debt Moore's poetry owes to her religious upbringing and her knowledge of scripture and sacred music. In this review of O to Be a Dragon *Rukeyser finds grounds for comparing Moore to Emily Dickinson, whose letters Moore reviewed in 1933.*

"I feel that the form is the outward equivalent of a determining inner conviction," writes Miss Moore on the jacket of her new book, "and that the rhythm is the person." The trust in art has always been one of Miss Moore's convictions. Another is the love of the great as "pacific yet passionate," a conviction that informs her title poem, which may here be quoted in full:

If I, like Solomon . . .
could have my wish–

my wish . . . O to be a dragon
a symbol of the power of Heaven–
of silkworm
size or immense; at times invisible.
Felicitous phenomenon!

Two notes accompany this poem. One speaks of the definition of a "dragon" in that fine book "The Tao of Painting"; one gives Solomon's wish as "an understanding heart"–cut short from First Kings, Chapter 3.

The poem called "In the Public Garden" again displays those qualities of rhythm and conviction that one thinks of as Marianne Moore's signature. It also provides useful clues to the method and sources of many others of her poems. She is enchanted by her subject, the relation between art and the festival in Boston, and has brought to it loving memories–of Harvard, of the taxi driver, of the steeple-jack gliding the Faneuil Hall grasshopper, of entering King's Chapel

to hear them sing: "My work be
praise while others go and come.
No more a stranger or a guest
but like a child
at home.

In later lines of the same poem she finds silence "as unattainable/as freedom. And what is freedom for?/For 'self-discipline,' as our/hardest-working citizen has said."

Notes have often been important outriggers of Marianne Moore's poems, and there are three notes attached to this poem. Two speak of the steeple-jack and the grasshopper. The third is to "My work be praise," identifying it as "Psalm 23–traditional Southern tune, arranged by Virgil Thomson." But clearly these lines are not from the 23rd Psalm. The closest I could come was the line in the 22nd, "In the midst of the congregation I will praise thee." Certainly the last line of the Psalm says, "And I shall dwell in the house of the Lord forever"; but the style, the rhythm, the conviction, as Miss Moore puts it, are off; "No more a stranger or a guest" could never have been said by the Psalmist. Miss Moore was in King's Chapel, she said, to hear them sing. So it is a hymn, of course, and not a Psalm at all. My King James Bible has The New Congregational Hymn Book of 1855 bound in with it, and as "Psalm 24 (Psalm 23) C. M. Watts," I read the lines: "O may Thy house be mine abode,/And all my work be praise./There would I find a settled rest,/While others go and come;/No more a stranger or a guest,/But like a child at home."

There is more here than an attribution to Watt's hymn. The "C. M." before his name are the initials of the metre. There is in the back of this hymnal an index familiar to many, the "Index of Peculiar Metres." The listings here refer to identifications which must be old friends to many church-goers. Some of these forms are very close to the forms which have been, in Marianne Moore's poems, taken to be eccentric–or, as the jacket of this book claims, "in strictest accordance with poetic rules invented by and for herself." I suggest a reading of "No better than 'a withered daffodil' " and "Melchior Vulpius" with some of the old hymns of the same syllabic count. Look at the poem for the Dodgers, for example, and "Thou art gone to the grave! we no longer behold thee," or "Boston has a festival/ compositely for all" with "Rise, my soul, and stretch thy wings/Thy better portion trace."

Miss Moore *is* original, and scrupulously honest, too, I believe; she does not wish for a moment, I am sure, that her readers take the 23rd Psalm to be her "document." But her reputation has been built on accuracy, on scrupulosities. Elizabeth Bishop, for example, calls her (on this jacket) "the World's Greatest Living Observer."

Marianne Moore has had in all her writing life a deep connection with the Psalms and with the hymns made out of their translated spirit. She allows us many glimpses of this real relation: in this book, the sudden emergence in "Melchior Vulpius," "but best of all an anthem," and the anthem's two fine lines. There is a breakthrough of the ark here, too. But I remember it among the early poems, the first poems of hers I read, lines charged with both hymn (in their form) and Psalm (in their subject):

But David, if the heart
Be brass, what boots the art
Of exorcising wrong,
Of harping to a song?

Miss Moore has a whole reach of followers to whom this relation with hymns will open up new fertilities, as does a similar relation in Emily Dickinson.

The fact of this relation and what it may signify, the conviction here which is the form, have deep emotional components which are to be explored or disregarded, according to the way we care about poetry. Marianne Moore, in her superb reticences, in her skilful and flexible use of the document as part of poetry, in her knowledge that the poem begins with the first breath of the title has been a major influence on many people engaged in writing today. We can see her work now against the background of the time in which it was first presented, and in the present, which needs so much of poetry of which there is still hardly a sign anywhere. The living connections that are in her poems assume again, in this book, qualities for which she has always stood, and we admire them as they are here made new.

BOOK REVIEW:
Winfield Townley Scott, "A Sampler of Delights," *New York Herald Tribune Books,* November 26, 1961, p. 9.

When invited to choose material for a "reader," Moore made a characteristic selection of unusual pieces–poems she thought worthy of reprinting, prose concerning baseball, Brooklyn, and Henry James, translations from La Fontaine, and her correspondence with the Ford Motor Company over naming the Edsel.

Miss Moore has long since attained to that dangerous eminence: everybody loves her. Dr. Williams is up there too, these days. And yet–it strikes one–neither of these eminents is really in danger. Even now, William Carlos Williams is likely to sass somebody in a manner not customary among literary elder statesmen. And as for Marianne Moore she simply isn't "above" anything. The nimbleness of her excitements is a great part of her charm. She has, on the printed page as in person, continual presence but no side. Thus, quite naturally–but unlike most literary personages–she may glow one moment over the erstwhile Brooklyn Dodgers and glow at another over the poetry of Guido Cavalcanti.

Her insouciance as to what is "correct" in the literary world shines in the infinite variety of her quotations. Both in her prose and verse she loves to quote. ("I've always felt that if a thing had been said in the *best* way, how can you say it better? If I wanted to say something and somebody had said it ideally, then I'd take it but give the person credit for it.") Her allusions range from T. S. Eliot to the late Rev. S. Parkes Cadman, from Bernard Shaw to Willie Mays, from Mark Twain to a leaflet issued by the Bell Telephone Company. Yet all this is a part of the interests of Marianne Moore–there is no acting going on in these pages.

A magpie of a mind. Yes, but without sloppiness. Sometimes prim, spinsterish, fussy–in a word, peculiar? Yes, but as by right. Amidst all the variety, a fastidious mind–a fastidious writer. It is the precision of her mind which so beguiles us. Its clarity and honesty fuse to a great beauty.

There have been volumes of her selected poems, but now we are given samples of all her work. Apparently Miss Moore has made her own selections, and she contributes a Foreword. ("Prose: mine will always be 'essays' and verse of mine, 'observations.' ") So the business of a brief notice is to tell what this "Reader" contains:

Her recent slim books, "Like a Bulwark" and "O to Be a Dragon," are here complete, and five new books; also 40-odd pages selected from her "Collected Poems."

> ("THE MIND IS AN ENCHANTING THING
> like the glaze on a
> katydid wing
> subdivided by sun
> till the nettings are legion.
> Like Gieseking playing Scarlatti; . . .")

Selections from her translation of the "Fables of La Fontaine." ("And if I have failed to give you real delight/My reward must be that I had hoped I might.")

Essays and reviews. (Her interests include Henry James, the City of Brooklyn, Abraham Lincoln, Edith Sitwell, a talented crow named Pluto.)

The correspondence with the Ford Motor Company over naming a new car which they–not Miss Moore–eventually christened Edsel. ("I am complimented to be recruited in this high matter.")

Finally, in the fine tradition of the Paris Review, an interview by Donald Hall with Miss Moore. ("I certainly never intended to write poetry. . . . And now, too, I think each time I write that it may be the last time; then I'm charmed by something and seem to have to say something.")

Along with Elizabeth Bishop, we all want Miss Moore to please come flying over Brooklyn Bridge–on and on.

INTERVIEW:
Brian O'Dougherty, "Telephone Interview with Busy Poet Produces Her Views on Baseball, Floyd Patterson, and Verse Style," *New York Times,* 15 November 1962, p. 39.

Moore was an ardent and informed baseball fan. Her poem about the Brooklyn Dodgers, "Hometown Piece," had graced the front page of the New York Herald Tribune *a few years earlier. Sports writer George Plimpton took her to a prizefight and to ballgames just to hear her descriptions of the athletes' techniques.*

"If you can't catch the attention at the start and hold it, there no use going on, whether it's biography, drama, verse, whatever it is," said Marianne Moore, one of America's leading poets. "In a poem the excitement has to maintain itself."

Miss Moore, who is 75 years old today, was talking on the telephone, as she was too busy helping other people celebrate her birthday for a face-to-face encounter. She was, among other things, preparing a speech for tonight's tribute to be given her by the National Institute of Arts and Letters. She had just returned from another celebration at Harvard, where, after an elaborate dinner, she read some of her poems. Since Miss Moore was not visible through the telephone, she was asked how she looked, and if she were wearing her famous hat.

"No," she said. "I'm not wearing my hat. I look like an Old English sheepdog at the moment–I've just washed my hair."

In her conversation Miss Moore covered her usual wide area–meditations on the craft of verse, a discourse on the character of Floyd Patterson, and of course, as the poet laureate of baseball, she had a few things to say about the national sport. She was asked if she had ever played it.

"I played in left field as a youngster," said Miss Moore, whose poetry seems to have been created right there. "But I was no asset at all. I was apprehensive when in line for fast balls. Batting? Not so good. I think it's a great thing to connect with the ball.

"These men are really artists," she went on, warming to her subject. "Why, I remember Don Zimmer playing at third base. He was moving toward the home plate when a fly came toward

LG-3276-6404

The Gay Nineties (1892) - Gala Amusement Park, North Beach, Long Island. It later became the site of a 105-acre private flying field, the Glenn H. Curtiss Airport. The new LaGuardia Airport comprises 575 acres.

On 16 April 1964 Brendan Gill of the New Yorker *sent Moore this photograph of an amusement park that had once stood on the site of LaGuardia Airport and suggested, "Why don't you write a poem about that boy leaning against the post on the curb in the left-hand margin of the picture?" That summer Moore wrote "Old Amusement Park," which appeared in the 29 August 1964 issue of the* New Yorker *and was collected in* Tell Me, Tell Me *(1966).*

him. He had to get back to third and he backhanded it with the left hand."

Regarding Floyd Patterson, it is not unlikely that he will turn up in verse. "His book, 'Victory Over Myself,' I regard as a manual for descriptive writing about how to exhibit yourself without repelling the reader. I read the book very carefully and annotated it at the back. It was delicately done. And his story is a model of modesty and tenacity. I got medals blessed by the Pope for Sandra and him, and I'd like to give them to him. I think he has the art of riveting the attention on the text. Zanthes wrote that "The bird of attention is a capricious one. If he slumbers, silence alone will awake him.' "

Miss Moore, a master of catching attention with the first lines of her poems, was asked about that.

"I'm very careful with my first lines," she said. "I put it down, I scrutinize it. I test it. I evaluate it.

Miss Moore feels strongly about the patterns and rhythm of her verse, which is at times as lopsidedly elegant as a tightrope walker with a limp.

"I think the thing that attracted me to put things in verse was the rhythm. Someone said the accents should be set so it would be impossible for the reader to get them wrong. If you can read it in 10 different ways, it's no good. That's very important to me. There are patterns in verse, just as you have restatement after contrast in music–as you have in Bach, particularly. Also I admire the legerdemain of saying alot in a few words."

Miss Moore has some definite prejudices against the maltreatment of poetry. "I'm very doubtful about scholasticizing poetry," she said, "I feel very strongly that poetry should be not an assignment but a joy."

"By the way," said Miss Moore, who had been thinking about it, "would it be permissible to ask what is Floyd Patterson's address? I'm a great fan of his. I think he's a wonderful chap."

REMINISCENCE:

Monroe Wheeler, "Reminiscence," from *Festschrift for Marianne Moore's Seventy Seventh Birthday,* edited by Tambimuttu (New York: Tambimuttu & Mass, 1964), pp. 127-130.

Monroe Wheeler, publisher of Harrison of Paris in the 1930s and afterward in charge of exhibitions and publications at the Museum of Modern Art in New York, became aware of Moore's collage technique when he published her poem "Marriage," comparing her work to that of Pablo Picasso and Georges Braque.

I began to enjoy the poems of Marianne Moore when I was a very young man in Evanston, Illinois. I remember copying them out from *Poetry Magazine.* In 1921, I came to New York on my way to London with my friend Glenway Wescott and Miss Moore and her beautiful mother received us with old-fashioned hospitality and with an extraordinary mingling of grace and wit and singularity.

I went on from London to Germany, and from there I wrote to her asking if I might have a poem to publish in a little series of pamphlets called *Manikin.* With her fabulous liberality and her aptness to surprise, she sent me the poem called "Marriage," which you all know: one of her longest poems, though the lines are short. I shall never forget my amusement when I read the passage about Adam and Eve:

(I quote)

. . . stipulating quiet:
'I should like to be alone';
to which the visitor replies,
'I should like to be alone;
why not be alone together?'
And later:
'I am such a cow,
if I had a sorrow
I should feel it a long time;
I am not one of those
who have a great sorrow
in the morning
and a great joy at noon;'

There are little mysteries in Miss Moore's work. For example, she uses both single quotes and double quotes. What I have just quoted is in single quotes, and I can't remember who it is quoted from. There are altogether about 30 quotations in this poem, magically woven into the fibre of her own thought. This method reminds me of the technique of *collage,* so brilliantly practised by Picasso, Braque and Kurt Schwitters: pictures made up of disparate images, cut and pasted, sometimes redrawn and recolored. Miss Moore does this with other people's words, from newspaper clippings to the most recondite medieval texts, all unified by her personal tone and turn of mind.

One thing that charms her friends is her being prompted, again and again, to extraordinary little adventures, many of which turn up later in her poems. It is what is called "saying YES to life." It is a kind of rehearsal of her work of imagination, in everyday amusement or inquisitiveness.

She once heard on the radio that a dancing school in Brooklyn was offering a free tango lesson. She telephoned at once. She received instructions for getting there, and took the lesson. But she resisted the teacher's efforts to sign her up for the course.

Before she had a television, she would go to the basement apartment of her building superintendent to watch the baseball games. That was long before her famous poem about the Dodgers, which was printed on the opening day of the World Series at the top of the front page of the *New York Herald Tribune:* the first and last time that an American poet has been thus honored.

I have tried to list in my mind some of the now famous virtues of my old friend: her indeflectable pursuit of merit; her indefatigable kindness and compassion; a bubbling sense of humor; her strength of mind, both in enthusiasm and prejudice; the flexibility of her thought, lighthearted, as a rule, but sometimes indignant, sometimes a little mischievous.

Some years ago she wrote in a letter, "Better be meek than attempt fireworks and produce only fragments." Thank heaven, she has not always been meek. She emits fireworks nearly every time she speaks, and her fragments are like jewels, and sometimes like seeds. The originality of her mind and spirit is equally apparent in her behaviour and in everything she says and writes.

The living room in Moore's apartment at 35 West Ninth Street in Greenwich Village, where she lived from 1965 until her death in 1972. She bequeathed the furnishings to the Rosenbach Museum & Library, where this room has been re-created.

Once, when she was dining with me in my flat, she lost a little gold bracelet which had been her mother's. She was in despair. The next day she retraced every step she had taken. She telephoned subway and taxi lost-and-found departments. She advertised in newspapers. And she grieved. Two weeks later my maid found the bracelet behind some pictures in the coat closet. When I telephoned Marianne the good news, she said, "Monroe, I am so elated I could jump out the window, and jump back in again."

One day when she had complained a little of certain changes that had taken place in the last 40 years, she suddenly checked herself, and said, "I ought to be thrown off a high tower and not picked up."

Here we have two images of defenestration: one joyous, the other self-reproachful.

She has written at length about humility, and she practices what she preaches. She once said she thought "artists and writers should be jailed for their necessitousness about their products. I look upon mine as kitchenware."

In one of her finest poems she wrote: "Blessed the geniuses who know that egomania is not a duty."

In the early years of her literary life, on principle she would deter publishers from making books of her poems. Her first book was issued without her consent. She said, "I thought I should be allowed to be eccentric anonymously."

But with this true humility there is a mingling of whimsical pride. I remember when she was asked for a special contribution to the anniversary number of a magazine, and the editor told her the renumeration would be "rather sensational." Marianne said, "I didn't like his putting it that way. I would rather he said, "I'll give you $500 for ten words, and be done with it." He told her she could write on any subject, and she chose music, particularly the work of a sixteenth-century contrapuntalist. "I thought that would be as near to it as I could hit," she said. "I firmly expected it not to be used. I never refute the umpire."

When Wystan Auden was asked to pay a tribute to Miss Moore at her 75th birthday dinner, he told me he was going to use only her own words. He found a passage in one of her poems saying that all one asked for was "a right good salvo of barks and few strong wrinkles puckering the skin between the eyes." He added that he had stolen from her more treasure than he could accurately assess.

And on this same occasion, Robert Lowell said, "She stands with Sappho and Emily Dickinson in her density."

One of the aptest characterizations of her is that of an English admirer, Cyril Connolly:

> *"Miss Moore is the outstanding woman poet of America . . . She is a metaphysical poet; her eye is a magnifying glass, constantly fixed on animals, plants, china, and other small objects; it enlarges each detail until it gives up a secret. Her language is bare and exact, her familiar emotions are aesthetic pleasure, curiously gratified, and truthfulness, with considerable humor and occasional indignation. Reading her poems is like daydreaming to Scarlatti."*

ADDRESS:

Malcolm Cowley, "Speech Delivered at Dinner Meeting of the National Institute of Arts and Letters on the Occasion of Marianne Moore's 75th Birthday, November 15, 1962," from *Festschrift for Marianne Moore's Seventy Seventh Birthday,* pp. 120-121.

Cowley salutes Moore's tenacity as an editor at the Dial.

In the remarks so far we can find the keynote of the evening which is a true keynote: respect and affection.

Affection and respect, both are feelings I am proud to share. I have known Marianne Moore longer than most people here. Perhaps Bill Zorack knew her earlier. I doubt that many others did. In the year 1920 my wife came back from her visit to a branch library far down on the West Side, where she had gone to borrow some books. "I said I was Mrs. Malcolm Cowley," she reported, and the librarian said, "Oh, yes, I know his name. I liked his poem in ----!" In what magazine I now forget, but it was a very little one for very young authors, and of course the librarian who had seen my poems there was Marianne Moore.

That same year we went to a poets' party in a studio on Sixteenth St.; Marianne says the studio belonged to Alfred Kreymborg's sister-in-law. Bill Williams was there, and Emmanuel Carnevali, and Marianne of course, all reading their latest poems. I still remember that, and I remember the years when Marianne was editor of *The Dial,* the fifth editor since the magazine had been reincarnated as a monthly in January 1920. First came Stewart Mitchell (Harvard '18), then Gilbert Seldes (Harvard '14), then briefly Kenneth Burke; then Alyse Gregory, then Marianne took over the editorial chair, deferently, modestly, but with what firm notions about the English language! As a contributor from the early days, I had my notions about the English language too, and sometimes they came into conflict with Marianne's.

There was one occasion, though I hate to recall it on her birthday, when she almost caused my death. I was in a Pittsburgh hospital waiting to have a pretty serious operation. In the morning mail came a big envelope from *The Dial* enclosing the manuscript of a review I had just written. Marianne wanted me to look at it again because of a grammatical question; should I have said "compared to" on the second page? Wouldn't the proper expression be "compared with?" I spent the morning on a long letter explaining what I thought was the difference between "compared to" and "compared with," and insisting that my choice of the first was in perfect consonance with the spirit of the English language. The letter had just been finished, and given to a nurse to mail, when I was wheeled into the operating room. I was very slow in recovering and *The Dial* was very fast in submitting proof. I read it on the first morning that my hand was strong enough to hold a pencil. Then I found that "compared with" was in the printed version in spite of all my protests, and I went into shock. My temperature rose to 106. Interns and nurses clustered round my bedside with grave faces. Faint heavenly music played and angels materialized on the ceiling.

Well, perhaps I exaggerate. Perhaps Marianne was right about "compared with," though after forty-five years I find it hard to admit I might have been wrong. But there is one thing I am delighted to admit; that at every moment, whether or not one agreed with Marianne on a given phrase, she filled one with perfect assurance of her discriminating taste and complete integrity. She was an editor like no other, just as she has always been a poet like no other. Today it is marvelous to find that a reputation she had

Moore in her apartment at 35 West Ninth Street

won among perhaps twenty persons in 1920, and perhaps two thousand in 1930, has extended over the country, and that we can no longer estimate the number of those who regard her with respect and affection, affection and respect.

BOOK REVIEW:

James Dickey, "What the Angels Missed," *New York Times Book Review*, 25 December 1966, pp. 1, 16.

In reviewing Tell Me, Tell Me: Granite, Steel, and Other Topics, *Dickey takes the occasion of noticing how Moore's penultimate book shows that the poet has never moved through phases in her writing but rather deepens her mastery of consistent particularities.*

Heaven is a vision, and so is earth; or at least it can be. Of one of these we know something; about the other we have to speculate. A question: What poet would we most like to have construct a Heaven for us, out of the things we already have? Construct it from his way of being, his particular method of putting the world together and endowing it with consequence? And what would we end up with, picking one rather than another? Would we prefer to inherit the cowled, ecclesiastical, distantly murmuring twilight of Eliot? Should the angels sing in a mixture of Provençal, Greek and frontier American, presided over by the perfect Confucian governor, as Ezra Pound might have it? Or would Paradise be the Artificial one of Baudelaire, a place like nocturnal Paris; a Heaven which–the maker might argue–contains those elements of Hell without which our joy could not exist?

If the question were put to me, I would choose Marianne Moore. And I suspect that this is so because of her persuasiveness in getting the things of this world to live together as if they truly belonged that way, and because the communal vividness of her poems suggests to me order of an ideal kind. In a way, she has spent her life in remaking—or making—our world from particulars that we have never adequately understood on our own.

Well, what kind of Heaven would Miss Moore's be? Much, most probably, like the earth as it is, but refined by responsiveness and intellect into a state very far from the present one; a state of utter consequentiality. For what is Heaven, anyway, but the power of dwelling eternally among objects and actions of consequence? Miss Moore's Heaven would have a means of recording such objects and actions; it would have a history, and a way of preserving its discoveries and happenings; it would have books. But it would be, first of all, a realm of Facts: it would include an enormous amount of matter for there to be opinions about, and so it would make possible vivid and creative and personal parallels between things, and conclusions unforeseeable until they were made. It would take forever from Fact the deadness of being *only* fact, for it would endow what Is with the joyous conjunctions that only a personality itself profoundly creative, profoundly accessible to experience—a personality called a soul—can find among them. Truly, would we have it otherwise in the Eternal City?

This is how Miss Moore might do it. Or, more truthfully, how she has done it, by taking—literally—everything as her province, as the province of her poems. Her Heaven would be not only an artist's Heaven—though it would be that with a magnificent authority—but a Heaven to show the angels what they have missed. Missed, for example, by not knowing, or caring *enough*, about the story in Meyer Berger's "Brooklyn Bridge: Fact and Symbol" of the young reporter of the 1870's who, drawn by some unknown imperative, climbed one of the cables of the bridge, became spellbound to the extent that he couldn't come down, and simply hung there all night. Who ever knew this but Mr. Berger, the reporter, and Miss Moore? Miss Moore knew it not only because she encountered it, but because she *cared* to encounter it, and then came to possess it, first by knowing it and then by using it.

Each of her poems employs items that Miss Moore similarly encountered and to which she gave a new, Mooreian existence in a new cosmos of consequential relationships. What seems to me to be the most valuable point about Miss Moore is that such receptivity as hers—though it reaches perhaps its highest degree in her example—is not Miss Moore's exclusive property. Every poem of hers lifts us toward our own discovery-prone lives. It does not state, in effect, that I am more intelligent than you, more creative because I found this item and used it and you didn't. It seems to say, rather, I found this, and what did you find? Or, better, what *can* you find?

Miss Moore's critical intelligence is not destructive, as criticism is almost always taken to be, but positive in the richest and best sense. As a result of its use, who knows better than she how sheerly *experienceable* the world is, and in how many ways and on how many levels? She has asked, and the world has answered, for it understands, in all its billions of parts, how to answer when questions are rightly put.

This is Miss Moore's first book of poems since 1959, and it is probably the finest of them all. It is, of course, much like her others, for she is not the kind of writer who goes through phases, but rather one who deepens down into what she already was: a poet of surprising particulars that also happen to be true. Here, some of her particulars are large, like the Brooklyn Bridge, and some are small, like the bear in the old Frank Buck animal-trapping film she saw. (And, come to think of it, "Bring 'Em Back Alive" is not an unrevealing way to characterize Miss Moore's poetic method, either.) What you find out from these new poems is what Miss Moore has learned from in the last seven years: what she has read, what ball-players she has watched, what museums and zoos she has gone to, what people she has talked to.

In one poem, for example, she juxtaposes a quotation from Sir Kenneth Clark's "Leonardo da Vinci," another from da Vinci's own notebooks and a statement by da Vinci that Henry Noss, a history professor at New York University, cited in a television lecture. These become entities which strike whole showers of fresh sparks from each other, and one feels that their conjunction is possible only because Miss Moore so thoroughly understands, by an act of the acutest intelligence, these quotations in all their expressive possibilities, and not simply in the contexts in which they originally occurred: she knows what

Moore at 35 West Ninth Street, dressed for Truman Capote's "Black and White Dance," at the Plaza Hotel on 28 November 1966

they are *all* about, instead of merely what they think they are all about.

Informing Miss Moore's work is a lovely, discriminating and enthusiastic involvement with the way things are: *are*. In her poem to the Brooklyn Bridge, it is part of her involvement to know as much as she can learn about the engineer who built the bridge, and also something of the purely technical problems of its construction: to know what a "catenary curve" is. As it turns out, this "curve formed by a rope or a cable hanging freely between two fixed points of support" is not only interesting in itself, it becomes a poetic as well as an engineering term: the next time you ride by it or on it or see a picture of it, feel how the bridge deepens not only its structural Thereness for you, but its range of suggestiveness as well, being now a construction as much like a poem as a bridge, and requiring on both levels its own lawns, its own initiates.

In her "burning desire to be explicit," Miss Moore tells us that facts make her feel "profoundly grateful." This is because knowledge, for her, is not power but love, and in loving it is important to know *what* you love, as widely and as deeply and as well as possible. In paying so very much attention to the things of this earth that she encounters, or that encounter her, Miss Moore urges us to do the same, and thus gives us back, in strict syllabics, the selves that we had contrived to lose. She persuades us that the human mind is nothing more or less than an organ for loving things in both complicated and blindingly simple ways, and is organized so as to be able to love in an unlimited number of fashions and for an unlimited number of reasons. This seems to me to constitute the correct poetic attitude, which is essentially a life-attitude, for it stands forever against the notion that the earth is an apathetic limbo lost in space.

Who knows of Heaven? It may be only the convenient fiction of a reviewer, after all. But whatever her labors in the realm of the celestial–and I personally would never discount the possibility of their existence–one thing is certain: Miss Moore is making our earth.

BOOK REVIEW:
John Ashbery, "Straight Lines over Rough Terrain," *New York Times Book Review,* 26 November 1967, pp. 1, 42.

With the appearance of her Complete Poems *in 1967, Moore entered her eighth decade, continuing to write, give readings, and attract critics such as the poet John Ashbery. However, in offering a "complete" poems, she teased her readers by including only 120 of her 190 published poems. Moore's tendency to revise by deletion never left her.*

It is more than 30 years since Marianne Moore published her "Selected Poems"; 15 years ago she gave us her "Collected Poems," and now, in the month of her 80th birthday, "Complete Poems" appears. If this sounds inexorable, one should note that Miss Moore shows no sign of abandoning poetry: the new book has new poems and new versions of old ones (notably a reworking of "The Steeple-Jack" which not only restores the drastic cuts made in the "Collected Poems" version, but actually adds to and improves on the seemingly unbeatable 1935 text of this masterpiece). There seems no reason not to look forward to "More Complete Poems"; as long as we can ask, like the student in her poem of that title, "When will your experiment be finished? we may expect the reply, "Science is never finished."

In reviewing her last collection a year ago, I wrote that "Marianne Moore is, with the possible exception of Pound and Auden, the greatest living poet in English." After rereading her in this magnificent volume (which reprints all her books of poetry starting with "Selected Poems" as well as a handful of uncollected poems and selections from the La Fontaine translations), I am tempted simply to call her our greatest modern poet. This despite the obvious grandeur of her chief competitors, including Wallace Stevens and William Carlos Williams. It seems we can never remind ourselves too often that universality and depth are not the same thing. Marianne Moore has no *Arma virumque cano* prefacing her work: she even avoids formal beginnings altogether by running the first line in as a continuation of the title. But her work will, I think, continue to be read as poetry when much of the major poetry of our time has become part of the history of literature.

Yet it seems to me that we underestimate Miss Moore. True, Eliot placed her work in "that small body of durable poetry written in our time," and others have concurred; but there is a point at which her importance gets lost in the welter of minutiae that people her poems, and in the unassuming but also rather unglamorous wisdom that flashes out between descriptions of bizarre fauna and rare artifacts. Is she not a sort of Mary Poppins of poetry, or, to state the case against her as quickly as possible, an American La Fontaine, who, great poet that he is, always seems on the verge of becoming a tiresome moralist like Joubert or even Poor Richard? Prudence and good judgment are not virtues we associate with the highest poetry, and here is Miss Moore telling us that she distrusts "merits" (so do we); that "A mirror-of-steel uninsistence should countenance / continence"; that "Truth is no Apollo / Belvedere, no formal thing"; that "the deepest feeling always shows itself in silence; / not in silence, but restraint."

Caution, healthy disrespect, restraint: is this the way of poetry? She is the opposite of a mystic, and it is hard to believe that there can be poetry without a grain of mysticism, a dark corner somewhere. But Miss Moore is explicit:

complexity is not a crime,
but carry it to the point of murkiness
and nothing is plain. Com-
plexity, moreover, that has been
committed to darkness, instead of

granting itself to be the pestilence
that it is, moves all a-
bout as if to bewilder us with the
dismal
fallacy that insistence
is the measure of achievement
and that all truth must be dark.

And again:

The opaque allusion, the simulated
flight upward, accomplishes
nothing.

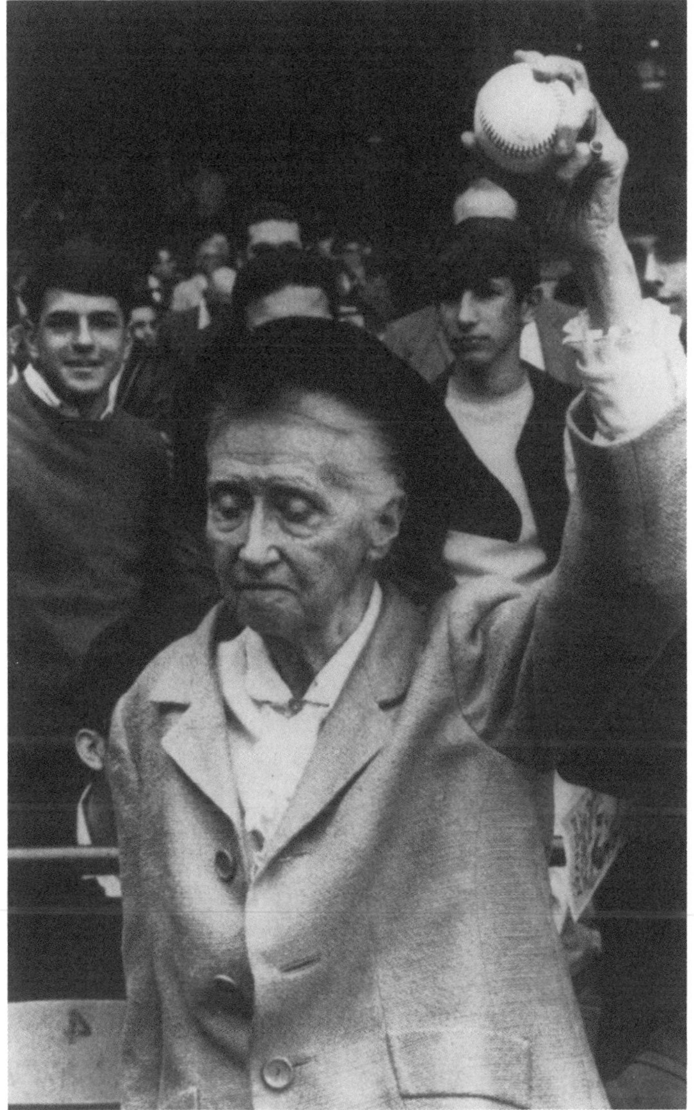

Moore throwing out the first ball on opening day at Yankee Stadium, 1968

This is strong language, but strong not exactly in the way we expect from great poetry, which has never, including Milton, been overly concerned with setting the record straight and sending the reader about his business. Without, however, suggesting that there is in Miss Moore's work a strain counter to the sentiments she *seems* to be expressing here (and of course, we should not assume that they are hers merely because she uses the form of direct address), that the swarming details, each one crystal clear, often add up not merely to complexity but to a "darkness" which gives contours to her "truth"–without going this far, one can still note that all here is not so modest, cheerful and brightly lit as the lines I have quoted seem to imply. She is not a moralist or an antiquarian, but a poet writing on many levels at once to produce work of an irreducible symphonic texture. If "restraint" is really an animating force in her poetry, then it is a strange kind of restraint indeed.

When we examine any of the poems that comprise the Moore canon–poems like "The Steeple-Jack," "The Fish," "Novices," "Marriage," "The Monkeys," "Bowls," "In the Days of Prismatic Color"–we are brought up against a mastery which defies attempts to analyze it, an intelligence which plays just beyond our reach. They start smoothly and calmly enough ("The monkeys winked too much and were afraid of the snakes") like a ride on a roller coaster, and in no time at all one is clutching the bar with both hands, excited and dismayed at the prospect of "ending up in the decor," as the French say of a car that drives off the road. And, not infrequently, this happens. I will never be entirely certain of what "it" is in "The Fish."

Repeated
evidence has proved that it
can live
on what can not revive
its youth. The sea
grows old in it.

And there are other cases in which I become aware before the end of a poem that Miss Moore and I have parted company somewhat further back. Sometimes, as in "The Jerboa," the author has her say and retires, leaving you in the company of some curious little rodent. And her mode of address can be misleading: toward the end of "To Statecraft Embalmed" you become aware that she is no longer addressing an ibis, or even you, the reader; for the last minute she has been gazing absently at something terribly important just over your left ear.

These are not the manners of a governess, whether endowed with magic powers or not. "There is something attractive about a mind that moves in a straight line," and though Marianne Moore's mind moves in a straight line, it does so over a terrain that is far from level. Only something like alchemy could account for the miracle of some of these poems, such as "An Octopus" which is for me perhaps the greatest of all of them. We start with an octopus, evoked with the customary precision ("dots of cyclamen-red and maroon on its clearly defined pseudopodia"), but the creature seems to be a glacier or else the two are superimposed, for now we are in a landscape of sierras and fir trees, while the author continues tacking imperturbably among excerpts from Ruskin, The Illustrated London News, The London Graphic, The National Parks Portfolio and a remark overheard at the circus, switching landscapes, language and levels with breathtaking abruptness, rising from botanical note-taking to pinpoint emblems of supernatural clarity that could be out of Shelley:

the white volcano with no
weather side;
the lightning flashing at its
base,
rain falling in the valleys, and
snow falling on the peak–

We can now appreciate the full extent of her disdain for "the simulated flight upward."

Perhaps it is in her translations of La Fontaine, which I confess I prefer to the originals, that one sees most clearly her gift for language making, for creating something where nothing was before. This sounds like a paradox since the poems are after all translations, but in trying to find an equivalent tone for La Fontaine's she happened on a new language–new to poetry and new to her, since she had to abandon her glittering, allusive style to hoe the straight row of the original. And yet her speech, strict as it is, resounds with allusions and untapped possibilities. At the same time she has laid the hardheaded, bourgeois ghost that hovers over the "Fables" even at their happiest–Miss Moore's verses are snug but not smug. And the earlier poems tell us why: it is not La Fontaine who would have appended this moral to a poem: "The passion for setting people right is in itself an afflictive disease / Distaste which takes no credit to itself is best." Nor would he have written: "one is not rich but poor / when one can always seem so right."

In short one can never be sure precisely what she is up to; like the unidentified protagonist of "In This Age of Hard Trying, Nonchalance Is Good And . . ." whose "byplay was more terrible in its effectiveness / than the fiercest frontal attack," she has set about poetry with all the tools at her disposal. Common sense is just one, so are intelligence and integrity that dazzle, an eye and ear that are almost magical in their power to recreate reality for us, and a mastery of form that outpaces the most devoted reader. All of these are brought to bear, as through a prism, on the amorphous "world" that surrounds us; the result is poetry in the almost-satisfactory definition of Théodore de Banville, which Gide quotes in the preface to his "Anthology of French Poetry": "That magic which consists in awakening sensations with the help of a combination of sounds . . . that sorcery by which ideas are necessarily communicated to us, in a definite way, by words which nevertheless do not express them." Or, as Miss Moore says more succinctly: "Ecstasy affords the occasion and expediency determines the form."

OBITUARY:

"Marianne Moore, Pulitzer Poet, Dies; Laureate of '52 Often Hailed Baseball," with Alden Whitman, "Shaper of Subtle Images," *New York Times*, 7 February 1972, p. 40.

Moore suffered several strokes in her last years, but observers noted that even after she could no longer speak, her spirit remained undaunted. When he received a cable announcing her death, Ezra Pound, aged eighty-six, organized a memorial service for Moore in Venice. Pound chose to read Moore's poem "What Are Years" at the service.

Marianne Moore, the prize-winning poet, died in her sleep Saturday at her home, 35 West Ninth Street. She was 84 years old last Nov. 15.

For nearly two years, Miss Moore had been a semi-invalid following a series of strokes and two nurses attended her, each taking a 12-hour shift.

The body will be on view in the Alexander chapel of the First Presbyterian Church, 7 West 11th Street, from 4 to 6 P. M. and 7 to 9 P. M. tomorrow.

It will be on view on Tuesday from 9:30 to 11:30 A. M. in the Underwood chapel of the Lafayette Avenue Presbyterian Church, Lafayette Avenue and Oxford Street, Brooklyn.

The funeral service will take place in the Brooklyn church at 1 P.M. on Tuesday.

Miss Moore told Mr. Driver some time ago that she wanted no flowers at the service. Instead she asked that funds be given to the Camperdown Foundation, 104 Prospect Park West, Brooklyn, for the purpose of planting and care of trees in Prospect Park in Brooklyn and Central Park in Manhattan.

Miss Moore is survived by a brother, Capt. John Warner Moore, Navy, retired, of Greenwich, Conn.

Shaper of Subtle Images

A writer with the dazzling ability to describe things as if she were observing them for the first time and with a remarkable talent for subtle imagery, Marianne Craig Moore was one of the country's most laureled poets and among its most ingenuous talkers and public personalities.

Indeed, Miss Moore, the personality, was more extensively known than Miss Moore, the poet, for she was an inveterate frequenter of concerts, balls, parties, fashion shows, unveilings, public receptions, lecture platforms, grocery shops, department stores, subway trains, baseball parks, exhibitions of boxing and literary salons.

A slight (5 feet 3 1/2 inches) woman with luminous, inquisitive blue-gray eyes, she was immediately recognizable for her invariable attire–a cape and a tricorn hat. "I like the tricorn shape," she explained, "because it conceals the defects of the head."

Her tricorn (she had dozens that shape) was, after middle age, perched on a braid of gray hair that she wrapped around her head and held in place with a celluloid hairpin. Her face, likened to that of an angelic Mary Poppins, was once round and soft, and although lines of age creased it over the years, it never lost its glow.

Her conversation, which tended to breakneck monologue, was notable for its diversity. Sometimes it seemed that she was as discursive and as superficial as a teen-ager, but this was deceptive, for her associative mode of thought had a way of coming to a profound (or at least important) point by the time she stopped talking. Her remarks, delivered in a Middle Western drawl, charmed and enthralled persons as disparate as Casey Stengel, E. E. Cummings and John Hay Whitney, about whose horse Tom Fool she wrote a poem. It read in part:

"You've the beat of a dancer to a measure or harmonious rush of a porpoise at the prow where the racers all win easily."

Saw Herself as 'Observer'

Although T. S. Eliot, expressing a generally held view, once remarked that "her poems form part of the small body of durable poetry written in our time," and although W. H. Auden confessed to pilfering from her, Miss Moore did not think of herself as a poet in the popular sense, one who wrote resonant sonnets, epics and odes. She was "an observer," she said, who put down what she saw.

"In fact, the only reason I know for calling my work poetry at all is that there is no other category in which to put it," she said on one occasion, adding:

"I'm a happy hack as a writer."

Few agreed with this self-disparagement, for Miss Moore was a painstaking craftsman whose verse, which she composed in a spidery hand, was notable for its rhythms and for its use of homely speech.

"I think the thing that attracted me to put things in verse was rhythm," she told an interviewer on her 75th birthday in 1962. "Someone

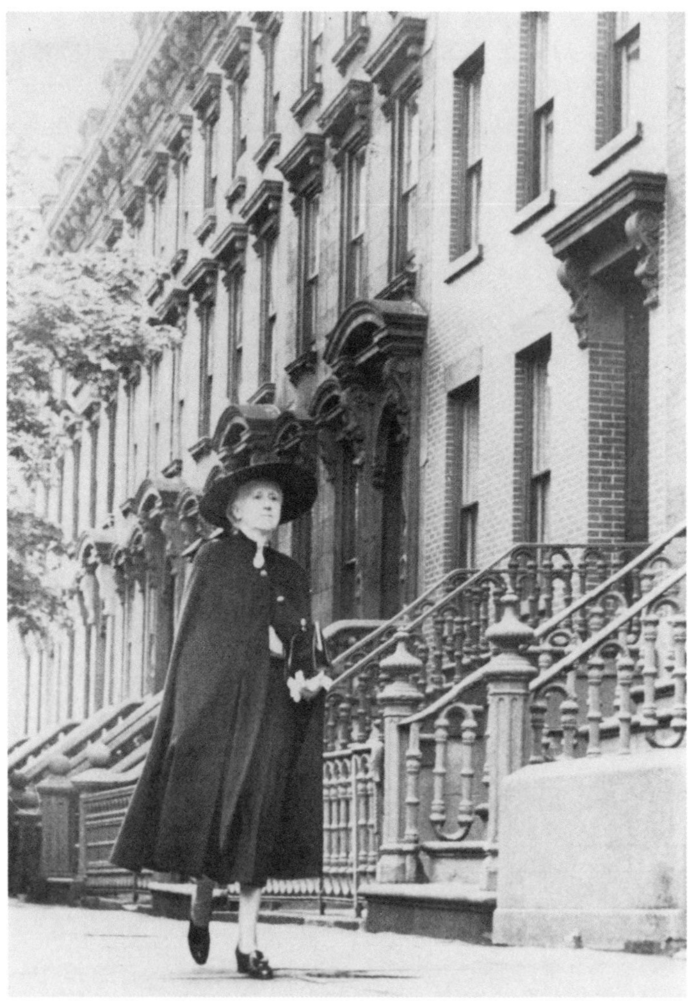

Marianne Moore

said the accents should be set so it would be impossible for any reader to get them wrong. If you can read it in 10 different ways, it's no good. That's very important to me.

"There are patterns in verse, just as you have restatement after contrast in music–as you have in Bach particularly. Also, I admire the legerdemain of saying a lot in a few words."

Miss Moore's poems utilized rhythms to create moods as well as to convey her admiration of such no-nonsense virtues as patience, firmness, courage, loyalty, modesty and independence. Much of her writing in this vein was a wry but gentle criticism of human conduct, literature and art, sometimes presented in unusual or baffling typographical arrangements. She made her point obliquely, for animals and plants rather then people were usually the formal subjects of her verse.

Some thought her poetry cold and austere because it seemed so detached from human life, but Miss Moore insisted that she wrote with affection. "She is a naturalist without pedantry, and a moralist without harshness," was the verdict of Louise Bogan, the critic.

Miss Moore's compact verse was not always easy to read or to comprehend, even though she professed "a burning desire to be explicit"; but for those who might have preferred the obvious she has this answer.

"It ought to be work to read something that was work to write."

Miss Moore took pride in catching attention with the first lines of her poems. "I am very careful with my first lines," she advised a questioner. "I put it down. I scrutinize it. I test it. I evaluate it."

One of her poems, "Values in Use," illustrates her concept of a catchy opening, as well as her economy of phrase and her use of aphorism to make an ironic and faintly pessimistic thrust. It reads:

I attended school and I liked the place–
grass and little locust-leaf shadows like lace.
Writing was discussed. They said, "We create
values in the process of living. daren't await
their historical progress." Be abstract
and you'll wish you'd been specific; it's a fact.
What was I studying? Values in use,
"Judged on their own ground." Am I still abstruse?
Walking along, a student said offhand,
" 'Relevant' and 'plausible' were words I understand."
A pleasing statement, anonymous friend.
Certainly the means must not defeat the end.

In some of her other verse the poet celebrated the weak as standing off a hostile natural environment, as she did in this fragment from "Nevertheless":

The weak overcomes its
menace, the strong over-
comes itself. What is there
like fortitude! What sap
went through the little thread
to make the cherry red?

As poets go, Miss Moore was unprolific. Only 120 poems, occupying 242 pages, were in "The Complete Poems of Marianne Moore," published by Viking Press and Macmillan for her 80th birthday in 1967. In addition to this fruit of more than 50 years, there were nine translations in verse from "The Fables of La Fontaine."

She labored to compose, "fiddling," she called it, going over and over each poem until she was satisfied of its perfection for her. This accounted for much of the intricate detail in the verse, its quality of seeming like an exquisite needle-point embroidery.

Miss Moore's gift for magical words was enlisted in 1955 by the Ford Motor Company in a quest for a name "for a rather important new series of cars." In the exchange of letters, subsequently published in The New Yorker magazine, she suggested The Ford Silver Sword, Hurricane Hirundo, The Impeccable, The Ford Fabergé, The Resilient Bullet, The Intelligent Whale, The Arcenciel, Regna Racer, Varsity Stroke, Cresta Lark, Chaparral and The Turtletopper.

Final Letter

The final letter in the exchange, from Ford, said:

"We have chosen a name [that] fails somewhat of the resonance, gaiety and zest we were seeking. But it has a personal dignity and meaning to many of us here. Our name, dear Miss Moore, is –Edsel. I hope you will understand."

(Edsel was a son of Henry Ford, founder of the company. The car that bore his name failed for lack of sales.)

For 37 years, from 1929 to 1966, the poet lived in a snug fifth-floor apartment at 260 Cumberland Street, in the Fort Greene section of Brooklyn. It was crammed with books and bric-a-brac–porcelain and ivory animals, a walrus tusk, prints and paintings, shells and feathers, old coins.

The kitchen, though, was sparsely furnished ("I cook only the essentials–meat and potatoes. I've never baked a pie") but it contained a vegetable squeezer in which Miss Moore made her own carrot juice, a libation of which she was fond. "Carrot juice increases vigor," she explained.

As Miss Moore's renown increased, her apartment was seldom without visitors–poets, artists, critics, admirers. Reluctantly, when the neighborhood became unsafe, she moved to Ninth Street in Greenwich Village in June, 1966.

Miss Moore's rise to eminence was slow. She was the daughter of John Milton and Mary Warner Moore and was born in Kirkwood, Mo., a suburb of St. Louis, on Nov. 15, 1887. She never knew her father, a construction engineer, who was institutionalized before her birth. After a brief stay with relatives, Mrs. Moore took Marianne and John, her elder brother, to Carlisle, Pa., where the mother taught in Metzger Institute, now a part of Dickinson College.

Marianne was sent to Bryn Mawr, where for lack of aptitude in English she studied biology and contributed some ephemeral verse to the literary monthly. Upon graduation in 1909 she took courses in typing and shorthand at the Carlisle Commercial College and then got a job teaching these subjects at the Carlisle Indian School. One of her pupils, before she resigned in 1916, was Jim Thorpe, the athlete.

Her Brother a Chaplain

Miss Moore moved to Chatham, N.J., to help keep house for her brother, a Presbyterian minister and later a Navy chaplain. In 1918, when he joined the Navy, she and her mother went to New York, where they lived for 11 years in an apartment on St. Luke's Place in Greenwich Village.

After a stint as secretary to a girls' school, Miss Moore became, in 1921, assistant librarian at the Hudson Park Branch of the New York Public Library, a post she filled until 1925.

Meanwhile, her first serious verse was published in The Egoist, a London magazine in which the Imagists were influential, and in Harriet Monroe's Poetry magazine in Chicago. The poems had a select, but impressed, readership, and in 1921 H.D. (Hilda Doolittle) and Bryher (Winifred Ellerman), the historical novelist, collected and published these works in a small volume called "Poems." It was issued in London without Miss Moore's knowledge.

The poems, with some later additions, were printed as "Observations" in the United States in 1925, winning for their author her first literary prize, the Dial Award, and enthusiastic critical notices. Edwin Seaver's review in The Nation, which was typical, said:

"In respect to her work Miss Moore hews to an ideology that is aristocratic and severe and pure. Against the commonplace and the easy her subtlety of sarcasm is devastating."

Now an established writer, Miss Moore left her library job to join the staff of The Dial, first as acting editor and then as editor. She remained with the magazine, one of the great literary periodicals of its day, until it expired in 1929.

After moving to Brooklyn that year with her mother, Miss Moore devoted herself to writing and published "Selected Poems" in 1935, winning the Ernest Hartsock Memorial Prize. The verses, The New York Times said, were "positive and exhilarating."

More encomiums greeted "What Are Years" when it appeared in 1941. Malcolm Cowley, for example, described the title poem as "among the noblest lyrics of our time."

With each succeeding slim book, Miss Moore fattened the list of her awards–the Harriet Monroe Poetry Award in 1944, a Guggenheim Fellowship in 1945, a joint grant from the American Academy of Arts and Letters and the National Institute of Arts and Letters in 1946, the Bollingen Prize in Poetry in 1952, the National Book Award for Poetry and the Pulitzer Prize the same year, the M. Carey Thomas Memorial Award in 1953, the Gold Medal of the National Institutes of Arts and Letters in 1953, the MacDowell Medal in 1967.

Honored for Translation

In addition, France gave her the Croix de Chevalier des Arts et Lettres for her translation of "The Fables of La Fontaine." She also held honorary degrees from at least eight colleges.

Despite all these honors, Miss Moore remained unaffected, saying, "There's nothing very special about me." She played tennis with neighborhood children in Fort Greene Park, rode the subway to and from appointments and became a fiery rooter for the Brooklyn Dodgers baseball team, whose feats she extolled in verse. When the Dodgers deserted Brooklyn for Los Angeles she changed her allegiance to the Yankees.

Miss Moore had become hooked on the Dodgers (and on baseball) after a friend had taken her to Ebbets Field in 1949. "These men are natural artists," she recalled in 1962. "Why, I remember Don Zimmer playing at third base. He was moving toward the home plate when a fly came toward him. He had to get back to third and he backhanded it with his left hand."

Miss Moore was as cryptic a lecturer as she was a conversationalist, and she appeared to enjoy herself immensely, whether she talked at Harvard or to a woman's club. At one woman's club meeting she read some of her verse that included a line dealing with "metaphysical newmown hay." Afterward, a listener demanded to know what kind of hay that was.

In a patient tone of voice, the poet replied:

"Oh, something like a sudden whiff of fragrance in contrast with a doggedly continuous opposition to spontaneous conversation that had gone before."

Cumulative Index

DLB before number: *Dictionary of Literary Biography,* Volumes 1-90
Y before number: *Dictionary of Literary Biography Yearbook,* 1980-1988
DS before number: *Dictionary of Literary Biography Documentary Series,* Volumes 1-7

Cumulative Index

Dictionary of Literary Biography, Volumes 1-90
Dictionary of Literary Biography Yearbook, 1980-1988
Dictionary of Literary Biography Documentary Series, Volumes 1-7

Cumulative Index

DLB before number: *Dictionary of Literary Biography,* Volumes 1-90
Y before number: *Dictionary of Literary Biography Yearbook,* 1980-1988
DS before number: *Dictionary of Literary Biography Documentary Series,* Volumes 1-7

A

Abbey Press....DLB-49
The Abbey Theatre and Irish Drama, 1900-1945....DLB-10
Abbot, Willis J. 1863-1934....DLB-29
Abbott, Jacob 1803-1879....DLB-1
Abbott, Lyman 1835-1922....DLB-79
Abbott, Robert S. 1868-1940....DLB-29
Abelard-Schuman....DLB-46
Abell, Arunah S. 1806-1888....DLB-43
Abercrombie, Lascelles 1881-1938....DLB-19
Abrams, M. H. 1912- DLB-67
Abse, Dannie 1923- DLB-27
Academy Chicago Publishers....DLB-46
Ace Books....DLB-46
Acorn, Milton 1923-1986....DLB-53
Acosta, Oscar Zeta 1935?- DLB-82
Actors Theatre of Louisville....DLB-7
Adair, James 1709?-1783?....DLB-30
Adame, Leonard 1947- DLB-82
Adamic, Louis 1898-1951....DLB-9
Adams, Alice 1926- Y-86
Adams, Brooks 1848-1927....DLB-47
Adams, Charles Francis, Jr. 1835-1915....DLB-47
Adams, Douglas 1952- Y-83
Adams, Franklin P. 1881-1960....DLB-29
Adams, Henry 1838-1918....DLB-12, 47
Adams, Herbert Baxter 1850-1901....DLB-47
Adams, J. S. and C. [publishing house]....DLB-49
Adams, James Truslow 1878-1949....DLB-17
Adams, John 1735-1826....DLB-31
Adams, John Quincy 1767-1848....DLB-37
Adams, Léonie 1899-1988 ....DLB-48
Adams, Samuel 1722-1803....DLB-31, 43
Adams, William Taylor 1822-1897....DLB-42
Adcock, Fleur 1934- DLB-40
Ade, George 1866-1944....DLB-11, 25
Adeler, Max (see Clark, Charles Heber)
Advance Publishing Company....DLB-49
AE 1867-1935....DLB-19
Aesthetic Poetry (1873), by Walter Pater....DLB-35
Afro-American Literary Critics: An Introduction....DLB-33
Agassiz, Jean Louis Rodolphe 1807-1873....DLB-1
Agee, James 1909-1955....DLB-2, 26
Aichinger, Ilse 1921- DLB-85
Aiken, Conrad 1889-1973....DLB-9, 45
Ainsworth, William Harrison 1805-1882....DLB-21
Aitken, Robert [publishing house]....DLB-49
Akins, Zoë 1886-1958....DLB-26
Alain-Fournier 1886-1914....DLB-65
Alba, Nanina 1915-1968....DLB-41
Albee, Edward 1928- DLB-7
Alcott, Amos Bronson 1799-1888....DLB-1
Alcott, Louisa May 1832-1888....DLB-1, 42, 79
Alcott, William Andrus 1798-1859....DLB-1
Alden, Henry Mills 1836-1919....DLB-79
Alden, Isabella 1841-1930....DLB-42
Alden, John B. [publishing house]....DLB-49
Alden, Beardsley and Company....DLB-49
Aldington, Richard 1892-1962....DLB-20, 36
Aldis, Dorothy 1896-1966....DLB-22
Aldiss, Brian W. 1925- DLB-14
Aldrich, Thomas Bailey 1836-1907 ....DLB-42, 71, 74, 79
Alexander, Charles Wesley [publishing house]....DLB-49

Alexander, James 1691-1756 ....DLB-24
Alexander, Lloyd 1924- DLB-52
Alger, Horatio, Jr. 1832-1899 ....DLB-42
Algonquin Books of Chapel Hill DLB-46
Algren, Nelson 1909-1981 ....DLB-9; Y-81, 82
Allan, Andrew 1907-1974 ....DLB-88
Allan, Ted 1916- DLB-68
Allbeury, Ted 1917- DLB-87
Alldritt, Keith 1935- DLB-14
Allen, Ethan 1738-1789 ....DLB-31
Allen, George 1808-1876 ....DLB-59
Allen, Grant 1848-1899 ....DLB-70
Allen, Henry W. 1912- Y-85
Allen, Hervey 1889-1949 ....DLB-9, 45
Allen, James 1739-1808 ....DLB-31
Allen, James Lane 1849-1925 ....DLB-71
Allen, Jay Presson 1922- DLB-26
Allen, John, and Company DLB-49
Allen, Samuel W. 1917- DLB-41
Allen, Woody 1935- DLB-44
Allingham, Margery 1904-1966 ....DLB-77
Allingham, William 1824-1889 ....DLB-35
Allison, W. L. [publishing house] DLB-49
Allott, Kenneth 1912-1973 ....DLB-20
Allston, Washington 1779-1843 ....DLB-1
Alsop, George 1636-post 1673 ....DLB-24
Alsop, Richard 1761-1815 ....DLB-37
Altemus, Henry, and Company DLB-49
Altenberg, Peter 1885-1919 ....DLB-81
Alurista 1947- DLB-82
Alvarez, A. 1929- DLB-14, 40
Ambler, Eric 1909- DLB-77
America: or, a Poem on the Settlement of the British Colonies (1780?), by Timothy Dwight DLB-37
American Conservatory Theatre DLB-7
American Fiction and the 1930s DLB-9
American Humor: A Historical Survey
East and Northeast
South and Southwest
Midwest
West DLB-11
American News Company DLB-49
The American Poets' Corner: The First Three Years (1983-1986) Y-86
American Publishing Company DLB-49
American Stationers' Company DLB-49
American Sunday-School Union DLB-49
American Temperance Union DLB-49
American Tract Society DLB-49
The American Writers Congress (9-12 October 1981) Y-81
The American Writers Congress: A Report on Continuing Business Y-81
Ames, Fisher 1758-1808 ....DLB-37
Ames, Mary Clemmer 1831-1884 ....DLB-23
Amini, Johari M. 1935- DLB-41
Amis, Kingsley 1922- DLB-15, 27
Amis, Martin 1949- DLB-14
Ammons, A. R. 1926- DLB-5
Amory, Thomas 1691?-1788 ....DLB-39
Anaya, Rudolfo A. 1937- DLB-82
Andersch, Alfred 1914-1980 ....DLB-69
Anderson, Margaret 1886-1973 ....DLB-4
Anderson, Maxwell 1888-1959 ....DLB-7
Anderson, Patrick 1915-1979 ....DLB-68
Anderson, Paul Y. 1893-1938 ....DLB-29
Anderson, Poul 1926- DLB-8
Anderson, Robert 1917- DLB-7
Anderson, Sherwood 1876-1941 ....DLB-4, 9, 86; DS-1
Andreas-Salomé, Lou 1861-1937 ....DLB-66
Andres, Stefan 1906-1970 ....DLB-69
Andrews, Charles M. 1863-1943 ....DLB-17
Andrews, Miles Peter ?-1814 ....DLB-89
Andrieux, Louis (see Aragon, Louis)
Andrian, Leopold von 1875-1951 ....DLB-81
Andrus, Silas, and Son DLB-49
Angell, James Burrill 1829-1916 ....DLB-64
Angelou, Maya 1928- DLB-38
The "Angry Young Men" DLB-15
Anhalt, Edward 1914- DLB-26
Anners, Henry F. [publishing house] DLB-49
Anthony, Piers 1934- DLB-8

Anthony Burgess's *99 Novels:* An Opinion Poll Y-84
Antin, Mary 1881-1949 ......Y-84
Antschel, Paul (see Celan, Paul)
Apodaca, Rudy S. 1939- DLB-82
Appleton, D., and Company DLB-49
Appleton-Century-Crofts DLB-46
Apple-wood Books DLB-46
Aquin, Hubert 1929-1977 ......DLB-53
Aragon, Louis 1897-1982 ......DLB-72
Arbor House Publishing Company DLB-46
Arcadia House DLB-46
Arce, Julio G. (see Ulica, Jorge)
Archer, William 1856-1924 ......DLB-10
Arden, John 1930- DLB-13
Arden of Faversham DLB-62
The Arena Publishing Company DLB-49
Arena Stage DLB-7
Arensberg, Ann 1937- Y-82
Arias, Ron 1941- DLB-82
Arland, Marcel 1899-1986 ......DLB-72
Arlen, Michael 1895-1956 ......DLB-36, 77
Armed Services Editions DLB-46
Arndt, Ernst Moritz 1769-1860 ......DLB-90
Arnim, Achim von 1781-1831 ......DLB-90
Arnim, Bettina von 1785-1859 ......DLB-90
Arno Press DLB-46
Arnold, Edwin 1832-1904 ......DLB-35
Arnold, Matthew 1822-1888 ......DLB-32, 57
Arnold, Thomas 1795-1842 ......DLB-55
Arnow, Harriette Simpson 1908-1986 ......DLB-6
Arp, Bill (see Smith, Charles Henry)
Arthur, Timothy Shay 1809-1885 ......DLB-3, 42, 79
Artmann, H. C. 1921- DLB-85
As I See It, by Carolyn Cassady DLB-16
Asch, Nathan 1902-1964 ......DLB-4, 28
Ash, John 1948- DLB-40
Ashbery, John 1927- DLB-5; Y-81
Asher, Sandy 1942- Y-83
Ashton, Winifred (see Dane, Clemence)
Asimov, Isaac 1920- DLB-8
Atheneum Publishers DLB-46
Atherton, Gertrude 1857-1948 ......DLB-9, 78
Atkins, Josiah circa 1755-1781 ......DLB-31
Atkins, Russell 1926- DLB-41
The Atlantic Monthly Press DLB-46
Attaway, William 1911-1986 ......DLB-76
Atwood, Margaret 1939- DLB-53
Aubert, Alvin 1930- DLB-41
Aubin, Penelope 1685-circa 1731 ......DLB-39
Aubrey-Fletcher, Henry Lancelot (see Wade, Henry)
Auchincloss, Louis 1917- DLB-2; Y-80
Auden, W. H. 1907-1973 ......DLB-10, 20
Audio Art in America: A Personal Memoir Y-85
Auernheimer, Raoul 1876-1948 ......DLB-81
Austin, Alfred 1835-1913 ......DLB-35
Austin, Mary 1868-1934 ......DLB-9, 78
Austin, William 1778-1841 ......DLB-74
The Author's Apology for His Book (1684), by John Bunyan DLB-39
An Author's Response, by Ronald Sukenick Y-82
Authors and Newspapers Association DLB-46
Authors' Publishing Company DLB-49
Avalon Books DLB-46
Avendaño, Fausto 1941- DLB-82
Avison, Margaret 1918- DLB-53
Avon Books DLB-46
Ayckbourn, Alan 1939- DLB-13
Aymé, Marcel 1902-1967 ......DLB-72
Aytoun, William Edmondstoune 1813-1865 ......DLB-32

B

Babbitt, Irving 1865-1933 ......DLB-63
Babbitt, Natalie 1932- DLB-52
Babcock, John [publishing house] DLB-49
Bache, Benjamin Franklin 1769-1798 ......DLB-43
Bachmann, Ingeborg 1926-1973 ......DLB-85
Bacon, Delia 1811-1859 ......DLB-1
Bacon, Thomas circa 1700-1768 ......DLB-31
Badger, Richard G., and Company DLB-49
Bage, Robert 1728-1801 ......DLB-39

Bagehot, Walter 1826-1877 ....DLB-55
Bagley, Desmond 1923-1983 ....DLB-87
Bagnold, Enid 1889-1981 ....DLB-13
Bahr, Hermann 1863-1934 ....DLB-81
Bailey, Alfred Goldsworthy 1905- DLB-68
Bailey, Francis [publishing house] DLB-49
Bailey, H. C. 1878-1961 ....DLB-77
Bailey, Paul 1937- DLB-14
Bailey, Philip James 1816-1902 ....DLB-32
Baillargeon, Pierre 1916-1967 ....DLB-88
Baillie, Hugh 1890-1966 ....DLB-29
Bailyn, Bernard 1922- DLB-17
Bainbridge, Beryl 1933- DLB-14
Baird, Irene 1901-1981 ....DLB-68
The Baker and Taylor Company DLB-49
Baker, Houston A., Jr. 1943- DLB-67
Baker, Walter H., Company ("Baker's Plays") DLB-49
Bald, Wambly 1902- DLB-4
Balderston, John 1889-1954 ....DLB-26
Baldwin, James 1924-1987 ....DLB-2, 7, 33; Y-87
Baldwin, Joseph Glover 1815-1864 ....DLB-3, 11
Ballantine Books DLB-46
Ballard, J. G. 1930- DLB-14
Ballou, Maturin Murray 1820-1895 ....DLB-79
Ballou, Robert O. [publishing house] DLB-46
Bambara, Toni Cade 1939- DLB-38
Bancroft, A. L., and Company DLB-49
Bancroft, George 1800-1891 ....DLB-1, 30, 59
Bancroft, Hubert Howe 1832-1918 ....DLB-47
Bangs, John Kendrick 1862-1922 ....DLB-11, 79
Banks, John circa 1653-1706 ....DLB-80
Bantam Books DLB-46
Banville, John 1945- DLB-14
Baraka, Amiri 1934- DLB-5, 7, 16, 38
Barber, John Warner 1798-1885 ....DLB-30
Barbour, Ralph Henry 1870-1944 ....DLB-22
Barbusse, Henri 1873-1935 ....DLB-65
Barclay, E. E., and Company DLB-49
Bardeen, C. W. [publishing house] DLB-49
Baring, Maurice 1874-1945 ....DLB-34
Barker, A. L. 1918- DLB-14
Barker, George 1913- DLB-20
Barker, Harley Granville 1877-1946 ....DLB-10
Barker, Howard 1946- DLB-13
Barker, James Nelson 1784-1858 ....DLB-37
Barker, Jane 1652-1727? DLB-39
Barks, Coleman 1937- DLB-5
Barlach, Ernst 1870-1938 ....DLB-56
Barlow, Joel 1754-1812 ....DLB-37
Barnard, John 1681-1770 ....DLB-24
Barnes, A. S., and Company DLB-49
Barnes, Djuna 1892-1982 ....DLB-4, 9, 45
Barnes, Margaret Ayer 1886-1967 ....DLB-9
Barnes, Peter 1931- DLB-13
Barnes, William 1801-1886 ....DLB-32
Barnes and Noble Books DLB-46
Barney, Natalie 1876-1972 ....DLB-4
Baron, Richard W., Publishing Company DLB-46
Barr, Robert 1850-1912 ....DLB-70
Barrax, Gerald William 1933- DLB-41
Barrie, James M. 1860-1937 ....DLB-10
Barrio, Raymond 1921- DLB-82
Barry, Philip 1896-1949 ....DLB-7
Barse and Hopkins DLB-46
Barstow, Stan 1928- DLB-14
Barth, John 1930- DLB-2
Barthelme, Donald 1931-1989 ....DLB-2; Y-80
Barthelme, Frederick 1943- Y-85
Bartlett, John 1820-1905 ....DLB-1
Bartol, Cyrus Augustus 1813-1900 ....DLB-1
Bartram, John 1699-1777 ....DLB-31
Bartram, William 1739-1823 ....DLB-37
Basic Books DLB-46
Bass, T. J. 1932- Y-81
Bassett, John Spencer 1867-1928 ....DLB-17
Bassler, Thomas Joseph (see Bass, T. J.)
Bate, Walter Jackson 1918- DLB-67
Bates, Katharine Lee 1859-1929 ....DLB-71
Baum, L. Frank 1856-1919 ....DLB-22
Baum, Vicki 1888-1960 ....DLB-85
Baumbach, Jonathan 1933- Y-80

Bawden, Nina 1925- DLB-14
Bax, Clifford 1886-1962 ....DLB-10
Bayer, Eleanor (see Perry, Eleanor)
Bayer, Konrad 1932-1964 ....DLB-85
Bazin, Hervé 1911- DLB-83
Beach, Sylvia 1887-1962 ....DLB-4
Beacon Press DLB-49
Beadle and Adams DLB-49
Beagle, Peter S. 1939- Y-80
Beal, M. F. 1937- Y-81
Beale, Howard K. 1899-1959 ....DLB-17
Beard, Charles A. 1874-1948 ....DLB-17
A Beat Chronology: The First Twenty-five Years, 1944-1969 ....DLB-16
Beattie, Ann 1947- Y-82
Beauchemin, Yves 1941- DLB-60
Beaulieu, Victor-Lévy 1945- DLB-53
Beaumont, Francis circa 1584-1616 and Fletcher, John 1579-1625 ....DLB-58
Beauvoir, Simone de 1908-1986 ....Y-86, DLB-72
Becher, Ulrich 1910- DLB-69
Becker, Carl 1873-1945 ....DLB-17
Becker, Jurek 1937- DLB-75
Becker, Jürgen 1932- DLB-75
Beckett, Samuel 1906- DLB-13, 15
Beckford, William 1760-1844 ....DLB-39
Beckham, Barry 1944- DLB-33
Beecher, Catharine Esther 1800-1878 ....DLB-1
Beecher, Henry Ward 1813-1887 ....DLB-3, 43
Beer, George L. 1872-1920 ....DLB-47
Beer, Patricia 1919- DLB-40
Beerbohm, Max 1872-1956 ....DLB-34
Beer-Hofmann, Richard 1866-1945 ....DLB-81
Beers, Henry A. 1847-1926 ....DLB-71
Behan, Brendan 1923-1964 ....DLB-13
Behn, Aphra 1640?-1689 ....DLB-39, 80
Behn, Harry 1898-1973 ....DLB-61
Behrman, S. N. 1893-1973 ....DLB-7, 44
Belasco, David 1853-1931 ....DLB-7
Belford, Clarke and Company DLB-49
Belitt, Ben 1911- DLB-5
Belknap, Jeremy 1744-1798 ....DLB-30, 37
Bell, James Madison 1826-1902 ....DLB-50
Bell, Marvin 1937- DLB-5
Bell, Robert [publishing house] DLB-49
Bellamy, Edward 1850-1898 ....DLB-12
Bellamy, Joseph 1719-1790 ....DLB-31
Belloc, Hilaire 1870-1953 ....DLB-19
Bellow, Saul 1915- DLB-2, 28; Y-82; DS-3
Belmont Productions DLB-46
Bemelmans, Ludwig 1898-1962 ....DLB-22
Bemis, Samuel Flagg 1891-1973 ....DLB-17
Benchley, Robert 1889-1945 ....DLB-11
Benedictus, David 1938- DLB-14
Benedikt, Michael 1935- DLB-5
Benét, Stephen Vincent 1898-1943 ....DLB-4, 48
Benét, William Rose 1886-1950 ....DLB-45
Benford, Gregory 1941- Y-82
Benjamin, Park 1809-1864 ....DLB-3, 59, 73
Benn, Gottfried 1886-1956 ....DLB-56
Bennett, Arnold 1867-1931 ....DLB-10, 34
Bennett, Charles 1899- DLB-44
Bennett, Gwendolyn 1902- DLB-51
Bennett, Hal 1930- DLB-33
Bennett, James Gordon 1795-1872 ....DLB-43
Bennett, James Gordon, Jr. 1841-1918 ....DLB-23
Bennett, John 1865-1956 ....DLB-42
Benoit, Jacques 1941- DLB-60
Benson, Stella 1892-1933 ....DLB-36
Bentley, E. C. 1875-1956 ....DLB-70
Benton, Robert 1932- and Newman, David 1937- DLB-44
Benziger Brothers DLB-49
Beresford, Anne 1929- DLB-40
Beresford-Howe, Constance 1922- DLB-88
Berford, R. G., Company DLB-49
Berg, Stephen 1934- DLB-5
Bergengruen, Werner 1892-1964 ....DLB-56
Berger, John 1926- DLB-14
Berger, Meyer 1898-1959 ....DLB-29
Berger, Thomas 1924- DLB-2; Y-80
Berkeley, Anthony 1893-1971 ....DLB-77

Berkeley, George 1685-1753 .... DLB-31
The Berkley Publishing Corporation DLB-46
Bernal, Vicente J. 1888-1915 .... DLB-82
Bernanos, Georges 1888-1948 .... DLB-72
Bernard, John 1756-1828 .... DLB-37
Bernhard, Thomas 1931-1989 .... DLB-85
Berrigan, Daniel 1921- DLB-5
Berrigan, Ted 1934-1983 .... DLB-5
Berry, Wendell 1934- DLB-5, 6
Berryman, John 1914-1972 .... DLB-48
Bersianik, Louky 1930- DLB-60
Berton, Pierre 1920- DLB-68
Bessette, Gerard 1920- DLB-53
Bessie, Alvah 1904-1985 .... DLB-26
Bester, Alfred 1913- DLB-8
The Bestseller Lists: An Assessment Y-84
Betjeman, John 1906-1984 .... DLB-20; Y-84
Betts, Doris 1932- Y-82
Beveridge, Albert J. 1862-1927 .... DLB-17
Beverley, Robert circa 1673-1722 .... DLB-24, 30
Bichsel, Peter 1935- DLB-75
Bickerstaff, Isaac John 1733-circa 1808 .... DLB-89
Biddle, Drexel [publishing house] DLB-49
Bidwell, Walter Hilliard 1798-1881 .... DLB-79
Bienek, Horst 1930- DLB-75
Bierbaum, Otto Julius 1865-1910 .... DLB-66
Bierce, Ambrose 1842-1914?......DLB-11, 12, 23, 71, 74
Biggle, Lloyd, Jr. 1923- DLB-8
Biglow, Hosea (see Lowell, James Russell)
Billings, Josh (see Shaw, Henry Wheeler)
Binding, Rudolf G. 1867-1938 .... DLB-66
Bingham, Caleb 1757-1817 .... DLB-42
Binyon, Laurence 1869-1943 .... DLB-19
Biographical Documents I Y-84
Biographical Documents II Y-85
Bioren, John [publishing house] DLB-49
Bird, William 1888-1963 .... DLB-4
Birney, Earle 1904- DLB-88
Bishop, Elizabeth 1911-1979 .... DLB-5
Bishop, John Peale 1892-1944 .... DLB-4, 9, 45
Bissett, Bill 1939- DLB-53
Black, David (D. M.) 1941- DLB-40
Black, Walter J. [publishing house] DLB-46
Black, Winifred 1863-1936 .... DLB-25
The Black Arts Movement, by Larry Neal DLB-38
Black Theaters and Theater Organizations in America, 1961-1982: A Research List DLB-38
Black Theatre: A Forum [excerpts] DLB-38
Blackamore, Arthur 1679-? DLB-24, 39
Blackburn, Alexander L. 1929- Y-85
Blackburn, Paul 1926-1971 .... DLB-16; Y-81
Blackburn, Thomas 1916-1977 .... DLB-27
Blackmore, R. D. 1825-1900 .... DLB-18
Blackmur, R. P. 1904-1965 .... DLB-63
Blackwood, Caroline 1931- DLB-14
Blair, Eric Arthur (see Orwell, George)
Blair, Francis Preston 1791-1876 .... DLB-43
Blair, James circa 1655-1743 .... DLB-24
Blair, John Durburrow 1759-1823 .... DLB-37
Blais, Marie-Claire 1939- DLB-53
Blaise, Clark 1940- DLB-53
Blake, Nicholas 1904-1972 .... DLB-77
(see also Day Lewis, C.)
The Blakiston Company DLB-49
Blanchot, Maurice 1907- DLB-72
Bledsoe, Albert Taylor 1809-1877 .... DLB-3, 79
Blelock and Company DLB-49
Blish, James 1921-1975 .... DLB-8
Bliss, E., and E. White [publishing house] DLB-49
Bloch, Robert 1917- DLB-44
Block, Rudolph (see Lessing, Bruno)
Blondal, Patricia 1926-1959 .... DLB-88
Bloom, Harold 1930- DLB-67
Bloomer, Amelia 1818-1894 .... DLB-79
Blume, Judy 1938- DLB-52
Blunck, Hans Friedrich 1888-1961 .... DLB-66
Blunden, Edmund 1896-1974 .... DLB-20
Blunt, Wilfrid Scawen 1840-1922 .... DLB-19
Bly, Nellie (see Cochrane, Elizabeth)
Bly, Robert 1926- DLB-5
Boaden, James 1762-1839 .... DLB-89
The Bobbs-Merrill Company DLB-46

Bobrowski, Johannes 1917-1965 ......DLB-75
Bodenheim, Maxwell 1892-1954 ......DLB-9, 45
Bodkin, M. McDonnell 1850-1933 ......DLB-70
Bodmershof, Imma von 1895-1982 ......DLB-85
Bodsworth, Fred 1918- DLB-68
Boehm, Sydney 1908- DLB-44
Boer, Charles 1939- DLB-5
Bogan, Louise 1897-1970 ......DLB-45
Bogarde, Dirk 1921- DLB-14
Boland, Eavan 1944- DLB-40
Böll, Heinrich 1917-1985 ......Y-85, DLB-69
Bolling, Robert 1738-1775 ......DLB-31
Bolt, Carol 1941- DLB-60
Bolt, Robert 1924- DLB-13
Bolton, Herbert E. 1870-1953 ......DLB-17
Bonaventura DLB-89
Bond, Edward 1934- DLB-13
Boni, Albert and Charles [publishing house] DLB-46
Boni and Liveright DLB-46
Robert Bonner's Sons DLB-49
Bontemps, Arna 1902-1973 ......DLB-48, 51
The Book League of America DLB-46
Book Reviewing in America: I Y-87
Book Reviewing in America: II Y-88
Book Supply Company DLB-49
The Booker Prize
Address by Anthony Thwaite, Chairman of the Booker Prize Judges
Comments from Former Booker Prize Winners Y-86
Boorstin, Daniel J. 1914- DLB-17
Booth, Mary L. 1831-1889 ......DLB-79
Booth, Philip 1925- Y-82
Booth, Wayne C. 1921- DLB-67
Borchardt, Rudolf 1877-1945 ......DLB-66
Borchert, Wolfgang 1921-1947 ......DLB-69
Borges, Jorge Luis 1899-1986 ......Y-86
Börne, Ludwig 1786-1837 ......DLB-90
Borrow, George 1803-1881 ......DLB-21, 55
Bosco, Henri 1888-1976 ......DLB-72
Bosco, Monique 1927- DLB-53
Botta, Anne C. Lynch 1815-1891 ......DLB-3
Bottomley, Gordon 1874-1948 ......DLB-10
Bottoms, David 1949- Y-83
Bottrall, Ronald 1906- DLB-20
Boucher, Anthony 1911-1968 ......DLB-8
Boucher, Jonathan 1738-1804 ......DLB-31
Boudreau, Daniel (see Coste, Donat)
Bourjaily, Vance Nye 1922- DLB-2
Bourne, Edward Gaylord 1860-1908 ......DLB-47
Bourne, Randolph 1886-1918 ......DLB-63
Bousquet, Joë 1897-1950 ......DLB-72
Bova, Ben 1932- Y-81
Bove, Emmanuel 1898-1945 ......DLB-72
Bovard, Oliver K. 1872-1945 ......DLB-25
Bowen, Elizabeth 1899-1973 ......DLB-15
Bowen, Francis 1811-1890 ......DLB-1, 59
Bowen, John 1924- DLB-13
Bowen-Merrill Company DLB-49
Bowering, George 1935- DLB-53
Bowers, Claude G. 1878-1958 ......DLB-17
Bowers, Edgar 1924- DLB-5
Bowles, Paul 1910- DLB-5, 6
Bowles, Samuel III 1826-1878 ......DLB-43
Bowman, Louise Morey 1882-1944 ......DLB-68
Boyd, James 1888-1944 ......DLB-9
Boyd, John 1919- DLB-8
Boyd, Thomas 1898-1935 ......DLB-9
Boyesen, Hjalmar Hjorth 1848-1895 ......DLB-12, 71
Boyle, Kay 1902- DLB-4, 9, 48, 86
Boyle, Roger, Earl of Orrery 1621-1679 ......DLB-80
Boyle, T. Coraghessan 1948- Y-86
Brackenbury, Alison 1953- DLB-40
Brackenridge, Hugh Henry 1748-1816 ......DLB-11, 37
Brackett, Charles 1892-1969 ......DLB-26
Brackett, Leigh 1915-1978 ......DLB-8, 26
Bradburn, John [publishing house] DLB-49
Bradbury, Malcolm 1932- DLB-14
Bradbury, Ray 1920- DLB-2, 8
Braddon, Mary Elizabeth 1835-1915 ......DLB-18, 70
Bradford, Andrew 1686-1742 ......DLB-43, 73
Bradford, Gamaliel 1863-1932 ......DLB-17

Bradford, John 1749-1830 ....DLB-43
Bradford, Roark 1896-1948 ....DLB-86
Bradford, William 1590-1657 ....DLB-24, 30
Bradford, William III 1719-1791 ....DLB-43, 73
Bradlaugh, Charles 1833-1891 ....DLB-57
Bradley, David 1950- DLB-33
Bradley, Ira, and Company DLB-49
Bradley, J. W., and Company DLB-49
Bradley, Marion Zimmer 1930- DLB-8
Bradley, William Aspenwall 1878-1939 ....DLB-4
Bradstreet, Anne 1612 or 1613-1672 ....DLB-24
Brady, Frederic A. [publishing house] DLB-49
Bragg, Melvyn 1939- DLB-14
Brainard, Charles H. [publishing house] DLB-49
Braine, John 1922-1986 ....DLB-15; Y-86
Braithwaite, William Stanley 1878-1962 ....DLB-50, 54
Bramah, Ernest 1868-1942 ....DLB-70
Branagan, Thomas 1774-1843 ....DLB-37
Branch, William Blackwell 1927- DLB-76
Branden Press DLB-46
Brault, Jacques 1933- DLB-53
Braun, Volker 1939- DLB-75
Brautigan, Richard 1935-1984 ....DLB-2, 5; Y-80, 84
Braxton, Joanne M. 1950- DLB-41
Bray, Thomas 1656-1730 ....DLB-24
Braziller, George [publishing house] DLB-46
The Bread Loaf Writers' Conference 1983 ....Y-84
The Break-Up of the Novel (1922), by John Middleton Murry DLB-36
Breasted, James Henry 1865-1935 ....DLB-47
Brecht, Bertolt 1898-1956 ....DLB-56
Bredel, Willi 1901-1964 ....DLB-56
Bremser, Bonnie 1939- DLB-16
Bremser, Ray 1934- DLB-16
Brentano, Bernard von 1901-1964 ....DLB-56
Brentano, Clemens 1778-1842 ....DLB-90
Brentano's DLB-49
Brenton, Howard 1942- DLB-13
Breton, André 1896-1966 ....DLB-65
Brewer, Warren and Putnam DLB-46
Brewster, Elizabeth 1922- DLB-60
Bridgers, Sue Ellen 1942- DLB-52
Bridges, Robert 1844-1930 ....DLB-19
Bridie, James 1888-1951 ....DLB-10
Briggs, Charles Frederick 1804-1877 ....DLB-3
Brighouse, Harold 1882-1958 ....DLB-10
Brimmer, B. J., Company DLB-46
Brinnin, John Malcolm 1916- DLB-48
Brisbane, Albert 1809-1890 ....DLB-3
Brisbane, Arthur 1864-1936 ....DLB-25
Broadway Publishing Company DLB-46
Broch, Hermann 1886-1951 ....DLB-85
Brochu, André 1942- DLB-53
Brock, Edwin 1927- DLB-40
Brod, Max 1884-1968 ....DLB-81
Brodhead, John R. 1814-1873 ....DLB-30
Brome, Richard circa 1590-1652 ....DLB-58
Bromfield, Louis 1896-1956 ....DLB-4, 9, 86
Broner, E. M. 1930- DLB-28
Brontë, Anne 1820-1849 ....DLB-21
Brontë, Charlotte 1816-1855 ....DLB-21
Brontë, Emily 1818-1848 ....DLB-21, 32
Brooke, Frances 1724-1789 ....DLB-39
Brooke, Henry 1703?-1783 ....DLB-39
Brooke, Rupert 1887-1915 ....DLB-19
Brooker, Bertram 1888-1955 ....DLB-88
Brooke-Rose, Christine 1926- DLB-14
Brookner, Anita 1928- Y-87
Brooks, Charles Timothy 1813-1883 ....DLB-1
Brooks, Cleanth 1906- DLB-63
Brooks, Gwendolyn 1917- DLB-5, 76
Brooks, Jeremy 1926- DLB-14
Brooks, Mel 1926- DLB-26
Brooks, Noah 1830-1903 ....DLB-42
Brooks, Richard 1912- DLB-44
Brooks, Van Wyck 1886-1963 ....DLB-45, 63
Brophy, Brigid 1929- DLB-14
Brossard, Chandler 1922- DLB-16
Brossard, Nicole 1943- DLB-53
Brother Antoninus (see Everson, William)
Brougham, John 1810-1880 ....DLB-11

Broughton, James 1913- DLB-5
Broughton, Rhoda 1840-1920............................DLB-18
Broun, Heywood 1888-1939..............................DLB-29
Brown, Alice 1856-1948....................................DLB-78
Brown, Bob 1886-1959.................................DLB-4, 45
Brown, Cecil 1943- DLB-33
Brown, Charles Brockden 1771-1810.....DLB-37, 59, 73
Brown, Christy 1932-1981.................................DLB-14
Brown, Dee 1908- Y-80
Browne, Francis Fisher 1843-1913 ....DLB-79
Brown, Frank London 1927-1962 ....DLB-76
Brown, Fredric 1906-1972 ....DLB-8
Brown, George Mackay 1921- DLB-14, 27
Brown, Harry 1917-1986 ....DLB-26
Brown, Marcia 1918- DLB-61
Brown, Margaret Wise 1910-1952 ....DLB-22
Brown, Morna Doris (see Ferrars, Elizabeth)
Brown, Oliver Madox 1855-1874.......................DLB-21
Brown, Sterling 1901-1989 ....DLB-48, 51, 63
Brown, T. E. 1830-1897.....................................DLB-35
Brown, William Hill 1765-1793..........................DLB-37
Brown, William Wells 1814-1884..................DLB-3, 50
Browne, Charles Farrar 1834-1867....................DLB-11
Browne, Michael Dennis 1940- DLB-40
Browne, Wynyard 1911-1964.............................DLB-13
Brownell, W. C. 1851-1928...............................DLB-71
Browning, Elizabeth Barrett 1806-1861 ....DLB-32
Browning, Robert 1812-1889.............................DLB-32
Brownjohn, Allan 1931- DLB-40
Brownson, Orestes Augustus
1803-1876...DLB-1, 59, 73
Bruce, Charles 1906-1971 ....DLB-68
Bruce, Leo 1903-1979 ....DLB-77
Bruce, Philip Alexander 1856-1933....................DLB-47
Bruce Humphries [publishing house] DLB-46
Bruce-Novoa, Juan 1944- DLB-82
Bruckman, Clyde 1894-1955.............................DLB-26
Brundage, John Herbert (see Herbert, John)
Bryant, William Cullen 1794-1878...........DLB-3, 43, 59
Buchan, John 1875-1940..............................DLB-34, 70
Buchanan, Robert 1841-1901 ....DLB-18, 35
Buchman, Sidney 1902-1975 ....DLB-26
Buck, Pearl S. 1892-1973 ....DLB-9
Buckingham, Joseph Tinker 1779-1861 and
Buckingham, Edwin 1810-1833..................DLB-73
Buckler, Ernest 1908-1984................................DLB-68
Buckley, William F., Jr. 1925- Y-80
Buckminster, Joseph Stevens 1784-1812............DLB-37
Buckner, Robert 1906- DLB-26
Budd, Thomas ?-1698..DLB-24
Budrys, A. J. 1931- DLB-8
Buechner, Frederick 1926- Y-80
Buell, John 1927- DLB-53
Buffum, Job [publishing house]..........................DLB-49
Bukowski, Charles 1920- DLB-5
Bullins, Ed 1935- DLB-7, 38
Bulwer-Lytton, Edward (also Edward Bulwer)
1803-1873 ....DLB-21
Bumpus, Jerry 1937- Y-81
Bunce and Brother DLB-49
Bunner, H. C. 1855-1896 ....DLB-78, 79
Bunting, Basil 1900-1985..................................DLB-20
Bunyan, John 1628-1688..................................DLB-39
Burch, Robert 1925- DLB-52
Burciaga, José Antonio 1940- DLB-82
Burgess, Anthony 1917- DLB-14
Burgess, Gelett 1866-1951 ....DLB-11
Burgess, John W. 1844-1931.............................DLB-47
Burgess, Thornton W. 1874-1965 ....DLB-22
Burgess, Stringer and Company.........................DLB-49
Burk, John Daly circa 1772-1808.......................DLB-37
Burke, Kenneth 1897- DLB-45, 63
Burlingame, Edward Livermore 1848-1922.......DLB-79
Burnett, Frances Hodgson 1849-1924...............DLB-42
Burnett, W. R. 1899-1982...................................DLB-9
Burney, Fanny 1752-1840 ....DLB-39
Burns, Alan 1929- DLB-14
Burns, John Horne 1916-1953...............................Y-85
Burnshaw, Stanley 1906- DLB-48
Burr, C. Chauncey 1815?-1883..........................DLB-79
Burroughs, Edgar Rice 1875-1950 ....DLB-8
Burroughs, John 1837-1921..............................DLB-64

Burroughs, Margaret T. G. 1917- DLB-41
Burroughs, William S., Jr. 1947-1981 ....DLB-16
Burroughs, William Seward 1914- DLB-2, 8, 16; Y-81
Burroway, Janet 1936- DLB-6
Burt, A. L., and Company DLB-49
Burt, Maxwell S. 1882-1954...............................DLB-86
Burton, Miles (see Rhode, John)
Burton, Richard F. 1821-1890............................DLB-55
Burton, Virginia Lee 1909-1968.........................DLB-22
Burton, William Evans 1804-1860......................DLB-73
Busch, Frederick 1941- DLB-6
Busch, Niven 1903- DLB-44
Butler, E. H., and Company..............................DLB-49
Butler, Juan 1942-1981 ....DLB-53
Butler, Octavia E. 1947- DLB-33
Butler, Samuel 1835-1902.............................DLB-18, 57
Butor, Michel 1926- DLB-83
Butterworth, Hezekiah 1839-1905.....................DLB-42
B. V. (see Thomson, James)
Byars, Betsy 1928- DLB-52
Byatt, A. S. 1936- DLB-14
Byles, Mather 1707-1788....................
...............DLB-24
Bynner, Witter 1881-1968..................................DLB-54
Byrd, William II 1674-1744 ....DLB-24
Byrne, John Keyes (see Leonard, Hugh)

C

Cabell, James Branch 1879-1958....................DLB-9, 78
Cable, George Washington 1844-1925.........DLB-12, 74
Cahan, Abraham 1860-1951.....................DLB-9, 25, 28
Cain, George 1943- DLB-33
Caldwell, Ben 1937- DLB-38
Caldwell, Erskine 1903-1987 ....DLB-9, 86
Caldwell, H. M., Company.................................DLB-49
Calhoun, John C. 1782-1850 ....DLB-3
Calisher, Hortense 1911- DLB-2
Callaghan, Morley 1903- DLB-68
Callaloo..Y-87
A Call to Letters and an Invitation to the Electric Chair, by Siegfried Mandel DLB-75
Calmer, Edgar 1907- DLB-4
Calverley, C. S. 1831-1884 ....DLB-35
Calvert, George Henry 1803-1889 ....DLB-1, 64
Cambridge Press DLB-49
Cameron, Eleanor 1912- DLB-52
Camm, John 1718-1778 ....DLB-31
Campbell, Gabrielle Margaret Vere (see Shearing, Joseph)
Campbell, James Edwin 1867-1896 ....DLB-50
Campbell, John 1653-1728 ....DLB-43
Campbell, John W., Jr. 1910-1971 ....DLB-8
Campbell, Roy 1901-1957 ....DLB-20
Campion, Thomas 1567-1620............................DLB-58
Camus, Albert 1913-1960 ....DLB-72
Candelaria, Cordelia 1943- DLB-82
Candelaria, Nash 1928- DLB-82
Candour in English Fiction (1890), by Thomas Hardy DLB-18
Canetti, Elias 1905- DLB-85
Cannan, Gilbert 1884-1955................................DLB-10
Cannell, Kathleen 1891-1974...............................DLB-4
Cannell, Skipwith 1887-1957 ....DLB-45
Cantwell, Robert 1908-1978.................................DLB-9
Cape, Jonathan, and Harrison Smith [publishing house] DLB-46
Capen, Joseph 1658-1725 ....DLB-24
Capote, Truman 1924-1984..................DLB-2; Y-80, 84
Cardinal, Marie 1929- DLB-83
Carey, Henry circa 1687-1689-1743 ....DLB-84
Carey, M., and Company DLB-49
Carey, Mathew 1760-1839 ....DLB-37, 73
Carey and Hart...DLB-49
Carlell, Lodowick 1602-1675 ....DLB-58
Carleton, G. W. [publishing house] DLB-49
Carossa, Hans 1878-1956...................................DLB-66
Carr, Emily 1871-1945 ....DLB-68
Carrier, Roch 1937- DLB-53
Carlyle, Jane Welsh 1801-1866 ....DLB-55
Carlyle, Thomas 1795-1881 ....DLB-55
Carpenter, Stephen Cullen ?-1820?....................DLB-73

Carroll, Gladys Hasty 1904- DLB-9
Carroll, John 1735-1815....DLB-37
Carroll, Lewis 1832-1898....DLB-18
Carroll, Paul 1927- DLB-16
Carroll, Paul Vincent 1900-1968....DLB-10
Carroll and Graf Publishers....DLB-46
Carruth, Hayden 1921- DLB-5
Carryl, Charles E. 1841-1920....DLB-42
Carswell, Catherine 1879-1946....DLB-36
Carter, Angela 1940- DLB-14
Carter, Henry (see Leslie, Frank)
Carter, Landon 1710-1778....DLB-31
Carter, Lin 1930- Y-81
Carter, Robert, and Brothers....DLB-49
Carter and Hendee....DLB-49
Caruthers, William Alexander 1802-1846....DLB-3
Carver, Jonathan 1710-1780....DLB-31
Carver, Raymond 1938-1988....Y-84, 88
Cary, Joyce 1888-1957....DLB-15
Casey, Juanita 1925- DLB-14
Casey, Michael 1947- DLB-5
Cassady, Carolyn 1923- DLB-16
Cassady, Neal 1926-1968....DLB-16
Cassell Publishing Company....DLB-49
Cassill, R. V. 1919- DLB-6
Castlemon, Harry (see Fosdick, Charles Austin)
Caswall, Edward 1814-1878....DLB-32
Cather, Willa 1873-1947....DLB-9, 54, 78; DS-1
Catherwood, Mary Hartwell 1847-1902....DLB-78
Catton, Bruce 1899-1978....DLB-17
Causley, Charles 1917- DLB-27
Caute, David 1936- DLB-14
Cawein, Madison 1865-1914....DLB-54
The Caxton Printers, Limited....DLB-46
Cayrol, Jean 1911- DLB-83
Celan, Paul 1920-1970....DLB-69
Céline, Louis-Ferdinand 1894-1961....DLB-72
Center for the Book Research....Y-84
Centlivre, Susanna 1669?-1723....DLB-84
The Century Company....DLB-49
Cervantes, Lorna Dee 1954- DLB-82
Chacón, Eusebio 1869-1948....DLB-82
Chacón, Felipe Maximiliano 1873-?....DLB-82
Challans, Eileen Mary (see Renault, Mary)
Chalmers, George 1742-1825....DLB-30
Chamberlain, Samuel S. 1851-1916....DLB-25
Chamberland, Paul 1939- DLB-60
Chamberlin, William Henry 1897-1969....DLB-29
Chambers, Charles Haddon 1860-1921....DLB-10
Chamisso, Albert von 1781-1838....DLB-90
Chandler, Harry 1864-1944....DLB-29
Chandler, Raymond 1888-1959....DS-6
Channing, Edward 1856-1931....DLB-17
Channing, Edward Tyrrell 1790-1856....DLB-1, 59
Channing, William Ellery 1780-1842....DLB-1, 59
Channing, William Ellery II 1817-1901....DLB-1
Channing, William Henry 1810-1884....DLB-1, 59
Chaplin, Charlie 1889-1977....DLB-44
Chapman, George 1559 or 1560-1634....DLB-62
Chappell, Fred 1936- DLB-6
Charbonneau, Robert 1911-1967....DLB-68
Charles, Gerda 1914- DLB-14
Charles, William [publishing house]....DLB-49
The Charles Wood Affair: A Playwright Revived....Y-83
Charlotte Forten: Pages from her Diary....DLB-50
Charteris, Leslie 1907- DLB-77
Charyn, Jerome 1937- Y-83
Chase, Borden 1900-1971....DLB-26
Chase-Riboud, Barbara 1936- DLB-33
Chauncy, Charles 1705-1787....DLB-24
Chávez, Fray Angélico 1910- DLB-82
Chayefsky, Paddy 1923-1981....DLB-7, 44; Y-81
Cheever, Ezekiel 1615-1708....DLB-24
Cheever, George Barrell 1807-1890....DLB-59
Cheever, John 1912-1982....DLB-2; Y-80, 82
Cheever, Susan 1943- Y-82
Chelsea House....DLB-46
Cheney, Ednah Dow (Littlehale) 1824-1904....DLB-1
Cherry, Kelly 1940....Y-83
Cherryh, C. J. 1942- Y-80

Chesnutt, Charles Waddell 1858-1932...DLB-12, 50, 78
Chester, George Randolph 1869-1924...DLB-78
Chesterton, G. K. 1874-1936...DLB-10, 19, 34, 70
Cheyney, Edward P. 1861-1947...DLB-47
Chicano History...DLB-82
Chicano Language...DLB-82
Child, Francis James 1825-1896...DLB-1, 64
Child, Lydia Maria 1802-1880...DLB-1, 74
Child, Philip 1898-1978...DLB-68
Childers, Erskine 1870-1922...DLB-70
Children's Book Awards and Prizes...DLB-61
Childress, Alice 1920- ...DLB-7, 38
Childs, George W. 1829-1894...DLB-23
Chilton Book Company...DLB-46
Chittenden, Hiram Martin 1858-1917...DLB-47
Chivers, Thomas Holley 1809-1858...DLB-3
Chopin, Kate 1850-1904...DLB-12, 78
Choquette, Adrienne 1915-1973...DLB-68
Choquette, Robert 1905- ...DLB-68
The Christian Publishing Company...DLB-49
Christie, Agatha 1890-1976...DLB-13, 77
Church, Benjamin 1734-1778...DLB-31
Church, Francis Pharcellus 1839-1906...DLB-79
Church, William Conant 1836-1917...DLB-79
Churchill, Caryl 1938- ...DLB-13
Ciardi, John 1916-1986...DLB-5; Y-86
Cibber, Colley 1671-1757...DLB-84
City Lights Books...DLB-46
Cixous, Hélène 1937- ...DLB-83
Clapper, Raymond 1892-1944...DLB-29
Clare, John 1793-1864...DLB-55
Clark, Alfred Alexander Gordon (see Hare, Cyril)
Clark, Ann Nolan 1896- ...DLB-52
Clark, C. M., Publishing Company...DLB-46
Clark, Catherine Anthony 1892-1977...DLB-68
Clark, Charles Heber 1841-1915...DLB-11
Clark, Davis Wasgatt 1812-1871...DLB-79
Clark, Eleanor 1913- ...DLB-6
Clark, Lewis Gaylord 1808-1873...DLB-3, 64, 73
Clark, Walter Van Tilburg 1909-1971...DLB-9
Clarke, Austin 1896-1974...DLB-10, 20
Clarke, Austin C. 1934- ...DLB-53
Clarke, Gillian 1937- ...DLB-40
Clarke, James Freeman 1810-1888...DLB-1, 59
Clarke, Rebecca Sophia 1833-1906...DLB-42
Clarke, Robert, and Company...DLB-49
Clausen, Andy 1943- ...DLB-16
Claxton, Remsen and Haffelfinger...DLB-49
Clay, Cassius Marcellus 1810-1903...DLB-43
Cleary, Beverly 1916- ...DLB-52
Cleaver, Vera 1919- and
Cleaver, Bill 1920-1981...DLB-52
Cleland, John 1710-1789...DLB-39
Clemens, Samuel Langhorne
1835-1910...DLB-11, 12, 23, 64, 74
Clement, Hal 1922- ...DLB-8
Clemo, Jack 1916- ...DLB-27
Clifton, Lucille 1936- ...DLB-5, 41
Clode, Edward J. [publishing house]...DLB-46
Clough, Arthur Hugh 1819-1861...DLB-32
Cloutier, Cécile 1930- ...DLB-60
Coates, Robert M. 1897-1973...DLB-4, 9
Coatsworth, Elizabeth 1893- ...DLB-22
Cobb, Jr., Charles E. 1943- ...DLB-41
Cobb, Frank I. 1869-1923...DLB-25
Cobb, Irvin S. 1876-1944...DLB-11, 25, 86
Cobbett, William 1762-1835...DLB-43
Cochran, Thomas C. 1902- ...DLB-17
Cochrane, Elizabeth 1867-1922...DLB-25
Cockerill, John A. 1845-1896...DLB-23
Cocteau, Jean 1889-1963...DLB-65
Coffee, Lenore J. 1900?-1984...DLB-44
Coffin, Robert P. Tristram 1892-1955...DLB-45
Cogswell, Fred 1917- ...DLB-60
Cogswell, Mason Fitch 1761-1830...DLB-37
Cohen, Arthur A. 1928-1986...DLB-28
Cohen, Leonard 1934- ...DLB-53
Cohen, Matt 1942- ...DLB-53
Colden, Cadwallader 1688-1776...DLB-24, 30
Cole, Barry 1936- ...DLB-14
Colegate, Isabel 1931- ...DLB-14
Coleman, Emily Holmes 1899-1974...DLB-4

Coleridge, Mary 1861-1907 ....DLB-19
Colette 1873-1954 ....DLB-65
Colette, Sidonie Gabrielle (see Colette)
Collier, John 1901-1980 ....DLB-77
Collier, P. F. [publishing house] DLB-49
Collin and Small DLB-49
Collins, Isaac [publishing house] DLB-49
Collins, Mortimer 1827-1876 ....DLB-21, 35
Collins, Wilkie 1824-1889 ....DLB-18, 70
Collyer, Mary 1716?-1763? DLB-39
Colman, Benjamin 1673-1747 ....DLB-24
Colman, George, the Elder 1732-1794 ....DLB-89
Colman, George, the Younger 1762-1836 ....DLB-89
Colman, S. [publishing house] DLB-49
Colombo, John Robert 1936- DLB-53
Colter, Cyrus 1910- DLB-33
Colum, Padraic 1881-1972 ....DLB-19
Colwin, Laurie 1944- Y-80
Comden, Betty 1919- and Green, Adolph 1918- DLB-44
The Comic Tradition Continued [in the British Novel] DLB-15
Commager, Henry Steele 1902- DLB-17
The Commercialization of the Image of Revolt, by Kenneth Rexroth DLB-16
Community and Commentators: Black Theatre and Its Critics DLB-38
Compton-Burnett, Ivy 1884?-1969 ....DLB-36
Conference on Modern Biography Y-85
Congreve, William 1670-1729 ....DLB-39, 84
Conkey, W. B., Company DLB-49
Connell, Evan S., Jr. 1924- DLB-2; Y-81
Connelly, Marc 1890-1980 ....DLB-7; Y-80
Connolly, James B. 1868-1957 ....DLB-78
Connor, Tony 1930- DLB-40
Conquest, Robert 1917- DLB-27
Conrad, John, and Company DLB-49
Conrad, Joseph 1857-1924 ....DLB-10, 34
Conroy, Jack 1899- Y-81
Conroy, Pat 1945- DLB-6
The Consolidation of Opinion: Critical Responses to the Modernists DLB-36
Constantine, David 1944- DLB-40
Contempo Caravan: Kites in a Windstorm Y-85
A Contemporary Flourescence of Chicano Literature Y-84
The Continental Publishing Company DLB-49
A Conversation with Chaim Potok Y-84
Conversations with Publishers I: An Interview with Patrick O'Connor Y-84
The Conversion of an Unpolitical Man, by W. H. Bruford DLB-66
Conway, Moncure Daniel 1832-1907 ....DLB-1
Cook, David C., Publishing Company DLB-49
Cook, Ebenezer circa 1667-circa 1732 ....DLB-24
Cook, Michael 1933- DLB-53
Cooke, George Willis 1848-1923 ....DLB-71
Cooke, Increase, and Company DLB-49
Cooke, John Esten 1830-1886 ....DLB-3
Cooke, Philip Pendleton 1816-1850 ....DLB-3, 59
Cooke, Rose Terry 1827-1892 ....DLB-12, 74
Coolbrith, Ina 1841-1928 ....DLB-54
Coolidge, George [publishing house] DLB-49
Coolidge, Susan (see Woolsey, Sarah Chauncy)
Cooper, Giles 1918-1966 ....DLB-13
Cooper, James Fenimore 1789-1851 ....DLB-3
Cooper, Kent 1880-1965 ....DLB-29
Coover, Robert 1932- DLB-2; Y-81
Copeland and Day DLB-49
Coppel, Alfred 1921- Y-83
Coppola, Francis Ford 1939- DLB-44
Corcoran, Barbara 1911- DLB-52
Corelli, Marie 1855-1924 ....DLB-34
Corle, Edwin 1906-1956 ....Y-85
Corman, Cid 1924- DLB-5
Cormier, Robert 1925- DLB-52
Corn, Alfred 1943- Y-80
Cornish, Sam 1935- DLB-41
Cornwell, David John Moore (see le Carré, John)
Corpi, Lucha 1945- DLB-82
Corrington, John William 1932- DLB-6

Corrothers, James D. 1869-1917 ....DLB-50
Corso, Gregory 1930- DLB-5, 16
Cortez, Jayne 1936- DLB-41
Corvo, Baron (see Rolfe, Frederick William)
Cory, William Johnson 1823-1892.....................DLB-35
Cosmopolitan Book Corporation.......................DLB-46
Costain, Thomas B. 1885-1965............................DLB-9
Coste, Donat 1912-1957 ....DLB-88
Cotter, Joseph Seamon, Sr. 1861-1949 ....DLB-50
Cotter, Joseph Seamon, Jr. 1895-1919 ....DLB-50
Cotton, John 1584-1652 ....DLB-24
Coulter, John 1888-1980......................................DLB-68
Cournos, John 1881-1966 ....DLB-54
Coventry, Francis 1725-1754 ....DLB-39
Coverly, N. [publishing house] DLB-49
Covici-Friede DLB-46
Coward, Noel 1899-1973 ....DLB-10
Coward, McCann and Geoghegan.......................DLB-46
Cowles, Gardner 1861-1946................................DLB-29
Cowley, Hannah 1743-1809 ....DLB-89
Cowley, Malcolm 1898-1989................DLB-4, 48; Y-81
Cox, A. B. (see Berkeley, Anthony)
Cox, Palmer 1840-1924 ....DLB-42
Coxe, Louis 1918- DLB-5
Coxe, Tench 1755-1824.......................................DLB-37
Cozzens, James Gould 1903-1978 ....DLB-9; Y-84; DS-2
Craddock, Charles Egbert (see Murfree, Mary N.)
Cradock, Thomas 1718-1770 ....DLB-31
Craig, Daniel H. 1811-1895 ....DLB-43
Craik, Dinah Maria 1826-1887 ....DLB-35
Cranch, Christopher Pearse 1813-1892..........DLB-1, 42
Crane, Hart 1899-1932 ....DLB-4, 48
Crane, R. S. 1886-1967 ....DLB-63
Crane, Stephen 1871-1900 ....DLB-12, 54, 78
Crapsey, Adelaide 1878-1914 ....DLB-54
Craven, Avery 1885-1980....................................DLB-17
Crawford, Charles 1752-circa 1815 ....DLB-31
Crawford, F. Marion 1854-1909.........................DLB-71
Crawley, Alan 1887-1975 ....DLB-68
Crayon, Geoffrey (see Irving, Washington)
Creasey, John 1908-1973 ....DLB-77
Creative Age Press..DLB-46
Creel, George 1876-1953 ....DLB-25
Creeley, Robert 1926- DLB-5, 16
Creelman, James 1859-1915 ....DLB-23
Cregan, David 1931- DLB-13
Creighton, Donald Grant 1902-1979.................DLB-88
Crèvecoeur, Michel Guillaume Jean de 1735-1813 ....DLB-37
Crews, Harry 1935- DLB-6
Crichton, Michael 1942- Y-81
A Crisis of Culture: The Changing Role of Religion in the New Republic DLB-37
Crispin, Edmund 1921-1978..............................DLB-87
Cristofer, Michael 1946- DLB-7
"The Critic as Artist" (1891), by Oscar Wilde....DLB-57
Criticism In Relation To Novels (1863), by G. H. Lewes DLB-21
Crockett, David (Davy) 1786-1836.................DLB-3, 11
Croft-Cooke, Rupert (see Bruce, Leo)
Crofts, Freeman Wills 1879-1957 ....DLB-77
Croly, Jane Cunningham 1829-1901 ....DLB-23
Crosby, Caresse 1892-1970 ....DLB-48
Crosby, Caresse 1892-1970 and Crosby, Harry 1898-1929 ....DLB-4
Crosby, Harry 1898-1929..................................DLB-48
Crossley-Holland, Kevin 1941- DLB-40
Crothers, Rachel 1878-1958.................................DLB-7
Crowell, Thomas Y., Company..........................DLB-49
Crowley, John 1942- Y-82
Crowley, Mart 1935- DLB-7
Crown Publishers...DLB-46
Crowne, John 1641-1712 ....DLB-80
Croy, Homer 1883-1965 ....DLB-4
Crumley, James 1939- Y-84
Cruz, Victor Hernández 1949- DLB-41
Csokor, Franz Theodor 1885-1969 ....DLB-81
Cullen, Countee 1903-1946......................DLB-4, 48, 51
Culler, Jonathan D. 1944- DLB-67
The Cult of Biography
Excerpts from the Second Folio Debate:

"Biographies are generally a disease of English Literature"–Germaine Greer, Victoria Glendinning, Auberon Waugh, and Richard Holmes Y-86
Cumberland, Richard 1732-1811 ....DLB-89
Cummings, E. E. 1894-1962 ....DLB-4, 48
Cummings, Ray 1887-1957 ....DLB-8
Cummings and Hilliard DLB-49
Cummins, Maria Susanna 1827-1866................DLB-42
Cuney, Waring 1906-1976................................DLB-51
Cuney-Hare, Maude 1874-1936........................DLB-52
Cunningham, J. V. 1911- DLB-5
Cunningham, Peter F. [publishing house]..........DLB-49
Cuomo, George 1929- Y-80
Cupples and Leon DLB-46
Cupples, Upham and Company........................DLB-49
Cuppy, Will 1884-1949 ....DLB-11
Currie, Mary Montgomerie Lamb Singleton, Lady Currie (see Fane, Violet)
Curti, Merle E. 1897- DLB-17
Curtis, George William 1824-1892................DLB-1, 43

D

D. M. Thomas: The Plagiarism Controversy Y-82
Dabit, Eugène 1898-1936..................................DLB-65
Daborne, Robert circa 1580-1628......................DLB-58
Daggett, Rollin M. 1831-1901...........................DLB-79
Dahlberg, Edward 1900-1977 ....DLB-48
Dale, Peter 1938- DLB-40
Dall, Caroline Wells (Healey) 1822-1912.............DLB-1
Dallas, E. S. 1828-1879......................................DLB-55
The Dallas Theater Center DLB-7
D'Alton, Louis 1900-1951 ....DLB-10
Daly, T. A. 1871-1948.......................................DLB-11
Damon, S. Foster 1893-1971 ....DLB-45
Damrell, William S. [publishing house].............DLB-49
Dana, Charles A. 1819-1897 ....DLB-3, 23
Dana, Richard Henry, Jr. 1815-1882 ....DLB-1
Dandridge, Ray Garfield DLB-51
Dane, Clemence 1887-1965...............................DLB-10
Danforth, John 1660-1730 ....DLB-24
Danforth, Samuel I 1626-1674 ....DLB-24
Danforth, Samuel II 1666-1727.........................DLB-24
Dangerous Years: London Theater, 1939-1945 ....DLB-10
Daniel, John M. 1825-1865 ....DLB-43
Daniel, Samuel 1562 or 1563-1619.....................DLB-62
Daniells, Roy 1902-1979...................................DLB-68
Daniels, Josephus 1862-1948 ....DLB-29
Danner, Margaret Esse 1915- DLB-41
Darwin, Charles 1809-1882...............................DLB-57
Daryush, Elizabeth 1887-1977 ....DLB-20
Dashwood, Edmée Elizabeth Monica de la Pasture (see Delafield, E. M.)
d'Aulaire, Edgar Parin 1898- and d'Aulaire, Ingri 1904- DLB-22
Davenant, Sir William 1606-1668.......................DLB-58
Davenport, Robert ?-? DLB-58
Daves, Delmer 1904-1977 ....DLB-26
Davey, Frank 1940- DLB-53
Davidson, Avram 1923- DLB-8
Davidson, Donald 1893-1968.............................DLB-45
Davidson, John 1857-1909.................................DLB-19
Davidson, Lionel 1922- DLB-14
Davie, Donald 1922- DLB-27
Davies, Robertson 1913- DLB-68
Davies, Samuel 1723-1761.................................DLB-31
Davies, W. H. 1871-1940...................................DLB-19
Daviot, Gordon 1896?-1952 ....DLB-10 (see also Tey, Josephine)
Davis, Charles A. 1795-1867..............................DLB-11
Davis, Clyde Brion 1894-1962.............................DLB-9
Davis, Dick 1945- DLB-40
Davis, Frank Marshall 1905-? DLB-51
Davis, H. L. 1894-1960..DLB-9
Davis, John 1774-1854 ....DLB-37
Davis, Margaret Thomson 1926- DLB-14
Davis, Ossie 1917- DLB-7, 38
Davis, Rebecca Harding 1831-1910...................DLB-74
Davis, Richard Harding 1864-1916 ....DLB-12, 23, 78, 79
Davis, Samuel Cole 1764-1809..........................DLB-37
Davison, Peter 1928- DLB-5

Davys, Mary 1674-1732 ....DLB-39
DAW Books DLB-46
Dawson, William 1704-1752 ....DLB-31
Day, Benjamin Henry 1810-1889 ....DLB-43
Day, Clarence 1874-1935 ....DLB-11
Day, Dorothy 1897-1980 ....DLB-29
Day, John circa 1574-circa 1640 ....DLB-62
Day, The John, Company DLB-46
Day Lewis, C. 1904-1972 ....DLB-15, 20
(see also Blake, Nicholas)
Day, Mahlon [publishing house] DLB-49
Day, Thomas 1748-1789 ....DLB-39
Deacon, William Arthur 1890-1977 ....DLB-68
Deal, Borden 1922-1985 ....DLB-6
de Angeli, Marguerite 1889-1987 ....DLB-22
De Bow, James Dunwoody Brownson 1820-1867 ....DLB-3, 79
de Bruyn, Günter 1926- DLB-75
de Camp, L. Sprague 1907- DLB-8
The Decay of Lying (1889), by Oscar Wilde [excerpt] DLB-18
Dedication, *Ferdinand Count Fathom* (1753), by Tobias Smollett DLB-39
Dedication, *Lasselia* (1723), by Eliza Haywood [excerpt] DLB-39
Dedication, *The History of Pompey the Little* (1751), by Francis Coventry DLB-39
Dedication, *The Wanderer* (1814), by Fanny Burney DLB-39
Defense of *Amelia* (1752), by Henry Fielding DLB-39
Defoe, Daniel 1660-1731 ....DLB-39
de Fontaiñe, Felix Gregory 1834-1896 ....DLB-43
De Forest, John William 1826-1906 ....DLB-12
de Graff, Robert 1895-1981 ....Y-81
Deighton, Len 1929- DLB-87
DeJong, Meindert 1906- DLB-52
Dekker, Thomas circa 1572-1632 ....DLB-62
Delafield, E. M. 1890-1943 ....DLB-34
de la Mare, Walter 1873-1956 ....DLB-19
Deland, Margaret 1857-1945 ....DLB-78
Delaney, Shelagh 1939- DLB-13
Delany, Martin Robinson 1812-1885 ....DLB-50
Delany, Samuel R. 1942- DLB-8, 33
de la Roche, Mazo 1879-1961 ....DLB-68
Delbanco, Nicholas 1942- DLB-6
De León, Nephtalí 1945- DLB-82
Delgado, Abelardo Barrientos 1931- DLB-82
DeLillo, Don 1936- DLB-6
Dell, Floyd 1887-1969 ....DLB-9
Dell Publishing Company DLB-46
delle Grazie, Marie Eugene 1864-1931 ....DLB-81
del Rey, Lester 1915- DLB-8
de Man, Paul 1919-1983 ....DLB-67
Demby, William 1922- DLB-33
Deming, Philander 1829-1915 ....DLB-74
Demorest, William Jennings 1822-1895 ....DLB-79
Denham, Sir John 1615-1669 ....DLB-58
Denison, T. S., and Company DLB-49
Dennie, Joseph 1768-1812 ....DLB-37, 43, 59, 73
Dennis, Nigel 1912-1989 ....DLB-13, 15
Dent, Tom 1932- DLB-38
Denton, Daniel circa 1626-1703 ....DLB-24
DePaola, Tomie 1934- DLB-61
Derby, George Horatio 1823-1861 ....DLB-11
Derby, J. C., and Company DLB-49
Derby and Miller DLB-49
Derleth, August 1909-1971 ....DLB-9
The Derrydale Press DLB-46
Desbiens, Jean-Paul 1927- DLB-53
des Forêts, Louis-René 1918- DLB-83
DesRochers, Alfred 1901-1978 ....DLB-68
Desrosiers, Léo-Paul 1896-1967 ....DLB-68
Destouches, Louis-Ferdinand (see Céline, Louis-Ferdinand)
De Tabley, Lord 1835-1895 ....DLB-35
Deutsch, Babette 1895-1982 ....DLB-45
Deveaux, Alexis 1948- DLB-38
The Development of Lighting in the Staging of Drama, 1900-1945 [in Great Britain] DLB-10
de Vere, Aubrey 1814-1902 ....DLB-35
The Devin-Adair Company DLB-46
De Voto, Bernard 1897-1955 ....DLB-9
De Vries, Peter 1910- DLB-6; Y-82

Dewdney, Christopher 1951- DLB-60
Dewdney, Selwyn 1909-1979 ....DLB-68
DeWitt, Robert M., Publisher DLB-49
DeWolfe, Fiske and Company.............................DLB-49
Dexter, Colin 1930- DLB-87
de Young, M. H. 1849-1925...............................DLB-25
The Dial Press..DLB-46
Diamond, I. A. L. 1920-1988 ....DLB-26
Di Cicco, Pier Giorgio 1949- DLB-60
Dick, Philip K. 1928- DLB-8
Dick and Fitzgerald DLB-49
Dickens, Charles 1812-1870....................DLB-21, 55, 70
Dickey, James 1923- DLB-5; Y-82; DS-7
Dickey, William 1928- DLB-5
Dickinson, Emily 1830-1886 ....DLB-1
Dickinson, John 1732-1808 ....DLB-31
Dickinson, Jonathan 1688-1747 ....DLB-24
Dickinson, Patric 1914- DLB-27
Dickinson, Peter 1927- DLB-87
Dickson, Gordon R. 1923- DLB-8
Didion, Joan 1934- DLB-2; Y-81, 86
Di Donato, Pietro 1911- DLB-9
Dillard, Annie 1945- Y-80
Dillard, R. H. W. 1937- DLB-5
Dillingham, Charles T., Company......................DLB-49
The G. W. Dillingham Company........................DLB-49
Dintenfass, Mark 1941- Y-84
Diogenes, Jr. (see Brougham, John)
DiPrima, Diane 1934- DLB-5, 16
Disch, Thomas M. 1940- DLB-8
Disney, Walt 1901-1966.......................................DLB-22
Disraeli, Benjamin 1804-1881.......................DLB-21, 55
Ditzen, Rudolf (see Fallada, Hans)
Dix, Dorothea Lynde 1802-1887 ....DLB-1
Dix, Dorothy (see Gilmer, Elizabeth Meriwether)
Dix, Edwards and Company DLB-49
Dixon, Paige (see Corcoran, Barbara)
Dixon, Richard Watson 1833-1900.....................DLB-19
Dobell, Sydney 1824-1874..................................DLB-32
Döblin, Alfred 1878-1957 ....DLB-66
Dobson, Austin 1840-1921 ....DLB-35
Doctorow, E. L. 1931- DLB-2, 28; Y-80
Dodd, William E. 1869-1940 ....DLB-17
Dodd, Mead and Company................................DLB-49
Doderer, Heimito von 1896-1968.......................DLB-85
Dodge, B. W., and Company.............................DLB-46
Dodge, Mary Mapes 1831?-1905 ....DLB-42, 79
Dodge Publishing Company DLB-49
Dodgson, Charles Lutwidge (see Carroll, Lewis)
Dodson, Owen 1914-1983..................................DLB-76
Doesticks, Q. K. Philander, P. B. (see Thomson, Mortimer)
Donahoe, Patrick [publishing house]..................DLB-49
Donald, David H. 1920- DLB-17
Donleavy, J. P. 1926- DLB-6
Donnadieu, Marguerite (see Duras, Marguerite)
Donnelley, R. R., and Sons Company DLB-49
Donnelly, Ignatius 1831-1901............................DLB-12
Donohue and Henneberry.................................DLB-49
Doolady, M. [publishing house]..........................DLB-49
Dooley, Ebon (see Ebon)
Doolittle, Hilda 1886-1961.............................DLB-4, 45
Dor, Milo 1923- DLB-85
Doran, George H., Company.............................DLB-46
Dorgelès, Roland 1886-1973.............................DLB-65
Dorn, Edward 1929- DLB-5
Dorr, Rheta Childe 1866-1948 ....DLB-25
Dorst, Tankred 1925- DLB-75
Dos Passos, John 1896-1970...................DLB-4, 9; DS-1
Doubleday and Company..................................DLB-49
Doughty, Charles M. 1843-1926..................DLB-19, 57
Douglas, Keith 1920-1944 ....DLB-27
Douglas, Norman 1868-1952 ....DLB-34
Douglass, Frederick 1817?-1895.........DLB-1, 43, 50, 79
Douglass, William circa 1691-1752 ....DLB-24
Dover Publications DLB-46
Dowden, Edward 1843-1913..............................DLB-35
Downes, Gwladys 1915- DLB-88
Downing, J., Major (see Davis, Charles A.)
Downing, Major Jack (see Smith, Seba)
Dowson, Ernest 1867-1900................................DLB-19
Doxey, William [publishing house].....................DLB-49

Doyle, Sir Arthur Conan 1859-1930 ....DLB-18, 70
Doyle, Kirby 1932- DLB-16
Drabble, Margaret 1939- DLB-14
Drach, Albert 1902- DLB-85
The Dramatic Publishing Company DLB-49
Dramatists Play Service....DLB-46
Draper, John W. 1811-1882....DLB-30
Draper, Lyman C. 1815-1891 ....DLB-30
Dreiser, Theodore 1871-1945 ....DLB-9, 12; DS-1
Drewitz, Ingeborg 1923-1986 ....DLB-75
Drieu La Rochelle, Pierre 1893-1945 ....DLB-72
Drinkwater, John 1882-1937 ....DLB-10, 19
The Drue Heinz Literature Prize
Excerpt from "Excerpts from a Report of the Commission," in David Bosworth's *The Death of Descartes*
An Interview with David Bosworth Y-82
Dryden, John 1631-1700....DLB-80
Duane, William 1760-1835....DLB-43
Dubé, Marcel 1930- DLB-53
Dubé, Rodolphe (see Hertel, François)
Du Bois, W. E. B. 1868-1963....DLB-47, 50
Du Bois, William Pène 1916- DLB-61
Ducharme, Réjean 1941- DLB-60
Dudek, Louis 1918- DLB-88
Duell, Sloan and Pearce DLB-46
Duffield and Green DLB-46
Duffy, Maureen 1933- DLB-14
Dugan, Alan 1923- DLB-5
Duhamel, Georges 1884-1966....DLB-65
Dukes, Ashley 1885-1959 ....DLB-10
Dumas, Henry 1934-1968 ....DLB-41
Dunbar, Paul Laurence 1872-1906 ....DLB-50, 54, 78
Duncan, Robert 1919-1988 ....DLB-5, 16
Duncan, Ronald 1914-1982....DLB-13
Dunigan, Edward, and Brother DLB-49
Dunlap, John 1747-1812 ....DLB-43
Dunlap, William 1766-1839....DLB-30, 37, 59
Dunn, Douglas 1942- DLB-40
Dunne, Finley Peter 1867-1936 ....DLB-11, 23
Dunne, John Gregory 1932- Y-80
Dunne, Philip 1908- DLB-26
Dunning, Ralph Cheever 1878-1930 ....DLB-4
Dunning, William A. 1857-1922....DLB-17
Plunkett, Edward John Moreton Drax, Lord Dunsany 1878-1957 ....DLB-10, 77
Durand, Lucile (see Bersianik, Louky)
Duranty, Walter 1884-1957....DLB-29
Duras, Marguerite 1914- DLB-83
Durfey, Thomas 1653-1723 ....DLB-80
Durrell, Lawrence 1912- DLB-15, 27
Durrell, William [publishing house] DLB-49
Dürrenmatt, Friedrich 1921- DLB-69
Dutton, E. P., and Company....DLB-49
Duvoisin, Roger 1904-1980....DLB-61
Duyckinck, Evert Augustus 1816-1878 ....DLB-3, 64
Duyckinck, George L. 1823-1863 ....DLB-3
Duyckinck and Company DLB-49
Dwight, John Sullivan 1813-1893 ....DLB-1
Dwight, Timothy 1752-1817 ....DLB-37
Dyer, Charles 1928- DLB-13
Dylan, Bob 1941- DLB-16

E

Eager, Edward 1911-1964....DLB-22
Earle, James H., and Company DLB-49
Early American Book Illustration, by Sinclair Hamilton DLB-49
Eastlake, William 1917- DLB-6
Eastman, Carol ?- DLB-44
Eberhart, Richard 1904- DLB-48
Ebner, Jeannie 1918- DLB-85
Ebner-Eschenbach, Marie von 1830-1916 ....DLB-81
Ebon 1942- DLB-41
Ecco Press....DLB-46
Edes, Benjamin 1732-1803....DLB-43
Edgar, David 1948- DLB-13
The Editor Publishing Company....DLB-49
Edmonds, Randolph 1900- DLB-51
Edmonds, Walter D. 1903- DLB-9
Edschmid, Kasimir 1890-1966 ....DLB-56

Edwards, Jonathan 1703-1758 ....DLB-24
Edwards, Jonathan, Jr. 1745-1801 ....DLB-37
Edwards, Junius 1929- DLB-33
Edwards, Richard 1524-1566 ....DLB-62
Effinger, George Alec 1947- DLB-8
Eggleston, Edward 1837-1902 ....DLB-12
Ehrenstein, Albert 1886-1950 ....DLB-81
Eich, Günter 1907-1972 ....DLB-69
Eichendorff, Joseph Freiherr von 1788-1857 ....DLB-90
1873 Publishers' Catalogues DLB-49
Eighteenth-Century Aesthetic Theories DLB-31
Eighteenth-Century Philosophical Background DLB-31
Eigner, Larry 1927- DLB-5
Eisenreich, Herbert 1925-1986 ....DLB-85
Eisner, Kurt 1867-1919 ....DLB-66
Eklund, Gordon 1945- Y-83
Elder, Lonne III 1931- DLB-7, 38, 44
Elder, Paul, and Company DLB-49
Elements of Rhetoric (1828; revised, 1846), by Richard Whately [excerpt] DLB-57
Elie, Robert 1915-1973 ....DLB-88
Eliot, George 1819-1880 ....DLB-21, 35, 55
Eliot, John 1604-1690 ....DLB-24
Eliot, T. S. 1888-1965 ....DLB-7, 10, 45, 63
Elizondo, Sergio 1930- DLB-82
Elkin, Stanley 1930- DLB-2, 28; Y-80
Elles, Dora Amy (see Wentworth, Patricia)
Ellet, Elizabeth F. 1818?-1877 ....DLB-30
Elliott, George 1923- DLB-68
Elliott, Janice 1931- DLB-14
Elliott, William 1788-1863 ....DLB-3
Elliott, Thomes and Talbot DLB-49
Ellis, Edward S. 1840-1916 ....DLB-42
The George H. Ellis Company DLB-49
Ellison, Harlan 1934- DLB-8
Ellison, Ralph 1914- DLB-2, 76
Ellmann, Richard 1918-1987 ....Y-87
The Elmer Holmes Bobst Awards in Arts and Letters Y-87
Emanuel, James Andrew 1921- DLB-41
Emerson, Ralph Waldo 1803-1882 ....DLB-1, 59, 73
Emerson, William 1769-1811 ....DLB-37
Empson, William 1906-1984 ....DLB-20
The End of English Stage Censorship, 1945-1968 ....DLB-13
Ende, Michael 1929- DLB-75
Engel, Marian 1933-1985 ....DLB-53
Engle, Paul 1908- DLB-48
English Composition and Rhetoric (1866), by Alexander Bain [excerpt] DLB-57
The English Renaissance of Art (1908), by Oscar Wilde DLB-35
Enright, D. J. 1920- DLB-27
Enright, Elizabeth 1909-1968 ....DLB-22
L'Envoi (1882), by Oscar Wilde DLB-35
Epps, Bernard 1936- DLB-53
Epstein, Julius 1909- and Epstein, Philip 1909-1952 ....DLB-26
Equiano, Olaudah circa 1745-1797 ....DLB-37, 50
Erichsen-Brown, Gwethalyn Graham (see Graham, Gwethalyn)
Ernst, Paul 1866-1933 ....DLB-66
Erskine, John 1879-1951 ....DLB-9
Ervine, St. John Greer 1883-1971 ....DLB-10
Eshleman, Clayton 1935- DLB-5
Ess Ess Publishing Company DLB-49
Essay on Chatterton (1842), by Robert Browning DLB-32
Estes, Eleanor 1906-1988 ....DLB-22
Estes and Lauriat DLB-49
Etherege, George 1636-circa 1692 ....DLB-80
Ets, Marie Hall 1893- DLB-22
Eudora Welty: Eye of the Storyteller Y-87
Eugene O'Neill Memorial Theater Center DLB-7
Eugene O'Neill's Letters: A Review Y-88
Evans, Donald 1884-1921 ....DLB-54
Evans, George Henry 1805-1856 ....DLB-43
Evans, M., and Company DLB-46
Evans, Mari 1923- DLB-41
Evans, Mary Ann (see Eliot, George)
Evans, Nathaniel 1742-1767 ....DLB-31
Evans, Sebastian 1830-1909 ....DLB-35

Everett, Alexander Hill 1790-1847....................DLB-59
Everett, Edward 1794-1865 ....DLB-1, 59
Everson, R. G. 1903- DLB-88
Everson, William 1912- DLB-5, 16
Every Man His Own Poet; or, The Inspired Singer's Recipe Book (1877), by W. H. Mallock DLB-35
Ewart, Gavin 1916- DLB-40
Ewing, Juliana Horatia 1841-1885.....................DLB-21
Exley, Frederick 1929- Y-81
Experiment in the Novel (1929), by John D. Beresford DLB-36

F

"F. Scott Fitzgerald: St. Paul's Native Son and Distinguished American Writer": University of Minnesota Conference, 29-31 October 1982...Y-82
Faber, Frederick William 1814-1863 ....DLB-32
Fair, Ronald L. 1932- DLB-33
Fairfax, Beatrice (see Manning, Marie)
Fairlie, Gerard 1899-1983 ....DLB-77
Fallada, Hans 1893-1947...................................DLB-56
Fancher, Betsy 1928- Y-83
Fane, Violet 1843-1905.......................................DLB-35
Fantasy Press Publishers DLB-46
Fante, John 1909-1983...Y-83
Farber, Norma 1909-1984..................................DLB-61
Farigoule, Louis (see Romains, Jules)
Farley, Walter 1920- DLB-22
Farmer, Philip José 1918- DLB-8
Farquhar, George circa 1677-1707 ....DLB-84
Farquharson, Martha (see Finley, Martha)
Farrar and Rinehart...DLB-46
Farrar, Straus and Giroux DLB-46
Farrell, James T. 1904-1979............DLB-4, 9, 86; DS-2
Farrell, J. G. 1935-1979......................................DLB-14
Fast, Howard 1914- DLB-9
Faulkner, William 1897-1962 ....DLB-9, 11, 44; DS-2; Y-86
Fauset, Jessie Redmon 1882-1961......................DLB-51
Faust, Irvin 1924- DLB-2, 28; Y-80
Fawcett Books DLB-46
Fearing, Kenneth 1902-1961................................DLB-9
Federal Writers' Project......................................DLB-46
Federman, Raymond 1928- Y-80
Feiffer, Jules 1929- DLB-7, 44
Feinberg, Charles E. 1899-1988 ....Y-88
Feinstein, Elaine 1930- DLB-14, 40
Fell, Frederick, Publishers..................................DLB-46
Fels, Ludwig 1946- DLB-75
Felton, Cornelius Conway 1807-1862 ....DLB-1
Fennario, David 1947- DLB-60
Fenno, John 1751-1798 ....DLB-43
Fenno, R. F., and Company...............................DLB-49
Fenton, James 1949- DLB-40
Ferber, Edna 1885-1968 ....DLB-9, 28, 86
Ferdinand, Vallery III (see Salaam, Kalamu ya)
Ferguson, Sir Samuel 1810-1886 ....DLB-32
Ferguson, William Scott 1875-1954 ....DLB-47
Ferlinghetti, Lawrence 1919- DLB-5, 16
Fern, Fanny (see Parton, Sara Payson Willis)
Ferrars, Elizabeth 1907- DLB-87
Ferret, E., and Company....................................DLB-49
Ferrini, Vincent 1913- DLB-48
Ferron, Jacques 1921-1985.................................DLB-60
Ferron, Madeleine 1922- DLB-53
Fetridge and Company.......................................DLB-49
Feuchtwanger, Lion 1884-1958...........................DLB-66
Fichte, Johann Gottlieb 1762-1814 ....DLB-90
Ficke, Arthur Davison 1883-1945.......................DLB-54
Fiction Best-Sellers, 1910-1945.............................DLB-9
Fiction into Film, 1928-1975: A List of Movies Based on the Works of Authors in *British Novelists, 1930-1959* DLB-15
Fiedler, Leslie A. 1917- DLB-28, 67
Field, Eugene 1850-1895 ....DLB-23, 42
Field, Nathan 1587-1619 or 1620.......................DLB-58
Field, Rachel 1894-1942................................DLB-9, 22
A Field Guide to Recent Schools of American Poetry Y-86
Fielding, Henry 1707-1754..........................DLB-39, 84

Fielding, Sarah 1710-1768 ....DLB-39
Fields, James Thomas 1817-1881 ....DLB-1
Fields, Julia 1938- DLB-41
Fields, W. C. 1880-1946 ....DLB-44
Fields, Osgood and Company DLB-49
Fifty Penguin Years Y-85
Figes, Eva 1932- DLB-14
Filson, John circa 1753-1788 ....DLB-37
Finch, Robert 1900- DLB-88
Findley, Timothy 1930- DLB-53
Finlay, Ian Hamilton 1925- DLB-40
Finley, Martha 1828-1909 ....DLB-42
Finney, Jack 1911- DLB-8
Finney, Walter Braden (see Finney, Jack)
Firbank, Ronald 1886-1926 ....DLB-36
Firmin, Giles 1615-1697 ....DLB-24
First Strauss "Livings" Awarded to Cynthia Ozick and Raymond Carver
An Interview with Cynthia Ozick
An Interview with Raymond Carver Y-83
Fish, Stanley 1938- DLB-67
Fisher, Clay (see Allen, Henry W.)
Fisher, Dorothy Canfield 1879-1958 ....DLB-9
Fisher, Leonard Everett 1924- DLB-61
Fisher, Roy 1930- DLB-40
Fisher, Rudolph 1897-1934 ....DLB-51
Fisher, Sydney George 1856-1927 ....DLB-47
Fisher, Vardis 1895-1968 ....DLB-9
Fiske, John 1608-1677 ....DLB-24
Fiske, John 1842-1901 ....DLB-47, 64
Fitch, Thomas circa 1700-1774 ....DLB-31
Fitch, William Clyde 1865-1909 ....DLB-7
FitzGerald, Edward 1809-1883 ....DLB-32
Fitzgerald, F. Scott 1896-1940 ....DLB-4, 9, 86; Y-81; DS-1
Fitzgerald, Penelope 1916- DLB-14
Fitzgerald, Robert 1910-1985 ....Y-80
Fitzgerald, Thomas 1819-1891 ....DLB-23
Fitzgerald, Zelda Sayre 1900-1948 ....Y-84
Fitzhugh, Louise 1928-1974 ....DLB-52
Fitzhugh, William circa 1651-1701 ....DLB-24
Flanagan, Thomas 1923- Y-80
Flanner, Hildegarde 1899-1987 ....DLB-48
Flanner, Janet 1892-1978 ....DLB-4
Flavin, Martin 1883-1967 ....DLB-9
Flecker, James Elroy 1884-1915 ....DLB-10, 19
Fleeson, Doris 1901-1970 ....DLB-29
Fleidser, Marieluise 1901-1974 ....DLB-56
Fleming, Ian 1908-1964 ....DLB-87
The Fleshly School of Poetry and Other Phenomena of the Day (1872), by Robert Buchanan DLB-35
The Fleshly School of Poetry: Mr. D. G. Rossetti (1871), by Thomas Maitland (Robert Buchanan) DLB-35
Fletcher, J. S. 1863-1935 ....DLB-70
Fletcher, John (see Beaumont, Francis)
Fletcher, John Gould 1886-1950 ....DLB-4, 45
Flieg, Helmut (see Heym, Stefan)
Flint, F. S. 1885-1960 ....DLB-19
Flint, Timothy 1780-1840 ....DLB-73
Follen, Eliza Lee (Cabot) 1787-1860 ....DLB-1
Follett, Ken 1949- Y-81, DLB-87
Follett Publishing Company DLB-46
Folsom, John West [publishing house] DLB-49
Foote, Horton 1916- DLB-26
Foote, Samuel 1721-1777 ....DLB-89
Foote, Shelby 1916- DLB-2, 17
Forbes, Calvin 1945- DLB-41
Forbes, Ester 1891-1967 ....DLB-22
Forbes and Company DLB-49
Force, Peter 1790-1868 ....DLB-30
Forché, Carolyn 1950- DLB-5
Ford, Charles Henri 1913- DLB-4, 48
Ford, Corey 1902-1969 ....DLB-11
Ford, Ford Madox 1873-1939 ....DLB-34
Ford, J. B., and Company DLB-49
Ford, Jesse Hill 1928- DLB-6
Ford, John 1586-? DLB-58
Ford, R. A. D. 1915- DLB-88
Ford, Worthington C. 1858-1941 ....DLB-47
Fords, Howard, and Hulbert DLB-49
Foreman, Carl 1914-1984 ....DLB-26
Forester, Frank (see Herbert, Henry William)

Fornés, María Irene 1930- DLB-7
Forrest, Leon 1937- DLB-33
Forster, E. M. 1879-1970....DLB-34
Forsyth, Frederick 1938- DLB-87
Forten, Charlotte L. 1837-1914....DLB-50
Fortune, T. Thomas 1856-1928....DLB-23
Fosdick, Charles Austin 1842-1915....DLB-42
Foster, Genevieve 1893-1979....DLB-61
Foster, Hannah Webster 1758-1840....DLB-37
Foster, John 1648-1681 ....DLB-24
Foster, Michael 1904-1956....DLB-9
Fouquë, Caroline de la Motte 1774-1831 ....DLB-90
Fouqué, Friedrich de la Motte 1777-1843 ....DLB-90
Four Essays on the Beat Generation, by John Clellon Holmes....DLB-16
Four Seas Company....DLB-46
Four Winds Press....DLB-46
Fournier, Henri Alban (see Alain-Fournier)
Fowler and Wells Company....DLB-49
Fowles, John 1926- DLB-14
Fox, John, Jr. 1862 or 1863-1919....DLB-9
Fox, Paula 1923- DLB-52
Fox, Richard K. [publishing house] DLB-49
Fox, Richard Kyle 1846-1922....DLB-79
Fox, William Price 1926- DLB-2; Y-81
Fraenkel, Michael 1896-1957....DLB-4
France, Richard 1938- DLB-7
Francis, C. S. [publishing house] DLB-49
Francis, Convers 1795-1863....DLB-1
Francis, Dick 1920- DLB-87
Francke, Kuno 1855-1930....DLB-71
Frank, Leonhard 1882-1961 ....DLB-56
Frank, Melvin (see Panama, Norman)
Frank, Waldo 1889-1967....DLB-9, 63
Franken, Rose 1895?-1988 ....Y-84
Franklin, Benjamin 1706-1790....DLB-24, 43, 73
Franklin, James 1697-1735 ....DLB-43
Franklin Library DLB-46
Frantz, Ralph Jules 1902-1979....DLB-4
Fraser, G. S. 1915-1980....DLB-27
Frayn, Michael 1933- DLB-13, 14
Frederic, Harold 1856-1898 ....DLB-12, 23
Freeling, Nicolas 1927- DLB-87
Freeman, Douglas Southall 1886-1953....DLB-17
Freeman, Legh Richmond 1842-1915....DLB-23
Freeman, Mary E. Wilkins 1852-1930....DLB-12, 78
Freeman, R. Austin 1862-1943....DLB-70
French, Alice 1850-1934 ....DLB-74
French, David 1939- DLB-53
French, James [publishing house]....DLB-49
French, Samuel [publishing house] DLB-49
Freneau, Philip 1752-1832....DLB-37, 43
Fried, Erich 1921-1988....DLB-85
Friedman, Bruce Jay 1930- DLB-2, 28
Friel, Brian 1929- DLB-13
Friend, Krebs 1895?-1967? DLB-4
Fries, Fritz Rudolf 1935- DLB-75
Fringe and Alternative Theater in Great Britain....DLB-13
Frisch, Max 1911- DLB-69
Frischmuth, Barbara 1941- DLB-85
Fritz, Jean 1915- DLB-52
Frost, Robert 1874-1963....DLB-54; DS-7
Frothingham, Octavius Brooks 1822-1895....DLB-1
Froude, James Anthony 1818-1894....DLB-18, 57
Fry, Christopher 1907- DLB-13
Frye, Northrop 1912- DLB-67, 68
Fuchs, Daniel 1909- DLB-9, 26, 28
The Fugitives and the Agrarians: The First Exhibition Y-85
Fuller, Charles H., Jr. 1939- DLB-38
Fuller, Henry Blake 1857-1929 ....DLB-12
Fuller, John 1937- DLB-40
Fuller, Roy 1912- DLB-15, 20
Fuller, Samuel 1912- DLB-26
Fuller, Sarah Margaret, Marchesa D'Ossoli 1810-1850 ....DLB-1, 59, 73
Fulton, Len 1934- Y-86
Fulton, Robin 1937- DLB-40
Furman, Laura 1945- Y-86

Furness, Horace Howard 1833-1912 .... DLB-64
Furness, William Henry 1802-1896 .... DLB-1
Furthman, Jules 1888-1966 .... DLB-26
The Future of the Novel (1899), by Henry James DLB-18

G

Gaddis, William 1922- DLB-2
Gág, Wanda 1893-1946 .... DLB-22
Gagnon, Madeleine 1938- DLB-60
Gaine, Hugh 1726-1807 .... DLB-43
Gaine, Hugh [publishing house] DLB-49
Gaines, Ernest J. 1933- DLB-2, 33; Y-80
Gaiser, Gerd 1908-1976 .... DLB-69
Galaxy Science Fiction Novels DLB-46
Gale, Zona 1874-1938 .... DLB-9, 78
Gallagher, William Davis 1808-1894 .... DLB-73
Gallant, Mavis 1922- DLB-53
Gallico, Paul 1897-1976 .... DLB-9
Galsworthy, John 1867-1933 .... DLB-10, 34
Galvin, Brendan 1938- DLB-5
Gambit DLB-46
Gammer Gurton's Needle DLB-62
Gannett, Frank E. 1876-1957 .... DLB-29
García, Lionel G. 1935- DLB-82
Gardam, Jane 1928- DLB-14
Garden, Alexander circa 1685-1756 .... DLB-31
Gardner, John 1933-1982 .... DLB-2; Y-82
Garis, Howard R. 1873-1962 .... DLB-22
Garland, Hamlin 1860-1940 .... DLB-12, 71, 78
Garneau, Hector de Saint-Denys 1912-1943 ...... DLB-88
Garneau, Michel 1939- DLB-53
Garner, Hugh 1913-1979 .... DLB-68
Garnett, David 1892-1981 .... DLB-34
Garraty, John A. 1920- DLB-17
Garrett, George 1929- DLB-2, 5; Y-83
Garrick, David 1717-1779 .... DLB-84
Garrison, William Lloyd 1805-1879 .... DLB-1, 43
Garve, Andrew 1908- DLB-87
Gary, Romain 1914-1980 .... DLB-83
Gascoyne, David 1916- DLB-20
Gaskell, Elizabeth Cleghorn 1810-1865 .... DLB-21
Gass, William Howard 1924- DLB-2
Gates, Doris 1901- DLB-22
Gates, Henry Louis, Jr. 1950- DLB-67
Gates, Lewis E. 1860-1924 .... DLB-71
Gauvreau, Claude 1925-1971 .... DLB-88
Gay, Ebenezer 1696-1787 .... DLB-24
Gay, John 1685-1732 .... DLB-84
The Gay Science (1866), by E. S. Dallas [excerpt] DLB-21
Gayarré, Charles E. A. 1805-1895 .... DLB-30
Gaylord, Charles [publishing house] DLB-49
Geddes, Gary 1940- DLB-60
Geddes, Virgil 1897- DLB-4
Geis, Bernard, Associates DLB-46
Geisel, Theodor Seuss 1904- DLB-61
Gelber, Jack 1932- DLB-7
Gélinas, Gratien 1909- DLB-88
Gellhorn, Martha 1908- Y-82
Gems, Pam 1925- DLB-13
A General Idea of the College of Mirania (1753), by William Smith [excerpts] DLB-31
Genet, Jean 1910-1986 .... Y-86, DLB-72
Genevoix, Maurice 1890-1980 .... DLB-65
Genovese, Eugene D. 1930- DLB-17
Gent, Peter 1942- Y-82
George, Henry 1839-1897 .... DLB-23
George, Jean Craighead 1919- DLB-52
Gerhardie, William 1895-1977 .... DLB-36
Germanophilism, by Hans Kohn DLB-66
Gernsback, Hugo 1884-1967 .... DLB-8
Gerould, Katharine Fullerton 1879-1944 .... DLB-78
Gerrish, Samuel [publishing house] DLB-49
Gerrold, David 1944- DLB-8
Geston, Mark S. 1946- DLB-8
Gibbon, Lewis Grassic (see Mitchell, James Leslie)
Gibbons, Floyd 1887-1939 .... DLB-25
Gibbons, William ?-? DLB-73
Gibson, Graeme 1934- DLB-53
Gibson, Wilfrid 1878-1962 .... DLB-19

Gibson, William 1914- DLB-7
Gide, André 1869-1951....................................DLB-65
Giguère, Diane 1937- DLB-53
Giguère, Roland 1929- DLB-60
Gilbert, Anthony 1899-1973 ....DLB-77
Gilbert, Michael 1912- DLB-87
Gilder, Jeannette L. 1849-1916....................................DLB-79
Gilder, Richard Watson 1844-1909 ....DLB-64, 79
Gildersleeve, Basil 1831-1924 ....DLB-71
Giles, Henry 1809-1882 ....DLB-64
Gill, William F., Company DLB-49
Gillespie, A. Lincoln, Jr. 1895-1950 ....DLB-4
Gilliam, Florence ?-?....................................DLB-4
Gilliatt, Penelope 1932- DLB-14
Gillott, Jacky 1939-1980 ....DLB-14
Gilman, Caroline H. 1794-1888 ....DLB-3, 73
Gilman, W. and J. [publishing house] DLB-49
Gilmer, Elizabeth Meriwether 1861-1951 ....DLB-29
Gilmer, Francis Walker 1790-1826 ....DLB-37
Gilroy, Frank D. 1925- DLB-7
Ginsberg, Allen 1926- DLB-5, 16
Ginzkey, Franz Karl 1871-1963 ....DLB-81
Giono, Jean 1895-1970....................................DLB-72
Giovanni, Nikki 1943- DLB-5, 41
Gipson, Lawrence Henry 1880-1971 ....DLB-17
Giraudoux, Jean 1882-1944 ....DLB-65
Gissing, George 1857-1903 ....DLB-18
Gladstone, William Ewart 1809-1898 ....DLB-57
Glaeser, Ernst 1902-1963 ....DLB-69
Glanville, Brian 1931- DLB-15
Glapthorne, Henry 1610-1643? DLB-58
Glasgow, Ellen 1873-1945....................................DLB-9, 12
Glaspell, Susan 1876-1948..........................DLB-7, 9, 78
Glass, Montague 1877-1934 ....DLB-11
Glassco, John 1909-1981 ....DLB-68
Glauser, Friedrich 1896-1938 ....DLB-56
F. Gleason's Publishing Hall DLB-49
Glück, Louise 1943- DLB-5
Godbout, Jacques 1933- DLB-53
Goddard, Morrill 1865-1937 ....DLB-25
Goddard, William 1740-1817 ....DLB-43
Godey, Louis A. 1804-1878 ....DLB-73
Godey and McMichael....................................DLB-49
Godfrey, Dave 1938- DLB-60
Godfrey, Thomas 1736-1763 ....DLB-31
Godine, David R., Publisher DLB-46
Godkin, E. L. 1831-1902....................................DLB-79
Godwin, Gail 1937- DLB-6
Godwin, Parke 1816-1904..............................DLB-3, 64
Godwin, William 1756-1836 ....DLB-39
Goes, Albrecht 1908- DLB-69
Goffe, Thomas circa 1592-1629..........................DLB-58
Goffstein, M. B. 1940- DLB-61
Gogarty, Oliver St. John 1878-1957 ....DLB-15, 19
Goines, Donald 1937-1974 ....DLB-33
Gold, Herbert 1924- DLB-2; Y-81
Gold, Michael 1893-1967 ....DLB-9, 28
Goldberg, Dick 1947- DLB-7
Golding, William 1911- DLB-15
Goldman, William 1931- DLB-44
Goldsmith, Oliver 1730?-1774 ....DLB-39, 89
Goldsmith Publishing Company DLB-46
Gomme, Laurence James
[publishing house] DLB-46
González-T., César A. 1931- DLB-82
The Goodman Theatre....................................DLB-7
Goodrich, Frances 1891-1984 and
Hackett, Albert 1900- DLB-26
Goodrich, S. G. [publishing house] DLB-49
Goodrich, Samuel Griswold 1793-1860 ...DLB-1, 42, 73
Goodspeed, C. E., and Company DLB-49
Goodwin, Stephen 1943- Y-82
Gookin, Daniel 1612-1687 ....DLB-24
Gordon, Caroline 1895-1981 ....DLB-4, 9; Y-81
Gordon, Giles 1940- DLB-14
Gordon, Mary 1949- DLB-6; Y-81
Gordone, Charles 1925- DLB-7
Gorey, Edward 1925- DLB-61
Görres, Joseph 1776-1848....................................DLB-90
Gosse, Edmund 1849-1928 ....DLB-57
Gotlieb, Phyllis 1926- DLB-88
Gould, Wallace 1882-1940 ....DLB-54

Goyen, William 1915-1983..........................DLB-2; Y-83
Gracq, Julien 1910- DLB-83
Grady, Henry W. 1850-1889..............................DLB-23
Graf, Oskar Maria 1894-1967.............................DLB-56
Graham, George Rex 1813-1894........................DLB-73
Graham, Gwethalyn 1913-1965..........................DLB-88
Graham, Lorenz 1902- DLB-76
Graham, Shirley 1896-1977...............................DLB-76
Graham, W. S. 1918- DLB-20
Graham, William H. [publishing house]............DLB-49
Graham, Winston 1910- DLB-77
Grahame, Kenneth 1859-1932...........................DLB-34
Gramatky, Hardie 1907-1979............................DLB-22
Granich, Irwin (see Gold, Michael)
Grant, George 1918-1988..................................DLB-88
Grant, Harry J. 1881-1963................................DLB-29
Grant, James Edward 1905-1966.......................DLB-26
Grass, Günter 1927- DLB-75
Grasty, Charles H. 1863-1924...........................DLB-25
Grau, Shirley Ann 1929- DLB-2
Graves, John 1920- Y-83
Graves, Richard 1715-1804...............................DLB-39
Graves, Robert 1895-1985.......................DLB-20; Y-85
Gray, Asa 1810-1888...DLB-1
Gray, David 1838-1861......................................DLB-32
Gray, Simon 1936- DLB-13
Grayson, William J. 1788-1863......................DLB-3, 64
The Great War and the Theater, 1914-1918
[Great Britain]..DLB-10
Greeley, Horace 1811-1872..........................DLB-3, 43
Green, Adolph (see Comden, Betty)
Green, Duff 1791-1875......................................DLB-43
Green, Gerald 1922- DLB-28
Green, Henry 1905-1973..................................DLB-15
Green, Jonas 1712-1767....................................DLB-31
Green, Joseph 1706-1780..................................DLB-31
Green, Julien 1900- DLB-4, 72
Green, Paul 1894-1981...........................DLB-7, 9; Y-81
Green, T. and S. [publishing house].................DLB-49
Green, Timothy [publishing house]...................DLB-49
Greenberg: Publisher..DLB-46
Green Tiger Press...DLB-46
Greene, Asa 1789-1838......................................DLB-11
Greene, Benjamin H. [publishing house]...........DLB-49
Greene, Graham 1904- DLB-13, 15, 77; Y-85
Greene, Robert 1558-1592.................................DLB-62
Greenhow, Robert 1800-1854............................DLB-30
Greenough, Horatio 1805-1852...........................DLB-1
Greenwell, Dora 1821-1882...............................DLB-35
Greenwillow Books..DLB-46
Greenwood, Grace (see Lippincott, Sara Jane Clarke)
Greenwood, Walter 1903-1974..........................DLB-10
Greer, Ben 1948- DLB-6
Greg, W. R. 1809-1881......................................DLB-55
Gregg Press...DLB-46
Persse, Isabella Augusta,
Lady Gregory 1852-1932...............................DLB-10
Gregory, Horace 1898-1982..............................DLB-48
Greville, Fulke, First Lord Brooke
1554-1628..DLB-62
Grey, Zane 1872-1939..DLB-9
Grier, Eldon 1917- DLB-88
Grieve, C. M. (see MacDiarmid, Hugh)
Griffith, Elizabeth 1727?-1793.....................DLB-39, 89
Griffiths, Trevor 1935- DLB-13
Griggs, S. C., and Company...............................DLB-49
Griggs, Sutton Elbert 1872-1930.......................DLB-50
Grignon, Claude-Henri 1894-1976....................DLB-68
Grigson, Geoffrey 1905- DLB-27
Grimké, Angelina Weld 1880-1958..............DLB-50, 54
Grimm, Hans 1875-1959...................................DLB-66
Grimm, Jacob 1785-1863..................................DLB-90
Grimm, Wilhelm 1786-1859..............................DLB-90
Griswold, Rufus Wilmot 1815-1857..............DLB-3, 59
Gross, Milt 1895-1953.......................................DLB-11
Grosset and Dunlap...DLB-49
Grossman Publishers...DLB-46
Groulx, Lionel 1878-1967..................................DLB-68
Grove Press...DLB-46
Grubb, Davis 1919-1980.....................................DLB-6
Gruelle, Johnny 1880-1938...............................DLB-22
Guare, John 1938- DLB-7

Guest, Barbara 1920- DLB-5
Guèvremont, Germaine 1893-1968 ....DLB-68
Guilloux, Louis 1899-1980.................................DLB-72
Guiney, Louise Imogen 1861-1920....................DLB-54
Guiterman, Arthur 1871-1943...........................DLB-11
Günderrode, Caroline von 1780-1806 ....DLB-90
Gunn, Bill 1934-1989..DLB-38
Gunn, James E. 1923- DLB-8
Gunn, Neil M. 1891-1973 ....DLB-15
Gunn, Thom 1929- DLB-27
Gunnars, Kristjana 1948- DLB-60
Gurik, Robert 1932- DLB-60
Gustafson, Ralph 1909- DLB-88
Gütersloh, Albert Paris 1887-1973 ....DLB-81
Guthrie, A. B., Jr. 1901- DLB-6
Guthrie, Ramon 1896-1973.................................DLB-4
The Guthrie Theater..DLB-7
Guy, Ray 1939- DLB-60
Guy, Rosa 1925- DLB-33
Gwynne, Erskine 1898-1948 ....DLB-4
Gysin, Brion 1916- DLB-16

H

H. D. (see Doolittle, Hilda)
Hackett, Albert (see Goodrich, Frances)
Hagelstange, Rudolf 1912-1984.........................DLB-69
Haggard, H. Rider 1856-1925............................DLB-70
Haig-Brown, Roderick 1908-1976 ....DLB-88
Hailey, Arthur 1920- DLB-88; Y-82
Haines, John 1924- DLB-5
Hake, Thomas Gordon 1809-1895 ....DLB-32
Haldeman, Joe 1943- DLB-8
Haldeman-Julius Company DLB-46
Hale, E. J., and Son...DLB-49
Hale, Edward Everett 1822-1909 ....DLB-1, 42, 74
Hale, Leo Thomas (see Ebon)
Hale, Lucretia Peabody 1820-1900....................DLB-42
Hale, Nancy 1908-1988 ....DLB-86; Y-80, 88
Hale, Sarah Josepha (Buell) 1788-1879...DLB-1, 42, 73
Haley, Alex 1921- DLB-38
Haliburton, Thomas Chandler 1796-1865.........DLB-11
Hall, Donald 1928- DLB-5
Hall, James 1793-1868 ....DLB-73, 74
Hall, Samuel [publishing house]........................DLB-49
Hallam, Arthur Henry 1811-1833.....................DLB-32
Halleck, Fitz-Greene 1790-1867 ....DLB-3
Hallmark Editions DLB-46
Halper, Albert 1904-1984 ....DLB-9
Halstead, Murat 1829-1908...............................DLB-23
Hamburger, Michael 1924- DLB-27
Hamilton, Alexander 1712-1756 ....DLB-31
Hamilton, Alexander 1755?-1804......................DLB-37
Hamilton, Cicely 1872-1952..............................DLB-10
Hamilton, Edmond 1904-1977 ....DLB-8
Hamilton, Gail (see Corcoran, Barbara)
Hamilton, Ian 1938- DLB-40
Hamilton, Patrick 1904-1962 ....DLB-10
Hamilton, Virginia 1936- DLB-33, 52
Hammett, Dashiell 1894-1961 ....DS-6
Hammon, Jupiter 1711-died between 1790 and 1806.......................................DLB-31, 50
Hammond, John ?-1663.....................................DLB-24
Hamner, Earl 1923- DLB-6
Hampton, Christopher 1946- DLB-13
Handel-Mazzetti, Enrica von 1871-1955 ....DLB-81
Handke, Peter 1942- DLB-85
Handlin, Oscar 1915- DLB-17
Hankin, St. John 1869-1909 ....DLB-10
Hanley, Clifford 1922- DLB-14
Hannah, Barry 1942- DLB-6
Hannay, James 1827-1873.................................DLB-21
Hansberry, Lorraine 1930-1965 ....DLB-7, 38
Harcourt Brace Jovanovich DLB-46
Hardenberg, Friedrich von (see Novalis)
Hardwick, Elizabeth 1916- DLB-6
Hardy, Thomas 1840-1928..........................DLB-18, 19
Hare, Cyril 1900-1958.......................................DLB-77
Hare, David 1947- DLB-13
Hargrove, Marion 1919- DLB-11

Harlow, Robert 1923- DLB-60

Harness, Charles L. 1915- DLB-8

Harper, Fletcher 1806-1877 ....DLB-79

Harper, Frances Ellen Watkins 1825-1911 ....DLB-50

Harper, Michael S. 1938- DLB-41

Harper and Brothers......................................DLB-49

Harris, Benjamin ?-circa 1720 ....DLB-42, 43

Harris, Christie 1907- DLB-88

Harris, George Washington 1814-1869..........DLB-3, 11

Harris, Joel Chandler 1848-1908.....DLB-11, 23, 42, 78

Harris, Mark 1922- DLB-2; Y-80

Harrison, Charles Yale 1898-1954 ....DLB-68

Harrison, Frederic 1831-1923............................DLB-57

Harrison, Harry 1925- DLB-8

Harrison, James P., Company..............................DLB-49

Harrison, Jim 1937- Y-82

Harrison, Paul Carter 1936- DLB-38

Harrison, Tony 1937- DLB-40

Harrisse, Henry 1829-1910................................DLB-47

Harsent, David 1942- DLB-40

Hart, Albert Bushnell 1854-1943 ....DLB-17

Hart, Moss 1904-1961 ....DLB-7

Hart, Oliver 1723-1795 ....DLB-31

Harte, Bret 1836-1902 ....DLB-12, 64, 74, 79

Hartlaub, Felix 1913-1945................................DLB-56

Hartley, L. P. 1895-1972.................................DLB-15

Hartley, Marsden 1877-1943 ....DLB-54

Härtling, Peter 1933- DLB-75

Hartman, Geoffrey H. 1929- DLB-67

Hartmann, Sadakichi 1867-1944 ....DLB-54

Harvey, Jean-Charles 1891-1967 ....DLB-88

Harwood, Lee 1939- DLB-40

Harwood, Ronald 1934- DLB-13

Haskins, Charles Homer 1870-1937.........................DLB-47

The Hatch-Billops Collection DLB-76

Hauff, Wilhelm 1802-1827 ....DLB-90

A Haughty and Proud Generation (1922), by Ford Madox Hueffer..............................DLB-36

Hauptmann, Carl 1858-1921 ....DLB-66

Hauptmann, Gerhart 1862-1946 ....DLB-66

Hauser, Marianne 1910- Y-83

Hawker, Robert Stephen 1803-1875 ....DLB-32

Hawkes, John 1925- DLB-2, 7; Y-80

Hawkins, Walter Everette 1883-?..........................DLB-50

Hawthorne, Nathaniel 1804-1864 ....DLB-1, 74

Hay, John 1838-1905 ....DLB-12, 47

Hayden, Robert 1913-1980.................................DLB-5, 76

Hayes, John Michael 1919- DLB-26

Hayne, Paul Hamilton 1830-1886...........................DLB-3, 64, 79

Haywood, Eliza 1693?-1756 ....DLB-39

Hazard, Willis P. [publishing house] DLB-49

Hazzard, Shirley 1931- Y-82

Headley, Joel T. 1813-1897 ....DLB-30

Heaney, Seamus 1939- DLB-40

Heard, Nathan C. 1936- DLB-33

Hearn, Lafcadio 1850-1904 ....DLB-12, 78

Hearst, William Randolph 1863-1951 ....DLB-25

Heath, Catherine 1924- DLB-14

Heath-Stubbs, John 1918- DLB-27

Hebel, Johann Peter 1760-1826............................DLB-90

Hébert, Anne 1916- DLB-68

Hébert, Jacques 1923- DLB-53

Hecht, Anthony 1923- DLB-5

Hecht, Ben 1894-1964.............DLB-7, 9, 25, 26, 28, 86

Hecker, Isaac Thomas 1819-1888 ....DLB-1

Hedge, Frederic Henry 1805-1890 ....DLB-1, 59

Hegel, Georg Wilhelm Friedrich 1770-1831 ....DLB-90

Heidish, Marcy 1947- Y-82

Heine, Heinrich 1797-1856................................DLB-90

Heinlein, Robert A. 1907- DLB-8

Heinrich, Willi 1920- DLB-75

Heidsenbüttel 1921- DLB-75

Heller, Joseph 1923- DLB-2, 28; Y-80

Hellman, Lillian 1906-1984...............................DLB-7; Y-84

Helprin, Mark 1947- Y-85

Helwig, David 1938- DLB-60

Hemingway, Ernest 1899-1961 ....DLB-4, 9; Y-81, 87; DS-1

Hemingway: Twenty-Five Years Later Y-85

Hemphill, Paul 1936- Y-87

Hénault, Gilles 1920- DLB-88
Henchman, Daniel 1689-1761 DLB-24
Henderson, Alice Corbin 1881-1949 DLB-54
Henderson, David 1942- DLB-41
Henderson, George Wylie 1904- DLB-51
Henderson, Zenna 1917- DLB-8
Henisch, Peter 1943- DLB-85
Henley, Beth 1952- Y-86
Henley, William Ernest 1849-1903 DLB-19
Henry, Buck 1930- DLB-26
Henry, Marguerite 1902- DLB-22
Henry, Robert Selph 1889-1970 DLB-17
Henry, Will (see Allen, Henry W.)
Henschke, Alfred (see Klabund)
Henty, G. A. 1832-1902 DLB-18
Hentz, Caroline Lee 1800-1856 DLB-3
Herbert, Alan Patrick 1890-1971 DLB-10
Herbert, Frank 1920-1986 DLB-8
Herbert, Henry William 1807-1858 DLB-3, 73
Herbert, John 1926- DLB-53
Herbst, Josephine 1892-1969 DLB-9
Herburger, Günter 1932- DLB-75
Hercules, Frank E. M. 1917- DLB-33
Herder, B., Book Company DLB-49
Hergesheimer, Joseph 1880-1954 DLB-9
Heritage Press DLB-46
Hermlin, Stephan 1915- DLB-69
Hernton, Calvin C. 1932- DLB-38
"The Hero as Man of Letters: Johnson, Rousseau, Burns" (1841), by Thomas Carlyle [excerpt] DLB-57
The Hero as Poet. Dante; Shakspeare (1841), by Thomas Carlyle DLB-32
Herrick, E. R., and Company DLB-49
Herrick, Robert 1868-1938 DLB-9, 12, 78
Herrick, William 1915- Y-83
Herrmann, John 1900-1959 DLB-4
Hersey, John 1914- DLB-6
Hertel, François 1905-1985 DLB-68
Hervé-Bazin, Jean Pierre Marie (see Bazin, Hervé)
Herzog, Emile Salomon Wilhelm (see Maurois, André)
Hesse, Hermann 1877-1962 DLB-66
Hewat, Alexander circa 1743-circa 1824 DLB-30
Hewitt, John 1907- DLB-27
Hewlett, Maurice 1861-1923 DLB-34
Heyen, William 1940- DLB-5
Heyer, Georgette 1902-1974 DLB-77
Heym, Stefan 1913- DLB-69
Heyward, Dorothy 1890-1961 and Heyward, DuBose 1885-1940 DLB-7
Heyward, DuBose 1885-1940 DLB-7, 9, 45
Heywood, Thomas 1573 or 1574-1641 DLB-62
Hiebert, Paul 1892-1987 DLB-68
Higgins, Aidan 1927- DLB-14
Higgins, Colin 1941-1988 DLB-26
Higgins, George V. 1939- DLB-2; Y-81
Higginson, Thomas Wentworth 1823-1911 DLB-1, 64
Highwater, Jamake 1942?- DLB-52; Y-85
Hildesheimer, Wolfgang 1916- DLB-69
Hildreth, Richard 1807-1865 DLB-1, 30, 59
Hill, Aaron 1685-1750 DLB-84
Hill, Geoffrey 1932- DLB-40
Hill, George M., Company DLB-49
Hill, "Sir" John 1714?-1775 DLB-39
Hill, Lawrence, and Company, Publishers DLB-46
Hill, Leslie 1880-1960 DLB-51
Hill, Susan 1942- DLB-14
Hill, Walter 1942- DLB-44
Hill and Wang DLB-46
Hilliard, Gray and Company DLB-49
Hillyer, Robert 1895-1961 DLB-54
Hilton, James 1900-1954 DLB-34, 77
Hilton and Company DLB-49
Himes, Chester 1909-1984 DLB-2, 76
Hine, Daryl 1936- DLB-60
Hinojosa-Smith, Rolando 1929- DLB-82
The History of the Adventures of Joseph Andrews (1742), by Henry Fielding [excerpt] DLB-39
Hirsch, E. D., Jr. 1928- DLB-67
Hoagland, Edward 1932- DLB-6
Hoagland, Everett H. III 1942- DLB-41
Hoban, Russell 1925- DLB-52

Hobsbaum, Philip 1932- DLB-40
Hobson, Laura Z. 1900- DLB-28
Hochman, Sandra 1936- DLB-5
Hodgins, Jack 1938- DLB-60
Hodgman, Helen 1945- DLB-14
Hodgson, Ralph 1871-1962 ....DLB-19
Hodgson, William Hope 1877-1918....DLB-70
Hoffenstein, Samuel 1890-1947....DLB-11
Hoffman, Charles Fenno 1806-1884 ....DLB-3
Hoffman, Daniel 1923- DLB-5
Hoffmann, E. T. A. 1776-1822 ....DLB-90
Hofmann, Michael 1957- DLB-40
Hofmannsthal, Hugo von 1874-1929....DLB-81
Hofstadter, Richard 1916-1970 ....DLB-17
Hogan, Desmond 1950- DLB-14
Hogan and Thompson DLB-49
Hohl, Ludwig 1904-1980 ....DLB-56
Holbrook, David 1923- DLB-14, 40
Holcroft, Thomas 1745-1809....DLB-39, 89
Holden, Molly 1927-1981 ....DLB-40
Hölderlin, Friedrich 1770-1843....DLB-90
Holiday House DLB-46
Holland, Norman N. 1927- DLB-67
Hollander, John 1929- DLB-5
Holley, Marietta 1836-1926 ....DLB-11
Hollingsworth, Margaret 1940- DLB-60
Hollo, Anselm 1934- DLB-40
Holloway, John 1920- DLB-27
Holloway House Publishing Company DLB-46
Holme, Constance 1880-1955 ....DLB-34
Holmes, Oliver Wendell 1809-1894....DLB-1
Holmes, John Clellon 1926-1988 ....DLB-16
Holst, Hermann E. von 1841-1904....DLB-47
Holt, Henry, and Company DLB-49
Holt, John 1721-1784....DLB-43
Holt, Rinehart and Winston....DLB-46
Holthusen, Hans Egon 1913- DLB-69
Home, Henry, Lord Kames 1696-1782....DLB-31
Home, John 1722-1808....DLB-84
Home Publishing Company DLB-49
Home, William Douglas 1912- DLB-13
Homes, Geoffrey (see Mainwaring, Daniel)
Honig, Edwin 1919- DLB-5
Hood, Hugh 1928- DLB-53
Hooker, Jeremy 1941- DLB-40
Hooker, Thomas 1586-1647 ....DLB-24
Hooper, Johnson Jones 1815-1862 ....DLB-3, 11
Hopkins, Gerard Manley 1844-1889....DLB-35, 57
Hopkins, John H., and Son DLB-46
Hopkins, Lemuel 1750-1801....DLB-37
Hopkins, Pauline Elizabeth 1859-1930....DLB-50
Hopkins, Samuel 1721-1803 ....DLB-31
Hopkinson, Francis 1737-1791 ....DLB-31
Horgan, Paul 1903- Y-85
Horizon Press....DLB-46
Horne, Frank 1899-1974....DLB-51
Horne, Richard Henry (Hengist) 1802 or 1803-1884....DLB-32
Hornung, E. W. 1866-1921....DLB-70
Horovitz, Israel 1939- DLB-7
Horton, George Moses 1797?-1883?....DLB-50
Horváth, Ödön von 1901-1938....DLB-85
Horwood, Harold 1923- DLB-60
Hosford, E. and E. [publishing house]....DLB-49
Hotchkiss and Company DLB-49
Hough, Emerson 1857-1923....DLB-9
Houghton Mifflin Company DLB-49
Houghton, Stanley 1881-1913 ....DLB-10
Household, Geoffrey 1900-1988....DLB-87
Housman, A. E. 1859-1936....DLB-19
Housman, Laurence 1865-1959....DLB-10
Houwald, Ernst von 1778-1845 ....DLB-90
Hovey, Richard 1864-1900....DLB-54
Howard, Maureen 1930- Y-83
Howard, Richard 1929- DLB-5
Howard, Roy W. 1883-1964....DLB-29
Howard, Sidney 1891-1939....DLB-7, 26
Howe, E. W. 1853-1937 ....DLB-12, 25
Howe, Henry 1816-1893 ....DLB-30
Howe, Irving 1920- DLB-67
Howe, Julia Ward 1819-1910....DLB-1
Howell, Clark, Sr. 1863-1936....DLB-25

Howell, Evan P. 1839-1905 ....DLB-23
Howell, Soskin and Company DLB-46
Howells, William Dean 1837-1920...DLB-12, 64, 74, 79
Hoyem, Andrew 1935- DLB-5
de Hoyos, Angela 1940- DLB-82
Hoyt, Henry [publishing house] DLB-49
Hubbard, Kin 1868-1930 ....DLB-11
Hubbard, William circa 1621-1704....................DLB-24
Huber, Therese 1764-1829 ....DLB-90
Huch, Friedrich 1873-1913 ....DLB-66
Huch, Ricarda 1864-1947 ....DLB-66
Huck at 100: How Old Is
Huckleberry Finn? Y-85
Hudson, Henry Norman 1814-1886 ....DLB-64
Hudson and Goodwin DLB-49
Huebsch, B. W. [publishing house] DLB-46
Hughes, David 1930- DLB-14
Hughes, John 1677-1720 ....DLB-84
Hughes, Langston 1902-1967 ....DLB-4, 7, 48, 51, 86
Hughes, Richard 1900-1976 ....DLB-15
Hughes, Ted 1930- DLB-40
Hughes, Thomas 1822-1896 ....DLB-18
Hugo, Richard 1923-1982 ....DLB-5
Hugo Awards and Nebula Awards DLB-8
Hull, Richard 1896-1973 ....DLB-77
Hulme, T. E. 1883-1917 ....DLB-19
Humboldt, Alexander von 1769-1859 ....DLB-90
Humboldt, Wilhelm von 1767-1835 ....DLB-90
Hume, Fergus 1859-1932 ....DLB-70
Humorous Book Illustration DLB-11
Humphrey, William 1924- DLB-6
Humphreys, David 1752-1818 ....DLB-37
Humphreys, Emyr 1919- DLB-15
Huncke, Herbert 1915- DLB-16
Huneker, James Gibbons 1857-1921 ....DLB-71
Hunt, Irene 1907- DLB-52
Hunt, William Gibbes 1791-1833 ....DLB-73
Hunter, Evan 1926- Y-82
Hunter, Jim 1939- DLB-14
Hunter, Kristin 1931- DLB-33
Hunter, N. C. 1908-1971 ....DLB-10
Hurd and Houghton DLB-49
Hurst and Company DLB-49
Hurst, Fannie 1889-1968 ....DLB-86
Hurston, Zora Neale 1901?-1960 ....DLB-51, 86
Huston, John 1906- DLB-26
Hutcheson, Francis 1694-1746 ....DLB-31
Hutchinson, Thomas 1711-1780 ....DLB-30, 31
Hutton, Richard Holt 1826-1897 ....DLB-57
Huxley, Aldous 1894-1963 ....DLB-36
Huxley, Elspeth Josceline
1907- DLB-77
Huxley, T. H. 1825-1895 ....DLB-57
Hyman, Trina Schart 1939- DLB-61

I

The Iconography of Science-Fiction Art DLB-8
Ignatow, David 1914- DLB-5
Iles, Francis (see Berkeley, Anthony)
Imbs, Bravig 1904-1946 ....DLB-4
Inchbald, Elizabeth 1753-1821 ....DLB-39, 89
Inge, William 1913-1973 ....DLB-7
Ingelow, Jean 1820-1897 ....DLB-35
The Ingersoll Prizes Y-84
Ingraham, Joseph Holt 1809-1860 ....DLB-3
Inman, John 1805-1850 ....DLB-73
Innerhofer, Franz 1944- DLB-85
Innis, Harold Adams 1894-1952 ....DLB-88
Innis, Mary Quayle 1899-1972 ....DLB-88
International Publishers Company DLB-46
An Interview with Peter S. Prescott Y-86
An Interview with Tom Jenks Y-86
Introduction to Paul Laurence Dunbar,
Lyrics of Lowly Life (1896),
by William Dean Howells DLB-50
Introductory Essay: *Letters of Percy Bysshe
Shelley* (1852), by Robert Browning DLB-32
Introductory Letters from the Second Edition
of *Pamela* (1741), by Samuel Richardson.....DLB-39
Irving, John 1942- DLB-6; Y-82
Irving, Washington
1783-1859 ....DLB-3, 11, 30, 59, 73, 74

Irwin, Grace 1907- DLB-68
Irwin, Will 1873-1948 ....DLB-25
Isherwood, Christopher 1904-1986..........DLB-15; Y-86
The Island Trees Case: A Symposium on School Library Censorship
An Interview with Judith Krug
An Interview with Phyllis Schlafly
An Interview with Edward B. Jenkinson
An Interview with Lamarr Mooneyham
An Interview with Harriet Bernstein Y-82
Ivers, M. J., and Company.................................DLB-49

J

Jackmon, Marvin E. (see Marvin X)
Jackson, Angela 1951- DLB-41
Jackson, Helen Hunt 1830-1885 ....DLB-42, 47
Jackson, Laura Riding 1901- DLB-48
Jackson, Shirley 1919-1965 ....DLB-6
Jacob, Piers Anthony Dillingham (see Anthony, Piers)
Jacobs, George W., and Company DLB-49
Jacobson, Dan 1929- DLB-14
Jahnn, Hans Henny 1894-1959 ....DLB-56
Jakes, John 1932- Y-83
James, Henry 1843-1916 ....DLB-12, 71, 74
James, John circa 1633-1729..............................DLB-24
James Joyce Centenary: Dublin, 1982....................Y-82
James Joyce Conference Y-85
James, P. D. 1920- DLB-87
James, U. P. [publishing house].........................DLB-49
Jameson, Fredric 1934- DLB-67
Jameson, J. Franklin 1859-1937 ....DLB-17
Jameson, Storm 1891-1986 ....DLB-36
Jarrell, Randall 1914-1965...........................DLB-48, 52
Jasmin, Claude 1930- DLB-60
Jay, John 1745-1829 ....DLB-31
Jeffers, Lance 1919-1985 ....DLB-41
Jeffers, Robinson 1887-1962.............................DLB-45
Jefferson, Thomas 1743-1826............................DLB-31
Jelinek, Elfriede 1946- DLB-85
Jellicoe, Ann 1927- DLB-13
Jenkins, Robin 1912- DLB-14
Jenkins, William Fitzgerald (see Leinster, Murray)
Jennings, Elizabeth 1926- DLB-27
Jens, Walter 1923- DLB-69
Jensen, Merrill 1905-1980.................................DLB-17
Jephson, Robert 1736-1803................................DLB-89
Jerome, Jerome K. 1859-1927 ....DLB-10, 34
Jesse, F. Tennyson 1888-1958............................DLB-77
Jewett, John P., and Company...........................DLB-49
Jewett, Sarah Orne 1849-1909......................DLB-12, 74
The Jewish Publication Society DLB-49
Jewsbury, Geraldine 1812-1880 ....DLB-21
Joans, Ted 1928- DLB-16, 41
John Edward Bruce: Three Documents.............DLB-50
John O'Hara's Pottsville Journalism.........................Y-88
John Steinbeck Research Center..............................Y-85
John Webster: The Melbourne Manuscript.............Y-86
Johnson, B. S. 1933-1973............................DLB-14, 40
Johnson, Benjamin [publishing house]..............DLB-49
Johnson, Benjamin, Jacob, and Robert [publishing house]...........................DLB-49
Johnson, Charles 1679-1748 ....DLB-84
Johnson, Charles R. 1948- DLB-33
Johnson, Charles S. 1893-1956 ....DLB-51
Johnson, Diane 1934- Y-80
Johnson, Edward 1598-1672..............................DLB-24
Johnson, Fenton 1888-1958 ....DLB-45, 50
Johnson, Georgia Douglas 1886-1966 ....DLB-51
Johnson, Gerald W. 1890-1980..........................DLB-29
Johnson, Helene 1907- DLB-51
Johnson, Jacob, and Company...........................DLB-49
Johnson, James Weldon 1871-1938 ....DLB-51
Johnson, Lionel 1867-1902 ....DLB-19
Johnson, Nunnally 1897-1977 ....DLB-26
Johnson, Owen 1878-1952 ....Y-87
Johnson, Pamela Hansford 1912- DLB-15
Johnson, Samuel 1696-1772..............................DLB-24
Johnson, Samuel 1709-1784..............................DLB-39
Johnson, Samuel 1822-1882.................................DLB-1
Johnson, Uwe 1934-1984 ....DLB-75
Johnston, Annie Fellows 1863-1931.....................DLB-42

Johnston, Basil H. 1929- DLB-60
Johnston, Denis 1901-1984....DLB-10
Johnston, George 1913- DLB-88
Johnston, Jennifer 1930- DLB-14
Johnston, Mary 1870-1936....DLB-9
Johnston, Richard Malcolm 1822-1898....DLB-74
Johnstone, Charles 1719?-1800?....DLB-39
Jolas, Eugene 1894-1952....DLB-4, 45
Jones, Charles C., Jr. 1831-1893....DLB-30
Jones, D. G. 1929- DLB-53
Jones, David 1895-1974....DLB-20
Jones, Ebenezer 1820-1860....DLB-32
Jones, Ernest 1819-1868....DLB-32
Jones, Gayl 1949- DLB-33
Jones, Glyn 1905- DLB-15
Jones, Gwyn 1907- DLB-15
Jones, Henry Arthur 1851-1929....DLB-10
Jones, Hugh circa 1692-1760....DLB-24
Jones, James 1921-1977....DLB-2
Jones, LeRoi (see Baraka, Amiri)
Jones, Lewis 1897-1939....DLB-15
Jones, Major Joseph (see Thompson, William Tappan)
Jones, Preston 1936-1979....DLB-7
Jones, William Alfred 1817-1900....DLB-59
Jones's Publishing House....DLB-49
Jong, Erica 1942- DLB-2, 5, 28
Jonke, Gert F. 1946- DLB-85
Jonson, Ben 1572?-1637....DLB-62
Jordan, June 1936- DLB-38
Joseph, Jenny 1932- DLB-40
Josephson, Matthew 1899-1978....DLB-4
Josiah Allen's Wife (see Holley, Marietta)
Josipovici, Gabriel 1940- DLB-14
Josselyn, John ?-1675....DLB-24
Joudry, Patricia 1921- DLB-88
Joyaux, Philippe (see Sollers, Philippe)
Joyce, Adrien (see Eastman, Carol)
Joyce, James 1882-1941....DLB-10, 19, 36
Judd, Orange, Publishing Company....DLB-49
Judd, Sylvester 1813-1853....DLB-1
June, Jennie (see Croly, Jane Cunningham)
Jünger, Ernst 1895- DLB-56
Justice, Donald 1925- Y-83

K

Kacew, Romain (see Gary, Romain)
Kafka, Franz 1883-1924....DLB-81
Kalechofsky, Roberta 1931- DLB-28
Kaler, James Otis 1848-1912....DLB-12
Kandel, Lenore 1932- DLB-16
Kanin, Garson 1912- DLB-7
Kant, Hermann 1926- DLB-75
Kantor, Mackinlay 1904-1977....DLB-9
Kaplan, Johanna 1942- DLB-28
Kasack, Hermann 1896-1966....DLB-69
Kaschnitz, Marie Luise 1901-1974....DLB-69
Kästner, Erich 1899-1974....DLB-56
Kattan, Naim 1928- DLB-53
Katz, Steve 1935- Y-83
Kauffman, Janet 1945- Y-86
Kaufman, Bob 1925- DLB-16, 41
Kaufman, George S. 1889-1961....DLB-7
Kavanagh, Patrick 1904-1967....DLB-15, 20
Kavanagh, P. J. 1931- DLB-40
Kaye-Smith, Sheila 1887-1956....DLB-36
Kazin, Alfred 1915- DLB-67
Keane, John B. 1928- DLB-13
Keating, H. R. F. 1926- DLB-87
Keats, Ezra Jack 1916-1983....DLB-61
Keble, John 1792-1866....DLB-32, 55
Keeble, John 1944- Y-83
Keeffe, Barrie 1945- DLB-13
Keeley, James 1867-1934....DLB-25
W. B. Keen, Cooke and Company....DLB-49
Keillor, Garrison 1942- Y-87
Keller, Gary D. 1943- DLB-82
Kelley, Edith Summers 1884-1956....DLB-9
Kelley, William Melvin 1937- DLB-33
Kellogg, Ansel Nash 1832-1886....DLB-23
Kellogg, Steven 1941- DLB-61

Kelly, George 1887-1974 .... DLB-7
Kelly, Hugh 1739-1777 .... DLB-89
Kelly, Piet and Company DLB-49
Kelly, Robert 1935- DLB-5
Kemble, Fanny 1809-1893 .... DLB-32
Kemelman, Harry 1908- DLB-28
Kempowski, Walter 1929- DLB-75
Kendall, Claude [publishing company] DLB-46
Kendell, George 1809-1867 .... DLB-43
Kenedy, P. J., and Sons DLB-49
Kennedy, Adrienne 1931- DLB-38
Kennedy, John Pendleton 1795-1870 .... DLB-3
Kennedy, Leo 1907- DLB-88
Kennedy, Margaret 1896-1967 .... DLB-36
Kennedy, William 1928- Y-85
Kennedy, X. J. 1929- DLB-5
Kennelly, Brendan 1936- DLB-40
Kenner, Hugh 1923- DLB-67
Kennerley, Mitchell [publishing house] DLB-46
Kent, Frank R. 1877-1958 .... DLB-29
Keppler and Schwartzmann DLB-49
Kerner, Justinus 1776-1862 .... DLB-90
Kerouac, Jack 1922-1969 .... DLB-2, 16; DS-3
Kerouac, Jan 1952- DLB-16
Kerr, Charles H., and Company DLB-49
Kerr, Orpheus C. (see Newell, Robert Henry)
Kesey, Ken 1935- DLB-2, 16
Kessel, Joseph 1898-1979 .... DLB-72
Kessel, Martin 1901- DLB-56
Kesten, Hermann 1900- DLB-56
Keun, Irmgard 1905-1982 .... DLB-69
Key and Biddle DLB-49
Keyserling, Eduard von 1855-1918 .... DLB-66
Kiely, Benedict 1919- DLB-15
Kiggins and Kellogg DLB-49
Kiley, Jed 1889-1962 .... DLB-4
Killens, John Oliver 1916- DLB-33
Killigrew, Thomas 1612-1683 .... DLB-58
Kilmer, Joyce 1886-1918 .... DLB-45
King, Clarence 1842-1901 .... DLB-12
King, Florence 1936 .... Y-85
King, Francis 1923- DLB-15
King, Grace 1852-1932 .... DLB-12, 78
King, Solomon [publishing house] DLB-49
King, Stephen 1947- Y-80
King, Woodie, Jr. 1937- DLB-38
Kinglake, Alexander William 1809-1891 .... DLB-55
Kingsley, Charles 1819-1875 .... DLB-21, 32
Kingsley, Henry 1830-1876 .... DLB-21
Kingsley, Sidney 1906- DLB-7
Kingston, Maxine Hong 1940- Y-80
Kinnell, Galway 1927- DLB-5; Y-87
Kinsella, Thomas 1928- DLB-27
Kipling, Rudyard 1865-1936 .... DLB-19, 34
Kirk, John Foster 1824-1904 .... DLB-79
Kirkconnell, Watson 1895-1977 .... DLB-68
Kirkland, Caroline M. 1801-1864 .... DLB-3, 73, 74
Kirkland, Joseph 1830-1893 .... DLB-12
Kirkup, James 1918- DLB-27
Kirsch, Sarah 1935- DLB-75
Kirst, Hans Hellmut 1914-1989 .... DLB-69
Kitchin, C. H. B. 1895-1967 .... DLB-77
Kizer, Carolyn 1925- DLB-5
Klabund 1890-1928 .... DLB-66
Klappert, Peter 1942- DLB-5
Klass, Philip (see Tenn, William)
Klein, A. M. 1909-1972 .... DLB-68
Kleist, Heinrich von 1777-1811 .... DLB-90
Kluge, Alexander 1932- DLB-75
Knapp, Samuel Lorenzo 1783-1838 .... DLB-59
Knickerbocker, Diedrich (see Irving, Washington)
Knight, Damon 1922- DLB-8
Knight, Etheridge 1931- DLB-41
Knight, John S. 1894-1981 .... DLB-29
Knight, Sarah Kemble 1666-1727 .... DLB-24
Knister, Raymond 1899-1932 .... DLB-68
Knoblock, Edward 1874-1945 .... DLB-10
Knopf, Alfred A. 1892-1984 .... Y-84
Knopf, Alfred A. [publishing house] DLB-46
Knowles, John 1926- DLB-6
Knox, Frank 1874-1944 .... DLB-29
Knox, John Armoy 1850-1906 .... DLB-23

Knox, Ronald Arbuthnott 1888-1957 ... DLB-77
Kober, Arthur 1900-1975 ... DLB-11
Koch, Howard 1902- ... DLB-26
Koch, Kenneth 1925- ... DLB-5
Koenigsberg, Moses 1879-1945 ... DLB-25
Koeppen, Wolfgang 1906- ... DLB-69
Koestler, Arthur 1905-1983 ... Y-83
Kolb, Annette 1870-1967 ... DLB-66
Kolbenheyer, Erwin Guido 1878-1962 ... DLB-66
Kolleritsch, Alfred 1931- ... DLB-85
Kolodny, Annette 1941- ... DLB-67
Komroff, Manuel 1890-1974 ... DLB-4
Konigsburg, E. L. 1930- ... DLB-52
Kopit, Arthur 1937- ... DLB-7
Kops, Bernard 1926?- ... DLB-13
Kornbluth, C. M. 1923-1958 ... DLB-8
Körner, Theodor 1791-1813 ... DLB-90
Kosinski, Jerzy 1933- ... DLB-2; Y-82
Kraf, Elaine 1946- ... Y-81
Krasna, Norman 1909-1984 ... DLB-26
Krauss, Ruth 1911- ... DLB-52
Kreisel, Henry 1922- ... DLB-88
Kreuder, Ernst 1903-1972 ... DLB-69
Kreymborg, Alfred 1883-1966 ... DLB-4, 54
Krieger, Murray 1923- ... DLB-67
Krim, Seymour 1922- ... DLB-16
Krock, Arthur 1886-1974 ... DLB-29
Kroetsch, Robert 1927- ... DLB-53
Krutch, Joseph Wood 1893-1970 ... DLB-63
Kubin, Alfred 1877-1959 ... DLB-81
Kubrick, Stanley 1928- ... DLB-26
Kumin, Maxine 1925- ... DLB-5
Kunnert, Günter 1929- ... DLB-75
Kunitz, Stanley 1905- ... DLB-48
Kunjufu, Johari M. (see Amini, Johari M.)
Kunze, Reiner 1933- ... DLB-75
Kupferberg, Tuli 1923- ... DLB-16
Kurz, Isolde 1853-1944 ... DLB-66
Kusenberg, Kurt 1904-1983 ... DLB-69
Kuttner, Henry 1915-1958 ... DLB-8
Kyd, Thomas 1558-1594 ... DLB-62
Kyger, Joanne 1934- ... DLB-16
Kyne, Peter B. 1880-1957 ... DLB-78

L

Laberge, Albert 1871-1960 ... DLB-68
Laberge, Marie 1950- ... DLB-60
Lacretelle, Jacques de 1888-1985 ... DLB-65
Ladd, Joseph Brown 1764-1786 ... DLB-37
La Farge, Oliver 1901-1963 ... DLB-9
Lafferty, R. A. 1914- ... DLB-8
Laird, Carobeth 1895- ... Y-82
Laird and Lee ... DLB-49
Lalonde, Michèle 1937- ... DLB-60
Lamantia, Philip 1927- ... DLB-16
Lambert, Betty 1933-1983 ... DLB-60
L'Amour, Louis 1908?- ... Y-80
Lamson, Wolffe and Company ... DLB-49
Lancer Books ... DLB-46
Landesman, Jay 1919- and Landesman, Fran 1927- ... DLB-16
Lane, Charles 1800-1870 ... DLB-1
The John Lane Company ... DLB-49
Lane, M. Travis 1934- ... DLB-60
Lane, Patrick 1939- ... DLB-53
Lane, Pinkie Gordon 1923- ... DLB-41
Laney, Al 1896- ... DLB-4
Langevin, André 1927- ... DLB-60
Langgässer, Elisabeth 1899-1950 ... DLB-69
Lanham, Edwin 1904-1979 ... DLB-4
Lanier, Sidney 1842-1881 ... DLB-64
Lapointe, Gatien 1931-1983 ... DLB-88
Lapointe, Paul-Marie 1929- ... DLB-88
Lardner, Ring 1885-1933 ... DLB-11, 25, 86
Lardner, Ring, Jr. 1915- ... DLB-26
Lardner 100: Ring Lardner Centennial Symposium ... Y-85
Larkin, Philip 1922-1985 ... DLB-27
La Rocque, Gilbert 1943-1984 ... DLB-60
Laroque de Roquebrune, Robert

(see Roquebrune, Robert de)
Larrick, Nancy 1910- DLB-61
Larsen, Nella 1893-1964 ....DLB-51
Lasker-Schüler, Else 1869-1945 ....DLB-66
Lasnier, Rina 1915- DLB-88
Lathrop, Dorothy P. 1891-1980 ....DLB-22
Lathrop, George Parsons 1851-1898 ....DLB-71
Lathrop, John, Jr. 1772-1820 ....DLB-37
Latimore, Jewel Christine McLawler (see Amini, Johari M.)
Laughlin, James 1914- DLB-48
Laumer, Keith 1925- DLB-8
Laurence, Margaret 1926-1987 ....DLB-53
Laurents, Arthur 1918- DLB-26
Laurie, Annie (see Black, Winifred)
Lavin, Mary 1912- DLB-15
Lawless, Anthony (see MacDonald, Philip)
Lawrence, David 1888-1973 ....DLB-29
Lawrence, D. H. 1885-1930 ....DLB-10, 19, 36
Lawson, John ?-1711 ....DLB-24
Lawson, Robert 1892-1957 ....DLB-22
Lawson, Victor F. 1850-1925 ....DLB-25
Layton, Irving 1912- DLB-88
Lea, Henry Charles 1825-1909 ....DLB-47
Lea, Tom 1907- DLB-6
Leacock, John 1729-1802 ....DLB-31
Lear, Edward 1812-1888 ....DLB-32
Leary, Timothy 1920- DLB-16
Leary, W. A., and Company DLB-49
Léautaud, Paul 1872-1956 ....DLB-65
Leavitt and Allen DLB-49
le Carré, John 1931- DLB-87
Lécavelé, Roland (see Dorgelès, Roland)
Lechlitner, Ruth 1901- DLB-48
Leclerc, Félix 1914- DLB-60
Le Clézio, J. M. G. 1940- DLB-83
Lectures on Rhetoric and Belles Lettres (1783), by Hugh Blair [excerpts] DLB-31
Leder, Rudolf (see Hermlin, Stephan)
Lederer, Charles 1910-1976 ....DLB-26
Ledwidge, Francis 1887-1917 ....DLB-20
Lee, Dennis 1939- DLB-53
Lee, Don L. (see Madhubuti, Haki R.)
Lee, George W. 1894-1976 ....DLB-51
Lee, Harper 1926- DLB-6
Lee, Harriet (1757-1851) and Lee, Sophia (1750-1824) DLB-39
Lee, Laurie 1914- DLB-27
Lee, Nathaniel circa 1645 - 1692 ....DLB-80
Lee, Vernon 1856-1935 ....DLB-57
Lee and Shepard DLB-49
Le Fanu, Joseph Sheridan 1814-1873 ....DLB-21, 70
Leffland, Ella 1931- Y-84
le Fort, Gertrud von 1876-1971 ....DLB-66
Le Gallienne, Richard 1866-1947 ....DLB-4
Legaré, Hugh Swinton 1797-1843 ....DLB-3, 59, 73
Legaré, James M. 1823-1859 ....DLB-3
Léger, Antoine-J. 1880-1950 ....DLB-88
Le Guin, Ursula K. 1929- DLB-8, 52
Lehman, Ernest 1920- DLB-44
Lehmann, John 1907- DLB-27
Lehmann, Rosamond 1901- DLB-15
Lehmann, Wilhelm 1882-1968 ....DLB-56
Leiber, Fritz 1910- DLB-8
Leinster, Murray 1896-1975 ....DLB-8
Leitch, Maurice 1933- DLB-14
Leland, Charles G. 1824-1903 ....DLB-11
Lemelin, Roger 1919- DLB-88
Le Moyne, Jean 1913- DLB-88
L'Engle, Madeleine 1918- DLB-52
Lennart, Isobel 1915-1971 ....DLB-44
Lennox, Charlotte 1729 or 1730-1804 ....DLB-39
Lenski, Lois 1893-1974 ....DLB-22
Lenz, Hermann 1913- DLB-69
Lenz, Siegfried 1926- DLB-75
Leonard, Hugh 1926- DLB-13
Leonard, William Ellery 1876-1944 ....DLB-54
LePan, Douglas 1914- DLB-88
Le Queux, William 1864-1927 ....DLB-70
Lerner, Max 1902- DLB-29
Lernet-Holenia, Alexander 1897-1976 ....DLB-85
LeSieg, Theo. (see Geisel, Theodor Seuss)

Leslie, Frank 1821-1880 ....DLB-43, 79

The Frank Leslie Publishing House DLB-49

Lessing, Bruno 1870-1940 ....DLB-28

Lessing, Doris 1919- DLB-15; Y-85

Lettau, Reinhard 1929- DLB-75

Letter to [Samuel] Richardson on *Clarissa* (1748), by Henry Fielding DLB-39

Lever, Charles 1806-1872 ....DLB-21

Levertov, Denise 1923- DLB-5

Levi, Peter 1931- DLB-40

Levien, Sonya 1888-1960 ....DLB-44

Levin, Meyer 1905-1981 ....DLB-9, 28; Y-81

Levine, Norman 1923- DLB-88

Levine, Philip 1928- DLB-5

Levy, Benn Wolfe 1900-1973 ....DLB-13; Y-81

Lewes, George Henry 1817-1878 ....DLB-55

Lewis, Alfred H. 1857-1914 ....DLB-25

Lewis, Alun 1915-1944 ....DLB-20

Lewis, C. Day (see Day Lewis, C.)

Lewis, Charles B. 1842-1924 ....DLB-11

Lewis, C. S. 1898-1963 ....DLB-15

Lewis, Henry Clay 1825-1850 ....DLB-3

Lewis, Janet 1899- Y-87

Lewis, Matthew Gregory 1775-1818 ....DLB-39

Lewis, Richard circa 1700-1734 ....DLB-24

Lewis, Sinclair 1885-1951 ....DLB-9; DS-1

Lewis, Wyndham 1882-1957 ....DLB-15

Lewisohn, Ludwig 1882-1955 ....DLB-4, 9, 28

The Library of America DLB-46

The Licensing Act of 1737 ....DLB-84

Liebling, A. J. 1904-1963 ....DLB-4

Lieutenant Murray (see Ballou, Maturin Murray)

Lilar, Françoise (see Mallet-Joris, Françoise)

Lillo, George 1691-1739 ....DLB-84

Lilly, Wait and Company DLB-49

Limited Editions Club DLB-46

Lincoln and Edmands DLB-49

Lindsay, Jack 1900- Y-84

Lindsay, Vachel 1879-1931 ....DLB-54

Linebarger, Paul Myron Anthony (see Smith, Cordwainer)

Link, Arthur S. 1920- DLB-17

Linn, John Blair 1777-1804 ....DLB-37

Linton, Eliza Lynn 1822-1898 ....DLB-18

Linton, William James 1812-1897 ....DLB-32

Lion Books DLB-46

Lionni, Leo 1910- DLB-61

Lippincott, J. B., Company DLB-49

Lippincott, Sara Jane Clarke 1823-1904 ....DLB-43

Lippmann, Walter 1889-1974 ....DLB-29

Lipton, Lawrence 1898-1975 ....DLB-16

Literary Documents: William Faulkner and the People-to-People Program Y-86

Literary Documents II: *Library Journal*– Statements and Questionnaires from First Novelists Y-87

Literary Effects of World War II [British novel] DLB-15

Literary Prizes [British] DLB-15

Literary Research Archives: The Humanities Research Center, University of Texas Y-82

Literary Research Archives II: Berg Collection of English and American Literature of the New York Public Library Y-83

Literary Research Archives III: The Lilly Library Y-84

Literary Research Archives IV: The John Carter Brown Library Y-85

Literary Research Archives V: Kent State Special Collections Y-86

Literary Research Archives VI: The Modern Literary Manuscripts Collection in the Special Collections of the Washington University Libraries Y-87

"Literary Style" (1857), by William Forsyth [excerpt] DLB-57

Literatura Chicanesca: The View From Without DLB-82

Literature at Nurse, or Circulating Morals (1885), by George Moore DLB-18

Littell, Eliakim 1797-1870 ....DLB-79

Littell, Robert S. 1831-1896 ....DLB-79

Little, Brown and Company DLB-49

Littlewood, Joan 1914- DLB-13

Lively, Penelope 1933- DLB-14

Livesay, Dorothy 1909- DLB-68

Livings, Henry 1929- DLB-13
Livingston, Anne Howe 1763-1841 ....DLB-37
Livingston, Myra Cohn 1926- DLB-61
Livingston, William 1723-1790 ....DLB-31
Lizárraga, Sylvia S. 1925- DLB-82
Llewellyn, Richard 1906-1983 ....DLB-15
Lobel, Arnold 1933- DLB-61
Lochridge, Betsy Hopkins (see Fancher, Betsy)
Locke, David Ross 1833-1888 ....DLB-11, 23
Locke, John 1632-1704.......................................DLB-31
Locke, Richard Adams 1800-1871......................DLB-43
Locker-Lampson, Frederick 1821-1895.............DLB-35
Lockridge, Ross, Jr. 1914-1948...............................Y-80
Locrine and *Selimus*..DLB-62
Lodge, David 1935- DLB-14
Lodge, George Cabot 1873-1909.......................DLB-54
Lodge, Henry Cabot 1850-1924 ....DLB-47
Loeb, Harold 1891-1974 ....DLB-4
Logan, James 1674-1751 ....DLB-24
Logan, John 1923- DLB-5
Logue, Christopher 1926- DLB-27
London, Jack 1876-1916..........................DLB-8, 12, 78
Long, H., and Brother DLB-49
Long, Haniel 1888-1956.....................................DLB-45
Longfellow, Henry Wadsworth 1807-1882....DLB-1, 59
Longfellow, Samuel 1819-1892............................DLB-1
Longley, Michael 1939- DLB-40
Longmans, Green and Company........................DLB-49
Longstreet, Augustus Baldwin 1790-1870 ....DLB-3, 11, 74
Longworth, D. [publishing house] DLB-49
Lonsdale, Frederick 1881-1954..........................DLB-10
A Look at the Contemporary Black Theatre Movement DLB-38
Loos, Anita 1893-1981 ....DLB-11, 26; Y-81
Lopate, Phillip 1943- Y-80
López, Diana (see Isabella, Ríos)
The Lord Chamberlain's Office and Stage Censorship in England DLB-10
Lorde, Audre 1934- DLB-41
Loring, A. K. [publishing house] DLB-49
Loring and Mussey DLB-46
Lossing, Benson J. 1813-1891 ....DLB-30
Lothar, Ernst 1890-1974 ....DLB-81
Lothrop, D., and Company................................DLB-49
Lothrop, Harriet M. 1844-1924.........................DLB-42
The Lounger, no. 20 (1785), by Henry Mackenzie DLB-39
Lounsbury, Thomas R. 1838-1915 ....DLB-71
Lovell, John W., Company................................DLB-49
Lovell, Coryell and Company DLB-49
Lovesey, Peter 1936- DLB-87
Lovingood, Sut (see Harris, George Washington)
Low, Samuel 1765-? DLB-37
Lowell, Amy 1874-1925.....................................DLB-54
Lowell, James Russell 1819-1891 ....DLB-1, 11, 64, 79
Lowell, Robert 1917-1977 ....DLB-5
Lowenfels, Walter 1897-1976...............................DLB-4
Lowndes, Marie Belloc 1868-1947.....................DLB-70
Lowry, Lois 1937- DLB-52
Lowry, Malcolm 1909-1957...............................DLB-15
Lowther, Pat 1935-1975 ....DLB-53
Loy, Mina 1882-1966.....................................DLB-4, 54
Lucas, Fielding, Jr. [publishing house]..............DLB-49
Luce, John W., and Company DLB-46
Lucie-Smith, Edward 1933- DLB-40
Ludlum, Robert 1927- Y-82
Ludwig, Jack 1922- DLB-60
Luke, Peter 1919- DLB-13
The F. M. Lupton Publishing Company DLB-49
Lurie, Alison 1926- DLB-2
Lyall, Gavin 1932- DLB-87
Lyly, John circa 1554-1606 ....DLB-62
Lyon, Matthew 1749-1822.................................DLB-43
Lytle, Andrew 1902- DLB-6
Lytton, Edward (see Bulwer-Lytton, Edward)
Lytton, Edward Robert Bulwer 1831-1891 ....DLB-32

M

Maass, Joachim 1901-1972 ....DLB-69
Mabie, Hamilton Wright 1845-1916..................DLB-71

Mac A'Ghobhainn, Iain (see Smith, Iain Crichton)

MacArthur, Charles 1895-1956................DLB-7, 25, 44

Macaulay, David 1945- DLB-61

Macaulay, Rose 1881-1958.................................DLB-36

Macaulay, Thomas Babington 1800-1859....DLB-32, 55

Macaulay Company..DLB-46

MacBeth, George 1932- DLB-40

MacCaig, Norman 1910- DLB-27

MacDiarmid, Hugh 1892-1978..........................DLB-20

MacDonald, George 1824-1905.........................DLB-18

MacDonald, John D. 1916-1986................DLB-8; Y-86

MacDonald, Philip 1899?-1980..........................DLB-77

Macdonald, Ross (see Millar, Kenneth)

MacEwen, Gwendolyn 1941- DLB-53

Macfadden, Bernarr 1868-1955.........................DLB-25

Machen, Arthur Llewelyn Jones 1863-1947.......DLB-36

MacInnes, Colin 1914-1976..............................DLB-14

MacInnes, Helen 1907-1985.............................DLB-87

MacKaye, Percy 1875-1956...............................DLB-54

Macken, Walter 1915-1967................................DLB-13

Mackenzie, Compton 1883-1972.......................DLB-34

Mackenzie, Henry 1745-1831............................DLB-39

Mackey, William Wellington 1937- DLB-38

Mackintosh, Elizabeth (see Tey, Josephine)

Macklin, Charles 1699-1797...............................DLB-89

MacLean, Katherine Anne 1925- DLB-8

MacLeish, Archibald 1892-1982.......DLB-4, 7, 45; Y-82

MacLennan, Hugh 1907- DLB-68

MacLeod, Alistair 1936- DLB-60

Macleod, Norman 1906- DLB-4

The Macmillan Company..................................DLB-49

MacNamara, Brinsley 1890-1963.......................DLB-10

MacNeice, Louis 1907-1963.........................DLB-10, 20

Macpherson, Jay 1931- DLB-53

Macpherson, Jeanie 1884-1946..........................DLB-44

Macrae Smith Company....................................DLB-46

Macy-Masius..DLB-46

Madden, David 1933- DLB-6

Maddow, Ben 1909- DLB-44

Madgett, Naomi Long 1923- DLB-76

Madhubuti, Haki R. 1942- DLB-5, 41

Madison, James 1751-1836................................DLB-37

Mahan, Alfred Thayer 1840-1914......................DLB-47

Maheux-Forcier, Louise 1929- DLB-60

Mahin, John Lee 1902-1984..............................DLB-44

Mahon, Derek 1941- DLB-40

Mailer, Norman 1923- DLB-2, 16, 28; Y-80, 83; DS-3

Maillet, Adrienne 1885-1963.............................DLB-68

Maillet, Antonine 1929- DLB-60

Main Selections of the Book-of-the-Month Club, 1926-1945..DLB-9

Main Trends in Twentieth-Century Book Clubs..DLB-46

Mainwaring, Daniel 1902-1977..........................DLB-44

Major, André 1942- DLB-60

Major, Clarence 1936- DLB-33

Major, Kevin 1949- DLB-60

Major Books...DLB-46

Makemie, Francis circa 1658-1708.....................DLB-24

The Making of a People, by J. M. Ritchie...DLB-66

Malamud, Bernard 1914-1986.......DLB-2, 28; Y-80, 86

Malleson, Lucy Beatrice (see Gilbert, Anthony)

Mallet-Joris, Françoise 1930- DLB-83

Mallock, W. H. 1849-1923..........................DLB-18, 57

Malone, Dumas 1892-1986................................DLB-17

Malraux, André 1901-1976................................DLB-72

Malzberg, Barry N. 1939- DLB-8

Mamet, David 1947- DLB-7

Mandel, Eli 1922- DLB-53

Mandiargues, André Pieyre de 1909- DLB-83

Manfred, Frederick 1912- DLB-6

Mangan, Sherry 1904-1961..................................DLB-4

Mankiewicz, Herman 1897-1953........................DLB-26

Mankiewicz, Joseph L. 1909- DLB-44

Mankowitz, Wolf 1924- DLB-15

Manley, Delarivière 1672?-1724..................DLB-39, 80

Mann, Abby 1927- DLB-44

Mann, Heinrich 1871-1950................................DLB-66

Mann, Horace 1796-1859.....................................DLB-1

Mann, Klaus 1906-1949.....................................DLB-56

Mann, Thomas 1875-1955.................................DLB-66

Manning, Marie 1873?-1945 ....DLB-29
Manning and Loring DLB-49
Mano, D. Keith 1942- DLB-6
Manor Books DLB-46
March, William 1893-1954 ....DLB-9, 86
Marchessault, Jovette 1938- DLB-60
Marcus, Frank 1928- DLB-13
Marek, Richard, Books DLB-46
Marion, Frances 1886-1973 ....DLB-44
Marius, Richard C. 1933- Y-85
The Mark Taper Forum DLB-7
Markfield, Wallace 1926- DLB-2, 28
Markham, Edwin 1852-1940 ....DLB-54
Markle, Fletcher 1921- DLB-68
Marlatt, Daphne 1942- DLB-60
Marlowe, Christopher 1564-1593 ....DLB-62
Marlyn, John 1912- DLB-88
Marmion, Shakerley 1603-1639 ....DLB-58
Marquand, John P. 1893-1960 ....DLB-9
Marquis, Don 1878-1937 ....DLB-11, 25
Marriott, Anne 1913- DLB-68
Marryat, Frederick 1792-1848 ....DLB-21
Marsh, George Perkins 1801-1882 ....DLB-1, 64
Marsh, James 1794-1842 ....DLB-1, 59
Marsh, Capen, Lyon and Webb DLB-49
Marsh, Ngaio 1899-1982 ....DLB-77
Marshall, Edward 1932- DLB-16
Marshall, James 1942- DLB-61
Marshall, Joyce 1913- DLB-88
Marshall, Paule 1929- DLB-33
Marshall, Tom 1938- DLB-60
Marston, John 1576-1634 ....DLB-58
Marston, Philip Bourke 1850-1887 ....DLB-35
Martens, Kurt 1870-1945 ....DLB-66
Martien, William S. [publishing house] DLB-49
Martin, Abe (see Hubbard, Kin)
Martin, Claire 1914- DLB-60
Martin du Gard, Roger 1881-1958 ....DLB-65
Martineau, Harriet 1802-1876 ....DLB-21, 55
Martínez, Max 1943- DLB-82
Martyn, Edward 1859-1923 ....DLB-10
Marvin X 1944- DLB-38
Marzials, Theo 1850-1920 ....DLB-35
Masefield, John 1878-1967 ....DLB-10, 19
Mason, A. E. W. 1865-1948 ....DLB-70
Mason, Bobbie Ann 1940- Y-87
Mason Brothers DLB-49
Massey, Gerald 1828-1907 ....DLB-32
Massinger, Philip 1583-1640 ....DLB-58
Masters, Edgar Lee 1868-1950 ....DLB-54
Mather, Cotton 1663-1728 ....DLB-24, 30
Mather, Increase 1639-1723 ....DLB-24
Mather, Richard 1596-1669 ....DLB-24
Matheson, Richard 1926- DLB-8, 44
Matheus, John F. 1887- DLB-51
Mathews, Cornelius 1817?-1889 ....DLB-3, 64
Mathias, Roland 1915- DLB-27
Mathis, June 1892-1927 ....DLB-44
Mathis, Sharon Bell 1937- DLB-33
Matthews, Brander 1852-1929 ....DLB-71, 78
Matthews, Jack 1925- DLB-6
Matthews, William 1942- DLB-5
Matthiessen, F. O. 1902-1950 ....DLB-63
Matthiessen, Peter 1927- DLB-6
Maugham, W. Somerset 1874-1965 ....DLB-10, 36, 77
Mauriac, Claude 1914- DLB-83
Mauriac, François 1885-1970 ....DLB-65
Maurice, Frederick Denison 1805-1872 ....DLB-55
Maurois, André 1885-1967 ....DLB-65
Maury, James 1718-1769 ....DLB-31
Mavor, Elizabeth 1927- DLB-14
Mavor, Osborne Henry (see Bridie, James)
Maxwell, H. [publishing house] DLB-49
Maxwell, William 1908- Y-80
May, Elaine 1932- DLB-44
May, Thomas 1595 or 1596-1650 ....DLB-58
Mayer, Mercer 1943- DLB-61
Mayer, O. B. 1818-1891 ....DLB-3
Mayes, Wendell 1919- DLB-26
Mayfield, Julian 1928-1984 ....DLB-33; Y-84
Mayhew, Henry 1812-1887 ....DLB-18, 55
Mayhew, Jonathan 1720-1766 ....DLB-31

Mayne, Seymour 1944- DLB-60
Mayor, Flora Macdonald 1872-1932..................DLB-36
Mayröcker, Friederike 1924- DLB-85
Mazursky, Paul 1930- DLB-44
McAlmon, Robert 1896-1956 ....DLB-4, 45
McBride, Robert M., and Company DLB-46
McCaffrey, Anne 1926- DLB-8
McCarthy, Cormac 1933- DLB-6
McCarthy, Mary 1912- DLB-2; Y-81
McCay, Winsor 1871-1934 ....DLB-22
McClatchy, C. K. 1858-1936 ....DLB-25
McClellan, George Marion 1860-1934 ....DLB-50
McCloskey, Robert 1914- DLB-22
McClure, Joanna 1930- DLB-16
McClure, Michael 1932- DLB-16
McClure, Phillips and Company.........................DLB-46
McClurg, A. C., and Company DLB-49
McCluskey, John A., Jr. 1944- DLB-33
McCollum, Michael A. 1946.....................................Y-87
McConnell, William C. 1917- DLB-88
McCord, David 1897- DLB-61
McCorkle, Jill 1958- Y-87
McCorkle, Samuel Eusebius 1746-1811 ....DLB-37
McCormick, Anne O'Hare 1880-1954...............DLB-29
McCormick, Robert R. 1880-1955 ....DLB-29
McCourt, Edward 1907-1972.............................DLB-88
McCoy, Horace 1897-1955...................................DLB-9
McCullagh, Joseph B. 1842-1896 ....DLB-23
McCullers, Carson 1917-1967...........................DLB-2, 7
McDonald, Forrest 1927- DLB-17
McDougall, Colin 1917-1984 ....DLB-68
McDowell, Obolensky...DLB-46
McEwan, Ian 1948- DLB-14
McFadden, David 1940- DLB-60
McFarlane, Leslie 1902-1977..............................DLB-88
McGahern, John 1934- DLB-14
McGeehan, W. O. 1879-1933.............................DLB-25
McGill, Ralph 1898-1969 ....DLB-29
McGinley, Phyllis 1905-1978........................DLB-11, 48
McGirt, James E. 1874-1930 ....DLB-50
McGough, Roger 1937- DLB-40
McGraw-Hill DLB-46
McGuane, Thomas 1939- DLB-2; Y-80
McGuckian, Medbh 1950- DLB-40
McGuffey, William Holmes 1800-1873 ....DLB-42
McIlvanney, William 1936- DLB-14
McIntyre, O. O. 1884-1938................................DLB-25
McKay, Claude 1889-1948........................DLB-4, 45, 51
The David McKay Company..............................DLB-49
McKean, William V. 1820-1903..........................DLB-23
McKinley, Robin 1952- DLB-52
McLaren, Floris Clark 1904-1978.......................DLB-68
McLaverty, Michael 1907- DLB-15
McLean, John R. 1848-1916 ....DLB-23
McLean, William L. 1852-1931...........................DLB-25
McLoughlin Brothers DLB-49
McLuhan, Marshall 1911-1980...........................DLB-88
McMaster, John Bach 1852-1932.......................DLB-47
McMurtry, Larry 1936- DLB-2; Y-80, 87
McNally, Terrence 1939- DLB-7
McNeil, Florence 1937- DLB-60
McNeile, Herman Cyril 1888-1937 ....DLB-77
McPherson, James Alan 1943- DLB-38
McPherson, Sandra 1943- Y-86
McWhirter, George 1939- DLB-60
Mead, Matthew 1924- DLB-40
Mead, Taylor ?- DLB-16
Medill, Joseph 1823-1899 ....DLB-43
Medoff, Mark 1940- DLB-7
Meek, Alexander Beaufort 1814-1865 ....DLB-3
Meinke, Peter 1932- DLB-5
Melançon, Robert 1947- DLB-60
Mell, Max 1882-1971..DLB-81
Meltzer, David 1937- DLB-16
Meltzer, Milton 1915- DLB-61
Melville, Herman 1819-1891 ....DLB-3, 74
Memoirs of Life and Literature (1920),
by W. H. Mallock [excerpt]..........................DLB-57
Mencken, H. L. 1880-1956.....................DLB-11, 29, 63
Méndez M., Miguel 1930- DLB-82
Mercer, Cecil William (see Yates, Dornford)
Mercer, David 1928-1980..................................DLB-13

Mercer, John 1704-1768 ....DLB-31
Meredith, George 1828-1909..................DLB-18, 35, 57
Meredith, Owen (see Lytton, Edward Robert Bulwer)
Meredith, William 1919- DLB-5
Meriwether, Louise 1923- DLB-33
Merriam, Eve 1916- DLB-61
The Merriam Company DLB-49
Merrill, James 1926- DLB-5; Y-85
Merrill and Baker..DLB-49
The Mershon Company DLB-49
Merton, Thomas 1915-1968 ....DLB-48; Y-81
Merwin, W. S. 1927- DLB-5
Messner, Julian [publishing house].....................DLB-46
Metcalf, J. [publishing house] DLB-49
Metcalf, John 1938- DLB-60
The Methodist Book Concern DLB-49
Mew, Charlotte 1869-1928 ....DLB-19
Mewshaw, Michael 1943- Y-80
Meyer, E. Y. 1946- DLB-75
Meyer, Eugene 1875-1959 ....DLB-29
Meynell, Alice 1847-1922...................................DLB-19
Meyrink, Gustav 1868-1932 ....DLB-81
Micheaux, Oscar 1884-1951...............................DLB-50
Micheline, Jack 1929- DLB-16
Michener, James A. 1907?- DLB-6
Micklejohn, George circa 1717-1818 ....DLB-31
Middleton, Christopher 1926- DLB-40
Middleton, Stanley 1919- DLB-14
Middleton, Thomas 1580-1627...........................DLB-58
Miegel, Agnes 1879-1964...................................DLB-56
Miles, Josephine 1911-1985 ....DLB-48
Milius, John 1944- DLB-44
Mill, John Stuart 1806-1873 ....DLB-55
Millar, Kenneth 1915-1983 ....DLB-2; Y-83; DS-6
Millay, Edna St. Vincent 1892-1950 ....DLB-45
Miller, Arthur 1915- DLB-7
Miller, Caroline 1903- DLB-9
Miller, Eugene Ethelbert 1950- DLB-41
Miller, Henry 1891-1980 ....DLB-4, 9; Y-80
Miller, J. Hillis 1928- DLB-67
Miller, James [publishing house] DLB-49
Miller, Jason 1939- DLB-7
Miller, May 1899- DLB-41
Miller, Perry 1905-1963 ....DLB-17, 63
Miller, Walter M., Jr. 1923- DLB-8
Miller, Webb 1892-1940 ....DLB-29
Millhauser, Steven 1943- DLB-2
Millican, Arthenia J. Bates 1920- DLB-38
Milne, A. A. 1882-1956...............................DLB-10, 77
Milner, Ron 1938- DLB-38
Milnes, Richard Monckton (Lord Houghton) 1809-1885 ....DLB-32
Minton, Balch and Company.............................DLB-46
Miron, Gaston 1928- DLB-60
Mitchel, Jonathan 1624-1668 ....DLB-24
Mitchell, Adrian 1932- DLB-40
Mitchell, Donald Grant 1822-1908.......................DLB-1
Mitchell, Gladys 1901-1983................................DLB-77
Mitchell, James Leslie 1901-1935........................DLB-15
Mitchell, John (see Slater, Patrick)
Mitchell, John Ames 1845-1918..........................DLB-79
Mitchell, Julian 1935- DLB-14
Mitchell, Ken 1940- DLB-60
Mitchell, Langdon 1862-1935 ....DLB-7
Mitchell, Loften 1919- DLB-38
Mitchell, Margaret 1900-1949..............................DLB-9
Mitchell, W. O. 1914- DLB-88
Mitterer, Erika 1906- DLB-85
Modern Age Books DLB-46
"Modern English Prose" (1876), by George Saintsbury DLB-57
The Modern Language Association of America Celebrates Its Centennial Y-84
The Modern Library..DLB-46
Modern Novelists–Great and Small (1855), by Margaret Oliphant.......................................DLB-21
"Modern Style" (1857), by Cockburn Thomson [excerpt].....................................DLB-57
The Modernists (1932), by Joseph Warren Beach..DLB-36
Modiano, Patrick 1945- DLB-83
Moffat, Yard and Company DLB-46
Monkhouse, Allan 1858-1936 ....DLB-10

Monro, Harold 1879-1932 ....DLB-19
Monroe, Harriet 1860-1936 ....DLB-54
Monsarrat, Nicholas 1910-1979 ....DLB-15
Montague, John 1929- DLB-40
Montgomery, John 1919- DLB-16
Montgomery, Marion 1925- DLB-6
Montgomery, Robert Bruce (see Crispin, Edmund)
Montherlant, Henry de 1896-1972 ....DLB-72
Moody, Joshua circa 1633-1697 ....DLB-24
Moody, William Vaughn 1869-1910 ....DLB-7, 54
Moorcock, Michael 1939- DLB-14
Moore, Catherine L. 1911- DLB-8
Moore, Clement Clarke 1779-1863 ....DLB-42
Moore, George 1852-1933 ....DLB-10, 18, 57
Moore, Marianne 1887-1972 ....DLB-45; DS-7
Moore, Mavor 1919- DLB-88
Moore, T. Sturge 1870-1944 ....DLB-19
Moore, Ward 1903-1978 ....DLB-8
Moore, Wilstach, Keys and Company DLB-49
The Moorland-Spingarn Research Center DLB-76
Moraga, Cherríe 1952- DLB-82
Morales, Alejandro 1944- DLB-82
Morency, Pierre 1942- DLB-60
Morgan, Berry 1919- DLB-6
Morgan, Charles 1894-1958 ....DLB-34
Morgan, Edmund S. 1916- DLB-17
Morgan, Edwin 1920- DLB-27
Morgner, Irmtraud 1933- DLB-75
Morison, Samuel Eliot 1887-1976 ....DLB-17
Morley, Christopher 1890-1957 ....DLB-9
Morley, John 1838-1923 ....DLB-57
Morris, George Pope 1802-1864 ....DLB-73
Morris, Lewis 1833-1907 ....DLB-35
Morris, Richard B. 1904-1989 ....DLB-17
Morris, William 1834-1896 ....DLB-18, 35, 57
Morris, Willie 1934- Y-80
Morris, Wright 1910- DLB-2; Y-81
Morrison, Arthur 1863-1945 ....DLB-70
Morrison, Toni 1931- DLB-6, 33; Y-81
Morrow, William, and Company DLB-46
Morse, James Herbert 1841-1923 ....DLB-71
Morse, Jedidiah 1761-1826 ....DLB-37
Morse, John T., Jr. 1840-1937 ....DLB-47
Mortimer, John 1923- DLB-13
Morton, John P., and Company DLB-49
Morton, Nathaniel 1613-1685 ....DLB-24
Morton, Sarah Wentworth 1759-1846 ....DLB-37
Morton, Thomas circa 1579-circa 1647 ....DLB-24
Mosley, Nicholas 1923- DLB-14
Moss, Arthur 1889-1969 ....DLB-4
Moss, Howard 1922- DLB-5
The Most Powerful Book Review in America [*New York Times Book Review*] Y-82
Motion, Andrew 1952- DLB-40
Motley, John Lothrop 1814-1877 ....DLB-1, 30, 59
Motley, Willard 1909-1965 ....DLB-76
Motteux, Peter Anthony 1663-1718 ....DLB-80
Mottram, R. H. 1883-1971 ....DLB-36
Mouré, Erin 1955- DLB-60
Movies from Books, 1920-1974 ....DLB-9
Mowat, Farley 1921- DLB-68
Mowrer, Edgar Ansel 1892-1977 ....DLB-29
Mowrer, Paul Scott 1887-1971 ....DLB-29
Mucedorus DLB-62
Muhajir, El (see Marvin X)
Muhajir, Nazzam Al Fitnah (see Marvin X)
Muir, Edwin 1887-1959 ....DLB-20
Muir, Helen 1937- DLB-14
Mukherjee, Bharati 1940- DLB-60
Muldoon, Paul 1951- DLB-40
Müller, Wilhelm 1794-1827 ....DLB-90
Mumford, Lewis 1895- DLB-63
Munby, Arthur Joseph 1828-1910 ....DLB-35
Munday, Anthony 1560-1633 ....DLB-62
Munford, Robert circa 1737-1783 ....DLB-31
Munro, Alice 1931- DLB-53
Munro, George [publishing house] DLB-49
Munro, H. H. 1870-1916 ....DLB-34
Munro, Norman L. [publishing house] DLB-49
Munroe, James, and Company DLB-49
Munroe, Kirk 1850-1930 ....DLB-42

Munroe and Francis....DLB-49
Munsell, Joel [publishing house]....DLB-49
Munsey, Frank A. 1854-1925....DLB-25
Munsey, Frank A., and Company....DLB-49
Murdoch, Iris 1919- DLB-14
Murfree, Mary N. 1850-1922....DLB-12, 74
Muro, Amado 1915-1971....DLB-82
Murphy, Arthur 1727-1805....DLB-89
Murphy, Beatrice M. 1908- DLB-76
Murphy, John, and Company....DLB-49
Murphy, Richard 1927- DLB-40
Murray, Albert L. 1916- DLB-38
Murray, Gilbert 1866-1957....DLB-10
Murray, Judith Sargent 1751-1820....DLB-37
Murray, Pauli 1910-1985....DLB-41
Muschg, Adolf 1934- DLB-75
Musil, Robert 1880-1942....DLB-81
Mussey, Benjamin B., and Company....DLB-49
Myers, Gustavus 1872-1942....DLB-47
Myers, L. H. 1881-1944....DLB-15
Myers, Walter Dean 1937- DLB-33

N

Nabbes, Thomas circa 1605-1641....DLB-58
Nabl, Franz 1883-1974....DLB-81
Nabokov, Vladimir 1899-1977....DLB-2; Y-80; DS-3
Nabokov Festival at Cornell....Y-83
Nafis and Cornish....DLB-49
Naipaul, Shiva 1945-1985....Y-85
Naipaul, V. S. 1932- Y-85
Nancrede, Joseph [publishing house]....DLB-49
Nasby, Petroleum Vesuvius (see Locke, David Ross)
Nash, Ogden 1902-1971....DLB-11
Nathan, Robert 1894-1985....DLB-9
The National Jewish Book Awards....Y-85
The National Theatre and the Royal Shakespeare Company: The National Companies....DLB-13
Naughton, Bill 1910- DLB-13
Neagoe, Peter 1881-1960....DLB-4
Neal, John 1793-1876....DLB-1, 59
Neal, Joseph C. 1807-1847....DLB-11
Neal, Larry 1937-1981....DLB-38
The Neale Publishing Company....DLB-49
Neely, F. Tennyson [publishing house]....DLB-49
"The Negro as a Writer," by G. M. McClellan....DLB-50
"Negro Poets and Their Poetry," by Wallace Thurman....DLB-50
Neihardt, John G. 1881-1973....DLB-9, 54
Nelson, Alice Moore Dunbar 1875-1935....DLB-50
Nelson, Thomas, and Sons....DLB-49
Nelson, William Rockhill 1841-1915....DLB-23
Nemerov, Howard 1920- DLB-5, 6; Y-83
Ness, Evaline 1911-1986....DLB-61
Neugeboren, Jay 1938- DLB-28
Neumann, Alfred 1895-1952....DLB-56
Nevins, Allan 1890-1971....DLB-17
The New American Library....DLB-46
New Directions Publishing Corporation....DLB-46
A New Edition of *Huck Finn*....Y-85
New Forces at Work in the American Theatre: 1915-1925....DLB-7
New Literary Periodicals: A Report for 1987....Y-87
New Literary Periodicals: A Report for 1988....Y-88
The New *Ulysses*....Y-84
The New Variorum Shakespeare....Y-85
A New Voice: The Center for the Book's First Five Years....Y-83
The New Wave [Science Fiction]....DLB-8
Newbolt, Henry 1862-1938....DLB-19
Newbound, Bernard Slade (see Slade, Bernard)
Newby, P. H. 1918- DLB-15
Newcomb, Charles King 1820-1894....DLB-1
Newell, Peter 1862-1924....DLB-42
Newell, Robert Henry 1836-1901....DLB-11
Newman, David (see Benton, Robert)
Newman, Frances 1883-1928....Y-80
Newman, John Henry 1801-1890....DLB-18, 32, 55
Newman, Mark [publishing house]....DLB-49

Newsome, Effie Lee 1885-1979 ....DLB-76
Newspaper Syndication of American Humor....DLB-11
Nichol, B. P. 1944- DLB-53
Nichols, Dudley 1895-1960 ....DLB-26
Nichols, John 1940- Y-82
Nichols, Mary Sargeant (Neal) Gove 1810-1884 ....DLB-1
Nichols, Peter 1927- DLB-13
Nichols, Roy F. 1896-1973 ....DLB-17
Nichols, Ruth 1948- DLB-60
Nicholson, Norman 1914- DLB-27
Ní Chuilleanáin, Eiléan 1942- DLB-40
Nicol, Eric 1919- DLB-68
Nicolay, John G. 1832-1901 and Hay, John 1838-1905 ....DLB-47
Niebuhr, Reinhold 1892-1971 ....DLB-17
Niedecker, Lorine 1903-1970 ....DLB-48
Nieman, Lucius W. 1857-1935 ....DLB-25
Niggli, Josefina 1910- Y-80
Niles, Hezekiah 1777-1839 ....DLB-43
Nims, John Frederick 1913- DLB-5
Nin, Anaïs 1903-1977 ....DLB-2, 4
1985: The Year of the Mystery: A Symposium Y-85
Nissenson, Hugh 1933- DLB-28
Niven, Larry 1938- DLB-8
Nizan, Paul 1905-1940 ....DLB-72
Nobel Peace Prize
The 1986 Nobel Peace Prize
Nobel Lecture 1986: Hope, Despair and Memory
Tributes from Abraham Bernstein, Norman Lamm, and John R. Silber Y-86
The Nobel Prize and Literary Politics Y-88
Nobel Prize in Literature
The 1982 Nobel Prize in Literature
Announcement by the Swedish Academy of the Nobel Prize
Nobel Lecture 1982: The Solitude of Latin America
Excerpt from *One Hundred Years of Solitude*
The Magical World of Macondo
A Tribute to Gabriel García Márquez Y-82
The 1983 Nobel Prize in Literature
Announcement by the Swedish Academy
Nobel Lecture 1983
The Stature of William Golding Y-83
The 1984 Nobel Prize in Literature
Announcement by the Swedish Academy
Jaroslav Seifert Through the Eyes of the English-Speaking Reader
Three Poems by Jaroslav Seifert Y-84
The 1985 Nobel Prize in Literature
Announcement by the Swedish Academy
Nobel Lecture 1985 ....Y-85
The 1986 Nobel Prize in Literature
Nobel Lecture 1986: This Past Must Address Its Present Y-86
The 1987 Nobel Prize in Literature
Nobel Lecture 1987 ....Y-87
The 1988 Nobel Prize in Literature
Nobel Lecture 1988 ....Y-88
Noel, Roden 1834-1894 ....DLB-35
Nolan, William F. 1928- DLB-8
Noland, C. F. M. 1810?-1858 ....DLB-11
Noonday Press DLB-46
Noone, John 1936- DLB-14
Nordhoff, Charles 1887-1947 ....DLB-9
Norman, Marsha 1947- Y-84
Norris, Charles G. 1881-1945 ....DLB-9
Norris, Frank 1870-1902 ....DLB-12
Norris, Leslie 1921- DLB-27
Norse, Harold 1916- DLB-16
North Point Press DLB-46
Norton, Alice Mary (see Norton, Andre)
Norton, Andre 1912- DLB-8, 52
Norton, Andrews 1786-1853 ....DLB-1
Norton, Caroline 1808-1877 ....DLB-21
Norton, Charles Eliot 1827-1908 ....DLB-1, 64
Norton, John 1606-1663 ....DLB-24
Norton, Thomas (see Sackville, Thomas)
Norton, W. W., and Company DLB-46
Nossack, Hans Erich 1901-1977 ....DLB-69
A Note on Technique (1926), by Elizabeth A. Drew [excerpts] DLB-36
Nourse, Alan E. 1928- DLB-8

Novalis 1772-1801 ....DLB-90

The Novel in [Robert Browning's] "The Ring and the Book" (1912), by Henry James DLB-32

The Novel of Impressionism, by Jethro Bithell DLB-66

Novel-Reading: *The Works of Charles Dickens, The Works of W. Makepeace Thackeray* (1879), by Anthony Trollope DLB-21

The Novels of Dorothy Richardson (1918), by May Sinclair DLB-36

Novels with a Purpose (1864), by Justin M'Carthy DLB-21

Nowlan, Alden 1933-1983 ....DLB-53

Noyes, Alfred 1880-1958 ....DLB-20

Noyes, Crosby S. 1825-1908 ....DLB-23

Noyes, Nicholas 1647-1717 ....DLB-24

Noyes, Theodore W. 1858-1946 ....DLB-29

Nugent, Frank 1908-1965 ....DLB-44

Nye, Edgar Wilson (Bill) 1850-1896 ....DLB-11, 23

Nye, Robert 1939- DLB-14

O

Oakes, Urian circa 1631-1681 ....DLB-24

Oates, Joyce Carol 1938- DLB-2, 5; Y-81

Oberholtzer, Ellis Paxson 1868-1936 ....DLB-47

O'Brien, Edna 1932- DLB-14

O'Brien, Fitz-James 1828-1862 ....DLB-74

O'Brien, Kate 1897-1974 ....DLB-15

O'Brien, Tim 1946- Y-80

O'Casey, Sean 1880-1964 ....DLB-10

Ochs, Adolph S. 1858-1935 ....DLB-25

O'Connor, Flannery 1925-1964 ....DLB-2; Y-80

O'Dell, Scott 1903- DLB-52

Odell, Jonathan 1737-1818 ....DLB-31

Odets, Clifford 1906-1963 ....DLB-7, 26

O'Donnell, Peter 1920- DLB-87

O'Faolain, Julia 1932- DLB-14

O'Faolain, Sean 1900- DLB-15

Off Broadway and Off-Off-Broadway DLB-7

Off-Loop Theatres DLB-7

Offord, Carl Ruthven 1910- DLB-76

O'Flaherty, Liam 1896-1984 ....DLB-36; Y-84

Ogilvie, J. S., and Company DLB-49

O'Grady, Desmond 1935- DLB-40

O'Hagan, Howard 1902-1982 ....DLB-68

O'Hara, Frank 1926-1966 ....DLB-5, 16

O'Hara, John 1905-1970 ....DLB-9, 86; DS-2

O. Henry (see Porter, William Sydney)

O'Keeffe, John 1747-1833 ....DLB-89

Old Franklin Publishing House DLB-49

Older, Fremont 1856-1935 ....DLB-25

Oliphant, Laurence 1829?-1888 ....DLB-18

Oliphant, Margaret 1828-1897 ....DLB-18

Oliver, Chad 1928- DLB-8

Oliver, Mary 1935- DLB-5

Ollier, Claude 1922- DLB-83

Olsen, Tillie 1913?- DLB-28; Y-80

Olson, Charles 1910-1970 ....DLB-5, 16

Olson, Elder 1909- DLB-48, 63

On Art in Fiction (1838), by Edward Bulwer DLB-21

On Learning to Write Y-88

On Some of the Characteristics of Modern Poetry and On the Lyrical Poems of Alfred Tennyson (1831), by Arthur Henry Hallam DLB-32

"On Style in English Prose" (1898), by Frederic Harrison DLB-57

"On Style in Literature: Its Technical Elements" (1885), by Robert Louis Stevenson DLB-57

"On the Writing of Essays" (1862), by Alexander Smith DLB-57

Ondaatje, Michael 1943- DLB-60

O'Neill, Eugene 1888-1953 ....DLB-7

Oppen, George 1908-1984 ....DLB-5

Oppenheim, E. Phillips 1866-1946 ....DLB-70

Oppenheim, James 1882-1932 ....DLB-28

Oppenheimer, Joel 1930- DLB-5

Optic, Oliver (see Adams, William Taylor)

Orczy, Emma, Baroness 1865-1947 ....DLB-70

Orlovitz, Gil 1918-1973 ....DLB-2, 5

Orlovsky, Peter 1933- DLB-16

Ormond, John 1923- DLB-27

Ornitz, Samuel 1890-1957 ....DLB-28, 44
Orton, Joe 1933-1967 ....DLB-13
Orwell, George 1903-1950 ....DLB-15
The Orwell Year Y-84
Osbon, B. S. 1827-1912 ....DLB-43
Osborne, John 1929- DLB-13
Osgood, Herbert L. 1855-1918 ....DLB-47
Osgood, James R., and Company DLB-49
O'Shaughnessy, Arthur 1844-1881 ....DLB-35
O'Shea, Patrick [publishing house] DLB-49
Oswald, Eleazer 1755-1795 ....DLB-43
Otero, Miguel Antonio 1859-1944 ....DLB-82
Otis, James (see Kaler, James Otis)
Otis, James, Jr. 1725-1783 ....DLB-31
Otis, Broaders and Company DLB-49
Ottendorfer, Oswald 1826-1900 ....DLB-23
Otway, Thomas 1652-1685 ....DLB-80
Ouellette, Fernand 1930- DLB-60
Ouida 1839-1908 ....DLB-18
Outing Publishing Company DLB-46
Outlaw Days, by Joyce Johnson DLB-16
The Overlook Press DLB-46
Overview of U.S. Book Publishing, 1910-1945 ....DLB-9
Owen, Guy 1925- DLB-5
Owen, John [publishing house] DLB-49
Owen, Wilfred 1893-1918 ....DLB-20
Owsley, Frank L. 1890-1956 ....DLB-17
Ozick, Cynthia 1928- DLB-28; Y-82

P

Pacey, Desmond 1917-1975 ....DLB-88
Pack, Robert 1929- DLB-5
Packaging Papa: *The Garden of Eden* Y-86
Padell Publishing Company DLB-46
Padgett, Ron 1942- DLB-5
Page, L. C., and Company DLB-49
Page, P. K. 1916- DLB-68
Page, Thomas Nelson 1853-1922 ....DLB-12, 78
Page, Walter Hines 1855-1918 ....DLB-71
Paget, Violet (see Lee, Vernon)
Pain, Philip ?-circa 1666 ....DLB-24
Paine, Robert Treat, Jr. 1773-1811 ....DLB-37
Paine, Thomas 1737-1809 ....DLB-31, 43, 73
Paley, Grace 1922- DLB-28
Palfrey, John Gorham 1796-1881 ....DLB-1, 30
Palgrave, Francis Turner 1824-1897 ....DLB-35
Paltock, Robert 1697-1767 ....DLB-39
Panama, Norman 1914- and Frank, Melvin 1913-1988 ....DLB-26
Pangborn, Edgar 1909-1976 ....DLB-8
"Panic Among the Philistines": A Postscript, An Interview with Bryan Griffin Y-81
Panneton, Philippe (see Ringuet)
Panshin, Alexei 1940- DLB-8
Pansy (see Alden, Isabella)
Pantheon Books DLB-46
Paperback Library DLB-46
Paperback Science Fiction DLB-8
Paquet, Alfons 1881-1944 ....DLB-66
Paradis, Suzanne 1936- DLB-53
Parents' Magazine Press DLB-46
Parisian Theater, Fall 1984: Toward A New Baroque Y-85
Parizeau, Alice 1930- DLB-60
Parke, John 1754-1789 ....DLB-31
Parker, Dorothy 1893-1967 ....DLB-11, 45, 86
Parker, James 1714-1770 ....DLB-43
Parker, Theodore 1810-1860 ....DLB-1
Parkman, Francis, Jr. 1823-1893 ....DLB-1, 30
Parks, Gordon 1912- DLB-33
Parks, William 1698-1750 ....DLB-43
Parks, William [publishing house] DLB-49
Parley, Peter (see Goodrich, Samuel Griswold)
Parrington, Vernon L. 1871-1929 ....DLB-17, 63
Parton, James 1822-1891 ....DLB-30
Parton, Sara Payson Willis 1811-1872 ....DLB-43, 74
Pastan, Linda 1932- DLB-5
Pastorius, Francis Daniel 1651-circa 1720 ....DLB-24
Patchen, Kenneth 1911-1972 ....DLB-16, 48
Pater, Walter 1839-1894 ....DLB-57
Paterson, Katherine 1932- DLB-52

Patmore, Coventry 1823-1896 ....DLB-35
Paton, Joseph Noel 1821-1901 ....DLB-35
Patrick, John 1906- DLB-7
Pattee, Fred Lewis 1863-1950 ....DLB-71
Pattern and Paradigm: History as Design, by Judith Ryan DLB-75
Patterson, Eleanor Medill 1881-1948 ....DLB-29
Patterson, Joseph Medill 1879-1946 ....DLB-29
Pattillo, Henry 1726-1801 ....DLB-37
Paul, Elliot 1891-1958 ....DLB-4
Paul, Peter, Book Company DLB-49
Paulding, James Kirke 1778-1860 ....DLB-3, 59, 74
Paulin, Tom 1949- DLB-40
Pauper, Peter, Press DLB-46
Paxton, John 1911-1985 ....DLB-44
Payn, James 1830-1898 ....DLB-18
Payne, John 1842-1916 ....DLB-35
Payne, John Howard 1791-1852 ....DLB-37
Payson and Clarke DLB-46
Peabody, Elizabeth Palmer 1804-1894 ....DLB-1
Peabody, Elizabeth Palmer [publishing house] DLB-49
Peabody, Oliver William Bourn 1799-1848 ....DLB-59
Peachtree Publishers, Limited DLB-46
Pead, Deuel ?-1727 ....DLB-24
Peake, Mervyn 1911-1968 ....DLB-15
Pearson, H. B. [publishing house] DLB-49
Peck, George W. 1840-1916 ....DLB-23, 42
Peck, H. C., and Theo. Bliss [publishing house] DLB-49
Peck, Harry Thurston 1856-1914 ....DLB-71
Peele, George 1556-1596 ....DLB-62
Pellegrini and Cudahy DLB-46
Pelletier, Aimé (see Vac, Bertrand)
Pemberton, Sir Max 1863-1950 ....DLB-70
Penguin Books DLB-46
Penn Publishing Company DLB-49
Penn, William 1644-1718 ....DLB-24
Penner, Jonathan 1940- Y-83
Pennington, Lee 1939- Y-82
Percy, Walker 1916- DLB-2; Y-80
Perec, Georges 1936-1982 ....DLB-83
Perelman, S. J. 1904-1979 ....DLB-11, 44
Periodicals of the Beat Generation DLB-16
Perkins, Eugene 1932- DLB-41
Perkoff, Stuart Z. 1930-1974 ....DLB-16
Permabooks DLB-46
Perry, Bliss 1860-1954 ....DLB-71
Perry, Eleanor 1915-1981 ....DLB-44
"Personal Style" (1890), by John Addington Symonds DLB-57
Perutz, Leo 1882-1957 ....DLB-81
Peter, Laurence J. 1919- DLB-53
Peterkin, Julia 1880-1961 ....DLB-9
Petersham, Maud 1889-1971 and Petersham, Miska 1888-1960 ....DLB-22
Peterson, Charles Jacobs 1819-1887 ....DLB-79
Peterson, Len 1917- DLB-88
Peterson, Louis 1922- DLB-76
Peterson, T. B., and Brothers DLB-49
Petry, Ann 1908- DLB-76
Pharr, Robert Deane 1916-1989 ....DLB-33
Phelps, Elizabeth Stuart 1844-1911 ....DLB-74
Philippe, Charles-Louis 1874-1909 ....DLB-65
Phillips, David Graham 1867-1911 ....DLB-9, 12
Phillips, Jayne Anne 1952- Y-80
Phillips, Stephen 1864-1915 ....DLB-10
Phillips, Ulrich B. 1877-1934 ....DLB-17
Phillips, Willard 1784-1873 ....DLB-59
Phillips, Sampson and Company DLB-49
Phillpotts, Eden 1862-1960 ....DLB-10, 70
Philosophical Library DLB-46
"The Philosophy of Style" (1852), by Herbert Spencer DLB-57
Phinney, Elihu [publishing house] DLB-49
Phoenix, John (see Derby, George Horatio)
PHYLON (Fourth Quarter, 1950), The Negro in Literature: The Current Scene DLB-76
Pickard, Tom 1946- DLB-40
Pictorial Printing Company DLB-49
Pike, Albert 1809-1891 ....DLB-74
Pilon, Jean-Guy 1930- DLB-60

Pinckney, Josephine 1895-1957 ....DLB-6
Pinero, Arthur Wing 1855-1934 ....DLB-10
Pinget, Robert 1919- DLB-83
Pinnacle Books DLB-46
Pinsky, Robert 1940- Y-82
Pinter, Harold 1930- DLB-13
Piontek, Heinz 1925- DLB-75
Piper, H. Beam 1904-1964 ....DLB-8
Piper, Watty DLB-22
Pisar, Samuel 1929- Y-83
Pitkin, Timothy 1766-1847 ....DLB-30
The Pitt Poetry Series: Poetry Publishing Today Y-85
Pitter, Ruth 1897- DLB-20
Pix, Mary 1666-1709 ....DLB-80
The Place of Realism in Fiction (1895), by George Gissing DLB-18
Plante, David 1940- Y-83
Platen, August von 1796-1835 ....DLB-90
Plath, Sylvia 1932-1963 ....DLB-5, 6
Platt and Munk Company DLB-46
Playboy Press DLB-46
Plays, Playwrights, and Playgoers DLB-84
Playwrights and Professors, by Tom Stoppard DLB-13
Playwrights on the Theater DLB-80
Plenzdorf, Ulrich 1934- DLB-75
Plessen, Elizabeth 1944- DLB-75
Plievier, Theodor 1892-1955 ....DLB-69
Plomer, William 1903-1973 ....DLB-20
Plumly, Stanley 1939- DLB-5
Plumpp, Sterling D. 1940- DLB-41
Plunkett, James 1920- DLB-14
Plymell, Charles 1935- DLB-16
Pocket Books DLB-46
Poe, Edgar Allan 1809-1849 ....DLB-3, 59, 73, 74
Poe, James 1921-1980 ....DLB-44
The Poet Laureate of the United States Statements from Former Consultants in Poetry Y-86
Pohl, Frederik 1919- DLB-8
Poirier, Louis (see Gracq, Julien)
Poliakoff, Stephen 1952- DLB-13
Polite, Carlene Hatcher 1932- DLB-33
Pollard, Edward A. 1832-1872 ....DLB-30
Pollard, Percival 1869-1911 ....DLB-71
Pollard and Moss DLB-49
Pollock, Sharon 1936- DLB-60
Polonsky, Abraham 1910- DLB-26
Poole, Ernest 1880-1950 ....DLB-9
Poore, Benjamin Perley 1820-1887 ....DLB-23
Popular Library DLB-46
Porlock, Martin (see MacDonald, Philip)
Porter, Eleanor H. 1868-1920 ....DLB-9
Porter, Henry ?-? DLB-62
Porter, Katherine Anne 1890-1980 ....DLB-4, 9; Y-80
Porter, Peter 1929- DLB-40
Porter, William Sydney 1862-1910 ....DLB-12, 78, 79
Porter, William T. 1809-1858 ....DLB-3, 43
Porter and Coates DLB-49
Portis, Charles 1933- DLB-6
Poston, Ted 1906-1974 ....DLB-51
Postscript to [the Third Edition of] *Clarissa* (1751), by Samuel Richardson DLB-39
Potok, Chaim 1929- DLB-28; Y-84
Potter, David M. 1910-1971 ....DLB-17
Potter, John E., and Company DLB-49
Pottle, Frederick A. 1897-1987 ....Y-87
Poulin, Jacques 1937- DLB-60
Pound, Ezra 1885-1972 ....DLB-4, 45, 63
Powell, Anthony 1905- DLB-15
Pownall, David 1938- DLB-14
Powys, John Cowper 1872-1963 ....DLB-15
Powys, T. F. 1875-1953 ....DLB-36
The Practice of Biography: An Interview with Stanley Weintraub Y-82
The Practice of Biography II: An Interview with B. L. Reid Y-83
The Practice of Biography III: An Interview with Humphrey Carpenter Y-84
The Practice of Biography IV: An Interview with William Manchester Y-85
The Practice of Biography V: An Interview with Justin Kaplan Y-86

The Practice of Biography VI: An Interview with David Herbert Donald Y-87
Praeger Publishers...DLB-46
Pratt, Samuel Jackson 1749-1814 ....DLB-39
Preface to *Alwyn* (1780), by Thomas Holcroft...DLB-39
Preface to *Colonel Jack* (1722), by Daniel Defoe..DLB-39
Preface to *Evelina* (1778), by Fanny Burney.......DLB-39
Preface to *Ferdinand Count Fathom* (1753), by Tobias Smollett DLB-39
Preface to *Incognita* (1692), by William Congreve...DLB-39
Preface to *Joseph Andrews* (1742), by Henry Fielding DLB-39
Preface to *Moll Flanders* (1722), by Daniel Defoe..DLB-39
Preface to *Poems* (1853), by Matthew Arnold..DLB-32
Preface to *Robinson Crusoe* (1719), by Daniel Defoe..DLB-39
Preface to *Roderick Random* (1748), by Tobias Smollett DLB-39
Preface to *Roxana* (1724), by Daniel Defoe........DLB-39
Preface to *St. Leon* (1799), by William Godwin......................................DLB-39
Preface to Sarah Fielding's *Familiar Letters* (1747), by Henry Fielding [excerpt]............DLB-39
Preface to Sarah Fielding's *The Adventures of David Simple* (1744), by Henry Fielding.......DLB-39
Preface to *The Cry* (1754), by Sarah Fielding.....DLB-39
Preface to *The Delicate Distress* (1769), by Elizabeth Griffin..DLB-39
Preface to *The Disguis'd Prince* (1733), by Eliza Haywood [excerpt] DLB-39
Preface to *The Farther Adventures of Robinson Crusoe* (1719), by Daniel Defoe....................DLB-39
Preface to the First Edition of *Pamela* (1740), by Samuel Richardson.....................................DLB-39
Preface to the First Edition of *The Castle of Otranto* (1764), by Horace Walpole.............DLB-39
Preface to *The History of Romances* (1715), by Pierre Daniel Huet [excerpts]......................DLB-39
Preface to *The Life of Charlotta du Pont* (1723), by Penelope Aubin DLB-39
Preface to *The Old English Baron* (1778), by Clara Reeve...DLB-39
Preface to the Second Edition of *The Castle of Otranto* (1765), by Horace Walpole.............DLB-39
Preface to *The Secret History, of Queen Zarah, and the Zarazians* (1705), by Delarivière Manley...DLB-39
Preface to the Third Edition of *Clarissa* (1751), by Samuel Richardson [excerpt]..................DLB-39
Preface to *The Works of Mrs. Davys* (1725), by Mary Davys DLB-39
Preface to Volume 1 of *Clarissa* (1747), by Samuel Richardson.......................................DLB-39
Preface to Volume 3 of *Clarissa* (1748), by Samuel Richardson.......................................DLB-39
Préfontaine, Yves 1937- DLB-53
Prelutsky, Jack 1940- DLB-61
Premisses, by Michael Hamburger DLB-66
Prentice, George D. 1802-1870...........................DLB-43
Prentice-Hall...DLB-46
Prescott, William Hickling 1796-1859......DLB-1, 30, 59
The Present State of the English Novel (1892), by George Saintsbury DLB-18
Preston, Thomas 1537-1598 ....DLB-62
Price, Reynolds 1933- DLB-2
Price, Richard 1949- Y-81
Priest, Christopher 1943- DLB-14
Priestley, J. B. 1894-1984 ....DLB-10, 34, 77; Y-84
Prime, Benjamin Young 1733-1791....................DLB-31
Prince, F. T. 1912- DLB-20
Prince, Thomas 1687-1758 ....DLB-24
The Principles of Success in Literature (1865), by George Henry Lewes [excerpt]....................DLB-57
Pritchett, V. S. 1900- DLB-15
Procter, Adelaide Anne 1825-1864 ....DLB-32
The Progress of Romance (1785), by Clara Reeve [excerpt]..DLB-39
Prokosch, Frederic 1906-1989 ....DLB-48
The Proletarian Novel..DLB-9
Propper, Dan 1937- DLB-16
The Prospect of Peace (1778), by Joel Barlow DLB-37
Proud, Robert 1728-1813...................................DLB-30
Proust, Marcel 1871-1922 ....DLB-65

Prynne, J. H. 1936- DLB-40
Przybyszewski, Stanislaw 1868-1927 ....DLB-66
The Public Lending Right in America
Statement by Sen. Charles McC. Mathias, Jr.
PLR and the Meaning of Literary Property
Statements on PLR by American Writers.........Y-83
The Public Lending Right in the United Kingdom
Public Lending Right: The First Year in the
United Kingdom Y-83
The Publication of English Renaissance
Plays DLB-62
Publications and Social Movements
[Transcendentalism] DLB-1
Publishers and Agents: The Columbia
Connection Y-87
Publishing Fiction at LSU Press Y-87
Pugin, A. Welby 1812-1852................................DLB-55
Pulitzer, Joseph 1847-1911 ....DLB-23
Pulitzer, Joseph, Jr. 1885-1955 ....DLB-29
Pulitzer Prizes for the Novel, 1917-1945 ....DLB-9
Purdy, Al 1918- DLB-88
Purdy, James 1923- DLB-2
Pusey, Edward Bouverie 1800-1882 ....DLB-55
Putnam, George Palmer 1814-1872 ....DLB-3, 79
Putnam, Samuel 1892-1950 ....DLB-4
G. P. Putnam's Sons DLB-49
Puzo, Mario 1920- DLB-6
Pyle, Ernie 1900-1945 ....DLB-29
Pyle, Howard 1853-1911 ....DLB-42
Pym, Barbara 1913-1980 ....DLB-14; Y-87
Pynchon, Thomas 1937- DLB-2
Pyramid Books...DLB-46
Pyrnelle, Louise-Clarke 1850-1907 ....DLB-42

Q

Quad, M. (see Lewis, Charles B.)
The Queen City Publishing House.....................DLB-49
Queneau, Raymond 1903-1976 ....DLB-72
The Question of American Copyright
in the Nineteenth Century
Headnote
Preface, by George Haven Putnam
The Evolution of Copyright, by Brander
Matthews
Summary of Copyright Legislation in the
United States, by R. R. Bowker
Analysis of the Provisions of the Copyright
Law of 1891, by George Haven Putnam
The Contest for International Copyright,
by George Haven Putnam
Cheap Books and Good Books,
by Brander Matthews....................DLB-49
Quin, Ann 1936-1973..DLB-14
Quincy, Samuel of Georgia ?-? DLB-31
Quincy, Samuel of Massachusetts 1734-1789.....DLB-31
Quintana, Leroy V. 1944- DLB-82
Quist, Harlin, Books..DLB-46
Quoirez, Françoise (see Sagan, Françoise)

R

Rabe, David 1940- DLB-7
Radcliffe, Ann 1764-1823 ....DLB-39
Raddall, Thomas 1903- DLB-68
Radiguet, Raymond 1903-1923..........................DLB-65
Radványi, Netty Reiling (see Seghers, Anna)
Raimund, Ferdinand Jakob 1790-1836..............DLB-90
Raine, Craig 1944- DLB-40
Raine, Kathleen 1908- DLB-20
Ralph, Julian 1853-1903....................................DLB-23
Ralph Waldo Emerson in 1982 ....Y-82
Rambler, no. 4 (1750), by Samuel Johnson
[excerpt] DLB-39
Ramée, Marie Louise de la (see Ouida)
Ramsay, David 1749-1815 ....DLB-30
Rand, Avery and Company................................DLB-49
Rand McNally and Company.............................DLB-49
Randall, Dudley 1914- DLB-41
Randall, Henry S. 1811-1876.............................DLB-30
Randall, James G. 1881-1953.............................DLB-17
The Randall Jarrell Symposium: A Small
Collection of Randall Jarrells
Excerpts From Papers Delivered at
the Randall Jarrell Symposium Y-86
Randolph, Anson D. F. [publishing house]........DLB-49
Randolph, Thomas 1605-1635...........................DLB-58
Random House DLB-46

Ranlet, Henry [publishing house]......................DLB-49
Ransom, John Crowe 1888-1974.................DLB-45, 63
Raphael, Frederic 1931- DLB-14
Raphaelson, Samson 1896-1983.........................DLB-44
Raskin, Ellen 1928-1984.....................................DLB-52
Rattigan, Terence 1911-1977.............................DLB-13
Rawlings, Marjorie Kinnan 1896-1953..........DLB-9, 22
Raworth, Tom 1938- DLB-40
Ray, David 1932- DLB-5
Ray, Henrietta Cordelia 1849-1916...................DLB-50
Raymond, Henry J. 1820-1869.....................DLB-43, 79
Raymond Chandler Centenary Tributes
from Michael Avallone, James Elroy, Joe Gores,
and William F. Nolan......................................Y-88
Reach, Angus 1821-1856....................................DLB-70
Read, Herbert 1893-1968 ....DLB-20
Read, Opie 1852-1939..DLB-23
Read, Piers Paul 1941- DLB-14
Reade, Charles 1814-1884.................................DLB-21
Reader's Digest Condensed Books DLB-46
Reading, Peter 1946- DLB-40
Reaney, James 1926- DLB-68
Rechy, John 1934- Y-82
Redding, J. Saunders 1906-1988.................DLB-63, 76
Redfield, J. S. [publishing house].......................DLB-49
Redgrove, Peter 1932- DLB-40
Redmon, Anne 1943- Y-86
Redmond, Eugene B. 1937- DLB-41
Redpath, James [publishing house]....................DLB-49
Reed, Henry 1808-1854....................................DLB-59
Reed, Henry 1914- DLB-27
Reed, Ishmael 1938- DLB-2, 5, 33
Reed, Sampson 1800-1880...................................DLB-1
Reese, Lizette Woodworth 1856-1935 ....DLB-54
Reese, Thomas 1742-1796 ....DLB-37
Reeve, Clara 1729-1807......................................DLB-39
Reeves, John 1926- DLB-88
Regnery, Henry, Company DLB-46
Reid, Alastair 1926- DLB-27
Reid, Christopher 1949- DLB-40
Reid, Helen Rogers 1882-1970..........................DLB-29
Reid, James ?-?..DLB-31
Reid, Mayne 1818-1883.....................................DLB-21
Reid, Thomas 1710-1796...................................DLB-31
Reid, Whitelaw 1837-1912................................DLB-23
Reilly and Lee Publishing Company DLB-46
Reimann, Brigitte 1933-1973............................DLB-75
Reisch, Walter 1903-1983..................................DLB-44
Remarque, Erich Maria 1898-1970....................DLB-56
"Re-meeting of Old Friends": The Jack Kerouac
Conference...Y-82
Remington, Frederic 1861-1909 ....DLB-12
Renaud, Jacques 1943- DLB-60
Renault, Mary 1905-1983......................................Y-83
Rendell, Ruth 1930- DLB-87
Representative Men and Women: A Historical
Perspective on the British Novel,
1930-1960 ....DLB-15
(Re-)Publishing Orwell Y-86
Reuter, Gabriele 1859-1941 ....DLB-66
Revell, Fleming H., Company............................DLB-49
Reventlow, Franziska Gräfin zu
1871-1918 ....DLB-66
Review of [Samuel Richardson's] *Clarissa* (1748),
by Henry Fielding DLB-39
The Revolt (1937), by Mary
Colum [excerpts] DLB-36
Rexroth, Kenneth 1905-1982............DLB-16, 48; Y-82
Rey, H. A. 1898-1977...DLB-22
Reynal and Hitchcock DLB-46
Reynolds, G. W. M. 1814-1879..........................DLB-21
Reynolds, Mack 1917- DLB-8
Reznikoff, Charles 1894-1976......................DLB-28, 45
"Rhetoric" (1828; revised, 1859), by
Thomas de Quincey [excerpt] DLB-57
Rhett, Robert Barnwell 1800-1876....................DLB-43
Rhode, John 1884-1964 ....DLB-77
Rhodes, James Ford 1848-1927 ....DLB-47
Rhys, Jean 1890-1979..DLB-36
Ricardou, Jean 1932- DLB-83
Rice, Elmer 1892-1967....................................DLB-4, 7
Rice, Grantland 1880-1954 ....DLB-29
Rich, Adrienne 1929- DLB-5, 67

Richards, David Adams 1950- DLB-53
Richards, George circa 1760-1814 ....DLB-37
Richards, I. A. 1893-1979 ....DLB-27
Richards, Laura E. 1850-1943 ....DLB-42
Richards, William Carey 1818-1892 ....DLB-73
Richardson, Charles F. 1851-1913 ....DLB-71
Richardson, Dorothy M. 1873-1957 ....DLB-36
Richardson, Jack 1935- DLB-7
Richardson, Samuel 1689-1761 ....DLB-39
Richardson, Willis 1889-1977 ....DLB-51
Richler, Mordecai 1931- DLB-53
Richter, Conrad 1890-1968 ....DLB-9
Richter, Hans Werner 1908- DLB-69
Rickword, Edgell 1898-1982 ....DLB-20
Riddell, John (see Ford, Corey)
Ridge, Lola 1873-1941 ....DLB-54
Ridler, Anne 1912- DLB-27
Riffaterre, Michael 1924- DLB-67
Riis, Jacob 1849-1914 ....DLB-23
Riker, John C. [publishing house] DLB-49
Riley, John 1938-1978 ....DLB-40
Rilke, Rainer Maria 1875-1926 ....DLB-81
Rinehart and Company DLB-46
Ringuet 1895-1960 ....DLB-68
Ringwood, Gwen Pharis 1910-1984 ....DLB-88
Rinser, Luise 1911- DLB-69
Ríos, Isabella 1948- DLB-82
Ripley, Arthur 1895-1961 ....DLB-44
Ripley, George 1802-1880 ....DLB-1, 64, 73
The Rising Glory of America: Three Poems DLB-37
The Rising Glory of America: Written in 1771 (1786), by Hugh Henry Brackenridge and Philip Freneau DLB-37
Riskin, Robert 1897-1955 ....DLB-26
Risse, Heinz 1898- DLB-69
Ritchie, Anna Mowatt 1819-1870 ....DLB-3
Ritchie, Anne Thackeray 1837-1919 ....DLB-18
Ritchie, Thomas 1778-1854 ....DLB-43
Rites of Passage [on William Saroyan] Y-83
The Ritz Paris Hemingway Award Y-85
Rivera, Tomás 1935-1984 ....DLB-82
Rivers, Conrad Kent 1933-1968 ....DLB-41
Riverside Press DLB-49
Rivington, James circa 1724-1802 ....DLB-43
Rivkin, Allen 1903- DLB-26
Robbe-Grillet, Alain 1922- DLB-83
Robbins, Tom 1936- Y-80
Roberts, Dorothy 1906- DLB-88
Roberts, Elizabeth Madox 1881-1941 ....DLB-9, 54
Roberts, Kenneth 1885-1957 ....DLB-9
Roberts Brothers DLB-49
Robertson, A. M., and Company DLB-49
Robinson, Casey 1903-1979 ....DLB-44
Robinson, Edwin Arlington 1869-1935 ....DLB-54
Robinson, James Harvey 1863-1936 ....DLB-47
Robinson, Lennox 1886-1958 ....DLB-10
Robinson, Mabel Louise 1874-1962 ....DLB-22
Robinson, Therese 1797-1870 ....DLB-59
Roblès, Emmanuel 1914- DLB-83
Rodgers, Carolyn M. 1945- DLB-41
Rodgers, W. R. 1909-1969 ....DLB-20
Rodriguez, Richard 1944- DLB-82
Roethke, Theodore 1908-1963 ....DLB-5
Rogers, Will 1879-1935 ....DLB-11
Rohmer, Sax 1883-1959 ....DLB-70
Roiphe, Anne 1935- Y-80
Rojas, Arnold R. 1896-1988 ....DLB-82
Rolfe, Frederick William 1860-1913 ....DLB-34
Rolland, Romain 1866-1944 ....DLB-65
Rolvaag, O. E. 1876-1931 ....DLB-9
Romains, Jules 1885-1972 ....DLB-65
Roman, A., and Company DLB-49
Romero, Orlando 1945- DLB-82
Roosevelt, Theodore 1858-1919 ....DLB-47
Root, Waverley 1903-1982 ....DLB-4
Roquebrune, Robert de 1889-1978 ....DLB-68
Rose, Reginald 1920- DLB-26
Rosei, Peter 1946- DLB-85
Rosen, Norma 1925- DLB-28
Rosenberg, Isaac 1890-1918 ....DLB-20
Rosenfeld, Isaac 1918-1956 ....DLB-28
Rosenthal, M. L. 1917- DLB-5

Ross, Leonard Q. (see Rosten, Leo)
Ross, Sinclair 1908- DLB-88
Ross, W. W. E. 1894-1966....DLB-88
Rossen, Robert 1908-1966 ....DLB-26
Rossetti, Christina 1830-1894....DLB-35
Rossetti, Dante Gabriel 1828-1882....DLB-35
Rossner, Judith 1935- DLB-6
Rosten, Leo 1908- DLB-11
Roth, Gerhard 1942- DLB-85
Roth, Henry 1906?- DLB-28
Roth, Joseph 1894-1939....DLB-85
Roth, Philip 1933- DLB-2, 28; Y-82
Rothenberg, Jerome 1931- DLB-5
Routier, Simone 1901-1987....DLB-88
Rowe, Elizabeth 1674-1737 ....DLB-39
Rowe, Nicholas 1674-1718 ....DLB-84
Rowlandson, Mary circa 1635-circa 1678....DLB-24
Rowley, William circa 1585-1626....DLB-58
Rowson, Susanna Haswell circa 1762-1824....DLB-37
Roy, Gabrielle 1909-1983....DLB-68
Roy, Jules 1907- DLB-83
The Royal Court Theatre and the English Stage Company....DLB-13
The Royal Court Theatre and the New Drama DLB-10
The Royal Shakespeare Company at the Swan....Y-88
Royall, Anne 1769-1854....DLB-43
The Roycroft Printing Shop DLB-49
Rubens, Bernice 1928- DLB-14
Rudd and Carleton....DLB-49
Rudkin, David 1936- DLB-13
Ruffin, Josephine St. Pierre 1842-1924....DLB-79
Ruggles, Henry Joseph 1813-1906 ....DLB-64
Rukeyser, Muriel 1913-1980 ....DLB-48
Rule, Jane 1931- DLB-60
Rumaker, Michael 1932- DLB-16
Rumens, Carol 1944- DLB-40
Runyon, Damon 1880-1946....DLB-11, 86
Rush, Benjamin 1746-1813 ....DLB-37
Ruskin, John 1819-1900....DLB-55
Russ, Joanna 1937- DLB-8
Russell, B. B., and Company DLB-49
Russell, Benjamin 1761-1845....DLB-43
Russell, Charles Edward 1860-1941 ....DLB-25
Russell, George William (see AE)
Russell, R. H., and Son DLB-49
Rutherford, Mark 1831-1913....DLB-18
Ryan, Michael 1946- Y-82
Ryan, Oscar 1904- DLB-68
Ryga, George 1932- DLB-60
Ryskind, Morrie 1895-1985 ....DLB-26

S

The Saalfield Publishing Company DLB-46
Saberhagen, Fred 1930- DLB-8
Sackler, Howard 1929-1982....DLB-7
Sackville, Thomas 1536-1608 and Norton, Thomas 1532-1584 ....DLB-62
Sackville-West, V. 1892-1962 ....DLB-34
Sadlier, D. and J., and Company....DLB-49
Saffin, John circa 1626-1710....DLB-24
Sagan, Françoise 1935- DLB-83
Sage, Robert 1899-1962 ....DLB-4
Sagel, Jim 1947- DLB-82
Sahkomaapii, Piitai (see Highwater, Jamake)
Sahl, Hans 1902- DLB-69
Said, Edward W. 1935- DLB-67
Saiko, George 1892-1962 ....DLB-85
St. Johns, Adela Rogers 1894-1988 ....DLB-29
St. Martin's Press DLB-46
Saint-Exupéry, Antoine de 1900-1944 ....DLB-72
Saint Pierre, Michel de 1916-1987....DLB-83
Saintsbury, George 1845-1933....DLB-57
Saki (see Munro, H. H.)
Salaam, Kalamu ya 1947- DLB-38
Salas, Floyd 1931- DLB-82
Salemson, Harold J. 1910-1988 ....DLB-4
Salinas, Luis Omar 1937- DLB-82
Salinger, J. D. 1919- DLB-2
Salt, Waldo 1914- DLB-44

Sampson, Richard Henry (see Hull, Richard)
Sanborn, Franklin Benjamin 1831-1917 ....DLB-1
Sánchez, Ricardo 1941- DLB-82
Sanchez, Sonia 1934- DLB-41
Sandburg, Carl 1878-1967 ....DLB-17, 54
Sanders, Ed 1939- DLB-16
Sandoz, Mari 1896-1966.......................................DLB-9
Sandys, George 1578-1644.................................DLB-24
Santayana, George 1863-1952 ....DLB-54, 71
Santmyer, Helen Hooven 1895-1986.......................Y-84
Sapper (see McNeile, Herman Cyril)
Sargent, Pamela 1948- DLB-8
Saroyan, William 1908-1981............DLB-7, 9, 86; Y-81
Sarraute, Nathalie 1900- DLB-83
Sarrazin, Albertine 1937-1967 ....DLB-83
Sarton, May 1912- DLB-48; Y-81
Sartre, Jean-Paul 1905-1980 ....DLB-72
Sassoon, Siegfried 1886-1967 ....DLB-20
Saturday Review Press..DLB-46
Saunders, James 1925- DLB-13
Saunders, John Monk 1897-1940 ....DLB-26
Savage, James 1784-1873 ....DLB-30
Savage, Marmion W. 1803?-1872 ....DLB-21
Savard, Félix-Antoine 1896-1982.......................DLB-68
Sawyer, Ruth 1880-1970 ....DLB-22
Sayers, Dorothy L. 1893-1957 ....DLB-10, 36, 77
Sayles, John Thomas 1950- DLB-44
Scannell, Vernon 1922- DLB-27
Scarry, Richard 1919- DLB-61
Schaeffer, Albrecht 1885-1950 ....DLB-66
Schaeffer, Susan Fromberg 1941- DLB-28
Schaper, Edzard 1908-1984 ....DLB-69
Scharf, J. Thomas 1843-1898 ....DLB-47
Schelling, Friedrich Wilhelm Joseph von 1775-1854 ....DLB-90
Schickele, René 1883-1940................................DLB-66
Schlegel, Dorothea 1763-1839 ....DLB-90
Schlegel, Friedrich 1772-1829............................DLB-90
Schleiermacher, Friedrich 1768-1834................DLB-90
Schlesinger, Arthur M., Jr. 1917- DLB-17
Schlumberger, Jean 1877-1968..........................DLB-65
Schmid, Eduard Hermann Wilhelm (see Edschmid, Kasimir)
Schmidt, Arno 1914-1979 ....DLB-69
Schmidt, Michael 1947- DLB-40
Schmitz, James H. 1911- DLB-8
Schnitzler, Arthur 1862-1931 ....DLB-81
Schnurre, Wolfdietrich 1920- DLB-69
Schocken Books DLB-46
The Schomburg Center for Research in Black Culture DLB-76
Schopenhauer, Arthur 1788-1860......................DLB-90
Schopenhauer, Johanna 1766-1838...................DLB-90
Schouler, James 1839-1920 ....DLB-47
Schrader, Paul 1946- DLB-44
Schreiner, Olive 1855-1920................................DLB-18
Schroeder, Andreas 1946- DLB-53
Schubert, Gotthilf Heinrich 1780-1860..............DLB-90
Schulberg, Budd 1914- DLB-6, 26, 28; Y-81
Schulte, F. J., and Company DLB-49
Schurz, Carl 1829-1906 ....DLB-23
Schuyler, George S. 1895-1977....................DLB-29, 51
Schuyler, James 1923- DLB-5
Schwartz, Delmore 1913-1966 ....DLB-28, 48
Schwartz, Jonathan 1938- Y-82
Science Fantasy...DLB-8
Science-Fiction Fandom and Conventions............DLB-8
Science-Fiction Fanzines: The Time Binders DLB-8
Science-Fiction Films DLB-8
Science Fiction Writers of America and the Nebula Awards DLB-8
Scott, Evelyn 1893-1963 ....DLB-9, 48
Scott, F. R. 1899-1985 ....DLB-88
Scott, Harvey W. 1838-1910 ....DLB-23
Scott, Paul 1920-1978 ....DLB-14
Scott, Sarah 1723-1795.......................................DLB-39
Scott, Tom 1918- DLB-27
Scott, William Bell 1811-1890............................DLB-32
Scott, William R. [publishing house] DLB-46
Scott-Heron, Gil 1949- DLB-41
Charles Scribner's Sons DLB-49
Scripps, E. W. 1854-1926 ....DLB-25

Scudder, Horace Elisha 1838-1902 ....DLB-42, 71
Scudder, Vida Dutton 1861-1954 ....DLB-71
Scupham, Peter 1933- DLB-40
Seabrook, William 1886-1945 ....DLB-4
Seabury, Samuel 1729-1796 ....DLB-31
Sears, Edward I. 1819?-1876 ....DLB-79
Sears Publishing Company DLB-46
Seaton, George 1911-1979 ....DLB-44
Seaton, William Winston 1785-1866...................DLB-43
Sedgwick, Arthur George 1844-1915 ....DLB-64
Sedgwick, Catharine Maria 1789-1867 ....DLB-1, 74
Seeger, Alan 1888-1916 ....DLB-45
Segal, Erich 1937- Y-86
Seghers, Anna 1900-1983 ....DLB-69
Seid, Ruth (see Sinclair, Jo)
Seidel, Frederick Lewis 1936- Y-84
Seidel, Ina 1885-1974 ....DLB-56
Séjour, Victor 1817-1874 ....DLB-50
Séjour Marcou et Ferrand, Juan Victor (see Séjour, Victor)
Selby, Hubert, Jr. 1928- DLB-2
Selden, George 1929- DLB-52
Selected English-Language Little Magazines and Newspapers [France, 1920-1939] DLB-4
Selected Humorous Magazines (1820-1950) DLB-11
Selected Science-Fiction Magazines and Anthologies DLB-8
Seligman, Edwin R. A. 1861-1939 ....DLB-47
Seltzer, Chester E. (see Muro, Amado)
Seltzer, Thomas [publishing house]....................DLB-46
Sendak, Maurice 1928- DLB-61
Sensation Novels (1863), by H. L. Manse...........DLB-21
Seredy, Kate 1899-1975 ....DLB-22
Serling, Rod 1924-1975 ....DLB-26
Settle, Mary Lee 1918- DLB-6
Seuss, Dr. (see Geisel, Theodor Seuss)
Sewall, Joseph 1688-1769 ....DLB-24
Sewell, Samuel 1652-1730 ....DLB-24
Sex, Class, Politics, and Religion [in the British Novel, 1930-1959] DLB-15
Sexton, Anne 1928-1974 ....DLB-5
Shaara, Michael 1929-1988 ....Y-83
Shadwell, Thomas 1641?-1692 ....DLB-80
Shaffer, Anthony 1926- DLB-13
Shaffer, Peter 1926- DLB-13
Shairp, Mordaunt 1887-1939..............................DLB-10
Shakespeare, William 1564-1616 ....DLB-62
Shange, Ntozake 1948- DLB-38
Shapiro, Karl 1913- DLB-48
Sharon Publications DLB-46
Sharpe, Tom 1928- DLB-14
Shaw, Bernard 1856-1950..............................DLB-10, 57
Shaw, Henry Wheeler 1818-1885 ....DLB-11
Shaw, Irwin 1913-1984 ....DLB-6; Y-84
Shaw, Robert 1927-1978 ....DLB-13, 14
Shay, Frank [publishing house]...........................DLB-46
Shea, John Gilmary 1824-1892 ....DLB-30
Shearing, Joseph 1886-1952...............................DLB-70
Shebbeare, John 1709-1788 ....DLB-39
Sheckley, Robert 1928- DLB-8
Shedd, William G. T. 1820-1894 ....DLB-64
Sheed, Wilfred 1930- DLB-6
Sheed and Ward DLB-46
Sheldon, Alice B. (see Tiptree, James, Jr.)
Sheldon, Edward 1886-1946 ....DLB-7
Sheldon and Company DLB-49
Shepard, Sam 1943- DLB-7
Shepard, Thomas I 1604 or 1605-1649 ....DLB-24
Shepard, Thomas II 1635-1677..........................DLB-24
Shepard, Clark and Brown DLB-49
Sheridan, Frances 1724-1766........................DLB-39, 84
Sheridan, Richard Brinsley 1751-1816 ....DLB-89
Sherriff, R. C. 1896-1975 ....DLB-10
Sherwood, Robert 1896-1955 ....DLB-7, 26
Shiels, George 1886-1949 ....DLB-10
Shillaber, B.[enjamin] P.[enhallow] 1814-1890 ....DLB-1, 11
Shine, Ted 1931- DLB-38
Ship, Reuben 1915-1975 ....DLB-88
Shirer, William L. 1904- DLB-4
Shirley, James 1596-1666 ....DLB-58
Shockley, Ann Allen 1927- DLB-33
Shorthouse, Joseph Henry 1834-1903................DLB-18

Showalter, Elaine 1941- DLB-67
Shulevitz, Uri 1935- DLB-61
Shulman, Max 1919-1988 ....DLB-11
Shute, Henry A. 1856-1943 ....DLB-9
Shuttle, Penelope 1947- DLB-14, 40
Sidney, Margaret (see Lothrop, Harriet M.)
Sidney's Press DLB-49
Siegfried Loraine Sassoon: A Centenary Essay Tributes from Vivien F. Clarke and Michael Thorpe Y-86
Sierra Club Books DLB-49
Sigourney, Lydia Howard (Huntley) 1791-1865 ....DLB-1, 42, 73
Silkin, Jon 1930- DLB-27
Silliphant, Stirling 1918- DLB-26
Sillitoe, Alan 1928- DLB-14
Silman, Roberta 1934- DLB-28
Silverberg, Robert 1935- DLB-8
Simak, Clifford D. 1904-1988 ....DLB-8
Simcox, George Augustus 1841-1905 ....DLB-35
Simenon, Georges 1903-1989 ....DLB-72
Simmel, Johannes Mario 1924- DLB-69
Simmons, Herbert Alfred 1930- DLB-33
Simmons, James 1933- DLB-40
Simms, William Gilmore 1806-1870 ....DLB-3, 30, 59, 73
Simon, Claude 1913- DLB-83
Simon, Neil 1927- DLB-7
Simon and Schuster DLB-46
Simons, Katherine Drayton Mayrant 1890-1969 ....Y-83
Simpson, Helen 1897-1940 ....DLB-77
Simpson, Louis 1923- DLB-5
Simpson, N. F. 1919- DLB-13
Sims, George 1923- DLB-87
Sims, George R. 1847-1922 ....DLB-35, 70
Sinclair, Andrew 1935- DLB-14
Sinclair, Jo 1913- DLB-28
Sinclair Lewis Centennial Conference Y-85
Sinclair, Lister 1921- DLB-88
Sinclair, May 1863-1946 ....DLB-36
Sinclair, Upton 1878-1968 ....DLB-9
Sinclair, Upton [publishing house] DLB-46
Singer, Isaac Bashevis 1904- DLB-6, 28, 52
Singmaster, Elsie 1879-1958 ....DLB-9
Siodmak, Curt 1902- DLB-44
Sissman, L. E. 1928-1976 ....DLB-5
Sisson, C. H. 1914- DLB-27
Sitwell, Edith 1887-1964 ....DLB-20
Skelton, Robin 1925- DLB-27, 53
Skinner, John Stuart 1788-1851 ....DLB-73
Skipsey, Joseph 1832-1903 ....DLB-35
Slade, Bernard 1930- DLB-53
Slater, Patrick 1880-1951 ....DLB-68
Slavitt, David 1935- DLB-5, 6
A Slender Thread of Hope: The Kennedy Center Black Theatre Project DLB-38
Slick, Sam (see Haliburton, Thomas Chandler)
Sloane, William, Associates DLB-46
Small, Maynard and Company DLB-49
Small Presses in Great Britain and Ireland, 1960-1985 ....DLB-40
Small Presses I: Jargon Society Y-84
Small Presses II: The Spirit That Moves Us Press Y-85
Small Presses III: Pushcart Press Y-87
Smart, Elizabeth 1913-1986 ....DLB-88
Smiles, Samuel 1812-1904 ....DLB-55
Smith, A. J. M. 1902-1980 ....DLB-88
Smith, Alexander 1829-1867 ....DLB-32, 55
Smith, Betty 1896-1972 ....Y-82
Smith, Carol Sturm 1938- Y-81
Smith, Charles Henry 1826-1903 ....DLB-11
Smith, Charlotte 1749-1806 ....DLB-39
Smith, Cordwainer 1913-1966 ....DLB-8
Smith, Dave 1942- DLB-5
Smith, Dodie 1896- DLB-10
Smith, Doris Buchanan 1934- DLB-52
Smith, E. E. 1890-1965 ....DLB-8
Smith, Elihu Hubbard 1771-1798 ....DLB-37
Smith, Elizabeth Oakes (Prince) 1806-1893 ....DLB-1
Smith, George O. 1911-1981 ....DLB-8
Smith, H. Allen 1907-1976 ....DLB-11, 29
Smith, Harrison, and Robert Haas [publishing house] DLB-46

Smith, Iain Crichten 1928- DLB-40
Smith, J. Allen 1860-1924 ....DLB-47
Smith, J. Stilman, and Company DLB-49
Smith, John 1580-1631 ....DLB-24, 30
Smith, Josiah 1704-1781 ....DLB-24
Smith, Ken 1938- DLB-40
Smith, Lee 1944- Y-83
Smith, Mark 1935- Y-82
Smith, Michael 1698-circa 1771 ....DLB-31
Smith, Red 1905-1982 ....DLB-29
Smith, Roswell 1829-1892 ....DLB-79
Smith, Samuel Harrison 1772-1845 ....DLB-43
Smith, Samuel Stanhope 1751-1819 ....DLB-37
Smith, Seba 1792-1868 ....DLB-1, 11
Smith, Stevie 1902-1971 ....DLB-20
Smith, Sydney Goodsir 1915-1975 ....DLB-27
Smith, W. B., and Company DLB-49
Smith, William 1727-1803 ....DLB-31
Smith, William 1728-1793 ....DLB-30
Smith, William Gardner 1927-1974 ....DLB-76
Smith, William Jay 1918- DLB-5
Smollett, Tobias 1721-1771 ....DLB-39
Snellings, Rolland (see Touré, Askia Muhammad)
Snodgrass, W. D. 1926- DLB-5
Snow, C. P. 1905-1980 ....DLB-15, 77
Snyder, Gary 1930- DLB-5, 16
Sobiloff, Hy 1912-1970 ....DLB-48
The Society for Textual Scholarship and *TEXT* Y-87
Solano, Solita 1888-1975 ....DLB-4
Sollers, Philippe 1936- DLB-83
Solomon, Carl 1928- DLB-16
Solway, David 1941- DLB-53
Solzhenitsyn and America Y-85
Sontag, Susan 1933- DLB-2, 67
Sorrentino, Gilbert 1929- DLB-5; Y-80
Soto, Gary 1952- DLB-82
Sources for the Study of Tudor and Stuart Drama DLB-62
Souster, Raymond 1921- DLB-88
Southerland, Ellease 1943- DLB-33
Southern, Terry 1924- DLB-2
Southern Writers Between the Wars DLB-9
Southerne, Thomas 1659-1746 ....DLB-80
Spark, Muriel 1918- DLB-15
Sparks, Jared 1789-1866 ....DLB-1, 30
Sparshott, Francis 1926- DLB-60
Späth, Gerold 1939- DLB-75
Spellman, A. B. 1935- DLB-41
Spencer, Anne 1882-1975 ....DLB-51, 54
Spencer, Elizabeth 1921- DLB-6
Spencer, Herbert 1820-1903 ....DLB-57
Spencer, Scott 1945- Y-86
Spender, Stephen 1909- DLB-20
Spicer, Jack 1925-1965 ....DLB-5, 16
Spielberg, Peter 1929- Y-81
Spier, Peter 1927- DLB-61
Spinrad, Norman 1940- DLB-8
Spofford, Harriet Prescott 1835-1921 ....DLB-74
Squibob (see Derby, George Horatio)
Stafford, Jean 1915-1979 ....DLB-2
Stafford, William 1914- DLB-5
Stage Censorship: "The Rejected Statement" (1911), by Bernard Shaw [excerpts] DLB-10
Stallings, Laurence 1894-1968 ....DLB-7, 44
Stallworthy, Jon 1935- DLB-40
Stampp, Kenneth M. 1912- DLB-17
Stanford, Ann 1916- DLB-5
Stanton, Elizabeth Cady 1815-1902 ....DLB-79
Stanton, Frank L. 1857-1927 ....DLB-25
Stapledon, Olaf 1886-1950 ....DLB-15
Star Spangled Banner Office DLB-49
Starkweather, David 1935- DLB-7
Statements on the Art of Poetry DLB-54
Steadman, Mark 1930- DLB-6
The Stealthy School of Criticism (1871), by Dante Gabriel Rossetti DLB-35
Stearns, Harold E. 1891-1943 ....DLB-4
Stedman, Edmund Clarence 1833-1908 ....DLB-64
Steele, Max 1922- Y-80
Steele, Richard 1672-1729 ....DLB-84
Steele, Wilbur Daniel 1886-1970 ....DLB-86

Steere, Richard circa 1643-1721 ....DLB-24
Stegner, Wallace 1909- DLB-9
Stehr, Hermann 1864-1940 ....DLB-66
Steig, William 1907- DLB-61
Stein, Gertrude 1874-1946 ....DLB-4, 54, 86
Stein, Leo 1872-1947 ....DLB-4
Stein and Day Publishers DLB-46
Steinbeck, John 1902-1968 ....DLB-7, 9; DS-2
Steiner, George 1929- DLB-67
Stephen, Leslie 1832-1904 ....DLB-57
Stephens, Alexander H. 1812-1883 ....DLB-47
Stephens, Ann 1810-1886 ....DLB-3, 73
Stephens, Charles Asbury 1844?-1931 ....DLB-42
Stephens, James 1882?-1950 ....DLB-19
Sterling, George 1869-1926 ....DLB-54
Sterling, James 1701-1763 ....DLB-24
Stern, Richard 1928- Y-87
Stern, Stewart 1922- DLB-26
Sterne, Laurence 1713-1768 ....DLB-39
Sternheim, Carl 1878-1942 ....DLB-56
Stevens, Wallace 1879-1955 ....DLB-54
Stevenson, Anne 1933- DLB-40
Stevenson, Robert Louis 1850-1894 ....DLB-18, 57
Stewart, Donald Ogden 1894-1980 ....DLB-4, 11, 26
Stewart, Dugald 1753-1828 ....DLB-31
Stewart, George R. 1895-1980 ....DLB-8
Stewart and Kidd Company DLB-46
Stickney, Trumbull 1874-1904 ....DLB-54
Stiles, Ezra 1727-1795 ....DLB-31
Still, James 1906- DLB-9
Stith, William 1707-1755 ....DLB-31
Stockton, Frank R. 1834-1902 ....DLB-42, 74
Stoddard, Ashbel [publishing house] DLB-49
Stoddard, Richard Henry 1825-1903 ....DLB-3, 64
Stoddard, Solomon 1643-1729 ....DLB-24
Stoker, Bram 1847-1912 ....DLB-36, 70
Stokes, Frederick A., Company DLB-49
Stokes, Thomas L. 1898-1958 ....DLB-29
Stone, Herbert S., and Company DLB-49
Stone, Lucy 1818-1893 ....DLB-79
Stone, Melville 1848-1929 ....DLB-25
Stone, Samuel 1602-1663 ....DLB-24
Stone and Kimball DLB-49
Stoppard, Tom 1937- DLB-13; Y-85
Storey, Anthony 1928- DLB-14
Storey, David 1933- DLB-13, 14
Story, Thomas circa 1670-1742 ....DLB-31
Story, William Wetmore 1819-1895 ....DLB-1
Storytelling: A Contemporary Renaissance Y-84
Stoughton, William 1631-1701 ....DLB-24
Stowe, Harriet Beecher 1811-1896 ....DLB-1, 12, 42, 74
Stowe, Leland 1899- DLB-29
Strand, Mark 1934- DLB-5
Stratemeyer, Edward 1862-1930 ....DLB-42
Stratton and Barnard DLB-49
Straub, Peter 1943- Y-84
Street, Cecil John Charles (see Rhode, John)
Street and Smith DLB-49
Streeter, Edward 1891-1976 ....DLB-11
Stribling, T. S. 1881-1965 ....DLB-9
Stringer and Townsend DLB-49
Strittmatter, Erwin 1912- DLB-69
Strother, David Hunter 1816-1888 ....DLB-3
Stuart, Jesse 1906-1984 ....DLB-9, 48; Y-84
Stuart, Lyle [publishing house] DLB-46
Stubbs, Harry Clement (see Clement, Hal)
The Study of Poetry (1880), by Matthew Arnold DLB-35
Sturgeon, Theodore 1918-1985 ....DLB-8; Y-85
Sturges, Preston 1898-1959 ....DLB-26
"Style" (1840; revised, 1859), by Thomas de Quincey [excerpt] DLB-57
"Style" (1888), by Walter Pater DLB-57
Style (1897), by Walter Raleigh [excerpt] DLB-57
"Style" (1877), by T. H. Wright [excerpt] DLB-57
"Le Style c'est l'homme" (1892), by W. H. Mallock DLB-57
Styron, William 1925- DLB-2; Y-80
Suárez, Mario 1925- DLB-82
Such, Peter 1939- DLB-60
Suckling, Sir John 1609-1642 ....DLB-58
Suckow, Ruth 1892-1960 ....DLB-9

Suggs, Simon (see Hooper, Johnson Jones)

Sukenick, Ronald 1932- Y-81

Suknaski, Andrew 1942- DLB-53

Sullivan, C. Gardner 1886-1965 ....DLB-26

Sullivan, Frank 1892-1976 ....DLB-11

Summers, Hollis 1916- DLB-6

Sumner, Henry A. [publishing house] DLB-49

Surtees, Robert Smith 1803-1864 ....DLB-21

A Survey of Poetry
Anthologies, 1879-1960 ....DLB-54

Surveys of the Year's Biography
A Transit of Poets and Others: American
Biography in 1982 ....Y-82
The Year in Literary Biography Y-83
The Year in Literary Biography Y-84
The Year in Literary Biography Y-85
The Year in Literary Biography Y-86
The Year in Literary Biography Y-87
The Year in Literary Biography Y-88

Surveys of the Year's Book Publishing
The Year in Book Publishing..............................Y-86

Surveys of the Year's Drama
The Year in Drama...Y-82
The Year in Drama...Y-83
The Year in Drama...Y-84
The Year in Drama...Y-85
The Year in Drama...Y-87
The Year in Drama...Y-88

Surveys of the Year's Fiction
The Year's Work in Fiction: A Survey.............Y-82
The Year in Fiction: A Biased View................Y-83
The Year in Fiction...Y-84
The Year in Fiction...Y-85
The Year in Fiction...Y-86
The Year in the Novel......................................Y-87
The Year in Short Stories.................................Y-87
The Year in the Novel......................................Y-88
The Year in Short Stories.................................Y-88

Surveys of the Year's Poetry
The Year's Work in American Poetry..............Y-82
The Year in Poetry Y-83
The Year in Poetry Y-84
The Year in Poetry Y-85
The Year in Poetry Y-86
The Year in Poetry Y-87
The Year in Poetry Y-88

Sutherland, John 1919-1956 ....DLB-68

Sutro, Alfred 1863-1933 ....DLB-10

Swados, Harvey 1920-1972 ....DLB-2

Swain, Charles 1801-1874 ....DLB-32

Swallow Press DLB-46

Swenson, May 1919- DLB-5

Swerling, Jo 1897- DLB-44

Swift, Jonathan 1667-1745 ....DLB-39

Swinburne, A. C. 1837-1909........................DLB-35, 57

Swinnerton, Frank 1884-1982..........................DLB-34

Swisshelm, Jane Grey 1815-1884 ....DLB-43

Swope, Herbert Bayard 1882-1958 ....DLB-25

Swords, T. and J., and Company DLB-49

Swords, Thomas 1763-1843 and
Swords, James ?-1844 ....DLB-73

Symonds, John Addington 1840-1893...............DLB-57

Symons, Arthur 1865-1945.........................DLB-19, 57

Symons, Julian 1912- DLB-87

Symons, Scott 1933- DLB-53

Synge, John Millington 1871-1909 ....DLB-10, 19

T

Tafolla, Carmen 1951- DLB-82

Taggard, Genevieve 1894-1948.........................DLB-45

Tait, J. Selwin, and Sons.................................DLB-49

Talvj or Talvi (see Robinson, Therese)

Taradash, Daniel 1913- DLB-44

Tarbell, Ida M. 1857-1944 ....DLB-47

Tarkington, Booth 1869-1946..............................DLB-9

Tashlin, Frank 1913-1972 ....DLB-44

Tate, Allen 1899-1979.............................DLB-4, 45, 63

Tate, James 1943- DLB-5

Tate, Nahum circa 1652-1715..........................DLB-80

Taylor, Bayard 1825-1878 ....DLB-3

Taylor, Bert Leston 1866-1921 ....DLB-25

Taylor, Charles H. 1846-1921 ....DLB-25

Taylor, Edward circa 1642-1729 ....DLB-24

Taylor, Henry 1942- DLB-5

Taylor, Sir Henry 1800-1886 ....DLB-32

Taylor, Mildred D. ?- DLB-52

Taylor, Peter 1917- Y-81

Taylor, William, and Company DLB-49

Taylor-Made Shakespeare? Or Is

"Shall I Die?" the Long-Lost Text of Bottom's Dream? Y-85
Teasdale, Sara 1884-1933 ..... DLB-45
The Tea-Table (1725), by Eliza Haywood [excerpt] DLB-39
Tenn, William 1919- DLB-8
Tennant, Emma 1937- DLB-14
Tenney, Tabitha Gilman 1762-1837 ..... DLB-37
Tennyson, Alfred 1809-1892 ..... DLB-32
Tennyson, Frederick 1807-1898 ..... DLB-32
Terhune, Albert Payson 1872-1942 ..... DLB-9
Terry, Megan 1932- DLB-7
Terson, Peter 1932- DLB-13
Tesich, Steve 1943- Y-83
Tey, Josephine 1896?-1952 ..... DLB-77
Thacher, James 1754-1844 ..... DLB-37
Thackeray, William Makepeace 1811-1863 ..... DLB-21, 55
Thanet, Octave (see French, Alice)
The Theater in Shakespeare's Time DLB-62
The Theatre Guild DLB-7
Theriault, Yves 1915-1983 ..... DLB-88
Thério, Adrien 1925- DLB-53
Theroux, Paul 1941- DLB-2
Thibaudeau, Colleen 1925- DLB-88
Thoma, Ludwig 1867-1921 ..... DLB-66
Thoma, Richard 1902- DLB-4
Thomas, Audrey 1935- DLB-60
Thomas, D. M. 1935- DLB-40
Thomas, Dylan 1914-1953 ..... DLB-13, 20
Thomas, Edward 1878-1917 ..... DLB-19
Thomas, Gwyn 1913-1981 ..... DLB-15
Thomas, Isaiah 1750-1831 ..... DLB-43, 73
Thomas, Isaiah [publishing house] DLB-49
Thomas, John 1900-1932 ..... DLB-4
Thomas, Joyce Carol 1938- DLB-33
Thomas, Lorenzo 1944- DLB-41
Thomas, R. S. 1915- DLB-27
Thompson, Dorothy 1893-1961 ..... DLB-29
Thompson, Francis 1859-1907 ..... DLB-19
Thompson, George Selden (see Selden, George)
Thompson, John 1938-1976 ..... DLB-60
Thompson, John R. 1823-1873 ..... DLB-3, 73
Thompson, Maurice 1844-1901 ..... DLB-71, 74
Thompson, Ruth Plumly 1891-1976 ..... DLB-22
Thompson, William Tappan 1812-1882 ..... DLB-3, 11
Thomson, James 1834-1882 ..... DLB-35
Thomson, Mortimer 1831-1875 ..... DLB-11
Thoreau, Henry David 1817-1862 ..... DLB-1
Thorpe, Thomas Bangs 1815-1878 ..... DLB-3, 11
Thoughts on Poetry and Its Varieties (1833), by John Stuart Mill DLB-32
Thurber, James 1894-1961 ..... DLB-4, 11, 22
Thurman, Wallace 1902-1934 ..... DLB-51
Thwaite, Anthony 1930- DLB-40
Thwaites, Reuben Gold 1853-1913 ..... DLB-47
Ticknor, George 1791-1871 ..... DLB-1, 59
Ticknor and Fields DLB-49
Tieck, Ludwig 1773-1853 ..... DLB-90
Ticknor and Fields (revived) DLB-46
Tietjens, Eunice 1884-1944 ..... DLB-54
Tilton, J. E., and Company DLB-49
Time and Western Man (1927), by Wyndham Lewis [excerpts] DLB-36
Time-Life Books DLB-46
Times Books DLB-46
Timothy, Peter circa 1725-1782 ..... DLB-43
Timrod, Henry 1828-1867 ..... DLB-3
Tiptree, James, Jr. 1915- DLB-8
Titus, Edward William 1870-1952 ..... DLB-4
Toklas, Alice B. 1877-1967 ..... DLB-4
Tolkien, J. R. R. 1892-1973 ..... DLB-15
Tolson, Melvin B. 1898-1966 ..... DLB-48, 76
Tom Jones (1749), by Henry Fielding [excerpt] DLB-39
Tomlinson, Charles 1927- DLB-40
Tomlinson, Henry Major 1873-1958 ..... DLB-36
Tompkins, Abel [publishing house] DLB-49
Tompson, Benjamin 1642-1714 ..... DLB-24
Tonks, Rosemary 1932- DLB-14
Toole, John Kennedy 1937-1969 ..... Y-81
Toomer, Jean 1894-1967 ..... DLB-45, 51

Tor Books DLB-46
Torberg, Friedrich 1908-1979 ....DLB-85
Torrence, Ridgely 1874-1950....DLB-54
Toth, Susan Allen 1940- Y-86
Tough-Guy Literature DLB-9
Touré, Askia Muhammad 1938- DLB-41
Tourgée, Albion W. 1838-1905....DLB-79
Tourneur, Cyril circa 1580-1626 ....DLB-58
Tournier, Michel 1924- DLB-83
Tousey, Frank [publishing house]....DLB-49
Tower Publications....DLB-46
Towne, Benjamin circa 1740-1793....DLB-43
Towne, Robert 1936- DLB-44
Tracy, Honor 1913- DLB-15
Train, Arthur 1875-1945....DLB-86
The Transatlantic Publishing Company DLB-49
Transcendentalists, American DS-5
Traven, B. 1882? or 1890?-1969?....DLB-9, 56
Travers, Ben 1886-1980 ....DLB-10
Tremain, Rose 1943- DLB-14
Tremblay, Michel 1942- DLB-60
Trends in Twentieth-Century Mass Market Publishing DLB-46
Trent, William P. 1862-1939....DLB-47
Trescot, William Henry 1822-1898....DLB-30
Trevor, William 1928- DLB-14
Trilling, Lionel 1905-1975 ....DLB-28, 63
Triolet, Elsa 1896-1970....DLB-72
Tripp, John 1927- DLB-40
Trocchi, Alexander 1925- DLB-15
Trollope, Anthony 1815-1882 ....DLB-21, 57
Trollope, Frances 1779-1863 ....DLB-21
Troop, Elizabeth 1931- DLB-14
Trotter, Catharine 1679-1749 ....DLB-84
Trotti, Lamar 1898-1952....DLB-44
Trottier, Pierre 1925- DLB-60
Troupe, Quincy Thomas, Jr. 1943- DLB-41
Trow, John F., and Company DLB-49
Trumbo, Dalton 1905-1976....DLB-26
Trumbull, Benjamin 1735-1820....DLB-30
Trumbull, John 1750-1831....DLB-31
T. S. Eliot Centennial Y-88
Tucholsky, Kurt 1890-1935....DLB-56
Tucker, George 1775-1861 ....DLB-3, 30
Tucker, Nathaniel Beverley 1784-1851 ....DLB-3
Tucker, St. George 1752-1827 ....DLB-37
Tuckerman, Henry Theodore 1813-1871 ....DLB-64
Tunis, John R. 1889-1975 ....DLB-22
Tuohy, Frank 1925- DLB-14
Tupper, Martin F. 1810-1889....DLB-32
Turbyfill, Mark 1896- DLB-45
Turco, Lewis 1934- Y-84
Turnbull, Gael 1928- DLB-40
Turner, Charles (Tennyson) 1808-1879 ....DLB-32
Turner, Frederick 1943- DLB-40
Turner, Frederick Jackson 1861-1932....DLB-17
Turner, Joseph Addison 1826-1868 ....DLB-79
Turpin, Waters Edward 1910-1968 ....DLB-51
Twain, Mark (see Clemens, Samuel Langhorne)
The 'Twenties and Berlin, by Alex Natan....DLB-66
Tyler, Anne 1941- DLB-6; Y-82
Tyler, Moses Coit 1835-1900 ....DLB-47, 64
Tyler, Royall 1757-1826 ....DLB-37
Tylor, Edward Burnett 1832-1917....DLB-57

U

Udall, Nicholas 1504-1556....DLB-62
Uhland, Ludwig 1787-1862 ....DLB-90
Uhse, Bodo 1904-1963....DLB-69
Ulibarrí, Sabine R. 1919- DLB-82
Ulica, Jorge 1870-1926....DLB-82
Under the Microscope (1872), by A. C. Swinburne....DLB-35
United States Book Company DLB-49
Universal Publishing and Distributing Corporation DLB-46
The University of Iowa Writers' Workshop Golden Jubilee Y-86
"The Unknown Public" (1858), by Wilkie Collins [excerpt]....DLB-57
Unruh, Fritz von 1885-1970 ....DLB-56

Upchurch, Boyd B. (see Boyd, John)
Updike, John 1932- DLB-2, 5; Y-80, 82; DS-3
Upton, Charles 1948- DLB-16
Upward, Allen 1863-1926 ....DLB-36
Urista, Alberto Baltazar (see Alurista)
Urzidil, Johannes 1896-1976 ....DLB-85
Ustinov, Peter 1921- DLB-13

V

Vac, Bertrand 1914- DLB-88
Vail, Laurence 1891-1968 ....DLB-4
Vailland, Roger 1907-1965 ....DLB-83
Vajda, Ernest 1887-1954 ....DLB-44
Valgardson, W. D. 1939- DLB-60
Van Allsburg, Chris 1949- DLB-61
Van Anda, Carr 1864-1945 ....DLB-25
Vanbrugh, Sir John 1664-1726 ....DLB-80
Vance, Jack 1916?- DLB-8
Van Doren, Mark 1894-1972 ....DLB-45
van Druten, John 1901-1957 ....DLB-10
Van Duyn, Mona 1921- DLB-5
Van Dyke, Henry 1852-1933 ....DLB-71
Van Dyke, Henry 1928- DLB-33
Vane, Sutton 1888-1963 ....DLB-10
Vanguard Press DLB-46
van Itallie, Jean-Claude 1936- DLB-7
Vann, Robert L. 1879-1940 ....DLB-29
Van Rensselaer, Mariana Griswold
1851-1934 ....DLB-47
Van Rensselaer, Mrs. Schuyler (see Van Rensselaer, Mariana Griswold)
Van Vechten, Carl 1880-1964 ....DLB-4, 9
van Vogt, A. E. 1912- DLB-8
Varley, John 1947- Y-81
Varnhagen von Ense, Karl August
1785-1858 ....DLB-90
Varnhagen von Ense, Rahel
1771-1833 ....DLB-90
Vassa, Gustavus (see Equiano, Olaudah)
Vega, Janine Pommy 1942- DLB-16
Veiller, Anthony 1903-1965 ....DLB-44
Venegas, Daniel ?-? DLB-82
Verplanck, Gulian C. 1786-1870 ....DLB-59
Very, Jones 1813-1880 ....DLB-1
Vian, Boris 1920-1959 ....DLB-72
Vickers, Roy 1888?-1965 ....DLB-77
Victoria 1819-1901 ....DLB-55
Vidal, Gore 1925- DLB-6
Viebig, Clara 1860-1952 ....DLB-66
Viereck, George Sylvester 1884-1962 ....DLB-54
Viereck, Peter 1916- DLB-5
Viewpoint: Politics and Performance, by David
Edgar DLB-13
Vigneault, Gilles 1928- DLB-60
The Viking Press DLB-46
Villanueva, Tino 1941- DLB-82
Villard, Henry 1835-1900 ....DLB-23
Villard, Oswald Garrison 1872-1949 ....DLB-25
Villarreal, José Antonio 1924- DLB-82
Villemaire, Yolande 1949- DLB-60
Villiers, George, Second Duke
of Buckingham 1628-1687 ....DLB-80
Viorst, Judith ?- DLB-52
Voaden, Herman 1903- DLB-88
Volkoff, Vladimir 1932- DLB-83
Volland, P. F., Company DLB-46
von der Grün, Max 1926- DLB-75
Vonnegut, Kurt 1922- DLB-2, 8; Y-80; DS-3
Voß, Johann Heinrich 1751-1826 ....DLB-90
Vroman, Mary Elizabeth circa 1924-1967 ....DLB-33

W

Wackenroder, Wilhelm Heinrich
1773-1798 ....DLB-90
Waddington, Miriam 1917- DLB-68
Wade, Henry 1887-1969 ....DLB-77
Wagoner, David 1926- DLB-5
Wah, Fred 1939- DLB-60
Waiblinger, Wilhelm 1804-1830 ....DLB-90
Wain, John 1925- DLB-15, 27
Wainwright, Jeffrey 1944- DLB-40

Waite, Peirce and Company DLB-49
Wakoski, Diane 1937- DLB-5
Walck, Henry Z. DLB-46
Walcott, Derek 1930- Y-81
Waldman, Anne 1945- DLB-16
Walker, Alice 1944- DLB-6, 33
Walker, George F. 1947- DLB-60
Walker, Joseph A. 1935- DLB-38
Walker, Margaret 1915- DLB-76
Walker, Ted 1934- DLB-40
Walker and Company DLB-49
Walker, Evans and Cogswell Company DLB-49
Walker, John Brisben 1847-1931 ....DLB-79
Wallace, Edgar 1875-1932 ....DLB-70
Wallant, Edward Lewis 1926-1962 ....DLB-2, 28
Walpole, Horace 1717-1797 ....DLB-39
Walpole, Hugh 1884-1941 ....DLB-34
Walrond, Eric 1898-1966 ....DLB-51
Walser, Martin 1927- DLB-75
Walser, Robert 1878-1956 ....DLB-66
Walsh, Ernest 1895-1926 ....DLB-4, 45
Walsh, Robert 1784-1859 ....DLB-59
Wambaugh, Joseph 1937- DLB-6; Y-83
Ward, Artemus (see Browne, Charles Farrar)
Ward, Arthur Henry Sarsfield (see Rohmer, Sax)
Ward, Douglas Turner 1930- DLB-7, 38
Ward, Lynd 1905-1985 ....DLB-22
Ward, Mrs. Humphry 1851-1920 ....DLB-18
Ward, Nathaniel circa 1578-1652 ....DLB-24
Ward, Theodore 1902-1983 ....DLB-76
Ware, William 1797-1852 ....DLB-1
Warne, Frederick, and Company DLB-49
Warner, Charles Dudley 1829-1900 ....DLB-64
Warner, Rex 1905- DLB-15
Warner, Susan Bogert 1819-1885 ....DLB-3, 42
Warner, Sylvia Townsend 1893-1978 ....DLB-34
Warner Books DLB-46
Warr, Bertram 1917-1943 ....DLB-88
Warren, John Byrne Leicester (see De Tabley, Lord)
Warren, Lella 1899-1982 ....Y-83
Warren, Mercy Otis 1728-1814 ....DLB-31
Warren, Robert Penn 1905-1989 ....DLB-2, 48; Y-80
Washington, George 1732-1799 ....DLB-31
Wassermann, Jakob 1873-1934 ....DLB-66
Wasson, David Atwood 1823-1887 ....DLB-1
Waterhouse, Keith 1929- DLB-13, 15
Waterman, Andrew 1940- DLB-40
Waters, Frank 1902- Y-86
Watkins, Tobias 1780-1855 ....DLB-73
Watkins, Vernon 1906-1967 ....DLB-20
Watmough, David 1926- DLB-53
Watson, James Wreford (see Wreford, James)
Watson, Sheila 1909- DLB-60
Watson, Wilfred 1911- DLB-60
Watt, W. J., and Company DLB-46
Watterson, Henry 1840-1921 ....DLB-25
Watts, Alan 1915-1973 ....DLB-16
Watts, Franklin [publishing house] DLB-46
Waugh, Auberon 1939- DLB-14
Waugh, Evelyn 1903-1966 ....DLB-15
Way and Williams DLB-49
Wayman, Tom 1945- DLB-53
Weatherly, Tom 1942- DLB-41
Weaver, Robert 1921- DLB-88
Webb, Frank J. ?-? DLB-50
Webb, James Watson 1802-1884 ....DLB-43
Webb, Mary 1881-1927 ....DLB-34
Webb, Phyllis 1927- DLB-53
Webb, Walter Prescott 1888-1963 ....DLB-17
Webster, Augusta 1837-1894 ....DLB-35
Webster, Charles L., and Company DLB-49
Webster, John 1579 or 1580-1634? DLB-58
Webster, Noah 1758-1843 ....DLB-1, 37, 42, 43, 73
Weems, Mason Locke 1759-1825 ....DLB-30, 37, 42
Weidman, Jerome 1913- DLB-28
Weinbaum, Stanley Grauman 1902-1935 ....DLB-8
Weisenborn, Günther 1902-1969 ....DLB-69
Weiß, Ernst 1882-1940 ....DLB-81
Weiss, John 1818-1879 ....DLB-1
Weiss, Peter 1916-1982 ....DLB-69
Weiss, Theodore 1916- DLB-5

Welch, Lew 1926-1971?..DLB-16
Weldon, Fay 1931- DLB-14
Wellek, René 1903- DLB-63
Wells, Carolyn 1862-1942....................................DLB-11
Wells, Charles Jeremiah circa 1800-1879 ....DLB-32
Wells, H. G. 1866-1946 ....DLB-34, 70
Wells, Robert 1947- DLB-40
Wells-Barnett, Ida B. 1862-1931........................DLB-23
Welty, Eudora 1909- DLB-2; Y-87
Wendell, Barrett 1855-1921 ....DLB-71
Wentworth, Patricia 1878-1961 ....DLB-77
Werfel, Franz 1890-1945 ....DLB-81
The Werner Company..DLB-49
Wersba, Barbara 1932- DLB-52
Wescott, Glenway 1901- DLB-4, 9
Wesker, Arnold 1932- DLB-13
Wesley, Richard 1945- DLB-38
Wessels, A., and Company DLB-46
West, Anthony 1914-1988 ....DLB-15
West, Dorothy 1907- DLB-76
West, Jessamyn 1902-1984 ....DLB-6; Y-84
West, Mae 1892-1980...DLB-44
West, Nathanael 1903-1940 ....DLB-4, 9, 28
West, Paul 1930- DLB-14
West, Rebecca 1892-1983 ....DLB-36; Y-83
West and Johnson DLB-49
Western Publishing Company DLB-46
Wetherell, Elizabeth (see Warner, Susan Bogert)
Wetzel, Friedrich Gottlob 1779-1819..................DLB-90
Whalen, Philip 1923- DLB-16
Whalley, George 1915-1983................................DLB-88
Wharton, Edith 1862-1937...................DLB-4, 9, 12, 78
Wharton, William 1920s?- Y-80
What's Really Wrong With Bestseller Lists Y-84
Wheatley, Dennis Yates 1897-1977 ....DLB-77
Wheatley, Phillis circa 1754-1784.................DLB-31, 50
Wheeler, Charles Stearns 1816-1843....................DLB-1
Wheeler, Monroe 1900-1988 ....DLB-4
Wheelock, John Hall 1886-1978..........................DLB-45
Wheelwright, John circa 1592-1679 ....DLB-24
Wheelwright, J. B. 1897-1940.............................DLB-45
Whetstone, Colonel Pete (see Noland, C. F. M.)
Whipple, Edwin Percy 1819-1886 ....DLB-1, 64
Whitaker, Alexander 1585-1617.........................DLB-24
Whitaker, Daniel K. 1801-1881 ....DLB-73
Whitcher, Frances Miriam 1814-1852 ....DLB-11
White, Andrew 1579-1656 ....DLB-24
White, Andrew Dickson 1832-1918....................DLB-47
White, E. B. 1899-1985 ....DLB-11, 22
White, Edgar B. 1947- DLB-38
White, Ethel Lina 1887-1944 ....DLB-77
White, Horace 1834-1916 ....DLB-23
White, Phyllis Dorothy James
(see James, P. D.)
White, Richard Grant 1821-1885........................DLB-64
White, Walter 1893-1955...................................DLB-51
White, William, and Company...........................DLB-49
White, William Allen 1868-1944 ....DLB-9, 25
White, William Anthony Parker
(see Boucher, Anthony)
White, William Hale (see Rutherford, Mark)
Whitechurch, Victor L. 1868-1933 ....DLB-70
Whitehead, James 1936- Y-81
Whitehead, William 1715-1785..........................DLB-84
Whitfield, James Monroe 1822-1871 ....DLB-50
Whiting, John 1917-1963 ....DLB-13
Whiting, Samuel 1597-1679 ....DLB-24
Whitlock, Brand 1869-1934 ....DLB-12
Whitman, Albert, and Company DLB-46
Whitman, Albery Allson 1851-1901 ....DLB-50
Whitman, Sarah Helen (Power) 1803-1878..........DLB-1
Whitman, Walt 1819-1892 ....DLB-3, 64
Whitman Publishing Company DLB-46
Whittemore, Reed 1919- DLB-5
Whittier, John Greenleaf 1807-1892 ....DLB-1
Whittlesey House DLB-46
Wideman, John Edgar 1941- DLB-33
Wiebe, Rudy 1934- DLB-60
Wiechert, Ernst 1887-1950.................................DLB-56
Wied, Martina 1882-1957...................................DLB-85
Wieners, John 1934- DLB-16
Wier, Ester 1910- DLB-52

Wiesel, Elie 1928- DLB-83; Y-87
Wiggin, Kate Douglas 1856-1923 ....DLB-42
Wigglesworth, Michael 1631-1705 ....DLB-24
Wilbur, Richard 1921- DLB-5
Wild, Peter 1940- DLB-5
Wilde, Oscar 1854-1900 ....DLB-10, 19, 34, 57
Wilde, Richard Henry 1789-1847 ....DLB-3, 59
Wilde, W. A., Company DLB-49
Wilder, Billy 1906- DLB-26
Wilder, Laura Ingalls 1867-1957 ....DLB-22
Wilder, Thornton 1897-1975 ....DLB-4, 7, 9
Wiley, Bell Irvin 1906-1980 ....DLB-17
Wiley, John, and Sons DLB-49
Wilhelm, Kate 1928- DLB-8
Wilkes, George 1817-1885 ....DLB-79
Wilkinson, Anne 1910-1961 ....DLB-88
Wilkinson, Sylvia 1940- Y-86
Wilkinson, William Cleaver 1833-1920 ....DLB-71
Willard, L. [publishing house] DLB-49
Willard, Nancy 1936- DLB-5, 52
Willard, Samuel 1640-1707 ....DLB-24
Williams, A., and Company DLB-49
Williams, C. K. 1936- DLB-5
Williams, Chancellor 1905- DLB-76
Williams, Emlyn 1905- DLB-10, 77
Williams, Garth 1912- DLB-22
Williams, George Washington 1849-1891 ....DLB-47
Williams, Heathcote 1941- DLB-13
Williams, Hugo 1942- DLB-40
Williams, Isaac 1802-1865 ....DLB-32
Williams, Joan 1928- DLB-6
Williams, John A. 1925- DLB-2, 33
Williams, John E. 1922- DLB-6
Williams, Jonathan 1929- DLB-5
Williams, Raymond 1921- DLB-14
Williams, Roger circa 1603-1683 ....DLB-24
Williams, Samm-Art 1946- DLB-38
Williams, Sherley Anne 1944- DLB-41
Williams, T. Harry 1909-1979 ....DLB-17
Williams, Tennessee 1911-1983 ....DLB-7; Y-83; DS-4
Williams, Valentine 1883-1946 ....DLB-77
Williams, William Appleman 1921- DLB-17
Williams, William Carlos 1883-1963 ....DLB-4, 16, 54, 86
Williams, Wirt 1921- DLB-6
Williams Brothers DLB-49
Williamson, Jack 1908- DLB-8
Willingham, Calder Baynard, Jr. 1922- DLB-2, 44
Willis, Nathaniel Parker 1806-1867 ...DLB-3, 59, 73, 74
Wilmer, Clive 1945- DLB-40
Wilson, A. N. 1950- DLB-14
Wilson, Angus 1913- DLB-15
Wilson, Arthur 1595-1652 ....DLB-58
Wilson, Augusta Jane Evans 1835-1909 ....DLB-42
Wilson, Colin 1931- DLB-14
Wilson, Edmund 1895-1972 ....DLB-63
Wilson, Ethel 1888-1980 ....DLB-68
Wilson, Harriet E. Adams 1828?-1863? DLB-50
Wilson, Harry Leon 1867-1939 ....DLB-9
Wilson, John 1588-1667 ....DLB-24
Wilson, Lanford 1937- DLB-7
Wilson, Margaret 1882-1973 ....DLB-9
Wilson, Michael 1914-1978 ....DLB-44
Wilson, Woodrow 1856-1924 ....DLB-47
Wimsatt, William K., Jr. 1907-1975 ....DLB-63
Winchell, Walter 1897-1972 ....DLB-29
Winchester, J. [publishing house] DLB-49
Windham, Donald 1920- DLB-6
Winsor, Justin 1831-1897 ....DLB-47
John C. Winston Company DLB-49
Winters, Yvor 1900-1968 ....DLB-48
Winthrop, John 1588-1649 ....DLB-24, 30
Winthrop, John, Jr. 1606-1676 ....DLB-24
Wirt, William 1772-1834 ....DLB-37
Wise, John 1652-1725 ....DLB-24
Wiseman, Adele 1928- DLB-88
Wisner, George 1812-1849 ....DLB-43
Wister, Owen 1860-1938 ....DLB-9, 78
Witherspoon, John 1723-1794 ....DLB-31
Wittig, Monique 1935- DLB-83
Wodehouse, P. G. 1881-1975 ....DLB-34
Wohmann, Gabriele 1932- DLB-75

Woiwode, Larry 1941- DLB-6
Wolcott, Roger 1679-1767 ....DLB-24
Wolf, Christa 1929- DLB-75
Wolfe, Gene 1931- DLB-8
Wolfe, Thomas 1900-1938....................DLB-9; DS-2; Y-85
Wollstonecraft, Mary 1759-1797 ....DLB-39
Wondratschek, Wolf 1943- DLB-75
Wood, Benjamin 1820-1900 ....DLB-23
Wood, Charles 1932- DLB-13
Wood, Mrs. Henry 1814-1887 ....DLB-18
Wood, Samuel [publishing house] DLB-49
Wood, William ?-?....................DLB-24
Woodberry, George Edward 1855-1930....................DLB-71
Woodbridge, Benjamin 1622-1684 ....DLB-24
Woodcock, George 1912- DLB-88
Woodhull, Victoria C. 1838-1927 ....DLB-79
Woodmason, Charles circa 1720-? DLB-31
Woodson, Carter G. 1875-1950 ....DLB-17
Woodward, C. Vann 1908- DLB-17
Woolf, David (see Maddow, Ben)
Woolf, Virginia 1882-1941 ....DLB-36
Woollcott, Alexander 1887-1943....................DLB-29
Woolman, John 1720-1772....................DLB-31
Woolner, Thomas 1825-1892....................DLB-35
Woolsey, Sarah Chauncy 1835-1905....................DLB-42
Woolson, Constance Fenimore 1840-1894....DLB-12, 74
Worcester, Joseph Emerson 1784-1865 ....DLB-1
The Works of the Rev. John Witherspoon (1800-1801) [excerpts]....................DLB-31
A World Chronology of Important Science Fiction Works (1818-1979) DLB-8
World Publishing Company DLB-46
Worthington, R., and Company....................DLB-49
Wouk, Herman 1915- Y-82
Wreford, James 1915- DLB-88
Wright, Charles 1935- Y-82
Wright, Charles Stevenson 1932- DLB-33
Wright, Frances 1795-1852 ....DLB-73
Wright, Harold Bell 1872-1944 ....DLB-9
Wright, James 1927-1980....................DLB-5
Wright, Jay 1935- DLB-41
Wright, Louis B. 1899-1984....................DLB-17
Wright, Richard 1908-1960 ....DS-2, DLB-76
Wright, Richard B. 1937- DLB-53
Wright, Sarah Elizabeth 1928- DLB-33
Writers and Politics: 1871-1918, by Ronald Gray....................DLB-66
Writers' Forum Y-85
Writing for the Theatre, by Harold Pinter........DLB-13
Wycherley, William 1641-1715 ....DLB-80
Wylie, Elinor 1885-1928....................DLB-9, 45
Wylie, Philip 1902-1971 ....DLB-9

Y

Yates, Dornford 1885-1960 ....DLB-77
Yates, J. Michael 1938- DLB-60
Yates, Richard 1926- DLB-2; Y-81
Yeats, William Butler 1865-1939 ....DLB-10, 19
Yep, Laurence 1948- DLB-52
Yerby, Frank 1916- DLB-76
Yezierska, Anzia 1885-1970....................DLB-28
Yolen, Jane 1939- DLB-52
Yonge, Charlotte Mary 1823-1901 ....DLB-18
A Yorkshire Tragedy DLB-58
Yoseloff, Thomas [publishing house] DLB-46
Young, Al 1939- DLB-33
Young, Stark 1881-1963 ....DLB-9
Young, Waldeman 1880-1938 ....DLB-26
Young, William [publishing house]....................DLB-49
Yourcenar, Marguerite 1903-1987....................DLB-72; Y-88
"You've Never Had It So Good," Gusted by "Winds of Change": British Fiction in the 1950s, 1960s, and After DLB-14

Z

Zamora, Bernice 1938- DLB-82
Zand, Herbert 1923-1970 ....DLB-85
Zangwill, Israel 1864-1926 ....DLB-10
Zebra Books DLB-46
Zebrowski, George 1945- DLB-8
Zech, Paul 1881-1946 ....DLB-56

Zelazny, Roger 1937- DLB-8
Zenger, John Peter 1697-1746....DLB-24, 43
Zieber, G. B., and Company....DLB-49
Zieroth, Dale 1946- DLB-60
Zimmer, Paul 1934- DLB-5
Zindel, Paul 1936- DLB-7, 52
Zolotow, Charlotte 1915- DLB-52
Zubly, John Joachim 1724-1781....DLB-31
Zu-Bolton II, Ahmos 1936- DLB-41
Zuckmayer, Carl 1896-1977....DLB-56
Zukofsky, Louis 1904-1978....DLB-5
zur Mühlen, Hermynia 1883-1951....DLB-56
Zweig, Arnold 1887-1968....DLB-66
Zweig, Stefan 1881-1942....DLB-81

(Continued from front endsheets)

71: *American Literary Critics and Scholars, 1880-1900,* edited by John W. Rathbun and Monica M. Grecu (1988)

72: *French Novelists, 1930-1960,* edited by Catharine Savage Brosman (1988)

73: *American Magazine Journalists, 1741-1850,* edited by Sam G. Riley (1988)

74: *American Short-Story Writers Before 1880,* edited by Bobby Ellen Kimbel, with the assistance of William E. Grant (1988)

75: *Contemporary German Fiction Writers,* Second Series, edited by Wolfgang D. Elfe and James Hardin (1988)

76: *Afro-American Writers, 1940-1955,* edited by Trudier Harris (1988)

77: *British Mystery Writers, 1920-1939,* edited by Bernard Benstock and Thomas F. Staley (1988)

78: *American Short-Story Writers, 1880-1910,* edited by Bobby Ellen Kimbel, with the assistance of William E. Grant (1988)

79: *American Magazine Journalists, 1850-1900,* edited by Sam G. Riley (1988)

80: *Restoration and Eighteenth-Century Dramatists,* First Series, edited by Paula R. Backscheider (1989)

81: *Austrian Fiction Writers, 1875-1913,* edited by James Hardin and Donald G. Daviau (1989)

82: *Chicano Writers,* First Series, edited by Francisco A. Lomelí and Carl R. Shirley (1989)

83: *French Novelists Since 1960,* edited by Catharine Savage Brosman (1989)

84: *Restoration and Eighteenth-Century Dramatists,* Second Series, edited by Paula R. Backscheider (1989)

85: *Austrian Fiction Writers After 1914,* edited by James Hardin and Donald G. Daviau (1989)

86: *American Short-Story Writers, 1910-1945,* First Series, edited by Bobby Ellen Kimbel (1989)

87: *British Mystery and Thriller Writers Since 1940,* First Series, edited by Bernard Benstock and Thomas F. Staley (1989)

88: *Canadian Writers, 1920-1959,* Second Series, edited by W. H. New (1989)

89: *Restoration and Eighteenth-Century Dramatists,* Third Series, edited by Paula R. Backscheider (1989)

90: *German Writers in the Age of Goethe, 1789-1832,* edited by James Hardin and Christoph E. Schweitzer (1989)

Documentary Series

1: *Sherwood Anderson, Willa Cather, John Dos Passos, Theodore Dreiser, F. Scott Fitzgerald, Ernest Hemingway, Sinclair Lewis,* edited by Margaret A. Van Antwerp (1982)

2: *James Gould Cozzens, James T. Farrell, William Faulkner, John O'Hara, John Steinbeck, Thomas Wolfe, Richard Wright,* edited by Margaret A. Van Antwerp (1982)

3: *Saul Bellow, Jack Kerouac, Norman Mailer, Vladimir Nabokov, John Updike, Kurt Vonnegut,* edited by Mary Bruccoli (1983)

4: *Tennessee Williams,* edited by Margaret A. Van Antwerp and Sally Johns (1984)

5: *American Transcendentalists,* edited by Joel Myerson (1988)

6: *Hardboiled Mystery Writers,* edited by Matthew J. Bruccoli and Richard Layman (1989)

7: *Modern American Poets,* edited by Karen L. Rood (1989)